# SAGE
# vantage

W0006006

## Course tools done right. Built to support your teaching. Designed to ignite learning.

**SAGE vantage** is an intuitive digital platform that blends trusted SAGE content with auto-graded assignments, all carefully designed to ignite student engagement and drive critical thinking. With evidence-based instructional design at the core, **SAGE vantage** creates more time for engaged learning and empowered teaching, keeping the classroom where it belongs—in your hands.

- **3-STEP COURSE SETUP** is so fast, you can complete it in minutes!

- Control over assignments, content selection, due dates, and grading **EMPOWERS** you to **TEACH YOUR WAY**.

- Dynamic content featuring applied-learning multimedia tools with built-in assessments, including video, knowledge checks, and chapter tests, helps **BUILD STUDENT CONFIDENCE**.

- eReading experience makes it easy to learn by presenting content in **EASY-TO-DIGEST** segments featuring note-taking, highlighting, definition look-up, and more.

- Quality content authored by the **EXPERTS YOU TRUST**.

**⑤SAGE vantage**™
engage. learn. soar.

**sagepub.com/vantage**

# The
# Hallmark
# Features

**Entrepreneurship: The Practice and Mindset** catapults students beyond the classroom by helping them develop an entrepreneurial mindset so they can create opportunities and take action in uncertain environments.

- A new chapter on DEVELOPING YOUR CUSTOMERS helps students gain a deeper understanding of market segmentation, customer personas, and the customer journey.

- 2 MINDSHIFT ACTIVITIES PER CHAPTER challenge students to take action outside the classroom and do entrepreneurship.

- 15 NEW CASE STUDIES and 16 NEW ENTREPRENEURSHIP IN ACTION PROFILES highlight a diverse range of entrepreneurs and start-ups.

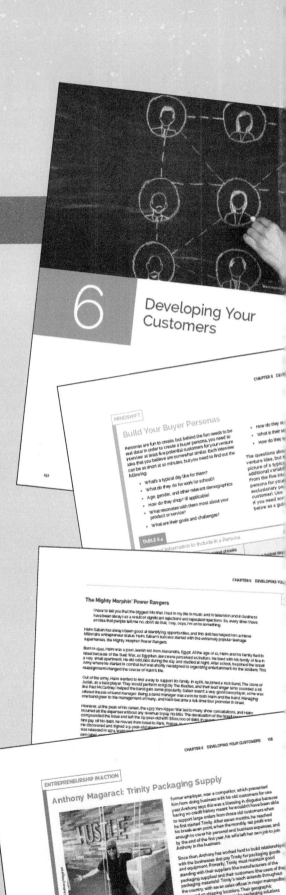

# SAGE Publishing:
# Our Story

At SAGE, we mean business. We believe in creating evidence-based, cutting-edge content that helps you prepare your students to succeed in today's ever-changing business world. We strive to provide you with the tools you need to develop the next generation of leaders, managers, and entrepreneurs.

- We invest in the right **AUTHORS** who distill research findings and industry ideas into practical applications.

- We keep our prices **AFFORDABLE** and provide multiple **FORMAT OPTIONS** for students.

- We remain permanently independent and fiercely committed to **QUALITY CONTENT** and **INNOVATIVE RESOURCES** .

# Entrepreneurship

Second Edition

We dedicate this book to future entrepreneurs of all types across the globe who will create opportunities and take action to change their world and the world of others. Embrace the journey and the learning, and take pride in knowing that you are moving society forward.

# Entrepreneurship

## The Practice and Mindset

### Second Edition

**Heidi M. Neck**
*Babson College*

**Christopher P. Neck**
*Arizona State University*

**Emma L. Murray**

Los Angeles | London | New Delhi
Singapore | Washington DC | Melbourne

FOR INFORMATION:

SAGE Publications, Inc.
2455 Teller Road
Thousand Oaks, California 91320
E-mail: order@sagepub.com

SAGE Publications Ltd.
1 Oliver's Yard
55 City Road
London EC1Y 1SP
United Kingdom

SAGE Publications India Pvt. Ltd.
B 1/I 1 Mohan Cooperative Industrial Area
Mathura Road, New Delhi 110 044
India

SAGE Publications Asia-Pacific Pte. Ltd.
18 Cross Street #10-10/11/12
China Square Central
Singapore 048423

Printed in the United States of America

Library of Congress Cataloging-in-Publication Data

Names: Neck, Heidi M., author. | Neck, Christopher P., author. | Murray, Emma L., author.

Title: Entrepreneurship : the practice and mindset / Heidi M. Neck, Babson College, Christopher P. Neck, Arizona State University, Emma L. Murray.

Description: Second Edition. | Thousand Oaks : SAGE Publishing, 2020. | Revised edition of the authors' Entrepreneurship, [2018] | Includes bibliographical references and index.

Identifiers: LCCN 2019031105 | ISBN 9781544354620 (paperback) | ISBN 9781544354637 (epub) | ISBN 9781544354644 (epub) | ISBN 9781544354651 (pdf)

Subjects: LCSH: Entrepreneurship.

Classification: LCC HB615 .N43297 2020 | DDC 658.4/21—dc23
LC record available at https://lccn.loc.gov/2019031105

Acquisitions Editor:  Maggie Stanley
Content Development Editor:  Lauren Gobell
Editorial Assistant:  Janeane Calderon
Production Editor:  Veronica Stapleton Hooper
Copy Editor:  Diana Breti
Typesetter:  C&M Digitals (P) Ltd.
Proofreader:  Talia Greenberg
Indexer:  Beth Nauman-Montana
Cover Designer:  Scott Van Atta
Marketing Manager:  Sarah Panella

23 24 25 26 27  10 9 8 7 6 5 4 3

# BRIEF CONTENTS

# DETAILED CONTENTS

© Peshkova/Shutterstock

## Part II. Creating and Developing Opportunities 55

## CHAPTER 3: Creating and Recognizing New Opportunities 56

## CHAPTER 4: Using Design Thinking 78

©iStockphoto.com/oatawa

©iStockphoto.com/marrio31

©iStockphoto.com/Gerasimov174

©iStockphoto.com/ipopba

©iStockphoto.com/utah778

©iStockphoto.com/PeopleImages

©iStockphoto.com/Gearstd

©iStockphoto.com/AndreyPopov

# CHAPTER 11: Anticipating Failure 256

## Part IV. Supporting New Opportunities 279

# CHAPTER 12: Bootstrapping and Crowdfunding for Resources 280

©iStockphoto.com/South_agency

Organic Valley (with permission)

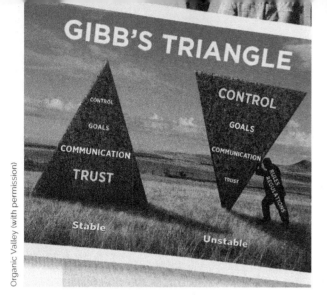

Organic Valley (with permission)

AP Photo/ Manish Swarup

# PREFACE

*Entrepreneurship: The Practice and Mindset* (2nd ed.) catapults students beyond the classroom to think and act more entrepreneurially in order to create opportunities and take action in uncertain environments. Based on the world-renowned Babson program, this text emphasizes practice and learning through action.

Entrepreneurship has historically and narrowly been defined as starting a new business, with little attention given to the individuals—the entrepreneurs of all types—who have the mindset, skillset, and toolset to create change, improve the world, and make a difference in their lives as well as the lives of others. The most current view of entrepreneurship is represented in this text. This is a view that entrepreneurship today is not reserved for the chosen few but is a life skill needed by all. The world will benefit not only from those who start new ventures but also from those who act entrepreneurially in all that they do. We are living in the entrepreneurial generation, and all students must get comfortable with creating and testing new ideas, navigating uncertain environments, and acting in order to learn rather than learning in order to act.

*Entrepreneurship: The Practice and Mindset* is a practice-based, realistic, and inclusive approach to entrepreneurship. It is a core textbook for college-level undergraduate and graduate students seeking methods for starting and running something new: a new business for-profit or nonprofit, inside a large corporation, or within a family business. Four points guide the philosophy of this book:

First, every student should be exposed to the practice of entrepreneurship regardless of major, discipline, or chosen career path. The life skill developed through the discipline of entrepreneurship is both necessary and differentiating. We have the innate ability to build, problem solve, lead, reflect, experiment, improvise, and empathize, but sometimes we lack the mindset (or have lost the mindset at some point) to do so in creative and ingenious ways. Our education system has deemphasized critical thinking in favor of right and wrong. In short, we have educated the human race to be less entrepreneurial than ever before. It's time to get those entrepreneurship skills back.

Second, students cannot simply read about entrepreneurship; they must *do* entrepreneurship. The text requires a lot of "doing" and, as a result, students develop courage to take action in highly ambiguous environments. Our vision in writing this book was to create a practice-based text that promotes active learning and engagement with the realities of entrepreneurship, encouraging students to think like entrepreneurs rather than passively learn about them.

Third, this textbook approaches learning entrepreneurship as a method that goes beyond simply understanding and knowing; it requires using, applying, and acting. We treat entrepreneurship as a method that demands practice. In fact we call it "the Entrepreneurship Method" throughout the book. Traditionally, entrepreneurship is taught as a process that typically involves traversing a linear pathway of identifying an opportunity, understanding resource requirements, acquiring resources, writing a business plan, implementing the plan, and then exiting the business at some point. In reality, entrepreneurship isn't that clean or clear cut. Additionally, the word *process* assumes known inputs and known outputs, as in a manufacturing process; it implies you will get to a specific destination. For example, building a car on an assembly line is a manufacturing process. You have all the parts; you know how they fit together; and you know the type of car you will have at the end because it was planned that way. A process is quite predictable. Entrepreneurship is not predictable and, therefore, cannot adequately be taught as a process. It's too messy for that and we need to embrace the messiness.

Fourth, students completing this text will be thinking and acting more entrepreneurially than when they started. Every action students take in this text will aid in building their entrepreneurial mindset. Every action is designed with intention so that students can experience and practice creative and nimble thinking, leading to a heightened level of experimentation where numerous iterations represent stages of learning rather than successes and failures or right and wrong answers. This text is a journey that encourages students to act their way into learning and knowing. It's about getting comfortable with uncertainty and developing the courage to act and find all the pieces of the puzzle.

It's about *being* entrepreneurial!

# NEW TO THIS EDITION

We have made several enhancements to this edition while retaining the unique mindset approach. In addition to updating the chapter references, we have updated all end of chapter case studies, provided new Entrepreneurship Meets Ethics features, new Research at Work features, new Mindshift features, new profiles for Entrepreneurship in Action features, and added new entrepreneurial research supported by the latest studies. Additionally, we have added a new chapter on developing your customers.

### Chapter 1: Practicing Entrepreneurship

- Chapters 1 (A Global Social Movement) and 2 (Practicing Entrepreneurship) from the first edition have been combined to create a new chapter
- New Entrepreneurship in Action: Juan Giraldo, Waku
- Expanded discussion on deliberate practice, including a new section on how deliberate practice shapes the brain
- New Entrepreneurship Meets Ethics: When to Practice Entrepreneurship
- New Case Study: Gyan-I Inc.

### Chapter 2: Activating an Entrepreneurial Mindset

- Chapter 3 (Developing an Entrepreneurial Mindset) from the first edition was retitled and renumbered as Chapter 2
- New Entrepreneurship in Action: Franklin Yancey, WME Entertainment and Yancey Realty
- Further detailed discussion on mindset featuring U.S. senator Corey Booker
- New Mindshift: Building Entrepreneurial Habits
- New Entrepreneurship Meets Ethics: Family and Friends Along for the Ride
- Expands on the dysfunctional side of passion by describing a recent Stanford study
- New Case Study: Doctory

### Chapter 3: Creating and Recognizing New Opportunities

- Chapter 5 (Generating New Ideas) from the first edition was retitled and renumbered as Chapter 3
- Added one new figure on increasing complexity and unknowingness in opportunity creation
- Added two new tables on discovering new opportunities and the IDEATE model for opportunity recognition
- New Entrepreneurship in Action: Jazmine Valencia, JV Agency
- New section on the four pathways to opportunity identification
- New Entrepreneurship Meets Ethics: The Ethics of Taking Someone's Idea

- New Mindshift: Practicing Identify in the IDEATE Model
- Research at Work: Testing IDEATE in the Entrepreneurial Classroom
- New Case Study: Yoee Baby

## Chapter 4: Using Design Thinking

- Chapter 6 from the first edition was renumbered as Chapter 4
- Added one new figure on insight statements
- Added three new tables on skills of designers, three phases of design thinking, and design thinking as a social technology
- New discussion of the four approaches of design company IDEO
- New Entrepreneurship in Action: Shaymaa Gaafar, Shay Jaffar
- New Mindshift: Needs Are Verbs; Solutions Are Nouns
- New example (Clean Team Ghana) to illustrate the three phases of design thinking in action
- New section explaining the four different types of observation
- Research at Work: Design Thinking Is a Social Technology
- Expanded discussion on preparing for an interview
- Expanded discussion on empathy using new IDEO example
- Detailed description of the interviewing process

## Chapter 5: Building Business Models

- Discussion of Massive Open Online Courses (MOOCs) and the Imitation Model as examples of different types of business models
- New Entrepreneurship in Action: Brandon Steiner, Steiner Sports
- New Entrepreneurship Meets Ethics: The Rights of Research Participants
- Discussion of business author Doug Hall's Three Laws of Marketing Physics: overt benefit, real reason to believe, and dramatic difference
- New Mindshift: The Overt Benefit, Real Reason to Believe, and Dramatic Difference
- Research at Work: Overt Benefit, Real Reason to Believe, and Dramatic Difference
- New Case Study: NatureBox

## Chapter 6: Developing Your Customers

- New Entrepreneurship in Action: Anthony Magaraci, Trinity Packaging Supply
- Expanded discussion on creating an end user profile, including psychographics
- New section Crossing the Chasm and explanation of "beachhead market"
- New example to illustrate customer journey mapping
- New Entrepreneurship Meets Ethics: Can You Sell Customer Information?
- New Mindshift: Build Your Buyer Personas
- New Mindshift: Creating a Customer Journey Map
- Research at Work: Emotional Motivators

- New example to illustrate market sizing
- New Case Study: The Mighty Morphin' Power Rangers

## Chapter 7: Testing and Experimenting With New Ideas

- New introduction featuring the benefits of experimentation
- New Entrepreneurship in Action: Karima Mariama-Arthur, WordSmithRapport
- New section explaining different types of experiments
- New section exploring prototypes in greater depth
- New Entrepreneurship Meets Ethics: When Links Break
- New example illustrating the six steps of scientific experimentation
- New example to explain the rules of experimentation in relation to stakeholders
- New Mindshift: Creating a Mockup
- New Research at Work: Why Overconfident Entrepreneurs Fail
- Introduces the five-dimensional model of curiosity created by Todd B. Kashan at George Mason University
- New section on building curiosity strength
- New Case Study: Stitch Fix

## Chapter 8: Developing Networks and Building Teams

- New Entrepreneurship in Action: Markesia Akinbami, Ducere Construction Services
- Introduces new research by the Economist Intelligence Unit on the benefits of informal professional networks and communities
- Introduction to the concept of implicit bias
- Adapted table: Top Organizations for Entrepreneurs
- New section on incubators and accelerators
- New Entrepreneurship Meets Ethics: Developing Networks and Building Teams
- New Mindshift: Building My Network
- Adapted table: LinkedIn Groups Dedicated to Entrepreneurs
- Adapted table: Facebook Groups for Entrepreneurs
- Discussion of Google's research on shared vision and management behaviors
- Research at Work: Don't Pitch Like a Girl
- New Case Study: AmeriCan Packaging

## Chapter 9: Creating Revenue Models

- New Entrepreneurship in Action: Kathey Porter, Porter Brown Associates
- Discussion on data brokers
- New Entrepreneurship Meets Ethics: How to Make an Ad
- New Mindshift: Revenue Model Pivot Practice
- Research at Work: The Dark Side of Entrepreneurship
- Provides detailed explanation of break-even analysis
- New Case Study: Invento Robotics

## Chapter 10: Planning for Entrepreneurs

- New Entrepreneurship in Action: Dr. Emmet C. (Tom) Thompson II, AFC Management
- New Entrepreneurship Meets Ethics: When to Be Transparent With Investors
- New section introducing the concept statement as an important part of planning
- New Mindshift: What Do You Know About Your Competition?
- Research at Work: Can We Think Ourselves Into (and out of) Planning?
- Additional tips for writing any type of business plan
- New Case Study: IoMob

## Chapter 11: Anticipating Failure

- New Entrepreneurship in Action: David James, K12 Landing
- Adapted table: Entrepreneurs Share Their Reasons for Failure
- Explores a study by CBI Insights on the number one reason for startup failure
- New Entrepreneurship Meets Ethics: From Tech Hero to Zero Net Worth
- New Mindshift: Go Get Rejected
- Research at Work: Overcoming the Stigma of Failure
- Updated figure: Fear of Failure Rates Around the World
- Updated figure: GEM Global Report
- New Case Study: Petwell Supply Co.

## Chapter 12: Bootstrapping and Crowdfunding for Resources

- New Entrepreneurship in Action: Bryanne Leeming, Unruly Studios
- Adapted table: Common Bootstrapping Strategies
- New Entrepreneurship Meets Ethics: When to Proclaim a Product Is Ready
- New Mindshift: Bootstrapping for Your Business
- Research at Work: The Informational Value of Crowdfunding for Music Entrepreneurs
- New Case Study: FUBU

## Chapter 13: Financing for Startups

- New Entrepreneurship in Action, Joel Barthelemy: GlobalMed
- Expanded discussion on splitting the ownership pie
- New section: The Age of the Unicorn
- Adapted table: Why Angels and Entrepreneurs Are Good for Each Other
- Updated table: Most Active Angel Groups in the U.S.
- Additional advice from the Angel Capital Association (ACA)
- Research at Work: Why Most Entrepreneurs Can't Access Capital
- Adapted table: Guidelines for Finding the Right VC for Your Startup
- New section: What About a Bank Loan?
- New section: The Due Diligence Process for VCs

- New Entrepreneurship Meets Ethics: Replacing the Founder CEO
- New Mindshift: Watch *Shark Tank* as an Investor
- New Case Study: Gravyty

## Chapter 14: Navigating Legal and IP Issues

- New Entrepreneurship in Action: Cameron Herold, 1-800-GOT JUNK? & COO Alliance
- Adapted table: Useful Online Legal Resources
- New section: The Founders' Agreement
- Adapted table: Resources for IP Information
- New section: Nondisclosure Agreement
- Updated Research at Work: Patent Trolls
- New Mindshift: Patent Battles
- New Entrepreneurship Meets Ethics: The Danger of Going on *Shark Tank*
- Expanded discussion of unpaid internships referencing the "primary beneficiary test" adopted by the Department of Labor
- New case: LULA

## Chapter 15: Engaging Customers Through Marketing

- Expanded introduction detailing how entrepreneurial marketing is different
- New Entrepreneurship in Action: Charlie Regan, Nerds on Site
- New Section: Marketing Trends
- Discusses new ideas for entrepreneurs to engage consumers through creating content
- New Section: How to Build Your Personal Brand
- Adapted table: Tips for Building Your Personal Brand
- New Entrepreneurship Meets Ethics: How Social Media Can Provide Marketing Headaches
- New Mindshift: What "About Us"?
- Research at Work: How a Pitch Can Help Build Your Brand
- New Case Study: RealPlay

## Chapter 16: Supporting Social Entrepreneurship

- New Entrepreneurship in Action: Organic Valley
- Discussion on the climate crisis drawing from studies from the University of Hawaii and information from the Intergovernmental Panel on Climate Change
- New Entrepreneurship Meets Ethics: How Social Entrepreneurs Can Be Unethical
- New Mindshift: How Entrepreneurship Is Saving the Planet
- Research at Work: United Nations Sustainable Development Goals
- Adapted table: Examples of Impact Investment Funds
- Expanded discussion on CSR initiatives drawing from the latest research

- New section: Social Entrepreneurship and Audacious Ideas
- Updated figure: Global Entrepreneurship Monitor Measuring Entrepreneurial Activity
- Updated figure: Global Entrepreneurship Monitor Measuring Rates by Gender
- New Case Study: 1854 Cycling Company

## What Makes Our Book Unique

- A focus on the **entrepreneurial mindset** helps students develop the discovery, thinking, reasoning, and implementation skills necessary to thrive in highly uncertain environments.

- An emphasis on the **Entrepreneurship Method**, in which entrepreneurship is approached as a method that requires doing. It's not a predictive or linear process. It's messy, but clarity comes with action and practice.

- Each chapter includes two **Mindshift activities** in which students take action outside the classroom in order to practice various aspects of entrepreneurship.

- Instructors are provided with **experiential learning activities** to use inside the classroom.

- A unique chapter on **learning from failure** helps students anticipate setbacks, develop grit, and understand the value of experimentation and iteration.

- A new chapter on **developing your customers** helps students gain a deeper understanding of their customers and explains how this knowledge is essential for early business success.

- **Cutting-edge topics** such as design thinking, business model canvas, bootstrapping, and crowdfunding are covered in depth, exposing students to the latest developments in the field.

## An Inclusive Approach

The media often exaggerate the meteoric rise of "overnight global sensations" such as Bill Gates (Microsoft), Steve Jobs (Apple), Mark Zuckerberg (Facebook), Elon Musk (Tesla), and Travis Kalanick (Uber). These stories have perpetuated the myth of the "tech entrepreneurial genius" and have captured the public imagination for decades. Although Bill Gates and his peers are certainly inspirational, we would argue that few can personally identify with the stories surrounding them, and they do little to represent the reality of entrepreneurship.

In *Entrepreneurship: The Practice and Mindset*, we deconstruct the myths and stories, which we believe limit others from becoming entrepreneurs. Dominant myths include that entrepreneurship is reserved for startups; that entrepreneurs have a special set of personality traits; that entrepreneurship can't be taught; that entrepreneurs are extreme risk takers; that entrepreneurs do not collaborate; that entrepreneurs devote large periods of time to planning; and that entrepreneurship is not a life skill.

With the support of extensive research, we show that the traditional view of the startup is not the only path for entrepreneurs; that there is no scientific evidence to suggest that entrepreneurs are any different from the rest of us in terms of personality traits or behaviors; that entrepreneurship can, indeed, be taught; that entrepreneurs are more calculated (rather than extreme) risk takers; that they collaborate more than they compete, act more than they plan, and perceive entrepreneurship as a life skill.

We also show that entrepreneurs do not have to come from a technology background to succeed. In *Entrepreneurship: The Practice and Mindset*, we include personal accounts of entrepreneurs from all types of disciplines, in the United States and around the world, including those in the fields of recruitment, science, food and beverage, tourism, engineering, finance, clothing, industrial design, pet services, fitness, costume design, sports, and promotional marketing.

These personal stories are intended to illustrate the realities of being an entrepreneur, detailing the unpredictability of entrepreneurship together with the highs and the lows; like famous U.S. entrepreneur computer designer Adam Osborne, we believe that "the most valuable thing you can make is a mistake—you can't learn anything from being perfect."

Entrepreneurship is all around us; everyone has the ability to think and act entrepreneurially, transform opportunity into reality, and create social and economic value. But as we show, practice is key to success, and learning is inseparable from doing.

## A Mindset and Action Approach

Mindset is the precursor to action. The work of researcher and Darden School of Business professor Saras D. Sarasvathy has added a new dimension to the field in understanding the entrepreneurial mindset. Sarasvathy discovered patterns of thinking, a theory she calls *effectuation,* which is the idea that the future is unpredictable yet controllable. In other words, because thinking can be changed and altered, we all have the ability to think and act entrepreneurially, and this thinking can be learned and taught. Moreover, entrepreneurship is not only about altering the way we think—it is about creating mindshifts to take action that yield significant change and value. And creating these mindshifts takes practice and experimentation.

We believe that it is very important to emphasize the mindset in the early development of entrepreneurship students. Often the mindset is either ignored or considered to be too difficult to teach. We introduce entrepreneurial mindset very early in the text, and then the mindset is further developed throughout the book based on the actions that students take and are required to practice throughout the book.

Knowing that an entrepreneurial mindset is needed is not sufficient for a strong entrepreneurship education. Practicing the mindset and helping students develop it over time are essential components of learning the discipline of entrepreneurship today. In her previous book, *Teaching Entrepreneurship,* Heidi Neck and her coauthors Candy Brush and Patti Greene encouraged educators to build classroom environments that encouraged students to play, create, experiment, empathize, and reflect in order to build a bias toward action and become more entrepreneurial. These elements are emphasized throughout this text.

# FEATURES

In each chapter, we include the following features that help students think and act like entrepreneurs:

- **Entrepreneurship in Action** at the beginning of each chapter includes interviews with entrepreneurs from many different businesses and disciplines both in the United States and around the world, demonstrating how the concepts discussed in the chapter are applied in real situations.

- Two **Mindshift** activities in each chapter provide instructors with exercises that encourage students to think and act outside of their comfort zones. These activities can be performed inside or outside the classroom, and the accompanying critical thinking questions promote further comprehension and analysis.

- **Entrepreneurship Meets Ethics** provides students with examples of ethical dilemmas and challenges related to topics discussed in the chapter. These real-world scenarios and the accompanying critical thinking questions guide students to think about how they would take action if confronted with a similar situation.

- **Research at Work** highlights recent seminal entrepreneurship studies and explores their impact on and application to the marketplace.

- Short **Case Studies** tell the stories of real companies from various sectors and markets to illustrate chapter concepts and encourage further exploration of these topics.
- **Summaries** and **Key Terms** recap important chapter information to aid with studying and comprehension.
- Topical **Supplements** offer greater depth of practice:
  - **Financial Statements and Projections for Startups** demonstrate how students can build financial projections based on sound data, using different types of financial statements.
  - **The Pitch Deck** provides an in-depth description of the pitch deck, includes sample slides, walks students through the preparation of their own pitch deck, and advises students on how to predict and prepare for the question-and-answer period that usually follows a pitch presentation.
- **VentureBlocks** simulation
  - In the VentureBlocks simulation, students start from scratch, with no resources or business ideas, and must explore a new, unknown market of bearlike pets called nanus. On their journey through the simulation, students learn how to interview customers to identify business opportunities based on their needs. Most students will complete VentureBlocks in 30 to 60 minutes. The simulation includes tutorials so they know what to do and how to navigate at all times. The simulation ends when they identify business opportunities that meet the needs of nanu owners.

## CONTENT AND ORGANIZATION

### Part I. Entrepreneurship Is a Life Skill

Chapter 1: Practicing Entrepreneurship describes the skills most important to the Entrepreneurship Method, how entrepreneurship is more of a method than a process, and the concept of deliberate practice.

Chapter 2: Activating an Entrepreneurial Mindset outlines the effectiveness of mindset in entrepreneurship and explains how to develop the habits of self-leadership, creativity, and improvisation.

### Part II. Creating and Developing Opportunities

Chapter 3: Creating and Recognizing New Opportunities explores the four pathways (design, effectuate, search, and find) toward explaining how entrepreneurs identify and exploit opportunities.

Chapter 4: Using Design Thinking describes the importance of design thinking in understanding customers and their needs, explains the four different types of observation, emphasizes the role of empathy in design thinking, and illustrates the key parts of the design thinking process and their relevance to entrepreneurs.

Chapter 5: Building Business Models examines the core areas of a business model, explores the importance of customer value propositions (CVPs), and illustrates the components of the business model canvas.

Chapter 6: Developing Your Customers explores different types of customers, customer segmentation, customer personas, the customer journey mapping process, and market sizing.

Chapter 7: Testing and Experimenting With New Ideas explains the benefits of experimentation, illustrates the six steps of scientific experimentation and how they apply to entrepreneurs, demonstrates how to test hypotheses, and discusses the five-dimensional model of curiosity.

Chapter 8: Developing Networks and Building Teams explains the importance of networks for building social capital, identifies the benefits of professional informal networks and communities, describes different ways of building networks, and describes how networking can help build a founding team.

## Part III. Evaluating and Acting on Opportunities

Chapter 9: Creating Revenue Models describes the different types of revenue models used by entrepreneurs and identifies different strategies entrepreneurs use when pricing their products and calculating prices.

Chapter 10: Planning for Entrepreneurs explains vision as an important part of entrepreneurial planning, the different types of plans used by entrepreneurs, and the types of questions to answer during planning, and provides advice for writing business plans.

Chapter 11: Anticipating Failure explores failure and its effect on entrepreneurs; the consequences of fear of failure; how entrepreneurs can learn from failure; and the significance of "grit" and its role in building tolerance for failure.

## Part IV. Supporting New Opportunities

Chapter 12: Bootstrapping and Crowdfunding for Resources describes the significance of bootstrapping and bootstrapping strategies for entrepreneurs and also discusses crowdfunding as a form of investment for entrepreneurial ventures.

Chapter 13: Financing for Startups outlines the stages of equity financing, explains the roles of angel investors and venture capital investors in financing entrepreneurs, and describes the due diligence process.

Chapter 14: Navigating Legal and IP Issues outlines the most common types of legal structures available to startups; describes IP, IP theft, and some IP traps experienced by entrepreneurs; and discusses the founders' agreement and nondisclosure agreements.

Chapter 15: Engaging Customers Through Marketing explores the principles of marketing and how they apply to new ventures, describes branding and how to build a personal brand, explains the value of social media for marketing opportunities, and discusses the different types of marketing tools available to entrepreneurs.

Chapter 16: Supporting Social Entrepreneurship defines social entrepreneurship, discusses the different types of social entrepreneurship, and explains how it can help to resolve wicked problems around the world that are connected to the United Nations Sustainable Development Goals.

# DIGITAL RESOURCES

## A Complete Teaching and Learning Package

*Engage, Learn, Soar* with **SAGE vantage**, an intuitive digital platform that delivers *Entrepreneurship: The Practice and Mindset, Second Edition*, textbook content in a learning experience carefully designed to ignite student engagement and drive critical thinking. With evidence-based instructional design at the core, SAGE vantage creates more time for engaged learning and empowered teaching, keeping the classroom where it belongs—in your hands.

Easy to access across mobile, desktop, and tablet devices, SAGE vantage enables students to engage with the material you choose, learn by applying knowledge, and soar with confidence by performing better in your course.

Highlights Include:

- **eReading Experience.** Makes it easy for students to study wherever they are—students can take notes, highlight content, look up definitions, and more!

- **Pedagogical Scaffolding.** Builds on core concepts, moving students from basic understanding to mastery.

- **Confidence Builder.** Offers frequent knowledge checks, applied-learning multimedia tools, and chapter tests with focused feedback to assure students know key concepts.
- **Time-saving Flexibility.** Feeds auto-graded assignments to your gradebook, with real-time insight into student and class performance.
- **Quality Content.** Written by expert authors and teachers, content is not sacrificed for technical features.
- **Honest Value.** Affordable access to easy-to-use, quality learning tools students will appreciate.

Favorite SAGE vantage Features

- **3-step course setup** is so fast you can complete it in minutes!
- **Control over assignments**, content selection, due dates, and grading empowers you to teach your way.
- **Quality content** authored by the experts you trust.
- **eReading experience** makes it easy to learn and study by presenting content in easy-to-digest segments featuring note-taking, highlighting, definition look-up, and more.
- **LMS integration provides single sign-on** with streamlined grading capabilities and course management tools.
- **Auto-graded assignments** include:
  - formative **knowledge checks** for each major section of the text that quickly reinforce what students have read and ensure they stay on track;
  - dynamic, hands-on **multimedia activities** that tie real world examples and motivate students to read, prepare for class;
  - summative **chapter tests** that reinforce important themes; and
  - **helpful hints and feedback** (provided with all assignments) that offer context and explain why an answer is correct or incorrect, allowing students to study more effectively.
- **Compelling polling questions** bring concepts to life and drive meaningful comprehension and classroom discussion.
- **Short-answer questions** provide application and reflection opportunities connected to key concepts.
- **Instructor reports** track student activity and provide analytics so you can adapt instruction as needed.
- **A student dashboard** offers easy access to grades, so students know exactly where they stand in your course and where they might improve.
- **Honest value** gives students access to quality content and learning tools at a price they will appreciate.

# ⑤SAGE coursepacks

## SAGE Coursepacks for Instructors

The **SAGE coursepack** for *Entrepreneurship: The Practice and Mindset, Second Edition* makes it easy to import our quality instructor materials and student resources into your school's learning management system (LMS), such as Blackboard, Canvas, Brightspace by D2L, or Moodle. Intuitive and simple to use, **SAGE coursepack** allows you to integrate only the content you need, with minimal effort, and requires no access code. Don't use an LMS platform? You can still access many of the online resources for *Entrepreneurship: The Practice and Mindset, Second Edition* via the **SAGE edge** site.

Available SAGE content through the coursepack includes:

- Pedagogically robust **assessment tools** that foster review, practice, and critical thinking and offer a more complete way to measure student engagement, including:
  - Diagnostic **coursepack chapter quizzes** that identify opportunities for improvement, track student progress, and ensure mastery of key learning objectives.
  - **Test banks** built on Bloom's taxonomy that provide a diverse range of test items.
  - **Activity and quiz options** that allow you to choose only the assignments and tests you want.
- Editable, chapter-specific **PowerPoint®** slides that offer flexibility when creating multimedia lectures so you don't have to start from scratch but can customize to your exact needs.
- **Instructions** on how to use and integrate the comprehensive assessments and resources provided.

# ⑤SAGE edge™

**SAGE edge** is a robust online environment featuring an impressive array of tools and resources for review, study, and further exploration, keeping both instructors and students on the cutting edge of teaching and learning. SAGE edge content is open access and available on demand. Learning and teaching has never been easier!

**SAGE edge for Students** at **https://edge.sagepub.com/neckentrepreneurship2e** provides a personalized approach to help students accomplish their coursework goals in an easy-to-use learning environment.

- **Learning objectives** reinforce the most important material
- Mobile-friendly **eFlashcards** strengthen understanding of key terms and concepts, and make it easy to maximize your study time, anywhere, anytime.
- Mobile-friendly practice **quizzes** allow you to assess how much you've learned and where you need to focus your attention.
- Carefully selected video resources bring concepts to life, are tied to learning objectives, and make learning easier.

**SAGE edge for Instructors** at **https://edge.sagepub.com/neckentrepreneurship2e** supports teaching by making it easy to integrate quality content and create a rich learning environment for students.

- The **Test bank**, built on Bloom's taxonomy (with Bloom's cognitive domain and difficulty level noted for each question), is created specifically for this text.
- **Sample course syllabi** provide suggested models for structuring your course.
- Editable, chapter-specific **PowerPoint® slides** offer complete flexibility for creating a multimedia presentation for the course, so you don't have to start from scratch but can customize to your exact needs.
- **Lecture Notes** features chapter summaries and outlines, providing an essential reference and teaching tool for lectures.
- Sample **answers to questions in the text** provide an essential reference.
- **Case notes** include summaries, analyses, and sample answers to assist with discussion.
- **Entrepreneurial exercises** written by Heidi Neck and other faculty from Babson College can be used in class to reinforce learning by doing.

- **Mindset Vitamins** are brief, fun, daily activities that can help you practice developing your entrepreneurial mindset every day

- **Suggested projects, experiential exercises, and activities** help students apply the concepts they learn to see how the work in various contexts, providing new perspectives.

- A set of all the **graphics from the text**, including all the maps, tables, and figures in PowerPoint formats are provided for class presentations.

- **Excel spreadsheets** accompany the supplement on financials.

- **Sample pitch decks** serve as examples to help students formulate their own pitch.

## SAGE Premium Video

*Entrepreneurship* offers premium video, available exclusively in the **SAGE vantage** digital option, produced and curated specifically for this text, to boost comprehension and bolster analysis.

## VentureBlocks Simulation

Practice interviewing customers and identifying their needs with VentureBlocks, a game-based simulation.

### Simulation Goals

1. **Develop** a better understanding of approaching opportunity creation through the identification of customer needs.
2. **Practice** interviewing potential customers:
   a. Approach strangers and start a conversation.
   b. Ask good open-ended questions to get useful and relevant information.
   c. Identify bad questions that would make real-world customer interviews unsuccessful.
   d. Feel rejection when someone does not want to engage in a conversation.
3. **Improve** listening and observation skills to identify the needs of potential customers and build strong customer insights.
4. **Cultivate** pattern recognition skills to identify potential opportunities that meet the needs of multiple customer types.
5. **Distinguish** between needs, customer insights, and solutions.

### What Is VentureBlocks?

In the VentureBlocks simulation, you start from scratch, with no resources or business ideas, and must explore a new, unknown market of bear-like pets called nanus. On your journey through the simulation, you learn how to identify business opportunities based on customer needs.

Most students will complete VentureBlocks in 30 to 60 minutes. The simulation includes tutorials so you know what to do and how to navigate at all times. Take your time, though, because this is a points-based competition. You will be able to see the top five performers at all times in your class on the real-time leaderboard!

**The nanu**

Here's a little bit more information about the simulation.

You assume the role of a nascent entrepreneur who lives in a small town called Trepton. A few years ago, scientists in Trepton created a new pet: the nanu. These cute bear-like pets are becoming popular fast. The number of nanu owners in Trepton is growing, and a few well-known veterinarians project nanu ownership to surpass dog ownership by the year 2040. This could be disruptive! The entrepreneur (you!) believes business opportunities exist but must learn more about nanus and their owners.

VentureBlocks is completed when you identify business opportunities that meet the needs of nanu owners. In order to do this, you must complete missions across eight levels of play. In Levels 1–4 you develop empathy for nanu owners by talking with them. In Levels 5–7, you generate customer insights that lead to business opportunities. A simulation learning summary occurs in Level 8. Figure 1 details the missions.

VentureBlocks represents early-stage entrepreneurial activity, and its foundations are rooted in design thinking that was introduced in this chapter. Figure 2 should look familiar: This is the human-centered approach framework presented in the chapter. Remember, strong opportunities are found at the intersection of feasibility, viability, and desirability. Feasibility answers the question, Can it be done from a technical or organizational perspective? Viability answers the question, Can we make money doing it? Desirability answers the question, What do people need?

## FIGURE 1

**VentureBlocks Missions**

| LEVEL | MANDATORY MISSION | LOCATION |
|---|---|---|
| 1 | Start a conversation and get rejected | Trepton Park |
| 2 | Trash a bad question while talking to people | Trepton Park |
| 3 | Talk to a nanu owner and earn 75 XP (experience points) | Trepton Park |
| 4 | Talk to a nanu owner and earn 110 XP (experience points) | Trepton Park |
| 5 | Go home and build 3 good insights | Home |
| 6 | Choose your top insight | Home |
| 7 | Create 2 business ideas based on your chosen insight | Home |

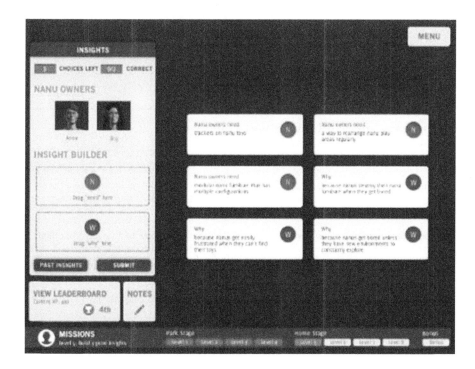

It is very common for entrepreneurship students to start with feasibility and viability. And these do represent two very important factors in building a sustainable business model, but sometimes we try to answer these questions too soon without giving adequate attention to what people need. As a result, VentureBlocks is designed to focus first on desirability: what nanu owners need.

### How to Use With This Text

Although the concepts students will practice in this simulation are most directly connected to concepts in Chapter 4: Using Design Thinking, they will also practice concepts from Chapter 3: Creating and Recognizing New Opportunities and Chapter 11: Learning From Failure. Figure 3 demonstrates how the chapter Learning Objectives align with the Simulation Goals.

### How to Access the Simulation

To access the VentureBlocks Simulation, visit sage.ventureblocks.com and enter your registration code. Your registration code will be available once your instructor sets up the course at sage.ventureblocks.com.

## FIGURE 2

### Design-Thinking Framework Revisited

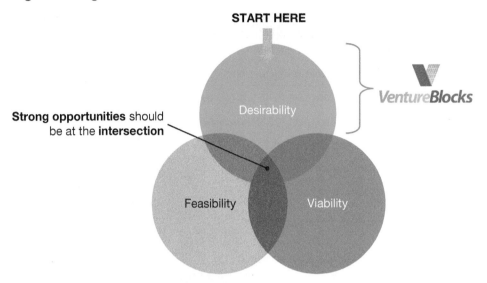

## FIGURE 3

### Simulation Goals and Chapter Learning Objectives

| SIMULATION GOALS | LEARNING OBJECTIVES |
| --- | --- |
| Develop a better understanding of approaching opportunity creation through the identification of customer needs. | 6.2 Demonstrate design thinking as a human-centered process focusing on customers and their needs. |
| Practice interviewing potential customers. | 6.6 Demonstrate how to interview potential customers in order to better understand their needs. |
| Improve listening and observation skills to identify the needs of potential customers and build strong customer insights. | 6.5 Demonstrate how to observe and convert observation data to insights. |
| Cultivate pattern recognition skills to identify potential opportunities that meet the needs of multiple customer types. | 5.4 Demonstrate how entrepreneurs find opportunities through active search and alertness.<br><br>5.3 Apply the two primary pathways to opportunity identification. |
| Distinguish between needs, customer insights, and solutions. | 5.5 Connect idea generation to opportunity recognition. |
| Apply learning from unsuccessful attempts to future attempts and develop an appreciation for the necessity of iteration. | 11.5 Describe the significance of "grit" and its role in building tolerance for failure. |
| Reflect on both successes and failures through built-in debrief questions. | 11.4 Explain the different ways entrepreneurs can learn from failure. |

# ACKNOWLEDGMENTS

The authors would like to thank the following people for their support in writing this book.

Heidi Neck would like to thank Dale Meyer, Candida Brush, Patricia Greene, Len Schlesinger, and the late Jeffry Timmons for the inspiration behind the book—all mentors and friends. She would also like to thank her research assistant and MBA '20, Gaurav Khemka; Anton Yakushin, her partner in VentureBlocks; and Babson College for their support in writing this book. Most important, she thanks the Timmons family and other Babson donors to the Jeffry A. Timmons endowed chair. This book would not have been possible without the resources provided by the Timmons endowed chair that Heidi Neck has held since 2008.

Chris Neck thanks Dean Amy Hillman at Arizona State (W. P. Carey School of Business) and Kevin Corley (department head, Department of Management and Entrepreneurship, Arizona State University) for their encouragement of his teaching and research efforts. He thanks Duane Roen (dean of the College of Integrative Sciences and Arts at Arizona State University) for his steadfast support and encouragement to excel in the classroom. He also thanks Mike Goldsby, Jeff Houghton, Stuart Mease, and Jay Heiler for their steadfast support for the book and other projects over the years.

He'd also like to thank those behind-the-scenes individuals who assisted in the research, development, and/or editing of various parts of this book. Specifically, he thanks Alex Stanley, Kevin Murphy, Tristan Gaynor, George Heiler, Rose Mary Sanders, and Sarah Hohmann. Their contributions to this book made the book even better.

We'd also like to thank Shyam Devnani, Brad George, Patti Greene, Candy Brush, Dennis Ceru, Matt Allen, Andrew Corbett, and Erik Noyes for their contributions to the experiential exercises featured on the instructor website.

We are indebted to the entrepreneurship faculty at Babson College and the University of Arizona's McGuire Center for Entrepreneurship, who were some of the earliest supporters of this book. Thank you Carlos J. Alsua, Randy M. Burd, K. Krasnow Waterman, Mark Peterson, Tristan Reader, and Richard Eric Yngve for your insightful feedback on the test bank. Your comments have helped us develop a better product, and for that we are very grateful. Additionally, we thank the countless adopters of the first edition who gave us both accolades and critical feedback to make the second edition an even better product. Special gratitude is given to Dan Cohen at Wake Forest University, who allowed us to build his IDEATE methodology into the book.

We also want to thank Ronda Taylor Bullock, Carly Erickson, April Kensington, Alex Smereczniak, Mark Aznavourian, Dana and Dave Lafleur, and Kevin Keller, who graciously allowed us to feature them in the new videos accompanying the second edition.

Writing a textbook is a huge undertaking that extends far beyond the author team. We would like to thank the incredibly committed team at SAGE for their constant encouragement, endless patience, and thoughtful suggestions. Their passion and enthusiasm has helped to deliver a textbook of which we are extremely proud.

Maggie Stanley, our acquisitions editor, has championed this book every step of the way, and we are enormously grateful for her considerate input and constant support. Content development editor Lauren Gobell has been a welcome driving force, encouraging us to explore and consider new ideas. Our talented editor Elsa Peterson helped clarify and refine the material and has significantly contributed to the quality of this textbook. Diana Breti, our copy editor, has been meticulous in her work, for which we are very appreciative. Veronica Stapleton Hooper, our production editor, oversaw the entire production process and, thanks to her, the whole project was kept on track. We'd also like to thank marketing manager Sarah Panella and marketing associate Kerstin Christiansen for their efforts promoting the book, editorial assistant Janeane Calderon for handling a number of tasks during development and production, permissions assistant Tyler Huxtable for his work helping secure permission to use a number of items included in the text, and senior graphic designer Scott Van Atta for creating a stunning interior and cover design.

For their thoughtful and helpful comments and ideas on our manuscript, we sincerely thank the following reviewers. Our book is a better product because of their insightful suggestions.

Jay A. Azriel, York College of Pennsylvania

Henry Balfanz, Alma College

Melissa S. Baucus, Texas State University

Sara Bliss Kiser, Alabama State University

Robert H. Epstein, University of Central Oklahoma

Mary Goebel-Lundholm, Peru State College

Jim Jindrick, University of Arizona Research, Discovery, and Innovation

Lori K. Long, Baldwin Wallace University

Vincent E. Mangum, Atlanta Metropolitan State College

Elizabeth A. McCrea, Stillman School of Business, Seton Hall University

Wallace W. Meyer Jr., University of Kansas

Mark B. Mondry, Virginia Polytechnic Institute and State University

Vitaliy Skorodziyevskiy, Texas Tech University

Jeffrey D. Stone, California State University Channel Islands

Sam Vegter, Western Piedmont Community College

Bill Wales, University at Albany, SUNY

We are also enormously grateful for the reviewers who provided valuable feedback on the first edition:

Anuradha Basu, San Jose State University

Susan Berston, City College of San Francisco

Constant D. Beugre, Delaware State University

Martin Bressler, Southeastern Oklahoma State University

Candida Brush, Babson College

Jacqueline H. Bull, Immaculata University

Kimble Byrd, Rowan University

C. S. Richard Chan, Stony Brook University

Shih Yung Chou, The University of Texas of the Permian Basin

Diane Denslow, University of North Florida

Art Diaz, University of Texas at El Paso

Robert S. D'Intino, Rowan University

Steven Edelson, Walsh University

Kevin Ernst, Ohio Northern University

Frances Fabian, University of Memphis

David J. Gavin, Marist College

Ranjan George, Simpson University

Peter Gianiodis, Duquesne University

Amy R. Gresock, University of Michigan—Flint

Maurice Haff, University of Central Oklahoma

Sheila Hanson, University of North Dakota

Lerong He, State University of New York at Brockport

Kirk Heriot, Columbus State University

Laurent Josien, SUNY Plattsburgh

Ryan Kauth, University of Wisconsin—Green Bay

Ram Kesavan, University of Detroit Mercy

Sara Kiser, Alabama State University

Rebecca Knapp, Saddleback College

Jon Krabill, Columbus State Community College

Nancy Kucinski, Hardin-Simmons University

Thomas Lachowicz, Radford University

Denise Lefort, Arapahoe Community College

Ada Leung, Penn State Berks

Martin Luytjes, Jacksonville University

Michele K. Masterfano, Drexel University

Sue McNamara, SUNY Fredonia

Stuart Mease, Virginia Tech

Wallace W. Meyer Jr., University of Kansas

John Edward Michaels, California University of Pennsylvania

Erik Monsen, University of Vermont

Charlie Nagelschmidt, Champlain College

David M. Nemi, Niagara County Community College

Laurel F. Ofstein, Western Michigan University

Bill Petty, Baylor University

Jonathan Phillips, Belmont University

Marlene Reed, Baylor University

Maija Renko, University of Illinois at Chicago

Rodney Ridley, Wilkes University

Timothy Ritter, Western Kentucky University

Robert W. Robertson, Independence University

Linda Wabschall Ross, Rowan University

Jacqueline Schmidt, John Carroll University

Darrell Scott, Idaho State University

Sally Sledge, Norfolk State University

Frank R. Spitznogle, Northern Arizona University

Joseph R. Stasio Jr., Merrimack College

Sunny Li Sun, University of Missouri—Kansas City

Lauren Talia, Independence University

Keith Ward, St. Edward's University

Paula A. White, Independence University

Lei Xu, Texas Tech University

Bill Zannini, Northern Essex Community College

Thanks are also due to the individuals who developed the digital resources that accompany this book: Steven Edelson, Jordan Jensen, Eva Mika, Colette Rominger, Sally Sledge, Tristan Gaynor, Paula A. White, and Cecilia Williams.

# ABOUT THE AUTHORS

## HEIDI M. NECK, PHD

**Heidi M. Neck**, PhD, is a Babson College professor and the Jeffry A. Timmons Professor of Entrepreneurial Studies. She has taught entrepreneurship at the undergraduate, MBA, and executive levels. She is the academic director of the Babson Academy, a dedicated unit within Babson that inspires change in the way universities, specifically their faculty and students, teach and learn entrepreneurship. The Babson Academy builds on Neck's work starting the Babson Collaborative, a global institutional membership organization for colleges and universities seeking to increase their capability and capacity in entrepreneurship education, and her leadership of Babson's Symposia for Entrepreneurship Educators (SEE), programs designed to inspire faculty from around the world to teach more experientially and entrepreneurially as well as build world-class entrepreneurship programs. Neck has directly trained more than 3,000 faculty around the world in the art and craft of teaching entrepreneurship. An award-winning teacher, Neck has been recognized for teaching excellence at Babson for undergraduate, graduate, and executive education. She has also been recognized by international organizations, the Academy of Management and USASBE, for excellence in pedagogy and course design. Most recently, in 2016 The Schulze Foundation awarded her Entrepreneurship Educator of the Year for pushing the frontier of entrepreneurship education in higher education.

Her research interests include entrepreneurship education, entrepreneurship inside organizations, and creative thinking. Neck is the lead author of *Teaching Entrepreneurship: A Practice-Based Approach* (Elgar), a book written to help educators teach entrepreneurship in more experiential and engaging ways. Additionally, she has published 40+ book chapters, research monographs, and refereed articles in such journals as *Journal of Small Business Management, Entrepreneurship Theory & Practice*, and *International Journal of Entrepreneurship Education*. She is on the editorial board of the *Academy of Management Learning & Education* journal.

Neck speaks and teaches internationally on cultivating the entrepreneurial mindset and espousing the positive force of entrepreneurship as a societal change agent. She consults and trains organizations of all sizes on building entrepreneurial capacity. She is the cofounder of VentureBlocks, an entrepreneurship education technology company, and was co-owner of FlowDog, a canine aquatic fitness and rehabilitation center that was located just outside of Boston. Heidi earned her PhD in strategic management and entrepreneurship from the University of Colorado at Boulder. She holds a BS in marketing from Louisiana State University and an MBA from the University of Colorado, Boulder.

## CHRISTOPHER P. NECK, PHD

**Dr. Christopher P. Neck** is currently an associate professor of management at Arizona State University, where he held the title "University Master Teacher." From 1994 to 2009, he was part of the Pamplin College of Business faculty at Virginia Tech. He received his PhD in management from Arizona State University and his MBA from Louisiana State University. Neck is author of the books *Self-Leadership: The Definitive*

*Guide to Personal Excellence* (2016, SAGE); *Fit to Lead: The Proven 8-Week Solution for Shaping up Your Body, Your Mind, and Your Career* (2004, St. Martin's Press; 2012, Carpenter's Sons); *Mastering Self-Leadership: Empowering Yourself for Personal Excellence* (6th ed., 2013, Pearson); *The Wisdom of Solomon at Work* (2001, Berrett-Koehler); *For Team Members Only: Making Your Workplace Team Productive and Hassle-Free* (1997, Amacom Books); and *Medicine for the Mind: Healing Words to Help You Soar* (4th ed., 2012, Wiley). Neck is also the coauthor of the principles of management textbook *Management: A Balanced Approach to the 21st Century* (2013, 2017, Wiley); the introductory entrepreneurship textbook *Entrepreneurship* (2017, SAGE); and the introductory organizational behavior textbook *Organizational Behavior* (2016, SAGE).

Dr. Neck's research specialties include employee/executive fitness, self-leadership, leadership, group decision-making processes, and self-managing teams. He has more than 100 publications in the form of books, chapters, and articles in various journals. The outlets in which Neck's work has appeared include *Organizational Behavior and Human Decision Processes, The Journal of Organizational Behavior, The Academy of Management Executive, Journal of Applied Behavioral Science, The Journal of Managerial Psychology, Executive Excellence, Human Relations, Human Resource Development Quarterly, Journal of Leadership Studies, Educational Leadership*, and *The Commercial Law Journal*.

Due to Neck's expertise in management, he has been cited in numerous national publications, including *The Washington Post, The Wall Street Journal, The Los Angeles Times, The Houston Chronicle,* and the *Chicago Tribune.* Additionally, each semester Neck teaches an introductory management course to a single class of anywhere from 500 to 1,000 students.

Dr. Neck was the recipient of the 2007 *Business Week* Favorite Professor Award. He is featured on www.businessweek.com as one of the approximately 20 professors from across the world receiving this award.

Neck currently teaches a mega section of Management Principles to approximately 500 students at Arizona State University. Neck received the Order of Omega Outstanding Teaching Award for 2012. This award is granted to one professor at Arizona State by the Alpha Lambda chapter of this leadership fraternity. His class sizes at Virginia Tech filled rooms up to 2,500 students. He received numerous teaching awards during his tenure at Virginia Tech, including the 2002 Wine Award for Teaching Excellence. Also, Neck was the 10-time winner (1996, 1998, 2000, 2002, 2004, 2005, 2006, 2007, 2008, and 2009) of the Students' Choice Teacher of The Year Award (voted by the students for the best teacher of the year within the entire university). Also, the organizations that have participated in Neck's management development training include GE/Toshiba, Busch Gardens, Clark Construction, the United States Army, Crestar, American Family Insurance, Sales and Marketing Executives International, American Airlines, American Electric Power, W. L. Gore & Associates, Dillard's Department Stores, and Prudential Life Insurance. Neck is also an avid runner. He has completed 12 marathons, including the Boston Marathon, the New York City Marathon, and the San Diego Marathon. In fact, his personal record for a single long-distance run is 40 miles.

# EMMA L. MURRAY, BA, HDIP, DBS IT

**Emma L. Murray** completed a bachelor of arts degree in English and Spanish at University College Dublin in County Dublin, Ireland. This was followed by a higher diploma (Hdip) in business studies and information technology at the Michael Smurfit Graduate School of Business in County Dublin, Ireland. Following her studies, Emma spent nearly a decade in investment banking before becoming a full-time writer and author.

As a writer, Emma has worked on numerous texts, including business and economics, self-help, and psychology. Within the field of higher education, Emma worked with Dr. Christopher P. Neck and Dr. Jeffery D. Houghton on *Management* (2013, Wiley) and is the coauthor of the principles of management textbook *Management: A Balanced Approach to the 21st Century* (2013, 2017, Wiley) and the coauthor of *Organizational Behavior* (2017, SAGE).

She is the author of *The Unauthorized Guide to Doing Business the Alan Sugar Way* (2010, Wiley-Capstone) and the lead author of *How to Succeed as a Freelancer in Publishing* (2010, How To Books). She lives in London.

# An Open Letter to All Students

Dear Student,

We suspect you are reading this now because you are on a journey—a journey in search of meaning, a desire to make a significant impact on the world, an itch to bring something new to market, a yearning not simply to find yourself but also to create yourself. Many believe that entrepreneurship can be a path to all of this. For some it can be, but it takes a lot of dedication and a lot of practice. That's what this book is all about: practicing entrepreneurship.

You are going to hear about the concept of practice throughout this entire book, and we want to take a minute to put this word in perspective. Think about a sport you're pretty good at or a musical instrument you have mastered. Even if you love the idea of playing the piano, it's very difficult to sit at the piano and start playing a piece that others really want to hear. You may be a very good soccer player today, but when you started playing, we're sure the coach didn't put you in the game immediately and say, "Go play, kid!" Similarly, you could destroy a golf course if you didn't know the basics of hitting that little white ball. Before we play the music piece in front of others, or play in our first competitive soccer game, and before we tee up on the first hole of a prestigious golf course, we have to practice.

Rarely do we perform the entire piece of music, or play the actual game, or get on the actual golf course before practicing parts of the experience. You practice scales on the piano, then you learn how to read the music, then you play simple pieces, then more complex compositions, and so on. In soccer, you work on fundamentals of kicking the ball, foot coordination, passing, heading, and tackling. A golfing instructor will make you swing different clubs for hours before you are allowed to try to hit the golf ball. Yes, just swinging. No hitting! You may also recognize in practicing these different experiences that you have to take action. We don't just read about playing the piano or soccer or golf. We have to do in order to learn. We have to take action in order to practice, and it is through practice that we can progress.

By practicing entrepreneurship, you will hone your skills and become proficient so that you can take action to reach your goals. Whether you have a concrete plan to bring something new to market or just a passion for finding ways to make the world a better place, we hope this book will help you on your journey.

Enjoy the journey and don't forget to practice!

The Authors

# PART I

## Entrepreneurship Is a Life Skill

# 1

# Practicing Entrepreneurship

"The best way to predict the future is to create it."

—Peter Drucker

# Chapter Outline

# Learning Objectives

1.1    Explain the importance of action and practice in entrepreneurship.

1.2    List the seven lesser-known truths about entrepreneurship.

1.3    Compare and contrast the different forms of entrepreneurship in practice today.

1.4    Distinguish between entrepreneurship as a method and as a process.

1.5    Compare and contrast the prediction and creation approaches to entrepreneurship.

1.6    Illustrate the key components of the Entrepreneurship Method.

1.7    Assess the role of deliberate practice in achieving mastery.

1.8    Propose different ways in which this book can help you practice entrepreneurship.

There's no doubt that we are living in unpredictable times: High schools and colleges are struggling to keep up with the ever-changing job market; underemployment rates are skyrocketing, especially among younger people; those halfway through their careers are asking what else is possible; mature workers are wondering what comes next; and seniors are postponing their retirement to stay relevant. The traditional concept of staying in one job for your entire working life is a thing of the past, especially when people are being asked to reinvent themselves every 5 years. In a world full of uncertainty, rapid change is the only constant.

Although the future of the traditional workplace may be unclear, the climate is ripe for entrepreneurship. Traditionally, entrepreneurship has been associated with launching new businesses. However, many individuals and institutions are beginning to think of entrepreneurship as a vital life skill that extends far beyond the ability to launch a venture, a life skill that prepares individuals to deal with an ambiguous and uncertain future. In other words, you don't need to build your own company to think and act like an entrepreneur! Entrepreneurship embodies methods for thinking, acting, identifying opportunities, and approaching problems that enable people to manage change, adjust to new conditions, and take control of actualizing personal goals, aspirations, and even dreams. It's also a vehicle for developing a set of skills—financial, social, communication, marketing, problem solving, and creative thinking, to name a few—that are applicable across many fields. Taken together, these are mindsets and skillsets that not only enable you to start a venture, but will also distinguish you in a variety of traditional and nontraditional life paths. To be entrepreneurial is to be empowered to create and act on opportunities of all kinds for yourself.

## 1.1 ENTREPRENEURSHIP REQUIRES ACTION AND PRACTICE

>> LO 1.1  **Explain the importance of action and practice in entrepreneurship.**

Entrepreneurship is a way of thinking, acting, and being that combines the ability to find or create new opportunities with the courage to act on them.

The pursuits of entrepreneurs have touched every corner of our lives, affecting every aspect of the way we live—from electricity, to music, to transport, to agriculture, to manufacturing, to technology, and many more. Although it can be difficult to see

**Entrepreneurship:** a way of thinking, acting, and being that combines the ability to find or create new opportunities with the courage to act on them.

Master the content at **edge.sagepub.com/ neckentrepreneurship2e**

**The first automatic dishwasher, invented by Josephine Cochrane**

entrepreneurial possibilities in the midst of unemployment, economic recession, war, and natural disasters, it is this sort of turbulence that often pushes us into creating new opportunities for economic progress. History shows us that in spite of the obstacles in their paths, all kinds of entrepreneurs have consistently taken action to change the world. For instance, Benjamin Franklin successfully invented the lightning rod (1749); George Crum created the potato chip (1853); and Josephine Cochrane invented the first automatic dishwasher (1893). This text is about creating the next page of history. It's time to bring the voices of today's entrepreneurs into the conversation. It's also time to bring *your* voice into the conversation. What kind of entrepreneur do you want to be?

# 1.2 ENTREPRENEURSHIP MAY BE DIFFERENT FROM WHAT YOU THINK

>> **LO 1.2**   **List the seven lesser-known truths about entrepreneurship.**

Our belief is that by taking action and putting ideas into practice, everyone "has what it takes" to be an entrepreneur. However, this is not necessarily the same message that is delivered by popular media. Let's examine some popular images of entrepreneurs. What is the truth behind these images?

## Media Images of Entrepreneurs

The media often exaggerate the meteoric rise of "overnight global sensations" such as Bill Gates (Microsoft), Steve Jobs (Apple), Mark Zuckerberg (Facebook), Elon Musk (Tesla), Jack Ma (Alibaba), Oprah Winfrey (Harpo Group), and Travis Kalanick (Uber). The likes of Bill Gates and his peers are certainly inspirational, but we would argue that few can personally identify with the stories surrounding them, and they do little to represent the reality of entrepreneurship.

The truth is there is no such thing as an overnight success.

## Debunking the Myths of Entrepreneurship

Rather than focusing on the myth of the overnight success story, let's take a look at some truths, illustrated in Table 1.1. Separating truth from fiction can be difficult, especially when some of these truths collide with the stories we read about in the media. Let's explore these truths in more detail to further understand how entrepreneurship can be a path for many.

**TABLE 1.1**

The Truths About Entrepreneurship

| | |
|---|---|
| Truth 1 | Entrepreneurship is not reserved for startups. |
| Truth 2 | Entrepreneurs do not have a special set of personality traits. |
| Truth 3 | Entrepreneurship can be taught (it's a method that requires practice). |
| Truth 4 | Entrepreneurs are not extreme risk takers. |
| Truth 5 | Entrepreneurs collaborate more than they compete. |
| Truth 6 | Entrepreneurs act more than they plan. |
| Truth 7 | Entrepreneurship is a life skill. |

## ENTREPRENEURSHIP IN ACTION

# Juan Giraldo, Waku

Photo Courtesy of Juan Giraldo

**Juan Giraldo, founder of Waku**

Entrepreneurs are seeing many opportunities in the market for health drinks: no sugar, low sugar, vitamin-infused waters, carbonated, not carbonated, healthy teas, fermented teas, drinkable yogurt, cold brew coffees, smoothies—it seems that we are all craving tasty yet healthy replacements for soda. Dozens of new beverages have emerged in the marketplace to satisfy the latest health trends, serving consumers' needs to feed mind, body, and spirit. We are in the midst of a generational shift that has created an industry with exponential growth. Take kombucha tea, for instance: This fermented tea, which is claimed to provide significant health benefits, is expected to be a $5 billion industry by 2025.

Juan Giraldo, an Ecuador-born entrepreneur, has been capitalizing on these trends with his company, Waku. Waku produces and sells wellness teas made with 20 super herbs from the Andes Mountains. They compete directly with kombucha-style drinks, but, Juan claims, "Waku tastes much better." Traditional kombucha is a lightly fermented beverage that boasts great health benefits derived from various probiotics. "Waku's wellness teas are also delicious and nutritious, but the health benefits stem from the medicinal benefits of the herbs used in the ingredients. The drinks are not fermented and are excellent for one's digestive system."

Juan has been an entrepreneur since he was 19 years old. His first company was an advertising firm that he sold to his business partner, and his next venture was an online fashion

outlet, which went bankrupt within 18 months. After that, he became CEO of a small IT consulting firm before founding Waku. The idea for Waku arose when Juan and his friend, Nicolas Estrella, exchanged fond memories of the "wellness tea" they used to drink in their homeland of Ecuador. After both moved to Boston, they decided to produce their own version of this beverage and sell it in the Boston area. The initial production of the tea helped support the businesses of approximately six independent Andes farmers who grew the medicinal herbs and flowers used to produce the product. What exactly is Waku? It is a filtered water brew blend of 20 herbs and flowers. The name comes from the Quechua word *wanku* (together), which represents the combining of the ingredients as well as the team effort that goes into the production of the product.

Juan's first step was to travel to Ecuador to source the right ingredients in order to test his concept. Back in the United States, the Waku team began developing prototypes. At the same time he was developing Waku, Juan was also earning his MBA at Babson College. Thinking that millennials were his target market, he felt surrounded by his potential customers and used them as resources. Juan would buy rival tea products and conduct countless taste tests to compare his Waku recipes to the competition. By developing early prototypes and conducting taste tests, he was able to interact with potential customers and get valuable feedback. Juan quickly learned that his target customers were not millennials who were well educated and well traveled, but women between the ages of 40 and 60 who wanted to live a healthier lifestyle.

The early growth of Waku created supply challenges. As the company grew from shipping one pallet of ingredients from Ecuador to ordering one full container (11 pallets) a month, Waku altered its strategy for paying its suppliers. Originally, Juan was expected to pay for all ingredients at the time of purchase, but that required a lot of cash up front. At the same time, Waku needed the ingredients from its suppliers to effectively meet forecasted demand. To find a solution, Juan traveled to Ecuador to work out a deal with the suppliers. After building trust with his suppliers, he proposed that they give Waku 180 days of credit to pay for ingredients. This would allow Waku the time to get the ingredients, produce the teas, sell the teas, and then pay its suppliers. As Juan explains, "At first the suppliers were hesitant, but after I showed them Waku's plans for payment and how important the suppliers were to the brand, they agreed."

With $200,000 in annual revenues, Juan believes the product has the potential to be a legitimate contender for market share as the business grows. Although Juan is certainly concerned with profits, that is not his only motive. His business offers beverages that he grew up with, and

*(Continued)*

(Continued)

he truly believes in the brand because of how much it hits home. "I want to provide opportunities for the people back in Ecuador. Producing top-quality ingredients is what we are known for in the rural parts of my country." Today, Waku has four full-time employees, an intern, and a strategic consultant. It also provides steady, reliable business to many farmers throughout rural Ecuador. As Waku continues to grow, many people in Ecuador will reap the benefits through an influx of capital and job creation.

Although he has been an entrepreneur for a long time, Juan admits that he didn't know much about the healthy beverage sector and needed a lot of advice. "I sent out emails to the top competitors in the industry, simply asking for advice. And many were more than willing to offer it!" Juan recalled. His advice to other entrepreneurs? "Don't be shy to ask for help. Mentors can have huge impacts on your performance. Reach out to the superstars in your industry.

You will be amazed how many people will want to help a young entrepreneur who has the burning desire to succeed."

### Critical Thinking Questions

1.   What differentiates Waku from other health beverages on the market today?

2.   Why was Juan able to approach his suppliers with the request he made regarding payment?

3.   Does Waku have a responsibility to the region of the world in which it sources its ingredients and finds its inspiration? ●

**Sources:**

Juan Giraldo (interview with author, October 22, 2018).
https://www.grandviewresearch.com/press-release/global-kombucha-market
https://livewaku.com/
https://www.bostonglobe.com/lifestyle/food-dining/2018/10/15/waku-well-ness-tea-with-roots-ecuador/23cPv5lwSkwLrkdhcNSrnN/story.html

## Truth 1: Entrepreneurship Is Not Reserved for Startups

The term *startup* came into vogue during the 1990s dot-com bubble, when a plethora of web-based companies were born. The term has various meanings, but we subscribe to Steve Blank's definition of **startup**: a temporary organization in search of a scalable business model.[1] In the traditional view of startups, anyone who starts a business is called an entrepreneur. The entrepreneur creates a business based on research to assess the validity of an idea or business model. The business may be partially funded by seed money from family members or investors, but usually the majority is funded by the entrepreneurs themselves.

**Startup:** a temporary organization in search of a scalable business model.

If the business is successful, the startup does not remain a startup. It can develop into its own formal organization, be merged with another organization, or be bought by another company. This traditional view of the startup, however, is not the only path for entrepreneurs. The truth is that entrepreneurs are everywhere, from corporations to franchises, to for-profit and nonprofit organizations, to family enterprises. We will explore these different types of entrepreneurs in more detail later in the chapter.

## Truth 2: Entrepreneurs Do Not Have a Special Set of Personality Traits

There is no evidence to suggest that entrepreneurs have a special set of personality characteristics that distinguishes them from the rest of us.

Early research identified four main traits that are ascribed to entrepreneurs: a need for achievement, an innate sense of having the ability to influence events, a tendency to take risks, and a tolerance for ambiguity. Yet there is no scientific evidence to confirm whether these traits are a result of nature or nurture or any proven patterns in the behavior of entrepreneurs versus nonentrepreneurs.[2] Academics researching traits of entrepreneurs seem to have a prevailing fascination with defining "who" the entrepreneur is, rather than what he or she does.

However, over the last couple of decades, researchers have moved away from the traits perspective in favor of examining how entrepreneurs think and act and have discovered that there are patterns in how entrepreneurs think. This means we can change how we think and that all of us have the ability to act and think entrepreneurially with practice.

In particular, the work of researcher Saras Sarasvathy has added a new understanding of the entrepreneurial mindset. Through a study involving serial entrepreneurs—entrepreneurs who start several businesses, either simultaneously or consecutively—Sarasvathy discovered patterns of thinking and developed a theory she calls **effectuation**, which is the idea that the future is unpredictable yet controllable. Entrepreneurs create and obtain control by taking actions to learn, collecting information, and reducing risk and uncertainty, and they are able to take action with resources that are available at a particular point in time.[3] In other words, it's about starting small with what you have, rather than what you think

**Effectuation theory:** an entrepreneurial approach to taking quick action using resources you have available to get early traction on new ideas.

you need. As the entrepreneur starts, very small actions lead to other actions and new resources. See Research at Work for more on effectuation theory.

Sarasvathy believes that effectual entrepreneurs focus on creating a future rather than predicting it. This means they create new opportunities, make markets rather than find them, accept and learn from failure, and build relationships with a variety of stakeholders. Effectual entrepreneurs use their own initiative and resources to fulfill their vision of the future.

We strongly believe that the mindset is the precursor to action. To us, it makes sense that if entrepreneurs are in the right frame of mind, there is greater confidence, intentionality, and vision to bring ideas from the whiteboard to the real world. We are not born with an entrepreneurial mindset; we have to work to develop it. As a result, and because it's so important, we devote a whole chapter to it (see Chapter 2).

## Truth 3: Entrepreneurship Can Be Taught (It's a Method That Requires Practice)

Because so many people tend to believe that "entrepreneurs are born and not made," those same people question whether entrepreneurship can be taught. If it were true that entrepreneurs have a certain set of innate personality traits, then entrepreneurship could not be taught. But, remember, there is no proven set of traits. What has been proven, instead, is that entrepreneurs exhibit common patterns in how they think, and our thinking can be changed and altered.[4] As a result, entrepreneurship can be taught. Furthermore, it's being taught everywhere around the globe. It would be difficult to find a college or university not offering at least one entrepreneurship course today (see Figure 1.1). Many of these courses teach entrepreneurship as a linear process, which involves identifying an opportunity, understanding resource requirements, acquiring resources, planning, implementing, and harvesting (exiting a business).[5] But the word *process* assumes known inputs and known outputs—a process is quite predictable.

Entrepreneurship is not predictable and, therefore, cannot adequately be taught as a process. Instead, approaching entrepreneurship as a method, as advocated in this text, results in a body of skills that—when developed through practice over time—constitute a toolkit for entrepreneurial action.[6] The entrepreneurial method requires consistent practice so that knowledge and expertise can be continuously developed and applied to future endeavors. More on this a bit later in the chapter!

## Truth 4: Entrepreneurs Are Not Extreme Risk Takers

Contrary to the stereotype that entrepreneurs like to gamble when the stakes are high, there is no evidence to suggest that entrepreneurs take more risks than anyone else. In fact, entrepreneurs with gambling tendencies are usually not successful, simply because they are leaving too much to chance.[7] Risk is very personal and relative. Things always seem more risky from the outside looking in because we really don't know what calculations were made to take the first step, then the second, then the third, and so on. In fact, most entrepreneurs are very calculated risk takers and gauge what they are willing to lose with every step taken. They practice a cycle of act-learn-build that encourages taking small actions in order to learn and build that learning into the next action (see Figure 1.2).[8] Entrepreneurship should never be a zero-sum game; it's never an all-or-nothing decision. It's not about ascending the summit of Mount Everest without ropes or oxygen. It just looks that way from the outside!

**Steve Jobs and Bill Gates collaborated on the Apple Mac despite being fierce competitors.**

## Truth 5: Entrepreneurs Collaborate More Than They Compete

Community and networking play important roles in entrepreneurship. No entrepreneur is an island and building strong connections with others is key to business success. Networking is so important to entrepreneurship that we have devoted an entire chapter

**FIGURE 1.1**

## Millennials—A Highly Educated and Entrepreneurial Generation

### Change in the Percentage of 25- to 29-Year-Olds With Selected Levels of Educational Attainment, 2007–2013

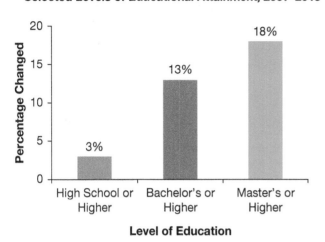

### Entrepreneurship Courses Offered

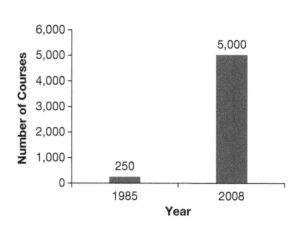

### Business School Alumni Who Began Businesses After Graduation

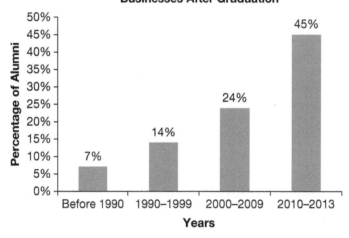

**FIGURE 1.2**

## Act-Learn-Build

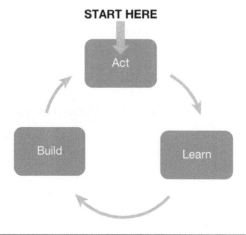

to it (see Chapter 8). Entrepreneurs draw on shared experiences and desire to learn from others facing similar challenges. It can be hard to know what entrepreneurship is all about until you are actually in the throes of it, so it becomes very important to have a support group of like-minded entrepreneurs willing to help one another out with a "pay it forward" attitude—collaborating for the greater good.[9]

Not only do successful entrepreneurs collaborate with other entrepreneurs, they also collaborate with their target customers to test new ideas, potential investors to build trust, and family and friends for support. In fact, recent studies have shown that collaboration and information sharing are more important in entrepreneurship than skills like determination or opportunity recognition.[10]

### Truth 6: Entrepreneurs Act More Than They Plan

Does every entrepreneur need a business plan to succeed? Not necessarily. Research revealed that fewer than half of Inc. 500 founders wrote formal business plans prior to launching their companies, and nearly 30% had only basic plans.[11] So, how did they do it? They acted: They went out and talked to other people, connected with their customers, generated buzz about their product or service, and built a strong network. With every action, they collected real data that informed the next step. In short, they each practiced being an entrepreneur.

Today's investors want to know what the entrepreneur has done, milestones met, action completed, customers sold, and overall traction. Planning and research is important but the creation of a formal business plan is not. Spending too much time writing a business plan means you are not spending enough time taking action on your idea in order to really learn whether it can work.

### Truth 7: Entrepreneurship Is a Life Skill

As we discussed in the introduction to this chapter, traditionally, entrepreneurship has been associated mostly with launching new businesses. However, these days, the meaning of entrepreneurship has transcended into something more than just the ability to begin a new business. Many individuals and institutions perceive entrepreneurship as

---

## Tell Me Your Story

Every entrepreneur has a story. What beliefs and expectations do you have about entrepreneurs' stories? To what extent do you think they conform to media images of entrepreneurs? In what ways might you expect them to be different? Here is an activity to help you examine your beliefs and expectations.

Find and introduce yourself to an entrepreneur—any type of entrepreneur is fine. Ask for 20 minutes of his or her time, and simply start with the opening question: *Tell me the story of how you became an entrepreneur.*

As the story unfolds, you may want to ask other questions, such as

> *What worried you the most as you started the venture?*
>
> *What excited you most about starting the venture?*
>
> *What resources did you use to start? Where did they come from?*

> *What moments do you remember most?*
>
> *Who helped you most along the way?*
>
> *How do you describe yourself to others?*
>
> *What advice do you have for me as a student of entrepreneurship?*

After having this 20-minute conversation, reflect on the beliefs and expectations you started with and answer the Critical Thinking Questions.

### Critical Thinking Questions

1. In what ways did your chosen entrepreneur confirm your beliefs and expectations?

2. In what ways did the story motivate you (or not)?

3. What did you learn that was most unexpected?

a life skill that helps people to deal with an uncertain future by providing them with the methods to think, act, identify opportunities, approach problems in a specific way, adapt to new conditions, and take control of personal goals and ambitions. It also provides people with a set of skills that can be applied to many other fields. Being entrepreneurial empowers us to create opportunities and reach our goals.[12] Remember the definition of entrepreneurship: a way of thinking, acting, and being that combines the ability to find or create new opportunities with the courage to act on them.

Now that we have separated the truths from the myths, it is time to create a new narrative. Our economic future depends on entrepreneurs, and the traditional, narrow definition has stifled what it really means to be an entrepreneur. But to create a new story, we need to know more about the different types of entrepreneurs in the workplace today.

# 1.3 TYPES OF ENTREPRENEURSHIP

>> **LO 1.3**   **Compare and contrast the different forms of entrepreneurship in practice today.**

Now that we have explored the truths about entrepreneurship, let's take a look at the types of entrepreneurship that are most commonly in practice today.

## Corporate Entrepreneurship

**Corporate entrepreneurship (or intrapreneurship):** a process of creating new products, ventures, processes, or renewal within large organizations.

Corporate entrepreneurship (also known as intrapreneurship) is a process of creating new products, ventures, processes, or renewal within large corporations.[13] It is typically carried out by employees working in units separate from the mainstream areas of the corporation who create and test innovations that are then assimilated into the broader corporation.

Corporate entrepreneurs tend to explore new possibilities and seek ways in which the organization's current structure and process can enable innovation. Similar to external entrepreneurs, corporate entrepreneurs identify opportunities, build teams, and create something of value in order to enhance competitive position and organizational profitability. Deloitte-owned design consultancy Market Gravity, based in the United Kingdom, celebrates the achievement of corporate entrepreneurs by holding an annual Corporate Entrepreneur Awards (CAE) ceremony.[14] Categories include awards for those who dare to "throw out the rule book" to achieve their goals; those with a proven concept who have succeeded in making their goals a reality; and those who have turned an idea into something groundbreaking. Past winners for corporate entrepreneurship have included employees from LEGO, Reebok, and Xerox.

© Helen H. Richardson/Contributor/Getty Images

**LEGO is an example of a company that embraces entrepreneurship.**

Corporations like Google, Apple, Virgin, and Zappos are also known for encouraging an entrepreneurial spirit. However, not all corporations are as enthusiastic about employees acting entrepreneurially inside the company. Some companies fear that if employees are encouraged to be more entrepreneurial, they will leave the company and start their own business. This is really an outdated view, though. Most corporations realize that they no longer have long-term employees.

## Entrepreneurship Inside

**Entrepreneurs inside:** entrepreneurs who think and act entrepreneurially within organizations.

Entrepreneurs inside are employees who think and act entrepreneurially within different types of organizations. Although this sounds similar to corporate entrepreneurs (employees who work for large corporations), there is an important difference: Entrepreneurs inside can exist and function in any type of organization, big or small, including government agencies, nonprofits, religious entities, self-organizing entities, and cooperatives.[15] These types of entrepreneurs often need inside support from senior managers or other team members for their initiatives, which can be difficult if those people tend to resist new ideas or are keen to simply "stick to the company brief" rather than push boundaries. Building a tribe of willing supporters is essential for getting buy-in to their ideas and proving there is a market for them.

The headquarters of MITRE in McLean, Virginia

What inside entrepreneurs have in common with other entrepreneurs is the desire to create something of value, be it a groundbreaking initiative or a new department, product, service, or process. When this happens, there is very little separation between who they are and what they do. Peter Modigliani is a defense department acquisition analyst at Massachusetts-based MITRE, a not-for-profit organization that provides guidance to the federal government. He breaks the traditional boundaries set by the chain of command by liaising with people inside and outside the organization to generate different perspectives. He says, "The more you can regularly connect with folks from other divisions, skillsets, and customers, the increased chances someone can offer you a fresh perspective or connection."[16]

## Franchising

A **franchise** is a type of license purchased by an individual (franchisee) from an existing business (franchisor) that allows the franchisee to trade under the name of that business.[17] In this type of entrepreneurship, both the franchisor (the founder of the original business) and the franchisee are entrepreneurs. Franchising can be a beneficial way for entrepreneurs to get a head start in launching their own businesses, as they do not have to spend the same amount of time on marketing, building the brand, developing processes, and sourcing product.

A 7-Eleven franchise location

A franchise is often referred to as a "turnkey operation." In other words, the franchisee turns the key to open the door and is ready for business. A franchisee not only pays the franchisor a lump sum to buy the franchise but also has to pay **royalties**, which are calculated as a percentage of monthly sales revenue. According to results of *Entrepreneur* magazine's annual Franchise 500, announced in 2017, 7-Eleven, McDonald's, Dunkin' Donuts, and the UPS Store are among the most popular franchises in the United States.[18] Today there are more than 740,000 franchise establishments in the United States. Table 1.2 describes the pros and cons of owning a franchise.[19]

**Franchise:** a type of license purchased by a franchisee from an existing business called a franchisor to allow them to trade under the name of that business.

**Royalties:** a share of the income of a business paid by a franchisee to the franchisor.

## Buying a Small Business

Buying a small business is another way to enter the world of entrepreneurship. In this arrangement, the entrepreneur is buying out the existing owner(s) and taking over operations. For some entrepreneurs this is a less risky approach than starting from scratch.[20] Chris Cranston was the owner of FlowDog, a canine aquatic and rehabilitation center outside of Boston. In 2009 she bought the business, which was called Aquadog at the time, from the previous owner. Cranston changed the name but subsumed a loyal customer base, pool equipment, location, some employees, and a favorable lease. In Cranston's words, "Starting from a blank slate was too overwhelming for me. I needed something that I could build upon. That I could handle!"[21] And handle it she has. FlowDog grew an average of 20% each year between 2009 and 2018, when Chris sold it to a large animal hospital in Boston.

**TABLE 1.2**

Pros and Cons of Owning a Franchise

| PROS | CONS |
|---|---|
| Ready-made business systems to help the franchise to become operational right away. | Franchise fee to be paid upfront. |
| Formal training program (online modules, formal training class) after franchise agreement signed. | Royalties (percentage of sales) to be paid to franchisor every month. |
| Technology designed to help manage customers and administrative processes. | Strict franchisors' rules with no wiggle room. |
| Marketing/advertising already in place to help launch your franchise. | Requirement to pay a percentage of gross sales into the franchisor's marketing fund. |
| Excellent support systems (in-house personnel, field reps, etc.). | Most products and supplies need to be purchased from the franchisor. |
| Real estate resources to help source best location for franchise. | Sale of franchise requires approval from the franchisor. |
| A whole franchisee network to reach out to for help and advice. | Potential competition from other franchisees in the network. |

**Source:** Based on material in Libava, J. (2015, February 16). The pros and cons of owning a franchise. *Entrepreneur.* Retrieved from https://www.entrepreneur.com/article/242848. Originally appeared at http://www.thefranchiseking .com/franchise-ownership-pros-cons

## Social Entrepreneurship

Since the beginning of the 21st century, social entrepreneurship has become a global movement, with thousands of initiatives launched every year to improve social problems such as water shortages, lack of education, poverty, and global warming.

There has been considerable debate as to how to define social entrepreneurship. Some argue that all types of entrepreneurship are social, while others define it as purely an activity of the nonprofit sector. These blurred lines imply that entrepreneurs are forced to choose between making a social or an economic impact. We contend that social entrepreneurs can do both. It is possible to address a social issue and make a profit—keeping a company economically stable ensures its capability to consistently meet the needs of its customers without relying on fundraising or other methods to keep it afloat.[22] We therefore define social entrepreneurship as the process of sourcing innovative solutions to social and environmental problems.[23]

A subcategory of social entrepreneurship is the benefit corporation, or B Corp. This is a form of organization certified by the nonprofit B Lab that ensures that strict standards of social and environmental performance, accountability, and transparency are met.[24] The voluntary certification is designed for for-profit companies aiming to achieve social goals alongside business ones. To be certified as a B Corp, the organization is rated on how its employees are treated, its impact on the environment, and how it benefits the community in which it operates.[25] B Corp certification ensures that the for-profit company fulfills its social mission, and the certification protects it from lawsuits from stakeholders that may claim that the company is spending more time or resources on social issues rather than maximizing profit.

B Corp members include Betterworld Books, which donates a book to someone in need every time a book is purchased; Revolution Foods, which provides affordable, freshly prepared meals to school children from low-income households; and the UK-based Toast Ale, which is tackling food waste by making beer from leftover bread from bakeries and supermarkets that would otherwise have been thrown away.[26]

**Social entrepreneurship:** the process of sourcing innovative solutions to social and environmental problems.

**Benefit corporation (or B Corp):** a form of organization certified by the nonprofit B Lab that ensures strict standards of social and environmental performance, accountability, and transparency are met.

## Family Enterprising

A family enterprise is a business that is owned and managed by multiple family members, typically for more than one generation. What makes family enterprising part of the portfolio of entrepreneurship types is that each generation has an opportunity to bring the organization forward in new, innovative ways.[27] Family-owned businesses are hugely important for the U.S. economy and account for 60% of employment, 78% of new jobs, and 65% of total wages (see Figure 1.3).[28]

An entrepreneurial agenda to move the family business forward is essential to business survival, as demonstrated by their low survival rate: For instance, approximately 70% of family businesses fail or are sold before the second generation reaches a position to take over.[29]

Many leading organizations that are family businesses are generally considered to be more stable, not only because of their history and experience, but because of their ability to take a long-term view, which inspires commitment and loyalty from their employees. Yet a long-term view that becomes stagnant is detrimental and can lead the company into a downward spiral.

Widely known businesses such as Walmart in the United States, auto company Volkswagen in Germany, and health care company Roche in Switzerland are all long-standing family businesses that continue to go from strength to strength. To continue their cycle of growth and continuity, family members must pass on their entrepreneurial mindsets as well as their business ethos. It is this mindset that ensures the survival of the family business for many years to come.

**Family enterprise:** a business that is owned and managed by multiple family members, typically for more than one generation.

## Serial Entrepreneurship

Serial entrepreneurs, also known as habitual entrepreneurs, are people who start several businesses, either simultaneously or consecutively. Not satisfied with just focusing on one business, serial entrepreneurs are constantly looking out for the next big thing or

**Serial entrepreneurs (or habitual entrepreneurs):** entrepreneurs who start several businesses, either simultaneously or consecutively.

**FIGURE 1.3**

**Percentage of Family-Owned Businesses**

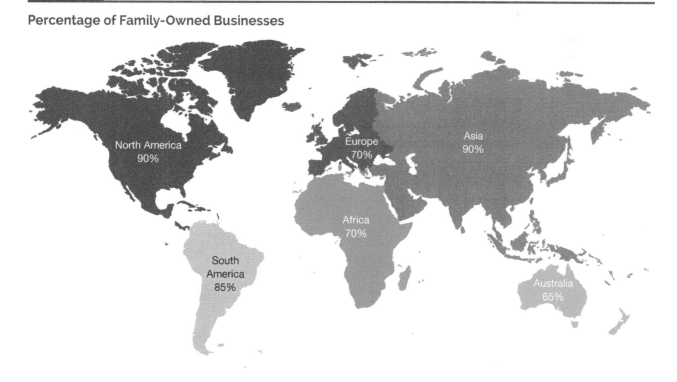

North America 90%

Europe 70%

Asia 90%

Africa 70%

South America 85%

Australia 65%

**Natalie Campbell, founder of Morgan de Toi and cofounder of A Very Good Company**

exploring ways to implement their diverse range of ideas. Natalie Campbell is a good example of a serial entrepreneur. While at university, she started her first venture running a franchise of fashion chain Morgan de Toi before going on to cofound social innovation agency A Very Good Company.[30]

# 1.4 ENTREPRENEURSHIP IS A METHOD, NOT A PROCESS

>> **LO 1.4   Distinguish between entrepreneurship as a method and as a process.**

A method is a systematic way of approaching a task, whereas a process is a series of steps taken to achieve a particular end. Traditionally, entrepreneurship has been viewed as a process of sequential steps that lead to a successful business (as in Table 1.3).

The process approach to entrepreneurship emphasizes planning and prediction—from firm creation right up until firm exit. It suggests that if you follow the 10 steps correctly, your new venture is more likely to succeed and that if you use proven business models, your risk of failure is reduced. There is no doubt that such a process works for larger organizations and corporations—but entrepreneurial ventures are not just smaller versions of large corporations.[31] The 10-step process isn't enough for entrepreneurial ventures. Why? Because it relies too much on history to predict the future, and a new venture with a new innovation does not have any history to draw from. And, simply stated, there are no steps or rules; it's just not that clean!

Entrepreneurship is nonlinear and unpredictable; it is ill-defined, unstructured, and complex. In fact, some statistics show that more than 50% of startups fail after 5 years of business.[32] There are several reasons for the extraordinary failure rate, such as lack of entrepreneurship education and not developing the ability to work through the messiness, accept ambiguity, and take action even when you are not really sure what to do. The interesting side of failure is that research has shown that if entrepreneurs who have failed

---

**TABLE 1.3**

The Entrepreneurship Process: An Outdated View

| Step 1 | Think of a product or service to sell |
|--------|----------------------------------------|
| Step 2 | Do market research |
| Step 3 | Get some financial projections |
| Step 4 | Find a partner/team |
| Step 5 | Write a business plan |
| Step 6 | Get financing |
| Step 7 | Find space, build a prototype, hire people |
| Step 8 | Bring your product/service to market |
| Step 9 | Manage the business |
| Step 10 | Plan an exit |

try again, they are far more likely to be successful in their second venture—even if the second venture is completely different from the first. The point of these statistics is not to scare you but to show you how unpredictable, complex, and chaotic entrepreneurship can be. The environment for entrepreneurship is fluid, dynamic, uncertain, and ambiguous. Doesn't it make sense that the way we learn entrepreneurship needs to help us manage such "craziness"? The good news is there is a way to manage the chaos and craziness, and we call this the Entrepreneurship Method. Viewing entrepreneurship as a method does not guarantee success or a fixed outcome, but it does help guide you through the craziness of entrepreneurship and increase your chances of success. Table 1.4 illustrates some key points about the Entrepreneurship Method.[33]

From this we can see that entrepreneurship is less an aptitude than it is a practice and mindset, and realizing that entrepreneurship is more of a method than a process is the first step in this journey we call entrepreneurship. Viewing entrepreneurship as a method caters to its uncertain and unpredictable nature. It represents a body of skills that together comprise a toolkit for entrepreneurial action.[34] Table 1.5 summarizes the differences between entrepreneurship as a method and entrepreneurship as a process.

Approaching entrepreneurship as a method gives us comfort and direction, but it is not a recipe. Part of the Method is learning and practicing as you go and consciously reflecting on events as and when they take place. Part of the Method is iterative. The entire Method, however, is action based and, of course, requires practice.

## TABLE 1.4

Assumptions Underlying the Entrepreneurship Method

| |
|---|
| It applies to novices and experts regardless of experience levels. |
| It is inclusive, which means it works for any organization at any stage of business. |
| It requires continuous practice with a focus on doing in order to learn. |
| It is designed for an unpredictable environment. |
| It changes how we think and act in ambiguous situations. |
| It helps you get unstuck when you are trying to start something new. |

**Source:** Adapted from Neck, H. M., & Greene, P. G. (2011). Entrepreneurship education: Known worlds and new frontiers. *Journal of Small Business Management, 49*(1), 55–70. Reprinted with permission from John Wiley & Sons.

## TABLE 1.5

Method Versus Process

| ENTREPRENEURSHIP AS A METHOD | ENTREPRENEURSHIP AS A PROCESS |
|---|---|
| A set of practices | Known inputs and predicted outputs |
| Phases of learning | Steps to complete |
| Iterative | Linear |
| Creative | Predictive |
| Action focus | Planning focus |
| Investment for learning | Expected return |
| Collaborative | Competitive |

**Source:** Neck, H. M., Greene, P. G., & Brush, C. (2014). *Teaching entrepreneurship: A practice-based approach.* Northampton, MA: Edward Elgar.

# 1.5 THE METHOD INVOLVES CREATING THE FUTURE, NOT PREDICTING IT

> **>> LO 1.5** **Compare and contrast the prediction and creation approaches to entrepreneurship.**

Earlier, we examined the truths behind some common images of entrepreneurs. As we just discussed, entrepreneurship is no longer about a path of starting and growing a venture using a linear, step-by-step process. Instead, it is a much messier, ongoing method of creating opportunities, taking smart action, learning and iterating, and using a portfolio of skills to navigate an ever-changing world.

The skills and mindset presented in this book are essential to the Entrepreneurship Method. There is no magic formula for success, but if you develop the skills and mindset, you will learn to work smarter and faster and be able to make decisions based on reality instead of guesses. As we will repeat many times throughout this book, entrepreneurship is a method that requires practice, and action trumps everything. The Method starts with the mindset. Even though our next chapter is devoted to the entrepreneurial mindset, let's do a quick lesson now on entrepreneurial thinking.

This chapter's Entrepreneurship in Action feature describes how Juan Giraldo, founder of Waku, created opportunities and took action to get his venture off the ground. How can Giraldo predict that his wellness tea business is going to succeed? The truth is, he can't; his focus is on creating a future rather than predicting it. But, by creating what he wants and what he believes his customers need, he's in control.

## Managerial Versus Entrepreneurial Thinking

Entrepreneurial ventures are not smaller versions of large corporations. Take this a little further and think about this: Managers lead corporations but entrepreneurs lead startups. Leading in a corporate environment is very different from leading a startup environment. Why? Because there is a lot more uncertainty and risk in the startup environments *and* a lot less information and data.

Managerial thinking works best in times of certainty and when there is access to information and data on which to base decisions. Managerial thinking is the dominant logic of large, established organizations, where goals are predetermined, issues are transparent, and information is reliable and accessible. Under these circumstances, it is relatively straightforward to analyze a situation, define problems and opportunities, and diagnose and find solutions. Big organizations can use sophisticated planning tools to analyze past and present data in order to predict any shifts in the business landscape. Yet this process is by no means foolproof, as demonstrated by many well-planned initiatives backed by large companies that do not succeed. Those same companies want to be more entrepreneurial.

An early entrepreneurial venture is unlikely to have access to sophisticated predictive tools, nor does it have access to the data.[35]

A simple dinner party example can quickly illustrate the difference between entrepreneurial and managerial thinking. If you are throwing a dinner party for a group of friends, you might choose a recipe or draw up a menu, buy the ingredients, and cook the meal according to a set of instructions provided to you in the cookbook. Here you are approaching the dinner party as a manager. In contrast, you might invite some friends over and ask each person to bring one ingredient but not tell them what to bring. Let's say 10 people show up and the ingredients are French bread, fresh pasta, potatoes, spinach, a few different types of cheeses, steak, salmon, romaine lettuce, avocado, and kale. These ingredients plus the ingredients you already have in your kitchen are what you have to cook with. Now, the group must come together, use the ingredients, and create dinner! This is an example of entrepreneurial thinking—creating something without a concrete set of instructions. Though the two ways of thinking—managerial and entrepreneurial— seem polar opposites, the goal is the same: to cook a meal for your group of friends. It's how you approach the challenge and with what resources that is different.

In reality, entrepreneurs should and do employ both ways of thinking, but, in general, most of us possess the managerial skills depicted in Table 1.6. This is not surprising;

**TABLE 1.6**

Managerial Versus Entrepreneurial Thinking

| MANAGERIAL | ENTREPRENEURIAL |
|---|---|
| Big planning | Small actions |
| Wait until you get what you need | Start with what you have |
| Expected return | Acceptable loss |
| Linear | Iterative |
| Optimization | Experimentation |
| Avoid failure at all costs | Embrace and leverage failure |
| Competitive | Collaborative |
| Knowable | Unknowable |
| Plan to act | Act to learn |

**Source:** Sarasvathy, S. D. (2008). *Effectuation: Elements of entrepreneurial expertise.* Cheltenham, UK and Northampton, MA: Edward Elgar: Schlesinger, L., Kiefer, C., & Brown, P. (2012). *Just start: Take action, embrace uncertainty, create the future.* Cambridge, MA: Harvard Business School Press. http://www.e-elgar.com/

the fact is we have been honing these skills for years throughout primary school, then secondary, and now college. We actually did think more entrepreneurially when we were babies—a time when everything around us was a mystery and uncertain. The only way we learned as a baby was by trial and error. Traditional education, the need to find the correct answer, and the constant need for measurement and assessment have inhibited our entrepreneurial nature. So if you ever feel like you can't get unstuck and you're not really sure how to solve a problem, just remember that we were all born with the ability to think and act entrepreneurially. As social entrepreneur and Nobel Prize winner Muhammad Yunus says,

> We are all entrepreneurs. When we were in the caves we were all self-employed . . . finding our food, feeding ourselves. That's where the human history began. . . . As civilization came we suppressed it, and made into labor. . . . Because you stamped us, we are labor. We forgot that we are all entrepreneurs.[36]

Although managerial thinking has its advantages and is necessary, it is not enough in today's uncertain, complex, and chaotic business environment. Ideally, new ventures need both entrepreneurs and managers in order to function. And most of the time the manager and the entrepreneur are one and the same, so you need to develop skills in both entrepreneurial and managerial thinking. The secret is understanding when to act and think like an entrepreneur and when to act and think like a manager. In the beginning of anything new, you'll need to be thinking like an entrepreneur. You'll need to take small actions to collect your own data. You'll need to use the resources you have rather than wait for lots of resources to come to you. You'll need to fail in order to make progress, experiment with new ideas, collaborate with others, share your ideas, and realize that you might be in uncharted territory. And all of this is ok. Just keep moving forward and take smart action.

## Entrepreneurial and Managerial Thinking in Action

To further examine entrepreneurial and management thinking, here is an example based on a thought experiment called "Curry in a Hurry" devised by Darden School of Business professor Saras D. Sarasvathy.[37] Say you want to start an Indian restaurant in your

**Customers dining in a
small Indian restaurant**

hometown. You could begin by assessing your market through questionnaires, surveys, and focus groups to separate those people who love Indian food from those who don't. Then you could narrow the "love it" segment down to the customers whom you might be able to approach when your restaurant opens.

This approach would help you predict the type of diners who might become regulars at your restaurant. You could then continue your information-gathering process by visiting other Indian restaurants to gauge their business processes and contacting vendors to gauge prices and availability of goods. Having spent months acquiring all this knowledge, you could formulate a business plan, apply for bank loans and loans from investors, lease a building and hire staff, and start a marketing and sales campaign to attract people to your restaurant.

This is one way to go about starting a new business, but it is based on two big assumptions: (1) you have the finances and resources for research and marketing, and (2) you have the time to invest in intensive planning and research. Typically, this is the sort of path taken by novice entrepreneurs who navigate worlds that they perceive as certain; they spend huge amounts of time on planning and analysis and allow the market to take control while they take a back seat. In short, they spend lots of time and money taking a managerial approach to predict the future.

Given that the managerial approach to opening a new restaurant is time-consuming and expensive, what other approach could novice entrepreneurs take to carrying out the same task? If you followed the entrepreneurial approach to starting your Indian restaurant, you would be going down a very different path. To learn more about the entrepreneurial approach and the corresponding effectuation theory, see the *Research at Work* feature below.

To implement the entrepreneurial approach, first, you would take a look at what means you have to start the process. Let's assume you have only a few thousand dollars in the bank and very few other resources. You could start by doing just enough research to convince an established restaurateur to become a strategic partner, or persuade a local business owner to invest in your restaurant, or even create some dishes to bring to a local Indian restaurant and persuade them to let you set up a counter in their establishment to test a selection there.

Second, you could contact some of your friends who work in nearby businesses and bring them and their colleagues some samples of your food, which might lead to a lunch delivery service. Once the word is out and you have a large enough customer base, you might decide to start your restaurant.

Getting out in your community, meeting new people, and building relationships with customers and strategic partners can lead to all sorts of opportunities. Someone might suggest that you write an Indian cookbook and introduce you to a publishing contact; someone else might think you have just the right personality to host your own cooking show and connect you with someone in the television industry. Others might want to learn more about Indian culture and inspire you to teach classes on the subject; or they might express an interest in travel, inspiring you to organize a food-themed tour of different regions around India. Suddenly you have a wealth of different business ideas in widely varied industries. Your original goal of starting a restaurant has evolved and multiplied into several different streams, demonstrating how it is possible to change, shape, and construct ideas in practice through action (see Figure 1.4).

But who knows what the actual outcome will be? Let's say the majority of people just don't like your cooking, even though your close friends rave about it. If you are really determined to reach your initial goal, you could use their feedback to work hard at improving your recipes and try again. However, if you silently agree with your customer base, you haven't lost too much time and money in your idea—which means you have resources left over to focus on your next entrepreneurial pursuit.

**FIGURE 1.4**

**The Creation Approach in Action**

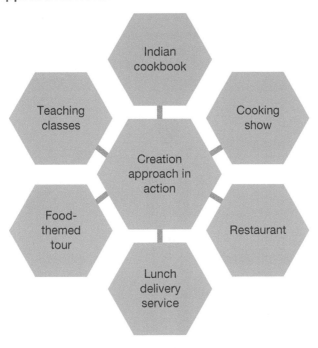

**Sources:**

Adapted from Schlesinger, L., Kiefer, C., & Brown, P. (2012). Just start: Take action, embrace uncertainty, create the future. Cambridge, MA: Harvard Business School Press.

Sarasvathy, S. D. (2008). Effectuation: Elements of entrepreneurial expertise. Northampton, MA: Edward Elgar.

Neck, H. M. (2011). Cognitive ambidexterity: The underlying mental model of the entrepreneurial leader. In D. Greenberg, K. McKone-Sweet, & H. J. Wilson (Eds.), The New entrepreneurial leader: Developing leaders who will shape social and economic opportunities (pp. 2442). San Francisco: Berrett-Koehler.

The creation approach to entrepreneurship is based on how entrepreneurs think. They navigate uncertain worlds to create rather than find opportunities; they make markets, learn from failure, and connect with a variety of stakeholders to fulfill their vision of the future.

# 1.6 THE KEY COMPONENTS OF THE ENTREPRENEURSHIP METHOD

>> **LO 1.6** **Illustrate the key components of the Entrepreneurship Method.**

The Entrepreneurship Method provides a way for entrepreneurs to embrace and confront uncertainty rather than to avoid it. It emphasizes smart action over planning. It emphasizes moving quickly from the whiteboard to the real world. It's a method that can be learned and should be repeated. There is no guarantee for success, but it does offer a few powerful assurances:

- You will act sooner, even when you don't know exactly what to do.
- Those things you can do, you will, and those things you can't, you will try.
- You will try more times because trying early is a low-cost experiment.
- You will fail sooner—enabling better, higher-quality information to be incorporated into the next iteration.
- You'll likely begin experimenting with many new ideas simultaneously.

The Method includes the two approaches that have already been addressed: prediction and creation. Prediction requires thinking about and analyzing existing information in order to predict the future, and creation is most concerned with acting and collecting

**FIGURE 1.5**

## The Entrepreneurship Method

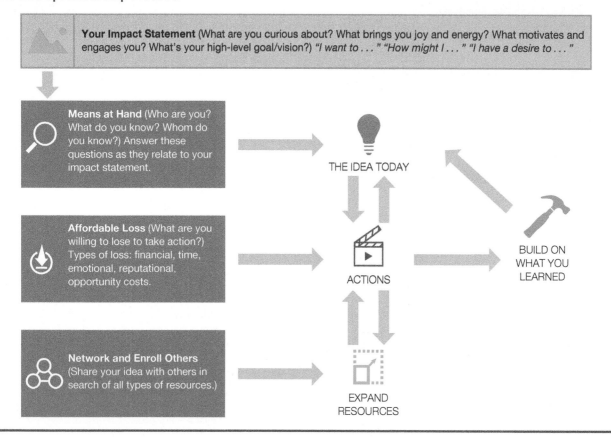

Adapted from the following sources:

Neck, H. M. (2011). Cognitive ambidexterity: The underlying mental model of the entrepreneurial leader. In D. Greenberg, K. McKone-Sweet, & H. J. Wilson (Eds.), *The new entrepreneurial leader: Developing leaders who will shape social and economic opportunities* (pp. 24–42). San Francisco, CA: Berrett-Koehler.

Sarasvathy, S. D. (2008). *Effectuation: Elements of entrepreneurial expertise.* Northampton, MA: Edward Elgar.

Schlesinger, L., Kiefer, C., & Brown, P. (2012). *Just start: Take action, embrace uncertainty, create the future.* Cambridge, MA: Harvard Business School Press.

new data—real and relevant data—in order to create the future. The prediction logic is better suited when we can deduce the future from the past, while the creation logic is the only choice under conditions of extreme uncertainty.

## Eight Components of the Entrepreneurship Method

Now that we understand the difference between a method and a process of entrepreneurship, it is time to take a deeper dive into the components of the Method, as illustrated in Figure 1.5. Let's examine each of them in more detail.

1.  **Identify your desired impact on the world** (see the Ted Talk at https://www .ted.com/talks/simon_sinek_how_great_leaders_inspire_ action?language=en). This is a simple statement that connects to your curiosity, drive, and motivation. To be successful at creating and building a new business, a new strategy, a new product, or anything radically new requires desire—you have to have a strong feeling to achieve something larger than yourself. Rarely is entrepreneurship about the money or the profit. Granted, fast-growth companies are primarily concerned with wealth creation, but the general reasons people start businesses go much deeper. Some pursue what they love, others value their autonomy and ability to control their work experience, and others have a strong desire to bring something new to

market.[38] The profit motive is simply not sustainable in the long run because entrepreneurship is hard work and requires satisfaction and desire that is derived from deep within. Ask yourself: What's my why?

2. **Start with the means at hand.**[39] Answer the following questions: Who am I? What do I know? Whom do I know? The composite answer will help you understand your current resource base—the resources you have available today that you can use for immediate action.

3. **Describe the idea today.** The idea is identified by connecting your means to your impact statement. What can you start to do today with what you have today?

4. **Calculate affordable loss.**[40] Leaving one's comfort zone is always perceived as risky, but risk is relative. What is considered high risk to one may not seem high risk to another; therefore, it can be quite difficult to calculate risk and use it as a valid decision-making criterion. Rather than calculating risk, think about taking action in terms of what you are willing to lose. What are you truly willing to give up in terms of money, reputation, time, and opportunity cost? By answering these questions, you take control rather than allowing yourself to be controlled by risk or the fear of failure.

5. **Take small action.** Nothing drastic . . . the first action is just a small start to get you going. No excuses here. You can do it. Once you calculate your affordable loss, you control all the risk.

6. **Network and enroll others in your journey.** The Entrepreneurship Method is about collaboration and cocreation rather than competition. Sharing your ideas and enrolling others in your journey will increase your resource base, expand the possibilities available, and validate your idea.

7. **Build on what you learn.** Assess performance of your action. Keep in mind that assessment is not about "killing" your new idea; it's about making the idea better. There is no right or wrong answer at this stage, just better. Expect and embrace setbacks, and celebrate the learning. When Thomas Watson, the founder of IBM, was asked about the key to success he responded, "Increase the rate of failure."

8. **Reflect and be honest with yourself.** One question always arises: How do I know when I should stop or keep going? The answer is easy. Quit only if you no longer have the desire inherent in your impact statement or if you have exceeded your affordable loss. Otherwise, the real question you have to answer now is "What are you going to do next?"

As you continue with the Entrepreneurship Method, you'll find that your affordable loss changes (usually increases) with each action. Why? Your idea receives greater validation, you have a solid and growing knowledge base, more people have joined your team, resource stocks increase, and your overall confidence in your ability to act grows. By practicing the Entrepreneurship Method, you will manage to deal with extreme uncertainty, control it, and use it to help you create what others cannot.

# 1.7 ENTREPRENEURSHIP REQUIRES DELIBERATE PRACTICE

>> **LO 1.7**  **Assess the role of deliberate practice in achieving mastery.**

In this section, we will explore the word *practice* so you better understand why we refer to the Entrepreneurship Method as both a mindset and a practice. We are surrounded by heroes in athletics, music, business, science, and entertainment who appear to exhibit astoundingly high levels of performance. How do they do it? How do musicians play complex pieces of music from memory, and how do professional sports players perform

# The 3-Hour Challenge

You may or may not have given a lot of thought to your entrepreneurial plans and goals. Either way, this activity will challenge you to clarify what plans and goals you have and why.

You can commit to doing a lot of things for only 3 hours, so give this Mindshift challenge a try. The 3 hours do not have to be spent in one continuous period. Doing it all at a stretch is probably not practical, so it is fine to spread out the time in 1-hour increments, but don't take longer than 3 days.

Hour 1: Write down your impact statement. Keep in mind that this is something that drives your curiosity, motivation to engage, and enthusiasm. Your impact statement is not an idea; it's a statement that expresses the type of impact you want to make as an entrepreneur. The following are examples of impact statements:

- I have a desire to help people age more gracefully.
- I have a desire to use video games to effect positive change.
- I have a desire to build greater community among different populations on my college campus.
- I have a desire to design clothes that help teenagers feel more confident.
- I have a desire to create healthy snack foods.

Take a full hour to write down your impact statement. Give it deep thought and really ask yourself, "What excites me?" Write it as clearly, sincerely, and completely as you can.

Hour 2: Share your impact statement with your classmates or others in your life, and try to find someone who shares a similar vision. Your goal is to find just one other person with a similar vision, but if you find more, that's great too!

Hour 3: Once you find your person, schedule a 1-hour meeting. Meet someplace unusual, not in the same coffee shop or restaurant where you always go. Share where your desired impact is coming from, and identify three potential business ideas that the two of you could pursue together to fulfill your desired impact. For example, if you both have a desire to create healthy snack foods, you may come up with an idea for vending machines that hold only fresh fruit and vegetables.

That's it . . . just craft your impact statement, find someone who shares your desire, and identify three potential business ideas. Don't judge the quality of your ideas at this point. There will be plenty of time for that.

## Critical Thinking Questions

1. What assumptions and beliefs did you have before starting the 3-hour challenge?

2. In what ways did the 3-hour challenge confirm your assumptions and beliefs? In what ways did it change them?

3. What did you learn about yourself that was unexpected or surprising? ●

---

seemingly unbelievable acts? And how do entrepreneurs move from being novices to expert serial entrepreneurs? The answer lies in a certain type of practice.

We have all heard the expression "practice makes perfect," but what does this really mean? We often associate practice with repetition and experience; for example, we picture a violinist playing a piece of music for hours every day or a basketball player shooting hoops for prolonged periods. However, research has shown that people who spend a lot of time simply repeating the same action on a regular basis reach a plateau of capability regardless of how many hours they have put in.[41] A golf enthusiast who spends a couple of days a week playing golf will reach a certain level, but she is unlikely to reach professional status solely through this form of practice. Performance does not improve purely as a result of experience. Similarly, as studies have shown, there is no evidence to suggest that world-class chess champions or professional musicians and sports players owe their success to genes or inheritance. How, then, do people advance from novice level to top performer?

Researchers have found that it all depends on *how* you practice. To achieve high levels of performance, high performers engage in **deliberate practice**, which involves carrying out carefully focused efforts to improve current performance.[42] The Mindshift features throughout this text are a useful way of deliberately practicing entrepreneurship. Table 1.7 lists the components of deliberate practice.

**Deliberate practice:** carrying out carefully focused efforts to improve current performance.

**TABLE 1.7**

Components of Deliberate Practice

| |
| --- |
| • Requires high levels of focus, attention, and concentration. |
| • Strengthens performance by identifying weaknesses and improving on them. |
| • Must be consistent and be maintained for long periods of time. |
| • Must be repeated to produce lasting results. |
| • Requires continuous feedback on outcomes. |
| • Involves setting goals beforehand. |
| • Involves self-observation and self-reflection after practice sessions are completed. |

**Source:** Baron, R. A., & Henry, R. A. (2010). How entrepreneurs acquire the capacity to excel: Insights from research on expert performance. *Strategic Entrepreneurship Journal, 4,* 49–65. Reprinted with permission from John Wiley & Sons.

Although aspects of deliberate practice exist in activities such as sport, chess, and music, it is also present in such diverse pursuits as typing, economics, and medicine. One study explored the use of deliberate practice by identifying the study habits of medical students when learning clinical skills. Researchers found that over time, students who used deliberate practice were able to make more efficient use of their time, energy, and resources.[43] In short, they seemed to "learn how to learn."

You might not be conscious of it, but chances are you probably already use some of the elements of deliberate practice. Think of when you first played a sport or picked up a musical instrument. You may have played the instrument for only 15 minutes a few times a week, or played football for 30 minutes twice a week, but without knowing it, during those short sessions, you were fully focused on what you were doing and intentionally repeating the activity, with a goal of improving your performance.

World-renowned sushi chef Jiro Ono has engaged in deliberate practice all his life by mastering the art of making sushi.[44] Of course, Ono cannot do it all by himself, so he has a number of apprentices under his careful watch. He starts off each apprentice with a small part of the sushi-making process—how to use a knife, how to cut fish, and so on. The apprentices are only permitted to move on to the next stage of the process once they have mastered each task. To put this into context, one of Ono's apprentices was only allowed to cook eggs for the first time after training under Ono for 10 years. Not only has Ono perfected the art of sushi making, but his commitment to deliberate practice has almost certainly benefited his brain.

## Deliberate Practice Shapes the Brain

Engaging in deliberate practice is even more worthwhile when you consider the effect it has on the brain.[45] When certain brain cells sense a lot of focused repeated activity, chemicals are produced to create myelin—a fatty, white tissue that increases the speed and strength of neural impulses, thereby improving performance. In contrast, regular practice without focused effort, consistent feedback, and guidance only reinforces mindless, automatic habits. For example, when you first learned to drive, you probably really concentrated on how to control the car, but after many instances of driving, you will find that you perform every step of the process without even thinking about it. You may think regular practice is sufficient for completing certain tasks, but you will have little chance of mastering them without systematic, deliberate practice. There is a big difference between practicing out of habit and using your head. For instance, virtuoso violinist Nathan Milstein was concerned that he wasn't practicing enough—everyone else seemed to be practicing all day long but he wasn't.[46] When he asked his professor for advice, Milstein was told, "It really doesn't matter how long. If you practice with your fingers, no amount is enough. If you practice with your head, two hours is plenty."

## Deliberate Practice and Entrepreneurs

What does deliberate practice mean for entrepreneurs? Sustained effort, concentration, and focus have important cognitive benefits such as enhancing perception, memory, intuition, and the way in which we understand our own performance (or metacognition). Expert entrepreneurs who engage in deliberate practice are generally more skilled at perceiving situations, understanding the meaning of complex patterns, and recognizing the differences between relevant and irrelevant information.

Entrepreneurs who engage in deliberate practice are better at storing new information and retrieving it when they need to, which helps them to plan, adapt, and make decisions more quickly in changing situations. Deliberate practice also enables entrepreneurs to realize what they know and don't know. Among the most common mistakes entrepreneurs make are getting blindsided by passion, which makes them overly optimistic and overconfident in their skills and abilities, and underestimating their resources—mistakes that often lead to unnecessary risk and failure.[47] Although passion is an important quality to possess, it is best guided by awareness of your own capabilities and knowledge. These sorts of mistakes can be overcome by receiving continual feedback on your performance from an expert in the field.[48] This is why it is so important for entrepreneurs to seek out mentors, coaches, or even a good friend whose business sense you admire and who will work with you, offer feedback, and help guide you in your decision making.

Finally, expert entrepreneurs who have consistently used deliberate practice over a number of years tend to have a higher sense of intuition, which enables them to make decisions more speedily and accurately based on knowledge and experience.

"Years of deliberate practice" may sound daunting, but you probably already have a head start! The cognitive skills that you developed through deliberate practice (e.g., by playing a musical instrument or sport, creative writing, or anything else that requires strong focus and effort) are all transferable to entrepreneurship. You have the capability to enhance your skills and become a lifelong learner—and you can demonstrate this by creating your own entrepreneurship portfolio.

---

**RESEARCH AT WORK**

# How Entrepreneurs Think

The Entrepreneurship Method in this text aligns with the work of Dr. Saras Sarasvathy and her theory of effectuation,[49] which is based on the idea that because the future is unpredictable yet controllable, entrepreneurs can affect the future. Sarasvathy believes it is futile for entrepreneurs to try to predict the future.

In 1997, Dr. Sarasvathy traveled to 17 states across the United States to interview 30 entrepreneurs from different types and sizes of organizations and from a variety of industries to assess their thinking patterns. The aim of her research was to understand their methods of reasoning about specific problems. Each entrepreneur was given a 17-page problem that involved making decisions to build a company from a specific product idea. By the end of the study, Sarasvathy discovered that 89% of the more experienced, serial entrepreneurs used more creative, effectual thinking more often than its contrary—predictive or causal thinking.[50]

Until Dr. Sarasvathy's study, we really didn't know how entrepreneurs think—at least, previous research didn't

identify such salient patterns as her work. She found that entrepreneurs, especially those entrepreneurs who had started businesses multiple times, exhibited specific thinking patterns. Thus, we are able to demonstrate that entrepreneurship can be taught because we can train ourselves to think differently—and how we think is the antecedent to how we act.

## Critical Thinking Questions

1. What strengths and weaknesses do you see in Sarasvathy's effectuation theory of entrepreneurship? Give some examples that would apply to real life.

2. If you were asked to participate in Dr. Sarasvathy's study, how might she classify your ways of thinking and problem solving?

3. What additional research questions can you suggest that would shed light on how entrepreneurs think and solve problems? ●

# 1.8 HOW THIS BOOK WILL HELP YOU PRACTICE ENTREPRENEURSHIP

>> **LO 1.8** **Propose different ways in which this book can help you practice entrepreneurship.**

By now, we hope that we have proved to you that becoming an entrepreneur is a pathway for many and that the world needs more entrepreneurs of all kinds. To reinforce our message, the following are some fundamental beliefs that form the main ethos of this book.

We believe that you as the student must take action and practice entrepreneurship at every opportunity. In each chapter of this book, you will find the following features, which are designed to challenge you to do just that.

- Entrepreneurship in Action: In entrepreneurship, there is no one right answer. Role models are very important because, by learning from others, you can develop empathy for entrepreneurs around the world who may be doing the same as you someday. Entrepreneurship in Action includes interviews with entrepreneurs from many different businesses and disciplines in the United States and around the world.

---

ENTREPRENEURSHIP MEETS ETHICS

## When to Practice Entrepreneurship

Becoming great at any skill requires a considerable deal of practice. Psychology writer Malcolm Gladwell believes it takes 10,000 hours of practice to become great at any skill. However, in the course of acquiring those 10,000 hours, burgeoning entrepreneurs must find a way to support themselves, and that often means having a conventional, full-time job.

Is it ethical to work on entrepreneurial ventures during company time? Can your performance at your current workplace be hampered because of your dedication to personal ventures?

These questions must be addressed for any entrepreneur to become an effective manager of employees upon starting a new business. According to a CareerBuilder survey, 29% of workers have a side job, and that number grows for younger workers.

For entrepreneurial-spirited workers, a close review of the employment contract and company handbook should be the first step, to make sure there are no specific policies against having a side business or job, especially a noncompetition clause. If there is no language barring an additional business pursuit, then a worker is in the clear to act on different pursuits. Nevertheless, that does not mean an employer or supervisor will be wholly happy to hear of a side venture.

Thus, an entrepreneurial employee is left with two options: disclose the nature of a side venture or do not.

Understanding a company's culture may be the first step in solving this conundrum, which takes time and relationship building to figure out. There is a possibility that an employer may be particularly interested in how an employee's entrepreneurial venture may help that employee grow with regard to the primary job. If there could be any potential conflict down the road, disclosing basic information to a human resources representative could be the best form of action.

### Critical Thinking Questions

1. Should workers devote all of their energy to their primary paid job? Can the mere existence of a side job hurt a worker's performance in a primary job?

2. Is it unethical to hide a side job from an employer, even if it is legal?

3. Can employers benefit from having an employee who wishes to become an entrepreneur? Could this be a sought-after trait for recruiters? ●

**Sources:**

Baer, D. (2014, June 2). Malcolm Gladwell explains what everyone gets wrong about his "10,000 hour rule." *Business Insider.* Retrieved from http://www.businessinsider.com/malcolm-gladwell-explains-the-10000-hour-rule-2014-6

Bitte, R. (2018). 4 questions smart people ask about side gigs (so they don't lose their jobs). *The Muse.* Retrieved from https://www.themuse.com/advice/4-questions-smart-people-ask-about-side-gigs-so-they-dont-lose-their-jobs

Morad, R. (2016, September 29). Survey: More than one-third of working millennials have a side job. *Forbes.* Retrieved from https://www.forbes.com/sites/reneemorad/2016/09/29/survey-more-than-one-third-of-working-millennials-have-a-side-job/#180359d6132f

- Mindshift: Because entrepreneurship requires action, there are two Mindshift features in each chapter that require you to close the textbook and go and act. This is when you will deliberately practice entrepreneurship.

- Entrepreneurship Meets Ethics: Entrepreneurs sometimes face complex ethical challenges that cause conflict. Peppered with situations faced by real-world entrepreneurs, the Entrepreneurship Meets Ethics feature challenges you to think about how you would take action if you were confronted with a similar ethical dilemma.

- Research at Work: This feature highlights recent seminal entrepreneurship studies and their impact on and application to the real world. This will allow you to view how the latest research applies to real-life settings.

- Case Study: Finally, witness the content of the chapter come alive in a short case study presented at the end of each chapter. These case studies are based on real companies of all kinds—for-profit, nonprofit, technology, social, product-based, service-based, online, and others—that have been started by entrepreneurs of all types.

Entrepreneurship is all around us—everyone has the ability to think and act entrepreneurially, to transform opportunity into reality, and to create social and economic value. But remember, practice is key—learning is inseparable from doing. So, let's get started! ●

---

Get the tools you need to sharpen your study skills. SAGE edge offers a robust online environment featuring an impressive array of free tools and resources.

- Access practice quizzes, eFlashcards, video, and multimedia at
  **edge.sagepub.com/neckentrepreneurship2e**

---

## SUMMARY

**1.1   Explain the importance of action and practice in entrepreneurship.**

Practice and action make it possible to achieve success. Many of the successful entrepreneurs behind major corporations today established their companies by acting, learning, and building what they learned into their next actions. Many entrepreneurs have learned entrepreneurship by doing entrepreneurship, but this text is designed to help you practice the essentials in the hope that you can avoid some of the more common pitfalls.

**1.2   List the seven lesser-known truths about entrepreneurship.**

There are seven lesser-known truths about entrepreneurship: (1) entrepreneurship is not reserved for startups; (2) entrepreneurs do not have a special set of personality traits; (3) entrepreneurship can be taught and it is a method that requires practice; (4) entrepreneurs are not extreme risk takers; (5) entrepreneurs collaborate more than they compete; (6) entrepreneurs act more than they plan; (7) entrepreneurship is a life skill.

**1.3   Compare and contrast the different forms of entrepreneurship in practice today.**

Corporate entrepreneurship (or intrapreneurship) is entrepreneurship within large corporations. Inside entrepreneurs are similar to corporate entrepreneurs, but they can be found in any type of organization, large or small, nonprofit or for-profit, and even among governing bodies. Franchising and buy-outs are popular ways to start relatively near the ground level. Social entrepreneurship—entrepreneurship focused on making the world a better place—is manifested in nonprofit and large, for-profit firms alike. A form of social entrepreneurship is the Benefit Corporation, or B Corp, which designates for-profit firms that meet high standards of corporate social responsibility. Family enterprises, entrepreneurship started within the family, remain a dominant form of business development in the United States and abroad. Serial entrepreneurs are so committed to entrepreneurship that they're constantly on the move creating new businesses.

**1.4   Distinguish between entrepreneurship as a method and as a process.**

The Entrepreneurship Method outlines the tools and practices necessary to take action. Entrepreneurship as a process, instead, guides would-be creators along a thorough but static path from inception to exit.

**1.5   Compare and contrast the prediction and creation approaches to entrepreneurship.**

The two main perspectives on entrepreneurship are the predictive logic, the older and more traditional view; and the creation logic, which has been developed through recent advances in the field. Prediction is the opposite of creation. Whereas prediction thinking is used in situations of certainty, the creation view is used when the future is unpredictable.

**1.6   Illustrate the key components of the Entrepreneurship Method.**

The Entrepreneurship Method is designed so entrepreneurs can embrace and confront uncertainty rather than avoid it. The eight components are identify your desired impact on the world; start with the means at hand; describe the idea today; calculate affordable loss; take small action; network and enroll others in your journey; build on what you learn; and reflect and be honest with yourself.

**1.7   Assess the role of deliberate practice in achieving mastery.**

Practice doesn't make perfect; rather, deliberate practice makes perfect. Starting with specific goals, deliberate practice involves consistent, targeted efforts for improvement. Feedback and self-reflection are necessary for meaningful improvement, and repetition is required to achieve lasting results.

**1.8   Propose different ways in which this book can help you practice entrepreneurship.**

The tools for success and methods to hone entrepreneurial skills will be available in every chapter. Thought and action exercises alike will be employed, and research and testimonials from proven academics and entrepreneurs will be provided as we move through the text. As a final test of application, case studies will follow every chapter, giving you the opportunity to employ what you've learned, a chance for entrepreneurship within a unique and real-world context.

## KEY TERMS

Benefit corporation
(or B Corp)   12

Corporate entrepreneurship (or intrapreneurship)   10

Deliberate practice   22

Effectuation theory   6

Entrepreneurs inside   10

Entrepreneurship   3

Family enterprise   13

Franchise   11

Inbound marketing   28

Outbound marketing   28

Royalties   11

Serial entrepreneurs (or habitual entrepreneurs)   13

Social entrepreneurship   12

Startup   6

## CASE STUDY

## Saurbh Gupta, founder, Gyan-I Inc.

Before you start your entrepreneurship journey, make sure you validate your reason and motivation for doing so. If you are convinced that you are doing this for the right reasons, whatever it may be, you shall be able to take on whatever comes your way.

—Saurabh Gupta, founder of Gyan-I Inc.

The name of Saurabh Gupta's company, Gyan-I, means "knowledgeable one" in Hindi. Having always wanted to be his own boss, Saurabh's entrepreneurship journey began when he came across an opportunity while working for a very large charitable foundation called Daniels Fund. Daniels Fund is headquartered in Denver, Colorado, and is dedicated to providing grants, scholarship programs, and ethics education in Colorado, New Mexico, Utah, and Wyoming. As vice president of IT, Saurabh oversaw the end-to-end management of the organization's entire IT infrastructure. This included vendor negotiations, department budgeting, project planning, and execution. Daniels Fund manages assets of more than 1 billion dollars, but Saurabh realized that smaller, less wealthy nonprofit organizations faced similar IT issues and technological challenges. He identified a real unmet need: IT services for nonprofit organizations that did not have the infrastructure or money to support a full-time IT staff. Saurabh felt that meeting this need would fit perfectly with his skillset and experience and would be a good way to finally fulfill his dream of becoming an entrepreneur.

Though he toyed with the idea of starting Gyan-I Inc. for years, he could only take the leap after he received his U.S. green card in 2011. The CEO of Daniels Fund was supportive of Saurabh's decision to start his own company and was also his first customer! His former CEO continues to be his mentor and a pillar of support today.

Gyan-I Inc. provides technology consulting and managed IT services primarily for nonprofit and small-business organizations. As Saurabh explains it,

For an organization with 10 to 100 people, it doesn't really make sense to hire a techie. What we do is that we run the basics around the network, website, online infrastructure, and even consult companies to give them new ideas and improve overall operations using IT. Most of the work is remote and our clients sometimes like us to operate out of their offices. While the five-member team usually works out of Denver, people are all over the country. Recently, however, we have pivoted the business to focus on cybersecurity, and all the services I just mentioned are offered only to legacy clients.

Over the past 2 years, with the increasing number of cyber incidents, crime, and malware, cybersecurity in business infrastructure has gained significant importance.

The hacking of the 2016 U.S. elections was a watershed moment for us. While cybersecurity is a space that I personally really enjoyed, it is also a space that is gaining significant importance and is here to stay. The IT infrastructure around the world is changing with more offerings coming on the cloud, increasing exposure to the Internet, making cybersecurity even more necessary and relevant. We saw this as an opportunity to evaluate the strength of our team and internal resources, focus our offerings towards cybersecurity and move up the pecking order in our niche market segment.

Gyan-I Inc. now offers three services that help small businesses manage their cyber risk. First, they do an initial risk assessment and give a report on the risk businesses are likely to face and consult on how to overcome the risk. Second, they extend offerings by hand-holding the company and providing the necessary support to protect the companies from risk, analyze their security, and train employees on an ongoing basis. The third service is related to fast responses to cyber breaches. The response to these higher-margin services, Saurabh says, has been "good."

In 2011, when Saurabh started, he was alone and "bootstrapped" the business. Bootstrapping is entrepreneurship lingo for starting a business with very limited resources without outside investment. Saurabh believes his bootstrapping approach helped him start small but grow with intention. As people joined the team, the company began to grow organically and slowly, not to mention being profitable from Day 1. Bootstrapping the company presented Saurabh with its own sets of constraints. He felt that it would not be possible to deliver the services to his clients at a low cost and on time if he developed his own resources (IT infrastructure). Instead, he adopted existing software-as-a-service (SaaS) solutions that were not only tried and tested but also readily available (e.g., SaaS for payroll, project management software). Using these existing solutions allowed him to bundle and customize his offerings to address the specific needs of his customers, improving customer satisfaction.

**Inbound marketing:** bringing potential customers to your business by creating online content that addresses their needs, in order to build trust and brand awareness.

**Outbound marketing:** promoting your product or service through traditional activities such as advertising, trade shows, and cold calling.

Bootstrapping also meant that other overhead costs had to be minimized. His first office was in a co-op workspace in Denver. "Everything is an operational expense when you're bootstrapped," he quipped. The business developed organically and mostly through word of mouth. Because most of the leads resulted from inbound marketing, their sales cycles were extremely short, so they could contact the customer, pitch the product, and close the sale in less than one day. This enabled them to grow 30% every year. Gyan-I Inc. currently has 45 to 50 customers, and they have expanded their marketing efforts to include outbound marketing. They have recently hired a marketing professional to help grow the company base and brand.

Not everything was smooth sailing for Saurabh. He recalls an early misstep in the business around 2013, when he decided to focus on developing a SaaS product called Applyd (http://applyd.co/) from scratch. He noticed many of his nonprofit clients followed a paper-based approach to file requests for scholarships. He thought it was possible to streamline this process electronically, reducing the time spent on redundant activities for these 500 potential clients. Building a product from scratch was different from what Gyan-I had done so far. Saurabh, however, felt that he understood the problem and that the product he would build would be adopted by potential users almost immediately. He decided to dive in with both feet, allocated a budget, and spent a lot of time building and working on the concept. His budget was running out and he was spending more than he wanted to on building the product. He was able to scrape through and finished the software in 2014, but the product did not achieve expected sales. It reached only 2–3% of the addressable market. The clients simply didn't use it. He quickly realized that his clients were not early adopters and couldn't see the value in automation. Saurabh stopped pursuing Applyd in 2015.

Saurabh realized that the company successfully worked as an outsourced model. His customers needed IT support and not new IT products. Gyan-I worked because it had internal resources—knowledgeable people who offered quality service and attention. Clients knew their IT was in good, capable hands. Today Saurabh is confident that his boutique business has a sustainable model that is scalable. The small staff size of the company also positions it well to provide high-quality services.

When a client approaches us, the team is able to be nimble and efficient. We are able to fine-tune our offerings in real-time based on the feedback and requirements of the client. Some clients are hard pressed for time and want work to be completed within the week, while some don't mind spreading it over a few months. We are able to manage those expectations, a big advantage in this space.

Added to this is the awareness that Gyan-I Inc. has of the events affecting its industry, especially those related to cybersecurity. This nimble attitude has allowed it to pivot effectively and leverage and build on the existing strengths of the team.

Saurabh's journey as an entrepreneur has not been without a struggle. He says that starting and running a company has been a spiritual and philosophical journey for him. It has not only helped him become more observant and disciplined in his personal life, but he has also developed a sense of self-awareness—something that he is very thankful for. Although he's not able to spend as much time with his family as he would like, he has been able to strike a meaningful balance between family life and work life. The technology industry is constantly evolving, and Saurabh points out that he is always concerned about the company's ability to remain relevant to customer needs and wants as the managed IT services industry is experiencing a tectonic shift toward cloud-based computing and consumption. This means that he is continuously learning in order to stay ahead of the game.

## Critical Thinking Questions

1. How risky is it to start a technology services company today when technology is changing at such a rapid pace?

2. The Entrepreneurship Method is about taking action and trying new things. Do you see evidence of the Method during the creation of Gyan-I?

3. As you think about doing something entrepreneurial, today or someday, what is your motivation for doing so?

**Source:** Saurabh Gupta (interview with Babson MBA graduate assistant Gaurav Khemka, September 09, 2018.)

# 2 Activating an Entrepreneurial Mindset

"If you want something you've never had, you must be willing to do something you've never done."

—Thomas Jefferson

# Chapter Outline

# Learning Objectives

## 2.1 THE POWER OF MINDSET

>> **LO 2.1    Appraise the effectiveness of mindset in entrepreneurship.**

In Chapter 1, we learned about the Entrepreneurship Method. Part of the Method is being in the right mindset to start and grow a business. The words from "Rise and Shine" in Figure 2.1 have been transcribed from an athlete motivation video on YouTube. It is a good description of how our mindset operates. When we wake up in the morning we have a choice between the "easy" way and the "right" way. Depending on our mindset, we will choose one path or the other. In this chapter's Entrepreneurship in Action feature, we describe how Franklin Yancey's entrepreneurial mindset encouraged him to start his own business selling comfortable stadium seats for sporting events. Yancey credits his early entrepreneurial experiences, his college education, and supportive family for his success.

But what motivated Yancey to start his own business? After all, he was still in college and had plenty of time to think about what he wanted to do afterward. We could say that Yancey was in the right mindset to start a business. He saw a problem that needed to be fixed and he was curious about finding solutions. Thanks to prior experiences, he had the confidence to take action by knocking on doors and gaining support for his idea. He also believed enough to persist with his idea, even in the face of high financial risk. It was Yancey's entrepreneurial mindset that kept him on the right track and ultimately led to success in multiple businesses.

## 2.2 WHAT IS MINDSET?

>> **LO 2.2    Define "entrepreneurial mindset" and explain its importance to entrepreneurs.**

We emphasized mindset in Chapter 1 and it's also in the subtitle of this text, so perhaps it is time we stopped to examine what it actually means. It has traditionally been defined as "the established set of attitudes held by someone."[1] It's really our lens for viewing the world, interpreting what we see, and reacting or responding to what we hear. Our mindset subconsciously guides our reactions and decisions. Sometimes it's really hard to define mindset, so perhaps a quick story will better illustrate.[2,3] Corey Booker, a U.S. senator for the state of New Jersey, was a law student in 1997. He had great passion for the city of Newark, which at the time was one of the most

**SAGE edge™**

Master the content at
**edge.sagepub.com/
neckentrepreneurship2e**

# Franklin Yancey, WME Entertainment and Yancey Realty

Photo courtesy of Franklin Yancey

**Franklin Yancey, Founder of College Comfort and Yancey Realty**

As a young child growing up in Blackstone, Virginia, Franklin Yancey used to go out to the woods, dig up trees, pot them, and sell them to neighborhood families. He also sold stickers by cutting pictures out of skateboard magazines. You could say that Franklin developed an entrepreneurial mindset very early on. His father certainly helped. As Franklin said, "My father was a hard worker who came up from little means working in tobacco fields at a very early age. Later he started his own pharmacy. My strong work ethic comes from both of my parents." You could also say that athletics also contributed to his mindset. From a young age, Franklin, his brother, and his sister played sports at competitive levels and they all were inducted into their high school hall of fame. His brother even played golf on the PGA Tour.

While in college at Virginia Tech University in the mid-1990s, Franklin enrolled in a management course, which jumpstarted his interest in entrepreneurship. "I realized that I didn't want to work for someone else," Franklin said. While walking to the Virginia Tech football stadium for a game, Franklin noticed a pile of portable, dilapidated stadium seats. These were seat cushions with a back support that fans could rent for a sporting event to make sitting in the stadium more comfortable. "They were made from cheap material and had been badly maintained," recalled Franklin. Teaming up with his roommate, John Hite, he decided to make a better product to rent to the university. And so the two became the founders of College Comfort: a company that manufactured and rented comfortable stadium seats for sporting events and large stadium events.

To produce the seats, they found a local former Levi's plant and asked for quotes to stitch high-quality material with school colors onto the rental stadium seats. Their first high-stakes deal came shortly after when Franklin pitched contracts with both East Carolina University and Virginia Tech for stadium seat cushion rentals. It was essential to get both schools to sign on, in order to get cash to produce the product and build credibility for College Comfort. Luckily, they both signed.

Franklin worked hard to market the product in new places. The next year they signed eight additional customers. Thanks to friends and family, they didn't have lodging expenses while they traveled around the country sourcing more customers. In their third year of business, College Comfort signed on 12 more schools and the business has continued to grow ever since.

In early 2008, a large privately owned, multibillion-dollar entertainment company called WME-IMG Entertainment acquired College Comfort. Today, Franklin still works on this part of the business as a vice-president with WME-IMG. He leads a team of 10 people and has contracts with more than 100 universities, NASCAR, Major League Baseball, and others to provide thousands of rental stadium seat attachments for events.

While truly enjoying his work with WME-IMG, he still felt the entrepreneurship "itch" to start something else from scratch. So in 2016, he created a real estate company in Charlotte, N.C., called Yancey Realty that focuses on commercial real estate, residential real estate, and property management. He now has more than 30 agents in three locations. Franklin feels the autonomous nature of his WME-IMG job, combined with the use of technology, allows him to do both "jobs" well. He feels the secret sauce in his real estate business is his ability to empower his agents to get the job done by providing them with the resources they need to perform.

Franklin credits his entrepreneurial mindset for his ability to work hard. "I hear 'work smart, not hard,' and I understand the logic behind it. But the real mission is to work smart *and* to work longer and harder than others. You have to lead yourself before you can lead others, too!" Even after all of his success and at the age of 42, he still works many long nights, but it is all worth it to him. As he sees it, "There is only one title that matters: owner. Being an entrepreneur is about being an owner."

## Critical Thinking Questions

1. In what ways does his mindset play a role in Franklin's success?

2. What is the one key trait that all entrepreneurs must possess, according to Franklin?

3. Have you considered any products or services as solutions to problems while walking through your own college campus? If so, describe them. ●

**Source:** Franklin Yancey (interview with author, December 31, 2018)

## FIGURE 2.1

### Rise and Shine

**Athletes use a motivational mindset to achieve goals on the field.**

It's six am and your hand can't make it to the alarm clock fast enough before the voices in your head start telling you that it's too early, too cold, and too dark to get out of bed. Aching muscles lie still in rebellion pretending not to hear your brain commanding them to move. A legion of voices are shouting their permission for you to hit the snooze button and go back to dream land. But you didn't ask their opinion. The one voice you're listening to is a voice of defiance. The voice that says there's a reason you set that alarm in the first place. So sit up, put your feet on the floor, and don't look back—because we've got work to do.

**Source:** Red Productions. (2012, February 16). *TCU baseball 2012—The grind* [Video file]. Retrieved from https://www .youtube.com/watch?v=MNL_DAI19_I

economically depressed cities in the country. In his final year of Yale law school, he began working as a tenants' rights advocate in Newark—even moving to the harshest area of the city called the Central Ward. There he met Virginia Jones, the president of the Brick Towers tenants' association—a slum in the Central Ward. Corey expressed to Virginia his interest in helping the community. As the story goes, Virginia took Corey to the middle of the busy street outside of the Brick Towers. She told Corey to look around and describe what he saw. Corey looked around and responded with such things as, "I see a playground overgrown with weeds and the equipment is rusty. I see trash on the sides of the road. I see houses with their windows boarded up. I saw a drug deal happening on that corner last night. I see so many people out of work." The list could go on but Virginia Jones stopped Corey Booker and simply said, "You can't help this area." She paused. The petite Virginia Jones looked up at the broad-shouldered and tall young Corey Booker and said, "Boy, you need to understand that the world outside of you is a reflection of what you have inside of you, and if you're one of those people who only sees darkness, despair, that's all there's ever gonna be." This is an example of mindset—the mindset Corey had but also the mindset Corey needed. His life and mindset forever changed on that day.

Fortunately our mindset is not static; it can change, as evidenced by the Corey Booker story above. Research has shown that our mindset needn't be "set" at all. Stanford University psychologist Carol Dweck proposes that there are two different types of mindset: a fixed mindset and a growth mindset (see Figure 2.2).[4]

**FIGURE 2.2**

**What Kind of Mindset Do You Have?**

Growth Mindset

I can learn anything I want to.
When I'm frustrated, I persevere.
I want to challenge myself.
When I fail, I learn.
Tell me I try hard.
If you succeed, I'm inspired.
My effort and attitude determine everything.

Fixed Mindset

I'm either good at it, or I'm not.
When I'm frustrated, I give up.
I don't like to be challenged.
When I fail, I'm no good.
Tell me I'm smart.
If you succeed, I feel threatened.
My abilities determine everything.

**Source:** Created by Reid Wilson @wayfaringpath.

---

**Fixed mindset:** the assumptions held by people who perceive their talents and abilities as set traits.

**Growth mindset:** the assumptions held by people who believe that their abilities can be developed through dedication, effort, and hard work.

In a fixed mindset, people perceive their talents and abilities as set traits. They believe that brains and talent alone are enough for success, and they go through life with the goal of looking smart all the time. They take any constructive criticism of their capabilities very personally and tend to attribute others' success to luck (see Research at Work, below, for a study about luck) or some sort of unfair advantage. People with a fixed mindset will tell themselves they are no good at something to avoid challenge, failure, or looking dumb.

On the other hand, in a growth mindset, people believe that their abilities can be developed through dedication, effort, and hard work. They think brains and talent are not the key to lifelong success, but merely the starting point. People with a growth mindset are eager to enhance their qualities through lifelong learning, training, and practice. Unlike people with fixed mindsets, they see failure as an opportunity to improve their performance and to learn from their mistakes. Despite setbacks, they tend to persevere rather than give up.

Recent studies have found that being praised simply for our intelligence can create a fixed mindset. For example, using a series of puzzle tests, Dweck discovered that 5th-grade children who were praised for their hard work and effort on the first test were far more likely to choose the more difficult puzzle the next time. In contrast, children who were praised for being smart or intelligent after the first test chose the easy test the second time around.[5]

It seems that the children who had been praised for being smart wanted to keep their reputation for being smart and tended to avoid any challenge that would jeopardize this belief. Yet the children who had been praised for how hard they had worked on the first test had more confidence in their abilities to tackle a more challenging test and to learn from whatever mistakes they might make.[6]

Dweck observes the growth mindset in successful athletes, business people, writers, musicians—in fact, anyone who commits to a goal and puts in the hard work and practice to attain it. She believes that people with growth mindsets tend to be more successful and happier than those with fixed mindsets.[7]

Although many of us tend to exhibit one mindset or the other, it is important to recognize that mindsets can be changed. Even if your mindset is a fixed one, it is possible to learn a growth mindset and thereby boost your chances for happiness and success. How can you do this? By becoming aware of that "voice" in your head that questions your ability to take on a new challenge, by recognizing that you have a choice in how you interpret what that voice is telling you, by responding to that voice, and by taking action.

For example, say you want to start a new business, but you're a little unsure of your accounting skills. Following are some messages you might hear from the "voice" in your head and some responses you might make based on a growth mindset.[8]

FIXED MINDSET:  "Why do you want to start up a business? You need accounting skills. You were always terrible at math at school. Are you sure you can do it?"

GROWTH MINDSET:  **"I might not be any good at accounting at first, but I think I can learn to be good at it if I commit to it and put in the time and effort."**

FIXED MINDSET:  "If you fail, people will laugh at you."

GROWTH MINDSET:  **"Give me the name of one successful person who never experienced failure at one time or another."**

FIXED MINDSET:  "Do yourself a favor; forget the idea and hang on to your dignity."

GROWTH MINDSET:  **"If I don't try, I'll fail anyway. Where's the dignity in that?"**

Next, suppose that you enroll in an accounting course, but you score very low marks on your first exam. Once again, you're likely to hear messages from the "voice" in your head and respond to them as follows.

FIXED MINDSET:  "Dude! This wouldn't have happened if you were actually good at accounting in the first place. Time to throw in the towel."

GROWTH MINDSET:  **"Not so fast. Look at Oprah Winfrey and Jack Ma—they suffered lots of setback along the way, yet they still persevered."**

Now suppose that a friend who hears about your low exam score makes a joke about your performance.

FIXED MINDSET:  "Why am I being criticized for doing badly in the accounting exam? It's not my fault. I'm just not cut out for accounting, that's all."

GROWTH MINDSET:  **"I can own this setback and learn from it. I need to do more practicing, and next time, I will do better."**

If you listen to the fixed mindset voice, the chances are you will never persevere with the accounting process. If you pay attention to the growth mindset voice instead, the likelihood is that you will pick yourself up, dust yourself off, start practicing again, and put the effort in before the next exam.

Over time, the voice you listen to most becomes your choice. The decisions you make are now in your hands. By practicing listening and responding to each of these voices, you can build your willingness to take on new challenges, learn from your mistakes, accept criticism, and take action.

As we have explored, our mindset is not dependent on luck, nor is it fixed: We each have the capability to adjust our mindset to recognize and seize opportunities and take action, even under the most unlikely or uncertain circumstances, but it takes practice. This is why the mindset is essential to entrepreneurship.

# Study on Luck

In the early 1990s, British psychologist and researcher Richard Wiseman carried out an experiment on luck to determine what defines a lucky or unlucky person. Over several years, using advertisements in newspapers and magazines, Wiseman sought out people who felt consistently lucky or unlucky. He interviewed them and identified 400 volunteers whom he asked to participate in the following experiment.

The 400 participants were divided into two groups: those who considered themselves lucky and those who considered themselves unlucky. Both groups were given a newspaper and asked to count how many photographs it contained.

In took approximately 2 minutes, on average, for the unlucky people to count all the photos, but it only took a few seconds for the lucky people. Why? Because the lucky people spotted a large message occupying more than half of the newspaper's second page that stated, "Stop counting. There are 43 photographs in this newspaper." The unlucky people had missed this instruction because they were too focused on what they thought they were *supposed* to look for.

Wiseman concluded that unlucky people tend to miss opportunities because they are too focused on something else, whereas lucky people tend to be more open to recognizing opportunities.

Wiseman's overall findings have revealed that "although unlucky people have almost no insight into the real causes of their good and bad luck, their thoughts and behaviors are responsible for much of their fortune" (or misfortune).

## Critical Thinking Questions

1.  Identify a successful entrepreneur. Do you believe luck played a role in their success? Why or why not?

2.  Do you consider yourself a particularly lucky or unlucky person? Or do you fall somewhere in the middle? Give some reasons to support your answer.

3.  Can you think of an opportunity that came your way because you were open to it? How might you make yourself more open to "lucky" opportunities in the future? ●

### Sources

Wiseman, R. (2003, January 9). Be lucky—it's an easy skill to learn. *The Telegraph.* Retrieved from https://www.telegraph.co.uk/technology/3304496/Be-lucky-its-an-easy-skill-to-learn.html
Wiseman, R. (2003). *The luck factor: The four essential principles.* New York, NY: Hyperion.

## The Entrepreneurial Mindset

The growth mindset is essential to a mindset for entrepreneurship. In Chapter 1, we discussed the Entrepreneurship Method and how it requires a specific mindset so that entrepreneurs have the ability to see the endless possibilities in the world. Although there is no single definition of mindset and how it relates to entrepreneurs, we believe the most accurate meaning of an **entrepreneurial mindset** is the ability to quickly sense opportunities, take action, and get organized under uncertain conditions.[9] This also includes the ability to persevere, accept and learn from failure, and get comfortable with a high level of discomfort!

**Entrepreneurial mindset:** the ability to quickly sense, take action, and get organized under uncertain conditions.

Many successful entrepreneurs appear to be very smart, but it is often the way they use their intelligence that counts. Cognitive strategies are the techniques people use to solve problems, such as reasoning, analyzing, experimenting, and so forth. The entrepreneurial mindset employs various cognitive strategies to identify opportunities, consider alternatives, and take action. Because working in uncertain environments "goes with the territory" in entrepreneurship, the entrepreneurial mindset requires constant thinking and rethinking, adaptability, and self-regulation—the capacity to control our emotions and impulses.

**Metacognition:** our ability to understand and be aware of how we think and the processes we use to think.

In Chapter 1 we touched on the concept of **metacognition**, which is our ability to understand and be aware of how we think and the processes we use to think (see Figure 2.3). For example, say you are reading through a complex legal document; you might notice that you don't understand some of it. You might go back and re-read it, pause to think it through, note the elements that don't make sense to you, and then either come back to it later or find a way to clarify the parts you don't understand. In this example, you are using your metacognitive skills to monitor your own understanding of the text, rather than simply plowing through the document without having much comprehension at all.

FIGURE 2.3

## Metacognition

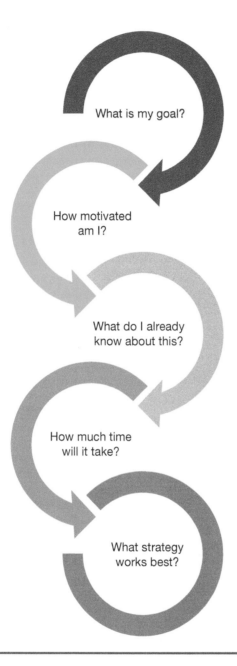

Entrepreneurs regularly engage in metacognitive processes to adapt to changing circumstances by thinking about alternative routes to take and choosing one or more strategies based on these options. Metacognitive awareness is part of the mindset, and it is not something that we are born with. It can be developed over time through continuous practice.

## Passion and Entrepreneurship

Among many elements of the entrepreneurial mindset, one of the most talked about is the element of passion. The entrepreneurial mindset is about understanding who you are and how you view the world. It deeply connects to your *desired impact* (described in Chapter 1), which some people equate with passion. In the past, researchers tended to use passion as a reason to explain certain behaviors displayed by entrepreneurs that were

# What Does Your Mindset Say About You?

Visit a place that you are unfamiliar with. It can be a park, somewhere on campus you haven't explored, a neighborhood, a new restaurant—really just about anywhere, provided you are not already familiar with the place. Bring with you a paper notepad and pen. Yes, real paper!

For 10 minutes, just look around and write down a description of what you observe. Make sure that when you write your observations, you use adjectives to describe what you see. For example, you may see a swing set in a park, but you need to describe that swing set. The swing set may be rusty, shiny, empty, broken, vibrant, or dull. A dog you see in the park may be big, cute, dirty, ugly, friendly, or hostile.

You must record your notes in writing, and you must observe for 10 minutes.

After you've finished, sit down and look at the list of words you've written. Circle all words that have a positive connotation. Using the park example above, you would circle shiny, vibrant, cute, and friendly. Now place a square

around all words that have a negative connotation. In our park example, this could be rusty, broken, dull, dirty, ugly, and hostile.

What's the point of all of this? Remember the Corey Booker story! What you see on the outside is a reflection of your mindset on the inside. If what you see in the world is predominantly negative, then your mindset for entrepreneurship needs to be further developed. If what you see in the world is more positive, it will be much easier for you to identify opportunities and make a difference.

## Critical Thinking Questions

1. In what ways did this 10-minute observation exercise confirm your existing assumptions and beliefs about your way of looking at the world? In what ways did it change them?

2. Did you learn anything about yourself that was unexpected or surprising?

3. What do you think would happen if you repeated this exercise in a different location? ●

© Bloomberg/Bloomberg/Getty Images

**Pierre Omidyar, founder of eBay**

**Passion:** an intense positive emotion, which is usually related to entrepreneurs who are engaged in meaningful ventures, or tasks and activities, and which has the effect of motivating and stimulating entrepreneurs to overcome obstacles and remain focused on their goals.

thought to be unconventional, such as perceived high risk taking, intense focus and commitment, and a dogged determination to fulfill a dream.[10] Indeed, many well-known entrepreneurs, such as Mark Zuckerberg (Facebook founder), Jeff Bezos (Amazon founder), and Pierre Omidyar (eBay founder), credit passion for their success.[11]

But what is passion, and is it really that important to entrepreneurial success? In the context of entrepreneurship, **passion** can be defined as an intense positive emotion, which is usually related to entrepreneurs who are engaged in meaningful ventures, or tasks and activities, and which has the effect of motivating and stimulating entrepreneurs to overcome obstacles and remain focused on their goals.[12] This type of passion is aroused by the pleasure of engaging in activities we enjoy. Studies have found that passion can also "enhance mental activity and provide meaning to everyday work,"[13] as well as fostering "creativity and recognition of new patterns that are critical in opportunity exploration and exploitation in uncertain and risky environments."[14]

Passion has also been associated with a wide range of positive effects, such as strength and courage, motivation, energy, drive, tenacity, strong initiative, resilience, love, pride, pleasure, enthusiasm, and joy—all of which can occur as part of the entrepreneurship process.

Passion is not all that is needed to be successful, but research has shown that positive feelings motivate entrepreneurs to persist and engage in tasks and activities in order to maintain those pleasurable emotions.[15]

However, there can also be a dysfunctional side to passion. As we explored in Chapter 1, it is possible to become blinded by passion and so obsessed by an idea or new venture that we fail to heed the warning signs or refuse to listen to negative information or feedback. This type of negative passion can actually curb business growth and limit the ability to creatively solve problems. Furthermore, a recent Stanford study carried out by postdoctoral fellow Paul O'Keefe and psychologists Carol Dweck and Gregory Walton shows that people who follow the old adage "find your passion" are less likely to try new things and tend to give up easily when they encounter obstacles. The researchers found that "develop your passion" through a growth mindset is a much more powerful approach to persevering in a particular area. As Dweck said, "My undergraduates, at first, get all starry-eyed about the idea of finding their passion, but over time they get far more excited about developing their passion and seeing it through. They come to understand that that's how they and their futures will be shaped and how they will ultimately make their contributions."[16]

Consumers are more likely to get into a "habit loop" of toothbrushing when the reward (the "tingling, clean feeling") is advertised.

## Entrepreneurship as a Habit

So far, we have discussed the meaning of mindset, the different types, and the importance of passion and positive thinking for success. As we have learned, mindset is not a predisposed condition; any one of us can develop a more entrepreneurial mindset, but how do we do it?

A good approach is to consider developing new habits. A habit is a sometimes unconscious pattern of behavior that is carried out often and regularly. Good habits can be learned through a "habit loop"—a process by which our brain decides whether or not a certain behavior should be stored and repeated. If we feel rewarded for our behavior, then we are more likely to continue doing it. For example, toothpaste companies instigate a habit loop in consumers by not just advertising the hygiene benefits of brushing teeth, but also the "tingling, clean feeling" we get afterwards—the reward. People are more likely to get into a toothbrushing habit loop as a result.[17]

In the sections that follow, we present three helpful habits to develop to build an entrepreneurial mindset: self-leadership, creativity, and improvisation. As with all good habits, they require practice.

**Habit:** a sometimes unconscious pattern of behavior that is carried out often and regularly.

## 2.3 THE SELF-LEADERSHIP HABIT

>> **LO 2.3**  **Explain how to develop the habit of self-leadership.**

In the context of entrepreneurship, self-leadership is a process whereby people can influence and control their own behavior, actions, and thinking to achieve the self-direction and self-motivation necessary to build their entrepreneurial business ventures.[18] Entrepreneurship requires a deep understanding of self and an ability to motivate oneself to act. You cannot rely on someone else to manage you, get you up in the morning, or force you to get the work done. It can be lonely, and often no one is around to give you feedback, reprimand you, or reward you! As a result, self-leadership is required. It consists of three main strategies: behavior-focused strategies; natural reward strategies; and constructive thought pattern strategies.

**Self-leadership:** a process whereby people can influence and control their own behavior, actions, and thinking to achieve the self-direction and self-motivation necessary to build their entrepreneurial business ventures.

## FIGURE 2.4

### Elements of Self-Leadership

Behavior-focused strategies help increase self-awareness to manage behaviors, particularly when dealing with necessary but unpleasant tasks. These strategies include self-observation, self–goal setting, self-reward, self-punishment, and self-cueing (see Figure 2.4).

Self-observation raises our awareness of how, when, and why we behave the way we do in certain circumstances. For example, twice a day, you could stop and deliberately ask yourself questions about what you are accomplishing; what you are not accomplishing; what is standing in your way; and how you feel about what is happening. This is the first step toward addressing unhelpful or unproductive behaviors in order to devise ways of altering them to enhance performance.

There has been much study regarding the importance of setting goals as a means of enhancing performance. Self–goal setting is the process of setting individual goals for ourselves. This is especially effective when it is accompanied by self-reward—ways in which we compensate ourselves when we achieve our goals. These rewards can be tangible or intangible; for example, you might mentally congratulate yourself when you have achieved your goal (intangible), or you might go out for a celebratory meal or buy yourself a new pair of shoes (tangible). Setting rewards motivates us to accomplish our goals.

Ideally, self-punishment or self-correcting feedback is a process that allows us to examine our mistakes before making a conscious effort not to repeat them. However, many of us have the tendency to beat ourselves up over perceived mistakes or failures; indeed, excessive self-punishment involving guilt and self-criticism can be very harmful to our performance.

Finally, we can use certain environmental cues as a way to encourage constructive behaviors and reduce or eliminate destructive ones through the process of self-cueing. These cues might take the form of making lists or notes or having motivational posters on your wall. They act as a reminder of your desired goals and keep your attention on what you are trying to achieve.

Rewarding ourselves is a beneficial way to boost our spirits and keep us committed to attaining our goals. Natural reward strategies endeavor to make aspects of a task or activity more enjoyable by building in certain features or by reshaping perceptions to focus on the most positive aspects of the task and the value it holds. For example, if you are working on a particularly difficult or boring task, you could build in a break to listen to some music or take a short walk outside. In addition, rather than dreading the nature of the work, you could refocus on the benefits of what you are doing and how good it will feel when it is done.

Much of our behavior is influenced by the way we think, and the habit of thinking in a certain way is derived from our assumptions and beliefs. **Constructive thought patterns** help us to form positive and productive ways of thinking that can benefit our performance. Constructive thought pattern strategies include identifying destructive beliefs and assumptions and reframing those thoughts by practicing self-talk and mental imagery.

As we observed earlier in this chapter, we can use positive self-talk to change our mindset and thought patterns by engaging in dialogue with that irrational voice in our heads that tells us when we can't do something. Similarly, we can engage in mental imagery to imagine ourselves performing a certain task or activity. In fact, studies show that people who visualize themselves successfully performing an activity before it actually takes place are more likely to be successful at performing the task in reality.[19]

These behavioral self-leadership strategies are designed to bring about successful outcomes through positive behaviors and suppress or eliminate those negative behaviors that lead to bad consequences. The concept of self-leadership has been related to many other areas, such as optimism, happiness, consciousness, and emotional intelligence. We believe self-leadership to be an essential process for helping entrepreneurs build and grow their business ventures.

©iStockphoto.com/Bobboz

**Motivational posters help us to stay focused on our goals.**

## 2.4 THE CREATIVITY HABIT

>> **LO 2.4** **Explain how to develop the habit of creativity.**

Creativity is a difficult concept to define, mainly because it covers such a wide breadth of processes and people—from artists, to writers, to inventors, to entrepreneurs—all of whom could be described as creative. Yet creativity can be elusive, and sometimes we spot it only after it is presented to us. Take the classic inventions, for instance. Sometimes, we look at these inventions and wonder why on Earth we hadn't thought of them ourselves. Post-it® notes, paper clips, zippers, and Velcro®—they all seem so obvious after the fact. But of course it is the simplest ideas that can change the world.

© Kim Kulish/Corbis News/Getty Images

**Employees at Facebook are encouraged to take breaks and play games in the office.**

**Constructive thought patterns:** models to help us to form positive and productive ways of thinking that can benefit our performance.

**Creativity:** the capacity to produce new ideas, insights, inventions, products, or artistic objects that are considered to be unique, useful, and of value to others.

Because of its elusiveness, there is no concrete or agreed definition of creativity; however, we like to define **creativity** as the capacity to produce new ideas, insights, inventions, products, or artistic objects that are considered to be unique, useful, and of value to others.[20] For example, Neide Sellin, founder of Brazilian company VixSystem, was among the winners of the 2018 Cartier Initiative Awards for creating Lysa, a robotic guide dog for the visually impaired.[21] In doing so, Sellin has created a solution that addresses the shortage of guide dogs for the millions of visually impaired people living in Brazil.

Human beings are inherently creative, but deeper creativity can be honed and developed. Studies have shown that people who are creative are open to experience, persistent, adaptable, original, motivated, self-reliant, and do not fear failure.

But what has creativity got to do with entrepreneurship? First, there is some evidence that entrepreneurs are more creative than others. A study published in 2008 found that students enrolled in entrepreneurship programs scored higher in personal creativity than students from other programs.[22] This tells us that although everyone has the capacity to

**Lysa, a robotic guide dog for the visually impaired, created by Neide Sellin of VixSystem**

be creative, entrepreneurs score higher on creativity simply because they are practicing the creative process more regularly.

Readers, use caution! We are about to talk about the 1980s! A classic film called *Dead Poets Society* was a huge hit in 1989. Yes, we know you weren't born yet, but the story is timeless. It is a story about a maverick English teacher named John Keating (played by Robin Williams) who challenges the strict academic structure of Welton, a traditional, exclusive all-boys college preparatory school. Mr. Keating urges his students to question the status quo, adjust their mindset, change their behaviors, live life to the fullest, and, famously, to seize the day (using the Latin phrase *carpe diem*). We feel one scene from the movie is an excellent example of unleashing creativity and especially relevant to entrepreneurs.

In one memorable scene, student Todd Anderson (played by Ethan Hawke)—a quiet, underconfident, insecure character who is full of self-doubt about his creative abilities—has not written a poem as assigned. Mr. Keating stands him at the front of the class and prods him to yell "Yawp!" like a barbarian would do, pointing to a picture on the wall of the famous poet Walt Whitman.[23] Then Keating encourages Anderson to improvise a poem by saying the first thing that pops into his head and using his imagination to describe what he sees. By doing so, Todd is able to let go of his insecurities and create in the moment.

As Mr. Keating demonstrates in this scene, creativity is something that can be unleashed even in the most reticent person. Many of us can identify with the Todd Anderson character. It is easy for us to become blocked when we are asked to do something creative, especially when we are put on the spot. Even though we know that every single one of us has the ability to be creative, like Todd, we still find ourselves stumbling against emotional roadblocks.

## The Fear Factor

James L. Adams, a Stanford University professor who specialized in creativity, identified six main emotional roadblocks preventing us from practicing creativity:

**Mr. Keating (played by Robin Williams) encourages underconfident student Todd Anderson (played by Ethan Hawke) to be creative.**

- fear,

- no appetite for chaos,

- preference for judging over generating ideas,

- dislike for incubating ideas,

- perceived lack of challenge, and

- inability to distinguish reality from fantasy.[24]

Of these six emotional roadblocks, it is fear that has the most detrimental effect on our capacity to be creative. Fear causes self-doubt, insecurity, and discomfort even before the beginning of the creative process. It can also block us from sharing our creativity with others because of the risk of failure, negative feedback, or ridicule.

Hamdi Ulukaya, the Turkish-born founder and CEO of the yogurt company Chobani, admitted feeling afraid every single day when he was building his multibillion-dollar business: "If I had failed, a lot of lives were going to be affected by it," he said.[25]

## A Creative Mind

The importance of creativity in navigating the uncharted waters of an uncertain world is also reflected in our biology. The human brain is divided into two hemispheres. Generally speaking, the left hemisphere controls movement, sensation, and perception on the right side of our body, and the right hemisphere does the same on the left side of our body. This is why an injury to the left side of the brain can result in impairment or paralysis on the right side of the body, and vice versa. In the 1960s, researchers proposed that each of the two hemispheres had its own distinct thinking and emotional functions. This idea was then further expanded to propose "left-brained" and "right-brained" orientations as though they were personality types (see Figure 2.5).

In his book *A Whole New Mind*, business and technology author Daniel Pink uses the right-brain/left-brain model to describe how today's society is moving from left-brain thinking to right-brain thinking.[26] Historically, Pink observes, people have tended to use left-brain thinking over right-brain thinking because most tasks and activities in the agricultural and industrial age demanded these attributes. Those were the times when jobs were more methodical and predictable. Today, many of the methodical tasks have been outsourced or have been taken over by computers. Pink holds that we now live in a "conceptual age" that requires us to use both the left and right sides of the brain to create new opportunities and possibilities—in other words, to succeed in today's world, we need a different way of thinking.

However, it is important to recognize that there has been little scientific support for the model of people being "left-brained" or "right-brained." In a 2012 study, researchers at the University of Utah analyzed brain scans from more than 1,000 people between the ages of 7 and 29. They found no evidence to suggest that one side of the brain was more dominant than the other in any given individual: "Our data are not consistent with a whole-brain phenotype of greater 'left-brained' or greater 'right-brained' network strength across individuals."[27] Study researcher Jared Nielsen, a graduate student in neuroscience at the university, concludes, "It may be that personality types have nothing to do with one hemisphere being more active, stronger, or more connected."[28]

Although personality traits are not "left-brained" or "right-brained," the idea of two different types of thinking can still be helpful in understanding how to foster creativity. A study carried out by psychology professor Mihaly Csikszentmihalyi between 1990

---

### FIGURE 2.5

**Left-Versus Right-Brain Orientation**

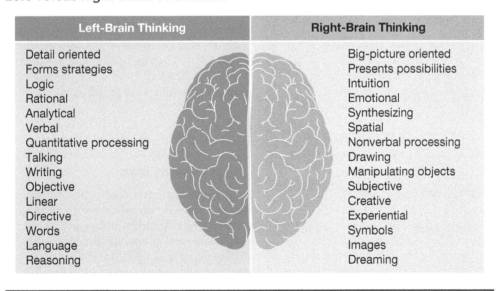

| Left-Brain Thinking | Right-Brain Thinking |
| --- | --- |
| Detail oriented | Big-picture oriented |
| Forms strategies | Presents possibilities |
| Logic | Intuition |
| Rational | Emotional |
| Analytical | Synthesizing |
| Verbal | Spatial |
| Quantitative processing | Nonverbal processing |
| Talking | Drawing |
| Writing | Manipulating objects |
| Objective | Subjective |
| Linear | Creative |
| Directive | Experiential |
| Words | Symbols |
| Language | Images |
| Reasoning | Dreaming |

*Source:* Neck, H. M. (2010). Idea generation. In B. Bygrave & A. Zacharakis (Eds.), *Portable MBA in entrepreneurship* (pp. 27–52; figure on p. 38). Hoboken, NJ: Wiley.

## TABLE 2.1

Csikszentmihalyi's Polarity of Creative Individuals

| | |
|---|---|
| High energy ● | ● Often quiet and at rest |
| Smart ● | ● Naïve |
| Disciplined ● | ● Playful |
| Strong sense of reality ● | ● Imagination and fantasy |
| Extroversion ● | ● Introversion |
| Proud ● | ● Humble |
| Traditionalist ● | ● Rebellious and independent |
| Masculine/feminine ● | ● Feminine/masculine |
| Objective ● | ● Passionate |
| Joy and bliss ● | ● Suffering and pain |

**Source:** Adapted from Neck, H. M. (2010). Idea generation. In B. Bygrave & A. Zacharakis (Eds.), *Portable MBA in entrepreneurship* (pp. 27–52; figure on p. 40). Hoboken, NJ: John Wiley & Sons; and adapted from Csikszentmihalyi, M. (1996). *Creativity: Flow and the psychology of discovery and invention.* New York: HarperCollins.

and 1995 shows an interesting paradox in the personality traits of creative people.[29] Csikszentmihalyi and a team of researchers identified 91 people over the age of 60 whom they considered highly creative, or "exceptional," in the fields of science, art, business, and politics. They discovered that although conflicting traits are not commonly found in the same person—for example, a person is typically introverted or extroverted, not both—they were present in many of the study participants. They exhibited seemingly polarized traits like discipline and playfulness, a strong sense of reality and a vivid imagination, and pride and humility (see Table 2.1). Csikszentmihalyi referred to these highly creative individuals as having "dialectic" personalities and concluded that for people to be creative, they need to operate at both ends of the poles.

If you compare the "polarized" traits in Table 2.1 with the left- and right-brain characteristics in Figure 2.5, you will see striking similarities, suggesting that creativity involves integrating "both sides" of the brain. In this sense, Csikszentmihalyi's study is consistent with Pink's argument that we are living in a conceptual age that requires us to tap into our creative potential and be "whole-brained" thinkers and doers.

Although successful entrepreneurs definitely do not fit into a single profile, there is some commonality in their mindset. They envision success while also preparing for failure. They value autonomy in deciding and acting and, therefore, assume responsibility for problems and failures. They have a tendency to be intolerant of authority, exhibit good salesmanship skills, have high self-confidence, and believe strongly in their abilities. They also tend to be both optimistic and pragmatic. They work hard and are driven by an intense commitment to the success of the organization. Here again, we see evidence that an entrepreneurial mindset requires more than one kind of thinking.

## 2.5 THE IMPROVISATION HABIT

>> **LO 2.5    Explain how to develop the habit of improvisation.**

Let's explore the third of the key habits for developing an entrepreneurial mindset: improvisation. Improvisation is the art of spontaneously creating something without preparation. Improvisation is connected to the entrepreneurial mindset because it helps us develop the cognitive ability to rapidly sense and act as well as change direction quickly.

For many of us, the word *improvisation* evokes images of people standing on stage in front of an audience under pressure to make them laugh or to entertain them. While it is true that world-famous comedy clubs like The Second City in Chicago offer classes in improvisation to aspiring actors—including Tina Fey, Stephen Colbert, and Jordan Peele—improvisational skills can be very useful to entrepreneurs of all types.

**Improvisation:** the art of spontaneously creating something without preparation.

The ability to function in an uncertain world requires a degree of improvisation. Entrepreneurs may begin with a certain idea or direction, but obstacles such as limited resources, unforeseen market conditions, or even conflicts with team members can prevent them from executing their initial plans. This means they need to find a way to quickly adapt to their circumstances, think on their feet, and create new plans to realize their vision. A recent study showed that entrepreneurs starting new ventures who displayed more signs of improvisational behavior tended to outperform those who did not have the same tendencies.[30]

There is a long tradition of improvisation techniques in theater and in music styles such as jazz, but improvisation has also been growing in popularity in business and entrepreneurship. For example, many major business schools, such as UCLA's Anderson School of Management, Duke University's Fuqua School of Business, MIT's Sloan School of Management, and Columbia Business School, offer business students courses on improvisation to teach skills such as creativity, leadership, negotiation, teamwork, and communication. Indeed, Columbia takes business students to a jazz club so they can engage with professional musicians regarding how they use improvisation on stage.[31]

Robert Kulhan, an assistant professor at Duke University's Fuqua School of Business, teaches improvisation to business students and executives. Kulhan asserts that "improvisation isn't about comedy, it's about reacting—being focused and present in the moment at a very high level."[32] In the world of business, teams from The Second City are often brought in to teach improvisation skills to staff working at the Chicago branch of Deloitte Consulting.[33]

Improvisation is especially relevant to the world of entrepreneurship when uncertainty is high and the ability to react is essential (see Table 2.2).

For those of you who may feel a little apprehensive about engaging in spontaneous creation, it may comfort you to know that anyone can improvise. In fact, you may not realize it, but each one of us has been improvising all our lives. Think about it: How could any one of us be prepared for everything life has to throw at us? Often, we are forced to react and create on the spot in response to certain events. There is simply no way we can prepare for every situation and every conversation before it takes place. We are naturally inclined to deal with the unexpected; now all we have to do is deliberately practice that ability.

**Comedic improvisers in action**

## TABLE 2.2

Improvisation Guidelines

- Improvisation is not just for actors or musicians.
- There's no such thing as being wrong.
- Nothing suggested is questioned or rejected (no matter how crazy it might sound!).
- Ideas are taken on board, expanded, and passed on for further input.
- Everything is important.
- It is a group activity—you will have the support of the group.
- You can trust that the group will solve a certain problem.
- It's about listening closely and accepting what you're given.
- It's about being spontaneous, imaginative, and dealing with the unexpected.

**Source:** http://iangotts.files.wordpress.com/2012/02/using-improv-in-business-e2-v1.pdf

However, many of us are apprehensive about sharing our ideas for fear of being shot down. One of the most useful improvisation exercises to address this fear is the "Yes, and" principle. This means listening to what others have to say and building on it by starting with the words, "Yes, and." Consider the following conversation among three friends.

Peter:     "I have a great idea for a healthy dried fruit snack for kids that contains less sugar than any other brand on the market."

Teresa:   "Hasn't this been done already? The market is saturated with these kinds of products."

Sami:     "I think it's an interesting idea, but I've heard that these products cost a fortune to manufacture and produce."

In this conversation, Peter has barely touched on his idea before it gets shot down by the others. Peter may not be conscious of it, but the reaction from his friends changes his mindset from positive to negative, instantly limiting his freedom to expand the idea further. Rather than helping Peter to build on his idea, Sami and Teresa rely on judgment and hearsay.

Now let's take a look at how the "Yes, and" principle can completely change the tone and output of the conversation.

Peter:     "I have a great idea for a healthy dried fruit snack for kids that contains less sugar than any other brand on the market."

Teresa:   "*Yes, and* each snack could contain a card with a fun fact or maybe some kind of riddle."

Sami:     "*Yes, and* if enough cards are collected, you could go online and win a small prize."

By using "Yes, and," Peter and his friends have managed to expand on his original idea and inject a bit of positivity into the conversation.

Why don't we practice improvisation more often? Self-doubt is the most common barrier to improvisation: "I don't want to pitch my idea. I hate speaking in public"; "What if I freeze up?"; and even worse, "What if I make a fool of myself?" The fear underlying the self-doubt is the fear of failure, which stems from not being able to plan in advance.

Yet people who engage in improvisation are actually more tolerant of failure because it helps us to break free of traditional structured thinking, releases our need for control, opens our minds, improves our listening skills, and builds our confidence by encouraging us to think quickly under pressure. Originally actors were trained in improvisational techniques so they could overcome forgetting their lines on stage during a performance.

Improvisation has a significant effect on our brain activity. Scientists studied the effects of improvisation on brain activity by asking six trained jazz pianists to play a combination of learned and improvised pieces of music while lying in an MRI machine with a miniature electronic keyboard. When it came to analyzing the brain scans, the scientists found that the musicians tended to switch off the self-censoring part of the brain, which gave them the ability to freely express themselves without restriction (see Figure 2.6).[34]

**FIGURE 2.6**

**MRI Scans From Jazz Improvisation**

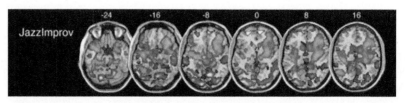

**Source:** Limb, C. J. Neural substrates of spontaneous musical performance: An fMRI study of jazz improvisation. *PLOS One*. Retrieved from http://journals.plos.org/plosone/article?id=10.1371/journal.pone.0001679

MINDSHIFT

# Building Entrepreneurial Habits

There are four tips to building new habits:

1.   Start with a small habit.

Make the habit so small you can't say no. Make the habit so easy you can get it done without a ton of motivation. Make the habit so small that you don't have to psych yourself up each day to do it. For example, say you want to start a habit of doing push-ups every day. Start with 5 push-ups a day instead of 50 per day.

2.   Increase your habit in very small ways.

After you start small, you need to gradually improve your habit. Even a 1% improvement can add up fairly quickly. With our push-up example, you could do five push-ups a day for a week, then go to six push-ups a day the following week.

3.   As you gradually build up your habit, break the habit into small chunks.

It is critical to keep each habit reasonable. Why? You need to keep momentum going and to make the behavior as easy as possible to accomplish. When you get your push-ups to 20 a day, you may want to do 10 push-ups, twice a day. This makes it an easier physical and mental challenge.

4.   Plan to fail.

The boxer Mike Tyson said, "Everyone has a plan until they get punched in the mouth." Understand that you probably will get punched in the face at times and fail. But you need to realize that this is ok in terms of practicing your new habit. Research shows that failing to do your habit once has very little impact on the long-term progress of performing your new habit. Even the best performers fail. The difference is that the best get back on the horse, so to speak, and keep riding, keep trying to do their new habit. So, if you don't have the motivation to do your push-ups one day, then don't think, "I've missed one day; I might as well miss the whole week." This is habit-defeating thinking. Instead say, "I missed today but it's no big deal; I'm going to get back on track tomorrow and do my 20 push-ups."

Now it's time to apply the four tips to an entrepreneurial habit of your choice. This could be looking at problems with a growth mindset or looking beyond what you are supposed to look at, as in the Research at Work feature Study on Luck. It could also be getting out of your comfort zone once a day or once a week. It could even be getting more comfortable with rejection or perhaps learning one impressive new piece of information every day. The possibilities are limitless, so use your imagination.

What amazing entrepreneurial habit do you want to build?

_____

How can you break it down into a smaller habit? What are you committing to do *this* week?

_____

_____

How can you increase the habit next week?

_____

_____

Is the habit "chunkable"? In what ways?

_____

_____

## Critical Thinking Questions

1.   At what point will you feel the habit has actually become a habit?

2.   At what moment did you experience failure, and how did the learning inform your next attempt?

3.   How can you apply the tips for building a habit to also breaking a habit? ●

**Source**: Clear, J. (2018). *Atomic habits: An easy & proven way to build good habits & break bad ones.* New York, NY: Avery.

In other words, we have a brain that is designed to generate unpredictable ideas when the self-monitoring part is suppressed.[35]

As we have learned, developing an entrepreneurial mindset requires practice in the areas of self-leadership, creativity, and improvisation. However, all this practice is meaningless unless your mindset is geared toward action.

# 2.6 THE MINDSET AS THE PATHWAY TO ACTION

>> **LO 2.6    Relate the mindset for entrepreneurship to entrepreneurial action.**

The mindset is the pathway to action. There is no entrepreneurship without action, and the mindset is antecedent to action. As we have seen in the preceding sections, the entrepreneurial mindset requires the habits of self-leadership, creativity, and improvisation. These habits create an emotional platform for entrepreneurial actions. You can have the best idea in the world, but without a mindset with a bias for action, there is nothing—no new venture, product, organization, or anything else. Taking action is the only way to get results. Even the process of changing and expanding your mindset involves taking action through deliberate practice.

But taking action requires a degree of confidence and belief in our abilities—an attribute known as self-efficacy. Let's take a look at how self-efficacy supports entrepreneurial activity.

## Self-Efficacy and Entrepreneurial Intentions

**Entrepreneurial self-efficacy (ESE):** the belief that entrepreneurs have in their own ability to begin new ventures.

There have been an increasing number of studies on entrepreneurial self-efficacy (ESE), which is the belief entrepreneurs have in their ability to begin new ventures. Self-efficacy is an essential part of the entrepreneurial mindset, and it is thought to be a good indicator of entrepreneurial intentions as well as a strong precursor to action.[36] In fact, recent research suggests that entrepreneurial self-efficacy can enable the entrepreneur to more effectively confront demands or stressors and thus improve entrepreneurial performance.[37] In other words, the research suggests that when we believe in our ability to succeed in something, we are more likely to actively take the steps to make it happen.

However, sometimes there is a fine line between self-confidence, self-efficacy, and arrogance. Arrogance leads a person to believe that he or she achieved success without help from others; further, the arrogant person may feel entitled to success and entitled to "bend the rules" to get ahead.

Kevin Plank, the CEO of the fitness apparel company Under Armour, believed in his vision so deeply that he invested all his savings—about $20,000—and took on an additional $40,000 of credit card debt just to fund the company. Thanks to his high degree of self-efficacy, Under Armour has taken in almost $2 billion in sales and has almost 6,000 employees.[38]

Like many other factors of entrepreneurship, researchers have found that ESE can be heightened through training and education.

In general, research shows that people with high levels of self-efficacy tend to put in more effort, persist with an idea, and persevere with a task more than those people who possess low levels of self-efficacy. For example, The General Self-Efficacy Scale (GSES; see Table 2.3) was designed by researchers to assess the degree to which we believe our actions are responsible for successful results.[39] It measures the belief we have in our ability to carry out difficult tasks, cope with adversity, persist in reaching our goals, and recover from setbacks.

The GSES has been used all over the world since the 1990s to measure the self-efficacy levels of a whole range of ages, nationalities, and ethnicities. It is thought to be an accurate way of testing self-efficacy levels. It consists of 10 items, takes 4 minutes to complete, and is scored on a range from 10 to 40; the higher the score, the stronger the belief in your ability to take action. Take 4 minutes and complete the scale.

Keep in mind that self-efficacy can change over time. The more you practice something, such as entrepreneurship, the greater the likelihood that your self-efficacy related to entrepreneurial action will increase.

## The Role of Mindset in Opportunity Recognition

As our mindset grows and expands through practicing self-leadership, creating, and improvising, we are more inclined to recognize and create opportunities. In fact, Richard Wiseman's study of luck, described in the Research at Work feature, shows us that people who consider themselves lucky are more open to recognizing opportunities.

**TABLE 2.3**

The General Self-Efficacy Scale (GSES)

| 1 | I can always manage to solve difficult problems if I try hard enough. |
|---|---|
| 2 | If someone opposes me, I can find the means and ways to get what I want. |
| 3 | It is easy for me to stick to my aims and accomplish my goals. |
| 4 | I am confident that I could deal efficiently with unexpected events. |
| 5 | Thanks to my resourcefulness, I know how to handle unforeseen situations. |
| 6 | I can solve most problems if I invest the necessary effort. |
| 7 | I can remain calm when facing difficulties because I can rely on my coping abilities. |
| 8 | When I am confronted with a problem, I can usually find several solutions. |
| 9 | If I am in trouble, I can usually think of a solution. |
| 10 | I can usually handle whatever comes my way. |

**Response Format**

1 = Not at all true. 2 = Hardly true. 3 = Moderately true. 4 = Exactly true.

**Source:** Schwarzer, R., & Jerusalem, M. (1995). Generalized self-efficacy scale. In J. Weinman, S. Wright, & M. Johnston (Eds.), *Measures in health psychology: A user's portfolio. Causal and control beliefs* (pp. 35–37). Windsor, UK: NFER-NELSON. Scale retrieved from http://userpage.fu-berlin.de/~health/engscal.htm

---

ENTREPRENEURSHIP MEETS ETHICS

# Family and Friends Along for the Ride

Switching to the realm of the entrepreneur means giving up the mindset of being an employee. Significant risks come with the change in lifestyle, and most notably, your steady paycheck disappears. For the avid entrepreneur, the risk to one's finances are often calculated, but what of the risk to those who are financially dependent on the entrepreneur, or even those who will be financially dependent in the future?

Conventional wisdom states that 9 out of 10 startups will fail (although the jury is still out on the accuracy of that number), and with such a high risk of failure, entrepreneurs face the daunting prospect of bankruptcy and poor credit before the businesses even take off. Taking precautions against the possibility of failure is a necessary step for any entrepreneur. Before beginning, it is important to decide just how much personal investment an entrepreneur should commit to, whether by using family savings or taking out loans.

It is easy to overlook the heavy financial risks for young entrepreneurs who have nobody financially dependent on them. But, the financial ruin of a failed venture has the capacity to follow an entrepreneur for many years to come. A poor credit situation and accumulated debt can take a toll on any future partner or child.

On the other side of the issue, perhaps financial stability and security do not build the strongest families. Children

who grow up with an entrepreneur for a parent might develop a stronger ability to overcome adversity and cope with hardship. Although the situation may be difficult in the short term, those children could grow into stronger adults.

## Critical Thinking Questions

1. How much patience should a spouse, child, or anyone financially dependent on an entrepreneur be forced to have during dire financial situations? How many failed ventures are too many for them to endure?

2. Is it fair to risk your family's financial security to pursue a dream?

3. Are the benefits of being an entrepreneur worth the heavy risk involved? Is the probability of failure too high to bet a family's future upon? ●

**Sources:**

Dholakiya, P. (2014, July 29). Don't fail when your business fails: Tips for bouncing back. *Fast Company.* Retrieved from https://www.fastcompany.com/3033622/dont-fail-when-your-business-fails-tips-for-bouncing-back

Griffith, E. (2017, June 27). Conventional wisdom says 90% of startups fail. Data say otherwise. *Fortune.* Retrieved from http://fortune.com/2017/06/27/startup-advice-data-failure/

Helmen, J. (2016, October 8). 3 things I learned growing up in a family of entrepreneurs. *Forbes.* Retrieved from https://www.forbes.com/sites/jillienehelman/2016/10/08/3-things-i-learned-growing-up-in-a-family-of-entrepreneurs/#6fefcb6b78c0

Think back to how Franklin Yancey started his original business, College Comfort. Alongside his friend John Hite, he identified an opportunity to make more comfortable stadium seating at a lower price than the competition by simply observing how the product was used. Through creativity and improvisation, both men succeeded in providing high-quality cushions to the sports and entertainment industry.

It is so easy to miss opportunities if we are not in the right mindset. Yancey and Hite could just as easily have casually exchanged remarks about the drabness of the seat cushions available and then simply moved on to a new topic of conversation, forgetting all about their initial observations. Even worse, one of them might have pointed out the opportunity to design new cushions, but the other could have discouraged him from persevering with the idea by saying that creating a new set of cushions would be time-consuming, expensive, and so on. Fortunately, both men were in the right mindset to identify a need for practical seating cushions and to support each other in their pursuit of the goal.

As we have explored, in order to develop an entrepreneurial mindset, we need to recognize its importance and consciously take the steps to nurture it through the practices of self-leadership, creativity, and improvisation. Working on those areas helps build higher levels of self-efficacy, which give us the confidence to create, share, and pursue our ideas. By building an entrepreneurial mindset, we are better able to identify exciting opportunities and to take action to begin new initiatives, start new businesses, and create new products and services. A continuously improving mindset is the key to successful entrepreneurship. ●

---

Get the tools you need to sharpen your study skills. SAGE edge offers a robust online environment featuring an impressive array of free tools and resources.

- Access practice quizzes, eFlashcards, video, and multimedia at
  **edge.sagepub.com/neckentrepreneurship2e**

---

## SUMMARY

### 2.1   Appraise the effectiveness of mindset in entrepreneurship.

Part of the Entrepreneurship Method is having the right mindset (or mental attitude) to start and grow a business. Entrepreneurs who have the right mindset are more likely to persist with ideas and act on potential opportunities.

### 2.2   Define "entrepreneurial mindset" and explain its importance to entrepreneurs.

An entrepreneurial mindset is the ability to quickly sense, take action, and get organized under certain conditions. Of the two mindsets proposed by Carol Dweck, the growth mindset represents a fundamental belief that failure is something to build on, and a learning mindset is essential for personal and professional growth.

### 2.3   Explain how to develop the habit of self-leadership.

Self-leadership is a process of self-direction that is developed by using behavior strategies, reward strategies, and constructive thought patterns.

### 2.4   Explain how to develop the habit of creativity.

Creativity is defined as the capacity to produce new ideas, insights, or inventions that are unique and of value to others. Developing the habit of creativity requires engaging in new experiences, making new associations, and letting go of fears and insecurities.

### 2.5   Explain how to develop the habit of improvisation.

Improvisation is the art of creating without preparation. Improvisation is recognized as a key skill not just for budding entrepreneurs, but for business practitioners of all types. Developing the habit of improvisation requires practice to quickly adapt to changing circumstances, think on your feet, and build on the ideas of others.

### 2.6   Relate the mindset for entrepreneurship to entrepreneurial action.

As entrepreneurship demands practice to achieve success, the right mindset is necessary for that practice to be successful. When people believe they can succeed, they're more likely to pursue the right activities to make that happen.

CASE STUDY

## Maliha Khalid, founder and CEO, Doctory

Before the inception of Doctory.pk, Maliha Khalid was accustomed to the regular routine of having a stable job in the corporate sector; however, she eventually found her work to be unfulfilling. "Sending emails to people on the same floor did not seem like the best way to spend the rest of my life," she recalled. She needed to see the impact of her actions. And her journey began. . . .

"The context in which we are working is of deprivation. There is still a large number of people in Pakistan that do not have access to proper health care," says Ayyaz Kiani, one of the three cofounders and CHO (chief health officer) of Doctory (www.doctory.pk), a platform that connects those with little or no access to the appropriate doctors, resources, and health care specialists all throughout the country of Pakistan. Maliha Khalid, the cofounder and CEO of Doctory, says, "Pakistan is a diverse country in terms of the socio-economic backgrounds of the health care consumers and in terms of diversity in geography and languages. There are a lot of people who cannot access quality health care, primarily due to financial reasons and the lack of access to the right information. This wide range of population belong in different categories and have different needs and Doctory is working towards serving them all."

Doctory's service aims to improve access among these people. It provides a free database of doctors segmented based on specialization and location on their website. People can look for a doctor or a specialist in their locality and reach out accordingly. However, 70% of the population live in non-urban areas and need to navigate unfamiliar territory to obtain health care. Doctory points toward the fact that because every person in the country has a mobile phone with an SIM card installed in it to call Doctory health centers, services such as food delivery and cab hailing have been able to take advantage of this. However, delivery of basic services such as health has been quite late in this regard, which seems quite surprising. By taking several doctors on board, Doctory has been able to tap this market by providing consultation services to the common person on the phone. The service is free of charge and doctors answer phone calls 12 hours a day for 5 days a week.

Public health indices (data regarding health indicators created and measured by the WHO wing of the UN) of Pakistan are not particularly favorable when compared to public health indices of its South Asian counterparts. Mother and infant mortality are pretty high even when the average income is steadily increasing. The rising middle class in big cities has also led to many big "5-star hospitals" opening up for those who can afford them. People travel long distances to cities like Islamabad (the capital of Pakistan) to get quality treatment. However, not everyone can afford to travel or use the services of these hospitals.

"There are three reasons why people don't go to doctors for treatment. One, they don't have the money required to access hospitals—they can't afford the trip, the fees of the doctor, the medicines. Two, people live in far-flung areas and health services networks set up in the early 1980s are now dysfunctional. You might find a primary health center in these areas but with no doctor or medicines. Lastly, people prefer to go to a religious or a traditional healer as doctors speak a difficult language," explains Ayyaz.

Lack of trust in the system is another hurdle. When Maliha was 17, she suffered from a mysterious series of symptoms. However, arriving at the right diagnosis of her condition was a "long and frustrating experience." The lack of information became a hurdle in her way of getting an adequate diagnosis. Even the information that she received from her personal network was incomplete and sometimes outdated and irrelevant. Each consultation with the doctor led her to another doctor resulting in more questions than answers. Maliha believes she is not alone in her experience, which causes millennials in Pakistan to avoid doctors altogether.

Maliha's journey into health care started with some insight from her uncle, Ayyaz Kiani. Having worked in consumer protection for a better part of his professional life, Ayyaz asked Maliha for her feedback on a consumer protection model in health care adopted from the United States (something similar to ZocDoc). She found this intriguing and started discussing this with her family and friends in order to understand the problem better. She was not only able to relate to her own experience but every new conversation got her more excited about solving this problem of access to health care professionals and resources.

"When we started, we never thought that this was going to be a startup or a social enterprise. We just started one day because we knew that there was a need and that we needed to work on it. It then turned into a social enterprise. It was exciting to imagine using technology to work for common good and solve a real-world problem," says Maliha. She cofounded Ezpz Sehat with Ayyaz in August 2014 with the vision to allow for informed decision making for those seeking health care.

Ezpz Sehat was aimed at addressing the problem Maliha had faced when she was unwell; it was a database giving details of all doctors in the vicinity along with a system to provide feedback on the services provided. It aimed to bridge the gap between doctors and patients by improving the quality of information provided. Maliha strived to address the disparity between the access to health care and the population distribution in Pakistan, and the culture that surrounded seeing health care services. "It is common in Pakistan for patients to visit specialists instead of General Physicians to seek consultation. Since people don't necessarily know what they need, they usually spend 80% of their time and money looking for the right doctor (usually the sixth doctor they meet)," Maliha explains. This approach found its roots in the lack of trust in public health services, making access to private health care very important. Maliha and Ayyaz are working to address the problem of accessibility and affordability through multiple prototypes they built over 3 years.

However, they ultimately realized that a technology product, such as a mobile or web app, would likely alienate a big portion of the population that were not comfortable browsing on the Internet. It was around this time (March to April 2018) at a startup accelerator program in Berlin that they met Mike LaVigne, the third cofounder and CPO (Chief Product Officer) of what then came to be called Doctory.pk. Having been the cofounder and CPO of Clue, a health app for women all over the world with over 10 million downloads, Mike had research, product design, and development experience that could prove crucial to Doctory's technological development.

The focus of Doctory shifted from not only providing access to information but providing access to high-quality health care while improving accountability. It aims to serve those people that are not properly served. With pockets of the populations not being able to afford even $0.70 in doctor's fees to treat their child, the team at Doctory demand accessibility to all. In the future, the team would also like to leverage the platform to review the services being provided by doctors. They believe that these reviews could be effective in altering the level of service provided by doctors as well as build greater trust between patients and doctors. "Once doctors and health care providers know that reviews might affect careers and business, it might affect their operations for the better," says Ayyaz. "If the doctor's practice suffers because of the negative comments received, he/she is likely to be motivated to provide a better service to the consumer. This sense of responsibility and empowerment of the consumer might help transform the industry for the better."

Since November 2017, Doctory has received a great response from its customers. Its first interaction with the market was through being featured on a radio program in Pakistan. The market reaction exceeded expectations. They received 500 calls the day they went on air, a busy day for the one doctor that they had employed then! This was a good start for Doctory and it has grown extensively by word of mouth, except for the occasional SMS campaigns. The number of calls received in the first 4 weeks was around 5,000. Doctory now employs six doctors who take calls based on their availability. Usually, a call is transferred to a doctor within 5 minutes. The act of talking to a professional over the phone not only provides the necessary counseling but even helps the patients navigate the health care system in Pakistan. Through their experience, the team has learned that 60–70% of all calls received usually require nonpharmaceutical remedies and that a simple conversation can help fix the problem. Their trained doctors provide valuable, accurate, and relevant advice for their patients' health concerns—everything from advice on the common cold, to diabetes, to sexual health.

Doctory's vision is one of creating maximum social impact. The databases of doctors are available for free online and are expected to remain free in the future. In the long run, Doctory is looking to provide a host of paid services, including concierge services to help generate revenue to fund the business while reaching as many people in Pakistan as possible. All in all, the people at Doctory have found their experience to be humbling. They are able to successfully direct their callers in ways that have not only saved patients money but also helped them avoid unnecessary medical procedures.

Maliha is very optimistic about the role the next generation can play in shaping the world as we know today. She says, "Millennials can create that impact and change that is needed to take the world to the next level!"

## Critical Thinking Questions

1. In your own words, how would you explain Maliha's entrepreneurial journey?

2. In what ways does Maliha Khalid's approach to life exemplify the entrepreneurial mindset advocated in this chapter? Does her approach differ in any ways?

3. Can you think of limitations you are placing on yourself that may be restricting your ability to achieve your goals? Name some specific examples.

4. How can you apply an entrepreneurial mindset to your life to help you break through these limitations in order to reach success?

**Source:** Maliha Khalid and Ayyaz Kiani (interview with the author, January 15, 2019)

# PART II

## Creating and Developing Opportunities

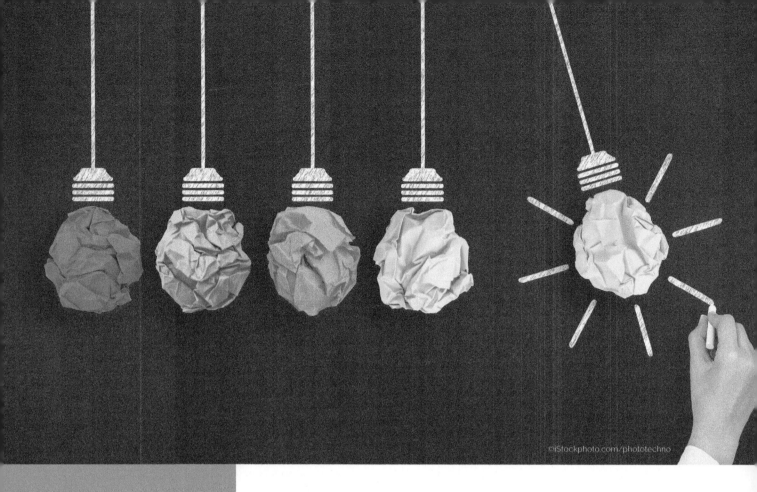

# 3 Creating and Recognizing New Opportunities

"Entrepreneurs see trends where others just see data; they connect dots when others just see dots. This ability to consistently recognize and seize opportunity does not develop overnight. It takes deliberate practice."

—Dan Cohen, entrepreneur and educator

# Chapter Outline

# Learning Objectives

## 3.1 THE ENTREPRENEURIAL MINDSET AND OPPORTUNITY RECOGNITION

>> **LO 3.1  Explain how the entrepreneurial mindset relates to opportunity recognition.**

In Chapter 2, we explored the concept of mindset and its importance to identifying opportunities. Applying what we have learned about mindset, it is evident that an entrepreneurial mindset positions you to identify opportunities and to take action. Entrepreneurship is all about openness to new ideas, new opportunities, and new ways of acting on them. Indeed, this is demonstrated time and again by countless entrepreneurs' stories, regardless of the diversity of their industries, whether for-profit or nonprofit, whether a startup or within an existing corporation. All the entrepreneurs featured throughout this text, including Juan Giraldo, founder of Waku; Saurabh Gupta, founder of Gyan-I; and Maliha Khalid, founder of Doctory, have found ways to identify new opportunities that address unmet needs in the marketplace. Let's take a closer look at what *opportunity* really means.

### What Is an Opportunity?

There are many definitions of opportunity, but most include references to three central characteristics: potential economic value, novelty or newness, and perceived desirability.[1] We define **opportunity** as a way of generating value through unique, novel, or desirable products, services, and even processes that have not been previously exploited in a particular context. Jazmine Valencia is a good example of an entrepreneur who found an opportunity to provide personalized services for musicians. For an opportunity to be viable, the idea must have the capacity to generate value.

Value can take many forms. The most common form of value is economic value: the capacity to generate profit. Two other forms of value—social value and environmental value—are less understood but equally important. An opportunity has social value if it helps to address a social need or creates social good. Environmental value exists if the opportunity protects or preserves the environment. We address this further in Chapter 16 on social entrepreneurship. Startup Bios Urn, headquartered in Spain, created a biodegradable urn in which to grow trees from human ashes, to address the environmental problems of a growing population (many people don't have the land to bury their loved ones) and the polluting effects of traditional burials.[2] All forms of value, however, are predicated on the assumption that there is a market populated with enough people to buy your product or service. This does not mean that a large market is required; there are countless examples of successful businesses that run on a small scale, catering to a market that is limited in one way or another. The key is to scale the business and its costs

**Opportunity:** a way of generating profit through unique, novel, or desirable products or services that have not been previously exploited.

# Jazmine Valencia, JV Agency

Photo courtesy of Jazmine Valencia

**Jazmine Valencia, founder, JV Agency**

Jazmine Valencia operates at the heart of one of the most disrupted and fastest-changing industries of the past decade. She has been on the cutting edge of the music industry since the beginning of her career. In 2012, she started from the bottom at the Island Def Jam Music Group label as an intern, working her way to director of digital marketing. During her 7 years at Island Def Jam, she witnessed the dawn of social media as an effective marketing tool before it was consolidated into the handful of platforms we have today, such as Facebook, YouTube, and Instagram. Jazmine saw the changes and she saw the possibilities. "In the beginning people didn't yet know exactly what social media could do for music marketing as it had yet to establish itself as a mainstream medium and it was not clear if major players would, but I wanted to be ready."

In 2014, Island Def Jam Music Group split into multiple labels and Jazmine's entire client list was shaken up. As Jazmine said, "It was like going through a divorce and we were all confused kids." Although her job was secure, her day-to-day had changed drastically, and many of the artists she had spent years building relationships with were no

longer hers. But Jazmine had skills that the artists needed, especially in this time of uncertainty. What those artists needed was help with marketing in this new world of music distribution. As a result, she left Island Def Jam in 2015 and started consulting with her clients who had been displaced in the split. She soon realized she was offering a little too much help for free. It was time, she thought, to "jump head first into starting my own music marketing agency."

It was an organic transition from Def Jam to her own business because it was easy to sell herself based on what she had already accomplished. There was no question of what she was capable of doing for musicians, and this made it easy to attract clients she had previously worked with as well as new ones. "It didn't seem like a risk to me; it felt easy and it happened by accident. I said to myself, 'Let me just go with this and see where it gets me.'"

Today, JV Agency is a marketing company handling campaigns for all levels of musicians from all genres. Jazmine leads and advises some of music's biggest artists, from indie rock band The Killers to Canadian singer-songwriter Shawn Mendes. She helps grow careers for some of the most talented musicians today using an artist-focused marketing approach to growth. This means she handles their digital marketing, social media, brand strategy, international distribution, and many other aspects of an artist's business. She credits her success in the industry to her creativity, confidence, and ability to thrive under pressure, all things she honed early on while at Island Def Jam. One thing Jazmine wishes everyone would do is replace the word "failure" with "lesson" because she feels that failure has such negative connotations. "I wish we could use a positive word for failure so people would be less afraid of making mistakes and more capable of learning lessons from their experiences." Jazmine knows that without failure and the associated learning, it's hard to see new opportunities. "Sometimes you have to learn lessons and pay the price in the short term and to realize that setbacks can be opportunities in disguise."

## Critical Thinking Questions

1. Why did Jazmine start her own business?

2. Why does she recommend doing what you are passionate about?

3. What is Jazmine's perspective on failure? ●

**Source:** Jazmine Valencia (interview with author, January 15, 2019)

to the size of the market—to balance supply with demand. Here again, the entrepreneurial mindset is what enables us to envision how a new product or service can generate value for a niche, an age group or interest segment, a geographic area, or a larger population.

In addition, a new idea that constitutes an opportunity, whether it is a product, service, or technology, must be new or unique or at least a variation on an existing theme that you are confident people will accept and adopt. The idea must involve something that people need, desire, and find useful or valuable. Or there must be a significant problem to solve. Finding solutions to problems and meeting customer needs are the essence of opportunity recognition.

## Innovation, Invention, Improvement, or Irrelevant?

Of course, all ideas are not created equal and not all ideas are venture opportunities. Part of recognizing an opportunity is the ability to evaluate ideas and identify those with the highest likelihood of success. One framework for doing this is to rate an idea on four different dimensions: The idea may be an *innovation*, an *invention*, an *improvement*, or *irrelevant*. Of these, innovations and inventions are high in novelty, while improvements and irrelevant ideas are low in novelty (see Figure 3.1).

A successful idea scores highly as an *innovation* if the product or service is novel, useful, and valuable. Today's smartphone, and the basic cellular phone of the 1980s, are both good examples of a product that meets all the requirements of a successful innovation.

Innovations and inventions are often paired together, but the difference between them lies in demand. *Inventions*, by definition, score highly for novelty, but if an invention does not reach the market or appeal to consumers, then it will be rendered useless. Inventions that succeed in finding a market move to the innovation stage.

**FIGURE 3.1**

### Idea Classification Matrix

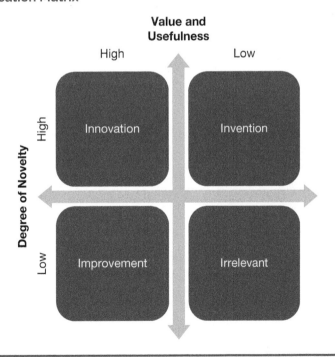

**Source:** Neck, H. M. (2010). Idea generation. In B. Bygrave & A. Zacharakis (Eds.), *Portable MBA in entrepreneurship* (pp. 27–52). Hoboken, NJ: John Wiley & Sons.

**Post-it® notes**

As an example of an invention that developed into an innovation, consider the story of Dr. Spencer Silver, the inventor of Post-it® notes.[3] More than 35 years ago, Silver was a scientist working for 3M. His task was to devise a new adhesive, something stronger and tougher that had never been seen before. During his experiments, he discovered an adhesive that was none of those things—although it did stick to surfaces, it didn't bond tightly to them. For years, Silver tried to persuade his colleagues that he had found something meaningful—the only problem was that he had no idea what the adhesive could be used for. Art Fry, another 3M scientist, had a problem of his own. Every time he tried to bookmark particular pages of the hymn book for choir practice with pieces of paper, they would fall out. Fry remembered Silver's discovery and they ended up working together to develop what we now know as the Post-it® note.

The Post-it® note took off because it was novel, useful, and practical—but it became an innovation of high value only when it hit the market. Yet ideas do not always need to be unique or novel to appeal to customers. There are many ideas that focus on *improvement* of existing products. Take folding sunglasses, serrated ice cream scoops, or liquid paper, for instance. Each product has been revisited and improved on. The products may not be high in novelty, but there is still a strong market for these products, as many people will find them useful to a degree.

Finally, there are ideas that fall into the *irrelevant* category, scoring low on both novelty and usefulness. The food and beverage industry, in particular, has experimented with some changes over the years that have failed to meet consumer expectations. Pepsi introduced a morning pick-me-up drink called Pepsi A.M., beverage giant Coors started selling mountain spring water, and soup company Campbell's combined soup and a sandwich into one frozen microwaveable meal—all of these are arguably examples of irrelevant ideas.[4]

However, it is difficult to fully pigeonhole ideas into neat categories. How can we really predict whether an idea is inventive, innovative, or irrelevant? Something we perceive as irrelevant and useless might appeal to someone else. For example, who would have thought fidget spinners would have been in such high demand? Or that Mood Rings would turn into such a trendy fashion item?[5] Or that the Slinky would make more than $3 billion?[6]

Even the most apparently bizarre inventions can find a home. Take Billy Bob Teeth, invented in the 1990s. Fake rotting teeth might seem absolutely ludicrous to some, but more than 20 million units have been sold, generating more than $50 million in profit.[7]

Opportunities spring from ideas, but not all ideas are opportunities. Although we all have the capability to generate a huge range of ideas, not everyone knows how to turn an idea into a valuable, revenue-generating opportunity. Making an idea a reality is a process that requires time, resources, commitment, and a great deal of work, which can seem a little daunting to many of us. But if it were easy, wouldn't everyone do it?

**Fidget Spinners.**

As the idea classification matrix illustrates, most opportunities in entrepreneurship demand high value and some degree of novelty. But how do we identify the right opportunities? The first step in the opportunity identification process is generating as many ideas as we can, for it is out of thousands of ideas that opportunities are born.

# 3.2 OPPORTUNITIES START WITH THOUSANDS OF IDEAS

>> LO 3.2 **Employ strategies for generating new ideas from which opportunities are born.**

The way to get good ideas is to get lots of ideas and throw the bad ones away. Different strategies can be employed and not all will work for you.

—Linus Pauling, Nobel Laureate in Chemistry

The first step in creating and identifying opportunities is idea generation; the more ideas we generate, the greater the likelihood we will find a strong opportunity. At this stage, it's important to embrace the openness of an entrepreneurial mindset to consider ideas that might seem impractical, obvious, wild, or even silly. On the surface, you never know what may turn out to be a good or bad idea.

## The Myth of the Isolated Inventor

Here's a quick exercise: Take a minute, close your eyes, and think of an idea for a new business. Ready? Think hard. How many ideas did you come up with? If you have come up with very few or no ideas at all, you are in good company. Ideas don't just spring fully formed into our minds, although the myth of the isolated inventor, working tirelessly from his or her workshop or laboratory, may lead us to think so.

In fact, as recent literature shows, history's greatest inventions occurred very differently from what we may have been taught. For instance, most of us learned in history class that Eli Whitney invented the cotton gin in 1793—except he didn't, really. In fact, he simply improved existing cotton gins by using coarse wire teeth instead of rollers. In other words, he took an existing product and enhanced it to make it more useful. The cotton gin was actually a result of the work of a group of different people who made improvements over a number of years, which finally resulted in a popular marketable innovation.[8]

Similarly, Thomas Edison did not invent the lightbulb—in fact, electric lighting and lightbulbs existed before he came along. Edison's discovery was a filament made of a certain species of bamboo that had a higher resistance to electricity than other filaments. Again, he took an existing product and made it more useful and valuable. Edison's biggest contribution to the lightbulb was making it more marketable.[9]

Many of the best-known inventions exist because of both a substantial number of people working on them simultaneously and improvements made by groups over the years or even centuries. Many sewage treatment plants and irrigation systems today use a rotating corkscrew type of pump known as Archimedes' screw, which dates back to the 3rd century BC. Although its invention is attributed to the Greek scientist Archimedes, chances are he did not devise it on his own—and even if he did, it has been modified and adapted in a multitude of ways around the world. Other inventions with long and varied histories include concrete (developed by the Romans around 300 BC); optical lenses (another ancient Roman discovery, made practical in 13th-century Europe); gunpowder (invented in the 9th century in China); and vaccination (first developed in the 1700s but not widely implemented until more than a century later). As history shows, there is very little reason to credit just one person for the creation of a novel product or service.[10]

Regardless of who is responsible for inventions and innovations, we can safely say that each of those successful products or services began with an idea. Opportunities emerge from thousands of ideas, but how can we learn to generate thousands of ideas? Let's take a look at some strategies we can use for idea generation. Keep in mind, however, that all ideas are equal! Later in the chapter, and certainly later in the text, we'll talk more about assessing whether good ideas are entrepreneurial opportunities.

# The Ethics of Taking Someone's Idea

Consider this scenario: You're on a public Internet forum or social networking site and someone has posted an idea for a really innovative new product. Despite the enthusiastic responses, the person tells the forum that he wants to work on the idea as a hobby rather than turn it into a business. You are one of those people who sees huge potential in the idea, but what do you do next? If you take the idea and run with it, would you consider this ethical?

The answer to this really depends on your own personal code of ethics, which varies from one person to another. In general, your personal code of ethics are the principles used to guide your decision making and identify what is right or wrong. One person's code could justify that if something is posted on a public forum, then the poster does not mind other people knowing about the idea and therefore the opportunity is there for the taking. Another person's code could be exactly the opposite. Still another person's code could be somewhere in the middle.

But what would happen if the message was posted on a private forum set up specifically for entrepreneurs to swap ideas in a secure environment based on trust? What do you do then? Using someone else's idea in this scenario may not be illegal, but exploiting an idea from one of those members could be considered a breach of trust and therefore unethical.

The online world is ripe with ethical quandaries. One way to make the right decision is to examine your own ethical standards and ask, If the situation were reversed, what would you think? Sometimes looking at your dilemma from the other person's point of view creates greater clarity in terms of right and wrong. Seeking advice from mentors you trust and respect are ways to test the efficacy of your actions. One rule of thumb to help you handle online ethical dilemmas is this: Ask yourself if your behavior was to be published on the front page of the *Wall Street Journal*, would you be ok with this?

## Critical Thinking Questions

1.  Put yourself in the shoes of the poster on the private forum. When they post, is there a risk of the idea being taken by others?

2.  Sharing ideas with others is part of the Entrepreneurship Method in this book. Is it possible to share new ideas and protect them at the same time?

3.  What other rules of thumb (besides the *Wall Street Journal* front page test) could be used to help you navigate ethical situations? ●

## Seven Strategies for Idea Generation

There are countless different ways to generate ideas—from the informal (but not very effective) type illustrated above, such as "close your eyes and think of an idea!" to more structured idea generation techniques, which we describe below.

Researchers have defined many formal methods for idea generation. Out of these, we have chosen seven main strategies that we believe are effective in the generation of entrepreneurial ideas:

- analytical strategies
- search strategies
- imagination-based strategies
- habit-breaking strategies
- relationship-seeking strategies
- development strategies
- interpersonal strategies[11]

Although not all of the strategies may suit everyone, each can help us forge new connections, think differently, and consider new perspectives in different ways. Let's take a closer look at each.

**Analytical strategies:** actions that involve taking time to think carefully about a problem by breaking it up into parts, or looking at it in a more general way, to generate ideas about how certain products or services can be improved or made more innovative.

Analytical strategies involve taking time to think carefully about a problem by breaking it up into parts, or looking at it in a more general way, to generate ideas about how certain products or services can be improved or made more innovative. In some cases, you may see very little correlation between problems until you think about them analytically. For example, in one study, a group was asked to think about different ways of stacking certain items. The ideas they came up with were then considered as ways to park cars. In another study, researchers found that artists who carried out critical analysis before they started their work, as well as during the task, were more successful than those who did not use the same analysis.

Search strategies involve using a stimulus to retrieve memories in order to make links or connections based on personal experience that are relevant to the current problem. For example, say you were asked to design a door hinge. Here, the door hinge is a stimulus—a starting point for searching for solutions to the problem. Although you may not have any prior experience of designing door hinges, you could search your memory to see if you can think of anything that you can associate with a door hinge to support the design process. For example, the search process may stimulate your memory of the opening and closing of a clam shell. By drawing on this memory, you could use your knowledge of the clam shell and apply it to the hinge design. This strategy illustrates our ability to be resourceful in generating associations between objects that at first appear to have no apparent relationship with each other.

Imagination-based strategies involve suspending disbelief and dropping constraints in order to create unrealistic states or fantasies. For example, the Gillette team used imagination to come up with a new shampoo by imagining themselves as human hairs. Though playful and even absurd, such freeing behavior allows our minds to think in ways we never thought possible.

One of the remarkable things about generating ideas, especially ideas that come from imagination-based strategies, is that one idea can lead to another, yielding a pipeline of great ideas that may impact the world. For example, scientists at NASA have needed to use a great deal of imagination to come up with tools, protective clothing, personal care items, foodstuffs, and other inventions that can be used in outer space. Along the way, these ideas led to other inventions that have changed many people's lives here on Earth; some of them are shown in Figure 3.2.

To think creatively, our mind needs to break out of its usual response patterns. Habit-breaking strategies are techniques that help to break our minds out of mental fixedness in order to bring about creative insights. One strategy is to think about the opposite of something you believe, in order to explore a new perspective. Another method focuses on taking the viewpoint of someone who may or may not be involved in the situation. A popular habit-breaking strategy is to take the role of a famous or admired individual and think about how he or she would perceive the situation. This is sometimes called the Napoleon technique, as in "What would Napoleon do?"

Relationship-seeking strategies involve consciously making links between concepts or ideas that are not normally associated with each other. For example, you could make a list of words that are completely unrelated to the problem you are trying to solve, then list the characteristics of each item on the list. Next, apply those characteristics to the problem in order to come up with ideas to solve the problem. The purpose of this exercise is to stimulate the mind into making connections that would otherwise have gone unnoticed.

Credit: ©iStockphoto.com/Gizmo

**Designing a door hinge may require use of search strategies as a stimulus.**

**Search strategies:** actions that involve using a stimulus to retrieve memories in order to make links or connections based on personal experience that are relevant to the current problem.

**Imagination-based strategies:** actions that involve suspending disbelief and dropping constraints in order to create unrealistic states or fantasies.

**Habit-breaking strategies:** actions that involve techniques that help to break our minds out of mental fixedness in order to bring about creative insights.

**Relationship-seeking strategies:** plans of action that involve consciously making links between concepts or ideas that are not normally associated with each other.

**FIGURE 3.2**

**Everyday Spinoffs From NASA**

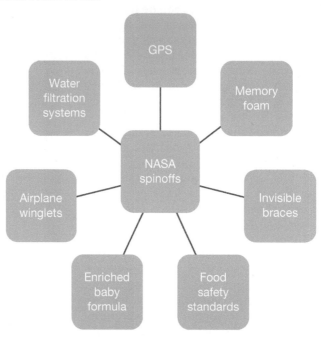

**Source:** Chino, M. (2014). You won't believe how many world-changing inventions came from NASA. *Inhabitat*. Retrieved from http://inhabitat.com/infographic-you-wont-believe-how-many-world-changing-inventions-came-from-nasa/; National Aeronautics and Space Administration. (2016). *Spinoff*. Retrieved from https://spinoff.nasa.gov/Spinoff2016/pdf/2016_Brochure_web.pdf

**Development strategies:** actions that involve enhancing and modifying existing ideas in order to create better alternatives and new possibilities.

**Interpersonal strategies:** actions that involve group members generating ideas and building on each other's ideas.

Development strategies are employed to enhance and modify existing ideas in order to create better alternatives and new possibilities. A common exercise in idea enhancement is to gather a group of four to six people together. Each person writes down three ideas, which are then passed around the group. Then every member spends 5 minutes suggesting improvements to the ideas to make them more feasible and effective. Group brainstorming is a good example of a development strategy.

Interpersonal strategies require group interaction; ideas are generated as a group and the group builds on each other's ideas. Brainstorming is a very common interpersonal tool for generating ideas that emphasize the creativity of the group over the individual.

The point of these seven strategies is to focus on generating enough ideas to eventually create pathways to new opportunities. Not all approaches will work for every person. Try a few and see what happens. As you try, you are training your brain to think more creatively!

## 3.3 FOUR PATHWAYS TO OPPORTUNITY IDENTIFICATION

>> **LO 3.3**   **Apply the four pathways to opportunity identification.**

When the famous explorer George Leigh Mallory was asked why he climbed Mount Everest, he answered, "Because it's there."[12] This indicates that Mallory took the opportunity to climb Everest simply because it was there for the taking. But how do entrepreneurs know when "the mountain" is there and when or if they should start to climb? In the case of Mallory, the idea was climbing Mount Everest, but it really wasn't an opportunity until he convinced himself that (1) the mountain was climbable and (2) he could do it. In previous sections we've talked about where ideas come from. Now it's time to shift our attention to turning ideas into marketable and valuable opportunities.[13]

# In Love With Your Idea?

Find some classmates and practice this quick brainstorming exercise. It's best to have a group of five or more. The more people you have, the more powerful the exercise will be. You'll need a few materials before you begin:

1. A sheet of paper for every group member

2. A pen or pencil for every group member

3. A paper clip that will not be used—or a picture of a paper clip, if you are working with a large group

4. A timer

Here are your instructions. They are quite simple: You have 5 minutes to brainstorm as many uses as you can for a paper clip. Yes, a paper clip!

Go for quantity, do not judge your ideas, and keep in mind that wild ideas are just as acceptable as are mundane ideas. Start the timer and go.

After 5 minutes have passed, stop brainstorming uses for a paper clip and count how many ideas each person has generated. Identify the person with the most ideas—the winner!

Ask the winner to identify his or her first and second idea. Then ask the other group members to raise their hands if their list included at least one of these two ideas. Usually most of the group will raise their hands.

The point of the exercise is you shouldn't fall in love with the first ideas that pop into your mind because most people will come up with those same ideas.

Now ask the winner to share an idea from the very bottom of his or her list. Typically, you will find that not many people in the room have that idea on their lists. The thoughts we

**Paper clips**

generate when we keep "digging," prodding ourselves to think of more and more ideas, are the ones that tend to be the most original and novel.

Brainstorming takes practice and it also takes energy, as it requires pushing beyond the easiest, most obvious ideas. Don't fall in love with the ideas at the top of your list. They won't be novel. Instead, keep going to get the most innovative ideas.

## Critical Thinking Questions

1. Reflect on your own idea generation methods. Do you tend to fall in love with your early ideas? Why or why not?

2. Which of the seven idea generation strategies was applied in this Mindshift?

3. In what ways did the exercise challenge your previous assumptions and beliefs? Did you learn anything that surprised you? ●

An opportunity can be a new product or service, new markets, new channels of distribution, new means of production or supply, or new ways of organizing.[14] Favorable opportunities are those that are valuable, rare, costly to imitate, and fit the capabilities of the entrepreneur.[15] *Valuable* means there is a market of customers; *rare* means they offer some novelty that doesn't currently exist for customers; *costly to imitate* creates barriers to entry to other entrepreneurs; and *fit* aligns with the skills and knowledge of the entrepreneur or founding team. In this section, we focus on different pathways that entrepreneurs use to identify opportunities. Think of these pathways as steps, and as you travel the steps, reflect on how the opportunity identified is a bit more complicated and the environment in which it's identified is a bit more uncertain. The increase in complexity and uncertainty may yield more valuable opportunities (see Figure 3.3).

## FIGURE 3.3

### Increasing Complexity and Unknowingness in Opportunity Creation

**DESIGN**

**EFFECTUATE**

**SEARCH**

**FIND**

*I wanted to create something innovative. I started looking around, observed, and talked to some people and identified new, unmet needs. Then I created something to meet those needs.*

*I thought about what I knew, my skills, experiences, and abilities and developed an idea that matched "me." I created something and just started testing it.*

*I knew I wanted to start a business but was unsure what business to start. I intentionally searched for different opportunities.*

*I saw a clear problem and developed a solution.*

**Source:** Neck, H. (2019). *Beyond the entrepreneurial mindset.* Keynote presentation for the Kern Entrepreneurial Engineering Network Annual Conference. January 5, 2019. Dallas, TX.

**Find pathway:** a pathway that assumes that opportunities exist independent of entrepreneurs and are waiting to be found.

Finding opportunities is the least complicated and perhaps most common way to identify new opportunities. The find pathway assumes that opportunities exist independent of entrepreneurs and are waiting to be found. Generally, an opportunity is found when the entrepreneur sees a clear problem and develops a solution. The problem is known to most, but the entrepreneur is the one who acts on the potential solution. Jason Craparo saw a clear problem. Paper business cards are passé. Most people forget to carry them or lose the ones they are given by others. However, connecting to new people at events in order to follow up with them later is essential to business and networking. He founded Contap, an online platform that enables users to connect and share information. Users can connect with one another by tapping the Contap logo on their phones when they meet. They can instantly share numbers, email addresses, websites, and any other connected social media accounts. Jason found a solution to the business card problem.

**Search pathway:** a pathway used when entrepreneurs are not quite sure what type of venture they want to start, so they engage in an active search to discover new opportunities.

The search pathway is used when entrepreneurs are not quite sure what type of venture they want to start, so they engage in an active search to discover new opportunities.[16] We all possess certain information sets or knowledge bases.[17] By actively searching these sets, we can access a wealth of information and uncover new opportunities. Typically, entrepreneurs find an area that they are interested in and then start searching for business opportunities. For example, Jen Gutman and Liz King met in the International Culinary Center pastry program. During their program, they would travel around Chinatown and other areas of New York City, tasting everything. They knew they wanted to start a pastry business together but were not sure what they wanted to do. They knew New York City didn't need another bon bon, but they wanted to turn the beloved Snickers bar into candy that capitalized on the artisanal food trend. Their idea? Recreate and make better Snickers and similar candy using high-quality, local, and organic ingredients.[18] They each had independent jobs until Liz discovered the Brooklyn Flea, a flea market for new food products. They began selling at the Brooklyn Flea in 2009 on weekends.[19] Then they set up a pop-up store for a month, and soon their business, Liddabit Sweets, was growing!

**CONTAP**

Contap founder Jason Craparo found a solution to paper business cards with his online platform that allows people to share their information virtually.

They developed an online store and even built a storefront in Brooklyn. Passion led their search, and their search led them to start Liddabit Sweets.

Effectuating opportunities involves using what you have (skills, knowledge, abilities) to uncover an opportunity that uniquely fits you. The opportunity builds on your experience, abilities, networks, and your confidence to act under conditions of uncertainty. Unlike finding and searching, the **effectuate pathway** is more about *creating* opportunities rather than simply uncovering them. To identify opportunities, this approach advocates using what you know, whom you know, and who you are. Your role as an entrepreneur is to take action and see how the market responds, recognize patterns, and learn from iteration to define the opportunity as it evolves. FlowDog, a canine aquatic and physical therapy facility for dogs, is a clear example of effectuation. Chris Cranston had deep knowledge of physical therapy, given her 13 years of practicing as a sports medicine physical-therapist. She also had a deep love for animals. Tired of dealing with the human side of medicine, she enrolled in a canine physical therapy course at the University of Tennessee. Armed with her extensive knowledge in sports medicine and her newfound knowledge in canine physical therapy, she began testing the market in the Boston area. She started a mobile practice to treat dogs in their homes, then she started a physical therapy clinic for an animal hospital outside of Boston, and she eventually bought a dog swimming facility and converted it to a therapeutic and physical therapy clinic for dogs. Each iteration of her business helped her create more experience, build deeper networks, and take confident action. In 2017, after 10 years of operating the clinic, she sold it to a large animal hospital in New England.

**Effectuate pathway:** a pathway that involves using what you have (skills, knowledge, abilities) to uncover an opportunity that uniquely fits you.

The final pathway, the **design pathway**, is one of the most complex, yet it can be the most value-creating approach. It can uncover high-value opportunities because the entrepreneur is focusing on unmet needs of customers—specifically, latent needs (needs we have but don't know we have). Design is at the top of the staircase in Figure 3.3 and is considered the most complicated pathway because of the practice and imagination it takes to uncover true unmet needs. As a matter of fact, we devote an entire chapter (Chapter 4) to this pathway! Design is another way to create opportunities because by identifying unmet needs, the entrepreneur is creating a new market. The most iconic example of using the design pathway to create a new market is the iPhone. The introduction of the iPhone (even though the BlackBerry existed) created a new global market of communication and connection. When we look back we can ask ourselves, did we need an iPhone? If the answer is "Well, I can't imagine living without one today," then you now understand what a latent need is!

**Design pathway:** a pathway that can uncover high-value opportunities because the entrepreneur is focusing on unmet needs of customers, specifically latent needs.

The four pathways can be classified as either a discovery approach or a creation approach (see Table 3.1).[20] The discovery approach assumes that opportunities exist and we rely on entrepreneurs to discover them. Creating, on the other hand, assumes that the entrepreneur creates the opportunity rather than simply uncovering it.

## TABLE 3.1

Discovering or Creating Opportunities

|  | DISCOVERY | CREATION |
|---|---|---|
| Opportunity pathways | Find and Search | Effectuate and Design |
| Assumptions | The opportunity exists and is waiting to be identified | The entrepreneur creates the opportunity |
| Role of the entrepreneur | Be alert to and scan the environment | Take action, build, iterate |
| Level of experience and prior knowledge needed to identify | Low | High |
| Potential value of opportunity | Lower | Higher |
| Action orientation | Risky | Uncertain |

**Source:** Alvarez, S. A., & Barney, J. B. 2007. Discovery and creation: Alternative theories of entrepreneurial actions. *Strategic Entrepreneurship Journal.* 1(1–2): 11–26.

# 3.4 ALERTNESS, PRIOR KNOWLEDGE, AND PATTERN RECOGNITION

>> **LO 3.4**   **Demonstrate how entrepreneurs find opportunities using alertness, prior knowledge, and pattern recognition.**

As we have discussed, access to the right information is one of the key influences of opportunity identification. However, access to information is not enough—it is how this information is used that makes the real impact.

## Alertness

**Alertness:** the ability some people have to identify opportunities.

To address the question of why some people spot opportunities and some don't, researchers have suggested that opportunities are everywhere waiting to be discovered, but discovery is made only by those entrepreneurs who have **alertness**, which is the ability to identify opportunities in their environment.[21] This means that entrepreneurs do not necessarily rationally and systematically search their environment or their particular information sets for opportunities. Rather, they become alert to existing opportunities through their daily activities—in some instances, they are even taken by surprise by what they observe.

Think back to Dr. Spencer Silver, the inventor of Post-its®, mentioned earlier in this chapter. Silver was not actively searching for an opportunity to invent a specific adhesive to create sticky notes, but he became alert to the idea through his scientific experiments. He then collaborated with a colleague to create a product that would prove to be a huge market success. Silver's experience adheres to this concept of alertness that suggests that we are capable of recognizing opportunities even when we are not looking for them.

The origin of the rugby football is another interesting example of alertness.[22] Until 1860, footballs were made of animal bladders, which were blown up into a plum or pear shape, then tied and sealed. Because the bladders were constantly exploding, shoemakers were often called upon to encase the bladders in leather to protect them from bursting so easily. A young shoemaker in the town of Rugby, England, named Richard Lindon was employed in this trade, and he enlisted the help of his wife to inflate the bladders by blowing air into them. However, after his wife died from an illness attributed to contact with infected pigs' bladders, Lindon started to look for a safer option. He found a way to replace the bladders with inflated rubber tubes and used a pump to inflate the footballs without any contact with the mouth. He is credited with inventing the oval rugby football we know today, as well as the hand air pump. The point is that although Lindon had not started out looking to revolutionize the football, he was able to recognize an opportunity when it appeared.

Some researchers believe that entrepreneurs may be more adept at spotting opportunities than non-entrepreneurs for several reasons:

Credit: Wikimedia Commons/Public Domain

**Richard Lindon with enhanced rugby balls**

- They have access to more information.

- They may be more prone to pursuing risks than avoiding them.

- They may possess different cognitive styles from those of non-entrepreneurs.

These reasons can be attributed to an entrepreneur's level of alertness as well as their persistence and optimism. Persistence helps entrepreneurs power through obstacles and optimism helps drive persistence.[23] The combination of persistence and optimism encourages a state of alertness and readiness to identify and act on new opportunities that others may miss or just don't see.

## Building Opportunities: Prior Knowledge and Pattern Recognition

There has been a great deal of research on measuring how entrepreneurs recognize opportunities. We have explored the importance of actively searching for opportunities, alertness to recognizing opportunities when they arise, and the importance of taking action to support the formation of opportunities. But once entrepreneurs have identified opportunities, how do they go about building on them?

Courtesy of SkratchLabs

**Allen Lim was able to use his prior knowledge to build his company, Skratch Labs.**

Researchers have identified two major factors in the building of opportunities: prior knowledge and pattern recognition.[24] As described in our earlier discussion of the finding approach, prior knowledge is information gained from a combination of life and work experience. Many studies indicate that entrepreneurs with knowledge of an industry or market, together with a broad network, are more likely to recognize opportunities than those who have less experience or fewer contacts.[25] Successful entrepreneurs often have prior knowledge with respect to a market, industry, or customers, which they can then apply to their own ventures.[26]

Allen Lim, founder of Skratch Labs, a company that provides tasty, natural hydrated food and drinks to athletes, was able to apply the knowledge he gained while working as a sports scientist and coach for professional cycling teams.[27]

Similarly, Sara Blakely, founder of Spanx, spent weeks researching the shapewear industry before using the knowledge she gained to create her seamless pantyhose product. Steve Sullivan, founder of functional and fashionable outdoor clothing company Stio, spent a number of years working in outdoor retailing before launching his venture.

These are just a few examples of how prior knowledge can be crucial in an entrepreneur's ability to build on an opportunity.

Another key factor in building and recognizing opportunities is **pattern recognition:** the process of identifying links or connections between apparently unrelated things or events. Pattern recognition takes place when people "connect the dots" in order to identify and then build on opportunities.[28] The "nine-dot exercise" (Figure 3.4) illustrates the limitations of our thinking. The challenge is to connect nine dots by drawing four

**Prior knowledge:** the information gained from a combination of life and work experience.

**Pattern recognition:** the process of identifying links or connections between apparently unrelated things or events.

---

## FIGURE 3.4

### Nine-Dot Exercise

Puzzle: Copy the above image to paper. Draw no more
than four straight lines (without lifting the pencil) and
connect all nine dots. No back-tracking either.

---

**Source:** Raudsepp, E., & Hough, G. (1977). *Creative growth games.* New York, NY: Jove. The nine-dot exercise is referred to as "Breaking Out" and is found on page 29. The solution is on page 113.

straight lines without lifting your pen from the paper and without backtracking. If you have difficulty completing the task, your mind may be blocked by the imaginary "box" created by the dots. Try to look beyond that imaginary constraint.

In a recent study, highly experienced entrepreneurs were asked to describe the process they used to identify opportunities.[29] Each entrepreneur reported using prior knowledge to make connections between seemingly unrelated events and trends. In cognitive science, pattern recognition is thought to be one of the ways in which we attempt to understand the world around us.

Some of the simplest ideas are born from making links from one event to the other. For example, keen travelers Selin Sonmez and Niko Georgantas were fed up with hauling their baggage around with them while waiting to check in to their accommodation. Sonmez said, "Niko and I always ended up schlepping our luggage around on the first and last days of our Airbnb stays. Similarly, we oftentimes wished to go to an event or go shopping but decided against it to because carrying bags around is a hassle. We hoped someone would find a solution to rid us of the burden. For months we wished. In the beginning of 2017, we decided to CREATE the solution."[30]

To solve this problem, Sonmez and Georgantas cofounded luggage storage company Knock Knock City, which partners with different shops to allow people to drop off their luggage for $2 an hour. Not only do travelers have the opportunity to explore new cities baggage-free, but the shops get to earn revenue by renting out unused space.

Moving from the idea to identifying an opportunity may seem like a daunting prospect, but we can all train ourselves to get better at recognizing opportunities. We do so by identifying changes in technology, markets, and demographics; engaging in active searches; and keeping our mind open to recognizing trends and patterns. And always look beyond the imaginary box!

## 3.5 FROM IDEA GENERATION TO OPPORTUNITY RECOGNITION

>> **LO 3.5**   **Connect idea generation to opportunity recognition.**

As we have explored, for an opportunity to be viable, the idea must be new or unique or at least a variation on an existing theme that you are confident people will accept and adopt. It must involve something that people need, desire, find useful, or find valuable, and it must have the capacity to generate profit. We cannot credit divine intervention as the source of new ideas, nor is every idea an opportunity. The best ideas are based on knowledge and the ability to transform the idea into a viable opportunity.

Let's take a look at the process that connects idea generation to opportunity recognition (see Figure 3.5). Typically, entrepreneurs go through three processes before they are able to identify an opportunity for a new business venture: idea generation, creativity, and opportunity recognition.

**FIGURE 3.5**

**Idea Generation, Creativity, and Opportunity Recognition**

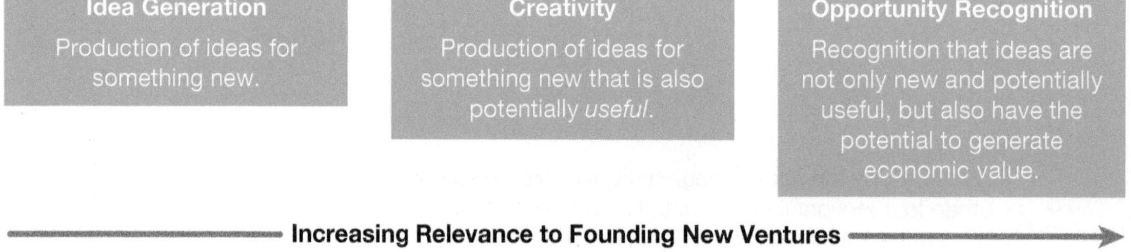

| Idea Generation | Creativity | Opportunity Recognition |
| --- | --- | --- |
| Production of ideas for something new. | Production of ideas for something new that is also potentially *useful*. | Recognition that ideas are not only new and potentially useful, but also have the potential to generate economic value. |

←——— **Increasing Relevance to Founding New Ventures** ———→

The journey from idea to opportunity is important to recognize because the difference between someone who comes up with an idea and an entrepreneur is that the entrepreneur turns this idea into an actionable opportunity that has the potential to become a viable business and generate profit. Figure 3.5 illustrates the journey from idea to opportunity. Though the goal is recognizing a value opportunity, the journey starts with lots of ideas—let's say 100 ideas. These ideas can be generated in many ways, potentially through the strategies we discussed earlier in the chapter. Of those 100 ideas, you need to determine which ones are the most useful for potential customers. Let's say, then, that the original 100 are narrowed to 25. Of the remaining 25 ideas, you then need to determine which ones can generate economic value, which is profit. Finally, the entrepreneur is the one who acts on the opportunity.

Along this continuum of idea generation to creativity to opportunity recognition depicted in Figure 3.5, educators and entrepreneurs Dan Cohen and Greg Pool have developed an empirically proven method for identifying and selecting high-potential ideas that can be converted to new opportunities. Their approach is called IDEATE: Identify, Discover, Enhance, Anticipate, Target, and Evaluate (see Table 3.2).[31]

Let's apply the IDEATE method to the evolution of the modern-day gourmet food truck.

The mobile food business is not a new concept, but traditionally street food has been associated with fast food such as burgers, hot dogs, and ice cream; these are the menu items often sold from food trucks, kiosks, and food carts. Yet in the past decade, the nature of the mobile food business has changed as the street food industry has become increasingly upscale and popular with "foodies." Using the Identify stage, we could observe that food trucks are popular but customers really want more healthy options. A possible concept could be a food truck that serves fresh seasonal salads and healthy grain bowls, with a menu that changes with the seasons.

Building on this food truck concept in the Discover stage, the opportunity could morph into an entirely different concept that takes into consideration social, demographic, political, or other environmental changes. For example, given that waste management is a significant issue in the world, and islands of plastic are forming in our oceans, the salad food truck mentioned above could promote itself not only as healthy for people but also healthy for the planet.[32] All plates, cups, and utensils would be compostable—even the straws! (see https://www.ecoproducts.com/compostable_straws.html). Note how the idea of the food truck has become a bit more innovative and meets the needs of customers, too.

**TABLE 3.2**

The IDEATE Model for Opportunity Recognition

| | |
|---|---|
| Identify | Identifying problems that customers are currently trying to solve, are spending money to solve, but are still not solved to the customers' satisfaction. Also identifying the underlying causes of the problem. |
| Discover | Actively searching for ideas in problem-rich environments where there is social and demographic change, technological change, political and regulatory change, and/or change in industry structure. |
| Enhance | Taking the ideas and expanding to new applications or adding innovative twists. Or simply enhancing existing ideas. |
| Anticipate | Studying change and analyzing future scenarios as they relate to social, technological, and other global changes and trends. |
| Target | Defining and understanding a particular target market, validating new ideas with early adopters. |
| Evaluate | Evaluating whether the solution solves a problem, size of target market, degree of personal interest by the entrepreneur, and skills and abilities of the entrepreneur. |

**Source:** Adapted from Cohen, D. Hsu, D. & Shinnar, R. (2018) Enhancing Opportunity Identification Skills In Entrepreneurship Education: A New Approach and Empirical Test (forthcoming); and Ideate: An empirically proven method for identifying and selecting high potential entrepreneurial ideas. Workbook.

# Practicing "Identify" in the IDEATE Model

Important to the IDEATE methodology is the ability to identify "headache problems." They are called headache problems because when one has a headache one usually buys aspirin. Consumers don't buy products or services; they buy solutions. In the case of a headache, the solution is an aspirin, so they buy aspirin. But other solutions could exist as well. What's important is your ability to identify headache problems *before* thinking about solutions. In this Mindshift, you are to identify five headache problems and then create five solutions per problem. We give you an example to help you get started:

Example headache problem: It's not easy to quickly exchange contact information and younger people don't carry business cards.

Possible solutions:

1. Contap (discussed in this chapter)
2. Phone bump attachment so when you bump phones the information is transferred automatically
3. QR code that can quickly be scanned
4. I look at my friend's phone and it recognizes me using iris recognition technology
5. Something connected to LinkedIn that recognizes all the people in your immediate vicinity and will send them requests to connect

At this point, we are not evaluating the ideas above. We are just helping you practice finding headache problems.

## Critical Thinking Questions

1. How difficult was it to identify headache problems?
2. How will you analyze whether some of your solutions have customers who are willing to buy?
3. Do a quick Google search for your solutions. How many already exist? What does that tell you? ●

PriceM/Shutterstock

**Food truck**

As you enter the Enhance stage, you could morph the food truck opportunity again. Enhancing the idea requires you to expand concepts to new applications or add innovative twists. Maybe the food truck turns into "fresh food" vending machines that are in strategic urban locations and the machines are restocked daily. Or maybe they could be placed in airports, where more and more people want access to healthy food to bring on their flights. Notice now that with the twists, our market just got bigger! We gain more customers by solving more headaches.

Applying the original food truck concept to the Anticipate stage could result in an entirely new concept. Here we are forced to think about future scenarios. Food deserts are becoming a serious problem. A food desert is an area that lacks access to affordable healthy food such as fruit, vegetables, grain, and other nonprocessed food. Most of these food deserts are in rural, minority, and low-income neighborhoods with very little access to supermarkets and fresh produce—places where there are more convenience stores than grocery stores.[33] Ultimately the health of these populations is at risk. How can we morph the food truck concept and anticipate the future? Now we can perhaps think about creating a fleet of food trucks that act as "mini" produce markets. These trucks travel through low-income areas selling healthy food at reasonable prices while also educating the public on how to eat healthy on tight budgets.

In the Target stage, you could take the food-truck-in-food-deserts concept and choose a low-income urban area in which to test the idea before investing in trucks. Or you could take the original food truck concept of seasonal salads and test it in downtown Denver, Colorado—one of the healthiest cities in the United States. The idea here is to find that niche market of early adopters who will help validate your idea.

# Testing IDEATE in the Entrepreneurial Classroom

Researchers Cohen, Shinnar, and Hsu (2019) set out to study the impact of the IDEATE method (discussed in Section 3.5 above) versus more traditional methods of opportunity identification. To compare the quality of ideas generated by each method, they took a group of U.S. undergraduate students enrolled in six sections of an Introduction to Entrepreneurship course. Out of the six sections of the course, three sections were taught the IDEATE method while the other three sections (the control group) learned a more traditional opportunity recognition method. Using the IDEATE method, the students were required to generate 100 high-quality ideas, or 25 ideas per IDEATE stage (see Mindshift: Practicing "Identify" in the IDEATE Model).

Because the IDEATE method is rooted in deliberate practice, the researchers hypothesized that this approach was more likely to sharpen students' skills in opportunity identification. When the experiment was complete, the researchers found "a significant correlation between the IDEATE teaching method and the innovativeness of the opportunities students identified"; they also discovered that "the students taught in sections using the IDEATE approach identified opportunities that were more innovative than the opportunities identified by students in the control sections." Overall, the researchers concluded that the IDEATE approach proved to be more effective in opportunity identification than any other of the methods tested.

## Critical Thinking Questions

1. What are the benefits of the IDEATE method versus the traditional methods of opportunity identification?
2. Which method would you choose to generate your ideas, and why?
3. What would you do with your ideas after you generated them? ●

**Source:** Cohen, D., Shinnar, R. S., & Hsu, D. K. (2019). *Enhancing opportunity recognition skills in entrepreneurship education: A new approach and empirical test.* 2019 Babson College Entrepreneurship Research Conference, Babson Park, MA.

Finally, the Evaluate stage encourages you to take all of the ideas and begin to "size" the problem:

1. food truck with salads and bowls
2. food truck (same as #1) that only uses compostable packaging and utensils
3. fresh food vending machine
4. fleet of trucks that offer "mini" produce markets in food deserts

For each concept, what is the size of the market? Is the customer reachable? Do I have the ability to reach the customer? Do I even want to work on any of these opportunities? Do I have the skills and ability to execute them? Do I know people who can help me? These are all questions we will be answering throughout this text.●

Get the tools you need to sharpen your study skills. SAGE edge offers a robust online environment featuring an impressive array of free tools and resources.

**$SAGE edge™**

- Access practice quizzes, eFlashcards, video, and multimedia at **edge.sagepub.com/neckentrepreneurship2e**

## SUMMARY

### 3.1   Explain how the entrepreneurial mindset relates to opportunity recognition.

Having the right entrepreneurial mindset is essential to identifying opportunities and taking action to start new ventures. It gives entrepreneurs the confidence to network and find unmet needs in the marketplace and the ability to persist with ideas and build on opportunities.

**3.2    Employ strategies for generating new ideas from which opportunities are born.**

Of the nearly countless ways of generating ideas, seven strategies have been outlined by researchers: analytical strategies, search strategies, imagination-based strategies, habit-breaking strategies, relationship-seeking strategies, development strategies, and interpersonal strategies.

**3.3    Apply the four pathways to opportunity identification.**

The four pathways (design, effectuate, search, and find) are useful for explaining how entrepreneurs identify and exploit opportunities.

**3.4    Demonstrate how entrepreneurs find opportunities using alertness, prior knowledge, and pattern recognition.**

To find opportunities, entrepreneurs need to be alert to random opportunities when they arise, possess knowledge based on past experience, and identify connections between seemingly unrelated things or events through pattern recognition.

**3.5    Connect idea generation to opportunity recognition.**

IDEATE (identify, discover, enhance, anticipate, target, and evaluate) is an empirically proven method for identifying and selecting high-potential ideas that can be converted to new opportunities.

## KEY TERMS

Alertness  68

Analytical strategies  63

Design pathway  67

Development strategies  64

Effectuate pathway  67

Find pathway  66

Habit-breaking strategies  63

Imagination-based strategies  63

Interpersonal strategies  64

Opportunity  57

Pattern recognition  69

Prior knowledge  69

Relationship-seeking strategies  63

Search pathway  66

Search strategies  63

## CASE STUDY

### Jillian Lakritz, founder, Yoee Baby

Jillian Lakritz's first job, after earning her MBA in 1997 from the University of Colorado–Boulder, was working on the national expansion of a chain of early childhood development centers called Crème de la Crème. These centers provide early education and childcare services for children up to 6 years old and after-school services for students between 5 and 12 years old. From her work at Crème de la Crème, Jillian learned that the most important window for cognitive development in children is the first 3 years of life, as a great deal of brain architecture is shaped during this period. This contributes directly to cognitive, linguistic, social, emotional, and motor development. Additionally, the earliest months of a baby's life also lay the foundation for all future learning, behavior, and health. Furthermore, Jillian said, "I also learned that playtime contributes significantly to this development and that it is important to make every moment count. These early play moments help build healthy brain architecture in babies, setting them up for a healthy future."

In 2009, Jillian gave birth to her daughter, Yoe. Of course, Jillian recalled her learnings during her time at Crème de la Crème and she knew that Yoe's early development needed help! "Yoe had lots of toys, but none that were really age appropriate," Jillian recalled. "Most toys are not meant for newborns. They are for children who can sit up and grab things." Jillian found herself looking for new ideas so she and Yoe could play, bond, and develop together.

Jillian started searching for play activities on popular websites and portals like babycenter.com. As she searched, she learned body awareness and sensory development are important in the first 6 months of life. One post on babycenter.com suggested that she take a feather or a piece of silk or velvet and gently caress her baby's body with it. When Jillian tried it for the first time, Yoe started laughing and smiling in a way Jillian had not seen before. "It was a really transformative moment for me because it was so joyful to see my new little baby smile. As new parents, we live for that smile—it makes your heart melt. Not only that, it was something we could do together," recalled Jillian. She also knew that while Yoe enjoyed the activity, it was also contributing to her body awareness and sensory development. Vision and hearing are the first sensory pathways that develop in a child. These are followed by early language skills and cognitive development. Sensory development is an important foundation for lifelong learning, behavior, and health. Feather playing became Jillian and Yoe's favorite pastime, but when Yoe turned 6 months old and started putting the feather in her mouth, Jillian said, "I was afraid that she would choke and this amazing activity that we did together could kill her!"

Jillian didn't want to put Yoe in danger, but she also didn't want to stop playing! That's when the "Aha!" moment occurred. She knew that if she could create a soft, irresistibly touchable baby-safe feather out of fabric, she could keep playing with her child and also share the same joy with as many new parents as possible around her. This is what inspired her to invent the product now called Yoee Baby.

After leaving Crème de la Crème in the early 2000s, Jillian worked as a product innovation, consumer insight, and brand strategy consultant for a consumer packaged goods company. Although she did not have any experience in designing and making toys, her experience in concept development enabled her to flesh out the idea. She first sketched the idea on paper, noting all the value she hoped the toy would capture. She then developed prototypes of the toy and looked long and hard for a toy designer. The initial idea was to create a character—a plush animal that had a feather-like tail. However, based on ongoing customer feedback, she made more than 15 prototypes that each tested different additions, like a handle or a teething ring. But, as Jillian says, "The feather had always been our 'holy grail.' How do you replicate nature's perfection and the gentle caress of the feather on your skin through manmade materials?"

After multiple brainstorming sessions, trying 50 types of fabrics and iterations, and early consumer testing, Jillian finally had a prototype ready to test with her consumers. Jillian also reached out to many other stakeholders to incorporate their feedback. She spoke to other manufacturers and distributors at trade shows, pediatricians, occupational therapists, neuroscientists, preschool teachers, and every other early childhood development expert she could find to help her get to a market-ready product (see image below).

**The Yoee Baby toy**

Around the fall of 2016, Jillian finally had a working prototype that she felt good about. She had invested close to $100,000 of her own money in product development. She raised a total of $535,000 from friends and family through convertible debt. An accelerator program in Colorado also invested $30,000. Also around this time, Jillian brought her Yoee Baby product to a trade show by the American Specialty Toy Retailers Association in Denver. The trade show further validated her idea. The show had many small, independent stores, and they all loved the product. She left the trade show with 40 orders for Yoee Baby.

With greater confidence in the product, she visited a factory in China that could produce the product while also launching a $25,000 Kickstarter campaign to raise additional funds. It became one of the highest funded baby toys in Kickstarter history as of 2016, surpassing her goal and raising almost $36,000. But Kickstarter was both a blessing and a curse. She was working to fulfill her Kickstarter promises during December 2016 when there was a major fabric failure: Big plugs of fabric were pulling out of the tail of the toy. She immediately started getting emails from Kickstarter backers complaining that Yoee Baby was a safety hazard. Jillian quickly recalled all products, hired a safety consultant to figure out what the issue was, and switched factories in China—twice—all in the first year of operations. Jillian said, "It was a huge challenge that took almost a year to work through. It was one of the most difficult times at Yoee Baby."

Jillian attributes her success, in general and on Kickstarter, to her network. She reached out to people for introductions and support. Jillian passionately believes that "People are everything!" She reached out to everyone she knew to help back her project. She has assembled a very impressive board of directors, including people from Mattel, Fisher Price, and Sesame Street. Jillian hopes to raise additional capital very soon, and she is quite hopeful about the future success of Yoee Baby. "The feedback we get from new parents is off the charts! Parents love the product and are writing to us every day, sending pictures and videos of how their babies are reacting to the product. It's amazing! I love it!" Jillian exclaims.

The journey continues for Jillian and Yoee Baby. "If you really want to do this," notes Jillian, "the P-words are the most important: persistence, passion, perseverance, patience." Today, Yoee Baby has a 4.5 average rating on Amazon. Jillian has positioned Yoee Baby as a product that enables bonding through play because she feels that bonding is one of the most important parts of a parent and child relationship. New products are on the horizon!

## Critical Thinking Questions

1. What strategy or strategies did Jillian employ to identify the Yoee Baby opportunity?

2. What headache problem is Jillian solving with the Yoee Baby toy?

3. What's more important, the idea or the network, to help you act on the idea?

**Sources:**

Jillian Lakritz (interview with Babson MBA graduate assistant Gaurav Khemka, September 28, 2018).

Center on the Developing Child at Harvard University. (2007). *The science of early childhood development.* Retrieved from http://www.developingchild.harvard.edu

Center on the Developing Child at Harvard University. (2013). *Early childhood mental health.* Retrieved from http://www.developingchild.harvard.edu

Center on the Developing Child at Harvard University. (2016). *8 things to remember about child development.* Retrieved from http://www.developingchild.harvard.edu

# 4

# Using Design Thinking

"Design can help to improve our lives in the present. Design thinking can help us chart a path into the future."

—Tim Brown, *Change by Design: How Design Thinking Transforms Organizations and Inspires Innovation*

# Chapter Outline

# Learning Objectives

4.1 Differentiate between design and design thinking.

4.2 Demonstrate design thinking as a human-centered process focusing on customers and their needs.

4.3 Describe the role of empathy in the design-thinking process.

4.4 Illustrate the key phases of the design-thinking process.

4.5 Demonstrate how to observe and convert observation data to insights.

4.6 Demonstrate how to interview potential customers in order to better understand their needs.

4.7 Identify and describe other approaches to design thinking.

## 4.1 WHAT IS DESIGN THINKING?

>> LO 4.1 **Differentiate between design and design thinking.**

What pops into your mind when you hear the word *design*? You might think of fashion design or graphic design or architectural design or industrial design. All of these types of "design" represent crafts that require specialized skills and deep knowledge of materials, visualization, user interface, and front-end development. For example, a graphic designer needs deep knowledge of typography, color theory, and even brain science. Architects need skills in drawing, math, engineering, and software. But there is a certain skillset held by designers that can apply to *all* disciplines—especially entrepreneurship. These skills constitute design thinking (see Table 4.1).[1] Design thinking is a toolkit for an entrepreneur to solve complex problems *for* people. Specifically, design thinking is a human-centered approach to innovation that brings together what people need with what is technologically feasible and economically viable. It also allows people who aren't trained as designers to use creative tools to address a vast range of challenges. Today, design thinking has taken a prominent role in entrepreneurship education. However, use caution! Design thinking is a tool of entrepreneurs. Design thinking is not entrepreneurship. This chapter will introduce you to some of the most commonly used design-thinking tools and profile some of the biggest pioneers of this groundbreaking approach. For instance, IDEO, a global design company, has popularized the use of design thinking over the past 20 years.

**Design thinking:** a human-centered approach to innovation that brings together what people need with what is technologically feasible and economically viable.

> Thinking like a designer can transform the ways organizations develop products, services, process, and strategy. This approach brings together what is desirable from a human point of view with what is technologically feasible and economically viable. It also allows people who aren't trained as designers to use creative tools to address a vast range of challenges.[2]

Design thinking works best at the fuzzy front end of creating something new—products, services, processes, whatever. It focuses on the people you are designing for, developing empathy for them, testing solutions on them—and, overall, creating something to meet their needs.

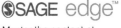

Master the content at **edge.sagepub.com/ neckentrepreneurship2e**

TABLE 4.1

Seven Skills of Designers That Entrepreneurs Should Have

| 1. **Observation** |
| --- |
| Designers are curious. They observe, always looking at the world through different lenses and making notes of things others overlook. |
| 2. **Listening** |
| Designers develop active listening skills so they are able to identify what really matters to others. The best designers never assume they know what is best for the user. |
| 3. **Desire Change** |
| Designers seek to solve problems and improve upon what may already exist. New products, services, and processes lead to change. |
| 4. **Context and Integration** |
| Designers design in context. Context helps us create meaning and understanding. Attention to context brings more relevance to a solution. For example, you design a chair for a room; a room for a house; a house for a neighborhood. |
| 5. **Solution-driven** |
| The goal of any designer is to solve a problem that was identified through observing and listening. |
| 6. **Consideration** |
| Good designers consider their impact of their work on people, the environment, and economies. |
| 7. **Unbound** |
| Great designers are unbound by the past and are open to the less-than-obvious solutions to problems. They ask "Why not?" when other people say it can't be done. |

**Source:** Adapted from Gibbons, W. (2016). 9 traits of a great designer. *Creative Bloq.* Retrieved from https://www.creativebloq.com/career/9-traits-great-designer-71613188

**Need:** a lack of something desirable, useful, or required that is uncovered through the design process.

Needs are a lack of something desirable, useful, or required that are uncovered through the design thinking process. Entrepreneurs who succeed in identifying and satisfying the needs of customers have a better chance of gaining traction in a market. Don't fall into the trap of "if you build it they will come." It's better to create something that people need because they are more likely to pay for something they need! Fashion entrepreneur Shaymaa Gaafar, featured in Entrepreneurship in Action, used design thinking to create a brand that encourages women to express themselves while staying true to their personal values.

For entrepreneurs, design thinking is a tool that focuses on different ways to solve problems to best meet the needs of the people for whom you are designing. In other words, how do you identify new solutions that meet the needs of a market? That is the essence of design thinking, and it can be taught to entrepreneurs.[3]

The concept of design thinking aligns with many of the facets of the Entrepreneurship Method, described in Chapter 1. Design thinking applies to everyone, regardless of experience levels; it involves getting out of the building and taking action; it requires continuous practice with a focus on doing in order to learn; and it works best in unpredictable environments. Design thinking incorporates the core elements of the Method and helps put the Method into action because it requires you to collaborate, cocreate, accept and expect setbacks, and build on what you learn.

One of the biggest obstacles to trying new things or generating new ideas is the fear of failure. What if the idea doesn't work out? What if the prototype fails to meet expectations? Design thinking does not see failure as a threat as long as it happens early and is used as a springboard for further learning—in other words, "Fail early to succeed sooner."[4] Design thinking is an iterative and often messy process that uses observation,

## Shaymaa Gaafar, Shay Jaffar

Photo courtesy of Shaymaa Gaafar

**Shaymaa Gaafar, founder of Shay Jaffar**

Fashion trends are ever-evolving and in the 21st century, some women have found themselves at odds with the modern, free-spirited, and revealing look that adorns social media and the front pages of fashion magazines. Although Western culture emphasizes individual expression, it also paradoxically encourages assimilating one's personal values into the current fashion trends in order to stay relevant. Times like this tend to give rise to independent thinkers who see things differently. This is Shaymaa Gaafar. She is a fashion entrepreneur who firmly believes that women can fully express themselves in fashion while remaining true to their personal values.

Born in Egypt and raised in the United Arab Emirates, Shaymaa grew up in a predominantly Muslim culture, where women were expected to dress modestly. As a little girl, Shaymaa never resented her culture; rather, it gave her a different lens through which beauty could be interpreted. She recalled, "As a little girl I would use all the colors to draw beautiful dresses and one day I asked my mother to help me make one." Together they sewed beautiful dresses for friends and family. Shaymaa started wearing her creations to school, and as she got older, she became aware that other girls didn't seem to have access to the same types of clothes. It was while she was studying computer science at Ain Shams University in Cairo, Egypt, that it really dawned upon Shaymaa that the fashion market was not reflecting what the women of the Middle East wanted. There was simply nothing available for women who wanted to dress modestly but also fashionably.

Although her enthusiasm for fashion never waned, Shaymaa's early career took her in a different direction. After college, she worked for IBM for more than 7 years. From there she landed an executive position at Pepsi. "People said I was crazy to leave that job," said Gaafar. "Corporate is great, but I had an inkling that maybe it wasn't for me."

After she left Pepsi, Shaymaa applied for a Fulbright Scholarship, which led her to the United States to pursue her MBA at Babson College in Massachusetts. This enabled her to seize the opportunity she had observed years before: to set up a clothing business catering to women seeking modest fashion.

While at Babson, she started her entrepreneurial fashion venture Shay Jaffar, now based in New York City.

Although Shaymaa had the idea and the passion necessary to start her own business, she admitted "that will only get a new venture so far." She received a small amount of seed money through a Babson incubator and used that money to start designing the type of fashion she dreamed of selling. However, she quickly faced challenges related to her target market. She said, "Shay Jaffar is a clothing line made for the global woman, and the end goal is to make it affordable for the everyday woman." Yet, at this stage in her startup, cash was very limited and she needed cash to fund operations. So she shifted her target market to more affluent women who had more money to spend: "A professional, accomplished woman. A woman that attends evening events and wants to be modest for any reason." Once the business is profitable, she intends to return to her original plan: "I'll design casual wear for the everyday hustle and bustle while staying true to my vision that you can be covered and be beautiful. There is no need to compromise if you want to remain modest."

Shaymaa initially tried to launch her startup in Egypt, but she soon found that the resources necessary for success were simply not as prevalent as they were in the United States. Additionally, the center of the fashion world is New York City, so Shay Jaffar is technically based in New York City, even though most of her work is done outside of Boston and sold online. Shay Jaffar is a lean operation that is very conscious of its cash. Shaymaa is not only the founder but the only employee: She relies on 22 different independent contractors to work with her on fabric and designs. This allows Shaymaa to keep costs to an absolute minimum while maintaining the quality she demands.

All in all, Shay Jaffar is a great example of a passion-turned-business. "This definitely wasn't easy. If you want to

*(Continued)*

(Continued)

be an entrepreneur, you need to learn to take action. It's always good to open some reports and understand your markets before doing something, but don't expect the reports and the textbooks to teach you everything. You will learn the most by taking action."

Even though most of today's fashion trends seem to veer in the opposite direction, Shaymaa understands the needs of her customers and is creating a new and growing fashion segment for women in the United States and around the world. As Shaymaa notes on her website,

> Shay Jaffar is the dream that I have been carrying for years. Today it is in full bloom. It is not only a brand, but a unique identity. An outspoken voice and an agent of change that will always

challenge limitations of conventions, while cherishing the value of modesty.

### Critical Thinking Questions

1. Who is Shay Jaffar's target customer?
2. What are the benefits of Shay Jaffar's current operating model?
3. For an entrepreneur, what are things that can hinder action? ●

#### Sources

Shaymaa Gaafar (interview with author, November 19, 2018).
Curran, S. (2019). Shay Jaffar: A brand born at Babson. *Babson Thought & Action.* Retrieved from http://entrepreneurship.babson.edu/shay-jaffar-a-brand-born-at-babson/
*Shay Jaffar.* (2019). Retrieved from https://shayjaffar.com/pages/our-story

interviewing, data synthesis, searching for and generating alternatives, critical thinking, feedback, visual representation, and creativity to yield valuable and innovative solutions. By using design thinking, entrepreneurs will be better able to identify and act on unique venture opportunities, solve complex problems, and create value across multiple groups of customers and stakeholders.

How do we become successful design thinkers? The first step is to focus on, even become obsessed with, who you are designing for.

## 4.2 DESIGN THINKING AS A HUMAN-CENTERED PROCESS

>> **LO 4.2**   **Demonstrate design thinking as a human-centered process focusing on customers and their needs.**

© Jon Shapley/Getty Images Entertainment/Getty Images

**Tim Brown, CEO of the design firm IDEO**

Typically, when new ideas are being vetted, we often jump to answer two questions: Can it be done? and Will it make money? But human-centered design thinking involves a different starting point in the creation process. The starting question focuses on humans: What do people need?[5]

As previously mentioned, IDEO has popularized design thinking and is featured several times in this chapter to illustrate design thinking in action. IDEO takes on all sorts of diverse design challenges—from developing new ways to optimize health care, to designing advertising campaigns, to finding different approaches to education, to designing new businesses. The CEO of IDEO, Tim Brown, credits one key phrase for sparking the design-thinking process: "How might we?" The "how" part presumes that the solutions to the problems already exist and they just need to be unearthed; the "might" part suggests that it is possible to put out ideas that may or may not work; and the "we" part means that the process will be a fruitful and collaborative one.[6] In short, "How might we?" encourages the design thinker to believe that anything is possible.

**FIGURE 4.1**

## Intersection of Desirability, Feasibility, and Viability

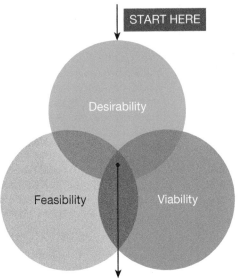

Final solutions should be at the intersection.

**Source:** IDEO. (2015). *The field guide to human-centered design.* San Francisco, CA: Author. Retrieved from http://
d1r3w4d5z5a88i.cloudfront.net/assets/guide/Field%20Guide%20to%20Human-Centered%20Design_IDEOorg_English-
ee47a1ed4b91f3252115b83152828d7e.pdf

Design thinkers welcome constraints and see them as opportunities to identify innovative solutions. An idea is deemed successful if it strikes a balance among three main criteria (see Figure 4.1):

- Feasibility—what can possibly be achieved in the near future?
- Viability—how sustainable is the idea in the long term?
- Desirability—who will want to use or buy the product or service?

The starting point is desirability—what do people need? It's not about building a new product and service and then searching for customers. It's about going to customers first, determining their needs, and then creating something to meet their needs. Even if you don't know who your customers are yet, find an opportunity space, a space that you are interested in, and watch and learn from people in this space to uncover needs. Remember, if you meet the needs of people, you are more likely to have customers.

Because design thinking is human centered, the focus is on what designers call "users." Users are those you are designing for. They are called "users" more often than "customers" because the users are not necessarily the buyer of the solution. For example, when IDEO was tasked by a medical device manufacturer to design a new device nurses could use to enter data before a surgical procedure, the client visualized an iPad-style device that the nurses would hold with two hands. Yet, when the IDEO team observed nurses (the users, in this case) during a standard medical procedure, they realized immediately that a two-handed device would not work because most nurses tend to hold the hand of patients who are anxious about undergoing surgery. Handling a two-handed device would not allow them to offer this comfort.[7] This is what's meant by design thinking being human centered. The IDEO team observed the nurses—the humans or users—to uncover the real need.

# Design Thinking Is a Social Technology

Professor Jeanne Liedtka at the Darden School of Business calls design thinking a "social technology" (see Table 4.2) because design thinking is leading to significant improvements in how we work and innovate. Liedtka evaluated 50 projects from a range of sectors and types of businesses (startups, NGOs, corporations) over a 7-year period. She discovered that from business and health care to social services, design thinking was changing how organizations approached and participated in innovation. She found that design thinking unleashed the creativity and imagination of people in ways she had not seen before. Design thinking and the tools associated with design thinking (user research, empathy, testing, and experimentation) helped teams break free of the fears and biases associated with working in new spaces. The structure of design thinking creates a system to explore problems in a human-centric way as well as permission to participate at all levels of the innovation process. As Liedtka concludes,

> Recognizing organizations as collections of human beings who are motivated by varying perspectives and emotions, design thinking emphasizes engagement, dialogue, and learning. By involving customers and other stakeholders in the definition of the problem and the development of solutions, design thinking garners a broad commitment to change. And by supplying a structure to the innovation process, design thinking helps innovators collaborate and agree on what is essential to the outcomes at every phase. *That* is social technology at work. (p. 79)

**Source:** Liedtka, J. (2018, September-October). Why design thinking works. *Harvard Business Review,* 72–79.

## TABLE 4.2

### Design Thinking as a Social Technology

| PROBLEM | DESIGN THINKING | IMPROVED OUTCOME |
| --- | --- | --- |
| Entrepreneurs are either trapped by their own expertise and experience or they have no expertise and experience. | Provides immersion in the user's experience | A better understanding of their customer and who they are designing for |
| Entrepreneurs are overwhelmed by the amount of data. | Makes sense of the data by organizing it into themes, patterns, and surprises | Leads to new insights, possibilities, and opportunities |
| Entrepreneurs are divided by different perspectives on the team. | Builds alignment because data and insights from actual users or customers don't lie | Convergence around what matters most to users and what their needs are |
| Entrepreneurs are confronted by too many ideas or ideas that are not innovative. | Encourages the emergence of fresh ideas and approaches, given the focus on customer inquiry and empathic understanding | A diverse set of potential new solutions that would not otherwise have been developed |
| Entrepreneurs lack feedback from users and may have the mentality of "if you build it they will come." | Offers user testing through very rough and early prototypes | Accurate feedback at a low cost that conveys what's most important to users |
| Entrepreneurs are afraid of uncertainty and ambiguity. | Delivers learning in action as experiments engage all stakeholders | A shared commitment and confidence in the desirability, viability, and feasibility of the idea |

**Source:** Liedtka, Jeanne (2018). Why Design Thinking Works. Harvard Business Review, September-October, pp. 72–79.

## Critical Thinking Questions

1. Given the definition of social technology provided above, can you identify other examples of social technology that emerged before or during your lifetime?

2. Why has design thinking helped so many people engage in the creative process?

3. Why are entrepreneurs, in particular, benefiting from design thinking as a social technology? ●

Rise Science, a sleep analytics startup that empowers elite performance from athletes, approached IDEO to help scale and rebrand the business and optimize its sleep training system for its customers.[8] The IDEO team collaborated with the Rise Science team to identify opportunities for change, particularly when it came to Rise Science's impersonal approach to onboarding customers to the new system. By the end of the process, IDEO had come up with the following strategy: A Rise Science employee introduces players and coaches to the value of sleep training. Players who agree to take part in the program receive a sleep-training kit, which includes a personalized sleep plan (designed according to their age, game schedule, and training load); a part-human, part-machine sleep coach that monitors progress and provides feedback; and sleeping products such as sleep masks and bed sensors. After just 1 week of using the freshly designed program, 97% of players reported getting almost an extra hour of quality sleep at night. Thanks to the new approach, the Chicago Bulls, Miami Dolphins, and the University of West Virginia have since signed up to Rise Science. By introducing a human element to the system, Rise Science was able to engage its target customer base from the very beginning.

The human approach ethos is not based just on thinking about what people need, but on exploring how they behave, asking them what they think, and empathizing with how they feel. By truly understanding the emotional and cultural realities of the people for whom you are designing, you will be more able to design a better solution with real value. This is why empathy is so important to the design process.

## 4.3 DESIGN THINKING REQUIRES EMPATHY

### >> LO 4.3  Describe the role of empathy in the design-thinking process.

Empathy is an essential skill for design thinkers and connects to both observation and listening. Developing our empathic ability allows us to better understand not only *how* people do things but *why*; their physical and emotional needs; the way they think and feel; and what is important to them.[9] In other words, to create meaningful solutions that people will buy, we need to know and care about the people who are using them.

We all have the ability to practice empathy, but how do we actually do it? The answer lies in observation, engaging people in conversation or interviewing, and watching and listening.[10] When the design thinkers at IDEO were approached by Dean Logan, county clerk for Los Angeles, to redesign the voting system, they jumped at the challenge. Los Angeles is the biggest voting jurisdiction in the United States, with a voter population that speaks more than a dozen languages. Logan wanted to make the voting system more accessible and to encourage more people to come to the ballot box.[11]

IDEO quickly realized that this wasn't a case of simply redesigning the voting system; it had more to do with using empathy to understand the complex social networks underlying

Old voting booth that IDEO is working to replace.

the act of voting. To that end, the IDEO team spent hundreds of hours observing, listening to, and interviewing people in an effort to understand the motivations behind voting. They met with people who suffered disabilities that prevented them from going to the ballot box and sought solutions to making voting more accessible—even Stevie Wonder took part in the testing and offered his advice. But the IDEO team didn't just stop with the voting community; they observed the people who delivered the voting machines to almost 5,000 polling locations and interviewed the volunteers who assembled the

# Empathy as an Ethical Challenge

**Embrace baby warmer sleeping bag for babies, created by Stanford students**

The practice of design thinking is fundamentally human centered and requires the innovator to uncover the feelings and actions of users as they experience a particular problem. These elements of empathy and user engagement make design thinking an inherently ethical endeavor. What could arouse more empathy than the death of an infant? Yet in developing countries, many premature and low-birthweight babies die from lack of warmth, or hypothermia. Is it ethical to turn a blind eye to these tragic deaths?

As a class project, Stanford graduate students Rahul Panicker, Jane Chen, Linus Liang, and Naganand Murty had been designing an intervention for at-risk babies that was low enough in cost to be used in developing countries. Their specific challenge was to create one that cost less than 1% of the cost of a state-of-the-art neonatal incubator. But when they created a prototype, collaborative field testing in Nepal with village families proved that the incubators were impractical because the families for whom the design was created lacked electricity. During their field testing, the students determined that the cold Nepal winters and limited heat sources resulted in frequent incidents of fatal hypothermia for low-birthweight babies.

Consequently, the students abandoned their electricity-powered incubator design. Instead, they began brainstorming creative solutions for a baby-warming device that didn't require electricity. The students eventually designed what looks like an infant-size sleeping bag. The bag is made of phase-change material that, after being heated, maintains its warmth for up to 6 hours, helping parents in remote villages give their vulnerable infants a chance to survive. Within 2 years of its pilot in 2011, the Embrace baby warmer had helped some 39,000 at-risk babies.

## Critical Thinking Questions

1. How can you design collaboratively and inclusively when resources are highly unequal?

2. Design thinking requires incorporation of user feedback and possibly scrapping your original designs. Have you ever had to throw away work you've spent weeks or months on and start over? Would you perceive this as progress or failure?

3. Provide an example of a time when empathy, or an emotional desire to help solve a problem, prompted you to think creatively. What did you do? What were the results? ●

**Sources**

Bajaj, H. (2014, March 13). *How to boost your innovation and stand out from the competition.* Retrieved from http://yourstory.com/2014/03/design-thinking-entrepreneurs/

Burnette, C. (2013, September 2). *The morals and ethics of a theory of design thinking.* Retrieved from http://www.academia.edu/4390557/The_Morals_and_Ethics_of_A_Theory_of_Design_Thinking

Embrace. (2019). *About us.* Retrieved from http://embraceglobal.org/about-us/

Fabian, C., & Fabricant, R. (2014, August 5). The ethics of innovation: An ethical framework can bridge the worlds of startup technology and international development to strengthen cross-sector innovation in the social sector. *Stanford Social Innovation Review.* Retrieved from http://ssir.org/articles/entry/the_ethics_of_innovation

Rodriguez, D., & Jacoby, R. (2007, May 16). *Embracing risk to grow and innovate.* Retrieved from http://www.bloomberg.com/bw/stories/2007-05-16/embracing-risk-to-grow-and-innovatebusinessweek-business-news-stock-market-and-financial-advice

Soule, S. A. (2013, December 30). How design thinking can help social entrepreneurs. *Stanford Business Graduate School.* Retrieved from http://www.gsb.stanford.edu/insights/sarah-soule-how-design-thinking-can-help-social-entrepreneurs

machines when they arrived, identifying any obstacles along the way. They combined all their findings with a review of issues relating to security and privacy and the complex nature of the regulatory environment.

Based on this research, the team created a working model based on a set of design principles guided by a single philosophy: One machine for all. IDEO will find out during the 2020 elections whether its new and improved voting devices will encourage more people to vote.

Although rationalism and analytical techniques are important when creating products and services, as we have seen, design thinking is very much a human-centered approach and looks at the emotional as well as the functional side of problems. For example, it allows us to put ourselves in the shoes of people who live with disabilities and think about how to make the voting experience a little easier. There are many ways in which we can use empathy to relate to the people around us. To encourage students to empathize with older people, researchers at the Massachusetts Institute of Technology (MIT) created the AGNES suit (Age Gain Now Empathy Suit), which is designed for the wearer to experience the physical discomfort that many elderly people have to deal with every day, such as joint stiffness, poor posture, bad eyesight and hearing, and lack of balance.[12] This is a very powerful means to encourage people to empathize with older people, in order to identify their needs. Given that our aging population is growing, there is ample opportunity for entrepreneurs to consider ways in which they can make the lives of the elderly more comfortable. This is yet another example of how empathy is one of the key elements of the design-thinking process used to solve complex problems and identify needs. As the previous examples have demonstrated, to develop empathy, design thinkers make use of two primary tools, interviewing and observation, which we will explore in greater depth later in this chapter. But first, let's take a look at the key phases of the design-thinking process.

## 4.4 THE DESIGN-THINKING PROCESS: INSPIRATION, IDEATION, IMPLEMENTATION

>> **LO 4.4** **Illustrate the key phases of the design-thinking process.**

In this section, we explore IDEO's version of the design-thinking process and its effectiveness in designing solutions. IDEO looks at the design-thinking process as a system of overlapping phases, rather than a linear process of going from step 1 to step 2 to step 3 and so on. The IDEO approach combines the power of empathy, creativity, and action and consists of three main phases: inspiration, ideation, and implementation (see Table 4.3).

The design-thinking process is based on two main types of thinking: divergence and convergence. **Divergent thinking** allows us to expand our view of the world to generate as many ideas as possible without being trapped by traditional problem-solving methods or predetermined constraints. This is a concept similar to the practice of play, which frees the imagination, opens up our minds to a wealth of opportunities and possibilities, and helps us to become more innovative. In fact, IDEO builds its whole culture around play and creating a fun environment for people to work in.[13]

The second type of thinking, **convergent thinking**, allows us to narrow down the number of ideas generated through divergent thinking in an effort to identify which ones have the most potential. These ways of thinking allow us to move from openness to understanding, from abstract to concrete, and from what is to what can be. Figure 4.2 incorporates these two types of thinking with the three phases of design thinking.

Let's explore the three phases of design thinking—inspiration, ideation, and implementation—in further detail.

### Inspiration

The **inspiration** phase involves two primary tasks: defining the design challenge and learning about the users you are designing for. The design challenge is the problem that stimulates the quest for a solution. It starts with a problem that is neither too narrow

**Divergent thinking:** a thought process that allows us to expand our view of the world to generate as many ideas as possible without being trapped by traditional problem-solving methods or predetermined constraints.

**Convergent thinking:** a thought process that allows us to narrow down the number of ideas generated through divergent thinking in an effort to identify which ones have the most potential.

**Inspiration:** the first phase of design thinking, when you develop the design challenge and acquire a deeper understanding of users.

**TABLE 4.3**

Design Thinking Phases and Outcomes

| DESIGN THINKING PHASE | OUTCOME |
| --- | --- |
| Inspiration | Design challenge and user needs |
| Ideation | Potential solutions to meet needs |
| Implementation | Prototyping and testing solutions |

**FIGURE 4.2**

**IDEO's Three Phases of Design Thinking**

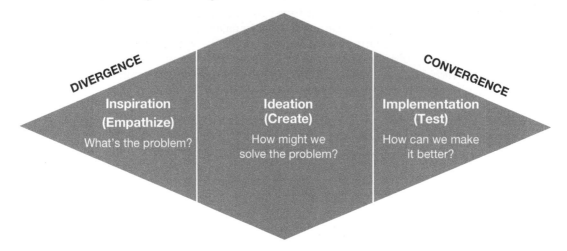

nor too broad and is framed in "How might we?" terms. We say neither too narrow nor too broad because a problem that is too narrow will not give you the freedom to create something innovative. Conversely, if the problem is too broad, there are no boundaries and it can be unwieldy or difficult to get started. Finding this sweet spot between broad and narrow is difficult, so some examples are offered.

Think about completing the "How might we?" question as you develop your design challenge statement. Here are some examples:

- How might we enhance the entrepreneurship education experience of students?

- How might we improve how the elderly live independently?

- How might we redesign how adults learn in virtual worlds?

- How might we reimagine how people get around in a town without cars?

*Reaching* **is considered a need while** *a ladder* **is considered a solution.**

Note that each of the design challenges above focus on a human, such as students, elderly people, adult learners, or people living in high-traffic, urban areas. Again, they are called "users." But in addition to defining the design challenge, we need to learn something about the users we hope to design for.

Let's imagine we are working on the following design challenge: How might we improve the customer experience in grocery stores? One way of understanding the users better is to observe and interview store customers while they are actually shopping in a grocery store. We'll talk more about observation and interviewing shortly, but for now let's imagine that you see a woman in a grocery store trying to reach something on a high shelf. You might conclude, "Hey, this woman needs a ladder." If you're thinking incrementally, next you may think about the type of ladder she needs. What if the woman is 80 years old? What does that ladder look like?

Now let's look at this from a broader perspective and help you think more creatively. Rather than simply saying the woman needs a ladder, what if we said, "How might we help customers reach products on a high shelf?"[14] Focusing on the needs that were uncovered through observing sets the stage for thinking creatively. By observing that woman trying to reach a high shelf in the store and not jumping too soon to solutions, we might come up with much more innovative ideas, such as robots, mini-elevators, or moving shelves. A simple way to think about needs versus solutions is that needs are verbs and solutions are nouns.[15] *Ladder* is a noun but *to reach* is a verb. In this phase of design thinking, we are *only* concerned with needs. No solutions at this point, please! It's too soon in the process.

Designers actively observe people in their environments to identify their real needs. By observing the actual experiences of real people as they go through their daily lives, entrepreneurs are able to imagine themselves in the shoes of the people for whom they are designing. This gives them an opportunity to develop empathy to better identify needs and, ultimately, develop solutions. It is also an excellent way to see the world differently in order to capitalize on potential opportunities that others have not yet recognized. This relates to the concept of alertness introduced in Chapter 3.

The inspiration phase of the design-thinking process is particularly useful for uncovering latent needs. **Latent needs** are needs we have but don't know we have. For example, we didn't know we needed an iPad or an iPhone until we held one. The late Steve Jobs, Apple CEO, was very good at identifying latent needs of customers, and he possessed great observation skills, yet he was often criticized for not talking to his customers. Latent needs are more easily identified by observing rather than talking because people can't always articulate what they really need. Additionally, if you can create solutions to meet latent needs, they are sometimes the most innovative, market-creating solutions.

**Latent needs:** needs we don't know we have.

---

MINDSHIFT

## Needs Are Verbs; Solutions Are Nouns

Entrepreneurs too quickly jump to solutions without first considering the needs of customers. The example used in this chapter of the woman reaching something on a high shelf immediately makes us think she needs a ladder. If we jump to the solution too fast, we might miss something really innovative. Below are some examples of needs versus solutions:

| NEED (VERB) | SOLUTIONS (NOUNS) |
|---|---|
| Relieve my aching back. | massage, better chair, shoes with special soles |
| Expand my professional network. | attend a conference, LinkedIn, set up informational interviews |
| Feed my dog when I'm not at home. | robot, professional pet sitter, auto-feeder |

As you can see from these examples, one need can lead to multiple solutions. Now it's time for you to practice writing needs as verbs and solutions as nouns.

Walk around a place for 30 minutes (no more and no less!). You can walk around campus, a mall, in the city, around a farm, wherever you want. You are to only look for needs in the form of verbs! To complete this Mindshift you need to record five needs and at least five solutions (existing or new) to meet those needs.

### Critical Thinking Questions

1. How did reframing a need as a verb impact how you viewed the world?

2. Why do we jump to solutions so quickly without first considering needs? ●

---

## Ideation

The second phase of the design-thinking process is ideation, which involves generating and developing new ideas to address needs (or latent needs), based on observations made during the inspiration process. Ideation is where empathy and creativity interact to generate solutions!

**Ideation:** a creative process that involves generating and developing new ideas to address needs.

The ideation process is in line with the creation view described in Chapter 1 as it requires a general openness to the world and involves using our creative ability to solve problems. This is also a period of divergent thinking in the design-thinking process. Remember, it is up to you to come up with the big ideas; you cannot depend on the people you have been observing to generate them for you. Instead, you use your observation data (see 4.5 Pathways Toward Observation and Insights, below) as a basis for coming up with ideas. During the ideation phase, ideas are often generated in collaboration with a diverse group of people whose experience spans many different disciplines. Within IDEO, it is not uncommon for a design team to consist of architects, psychologists, artists, and engineers, most of whom have also had some kind of experience in business or marketing, or who have completed an MBA. By combining different viewpoints, the team can generate a wide variety of ideas and engage in productive debates about competing ideas.

Here we will talk about brainstorming as a pathway to generating solutions to the needs identified in the inspiration phase, but also don't forget what you learned in Chapter 3 on generating new opportunities. Those skills can come in handy here. But for now, it's all about brainstorming in this phase. Though an old tool, it's still very good when the rules are followed! Brainstorming was created in the 1950s by writer and advertising executive Alex Osborne, who wrote about creativity in his text *Applied Imagination*. One of the key factors of brainstorming, in Osborne's model, was to "hold back criticism until the creative current has had every chance to flow." He considered the following four ground rules for brainstorming as pivotal to divergent thinking:

- suspending all judgment;
- being open to wild suggestions;
- generating as many ideas as possible; and
- putting ideas together and improving on them.[16]

Thus, the ideation phase uses brainstorming as a way to generate as many ideas as possible to meet the needs identified in the inspiration phase. Similarly, IDEO follows a set of rules for brainstorming (see Table 4.4); many of these are based on Osborne's four rules.

## TABLE 4.4

IDEO's Brainstorming Rules

| 1. | Avoid judging others. The whole idea of brainstorming is to make everyone comfortable enough to say whatever springs to mind. Remember, the more ideas out there, the more chance there is of building on those ideas to create the right solution. |
|----|----|
| 2. | Let the creativity flow. Always encourage ideas—no matter how outlandish they may be. Seemingly "crazy" ideas can often give rise to real solutions. |
| 3. | Be open to developing the ideas of others. However unlikely the idea may be, using positive language (use "and" rather than "but") when investigating an idea can achieve real breakthroughs. |
| 4. | Stay on topic. Keep your attention on the topic being discussed; otherwise, you risk exploring different paths that may go far beyond the scale of the project. |
| 5. | Follow the "one at a time" rule. There is more chance of the team developing ideas when full attention is focused on one person speaking at a time. |
| 6. | Use visuals. Visuals such as sticky notes or rough sketches are powerful ways to get an idea across to an audience. |
| 7. | Generate as many new ideas as possible. Try for up to 100 ideas in a 60-minute session, and then choose the ones worth developing. |

**Source:** Adapted from IDEO. (2015). *The field guide to human-centered design.* San Francisco, CA: Author. Retrieved from http://www.designkit.org/methods/28

## Implementation

Once you have used inspiration and ideation to identify some ideas that you think may have potential, it's time to enter the third phase of the design-thinking process: implementation.

Implementation seeks to answer the questions, "I have an idea, so how do I get feedback, how do I test it, how do I iterate, and how do I learn as quickly as possible whether there is a potential market?" During the implementation phase, ideas generated in the ideation phase are transformed into concrete actions that require user interaction. Note that the inspiration phase requires human interaction, but so does this phase. Again, design thinking is human centered and obsessed with users!

At the heart of the implementation process is low-cost experimentation through rapid prototyping, which creates an actual model of the product or service, which is then repeatedly tested for strengths and weaknesses until it leads from the project stage into people's lives. Prototypes need not be sophisticated or expensive.

For example, in a project with the German airline Lufthansa, to understand the growing demands of business class travelers, IDEO designers built a rapid prototype—a cheap mock-up of a plane using sturdy foam board for the plane business class seats.[17] Real passengers and crew were then invited to test them out and share their experiences, which provided the designers with valuable feedback that they could use in the next iteration of the prototype. Rapid prototypes are a time-saving, cost-effective way to learn how customers experience a product before too much money is spent on development.[18] From this example, it's clear that experimentation is relevant to the implementation phase, as it involves acting in order to learn, trying something new, learning from the attempt, and building that learning into the next iteration. This should sound familiar to the Entrepreneurship Method!

Rather than executing the ideas generated in the inspiration and ideation phases, the implementation phase focuses on early, fast, cheap testing to strengthen ideas and ensure that the design team is on the right path toward meeting the needs of the people for whom they are designing. This part is so important that we've devoted Chapter 7: Testing and Experimenting With New Ideas to this topic. Let's take a look at a real-life example of the three phases of design thinking in action.

**Implementation:** a process involving the testing of assumptions of new ideas to continuously shape them into viable opportunities.

Source: Courtesy of Water & Sanitation for the Urban Poor (WSUP).

**Woman in Ghana with a working toilet**

## The Three Phases of Design Thinking in Action

Millions of Ghana's urban poor live without indoor toilets. IDEO partnered with Unilever and Water and Sanitation for the Urban Poor (WSUP) and developed Clean Team Ghana, a waste removal service that delivers and maintains stand-alone rental toilets to low-income Ghanaians.[19] They used the three phases of design thinking to understand the design challenge.

During the *inspiration* phase, the IDEO team set out to define the problem and to identify any constraints. They interviewed sanitation experts, shadowed a toilet operator, and talked to many Ghanaians about how the new sanitation system might look. Early on, the team discovered an important historical fact: For a long time, night soil collectors used to collect waste from bucket latrines, but some of these collectors dumped the waste in the street. As a consequence, night soil collection was banned. By finding out this important fact, IDEO was able to learn more about in-home waste removal while ensuring that their new model didn't allow for illegal waste dumping. During the *ideation* phase, the team brought together what they had learned from their interviews and began to brainstorm. They developed several prototypes based on modifications of existing portable toilets and gave them to the Ghanaians for their input. During this phase, they learned about the technical limitations of their prototypes; for instance, the flush function would not work to full capacity due to water scarcity. The *implementation* phase focused on testing the design of the new toilet using parts from off-the-shelf cabin toilets to reduce costs. Since 2012, thousands of Ghanaians have been able to install indoor toilets in their homes

As we mentioned, the design-thinking process is not linear. It is not unusual to loop back through the three phases of inspiration, ideation, and implementation when exploring and testing new ideas. An initially successful idea, too, may need to be revisited. The concept might need a new round of inspiration, ideation, and implementation to identify key weaknesses and devise ways to remedy them. Because design thinking does not follow a strict pattern, it may at first seem like a chaotic process; however, there is structure in the chaos that serves to produce creative, meaningful results. The design challenge gives us direction, but through observation, we begin to uncover the real problems and needs. We will explore ideation and implementation in greater detail in later chapters, but here let's take a closer look at what happens during the inspiration phase.

## 4.5 PATHWAYS TOWARD OBSERVATION AND INSIGHTS

>> **LO 4.5**   **Demonstrate how to observe and convert observation data to insights.**

Two of the most important techniques that entrepreneurs use during the inspiration phase are observation and insight or need development. **Observation** is the action of closely monitoring the behavior and activities of users/potential customers in their own environment for greater empathic understanding. Many of us are so very accustomed to just seeing or simply talking to (or *at*) other people that we don't necessarily know how to observe. Because we are so used to our own environment, we tend to lose sight of the bigger picture or the things we miss seeing every day. It can be difficult to consciously stop and simply observe, yet observation is essential for gathering facts and identifying those latent needs previously discussed.

Observation leads to insight development, and insights are where we begin to articulate the needs of users. First, let's start with what an insight is *not*. The term is quite often misused. It is important to understand that insights and observations are not the same thing. Observations focus on the raw data that you have consciously recorded from all the things you have heard and seen, without any interpretation. An insight comes later: It is an interesting, nonobvious piece of information derived from interview or observation data that drives opportunities.

An insight is *not* just reporting what you heard in the conversations. An insight is *not* an idea. An insight *is* a statement that identifies a customer need and explains why. In other words, an **insight** is an interpretation of an observation or a sudden realization that provides us with a new understanding of a human behavior or attitude that results in some sort of action—for example, a new product or service to meet customer needs or even a new process to increase employee satisfaction.[20] Remember the grocery story example from earlier in the chapter? The need was to reach something on a higher shelf, but we didn't really address why she needed to reach something on a higher shelf. The insight in this case can be phrased as, *Grocery store customers need to reach products on higher shelves in a way that keeps them safe.* In general, an insight statement can be written using the following equation: User + Need + Why. Some useful "fill-in-the-blanks" to create powerful insight statements from your observations can be found in Figure 4.3.

Observations represent *what* we see and insights help us better understand *why* we are seeing what we are seeing. Insights are the patterns we observe; they help us identify the needs of the people we are observing. Probably one of the best ways to remember the definition of an insight is the following:

Q:   "Why is a good insight like a refrigerator?"

A:   "Because the moment you look into it, a light comes on."[21]

**Observation:** the action of closely monitoring the behavior and activities of users/potential customers in their own environment.

**Insight:** an interpretation of an observation or a sudden realization that provides us with a new understanding of a human behavior or attitude that results in the identification of a need.

**FIGURE 4.3**

### Fill in the Blank for Insight Statements

_____(users)_____ need ___(verb)_____ because_____(insert why)_____ .

Example: Surfers need to conveniently travel with their board because they like to explore new surfing areas.

_____(users)_____ need ___(verb)_____ in a way that _____(insert why)_____ .

Example: City drivers need to reduce their speed in a way that protects pedestrians and bikers.

_____(users)_____ need ___(verb)_____ so_____(insert why)_____ .

Example: College professors need to teach more experientially so that students are more engaged with course content.

In Chapter 3, we discussed pattern recognition, a process by which people identify links or connections, or "connect the dots," in order to identify and then build on opportunities between apparently unrelated events. You may remember Knock Knock City founders Selin Sonmez and Niko Georgantas, who connected the dots between hauling baggage around with them and empty, unused retail space.

Recognizing patterns generates *insights* that enable us to see everyday things in a new light. These insights can often take us by surprise. For example, in an effort to understand why bicycle helmets were so unpopular in Sweden, two Swedish students, Anna Haupt and Terese Alstin, spent years observing and gathering information from a whole range of adult cyclists. Their research showed that, on the surface, people attributed their reluctance to wear bicycle helmets to lack of safety, but the real reason lay in the aesthetics. It was this insight that led the women on a quest for a bicycle helmet that would be safe, comfortable, and aesthetically pleasing—a quest that led to their creation of the invisible bicycle helmet.

Insights are not ideas, but they help us generate innovative ideas, sometimes for new products or services that we didn't even know we needed. For example, how many of us have thought aloud, "Do you know what I really need? An invisible bicycle helmet!" Yet some of the greatest innovations of today have fulfilled a need that we had no idea we had—a latent need—such as the Internet or the iPhone. Instead of simply observing, Haupt and Alstin asked *why,* and they continued to ask why until they came up with a meaningful insight that led them to identify the primary need and to create the solution to meet the need. In other words, they had spotted the gap between where the customers are today and where they want to be.[22]

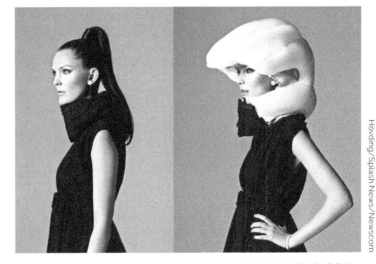

Hövding/Splash News/Newscom

**Model wearing invisible bicycle helmet made by Hövding, showing how the "air bag" mechanism looks when deployed.**

## Observation Techniques

Developing keen observation skills requires practice. Some may argue that we observe every day, so we already have strong observation skills. Observation requires looking *and* seeing. Although we look every day, we may not really be seeing. Seeing is an ability to understand more deeply what we are looking at. Seeing helps us make sense of what is in front of us, what it's about, and how it relates to other things in the environment. Looking isn't sufficient for observation. You need to also see. The more we practice observation, the greater the likelihood of our developing new, meaningful insights that can lead to

**TABLE 4.5**

Four Types of Observation

| 1.   Complete Observer |
|---|
| A complete observer is someone who is either hidden from view or is observing in plain sight but is not noticed by participants. For instance, you might go to a shopping mall to observe people's shopping habits. Other public places for this type of observation include airports, subway stations, or even public bathrooms. Although this observation technique is useful for noting how people behave—they are more likely to act naturally when they don't know they are being observed—consider the ethical implications of this approach. After all, how would you feel if you found out you were being watched without your consent? |
| 2.   Observer as Participant |
| In this case, the observer is known to the participants but maintains a neutral stance throughout. This type of observation may be useful to understand how people carry out certain activities, for instance, observing how people use certain software to achieve their goals. |
| 3.   Participant as Observer |
| Here, researchers are not only known by the participants, but considered more of a friend or a colleague. This method is often used when researchers visit remote indigenous populations or inner-city cultures to gather information on different cultural habits. |
| 4.   Complete Participant |
| A complete participant is almost like an undercover spy. The researcher fully engages with the participants and joins in with their activities, but they have no idea they are being observed. This technique is often used in customer research, such as the secret shopper role in the show *Undercover Boss*. It is a useful way to gather firsthand experience of how consumers operate. |

**Source:** Adapted from Sauro, J. (2015). 4 Types of Observational Research. Retrieved from https://measuringu.com/observation-role/

**AEIOU framework:**
acronym for *activities, environments, interactions, objects,* and *users*—a framework commonly used to categorize observations during fieldwork.

innovative solutions. There are four types of observation that can help us to focus on the things that are not necessarily visible or obvious at first glance (see Table 4.5).[23]

Another technique used to guide observation efforts is the **AEIOU framework**: an acronym for *activities, environments, interactions, objects,* and *users*.[24] This is a framework commonly used to categorize observations during fieldwork to help you make sense of what you are seeing. AEIOU is also the focus of the Mindshift exercise. Table 4.6 defines the five AEIOU dimensions.

**TABLE 4.6**

The Five AEIOU Dimensions

| |
|---|
| *Activities* are goal-directed sets of actions—pathways toward things that people want to accomplish. What activities and actions do people engage in when carrying out tasks? |
| *Environments* include the entire arena where activities take place. What is the function of the individual, shared, and overall space? Taking photographs or drawing sketches of the environment is also a useful way to record environmental cues. |
| *Interactions* take place between a person and something or someone else. What is the nature of these exchanges? Can you observe what the person enjoys the most or the least? |
| *Objects* are the building blocks or physical items that people interact with. What are the objects and devices that people use, and how do they relate to their activities? |
| *Users* are the people whose behaviors, needs, and preferences are being observed. What are their goals, values, motivations, roles, prejudices, and relationships? Who are they? |

**Source:** AEIOU framework. (n.d.). Retrieved from http://help.ethnohub.com/guide/aeiou-framework

In addition to the observations frameworks, there are small adjustments you can make to your own lifestyle to increase your powers of observation.[25] For example, you could deliberately change your routine. Do you always take the same route to class? Or go to the same grocery stores? If so, then try to take a different route or go to a different store, and see if you can make any observations based on these changes. Imagine you are seeing things for the first time, and see if you can discover anything new. Furthermore, the act of observation doesn't have to be a solitary activity. Bringing along someone else to help spot something you didn't notice before or offer a different point of view can be invaluable in developing new insights.

Here's a direct challenge. Once a day, stop and observe the ordinary. Look and see those everyday things that you normally take for granted, as if really seeing them for the first time. Why are manhole covers round, for instance? Why do we use forks? Why is a toothbrush the best tool for dental hygiene? Not only will this exercise improve your observation skills, but it will make you a better design thinker, for good design thinkers observe, but great design thinkers observe the ordinary in extraordinary ways.[26]

# 4.6 INTERVIEWING AS A USEFUL TECHNIQUE FOR IDENTIFYING NEEDS

>> **LO 4.6**  **Demonstrate how to interview potential customers in order to better understand their needs.**

Interviewing is an important part of the inspiration phase, second only to observation, to understand users and identify needs. It can be an alternative and/or complement to observation. It's simply another way to collect real and valuable data. A skilled interviewer is open minded, flexible, patient, observant, and a good listener. Like observation, interviewing is a skill that improves with practice.

It's very common for entrepreneurs to interview customers after they have purchased a product or service. This is called a feedback interview. But it's also common to use interviewing much earlier in the process to develop insights and identify needs. This is called a need-finding interview. Both follow similar protocols but their purposes are different. Regardless of the type of interview you are conducting, the following sections will help you develop your interviewing skills for maximum impact.

**Feedback interview:** an interview conducted to get feedback on an existing product or service.

**Need-finding interview:** an interview conducted to better understand the problems or needs of people or validate what you think a need or problem may be.

## Preparing for an Interview

First, think about whom you want to interview. Whom do you really want to learn from? Because we are still trying to identify needs, think about those people in the space you are interested in. For example, let's say you are interested in pet owners and whether there are unmet needs in this space. You might find people to talk to at a dog park or in a pet store or at a dog show. Try to stay away from people you know, even at this phase. Talking to strangers, which can be intimidating, will produce much better data than talking to people you already know. Now you need to consider why you want to talk to pet owners. What is the purpose of the conversation? In the need-finding phase you are trying to understand their lives with their pets. It's a very general goal, but that's the starting point with a need-finding interview. You should not walk into an interview thinking you already know what they need. This is the time for listening!

If the goal is to better understand pet owners' lives with their pets, then consider creating three very broad and open-ended questions to ask, such as,

1. Tell me about an average day with Fluffy.

2. Why did you adopt Fluffy?

3. How do other people in your life interact with Fluffy?

4. Tell me about some recurring "headaches" (problems) you have with Fluffy.

These four questions represent broad categories of the need-finding interview: day in the life, values related to pet ownership, connections to others, and pain points. Your role as an interviewer is to ask one broad question, listen, then probe. That's the formula: question—listen—probe!

# Observations to Insights

Now it's time to practice a little design thinking. When talking about observation as a core tenet of design thinking, it's easy to say, "I've observed all my life. I don't need to practice observing." Well, you haven't been observing your entire life; you've just been looking. When we observe with purpose and intention, we often see new things.

This Mindshift is about getting outside of the classroom, observing, and then building insights from your observation data. The AEIOU framework is a tool to help you do this.

First, identify an area of curiosity for you. This could be fitness, video gaming, food, travel, education—any human activity you are curious about. Once you have identified an area of curiosity, find a space that is related to this area. For example, if you are interested in food, you could observe waiters at a local restaurant. If you are interested in education, you could observe students in a class. If you are interested in travel, you could observe people in an airport or at a highway rest stop. What's most important is that you must observe *people*. Remember, design thinking is human centered, and desirability comes first. By observing people, you can identify what they need.

Observe for 2 hours and record your notes using a table like the one below. Using the AEIOU framework helps you organize your notes.

**OBSERVATION WORKSHEET**

**AEIOU FRAMEWORK**

| |
|---|
| **Activities** |
| What are people doing? |
| **Environment** |
| How are people using the environment? What's the role of the environment? |
| **Interactions** |
| Do you see any routines? Do you observe special interactions between people? Between people and objects? |
| **Objects** |
| What's there and being used or not used? Describe engagement with objects. Are there any work-arounds you can identify? |
| **Users** |
| Who are the users you are observing? What are their roles? Are there any extreme users? |

**Source:** Doblin, Inc. by Rick Robinson and Stef Norvaisis Available at http://help.ethnohub.com/guide/aeiou-framework

Now think about any insights arising from your observations. Remember, an insight is not an idea; it's a statement that drives your idea and identifies the needs of users. Use the fill-in-the-blank from Figure 4.3 to help you!

## Critical Thinking Questions

1.  Do you agree that observing and seeing are two different skills? In what ways, if any, are they different?

2.  In the AEIOU framework, which aspect of observation did you find the most useful? The most challenging? Explain your answers.

3.  What insight can you identify for the space you observed in this exercise? Does your insight relate to a need or a solution? Remember, insights are not solutions—they lead you to solutions. Why is separating needs and solutions important? ●

For example, let's say you were interviewing a college student who had a cocker spaniel dog and she lived in an apartment off campus. You may ask, "Why did you adopt Fluffy?" The student's response may be, "Because Fluffy helps me focus." Don't just move on to the next question. Now it's time to probe by saying, "Why does Fluffy help you focus?" From this probing question, you may learn that the student suffers from high anxiety that leads to an inability to focus on schoolwork. She doesn't want to take medication with side effects, and she learned that pets, specifically trained dogs, are very good at reducing anxiety in young people. The probing question is very important. How would you have learned the rest of the story without asking, "Why"? Always ask why! This method is called "peeling the onion," which is a way of delving into a problem one layer at a time. Begin with the challenges the person faces, and then continue to dig deeper in order to understand the root of the problem. Simply asking, "Why?" or saying, "Tell me more about _____" will help you gain a deeper understanding.

## Conducting the Interview

Once you have a short list of broad questions and you have thought about how you will probe, it's important to have an approach, especially when trying to talk to strangers. When you approach strangers, they do not want to be sold anything and they don't want to spend a lot of time with you. But, you will be surprised how many are willing to talk with you when they are interested. A good tip when approaching is simply saying, "Do you have 2 minutes to talk about….?" Don't say "Do you have time?" or "Do you have a few minutes?" Strangers will find it hard to say no to 2 minutes. For example, if you walk up to someone in a dog park, you might consider asking, "I'm trying to better understand the needs of pet owners. Do you have 2 minutes to talk about your dog?" Then you jump into your first question. Usually the stranger will give you more time, but if not, be thankful for the data you got in 2 minutes and then go find another stranger.

Take notes throughout, and if you are intending to also audio record the interview, make sure you ask permission first. Remember to use your questions as a guide only—it's best to keep the tone conversational and relaxed, but directed. The golden rule of interviewing is to actively listen to the other person. Practice a technique called parroting, which is repeating back what the person has said. Two things can happen with parroting.[27] The person may correct you because you have misrepresented what they said. Or, when the person hears what they actually said, they may change their answer a bit or provide more detail. In general, don't become so focused on your prepared questions that you neglect to pay attention to what the other person is telling you. Furthermore, when you reflect back or paraphrase what the other person has said, this shows that you are listening. However, do not interrupt or try to guess the answers. If there is a pause in the conversation, don't feel obliged to rush in and fill the space—your interviewee may be thinking about something or planning what to say next.

Finally, make sure you also record some basic facts about the person (gender, occupation, age, profession, industry, affluence). There is no need to ask these questions directly, as they can be offensive. Do your best to make some reasonable guesses.

Remember, your goal here is to learn as much as possible—you're not selling to the person (although, keep in mind that this person might well be a future customer of yours). The focus should be on the people you interview, getting to know them, the problems they have experienced and how they have tried to solve them (or not), and the outcome. If you are unclear about something or have a question, don't be afraid to seek clarification. In this way, you will come away from the interview with as much concise information as possible.

One of the most common interviewing mistakes is to seek validation for your ideas. Remember, at this stage, you either have a very early idea or may not even have an idea at all. Overall, you are trying to better understand the needs of various users. For example, let's say you have an idea to schedule and source a vast array of food trucks for corporate events. During an interview with a young financial analyst at an investment bank you learn that he and his colleagues think that food trucks are not high-end enough for corporate events. Don't get defensive and argue why you think food trucks are trendy and will appeal to a newer generation of professions. The aim here is to listen and understand why he doesn't think food trucks would be that appealing. His answers may not be the ones you are looking for, and sometimes the truth hurts, but his feedback may lead to new insights and ideas. Figure 4.4 provides examples of "bad" interview question types to avoid and "good" interview question types that are often helpful.

## After the Interview

As soon as the interview finishes, take some time to go through your notes and write down any additional observations or thoughts while the interaction is fresh in your mind.

## FIGURE 4.4

**Bad Questions to Avoid and Good Questions to Remember**

| BAD QUESTION REMINDERS | GOOD QUESTION REMINDERS |
|---|---|
| **Too Soon:** Asking a stranger for commitment or personal information before it's appropriate in the conversation | **Ask Permission:** Getting the customer's permission to conduct a short interview |
| **Leading:** Making assumptions about your customer that may be false and bringing your own biases into the conversation | **Customer Pain:** While exercising sensitivity, encouraging the customer talking about a problem or pain that they have |
| **Dead End:** Asking questions that can be answered with a "yes" or "no" and don't give your customer a chance to tell you anything meaningful | **Existing Alternatives:** Learning what the customer has tried to do to solve his or her problem in the past |
| **Poor Listener:** Showing that you clearly didn't listen to your customer's earlier responses | **Prioritize Pain:** Clarifying that alleviating the customer's pain is one of your top priorities |
| **Sales Pitch:** Asking your customer if they're interested in a product or service instead of listening and learning about them | **Dig Deep:** Following up a question to learn more |
| **Insulting:** Offending your customer so much that they end the conversation | **Get a Story:** Asking the customer to tell you a story about his or her situation |

**Source:** Heidi Neck & Anton Yakushin. 2015 VentureBlocks Teaching Note.

Try to craft insights from your notes by looking for themes and patterns based on responses to questions, body language, and tone of voice, and make note of any other questions or findings that have emerged. Develop your reflection skill; reflection is useful here, as it helps you to make sense of your feelings, the knowledge you have gained, what questions you may have, and what you need to consider as a result. Reflecting on the interview also gives you the opportunity to come up with new perspectives and conclusions. Also think about how you could improve the interview the next time. Practice makes perfect!

## The Empathy Map

One of the most useful ways to efficiently record the information from an interview is by completing an empathy map. An empathy map is a tool that helps you collate and integrate your interview data in order to discover surprising or unanticipated insights. It also enables you to uncover unmet needs, find the source of any frustrations, discover areas for improvement, explore different perspectives, and question your own assumptions and beliefs. In other words, empathy mapping gets you out of your head and into someone else's.[28]

Figure 4.5 is a template that illustrates the type of content that goes into an empathy map—you can either use this one or draw your own. The map contains four main components that help you organize data from people you interview: Say, Do, Think, and Feel.[29]

Drawing from the observations you have made during your interviews, write down the following:

*Say:* What sort of things did the person say? What struck you as being particularly significant? Are there any interesting quotes you can use?

*Do:* What sorts of actions and behavior were displayed by the person? Any particular body language that you noticed?

*Think:* What might the person be thinking? What sort of beliefs or attitudes might be relevant?

*Feel:* What sort of emotions do you think the person is experiencing?

**FIGURE 4.5**

### Empathy Map

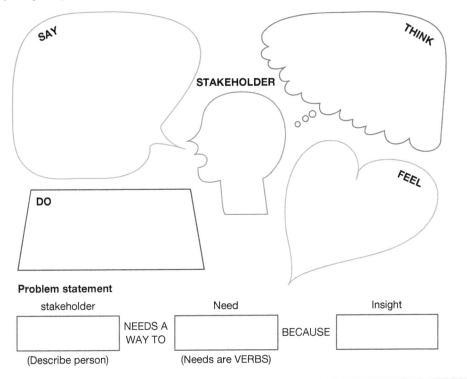

**Source:** The empathy map worksheet was part of the instructional materials for the Stanford University online course Design Thinking Action Lab, taught by Leticia Britos Cavagnaro in 2013 on the NovoEd platform (https://novoed.com/designthinking/). Credit to David Grey for the original empathy map framework. More context on the use of empathy map as part of a design thinking toolkit can be found at http://dschool.stanford.edu/use-our-methods/

When complete, the empathy map is a useful way for you to spot contradictions and certain tensions that can spark a whole host of interesting insights. Sometimes we have a tendency to say one thing and mean. Anna Haupt and Terese Alstin spotted this disconnect when people at first claimed lack of safety as the reason for not wearing bicycle helmets when the real reason was vanity. This triggered an idea to create a helmet that addressed both safety and aesthetics.

## 4.7 VARIATIONS OF THE DESIGN-THINKING PROCESS

### >> LO 4.7   Identify and describe other approaches to design thinking.

Earlier in the chapter, we described IDEO's three phases of design thinking (inspiration, ideation, and implementation), but it is important to recognize that there are also other schools of design thought. The authors of *Designing for Growth* suggest four questions that are useful to ask during the design-thinking process—all of which have periods of divergence and convergence:

- What is?
- What if?
- What wows?
- What works?[30]

**TABLE 4.7**

The Stanford Design School Five Phases of Design Thinking

| |
| --- |
| • *Empathy* is getting out and talking to your customers directly |
| • *Define* is defining a problem statement from that empathy work |
| • *Ideate* is brainstorming lots of ideas that could help you solve the problem you identified |
| • *Prototype* is building a crude version of the solution that you want to test with users |
| • *Test* is getting out and testing with users |

**Source:** Hasso Plattner Institute of Design at Stanford. (n.d.). *An introduction to design thinking: Process guide.*

*What is* encourages the entrepreneur to explore the current reality of the problem; *What if* encourages you to imagine all of the possibilities without regard to the reality of the ideas; *What wows* focuses on making decisions about what the customer really wants; and *What works* tests these solutions in the marketplace.

Another variation on the design-thinking process is from the Stanford Design School. Rather than IDEO's three phases or the four questions suggested by *Designing for Growth*, the Stanford Design School uses five phases: empathy, define, ideate, prototype, and test (see Table 4.7).

Finally, the Google Design Sprint method draws on design thinking by using its tools to develop hypotheses, prototype ideas, and run low-cost tests in a real environment.[31] Based on the Stanford Design School and IDEO methodology, the design sprint model aligns Google teams under a shared vision to move faster toward product launch.

Regardless of the variations inherent in design-thinking approaches, the themes and goals are similar. Each approach focuses on the importance of people and their needs; encourages entrepreneurs to get in front of real people in order to understand them; emphasizes the identification of needs before developing solutions; and recommends testing and experimentation, not for the purposes of killing an idea but to shape it and make it stronger.

Design thinking can be used to develop new products and services and also to build organizations, design strategy, and improve processes that all bring value and deliver meaningful results. By adopting some of the methods designers use when approaching problems, entrepreneurs will be better able to find effective solutions to complex problems.

So far, we have explored the different processes of design thinking, the power of design thinking in solving complex problems, and the importance of empathy, observation, and interviewing in the creation of successful design. In the next chapter, we will apply some of the concepts we have learned from design thinking to building business models. ●

---

Get the tools you need to sharpen your study skills. SAGE edge offers a robust online environment featuring an impressive array of free tools and resources.

• Access practice quizzes, eFlashcards, video, and multimedia at
  **edge.sagepub.com/neckentrepreneurship2e**

---

## SUMMARY

### 4.1   Differentiate between design and design thinking.

Many types of design are related to fashion, graphic, architectural design, or industrial design. Similar to the Entrepreneurship Method in many ways, design thinking is ultimately a constructive and collaborative process that merges the power of observation, synthesis, searching and generating alternatives, critical thinking, feedback, visual representation, creativity, problem solving, and value creation. There are seven design skills relevant to entrepreneurs: observation, listening, desire change, context and integration, solution-driven, consideration, and unbound.

**4.2** **Demonstrate design thinking as a human-centered process focusing on customers and their needs.**

Before business feasibility and economic sustainability are considered in the design process, entrepreneurs discover what people need. Products that achieve all three are bound to be the most successful, but the product or service must first be designed to provide a desired solution, or fulfill a need, for the design process to be considered human centered.

**4.3** **Describe the role of empathy in the design-thinking process.**

To create meaningful ideas and innovations, we need to know and care about the people who are using them. Developing our empathic ability enables us to better understand the way people do things and the reasons why; their physical and emotional needs; the way they think and feel; and what is important to them.

**4.4** **Illustrate the key phases of the design-thinking process.**

The design-thinking process consists of three main overlapping phases: inspiration, ideation, and implementation.

**4.5** **Demonstrate how to observe and convert observation data to insights.**

An insight, in this sense, is an interpretation of an event or observation that, importantly, provides new information or meaning. There are four different types of observation, and, like entrepreneurship, the ability to discern trends and patterns from each dimension is a skill that can be practiced and improved.

**4.6** **Demonstrate how to interview potential customers in order to better understand their needs.**

Interviews should be done for two reasons: (1) to develop a better understanding of user needs during the inspiration phase of design thinking and (2) to get feedback on ideas during the implementation phase. The interview must be well-prepared, the customer must be listened to and intelligent questions asked, and the interview must be evaluated when it is over.

**4.7** **Identify and describe other approaches to design thinking.**

The authors of *Designing for Growth* suggest four questions that are useful to ask during the design-thinking process, all of which have periods of divergence and convergence: What is? What if? What wows? What works?[33] Another variation on the design-thinking process is from the Stanford Design School, which uses five phases: empathy, define, ideate, prototype, and test. Finally, the Google Design Sprint method draws on design thinking by using its tools to develop hypotheses, prototype ideas, and run low-cost tests in a real environment.

KEY TERMS

AEIOU framework  94

Convergent thinking  87

Design thinking  79

Divergent thinking  87

Feedback interview  95

Ideation  89

Implementation  91

Insight  92

Inspiration  87

Latent needs  89

Need  80

Need-finding interview  95

Observation  92

CASE STUDY

## Anton Yakushin, cofounder and CEO, VentureBlocks

Anton Yakushin is the cofounder of an education technology (EdTech) startup called VentureBlocks. Founded in March of 2014, VentureBlocks is a game-based online simulation that teaches student entrepreneurs how to interview customers and identify their needs (VentureBlocks is described in more detail below).

A self-confessed "lifelong tech nerd," Anton began coding at a young age. After high school, he sought out roles that involved building software. For several years he worked as a software engineer for a variety of employers. During this time, Anton was also working on his degree at Babson College. He signed up for an entrepreneurship course, which he hoped would help him achieve his goal to be a tech entrepreneur. He was also keen to learn the business skills he felt he needed to capitalize on his vast range of tech knowledge.

After graduating from Babson in 2008, Anton had a variety of stints in consulting and startups, but in 2014, he returned to meet with his old entrepreneurship professor, Heidi Neck. He told Professor Neck that he wanted to make a difference in the way students were taught, specifically in the area of simulations. He says,

"When I was at college, I was always surprised how limited the simulations we used were. They were limited both in terms of topics covered and with what actions you could take while playing. More often than not, you could figure out a set of buttons to click consistently and win!"

He presented an idea to create a multiplayer online game in which students would compete with each other while operating retail businesses.

Professor Neck told him that although she wouldn't use it, he should interview some other professors to find out whether they were interested. Anton reflects, "After about a dozen initial conversations with professors at various business schools, I couldn't get one person to say they would use (and much less pay or have their students pay for) such a simulation."

However, the interviews had given Anton some valuable feedback, which he shared with Professor Neck, who ultimately signed on as a cofounder. Upon assessing this feedback, Neck introduced Anton to the idea of game-based learning in education. The first step was to identify how game-based simulations could be enhanced for learning purposes and who would use them. To do this, Anton needed to identify his target users and how to address their needs.

Anton started by interviewing hundreds of people in education, including students, professors, administrators, and high school students. It was during his interviews with a hundred entrepreneurship professors from different business schools that he quickly discovered a pattern. The biggest and most consistent pain point for most of the entrepreneurship professors was teaching students to identify customer needs. The reason was that each student had a different approach: Some were not listening to their customers and were asking the wrong questions, while others were being negatively influenced by existing biases. This made it very difficult for professors to teach customer development and need finding, especially when this topic was typically restricted to one or two classes.

This feedback from entrepreneurship professors would eventually lead to the creation of VentureBlocks, a tool that would prepare students to effectively interview customers in order to identify their needs. In addition, VentureBlocks provides a safe and fun space for students to compete with each other. Through the simulation, students also learn how to develop empathy and build stronger customer insights. Because students receive instant feedback as they are playing, they learn quickly from their mistakes.

Although Anton had not originally set out to create a simulation to sell to professors to aid student learning in this area of entrepreneurship, the interview feedback showed that there was potential to provide a solution to this pain point and create a business. Building on this knowledge, Anton created a low-cost prototype to demonstrate to professors and to give them something tangible to play, themselves.

Before writing a single line of code, Anton built the simulation as a paper prototype, which underwent about 50 iterations over the course of 6 months. Anton said, "Since we wanted to build a software simulation, we prototyped with a paper card–based one where I took on the role of the computer, doing what the simulation would have done. We found, through iteration, how to engage groups of players and how to embed the lessons most crucial to professors in a fun way."

In testing the prototype, Anton regularly went to the Babson College library, cafeteria, student center, and graduate school to play with undergraduate and MBA students as well as professors to get their feedback. He also contacted other colleges within driving distance to do the same and used Craigslist to find students willing to playtest the prototype during school vacation. He took time to complete the Business Model Canvas on several occasions, in order to prove that he had a product that people would buy before he went any further. After months of testing and feedback, Anton finally knew when he had a viable product to market. Though Anton did most of the coding himself using a platform called Unity, he coordinated a team of contractors to help with 3D graphics, scriptwriting, and user-interface design.

> We decided that our product met customer needs when students confirmed (1) that they learned what we set out teach them and (2) that the process of playing was engaging to them. We knew we achieved the first goal when a group of students told me that they were going to change their approach to identifying customer needs after playing the simulation in class. We knew we achieved our second goal when a group of professors was so engaged playing that they lost track of time and became quite competitive for top score!

Although the outlook seemed positive, Anton suffered an unexpected setback in the initial stages of launching the product. During the official launch at an entrepreneurship educators' conference, the product attracted the attention of a few early adopters, but the overriding response was quite negative. When Anton asked why, he was told that most professors were impressed by the quality of the simulation, but almost everyone was unhappy with the price for student access. Anton discovered that professors, though keen to use the product, were restricted by college budgets.

> The mistake we made with pricing was that we set it based on analyzing the competition (other simulations) and by talking to professors at a handful of private, relatively expensive colleges. We realized that we had set a price that limited the number of early adopters, and in doing so hurt our opportunity to grow and scale our user base—something critical for a brand new product in the market.

The idea itself has been completely overhauled many times in the first 6 months through customer interviews and prototypes. We completely overhauled the software simulation after the first year because of how much we learned from our early adopters. We also pivoted with our revenue model and our channels. We changed pricing and revenue type along the way and also changed how we reach potential customers and what we do when we reach them.

For Anton, VentureBlocks has been a labor of love, but his passion for the product is reflected in its success. To date, VentureBlocks is used by more than 10,500 students in 100 colleges and universities and is even available bundled with the textbook that you are reading. "It's great that a textbook publisher actually sees the value in VentureBlocks, and it will be helpful for the company to extend its reach both in the U.S. and around the world."

## Critical Thinking Questions

1. The three core components of design thinking are inspiration, ideation, and implementation. Can you identify these components in the evolution of VentureBlocks?

2. The journey of VentureBlocks is populated with many tests, experiments, and prototypes. Where do you think VentureBlocks would be today if Anton had simply written a business plan and started the business? Why?

3. How might you apply design thinking to your own academic endeavors to maximize your potential for success after graduation?

**Sources**

Anton Yakushin (interview with the author, April 22, 2019)

VentureBlocks website (http://ventureblocks.com/)

# 5 Building Business Models

"Startups have finite time and resources to find product/market fit before they run out of money. Therefore startups trade off certainty for speed, adopting "good enough decision making" and iterating and pivoting as they fail, learn, and discover their business model."

—Steve Blank, Silicon Valley entrepreneur

# Chapter Outline

# Learning Objectives

## 5.1 WHAT IS A BUSINESS MODEL?

>> **LO 5.1**   **Define the business model.**

In Chapter 1, we defined entrepreneurship as a way of thinking, acting, and being that combines the ability to find or create new opportunities with the courage to act on them. So far, we've focused on the finding and creating part of the definition, but now it's time to start thinking about the plausibility of some of your ideas. What additional actions do we need to take to convince ourselves and others that not only do we have something that customers need (see Chapter 4: Using Design Thinking) but also something that has economic feasibility and viability? Feasibility answers the question, "Can we do it?" Viability answers the question, "Can we make money doing it?" To begin answering these two questions, we must explore possible business models.

In this chapter, we will look at the different components of a business model and how each component represents assumptions and hypotheses that need further exploration. The business model as presented in this chapter is a journey to gather evidence and prove that the startup can be a sustainable business. Steve Blank, Silicon Valley entrepreneur, defines a startup as a temporary organization in search of a scalable business model. To move from temporary startup to scalable and sustainable venture requires evidence that is gathered from talking to people, investigating and asking lots of questions, testing assumptions, iterating, and learning continuously. In other words, it's a practice of hypothesizing, testing, and validating, just like the Entrepreneurship Method introduced in Chapter 1. The difference now is that we are using the Method to develop the business model. A business model is not created in a vacuum; it's built over time by collecting evidence that what you are creating works, has value for customers, is profitable, and is sustainable over the long term. This practice of hypothesizing, testing, and validating is often called **evidence-based entrepreneurship**. So, let's dig in and see if we can get beyond startup and to a scalable business model!

A **business model** describes the rationale of how a new venture creates, delivers, and captures value.[1] It includes a network of activities and resources that interact to deliver value to customers. Working through the components of a business model helps entrepreneurs better understand what they are doing, how they are doing it, for whom, and why. Value is better understood and generated in several ways: by fulfilling unmet needs in an existing market, by delivering existing products and services to existing customers but with unique differentiation, or by serving customers in new markets.

As Figure 5.1 illustrates, business models can create a whole new market in which new customers are offered a new product or service. Social media sites such as Facebook illustrate a type of business model known as Innovation. Business models can also disrupt existing markets by creating something entirely new for customers.

**Evidence-based entrepreneurship:** the practice of hypothesizing, testing, and validating to create a business model.

**Business model:** describes the rationale of how a new venture creates, delivers, and captures value.

Master the content at
**edge.sagepub.com/
neckentrepreneurship2e**

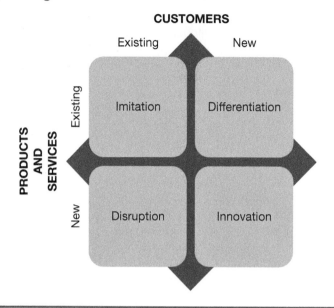

**Market Entry Strategies**

FIGURE 5.1

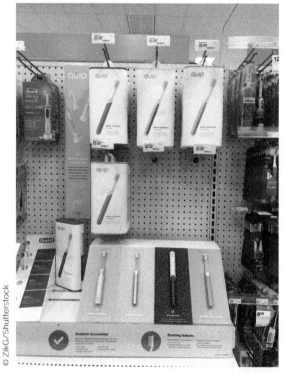

**Quip electric toothbrushes**

The emergence of MOOCs—Massive Open Online Courses—disrupted higher education when students opted for these free courses rather than paying tuition at colleges and universities. MOOCs are an example of the Disruption business model. Fulfilling unmet needs of customers using an existing product or service is called Differentiation. A good example of Differentiation is Quip, an electric toothbrush created by entrepreneur and inventor Simon Enever. Though there are plenty of electric toothbrushes available today, Quip differentiates itself by being simple, convenient, affordable, and portable.

Entrepreneurs like Enever use Differentiation to encourage existing customers to switch to their product or attract new customers to the product category. Finally, the Imitation business model should really be avoided. Imitation without Differentiation is not the greatest form of flattery. If you are going to offer something similar to an existing set of customers, the product needs to be better or not currently available to customers. Just because a Starbucks exists in your town does not mean that a new coffee shop would fail. Don't try to be Starbucks. Be uniquely you, in your own way, meeting customer needs not met by Starbucks. That's how you quickly move from Imitation to Differentiation.

Entrepreneurs like Brandon Steiner, profiled in the Entrepreneurship in Action feature, have the freedom to create, test, and adapt their business models until they find a compelling value proposition that meets the needs of most customers.

Because new businesses tend to be small in the beginning, it is much easier to be agile and make quick, efficient changes to the business model during the startup stage. Then, if successful, the business can scale as the young business model is tested and validated through early action. Equally, if the changes don't seem to work, then it is easy to spot the flaws and adjust them accordingly before large-scale investments are made. The most important thing before actually starting a business is to think through the business model,

# Brandon Steiner, Steiner Sports

Photo courtesy of Brandon Steiner

**Brandon Steiner, founder of Steiner Sports**

Entrepreneurs are often the first people who are willing to look at a fragmented industry and think about how to enter the industry and stand out among the fragments (other players), so to speak. Many facets of the sports industry have proven to be fragmented failures that entrepreneurs have tried to consolidate and conquer, most of them failing in their attempts. Brandon Steiner, founder of Steiner Sports, was successful in his attempt to bring some order to the sports memorabilia market and has, in turn, built a sports collectables empire worth hundreds of millions of dollars.

Brandon Steiner grew up in Flatbush, a neighborhood in the New York City borough of Brooklyn. He is the second of three brothers and his family did not come from money. After attending Syracuse University in upstate New York, Brandon started a traditional 9 to 5 job at Hyatt, in Baltimore. In 1984, he moved back to New York City and worked at the newly opened Hard Rock Cafe. Brandon made some close friends, with whom he started his own sports bar called Sporting Club. The bar proved to be a massive success, and it attracted the attention of some very prominent figures in the sports world who wanted to emulate its success. Professional superstar athletes like Mickey Mantle and Lawrence Taylor consulted Steiner, hoping to open their own successful sports bars. As he continued to build relationships in the sporting community, Steiner started to hire athletes to make appearances at the Sporting Club. This would obviously bring in a ton of business, but it ultimately helped him identify an opportunity to monetize a need.

After observing that athletes needed professional help marketing themselves as valuable business assets, Steiner used $8,000 in savings and started the sports marketing company Steiner Associates. The company employed a relatively new type of business model at the time, one that lacked formal agreements. Although Steiner did have a great idea and vision for his new company, he had to employ the "learn as you go" approach. According to Brandon,

> I thought we were doing really good in our first year, but we soon realized that we were about to go out of business. We didn't have formal compensation agreements with key staff members and almost half of them left. We were sprinting in the wrong direction. We were not placing enough emphasis on cash and we weren't managing our margins well. This was a wakeup call. I took out another mortgage on my house and adjusted.

Steiner now places a huge emphasis on something that is often overlooked by entrepreneurs: margins. He defines margins as the difference between revenues and expenses, and these are key indicators of success and excellent benchmarks to use when planning, according to him. Also, he feels that cash on hand is essential to ensure that the operations of a business do not cease. His view is that companies have the responsibility to pay their employees, and if they are unable to do that, the company needs to investigate whether it should close up shop, improve upon its existing business model, or follow a new model. Luckily for Steiner, he soon got his company back on track. He improved his new business model to focus on the company's financial viability; that is, he focused on the business's revenue and cost structures needed to meet its operating expenses and financial obligations.

By 1993, Steiner Sports was maintaining profits upwards of $5 million using a commission-based business model. In this model, Steiner Sports would act on the athlete's behalf and help him or her find endorsement deals, sell his or her authentic merchandise, or arrange public appearances and autograph signings. Steiner would then collect a percentage of the revenue paid to the athletes, often between 10% and 20%.

Today, Steiner Sports has 70 full-time employees and focuses most of its energies on the sports collectables market, as opposed to endorsement deals/appearances for athletes. It remains the largest sports memorabilia retailer in the world. As consumer preferences shift and demand changes, Steiner sports has been able to adapt well. Now it works with celebrities, not just athletes. For example, it will organize an auction to sell props from a certain film or sell clothes worn by a certain artist from a concert. Brandon maintains that his greatest difficulty is educating his clients on their own worth.

*(Continued)*

(Continued)

It's hard to get the clients to understand that "hey, these shoes might be worth something to someone; I should probably hold onto them." For celebrities and athletes it needs to become second nature for them because eventually their playing days will end, but that does not mean they can't still make money off of their performances.

From humble beginnings, Brandon Steiner created a sports empire. By 2005, Steiner Sports had reached deals with the University of Notre Dame, the New York Yankees, and the Dallas Cowboys. Per the deals, Steiner Sports has the license to sell a wide range of products including hats, game-used memorabilia, and jerseys. In 2009, in its most widely publicized deal, Steiner came to an agreement with the New York Yankees to be the chief broker of memorabilia from the old Yankee stadium. The road to get to this point was not an easy one for Brandon, but his business model was new and it brought a great amount of organization to a fragmented space. In his own words to aspiring entrepreneurs,

Don't necessarily try to be exclusively an inventor; try to be an improver. More often than not, people will try something and fail and then the next guy will come along and try that same thing and get rich. Opportunities to improve things are everywhere. The best entrepreneurs are able to make money by taking some invention and making it better.

**Critical Thinking Questions**

1. Consider Brandon's progression as an entrepreneur. Identify times when he jumped into a new opportunity and times when he pivoted and did something different.

2. Why should entrepreneurs be cash conscious?

3. Describe the Steiner Sports business model. ●

**Sources:**

Brandon Steiner (interview with author, November 20, 2018)
Van Riper, T. (2009). The selling of old Yankee Stadium. *Forbes.* Retrieved from https://www.forbes.com/2009/07/21/yankees-stadium-memorabilia-business-sports-jackson.html#2fad30ef3359

iterate, and gather evidence. However, the ability to tweak and change business models is not as quick or as efficient for larger or more established organizations, and some of them have ultimately failed because of their inability to change their business models. Consider BlackBerry, which stormed the business, government, and consumer markets with its smartphone technology in the early 2000s. Within a decade, BlackBerry failed to adapt to new competitors who were offering sleeker smartphones with additional functions such as touch interface and video/photo transmission, putting the company on the decline.[2] Similarly, Kodak failed to adapt to the digital camera revolution quickly enough, and Blockbuster did not respond in time to the growing threat of online media services provider Netflix. The point is that the business model in any company (big, small, new, old) must always be poised for adjustment and changes as new information is received and markets change.

But who says business models have to be reinvented at all? U.S.-based food company General Mills is entrepreneurial but also stays true to its business model by manufacturing food that meets the needs of its customers.[3] For instance, in response to the demand for less sugar and simpler ingredients, the company has introduced a new yogurt brand called YQ, which is targeted at key health influencers.

YQ may be considered a new innovation in yogurt products, but General Mills didn't need to change its business model to accommodate it—in fact, the product fit squarely within its existing business model of selling nutritional foods. As this example shows, the key to a successful business model is focusing on what customers want and where they are going.

## 5.2 THE FOUR PARTS OF A BUSINESS MODEL

>> **LO 5.2**   **Identify the four parts of a business model.**

Let's begin a deeper exploration of the business model by breaking it down into its four major components. The business model consists of four main interlocking parts that together create "the business": the *offering*, the *customers*, the *infrastructure*, and the *financial viability*.[4] Without these four parts, there is no business, no company, no opportunity. All must coexist, and none can be ignored; however, each can be a source of innovation and advantage over the competition. In other words, competitive advantage doesn't always come from the product or service you are offering. It can come from the other areas of the business as well.

## The Offering

The first part of the business model is the offering, which identifies what you are offering to a particular customer segment, the value generated for those customers, and how you will reach and communicate with them. The offering includes the customer value proposition (CVP), which describes why a customer should buy and use your product or service. The "value" part of the CVP means how much your product or service is worth to your customers. For instance, it might only cost a plumber $40 to fix a burst pipe at a customer's house ($5 for travel, $5 for materials, and $30 for an hour's labor), but the value to the customer for having the problem fixed is far greater, which is why the plumber can afford to charge more.[5]

The CVP explains how you can help customers do something more inexpensively, easily, effectively, or quickly than before. We will explore the concept of the CVP in greater detail later in this chapter.

**Offering:** what you are offering to a particular customer segment, the value generated for those customers, and how you will reach and communicate with them.

**Customer value proposition (CVP):** a statement that describes why a customer should buy and use your product or service.

## The Customers

Customers are the people who populate the segments of a market that your offering is serving (see Chapter 6: Developing Your Customers). They are the individuals or businesses willing to pay for what you are offering. Entrepreneurs typically can't serve everyone in a market, so you have to choose who you will target. In addition, you have to determine how you will reach those segments and how you will maintain a relationship with the customer. Bryan Bitticks is an entrepreneur and franchise owner of Great Clips hair salons, headquartered in Minneapolis.[6] Bitticks created a virtual online experience that enabled its customers to check in online and explore wait times. This approach has attracted thousands of younger tech-savvy customers who are more accustomed to booking appointments online. The convenience and comfort that Great Clips provides customers *before* they walk through the Great Clips door is all part of the customer experience and tied to the offering.

**Customers:** people who populate the segments of a market served by the offering.

## The Infrastructure

The infrastructure generally includes all the resources (people, technology, products, suppliers, partners, facilities) that an entrepreneur must have in order to deliver the CVP. For example, Justin Gold, founder of the nut butters brand Justin's, started off using limited resources, such as his own food processor, to make his nut butter in his own kitchen.[7] When he tried to scale his business, he realized that he could not afford the types of peanut butter mills used by manufacturers. The mills turn the peanuts or other nuts into the actual buttery product. Gold went out and bought the oldest food processors he could and started to produce perfect peanut butter that was impossible for the traditional manufacturers to mimic. By being resourceful, Gold was able to build competitive advantage and uniqueness into his infrastructure to create a successful business.

**Infrastructure:** the resources (people, technology, products, suppliers, partners, facilities) that an entrepreneur must have in order to deliver the CVP.

## Financial Viability

Financial viability defines the revenue and cost structures a business needs to meet its operating expenses and financial obligations: How much will it cost to deliver the offering to our customers? How much revenue can we generate from customers? And, of course, the difference between revenue and cost is profit.

For example, when Brandon Steiner, founder of Steiner Sports, realized the business wasn't managing its margins or meeting its financial obligations, he took out another mortgage on his house and made some changes to his business model to meet the needs of his customers (see Entrepreneurship in Action).

People often make a mistake in thinking that the business model is just about revenue and costs, but a business model is more than a financial model. It has to describe more than how you intend to make money; it needs to explain why a customer would give you money in the first place and what's in it for the customer. This is where the CVP comes in.

**Financial viability:** defines the revenue and cost structures a business needs to meet its operating expenses and financial obligations.

# The Rights of Research Participants

Credit: MARICE COHN BAND/Newscom

**Leanna Archer with her hair product**

Leanna Archer started her entrepreneurial venture when she was only 9 years old. Archer used her grandmother's homemade hair care products and received numerous compliments on the softness of her hair. Motivated to investigate starting her own hair care business, Archer obtained her grandmother's recipe, which used only natural, nonchemical ingredients. Her parents provided funding, and Archer began experimenting with different ingredients. Once several prototypes had been created, Archer sent samples to neighbors to get feedback. With the success of her trials and with family helping with bookkeeping and other administrative tasks, she launched the Leanna's Hair product lines. By the time she was ready to graduate from high school, her company was bringing in a six-figure income and the story of her "teenpreneurial" success had been featured in *Forbes*, *TIME*, and *INC Magazine*, among other international publications.

Entrepreneurs often conduct focus groups to see whether they are, in fact, providing value to customers. Before beginning testing and experimentation, the entrepreneur must consider some ethical concerns related to market research and the rights of research participants. Most notably, people participating in experiments have the right to informed consent; the right to be treated with dignity regardless of racial or ethnic background, sexual preference, or socioeconomic status; the right to privacy and confidentiality; and the right not to be deceived or harmed as a consequence of research participation. In addition, there are legal requirements for testing food items and personal care products that come into contact with the human body, as well as regulations on the use of animals in product testing.

As long as the researcher is able to conduct the market research ethically and laws are followed, research doesn't have to be expensive. For example, entrepreneurs may enlist a group of people to try out free samples of a product in exchange for submitting an evaluation or attending a focus group afterward. There are also many laboratories that perform testing for regulatory compliance, with various price structures to suit different budgets.

## Critical Thinking Questions

1. How would you find out what kinds of testing are required for an entrepreneurial product or service?

2. If your product or service was suitable for nonprofessional testing in people's homes or at a focus group, whom would you recruit to participate in your test? Explain how you would choose your best customer types to participate.

3. How would you ensure that the participants in your experiments were treated ethically and had their rights protected? ●

**Sources**

Al Smadi, S. (n.d.). *Ethics in market research: Concerns over rights of research participants.* Retrieved from http://wbiconpro.com/Marketing/Sami.pdf

Entrepreneur Media Inc. (2016). *Small business encyclopedia: Market testing.* Retrieved from http://www.entrepreneur.com/encyclopedia/market-testing

Snepenger, D. J. (2007, April 5). Marketing research for entrepreneurs and small business managers. *Montguide.* Retrieved from http://msucommunitydevelopment.org/pubs/mt9013.pdf

Tumati, P. (2010). Market research tips for startups. *Go4Funding.* Retrieved from http://www.go4funding.com/Articles/Market-Research-Tips-For-Startups.aspx

# 5.3 THE CUSTOMER VALUE PROPOSITION (CVP)

**>> LO 5.3   Explain the importance of the Customer Value Proposition.**

The CVP is perhaps the most important part of your business model. The key word in CVP is *customer*. The focus should always be on the value generated for the customer and how this value is then captured by the business in the form of profit.[8]

For your CVP to be truly effective, it needs three qualities:

- It must offer better value than the competition.

- It must be measurable in monetary terms (i.e., you must be able to prove that your CVP is better value than other offerings on the market).

- It must be sustainable (i.e., you must have the ability to execute it for a considerable length of time).[9]

In Chapter 4, we explored the concept of design thinking and the phases entrepreneurs go through to identify needs and develop solutions to meet those needs. As we have learned, design thinking is ultimately an iterative and collaborative process that combines the skills of observation, synthesis, searching and generating alternatives, critical thinking, feedback, visual representation, creativity, problem solving, and need finding. Design thinking helps you create a CVP that is unique and differentiating.[10] As with design thinking, the CVP means thinking about your business from the customer's viewpoint rather than from an organizational perspective. Your CVP must demonstrate that you are meeting the needs of various customer segments.

## Jobs, Pain Points, and Needs

The key to a successful CVP is a deep understanding of what the customer really wants or needs—not just how the customer does things now. It is an exciting opportunity to meet the needs of a real customer who wants to accomplish a goal, to get the job done.[11] Creating your CVP does not begin with trying to persuade customers to buy your product or service. Rather, it's about finding a goal—a job that the customer needs done—and then proposing a way to achieve that goal.[12] It's about uncovering what your customer needs and providing solutions to meet those needs. It's about relieving pain points. So, the CVP is that message that screams to a customer, "Hey! I can help you get a job done, relieve a pain point, or fulfill a need!" It's a promise to the customer—a promise of value.

Businesses start and survive because they successfully answer three questions for customers: What's in it for me? Why should I believe you? Why should I care? Best-selling business author Doug Hall calls these the overt benefit, real reason to believe, and dramatic difference, respectively.[13] The **overt benefit** is the one big benefit for the customer. Not the list of benefits—just the one big one. The marketplace is too cluttered and customers don't have time or want to figure out what's cool about your product or service. And if it's not clearly articulated, the benefit is really invisible. This means the CVP is also invisible. **Real reason to believe** provides evidence to the customer that you will do as you promise. You have to have credibility in the eyes of the customer, and this is more important than ever with the proliferation of online reviews. If you don't deliver on your promise, word travels fast online. **Dramatic difference** relates to uniqueness and how your product or service is different from the many other options that are likely available.

For example, the Swedish home-furnishings company IKEA understood the goal of customers who needed to furnish their rooms or apartments on a tight budget but did not want to settle for unattractive, worn, secondhand pieces. By providing do-it-yourself furniture kits at a lower cost than ready-made furniture sold in major furniture stores, IKEA solved the problem of obtaining good-quality, new, stylish furniture for a low price. IKEA is in the process of revamping its business model to meet the growing needs of its customers by providing affordable home delivery, renting furniture, opening stores in city center locations (rather than out of town), and using virtual reality to help people visualize home interiors.[14]

Similarly, FedEx made the job of transporting a letter or package overnight effortless in comparison with the regular mailing and parcel delivery services that existed in the 1970s when FedEx (then called Federal Express) was launched.[15]

In creating their CVPs, both IKEA and FedEx first focused on the jobs that the customer needed to get done before coming up with a solution to meet this need. The CVP also involves identifying ways in which your company best fits into customers' lifestyles;

**Overt benefit:** the one big benefit for your customer.

**Real reason to believe:** provides evidence to the customer that you will do as you promise.

**Dramatic difference:** the uniqueness of your product or service in relation to other available options.

# Overt Benefit, Real Reason to Believe, and Dramatic Difference

Doug Hall is a speaker, inventor, author, and researcher. He loves data and the power that data have to help startups get past the idea stage. He analyzed 4,000 concept descriptions for new products or services in order to answer the question, "What is going on in customers' minds when they are making buying decisions?" Hall and his team conceived the Three Laws of Marketing Physics, which "define and describe the universe of customer purchase behavior": overt benefit, real reason to believe, and dramatic difference. Then, by using complex statistical methods to identify patterns and recurring themes, Doug was able to model and predict the success of new products. "Success" is defined as a product or service that is actively on the market for at least 5 years.

Hall found that if the product or service had a high overt benefit, its probability of success was 38%. This is actually pretty high when compared to the probability of success with a low overt benefit, which was only 13%. If the product or service had a high reason to believe, the probability of success was 42% (versus 18% for low reason to believe). If the product or service had a high dramatic difference, the probability of success was 53% (versus 15% for low dramatic difference). According to Hall, when a strong overt benefit and real reason to believe was paired with a high dramatic difference, "sales and profits explode." ●

**Source:** Hall, D. (2005). *Jump start your business brain: The scientific way to make more money.* Cincinnati, OH: Eureka! Institute.

**The Tata Nano, the world's cheapest car**

it means analyzing the relationships you need to establish with customers versus the relationships your customers expect to establish with you; finally, it emphasizes how much customers are willing to pay for value, rather than trying to extract money from your customers.[16] To illustrate these points, let's look at an example of a successful CVP in action.

Tata Motors, an automotive manufacturing company in India previously known for building trucks and buses, created a CVP to provide radically low-cost cars for the people of India. Prior to the introduction in 2008 of Tata's highly affordable car, millions of citizens mostly used scooters to get around. Sometimes whole families would put themselves at risk by crowding onto a scooter, exposed to rain, wind, and traffic hazards. The problem was that many families could not afford to buy a car—even the cheapest car cost five times more than a scooter—so they had to make do with what they could afford.

Tata Motors created a CVP focused on providing an affordable, safer, more comfortable mode of transport for the low price of $2,500. This price was intended to make the car competitive with scooters, which its customer segments were currently buying.

Yet Tata Motors' existing business model did not allow the company to create a car at the price it wanted. Creating such a radically low-cost car would require a new business model that would support the low price point. Tata needed to find ways to cut the costs of manufacturing in order to make the car affordable for its customer segments.

How did Tata do it? First, it created a product design process that removed as much cost as possible from the car. Tata looked at eliminating everything it possibly could to reduce the number of parts used in the car. The resulting car has no air conditioning, no power steering, no power windows, no fabric covering the seats, no radio, no central locking of doors, and only the driver's seat is adjustable.[17] Tata also used 60% fewer suppliers than are needed for a typical economy car, thus giving more business to fewer suppliers and reducing coordination costs.

Tata then outsourced 83% of the car's components to find the lowest possible cost. What's more, Tata worked closely with its suppliers from the start, getting them involved in designing the components rather than merely building them to Tata's specifications. For example, instead of specifying, "build a windshield wiper X inches long with a Y diameter," Tata issued a more functional goal: "wipe water from the windshield." This allowed suppliers to come up with new, innovative, and low-cost ways to meet goals. In the case of the car's wipers, the suppliers came up with the idea of having only one wiper blade rather than the standard two wipers.

Next, Tata created a different manufacturing process that reduced the cost of final assembly. It made the innovative decision to save costs by not assembling its cars. Instead, Tata ships a "kit" with all the required parts in modules to a network of local entrepreneurs who assemble the cars on demand. The modules are designed to be glued together rather than welded because gluing is less expensive and doesn't require costly welding equipment. In addition to assembling the cars, the local entrepreneurs sell and service the cars.

By reinventing its business model to fulfill its CVP, Tata's innovative approach to the production, design, and manufacturing of cars opened up a whole new market to meet the needs of hundreds of thousands of people who previously couldn't afford cars.[18] Tata didn't simply create a low-cost car; the company created a car that delivered the value customers were willing to pay for. Tata Motors attacked the problem of affordability for its customers, but even the best-thought-out CVP is no guarantee for success. Though the Nano solved the problem of affordability, comfort, and safety, customer demand was less than expected.[19] Furthermore, increased regulation on emission requirements in India would require additional investment in production and design. Today the car will only be produced on demand.[20] Company insiders and executives suggest that marketing the Nano as the "world's cheapest car" backfired as the perception of poor quality overshadowed its value proposition.[21]

## Four Problems Experienced by Customers

Typically, customers face at least one of four problems that prevent them from getting a job done: lack of time, lack of money, lack of skills, or lack of access. As an entrepreneur, if you can find a new way to solve one of these problems, you're on your way to creating a strong CVP. Let's take a look at how some companies have resolved each of these problems with their own CVPs.

### Lack of Time

In the United States, people spend 1.1 billion hours obtaining medical care that equates to $52 billion in time lost. In other words, Americans are spending, on average, $43 of their own money (money that could be earned working) every time they go to the doctor.[22] Waiting to be seen by the doctor, hanging around for results, filling out paperwork, being seen by the doctor, and getting prescriptions filled takes up hours of valuable time. The ThedaCare hospital system in Wisconsin has found a solution to this time-wasting problem by ensuring that patients are seen more quickly and that results are dispatched before they leave, rather than days later. They implemented systems in which value to the patient is evaluated at every touchpoint, from check-in to discharge. From online medical records to continuous improvement processes, the patient is always their primary concern. Additionally, all levels of staff are required to innovate and experiment in ways that increase productivity and patient satisfaction.[23]

### Lack of Money

Delivering previously unaffordable products or services for less money can help beat the competition and open up a whole new market. Getting a taxi used to be a luxury until Uber came along; dining out was viewed as an unnecessary expense before Groupon started to offer restaurant deals and discounts; and staying in decent accommodation seemed like an impossibility for many until Airbnb launched its hospitality service. Uber, Groupon, and Airbnb are among thousands of startups that have succeeded in democratizing services previously reserved for a small portion of the population.

# Overt Benefit, Real Reason to Believe, and Dramatic Difference

Let's test Doug Hall's three laws (see p. 117): overt benefit, real reason to believe, and dramatic difference. Identify 15 products that currently exist in the food space. Go to a local grocery store but look for the lesser-known brands. In other words, look for the products of startup entrepreneurs. Whole Foods is a great place to look because they are known for carrying new and local brands, but any equivalent store will do. You can go online to Amazon and see Whole Foods offerings there because Amazon now owns Whole Foods, but it's actually more fun to go to the store . . . so get away from your computer!

Don't just randomly choose 15 products. First, choose five product categories, such as chips, nutrition bars, energy drinks, frozen pizza, herbal supplements, shampoo. Choose whatever categories interest you. For each of the five categories, identify three products and score each product as high, medium, or low on overt benefit; real reason to believe; and dramatic difference. Create a chart like the one below for your analysis. Extra action points are earned if you ask someone in the store which of the products you analyzed are the best sellers!

Product Category: _____

|  | OVERT BENEFIT I UNDERSTAND WHAT THE OBVIOUS BENEFIT OF THIS PRODUCT IS FOR THE CUSTOMER. | REASON TO BELIEVE IT'S CLEAR WHY THIS PRODUCT CAN DELIVER ON WHAT IT PROMISES TO DO. | DRAMATIC DIFFERENCE THE OVERT BENEFIT AND REASON TO BELIEVE REPRESENT SOMETHING NEW OR NOVEL TO THE WORLD. |
|---|---|---|---|
| Product 1: | High / Med / Low | High / Med / Low | High / Med / Low |
| Product 2: | High / Med / Low | High / Med / Low | High / Med / Low |
| Product 3: | High / Med / Low | High / Med / Low | High / Med / Low |

## Critical Thinking Questions

1. Did Hall's Three Laws stand up to your test? Why or why not?

2. How can you improve your own idea to increase its probability of success?

3. Did you really go ask someone at the store which of your analyzed products are the best sellers? If you didn't, what is preventing you from taking such action? If you did, well done. ●

## Lack of Skills

In many areas of life, people might like to accomplish a task but lack the specialized skills to get the job done. This common problem creates an opportunity to provide easy-to-use solutions that convert complex professional-level tools into consumer products.

In the mid-19th century, as fewer households had servants or custom tailors, many women wished to sew clothing for themselves and their families but lacked the skills to make a well-fitting garment based on a picture in a fashion magazine. The solution was the sewing pattern that was printed on tissue paper, sold in various sizes, and accompanied by instructions that a nonexpert could follow.

A more recent example of how ease of use transformed customers' lives is the shift from computers with arcane command-line interfaces to computers with graphical user interfaces like Apple's Macintosh or Microsoft's Windows. These new interfaces meant that you no longer had to have expertise in computer programming to use a computer. To solve another common problem—lack of writing skills—online grammar checking platform Grammarly enables users to communicate better. Since its launch in 2008, Grammarly has acquired almost 7 million daily users.[24]

## Lack of Access

Finally, people struggle with lack of access, which prevents them from getting a job done. For example, most of us think nothing of traveling on public transport to get to our chosen destinations, but millions of visually impaired people lack the ability to travel independently. UK-based nonprofit organization Wayfindr aims to solve this problem by providing an open standard (software that can be used by anyone) app that gives audio instructions to help vision-impaired people to navigate their journey without a human guide (https://www .wayfindr.net). This startup has set a goal to make Wayfindr available to the 285 million blind people living in the world today, thereby increasing their access to travel.

Another example of the lack-of-access problem is solar energy. The technology for small-scale solar collectors has been available since the 1970s, but it is generally suitable only for commercial buildings and homes with a large amount of roof space—and they need to be located where they receive direct sunlight for many hours per day. Moreover, it requires a sizable investment beyond the means of low-income homeowners, let alone rental tenants. To solve this problem of access, companies like Dvinci Energy, founded by entrepreneur Walid Halty, have devised a program to make solar energy affordable and accessible to everyone.[25]

Courtesy of www.standard.co.uk

**A user of the Wayfindr app**

# 5.4 DIFFERENT TYPES OF CVPs AND CUSTOMER SEGMENTS

>> **LO 5.4**   **Describe the different types of Customer Value Propositions and learn how to identify your customer segments.**

You may feel you have the greatest product or service idea in the world, but how do you convince others of its greatness? This is where many entrepreneurs fall short: They have the idea in mind but may not be so clear on the marketing or the execution. In fact, some entrepreneurs cannot even prove that customers want to buy their offering. This is where the CVP really fulfills its potential, as it delineates the value of your idea in meeting customer needs. In this section, we will explore different types of CVPs and learn how to identify your customer segments.

## Types of Value Propositions

Some CVPs are better than others. Let's explore three main approaches to creating value propositions: the all-benefits, points-of-difference, and resonating-focus approaches (see Figure 5.2).[26]

The **all-benefits** approach to CVP involves identifying and promoting all the benefits of your product or service to customer segments, with little regard for the competition or any real insight into what the customer really wants or needs. This is the least impactful approach for creating a value proposition because it's overly product focused. In other words, you are promoting features and benefits that customers may not even need.

The **points-of-difference** approach produces a stronger CVP than all-benefits because it focuses on your product or service relative to the competition and recognizes that your offering is unique and different from others on the market. However, although focusing on the differences may help you differentiate your business from the competition, it still doesn't provide evidence that customers will also find the differences valuable. Simply assuming that customers will find these points of difference favorable is not evidence enough to prove they will buy from you.

A CVP that uses the **resonating-focus** approach (also called "just what the customer wants" or **product–market fit**) is the "gold standard." All-benefits and points-of-difference CVPs each provide a laundry list of the presumed benefits to the customers,

**All-benefits:** a type of value proposition that involves identifying and promoting all the benefits of a product or service to customer segments, with little regard for the competition or any real insight into what the customer really wants or needs.

**Points-of-difference:** a type of value proposition that focuses on the product or service relative to the competition and how the offering is different from others on the market.

**Resonating-focus:** a type of value proposition that describes why people will really like your product and focuses on the customers and what they really need and value.

**Product–market fit:** an offering that meets the needs of customers.

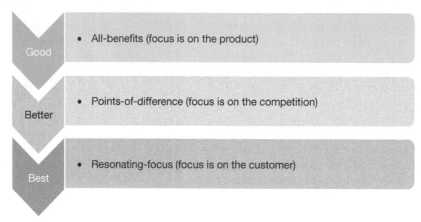

## FIGURE 5.2

### Three Types of Value Propositions

**Good** — All-benefits (focus is on the product)

**Better** — Points-of-difference (focus is on the competition)

**Best** — Resonating-focus (focus is on the customer)

Coca-Cola Zero advertising is aimed at men while Diet Coke is aimed at women.

© Anastasiia Marynych/Shutterstock

and the differences between your products or services in comparison with the competition, but a resonating-focus CVP drills down to what is most important to the customer. It describes why people will buy your product and focuses on the customers and what they really need and value. Your offering shows an understanding of your customers' problems and needs and describes how you intend to meet their demands.[27]

When it comes to defining your customer, you may be tempted to think that everyone will want to buy your product or service. In fact, trying to aim the CVP at "everyone" is a very common mistake made by young entrepreneurs. As a knowledgeable entrepreneur, you must realize that a major part of your business proposition is to figure out which customers to focus on and which ones to ignore. For example, if you're trying to sell luxury yachting experiences, you may target professionals between 30 and 65, with a high income, who live in a location close to water, and who have an interest in water sports. Remember, if you're not clear on your customer segment, your CVP will also not be clear.[28]

## Types of Customer Segments

Many products and services are attractive to more than one customer segment. How, then, can a "gold standard" CVP be developed if the focus is supposed to center on the customer? The answer is that businesses often have different CVPs for each customer segment. This is to ensure they are meeting the needs of the customers within each segment. In this section, we will explore how businesses adjust their CVPs to cater to different types of customer segments.

Consider Diet Coke and Coca-Cola Zero. The two products have very similar ingredients, but they are aimed at different target markets. Why? Market research indicated that young men shied away from Diet Coke because they associated it with women who were trying to lose weight.[29] In response, a new CVP was created, resulting in Coca-Cola Zero, which many people believe is aimed at men.[30] By understanding the motivations, desires, and unmet needs of your customers, you are better able to create a product or service that they will be willing to buy.

Customer segments targeted by different types of businesses include mass markets, niche markets, segmented markets, diversified markets, and multisided markets. Let's take a closer look at each of these.

A **mass market** is a large group of customers with very similar needs and problems. You may have heard of the phrase "It's gone mass market," which means a product or a service is being purchased by an enormous proportion of customers all looking for the same thing. Computers, soap, cars, insurance, and health care are examples of mass market products. Coke and Pepsi are mass market products because they target a wide range of customer groups, from youths to families.

A **niche market** is a small market segment consisting of customers with specific needs and requirements. The CVP is tailored to meet these particular needs. For example, entrepreneurs Carlton and Hazel Solle created the BioScarf as an alternative to the common filtration masks used in China to protect local citizens from breathing in the polluted air (https://www.bioscarf.com). The BioScarf is a more fashionable and comfortable filtration mask made from sustainable materials and protects its user from germs, pollen, and cigarette smoke. BioScarf also operates a Plus One program that donates a BioScarf to people in need for every one sold.

A **segmented market** is divided into groups according to customers' different needs and problems. For example, a bank might provide different services to its wealthier clients than to people with an average income, or offer different products for small versus large businesses. Segmenting customers is a good way of generating more business.

A **diversified market** offers a variety of services to serve two or more customer segments with different needs and problems that bear no relationship to each other. Amazon is a good example of an organization that diversified from its retail business—selling books and other tangible products—to sell cloud computing services, online storage space, and on-demand server usage. In short, Amazon adapted its CVP to cater to a whole new wave of customers, such as web companies, that would buy these computing services.[31]

**Multisided markets** are markets with two or more customer segments that are linked but are independent of each other. For example, a free newspaper caters to its readers by providing commuters with newsworthy content. The newspaper also needs to prove to advertisers that it has a large readership in order to get the revenue to produce and distribute the free publication. The newspaper is dependent on both of these two distinct customer segments in order to be successful.[32]

Matching the right CVP to targeted customer segments is essential to the development of a scalable business model.

Photo courtesy of BioScarf

**BioScarf, an alternative, fashionable air filtration mask**

**Mass market:** a large group of customers with very similar needs and problems.

**Niche market:** a small market segment that consists of customers with specific needs and requirements.

**Segmented market:** a market divided into groups according to customers' different needs and problems.

**Diversified market:** two or more customer segments with different needs and problems that bear no relationship to each other.

**Multisided markets:** markets with two or more customer segments that are mutually independent of each other.

**Business model canvas (BMC):** a one-page plan that divides the business model into nine components in order to provide a more thorough overview.

## 5.5 THE BUSINESS MODEL CANVAS (BMC)

**>> LO 5.5   Identify the nine components of the Business Model Canvas.**

As we have learned, there are four major parts of the business model: the offering, the customers, the infrastructure, and the financial viability. In this section, we further explore how a company creates, delivers, and captures value for customers through a more in-depth study of the **Business Model Canvas (BMC)**.[33] The BMC, introduced in 2008 by Swiss business theorist Alexander Osterwalder, divides the business model's four parts into nine components in order to provide a more thorough overview of the logic of the business model. When the four parts are divided into nine components, the result looks like this:

- The offering constitutes the (1) value proposition.
- Customers relate to (2) customer segments, (3) channels, and (4) customer relationships.

- Infrastructure includes (5) key activities, (6) key resources, and (7) key partners.
- Financial viability includes (8) cost structure and (9) revenue streams.

Figure 5.3 illustrates the nine components of a BMC using an idea for a new retail store that sells trendy T-shirts emblazoned with original designs by young, emerging artists.

Let's apply the T-shirt store example to some questions that each of the nine components must address.

1. **Customer Value Proposition:** As described earlier in this chapter, the CVP is designed to solve a customer problem or meet a need. With regard to your new T-shirt business, ask yourself the following: What value do we deliver? What bundle of products and services are we offering? What are we helping customers achieve by providing a new range of T-shirts?

2. **Customer Segments:** As defined above, a customer segment is a part of the customer grouping of a market. For example, "gluten-free" is a segment of the group of customers who buy food; another segment would be customers who are lactose intolerant. The customer segmentation questions for the T-shirt business are these: Who are your most important customers? What segment of the market would be most likely to buy your T-shirts?

3. **Channels:** The value proposition is delivered through communication, distribution, and sales channels. The core question here: What are all the ways in which you can reach your customers? For example, you could reach your customers online, through a brick-and-mortar store, and/or through word of mouth.

4. **Customer Relationships:** Relationships can be developed on a one-to-one basis in a brick-and-mortar T-shirt store and/or through a purely automated process of selling the T-shirts online. Customer relationships go beyond just buying and selling; they depend on engendering positive feelings about your business, building a sense of customer identity ("I am a so-and-so T-shirt customer"), and motivating customers to want to bring their friends into the relationship. The key here is one of the most important questions an entrepreneur can answer: How do you establish and maintain relationships with your customers?

5. **Key Activities:** What are the most important activities that the company participates in to get the job done? When running a T-shirt business, you will need to consider such activities as stock management, sales management, and T-shirt design selection.

6. **Key Resources:** Resources are what you need to develop the business, create products and services, and deliver on your CVP. Resources take many forms and include people, technology, information, equipment, and finances. How much and which resources will you need if your company has 1,000 customers or 1,000,000? What resources do you need to accomplish the key activities? If you're opening up a store, then you need to figure out the location and size; you also need people who are going to sell your T-shirts, space to store inventory, and a range of artists who will provide the designs for your T-shirts. You will also need to calculate how much money you will need to set up, as well as accumulate the skills, knowledge, and information you need to start your own business.

7. **Key Partners:** Entrepreneurs are not able to do everything by themselves, so partnering with suppliers, associates, and distributors is a logical option, not only for strategic purposes but also for efficiency. For example, you could partner with a designer who could advise you on the artwork of the T-shirts as well as provide you with a network of other designers. Could some activities be outsourced? Do you have a network of suppliers/buyers you could tap into or negotiate with?

8. **Revenue Streams:** Revenue is generated if a successful value proposition is delivered. Here you need to ask: How much are my customers willing to pay? How many customers do I need? How much cash can be generated through T-shirt sales in the store or T-shirt sales online? How much does each stream contribute to the total? (We will explore revenue models in further detail in Chapter 9.)

9. **Cost Structure:** The cost structure represents all expenses required to execute and run the business model. What are the most important costs inherent in the business model? Which resources are the most expensive to get? Which activities are the most expensive? Store rental, employee salaries, the cost of purchasing T-shirt materials and designs, and the cost of sales and marketing are all factors to consider when formulating a cost structure.

Remember, a business model is about creating, capturing, and delivering value. The BMC is a great tool to help you think about this. The right side of the BMC is about creating value and the left side is about delivering that value as efficiently as possible. Additionally, the BMC encourages you to find answers to the most important questions and think about them in a structured way, using the canvas to unlock your creativity. The process is iterative—you'll probably be moving back and forth between the boxes as you test ideas in relation to each other. Not only that, some of your ideas will need to be tested through experimentation before you have a solid answer.

To stay competitive, it is important to keep refining and revisiting your business model because, as we saw at the beginning of this chapter with the examples of BlackBerry, Blockbuster, and Kodak, leaving your model to stagnate can lead to business failure.

## FIGURE 5.3

### The Business Model Canvas

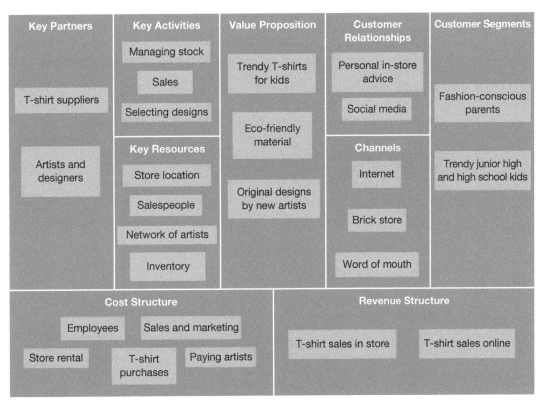

**Source:** Osterwalder, A., & Pigneur, Y. (2010). *Business model generation.* Hoboken, NJ: John Wiley & Sons. Retrieved from http://www.businessmodelgeneration.com/canvas/bmc

# Create Your Own BMC

Download a free copy of the Business Model Canvas from http://www.businessmodelgeneration.com/canvas/bmc.

Yes, we want you to fill out the canvas with one of the many business ideas you probably have at this stage. But most students don't know where to start. Do you start with the value proposition, key resources, or customer segments?

To answer this question, fold the canvas in half so there is a crease down the middle of the page. Now open the page to its original position. The area of the canvas to the right of the crease is all about *creating* value. The area of the canvas to the left of the crease is all about *delivering* that value in an efficient way.

In order to build an innovative and sustainable business model, always focus on the right (value creation) side of the canvas first. The left (value delivery) side of the canvas is operational and process oriented. Don't spend too much time on the left until you have established something truly valuable for customers.

Again, every completed box is just a guess. Once your canvas is completed, your job is to begin testing. Start by testing the value proposition with the customer segment you've identified—the product–market fit. Are you offering something people want?

Now you are ready to complete your first canvas. Take an idea and complete a canvas using the example in Figure 5.3 as a guide.

## Critical Thinking Questions

1. Why do you think this tool is called the Business Model Canvas?
2. In what ways does the division between value creation and value delivery help clarify the process of refining the business model?
3. In completing a BMC for your idea, which boxes were more difficult to fill out? Why? What are you going to do now with your completed BMC? ●

Thinking through all nine components of your business model helps you understand how the various parts work together: the value you'll create for customers, the processes you must implement to deliver value, the resources you need, and the way you'll make money. Overall, the goal is to lay out your assumptions so that you can test them. Be ready to change because your ideas will likely evolve before you get the formula right.

The common thread running through examples like IKEA, FedEx, and Tata Motors isn't that a particular set of processes is best. Each company has created its own processes and resource models to suit its CVP and industry. Tata Motors not only succeeded in creating their own tailored CVP but also gave some serious thought to how much money they would need to action their processes. Without sound financial models built into their respective business models, the companies never would have succeeded. One of the biggest considerations in building your own business model is money—it matters.

## The Lean Canvas: A Business Model Canvas Alternative

**Lean Canvas:** an adapted version of the BMC that was created to better address the needs of startup entrepreneurs.

There have been many adaptations of the BMC, and one has emerged as very popular for entrepreneurs: the Lean Canvas.[34] Unlike the BMC, the Lean Canvas

- Places less emphasis on customer segments but more emphasis on likely first adopters
- Begins with a problem rather than value proposition
- Addresses key metrics and suggests focusing on one key metric to track how your business is doing
- Addresses competitive advantage and uniqueness, called "unfair advantage"

The Lean Canvas ignores some of the boxes in the BMC. Key activities and resources, customer relationships, and key partners are eliminated. Key activities in the Lean Canvas are covered in the Solutions box. Customer relationships are covered in the Channels box. Key partners in the Lean Canvas were eliminated because it may be too early for the entrepreneurs to think about strategic partners when the business is not truly functioning yet. Let's take a look at the new boxes in the Lean Canvas (see Figure 5.4) that are not included in the BMC.

**Problem:** Startups too often build something that doesn't solve a problem, so problem understanding and validation is essential. If you already have a product or service in mind, then what is the problem you are solving for your customers? Is it a big enough problem? Conversely, start with the problem first, validate it's an actual problem, and then create a solution. We talked a lot about this in Chapters 3 and 4!

**Solution:** The Solution box is where you note potential solutions to the problems identified. The Lean Canvas purposely keeps this box small so you don't fall in love too quickly with an idea and you test the solution sooner rather than later.

**Key Metrics:** It's easy to get dizzy from information overload and drown in the numbers. The Lean Canvas encourages identifying what is most important for your stage of business and keeping track of that. Key metrics may be the cost of acquiring a new customer, revenue, activating new users, or retention rate.

**Unfair Advantage:** Unfair advantage is the same thing as competitive advantage; it just sounds a bit more hip for entrepreneurs! This box is important because as you test solutions, your advantage over the competition is likely to emerge. If there is no unfair advantage, long-term success is unlikely. Sources of unfair advantage may take the form of user friendliness, product design, service experience, influence on social media, and price.

Leanstack.com is a great free resource that will walk you through an online version of the Lean Canvas. You can develop your own there!

**FIGURE 5.4**

**The Lean Canvas**

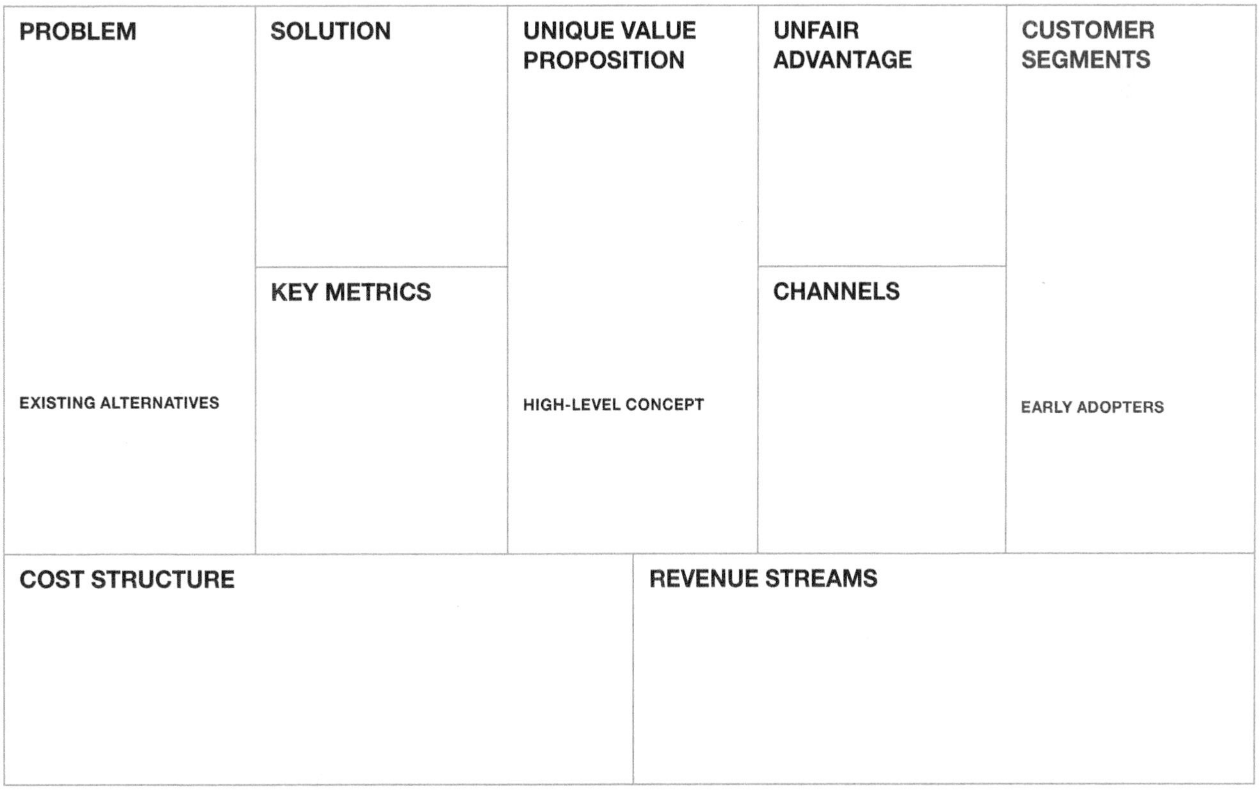

| PROBLEM | SOLUTION | UNIQUE VALUE PROPOSITION | UNFAIR ADVANTAGE | CUSTOMER SEGMENTS |
|---|---|---|---|---|
| | **KEY METRICS** | | **CHANNELS** | |
| EXISTING ALTERNATIVES | | HIGH-LEVEL CONCEPT | | EARLY ADOPTERS |
| **COST STRUCTURE** | | **REVENUE STREAMS** | | |

**Source:** Leanstack (2019). *The Lean Canvas.* Retrieved from https://leanstack.com/leancanvas

In general, the Lean Canvas works better for those at the very early stages of a startup when a solution to a particular problem has not been chosen, or a product has not yet been developed, or few actions have been taken. If the BMC is too complex for where you are in your startup, then the Lean Canvas may be a great alternative. Just as with the BMC, however, every box is a hypothesis that needs to be tested, validated, or changed. Both the BMC and Lean Canvas are tools to help you identify a model that will help you create a sustainable business. ●

---

**$SAGE edge™**

Get the tools you need to sharpen your study skills. SAGE edge offers a robust online environment featuring an impressive array of free tools and resources.

- Access practice quizzes, eFlashcards, video, and multimedia at **edge.sagepub.com/neckentrepreneurship2e**

---

## SUMMARY

### 5.1   Define the business model.

The business model is the framework for creating and delivering consumer value, while extracting value for the entrepreneur as well.

### 5.2   Identify the four core areas of a business model.

Each business model includes an offering, customers, infrastructure, and financial viability.

### 5.3   Explain the importance of the Customer Value Proposition.

The CVP outlines exactly how the firm will generate value, how it will generate it in excess of its competition, and how it will continue to do so in the future. As the true measure of any business is creating value, the true measure of a business model is its customer value proposition.

### 5.4   Describe the different types of Customer Value Propositions and learn how to identify your customer segments.

Businesses tend to have different CVPs for each customer segment. This is to ensure they are meeting the needs of the customers within each segment. Examples of different customer segments targeted by different types of businesses include mass market, niche market, segmented market, diversified market, and multisided markets. Types of CVPs include all-benefits, points of difference, and resonating focus.

### 5.5   Identify the nine components of the Business Model Canvas.

The four core elements of a business model can be expanded to nine business model components. Separating core elements into their respective components makes them easier to define and integrate with one another. The offering constitutes the (1) value proposition. Customers relate to (2) customer segments, (3) channels, and (4) customer relationships. Infrastructure includes (5) key activities, (6) key resources, and (7) key partners. Financial viability includes (8) cost structure and (9) revenue streams.

### 5.6   Explore the Lean Canvas as an alternative to the Business Model Canvas.

The Lean Canvas is an adapted version of the BMC and was created to better address the needs of startup entrepreneurs. The Lean Canvas replaces the BMC components of customer relationships, key activities, key resources, and key partners with unfair advantage, solution, key metrics, and problem, respectively. The focus of the Lean Canvas is problem and solution, whereas the BMC focuses more on value proposition and customer segments.

---

## KEY TERMS

All-benefits   115

Business model   105

Business model canvas (BMC)   117

Customer value proposition (CVP)   109

Customers   109

Diversified market   117

Evidence-based entrepreneurship   105

Financial viability   109

Infrastructure   109

Lean Canvas   120

Mass market   117

Multisided markets   117

Niche market   117

Offering   109

Points-of-difference   115

Product–market fit   115

Resonating-focus   115

Segmented market   117

## Gautam Gupta, cofounder, NatureBox

Gautam Gupta and his cofounder Ken Chen met during their time at Babson College and quickly became great friends. They bonded over everything related to entrepreneurship and decided to start a business together. In addition to their entrepreneurship obsession, they both had a passion for food. For Gautam, food was very personal. He struggled with obesity until he was 18 years old, when he started learning everything he could about diet and exercise. He eliminated all chips, candy, soda, and other junk food from his diet and started exercising regularly. His hard work resulted in a loss of 70 pounds before he started his first year at Babson College in August 2003.

Gautam's weight loss journey introduced him to nutrition science. He quickly discovered that snacking was one of the leading causes of obesity and the single greatest source of empty calories. He also noticed that all snacks deemed "healthy" didn't really taste very good. The market gap was clear—tasty healthy snacks. According to Gautam, "Snacking preferences differ from person to person, so we wanted to use technology to bring personalization to healthy snacking. We wanted to create a Netflix for food."

Gautam and Ken graduated from Babson and both had jobs, but they reserved time over weekends to develop NatureBox, a subscription-based healthy snack box delivery service. The part-time work on the business idea was taking too long and they were waffling on the decision to actually start a business. Gautam recalls,

> One weekend in 2011, we borrowed an office space from a friend from Babson and decided that we wouldn't leave until they made a decision about whether or not to start NatureBox. We put a box of healthy snacks together. We shot a photo of it and then we put that photo on our website and we drove some traffic through Facebook to that website.

By the end of that fateful weekend, they had 100 customers that were more than just friends and family who had actually paid for a product that didn't exist! They spent the rest of the weekend packing the 100 boxes of snacks for their first customers. When customers subscribed for more than 1 month, they knew that they were on to something.

NatureBox officially launched on January 1, 2012, providing monthly subscription boxes that included five snacks, such as nuts, trail mixes, and granola bars, under the NatureBox brand. During the early days of NatureBox, customers could not customize their snack boxes. Within the first year of operations, Gautam and Ken quickly learned that their "one size fits all" snack box did not provide a fully satisfying customer experience. When customers didn't like a snack in the box they were unlikely to keep their subscription because customers didn't want to pay for snacks that they wouldn't eat. NatureBox quickly transitioned to a more personal snacking model allowing customers to choose and customize their boxes. Over time they also learned that snacking is an impulse purchase. In 2016, customers were encouraged to purchase single, à la carte snacks in addition to the subscription option.

Gautam and Ken believe that NatureBox's most significant advantage has been their ability to understand and successfully adapt quickly to changing market conditions and customer needs. They make conscious effort to listen to the consumer and constantly gather feedback through customer reviews and online ratings. Rather than sourcing their products from other brands, their snack offerings are proprietary and developed in house. They have a membership model that allows members to subscribe to regular deliveries of snacks or make one-time purchases to try different products. They also offer a wide variety of quantities ranging from 1 ounce to 7 ounces for single serving items and bulk purchasing options of 70–80 ounces for the same snacks. Their offerings include a lot of interesting snacks such as popcorn and pretzels, cookies and bars, dried fruit, jerky, chips and crackers, trail mixes, breakfast snacks such as oatmeal and cereal, coffee, and a lot more. They also have a monthly "Discovery Box" that has a good mix of the snacks they have to offer. The January, 2019 Discovery Box, for instance, includes Crunchy BBQ Twists, Tropical Fruit Medley, Kettle Corn, Limited Edition Trail Mix Cookies, and Dark Chocolate Berry Trail Mix. Gautam and Ken want to build a brand around the healthy snacks they offer in addition to the actual box in which the snacks are contained. NatureBox links product development processes to customer feedback and their extensive network of natural product suppliers. This has helped them create more than 400 products that customers love!

A relentless customer focus has helped them understand their core customer and attract new segments. For example, the initial customer focus of NatureBox at launch was mothers looking for healthy snacking options for their children. However, they soon realized that millennial women were apt to subscribe to NatureBox for both home and work consumption. Individual, direct sales was the primary focus at NatureBox from 2011 to 2015, yet in 2016 they began selling snacking services to corporate offices. Businesses pay $20 per month per employee for an unlimited supply of snacks. This has expanded their distribution and provided a welcome new revenue stream.

In the packaged food industry, consumer feedback takes time and this lack of readily available real-time information usually extends the product innovation cycle in the perishable food industry to a few years, making both product innovation and the struggle to profitability very hard. It's not uncommon for food startups to burn through a lot of cash while channel distribution and retail partners take a huge part of the pie, making margins for food startups very thin. By successfully integrating real-time feedback into their supply chain, NatureBox has shortened the traditional multiyear product innovation roadmaps (from idea to product delivery) to 10 to 12 weeks and has constantly been adding new snacks to their product line based on consumer feedback (e.g., Sriracha Roasted Cashews, White Cheddar Caramel Popcorn, and Honey Dijon Pretzels). Developing these products in house not only enhances profitability, it also allows them to diversify the product line and therefore reach out to a broader consumer base.

Scaling NatureBox has required significant investment and most resources have come from within Gautam's network. Neither Gautam nor Ken were familiar with food manufacturing. While talking to a few of his friends in investment banking, Gautam learned of a food conference happening in Chicago. This conference introduced them to suppliers and manufacturers in the industry. Gautam's ex-employer and early-stage venture fund, General Catalyst Partners, was an early investor in NatureBox. That initial funding has led to other investors. NatureBox raised $58.5 million between 2012 and 2015. In addition to the funding, Gautam's network has been very helpful in getting NatureBox with the right people at the right time. He has leveraged his deep network of mentors and advisors to learn from their experience and expertise in order to get the business moving faster. This network has helped him hire the right people, scale up, and guide the business in the right direction.

The journey of NatureBox has been both exciting and challenging. "Making the decision to move away from only a subscription model in 2013 into one that offers both à la carte and subscription options was one of the most challenging pivots for the business," he recalls. "You can never be 100% sure as the data is never clear. It was a leap of faith!" That decision has helped the business greatly since then and has helped make the business a lot healthier. Additionally, the marketing mix has evolved over the years from only marketing on Facebook to being early adopters in channels such as podcasts. Today NatureBox is looking at narrowing down its marketing efforts back on Facebook where it has gathered over a million likes (https://www .facebook.com/NatureBox). Gautam and his team believe that the dynamic and ever-changing nature of marketing platforms makes it difficult to keep up with the trends, and a more focused approach will help make marketing activities more effective.

Gautam feels that 6 years after launching NatureBox, they are now truly delivering on its promise of a completely customizable healthy snack experience for its customers. Growth has not come easily, but Gautam says it's essential to stay calm and manage your mental state so as to not get caught up in the roller coaster ride called entrepreneurship! His advice to students and aspiring entrepreneurs is two-fold:

> First is to focus on the quality of the team, from the first person you start working with and every hire that comes on board. It is very easy to regress the quality of the team and you can only keep the bar high on talent by being personally involved. Secondly, as much fun as it is to execute the business, spend a lot of time, especially in the early stage of the business, thinking about the type of business you want to build and what it implies about the process that you need, the values of the organization. You should do as much planning on those things as much as executing. Often, entrepreneurs are quick to jump to action. The process of building a company is lot more than just offering a great product.

## Critical Thinking Questions

1. Describe the NatureBox business model. Could it be improved in some way?

2. There is a lot of competition for NatureBox today. How will the company compete in the future? Are there other directions in which the team could go?

3. Do you believe that Gautam and NatureBox are delivering on their customer value proposition of a customizable healthy snack experience? Why or why not?

**Sources:**

Interview with Babson MBA graduate assistant Gaurav Khemka, September 28, 2018.

Anastasia. (2015). NatureBox: Interview with its CEO & founder, Gautam Gupta. *Cleverism*. Retrieved from https://www.cleverism.com/naturebox-interview-ceo-co-founder-gautam-gupta

Crunchbase. (2019). NatureBox. Retrieved from https://www.crunchbase.com/organization/naturebox#section-investors

Vernon, L. (2017). Why food startups need to keep profitability in mind right now. *Ridgeline Ventures*. Retrieved from http://ridgelinevc .com/2017/09/19/food-startups-need-keep-profitability-mind-right-now

# Introducing…

# ⑤SAGE vantage™

## Course tools done right.

## Built to support teaching.
## Designed to ignite learning.

**SAGE vantage** is an intuitive digital platform that blends trusted SAGE content with auto-graded assignments, all carefully designed to ignite student engagement and drive critical thinking. Built with you and your students in mind, it offers easy course set-up and enables students to better prepare for class.

**SAGE vantage** enables students to engage with the material you choose, learn by applying knowledge, and soar with confidence by performing better in your course.

**PEDAGOGICAL SCAFFOLDING**

Builds on core concepts, moving students from basic understanding to mastery.

**CONFIDENCE BUILDER**

Offers frequent knowledge checks, applied-learning multimedia tools, and chapter tests with focused feedback.

**TIME-SAVING FLEXIBILITY**

Feeds auto-graded assignments to your gradebook, with real-time insight into student and class performance.

**QUALITY CONTENT**

Written by expert authors and teachers, content is not sacrificed for technical features.

**HONEST VALUE**

Affordable access to easy-to-use, quality learning tools students will appreciate.

©istockphoto.com/mario31

# 6 Developing Your Customers

"I've learned that people will forget what you said, people will forget what you did, but people will never forget how you made them feel."

—Maya Angelou

# Chapter Outline

# Learning Objectives

6.1    Define a customer and a market.

6.2    Describe the different types of customers entrepreneurs may encounter.

6.3    Identify your customers through segmentation.

6.4    Find your target customer.

6.5    Acquire a deeper understanding of your customer through personas.

6.6    Illustrate the customer journey mapping process.

6.7    Explain the importance of market sizing in growing your customer base.

## 6.1 CUSTOMERS AND MARKETS

**>> LO 6.1   Define a customer and a market.**

We're entering an age in which there is greater focus on the customer than ever before. Companies have realized that they must treat customers like members of a family through every stage of the journey to attract and retain their business. That means understanding and nurturing them from the very first interaction to long after the first purchase has been made. Of course, large corporations have big budgets and the staff to focus on understanding, developing, and retaining their customer base. But the good news is that even entrepreneurs with limited resources can use methods to identify and target their customers, estimate the potential of their market size, and create ways to gain a deeper understanding of exactly who is buying their products and why.

Businesses don't exist without customers, so gaining a deep understanding of your customers is absolutely essential to early business success. The truth is that no matter how great you think your product or service is, nobody will buy it unless you really understand what your customers want and need and you are providing more value than your competition. Once you have this knowledge, you can use it to attract more customers. But before the customer journey begins, let's explore what is meant by customers and markets.

Although we tend to use the terms *customer* and *consumer* interchangeably, they do not mean the same thing. A **customer** is someone who pays for a product or service. Customers become **consumers** when they actually use the product or service.

There can also be some confusion over the definition of a market.[1] Some people consider *market* to mean customers or customer demand, but that is only one part of it. A **market** is a place where people can sell goods and services (the supply) to people who wish to buy those goods and services (the demand). **Supply** refers to the sellers who compete for customers in the marketplace, while **demand** implies the prospective customers' desire for the goods and services available. A market can be a physical location, such as a farmer's market or supermarket, or a virtual one, such as the Internet or even a grouping of customers such as the "market for women's jeans." When supply meets demand, millions of successful exchanges take place every day. Generally, a market is:

- A set of actual or potential customers
- For a given set of products or services
- Who have a common set of needs or wants, and
- Who reference each other when making a buying decision[2]

**Customer:** someone who pays for a product or service.

**Consumers:** customers who actually use a product or service.

**Market:** a place where people can sell goods and services (the supply) to people who wish to buy those goods and services (the demand).

**Supply:** the sellers who compete for customers in the marketplace. There are four main elements that define a market:

**Demand:** prospective customers' desire for the goods and services available.

**$SAGE** edge™

Master the content at
**edge.sagepub.com/
neckentrepreneurship2e**

**TABLE 6.1**

Identifying Market Opportunities: Comparisons Between Novice and Experienced Entrepreneurs

| THE MAIN FOCUS OF NOVICE ENTREPRENEURS | THE MAIN FOCUS OF EXPERIENCED ENTREPRENEURS |
|---|---|
| the novelty of the idea | the degree to which their idea will solve a customer problem |
| the newness of the technology behind the idea | the potential for the product or service to generate cash flow |
| the superiority of the product or service | the speed at which revenue will be generated |
| the potential of the product or service to revolutionize the industry | the amount of risk involved |
| the tendency to make decisions based on intuition or gut feel | the people in their network who will support them in developing the venture |

**Source:** Nijssen, E. (2014). *Entrepreneurial marketing: An effectual approach* (p. 20). London: Routledge.

For example, family-owned dog food company The Honest Kitchen's customers are dog and cat owners who are concerned about the ingredients in their pet's food.[3] They want organic. They want natural. And they want whole food.

A big part of entrepreneurship is discovering a market opportunity for a new idea. A market opportunity is often identifiable by the degree of customer or market demand for a specific product application. A product application refers to the goods or services created to meet this demand, thereby providing a solution to a customer problem.[4] How entrepreneurs identify market opportunities very much depends on their experience. For example, novice entrepreneurs tend to focus on the novelty or newness of the idea, while experienced entrepreneurs focus on developing their idea into a viable product that will attract customers and generate money. The point is that novel ideas only go so far. If your idea doesn't solve a customer problem or meet a customer need there will be no customers at all.

Table 6.1 outlines more comparisons between novice and experienced entrepreneurs when it comes to identifying market opportunities. You will notice that the first three items listed in the table under "experienced entrepreneurs" relate to customers. This is because knowledgeable entrepreneurs realize the importance of keeping customers at the forefront of their minds from the very beginning.

In some respects, identifying a market opportunity or new venture idea is the easy part. What's most challenging is demonstrating that there is a large enough market (group of customers) willing to pay for your products and services. A logical starting point is understanding the different types of customers for your product or service. Anthony Magaraci, who is featured in Entrepreneurship in Action, works hard to evaluate the nature of the company's relationship with its customers by using a color-coding strategy.

**Market opportunity:** the degree of customer or market demand for a specific product application.

**Product application:** goods or services created to meet a demand, thereby providing a solution to a customer problem.

## 6.2 TYPES OF CUSTOMERS

>> **LO 6.2    Identify the different types of customers entrepreneurs may encounter.**

People often think of businesses having one type of customer, but instead of looking for a single customer, companies should identify the "chain of customers" composed of users, purchasers (buyers), and influencers.[5] Depending on the type of business you are in, the customer may play all three roles. For instance, a toy company producing toy cars may presume that its customers will be boys between the ages of 3 and 12. However, although

# Anthony Magaraci, Trinity Packaging Supply

Photo courtesy of Anthony Magaraci

**Anthony Magaraci, founder of Trinity Packaging Supply**

After receiving his undergraduate degree in entrepreneurship at Rowan University in New Jersey, Anthony went to work in sales at a packaging supply company. There he discovered he had a true talent for selling, and he achieved multiple promotions during his time there. His mission was to learn as much as he could about the packaging business. As he said, "I wanted to consume as much information as I possibly could." After 3 years of great success in sales, he became a manager and learned enough to start his own company, Trinity Packaging Supply, which he founded in 2010. Today, his company brings in $30 million in annual revenue.

Trinity Packaging Supply is a wholesale supplier of packaging and shipping supplies. The company specializes in stretch film, packaging tape, corrugated boxes, void fill, shrink film, and pallets, and it offers the full spectrum of packaging material and equipment. It has more than 18,000 items in stock and provides next-day delivery in most areas of the country. Trinity specializes in national account programs, in which a company with multiple locations can spend nationally, while having the support and services of local businesses, with one streamlined point of contact nationwide. The company also offers free packaging consultations, which involve touring a company's facility and recommending ways to save on their packaging needs and processes.

The early years of Trinity Packaging Supply were the most difficult. Anthony had a noncompete agreement with his former employer, now a competitor, which prevented him from doing business with his old customers for 1 year. Anthony says this was a blessing in disguise because having no credit history meant he wouldn't have been able to support large orders from those old customers when he first started Trinity. After 7 months, he reached his break-even point, when the monthly net profit was enough to cover his personal and business expenses, and by the end of the first year, his wife left her own job to join Anthony in the business.

Since then, Anthony has worked hard to build relationships with the businesses that pay Trinity for packaging goods and equipment. Primarily, Trinity must maintain good standing with their suppliers (the manufacturers of the packaging supplies) and their customers (the users of the packaging materials). Trinity's reach extends throughout the country, with seven sales offices in major metropolitan cities and 20 shipping locations. Their geographic distribution allows them to make packaging solutions cheaper and faster for clients.

Trinity's customers are product manufacturers and distributors. Their clients have products that need to be packaged and transported, and that need crosses a lot of different industries. Having such a diverse range of customer segments tends to "flat line" or reduce the volatility of industry-specific recessions. For example, when the housing market collapsed, home improvement and building products almost ceased distribution, while fast food and alcohol distribution skyrocketed. Anthony reflected on the last recession: "Unless someone invents a way to teleport products, our industry is relatively recession-proof."

Selling to customers is essential and fundamental for any entrepreneur. "It is important to work hard, but working hard does not just mean working long hours. You have to go out and get customers. If you can do that, you're going to be successful," he says. "The key to successful selling is spending quality time with the people who can make the decision to move forward with an order." But for Anthony, his relationship with customers is not simply a transaction.

> Our relationship with our customers is crucial. For every customer, we evaluate our relationship with them in five stages, using a different color for each. We use red for a defective relationship, orange for transactional, yellow for strategic, green for partnership, and blue for "BFF." Customer service is at the heart of our company, so we will be proactive in improving and reaching

*(Continued)*

(Continued)

the next level of our relationship with customers. We do this by increasing the frequency of our interactions with people, either in-person or via digital platforms. Building relationships is a core value of our company, and the mentality extends to nourishing any relationship within our organization and network.

Today, Trinity has a team of 32 people; offices in Philadelphia, Atlanta, Columbus, Chicago, Dallas, Houston, and Los Angeles; and is growing at breakneck pace.

### Critical Thinking Questions

1.  What is Anthony's secret in terms of customer service?
2.  Why is Trinity Packaging Supply recession-proof?
3.  What other industries do you think are recession-proof? Why? ●

**Sources:**
Anthony Magaraci (interview with author, September 18, 2018)
Harris, G. (2017). We asked 169,000 workers about what makes their workplace great. Here's their take. *Inc.com.* Retrieved from https://www.inc.com/magazine/201706/greg-harris/policies-perks-methodology-best-work-places-2017.html

boys might certainly be the "users" of the product, they might not necessarily be the buyers; the "purchasers" might actually be the parents. Similarly, the boys' "influencers" need to be taken into account, who could be close friends or family members. Identifying how customer types overlap is important when building a target base for your product or service. Table 6.2 illustrates five different types of customers: users, influencers, recommenders, economic buyers, and decision makers.[6] Let's take a closer look at each of these types.

**End users:** the type of customers who will use your product. Their feedback will help you refine and tweak the product.

**Influencers** (or **opinion leaders**): customers with a large following who have the power to influence our purchase decisions.

- **End users**: the customers who will actually use your product. They will buy it (or not), touch it, operate it, use it, and tell you whether they love it or hate it. Gaining a deeper insight into the needs and motivations of end users is essential in the experimentation period, as their feedback will help you refine and tweak the product.

- **Influencers** (or **opinion leaders**): customers with a large following who have the power to influence our purchase decisions. Sometimes the biggest influence on the success of a service or product comes from "customers" who have no involvement in it all. Celebrities, journalists, industry analysts, and bloggers have the power to influence our purchase decisions. Yet, increasingly, it is social media influencers—those without star status who have managed to establish credibility through their online platforms—who are becoming the new face of marketing. For example, in 2017, more than 400 social media influencers, including Kendall Jenner, supermodel Bella Hadid, and actor and model Emily Ratajkowski, were paid to promote the Fyre Festival—a "luxury music festival" in the Bahamas—on their Instagram accounts.[7] Thanks to these endorsements, more than 5,000 people bought the expensive festival tickets, only to find a disaster scene when they got there. The buzz leading up to the festival and the demand for tickets (some of

### TABLE 6.2

Five Types of Customers

| CUSTOMER | EXAMPLE |
| --- | --- |
| End User | Teen playing a video game |
| Influencer | Celebrity endorsing the video game in a commercial |
| Recommender | Blogger writing positive reviews for the video game on a website |
| Economic buyer | Buyer for GameStop who decided to stock the video game in the company's stores |
| Decision maker | CEO of the gaming company who decided to buy the game from the game designer |

which cost $75,000) show how powerful influencers can be. Make a list of all the outside influencers you would like to target and ways in which you can reach them, such as via social media or by attending events where your target influencers will be present.

- **Recommenders**: people who may evaluate your product and tell the public about it, such as bloggers or experts in an industry. Their opinions have the power to make or break your reputation. For example, a games blogger who recommends a new game could do wonders for a new product.

- **Economic buyers**: the customers who have the ability to approve large-scale purchases, such as buyers for retail chains, corporate office managers, and corporate VPs. Economic buyers have the power to put your product on the shelves, physically or virtually. Connecting with economic buyers brings you one step closer to the end-user customers you want to have the opportunity to buy your service or product.

- **Decision makers**: customers similar to economic buyers who have even more authority to make purchasing decisions as they are positioned higher up in the hierarchy. The ultimate decision makers do not need to be CEOs—they could also be "Mom" or "Dad," who have the power to approve purchases for their family.

Huda Kattan, founder of cosmetics line Huda Beauty, beauty blogger, and social media influencer with 23 million followers

In addition, entrepreneur and educator Steve Blank suggests that we do not ignore the *saboteurs*.[8] Saboteurs are anyone who can veto or slow down a purchasing decision—from top managers, to friends, spouses, to even children. Identify your saboteur customers and find out what's putting them off. You might learn a lot from their feedback.

## 6.3 CUSTOMER SEGMENTATION

**>> LO 6.3  Identify your customers through segmentation.**

In Chapter 5: Building Business Models, we defined customer segments as a part of the customer grouping of a market. As discussed, customer segmentation is one of the most important building blocks in the Business Model Canvas (BMC), so identifying the right customer segments for business is key to early business success.

Companies often group customers based on their common needs, common behaviors, or other attributes. This provides some insight into which customers would be more likely to buy from them. Once this has been achieved, the BMC can be tailored around the customers' needs. Customers can be divided in separate segments, if any of the following apply:

- Their needs validate an offering.

- They have different distribution channels.

- They call for different types of relationships.

- They have substantially different profitabilities.

- They are willing to pay for different aspects of the offer.

Overall, different customer segments have different needs, which require different approaches and more tailored solutions. This is why it is so important for entrepreneurs to define customer segments and become familiar with the type of customers most likely to buy their product or service.

**Recommenders:** people who may evaluate your product and tell the public about it, such as bloggers or experts in an industry.

**Economic buyers:** the customers who have the ability to approve large-scale purchases, such as buyers for retail chains, corporate office managers, and corporate VPs.

**Decision makers:** customers similar to economic buyers who have even more authority to make purchasing decisions as they are positioned higher up in the hierarchy.

Customer segments can be defined in four ways:[9]

1. Who are they? Find out their demographic (age, gender, education, income, etc.).

2. Where are they? Note your customers' locations.

3. How do they behave? List all behavioral or lifestyle habits demonstrated by your customers.

4. What are their needs? It is essential that you record your customers' needs to clarify your offering.

Once you have carried out the customer segmentation process, you can create an end-user profile of the person most likely to use your product or service.

## Creating an End User Profile

Typically, an end user profile consists of six items: demographics, psychographics, proxy product, watering holes, day in the life, and biggest fears and motivators.[10]

**Demographics:** Demographics are useful data in identifying your target end user, but they may not be entirely accurate when it comes to *understanding* your end user. For example, if you find out that your end users are all men in their 30s living in a particular geographic location, it doesn't tell you much about their attitudes or likes and dislikes. It is important to analyze demographics, but don't place too much emphasis on them.

**Psychographics:** Psychographics is a method used to describe the psychological attributes (attitudes, values, or fears) of your target end users. Unlike demographics, which provide basic information about your users, psychographics present a more detailed overview, such as their aspirations, whom they admire, what they believe, and so on. However, it is difficult to get psychographic data and even harder to analyze for accuracy. For example, Facebook may be able to give you some information about users' likes and dislikes, but it's more difficult to pinpoint in-depth detail like fears.

**Proxy product:** Proxy products give you an idea of what else the user is likely to buy. For example, people who already buy from high-end fashion brands are more likely to buy an expensive piece of clothing. Proxy products can also display some demographic and psychographic characteristics. For instance, people who buy from farmer's markets rather than from potentially cheaper supermarkets may be interested in promoting sustainability. This group might also be interested in eco-friendly products, such as clothes made from recycled fabric or homemade skincare merchandise.

**Watering holes:** Watering holes are the places where users meet and swap information. They are also the best spots for word-of-mouth recommendations. There are many different types of watering holes, both formal and informal. Formal meeting places include work conferences or business meetings, while less formal watering holes include bars, fitness classes, and social media.

**Day in the life:** One of the most useful ways entrepreneurs can create a profile of their end users is to walk in their shoes for a day. This method is particularly effective after you have spent some time observing and talking to a group of end users. Creating this real-world story puts all the data into perspective and provides a deeper insight into the behavior of your potential customers. As serial entrepreneur Les Harper says, "If you can get into their shoes and see their needs from their point of view, then you can take your experience and your entrepreneurial drive and really satisfy them."[11]

**Biggest fears and motivators:** Find out what keeps your end users awake at night and identify their top priorities in order to understand their biggest fears and motivators. This exercise is best carried out by sitting with a group of end users, making a comprehensive list of all their concerns, and asking them to score their priorities from highest to lowest. By the end of the exercise, you will have a list of their top five priorities, which will be a useful addition to all the research you have carried out so far.

When you have created your end user profile, you will have greater insight into how real people will use your product in the real world, and this is why it is worth spending time on. Segmenting your customers, and creating an end user profile, brings you one step closer to finding your real customer base and understanding which are the most important groups to target.

# 6.4 TARGET CUSTOMER GROUP

>> **LO 6.4**   **Find your target customer.**

To truly understand the targeting process, you must first understand the difference between how the targeting process works in traditional marketing and how it works in entrepreneurship. In traditional marketing, the most viable customer segment is identified and a new product is developed for it. But in entrepreneurship, many entrepreneurs start with the idea of the new product and then identify the target customer segment. Testing products with customers is a valuable way for entrepreneurs to find their target customer group (see Chapter 7: Testing and Experimenting With New Ideas).[12]

But finding your target customer group is only the beginning. The success or failure of your product or service depends on the response of your potential customers in the marketplace. Typically, people respond to new innovations in different ways. Understanding how people adopt or accept new innovations is key to success. The technology adoption life cycle, introduced by communications professor Everett Rogers, is a model that describes the process of acceptance of a new innovation over time, according to defined adopter groups. The model (see Figure 6.1) divides the market into five categories of potential customers: innovators, early adopters, early majority, late majority, and laggards.

**Innovators** (2.5% of customers): These are the first customers to try a new product. They are people who are enthusiastic about new technology and are willing to take the risk of product flaws or other uncertainties that may apply to early versions. In general, innovators are wealthier than other adopters; in other words, they can afford to take a risk on a new innovation.

**Early adopters** (next 13.5% of customers): This is the second group to adopt a product. Like innovators, they tend to buy new products shortly after they hit the market. However, unlike innovators, they are not motivated by their enthusiasm for new technology. Early adopters are usually influential people from business or government who make reasoned decisions as to whether or not to exploit the innovation for competitive advantage.

**Early majority** (next 34% of customers): People in this category tend to take interest in a new product as it begins to have mass market appeal. They are both practical and extremely risk averse, preferring to wait and see how others view the technology before they buy it themselves. As a consequence, they look for opinions from their peers or professional contacts to support them in their decision to invest. It is essential for entrepreneurs to appeal to this group, given that it makes up more than one-third of the life cycle.

**Late majority** (next 34% of customers): These customers are typically skeptical, pessimistic, risk averse, and less affluent than the previous groups. However, because this group makes up such a large portion of the life cycle, they cannot be ignored. It is possible for entrepreneurs to win over this group by providing simpler products or systems at an affordable cost.

**Laggards** (final 16% of customers): People in this final category are the last to adopt a new innovation. They tend to have a negative attitude toward technology in general and have a strong aversion to change. Despite their best efforts, entrepreneurs may never be able to persuade this group that their innovation is worth a first glance, never mind going so far as to purchase it.

In an ideal world, all five categories of customers in the adoption life cycle would adopt the new innovation, but of course, this is not the case. As the model shows, a product tends to go through different stages of adoption over time. Some customers may rush to

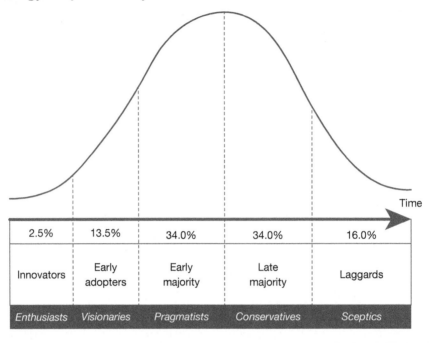

**FIGURE 6.1**

**Technology Adoption Life Cycle**

purchase a product as soon as it comes on the market, while others may not. Understanding this concept is essential when it comes to developing and growing your market, and it also explains why some products never really take off. Although the adoption life cycle is a useful way to win different groups of users, there are some cracks in the curve.

## Crossing the Chasm

High-tech and marketing expert Geoffrey Moore identified some cracks between each phase of the adoption life cycle (see Figure 6.2). According to Moore, the biggest difficulty is making the transition between early adopters and the early majority; he calls this the "chasm." Crossing the chasm involves focusing your resources on a single, primary market first, known as a *beachhead market*, before winning over that market and then using that momentum to dominate larger markets.[13]

The beachhead market takes its name from the battle of Normandy, which took place during World War II. During the battle, the Western allies stormed the beachheads of Normandy, enabling them to control what would turn out to be one of the most important battles of World War II. The beach became a stronghold from which the allies advanced into the rest of the territory. Without the offensive in Normandy, the Germans may well have been victorious.

Focusing on one market that is the most straightforward to capture is a particularly useful way for entrepreneurs who are typically short of money, time, and human capital to establish an early following. At first, the beachhead market may be a small segment of customers, but still enough to generate the cash flow needed to strategically position the product to win over other markets.

Finding your beachhead market is key to attacking other markets, which will generate a larger following.

There are three factors that define a beachhead market:

1.  The customers in that market buy similar products.

2.  Those customers have similar expectations of value.

3.  The customers use word of mouth to communicate to others in similar regions or professional organizations.[14]

Smart Skin Care is a good example of a company that successfully discovered a beachhead market.[15] Its founder, Pedro Valencia, patented a new technology that allowed for slow-release medication. Valencia and his team spent weeks trying to find a market for the new innovation. During this time, they found that the new technology could be applied to sunscreen—the slow release of sun-blocking chemicals over a certain period of time. Yet, further research showed that the sunscreen market was too large and diverse to enter. So, Valencia continued to find a smaller segment of the market to which he could sell his product. Finally, they landed their beachhead market: a segment of people in their 30s who engaged in extreme sports such as triathlons. Not only would the athletes benefit from slow-release sunscreen, but they also had the disposable income to spend on a more expensive version. Once Valencia conquered this segment of the market, it became much easier to launch the sunscreen product in other markets. This example shows that there is more than one path to success.

Once you have identified your beachhead market, then you can use the following three steps to successfully cross the chasm:

1. Create the entire product first.

   Your early adopters may be forgiving of a few bugs and glitches, but your early majority won't. This is why it is so important to make sure your product is as whole as possible before you launch it.

2. Position the product.

   As the early majority tend to be pragmatists, it is important to position your product to this audience by emphasizing its value. This might involve showcasing the market share captured to date, sharing details of third-party support, providing professional endorsements, and mentioning any press coverage.

3. Distribute the product through the right channels.

   Penetrating the initial target segment requires direct sales and support to explain the benefits of the product. Direct sales is the least expensive and best way to create demand.

Moore has further refined these three steps by using the analogy of a bowling alley. If you hit the first pin hard enough, the others will fall. So it's important to first identify your specific market segment (the first pin), or beachhead market, and then create a plan to expand from that segment to other segments before finally reaching the broader market (knocking down all the available pins). Facebook is a good example of a company that brilliantly executed the bowling pin strategy. It first started out at Harvard before spreading to other universities and eventually across the entire world. Yelp is another good example; it began by focusing on a niche market (San Francisco) before expanding into the mass market.[16]

**The Yelp app is used around the world.**

## The Tornado

Moore suggests that if the bowling strategy is executed successfully, your product and your business may enter a tornado. Being "in the tornado" means that your product is in high demand and your business is experiencing rapid growth. During this period, it is essential to meet customer demand and ship the product efficiently.

## Main Street

Following the tornado, your business is likely to enter a period of calm. Your product has proven to be a success in the market and has been widely adopted. However, there is still work to be done. Now is the time to leverage your market position by further enhancing your offering to ensure that your customers do not switch to a competitor.

**FIGURE 6.2**

## Critical Points in the Product Adoption Cycle

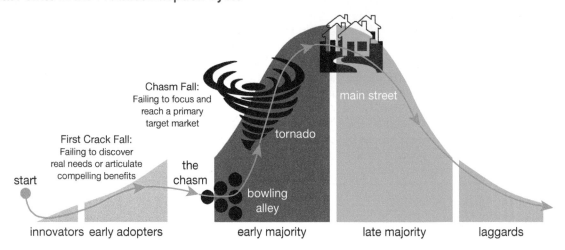

**Sources:**

Geoffrey A. Moore (2014) Crossing the Chasm (3rd ed). Harper Collins.

Geoffrey A. Moore (2004) Inside the Tornado. Harper Collins.

Jake Nielson (2014) https://www.ignitionframework.com/crossing-the-chasm-theory-how-to-market-sell-and-improve-your-new-invention/

## 6.5 CUSTOMER PERSONAS

>> **LO 6.5**  **Acquire a deeper understanding of your customer through personas.**

Earlier in the chapter, we explored the benefits of building an end user profile for gaining insight into your customer, but going a little deeper will provide you with greater customer understanding. Today's customers make buying decisions without the input of the actual seller. Using social networks and peer reviews is more commonplace. That's why it's more important than ever to understand your customer before you try to sell to that customer. In other words, how do you sell your product without you? How do you sell your product without sales representatives? The first step is to understand your buyer personas.

**Buyer personas** are profiles or representations of your ideal customers based on information and market research.[17] These personas help you to create strategies to connect with your target audience and promote product and services to people who will potentially buy them.

**Buyer personas:** profiles or representations of your ideal customers based on information and market research.

Building personas is an important exercise in understanding your customer; as you have read, demographics and psychographics will only take you so far. In fact, combined, they really only give you a buyer profile rather than a deeper insight into customer behavior. For example, the demographics may tell you where your customer lives, his or her age range, and marital status, but that information doesn't deliver any real insight into buying behavior. Similarly, the psychographics may capture the fact that your customer is a regular church-goer and good at managing but, again, that detail doesn't say much about how, when, and why your customer makes certain purchasing decisions.

Building personas is a powerful way to predict your buyers' behavior. The personas may be based on fictional characters, but they are based on real data and information, which makes them more meaningful (see Figure 6.3). As research shows, personas have the power to engage and help us to anticipate how these fictional characters might behave in different situations.[18]

The best way to build buyer personas is through real interviews with prospective customers (see Mindshift activity). By creating your buyer's story, you will be able to

FIGURE 6.3

### Cooper, the Stay-at-Home Dad

©istockphoto.com/gradyreese

**LIFESTYLE**

- Cooper is married to Jessica and they have three kids—2 boys (ages 8 and 10) and 1 girl (age 4)
- Jessica has a very demanding job as a lead research scientist with a biotechnology company and often works long hours.
- There are some financial pressures given that the family is living on one salary but they live in an area with strong public schools.
- Cooper gets the boys to school every day but also stays at home with his daughter. The older boys are starting to do more activities after school, which also requires a lot of scheduling and carpooling.
- Cooper, once a chef for a restaurant, also cooks all the meals.
- Cooper and Jessica love the outdoors and find themselves hiking and camping with the kids more often.

**BACKGROUND**

- Graduated from culinary school.
- Traveled through Italy after school to learn about Italian cuisine.
- Jessica, his wife, has a PhD in biology.
- They currently live in a suburb of Boston, Massachusetts, given that Boston is the hub of many biotech companies.

**CHALLENGES/PAIN POINTS**

- Jessica makes a good salary but the Boston area is expensive.
- Their youngest daughter will be in school soon, so Cooper is considering getting a job again but being a chef is not conducive to raising children given long work hours.
- Cooper is considering alternative lines of work but worries he may need to go back to school.

**VALUES**

- Cooper values family first. He was an acclaimed chef but when they had their first child, he knew he had to focus on the family.
- Values education and was very much attracted to Jessica because of her PhD.
- Has raised his kids to value diversity and be kind to all types of people.
- Both Cooper and Jessica are strong advocates of protecting the environment and educating their kids to do the same.

get closer to the people you are trying to influence. The information mined from those interviews, together with the data derived from your buyer profiles, will generate some key buying insights:

- The buyers who are interested in your product/service, as well as those who will never be interested, despite your best efforts

- The features of your solution that are relevant to them and those that are irrelevant

- The attitudes that put off your buyers from considering your offering. For example, perhaps they have had a negative experience with a similar product to yours, which prevents them from trying your offering.

- The kinds of resources your buyers trust when it comes to evaluating their options

- The types of buyers who are involved in the decision and the amount of influence they employ

Table 6.3 illustrates some key points for building a basic persona.

## Exclusionary Personas

Buyer personas are a good representation of your ideal customer, but it is also useful to create an exclusionary persona, which is a model of who you *don't* want as a customer.[19] Building exclusionary personas saves you time and valuable resources by identifying the people who will never buy from you, regardless of how much effort you put into sales and marketing (e.g., people who are too advanced for your product or service, students who only engage with the information you provide but don't buy from you, or people who only buy from you at rock bottom prices). This is not to say that you shouldn't engage

**TABLE 6.3**

Key Points for Building a Persona

| |
|---|
| Demographics (age, gender, salary, location, education, family) |
| Goals and challenges |
| Value and fears |
| Pain points or complaints |
| Hobbies |
| Where they get their news or other information |
| Blogs they read |
| Shopping preferences |
| Apps used most frequently |
| General lifestyle description |
| Day in their life |
| Work and/or school activities |
| Relationship with friends |
| Culture |
| Relationship with technology |
| How is free time spent? |
| Social media usage |
| Views on health and well-being |
| Quotes from interviews |

with those who fit into your exclusionary persona model (they could turn into influencers), but there is little point in trying to convert them into customers. The guidelines for creating your buyer personas also apply to creating an exclusionary persona. Identifying who your customers are *not* can actually help you further refine who your customers *are*.

Remember that a buyer profile alone will only tell you who your buyer is, but a buyer profile with buyer insights gives you a much clearer picture of the decisions you need to make to win their business.

## 6.6 CUSTOMER JOURNEY MAPPING PROCESS

**>> LO 6.6   Illustrate the customer journey mapping process.**

**Customer journey map:** a visual representation that captures customer experience across multiple touchpoints.

Customer journey maps are similar to personas in that they represent a typical customer experience. However, the main difference lies in the fact that personas focus on the buyer, while the customer journey map focuses on the buyer's experience. A **customer journey map** is a visual representation that captures customer experience across multiple touchpoints. It is designed to provide a holistic view of your customers' experience with your product or service while also allowing you to identify pain points. Journey mapping is a necessary process in the early stages of your startup so you can develop empathy for your customers as well as learn how to make their experience with your company or product a great one.

MINDSHIFT

# Build Your Buyer Personas

Personas are fun to create, but behind the fun needs to be real data! In order to create a buyer persona, you need to interview at least five potential customers for your venture idea that you believe are somewhat similar. Each interview can be as short as 10 minutes, but you need to find out the following:

- What's a typical day like for them?
- What do they do for work (or school)?
- Age, gender, and other relevant demographics
- How do they shop? (if applicable)
- What resonates with them most about your product or service?
- What are their goals and challenges?

- How do they stay connected?
- What is their social life like?
- How do they spend their free time?

The questions above can change based on your venture idea, but the goal is to get a complete picture of a typical customer (see Table 6.3 for additional variables to include in your personas). From the five interviews, create (1) a buyer persona for your own product/service and (2) an exclusionary persona (someone who should not be a customer). Use pictures as well as text. Be creative! If you need some help to get started, use Table 6.4 below as a guide. ●

## TABLE 6.4

Additional Information to Include in a Persona

| Is there a picture from a magazine that kind of looks like the customer you are personifying? Give the persona a name (e.g., Charlie) | What's a typical day for Charlie look like? | |
|---|---|---|
| Relevant demographics (age, gender, income, etc.) | What resonates with Charlie most about the product or service? What needs are being met? | What does Charlie care most about? |
| Job or school routines | | How does Charlie spend his free time? |
| How does Charlie stay connected? | Describe Charlie's social life. | How does Charlie shop? |

The benefits of customer journey mapping include the following:[20]

- Presents a clear picture of how your customers interact with your business, including their goals, needs, and expectations

- Clarifies what your customers think and how they feel about their experiences by identifying positive and negative emotions

- Confirms whether the customer journey is in a logical order

- Highlights the gaps between desired customer experience and the one actually experienced by your customers

- Allows you to connect to customers on an emotional level and provide the optimal customer experience by addressing and resolving key pain points

Overall, customer journey mapping is a good way to shift your perspective to your customers, to put yourself in their shoes, and think about how they can achieve their goals along their customer journey. Each touchpoint along the customer journey must be from their point of view and in the context of the goals they are trying to achieve. Then you layer on how they might be feeling when they encounter a problem. The visual

©istockphoto.com/skynesher

**Thinking about the guests' journey when planning events, such as a graduation party, can help enhance the guest experience.**

map charts the journey from the moment customers become aware of your product to the moment they stop being customers altogether. Customer journey mapping may sound like a lot of work, but not doing it runs the risk of unsatisfied customers and loss of opportunities to improve their experience.

For example, say you were throwing a graduation party for a group of friends.[21] You might think about the type of food and drink you will be serving, what time you would like your guests to arrive, and how many people you want to come. So far, everything is from your point of view. But now think about the party from your guests' perspective. The first touchpoint will be your guests receiving the invitation. With any luck, this will make them feel happy to be invited. But the invitation will also give rise to a number of questions: Who else is going to the party? What's the dress code? Do I need to bring snacks?

Closer to the date, you send out a reminder. That's the second touchpoint, which may prompt more questions: Where will I park? Do I need to pay for parking? Is it easy to find a parking spot?

The final touchpoint is the graduation party itself. They arrive at your house and may be asking themselves the following questions: Where do I put my coat? Where do I put the snacks I brought? How do I get a drink?

As the party host, you may have thought of some of these concerns, but not all of them because you have most likely been thinking of the party from your own perspective. This exercise is a really useful way to empathize with your customers and feel what it's like to be them.

You may wonder why journey mapping is necessary when you have already gathered lots of data on your customer base. The problem with data is that it often fails to communicate the frustrations and experiences of customers. For example, if you only analyze the data gathered from your party, you will know how much wine has been consumed, who had food and who didn't, how many guests showed up and how many didn't, but that doesn't tell you much about their experience of your party. Did they have a good time? Will they come to your next party? Will they talk to others about the party in a positive or negative way? On the other hand, a story such as the one told by a journey map is a wonderful way to engage and connect with your customers and find ways to improve their experience.

## Confirming Your Findings

However, certain data are useful in confirming the findings made from your journey map. There are many sources for data about your customers, including website analytics, social media tools, and direct customer contact.[22]

### Website Analytics

If your website is already up and running, then website analytics will provide you with lots of information, including your customers' location, the amount of traffic to your site, and the number of clicks on each page. Analytics also expose weaknesses in your site by showing you points in the process where your customer may have become frustrated and abandoned the site.

### Social Media Tools

Social media tools are also a useful source of data. For instance, SocialMention is a tool that searches blogs, comments, and videos for mentions of your brand and advises you whether those mentions are positive or negative. This type of customer feedback provides extremely useful insights into your customers' journey. You could also consider running a survey to find out your customers' questions, feelings, and thoughts.

### Direct Customer Contact

Sitting down and talking with your customers is one of the most valuable ways to get feedback about their customer experience. It can be difficult to organize but very worthwhile if you can manage it.

The customer journey map ranges from simple to extremely complicated. For fun, Google "customer journey maps" and see all the different types of maps available. We suggest you keep it simple in the beginning, using the six steps below.

## Six Steps to Creating Your Customer Journey Map

1.  Gather a whiteboard, sticky notes, and some felt-tip markers.

2.  Identify the segment of customers you would like to map.

3.  Write down as many touchpoints as you can think of for the entire journey, one on each sticky note, and post the notes on the whiteboard.

4.  Identify three or four aspects of the customer journey you would like to explore (e.g., emotional needs, pain points, obstacles to satisfaction).

5.  Think about how you can resolve these problems and improve the customer experience, and post these ideas on the whiteboard.

6.  When you're finished, create a visual representation that shows the customer going through the process, noting the pain points, emotions, and sources of convenience.[23] The visual representation can be as crude as using stick figures or a little more sophisticated, like a cartoon, or formal, using a computer-based diagram.

Another way to think about the customer journey uses the five typical stages of customer interaction with a company: discovery, research, purchase, delivery, and after the sale.[24] For example, let's say your customer, Darnell, is going on a short business trip and is looking for a stylish overnight bag.

1.  Discovery: A need has been identified by the customer. In this case, Darnell needs the right bag for his business trip.

2.  Research: Once the need has been identified, the research stage begins. In trying to find the right bag, Darnell starts researching luggage online, checks prices, compares brands, reads reviews, and asks his friends for their recommendations.

3.  Purchase: Darnell finds what he is looking for and makes a decision to purchase the bag.

4.  Delivery: With the payment made online, Darnell receives an email confirmation and the product is delivered a few days later.

5.  After sales: Darnell receives a thank you note and a discount coupon for future purchases.

Now it's time to practice your journey mapping skills with the following Mindshift.

Now you know the five stages of interaction, you can start layering some more information to find out more about your customer. Here are some factors to keep in mind while completing the journey map:[25]

Key Touchpoints: How does your user interact with your company?

Tasks: What is your customer trying to achieve?

Knowledge: What does your customer want to know?

# Create a Customer Journey Map

Using your own venture idea or just a business you really like, map the journey of a typical customer. Before actually drawing the journey, it may be helpful to complete the customer journey grid below (Table 6.5). Start with the five stages of customer interaction: discovery, research, purchase, delivery, and after the sale. Then consider the key touchpoints: what the customer is doing in each stage, information needed, the pain points in each stage, what's going well in each stage, customer emotions in each stage, and customer wish list. If you are applying the journey grid below to your own venture, the source of much of the data is your own research (customer journey through competitors) and your own interviews (as suggested in Mindshift: Build Your Buyer Personas). After completing the grid, try drawing a more visual representation of the journey.

Hint: When trying to find value in your customer experience, first grid and map the journey of a customer from your closest competitor (see Table 6.5). Then show how your customer experience is better. ●

**TABLE 6.5**

Customer Journey Grid

|  | DISCOVERY STAGE | RESEARCH STAGE | PURCHASE STAGE | AFTER THE SALE STAGE |
|---|---|---|---|---|
| Key touchpoints (points of interaction between the customer and company) |  |  |  |  |
| Tasks (what the customer is trying to get accomplished) |  |  |  |  |
| Knowledge (what the customer wants or needs to know) |  |  |  |  |
| Pain points (where the customer is disappointed) |  |  |  |  |
| Happy points (where the customer is satisfied) |  |  |  |  |
| Emotions (what the customer is likely feeling) |  |  |  |  |
| Wish list (what would make the customer experience awesome) |  |  |  |  |

Pain Points: How does your company disappoint the customer?

Happy Points: How does the company satisfy the customer?

Emotions: What is your customer feeling at each stage of the process?

Wish List: What would make the customer experience awesome?

Influencers: Who or what are the key influencers in your customer's decision-making process?

Additionally, mapping a journey also uncovers areas where you can think about generating more value for the customer. For example, in the case of Darnell above, maybe he wants to receive a text message when the product is delivered. Remember that the map won't stay static; it will change over time as long as you keep revisiting it. Besides, it is worth keeping, as it serves as a good reminder that customers should always be at the forefront of your thinking.

# Connecting With Customers on an Emotional Level

Researchers Scott Magids, Alan Zorfas, and Daniel Leemon suggest that connecting with the emotions of customers is integral to building sales, brand recognition, and customer loyalty. They researched hundreds of brands across a diverse group of product categories to identify "emotional motivators" that allow companies to connect on an emotional level with their customer in order to drive sales.

The researchers suggest that if companies can identify the most powerful emotional motivators for their customers, they are likely to have a competitive advantage:

> Our research stemmed from our frustration that companies we worked with knew customers' emotions were important but couldn't figure out a consistent way to define them, connect with them, and link them to results. We soon discovered that there was no standard lexicon of emotions, and so 8 years ago we set out to

create one, working with experts and surveying anthropological and social science research. We ultimately assembled a list of more than 300 emotional motivators. (p. 68)

It's complicated to measure emotion. The researchers used big customer datasets and applied extensive data analytics to identify emotional motivators. Though motivators change based on industry, brand, and customer touchpoints, the researchers were able to uncover 10 emotional motivators that crossed all the product categories and brands studied.

The research also suggests that customers who are both satisfied with the product and emotionally connected to the company or brand are 52% more valuable to the company than a customer who is only highly satisfied. ●

**Source:** Magids, S., Zorfas, A., & Leemon, D. (2015). The new science of customer emotions: A better way to drive growth and profitability. *Harvard Business Review*, November, 66–76.

## High-Impact Motivators

| EMOTIONAL MOTIVATOR | HOW ENTREPRENEURS CAN LEVERAGE THE MOTIVATOR |
|---|---|
| Stand out from the crowd | Project a unique social identity; be seen as special |
| Have confidence in the future | Perceive the future as better than the past; have a positive mental picture of what's to come |
| Enjoy a sense of well-being | Feel that life measures up to expectations and that balance has been achieved; seek a stress-free state without conflicts or threats |
| Feel a sense of freedom | Act independently, without obligations or restrictions |
| Feel a sense of thrill | Experience visceral, overwhelming pleasure and excitement; participate in exciting, fun events |
| Feel a sense of belonging | Have an affiliation with people they relate to or aspire to be in life; feel part of a group |
| Protect the environment | Sustain the belief that the environment is sacred; take action to improve their surroundings |
| Be the person I want to be | Fulfill a desire for ongoing self-improvement; live up to their ideal self-image |
| Feel secure | Believe that what they have today will be there tomorrow; pursue goals and dreams without worry |
| Succeed in life | Feel that they lead meaningful lives; find worth that goes beyond financial or socioeconomic measures |

**Source:** Scott Magids, Alan Zorfas, and Daniel Leemon. The New Science of Customer Emotions: A better way to drive growth and profitability. Harvard Business Review. November 2015, pp. 66-76.

# 6.7 MARKET SIZING

>> **LO 6.7   Explain the importance of market sizing in growing your customer base.**

Once you have identified your potential market segment and gained a good understanding of your customer, it is time to assess the size of your market.

Market sizing is a method of estimating the number of potential customers and possible revenue or profitability of a product or service. It is important for investors to

**Market sizing:** a method of estimating the number of potential customers and possible revenue or profitability of a product or service.

see that you have thought through the size of the market you intend to target. If you cannot prove that you have a good chance of penetrating the local market, then they will be unable to see the growth potential of your business.

When it comes to creating market opportunity, investors will want to see that you have thought through three important acronyms that represent different subgroups of the market: TAM, SAM, and SOM.

**TAM:** total available market; the total market demand for a product or service.

**SAM:** serviceable available market; the section of the TAM that your product or service intends to target.

**SOM:** share of market; the portion of SAM that your company is realistically likely to reach.

- **TAM**, or Total Available Market, refers to the total market demand for a product or service.

- **SAM**, or Serviceable Available Market, is the section of the TAM that your product or service intends to target.

- **SOM**, or Share of Market, is the portion of the SAM that your company is realistically likely to reach.

To explain these acronyms in further detail, let's take the example of an entrepreneur pitching a gourmet donut café. Let's call it The Gourmet Donut Co. The café will serve high-end coffee and tea and unique-flavored, gourmet donuts, such as maple bacon or ham and cheese, in addition to the traditional glazed and chocolate. The entrepreneur wants to locate the café in Baton Rouge, Louisiana.

The TAM is all the possible customers who visit donut shops or cafés in the United States. If you were to open coffee shops all over the United States, then you could potentially generate revenues from TAM. Although your intention is not to run your business to this scale, you could always produce this statistic to your audience as overall evidence of the popularity of donut shops and cafés.

The SAM is a little more specific than TAM as it describes the demand for your types of products within your reach; in this case, the café or donut market in the Baton Rouge area. In other words, if you had no competition in the Baton Rouge area, then you could potentially generate revenues from SAM. Keep in mind, however, that you always have competition.

The SOM describes the share of the market you can realistically reach with your café in Baton Rouge. This involves working out the percentage of SAM that you could potentially service. For example, in this case, SOM may be a particular geographic radius within the city of Baton Rouge. You would need to figure out how much market share you could capture, given the amount of competition and the geographic radius. To help your audience better visualize TAM, SAM, and SOM, you could use a graphic like Figure 6.4 in your presentation.

However, providing TAM, SAM, and SOM information to your investors is not enough; entrepreneurs need to know where this niche market is going in the future and how their business fits into it.[26] This involves understanding the deeper market dynamics at play, such as the competition and how it may evolve, any regulatory changes that might affect the product, and anything else that may impact future demand.

To really show evidence that the opportunity is a real business, entrepreneurs need to go beyond TAM, SAM, and SOM to establish a launch market.

## Launch Market

Creating a launch or niche market is similar to the beachhead and bowling pin strategies. It involves proving that you already have a group of launch customers who really want to buy your product.[27] This is an essential way to convince investors that you already have a real niche customer base ready and willing to buy your product as soon as it launches.

Overall, the entrepreneur needs to assess the viability and attractiveness of the chosen segment or segments. Table 6.6 lists the key questions entrepreneurs need to answer when assessing the potential of their own customer segments.

## FIGURE 6.4

### TAM, SAM, and SOM

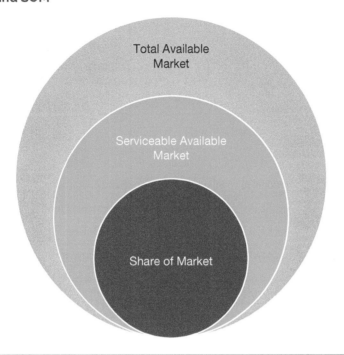

## TABLE 6.6

Key Questions Relating to Customer Segments

| 1.   What size is your customer segment? |
|---|
| The size of a segment is not just the number of customers, but also its potential to contribute to the growth of your company. |
| 2.   How much buying power do your customers have? |
| Your customers must be able to afford your product. Regardless of their enthusiasm, customers are no use to your company if they lack the resources to buy. |
| 3.   Can your customers be identified in the segment? |
| Although you might be able to identify your segment, you also need to be able to pinpoint and profile the people or businesses that are most likely to buy from you. |
| 4.   How accessible are the customers in your segment? |
| A key part of maintaining customer loyalty is being able to reach your customer base; only then will you know the most suitable marketing strategy to implement. This involves an insight to your customers' buying behavior and the types of media they might use. |
| 5.   How stable is your customer segment? |
| A stable customer segment is one that can be marketed to over a long period of time. Assessing the degree of stability of your customer segment is essential for the longevity of your product and your business. |

**Source:** Adapted from Nijssen, E. J. (2017). Entrepreneurial marketing: an effectual approach. Routledge. pp 33–34.

Once you have a good idea of the market potential, then you can start to build solid strategies to calculate the market size. Determining market size is absolutely essential for any startup; without this knowledge, you may find yourself operating in a market too small to make any money. It also helps you to differentiate between your TAM and SAM, thereby clarifying the potential customer demand for your product or service offering. Table 6.7 outlines more reasons behind the importance of market sizing.

---

**TABLE 6.7**

Why Market Sizing Is Important

| | |
|---|---|
| 1. | It estimates the number of sales and resulting profits of new products or customer segments. |
| 2. | It identifies growth opportunities in different product lines and customer segments. |
| 3. | It helps to pinpoint competitive threats and how to develop strategies for those threats. |
| 4. | It forces you to think about exit strategies or pivot points in the future. |
| 5. | It gives you a sense of market trends and their potential to impact your business in the future. |
| 6. | It is important for investors who want to see evidence of a large enough market to justify their investment. |

---

## Calculating Market Size

For a decent estimate of your market size, you will need to carry out the following:

1. Define your segment of the market.

   We have outlined in the sections above the importance of focusing on an initial pool of customers before you expand into other segments.

2. Conduct a top-down analysis.

   A **top-down analysis** involves determining the total market and then estimating your share of the market.[28] It typically uses demographic data like population, age, income, or location to calculate market share. For example, if your business involves selling video doorbells, you may reason that if there are 300,000 people in your area, then at least 5% of the market will buy your doorbell, in which case you will make 15,000 sales. Of course, this is just a rough estimate and further research must be carried out to produce more accurate results.

3. Conduct a bottom-up analysis.

   A **bottom-up analysis** involves estimating potential sales using calculations in order to arrive at total sales figure.[29] This type of analysis requires more effort than top-down analysis but is worth carrying out as it delivers more accurate results.

**Top-down analysis:** determining the total market using demographic data and then estimating your share of the market.

**Bottom-up analysis:** estimating potential sales using calculations in order to arrive at a total sales figure.

The following example illustrates how bottom-up analysis works. Let's say you have created a prototype for a new bicycle light that increases your visibility in the dark, and you want to find out if there is a profitable market for your business.[30] First, you can look at the places bicycle lights are typically sold. The lights will most likely be sold in bike shops, retailers, and online, but you decide to focus on just bike shops for now. Second, check out the number of bike shops in the United States (a quick search on the Internet should give you an idea of the number of bike shops). Third, talk to the bike shops and see if they are willing to stock your new light. Finally, check out the number of bike lights the shops usually sell in a year.

Once you have gathered all your data, remember to be conservative in your estimate. For instance, say 30 out of the 100 bike shops you have called agree to stock your product.

# Can You Sell Customer Information?

When customers buy products through an online company, they leave a lot of information behind, including their name and address and the types of products they have viewed while browsing. Partner companies often approach businesses to buy this type of data to find out more about customers' purchasing patterns. But is it right to sell customer information? And even if it is not sold, should it even be used in house?

David Hennessey, professor of marketing at Babson College, believes that using consumer information is a privacy and fairness issue if not a legal one, certainly because, in most cases, people believe they are making purchases anonymously or are somehow otherwise protected.

Hennessey suggests that companies unsure about their right to sell customer data should consult the company's code of ethics to determine how much information can be used internally and externally. He adds that the company could create its own policy to set standards around customer information and when it should or should not be shared. The American Marketing Association's set of standards are useful for determining this policy.

Overall, sometimes the most straightforward way to resolve this ethical dilemma is to put yourself in the shoes of your customers.

## Critical Thinking Question

1. How would you feel if an online company you had made purchases from sold your data to a third party? Would you view it as an invasion of privacy or a betrayal? Or both? ●

**Source:** Di Meglio, F. (n.d.). Ethics in marketing. *Monster.* Retrieved from https://www.monster.com/career-advice/article/ethics-in-marketing

---

Some of those deals may not come to pass, so better to halve the number. This means it's reasonable to presume that 15% of bike shops might commit to buying your product. If there are 4,000 bike shops in the United States, then your bike lights have the potential to be sold in 600 bike shops. Similarly, from your bike shop data, you can work out the average selling price of other bike lights on the market. You can also work out the approximate number sold every year. Again, remember to be realistic: Just because the bike shop sells 200 bike lights a year doesn't mean you will sell the same amount. Simply halve the figure of sales, and that will give you a more realistic result. Better to be conservative than wildly off target.

Once you have a good idea of your potential buyers (TAM), price, and annual consumption, then you can use SAM and SOM to estimate your market potential. For instance, to get the most accurate representation, you could use SOM, and to look at the bigger market you may eventually target, you could use SAM.

4. Don't forget to do sanity checks.

You might have gathered all your data and research, but don't neglect to carry out sanity checks during the calculations process. For instance, if you calculate a market size of 350 million cyclists, but the population of the United States is only 300 million, then you know you have gone wrong somewhere.

5. Check out the competition.

Do some research on your competition. Is your industry crowded? What companies are leading the way in selling products or services similar to yours? For example, an entirely new product or service that meets a specific need is likely to capture more market share than a product in a market that is already quite saturated.

As we have explored, in order for entrepreneurs to find, build, and grow their customer base, they must take the right steps to identify the different types of customers, understand that different customers have different needs, and devise the right strategies to create the most viable marketing opportunity. Only then will entrepreneurs be able to connect with their target audience in a meaningful way and promote their products and services to people who will potentially buy them. ●

**⑤SAGE edge™**

Get the tools you need to sharpen your study skills. SAGE edge offers a robust online environment featuring an impressive array of free tools and resources.

- Access practice quizzes, eFlashcards, video, and multimedia at **edge.sagepub.com/neckentrepreneurship2e**

## SUMMARY

### 6.1  Define a customer and market.

A customer is someone who pays for a product or service. Customers become consumers when they actually use the product or service.

A market is a place where people can sell goods and services (the supply) to people who wish to buy those goods and services (the demand). *Supply* refers to the sellers that compete for customers in the marketplace, while *demand* implies the desire held by prospective customers for the goods and services available.

### 6.2  Describe the different types of customers entrepreneurs may encounter.

Typically, there are five different types of customers: users, influencers, recommenders, economic buyers, and decision makers.

### 6.3  Identify your customers through segmentation.

Different customer segments have different needs, which require different approaches and more tailored solutions. Business success depends on defining customer segments and becoming familiar with the type of customers most likely to buy the product or service.

### 6.4  Find your target customer.

The success or failure of a product or service depends on the response of potential customers in the marketplace. The technology adoption life cycle model divides the market into five categories of potential customers: innovators, early adopters, early majority, late majority, and laggards. Entrepreneurs can also find target customers by focusing their resources on a single, primary market first, known as a *beachhead market*.

### 6.5  Acquire a deeper understanding of your customer through personas.

Buyer personas are profiles or representations of your ideal customers based on information and market research. These personas help you to create strategies to connect with your target audience and promote products and services to people who will potentially buy them.

### 6.6  Illustrate the customer journey mapping process.

A customer journey map is a visual representation that captures customer experience across multiple touchpoints of your business. Journey mapping is a necessary process in the early stages of your startup so you can develop empathy for your customers as well as learn how to make their experience with your company or product a great one.

### 6.7  Explain the importance of market sizing in growing your customer base.

Market sizing is a method of estimating the number of potential customers and possible revenue or profitability of a product or service. When it comes to creating market opportunity, investors will want to see that you have thought through three important acronyms that represent different subgroups of the market: TAM, SAM, and SOM.

## KEY TERMS

| | | |
|---|---|---|
| Bottom-up analysis  146 | Economic buyers  131 | Product application  128 |
| Buyer personas  136 | End users  130 | Recommenders  131 |
| Consumers  127 | Influencers (or opinion | SAM  144 |
| Customer  127 | leaders)  130 | SOM  144 |
| Customer journey map  138 | Market  127 | Supply  127 |
| Decision makers  131 | Market opportunity  128 | TAM  144 |
| Demand  127 | Market sizing  143 | Top-down analysis  146 |

## Haim Saban, The Mighty Morphin' Power Rangers

I have to tell you that the biggest hits that I had in my life in music and in television and in business have been always as a result of significant rejections and repeated rejections. So, every time I have an idea that people tell me no, don't do that, I say, oops, I'm on to something.

Haim Saban has always been good at identifying opportunities, and this skill has helped him achieve billionaire entrepreneur status. Haim Saban's success started with the extremely popular teenage superheroes, the *Mighty Morphin' Power Rangers.*

Born in 1944, Haim was a poor Jewish kid from Alexandria, Egypt. At the age of 12, Haim and his family fled to Israel because of the Suez War, as Egyptian Jews were perceived as traitors. He lived with his family of five in a very small apartment. He did odd jobs during the day and studied at night. After school, he joined the Israeli Army, where he started in combat but was shortly reassigned to organizing entertainment for the soldiers. This reassignment changed the course of Haim's life.

Out of the army, Haim wanted to find a way to support his family. In 1966, he joined a rock band, The Lions of Judah, as a bass player. They would perform songs by The Beatles, and their lead singer (who sounded a lot like Paul McCartney) helped the band gain some popularity. Saban wasn't a very good bass player, so he was offered the job of band manager. Being a band manager was a win for both Haim and the band. Managing one band grew to the management of many, and Haim became a full-time tour promoter in Israel.

However, at the peak of his career, the 1973 Yom Kippur War led to many show cancellations, and Haim incurred all the expenses without any revenue to pay his bills. The devaluation of the Israeli pound compounded the issue and left the 29-year-old with $600,000 of debt. In search of a larger market to help him pay off his debt, he moved from Israel to Paris, France, to expand his scope and access a larger market. He discovered and signed a 9-year-old singer, Noam Kaniel. Noam's first record ("Difficile De Choisir"), which was released in 1974, went platinum. Riding on this success, Haim started a production company, set up his own label, and sold more than 18 million records in a period of 8 years. During these years, Haim learned how to knock on doors of distributors and piece together all that is involved in setting up a record company. He decided to continue producing and distributing music in the United States, and in the early 1980s he moved to Studio City, California.

Before moving to the United States, Haim studied how music royalties were paid in America by representative collection agencies like the American Society of Composers, Authors and Publishers (ASCAP) and Broadcast Music, Inc. (BMI). He called them to learn how the system worked and discovered that producing music for cartoons was the most profitable. He learned that sitcoms only had music that cumulatively played for 2 or 3 minutes. Cartoons, on the other hand, had wall-to-wall music that would play for the entire length of a cartoon. Collection agencies paid royalties based on the number of unit minutes on the air, making cartoon music a lot more profitable than some of the highest rated sitcoms of the time. He reached out to different cartoon producers to "make them an offer they couldn't refuse." He told them that he would compose the music for free, if he was allowed to keep both the publisher's share and the composer's share of the royalty. Producers usually had to pay composers a fee in addition to the royalties. Free compositions were unheard of, and cartoon producers found this to be a good offer.

With an innovative business model, Saban Entertainment was born. The company produced music for cartoons like *Inspector Gadget, Heathcliff, He-Man,* and other iconic TV shows. The business grew and very soon he was running 12 studios that were all producing music for cartoon TV shows.

In 1984, Haim visited Japan and happened upon the *Mighty Morphin' Power Rangers* (then called *Zyuranger*) on his hotel room TV. He really liked the show and saw another opportunity. Haim believed that the American audience would love the show and that he could produce it at a much lower cost because the action sequences, which would probably cost the most to produce, were already available to use from the Japanese show. He could shoot the same show in America, with American kids, and use existing action sequences. Once the teenagers turned into the *Power Rangers*, with their masks and spandex costumes on, they could be "kicking monster butts" anywhere, Japan or America. Haim bought the rights to the show to bring it back to America.

However, distribution cable networks were not excited about the show at all. He tried to pitch the show to people for 8 years, with no success. Networks thought the show was "cheesy" and that Haim was embarrassing himself. However, Haim was confident that if the show could run successfully in Japan for 20 years, the likelihood of it working in the United States was very high. Margaret Loesch, a Fox executive, was the only one interested in giving the show a shot and ordered it to air in 1993. The management at Fox were not happy with her decision as they did not believe in the show. Margaret decided to air the *Power Rangers* in the early morning slot, in the summer, just to test it out with little risk to the viewership. Within a week, it became the highest rated kids show ever on Fox Kids, beating out *Batman* and *Looney Tunes.* The show was immediately moved to a prime-time slot. In 1994, Fox approached Haim with an offer to buy Saban Entertainment for $400 million. The network wanted an immediate presence in television for children and

Haim had the content and the distribution network to make it happen. Saban turned down the offer, but then Chase Carey, the COO of Fox Inc. and CEO of Fox Broadcasting Company, proposed a joint venture between Saban Entertainment and Fox Kids instead. Haim agreed to give them all his cartoons and his distribution network in exchange for half of the Fox Kids network. The deal was solidified in 1995 with Saban and News Corp. each getting 49.5%.

In 2000, Haim was ready for a change. His 1995 contract with Fox Kids allowed him to sell his 49.5% share in 5 years. Haim realized that it was time to sell the network as they had started competing with firms like Disney and Warner Brothers that were 10 times their size. He knew that there were two potential buyers, CBS and Disney. Disney was very interested in the assets of the company and bought the company for $5.3 billion. Haim's share was valued at $1.5 billion. In the fall of 2001, he set up an investment fund called Saban Capital Group, which he still runs today, that allows him to invest and help other ventures grow and prosper.

## Critical Thinking Questions

1. Identify and describe all the key decision makers who have influenced Haim's ventures.

2. What was most innovative about the business model of Saban Entertainment?

3. Who is the customer of Saban Entertainment? Who is the customer of the joint venture between Saban and Fox?

**Sources:**

Bruck, C. (2010). The influencer. *The New Yorker*. Retrieved from https://www.newyorker.com/magazine/2010/05/10/the-influencer

Dolan, K. A. (2001). Beyond Power Rangers. *Forbes*. Retrieved from https://www.forbes.com/global/2001/1126/050.html

Raz, G. (Producer). (2018, September 24). *Power Rangers: Haim Saban* [Audio podcast]. Retrieved from https://www.npr.org/templates/transcript/transcript.php?storyId=650524515

# Introducing...

# ⑤SAGE vantage™

## Course tools done right.

## Built to support teaching. Designed to ignite learning.

**SAGE vantage** is an intuitive digital platform that blends trusted SAGE content with auto-graded assignments, all carefully designed to ignite student engagement and drive critical thinking. Built with you and your students in mind, it offers easy course set-up and enables students to better prepare for class.

**SAGE vantage** enables students to **engage** with the material you choose, **learn** by applying knowledge, and **soar** with confidence by performing better in your course.

### PEDAGOGICAL SCAFFOLDING

Builds on core concepts, moving students from basic understanding to mastery.

### CONFIDENCE BUILDER

Offers frequent knowledge checks, applied-learning multimedia tools, and chapter tests with focused feedback.

### TIME-SAVING FLEXIBILITY

Feeds auto-graded assignments to your gradebook, with real-time insight into student and class performance.

### QUALITY CONTENT

Written by expert authors and teachers, content is not sacrificed for technical features.

### HONEST VALUE

Affordable access to easy-to-use, quality learning tools students will appreciate.

© iStockphoto.com/Gerasimov174

# 7

# Testing and Experimenting With New Ideas

"What good is an idea if it remains an idea? Try. Experiment. Iterate. Fail. Try again. Change the world."

—Simon Sinek

# Chapter Outline

# Learning Objectives

## 7.1 EXPERIMENTS: WHAT THEY ARE AND WHY WE DO THEM

>> **LO 7.1**  **Define experiments and describe why we do them.**

In Chapter 4, we explored the concept of design thinking as a process that helps us identify solutions to complex problems. We also described the three phases of the design-thinking process: inspiration, ideation, and implementation—a nonlinear approach that produces creative, meaningful results. In Chapter 4 we primarily focused on inspiration and ideation; now it's time to focus on testing the solutions generated in the ideation phase. In this chapter, we will explore in further detail the processes that take place during the implementation phase, specifically with regard to experimentation. The implementation phase focuses on early, fast, low-cost testing and experimentation to strengthen ideas and ensure that entrepreneurs are on the right path to meet the needs of their potential customers.

The implementation phase also ties in with developing the skill of experimentation as part of the Entrepreneurship Method, described in Chapter 1. This involves taking action, trying something new, and building that learning into the next iteration. Experimentation requires getting out of the building and collecting real-world information to test new concepts, rather than sitting at a desk searching databases for the latest research. It involves asking questions, validating assumptions, and taking nothing for granted.

An **experiment** is defined as a test designed to help you learn and answer questions related to the feasibility and viability of your venture. In Chapter 4 we talked about design thinking, which is focused primarily on desirability. Desirability answers the question, What do people need? Feasibility answers the question, Can we do it? Viability answers the question, Can we make money doing it or is it sustainable? (See Figure 7.1.) Experiments can help validate the needs, but they are mostly designed to determine whether the solution is doable and potentially profitable.

Experiments need to have a clear purpose, be achievable, and generate reliable results. Experiments guide us toward which customer opinions to listen to, what important product or service features should take priority, what might please or upset customers, and what should be worked on next.[1] They are essential when it comes to trying out new ideas, finding solutions, and providing answers to those "What if?" questions.[2] It is through experimentation that we start to address feasibility and viability. Table 7.1 outlines the reasons why all entrepreneurs should experiment.

An experiment begins with a **hypothesis**, which is an assumption that is tested through research and experimentation. In the Entrepreneurs in Action feature, Karima Mariama-Arthur, founder of boutique consulting firm WordSmithRapport,

**Experiment:** a method used to prove or disprove the validity of an idea or hypothesis.

**Hypothesis:** an assumption that is tested through research and experimentation.

Master the content at **edge.sagepub.com/ neckentrepreneurship2e**

**FIGURE 7.1**

**Feasibility and Viability Are Better Understood Through Experimentation**

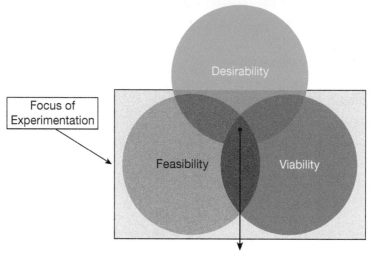

Final solutions should be at the intersection.

**Source:** Adapted from IDEO. (2015). *The field guide to human-centered design* (p. 14). Retrieved from http://d1r3w4d5z5a88i.cloudfront.net/assets/guide/Field%20Guide%20to%20Human-Centered%20Design_IDEOorg_English-ee47a1ed4b91f3252115b83152828d7e.pdf

**TABLE 7.1**

Five Characteristics of Good Experiments

| | |
|---|---|
| 1. | They are structured and follow a particular template. |
| 2. | They are focused and don't try to test too many things at the same time. Focus on a core hypothesis. |
| 3. | They are believable so you can trust what you learn. |
| 4. | They are flexible so you can make changes while in the experiment if necessary. |
| 5. | They are compact so you can learn quickly. |

**Source:** Reprinted with permission from Testing with Humans, by Giff Constable (Copyright Owner).

used experimentation to validate her hypothesis that people want more support in leadership development and organizational performance.

As Karima discovered, there are huge benefits to experimentation for entrepreneurs. Table 7.2 outlines the reasons why all entrepreneurs should experiment.

In the next section, we will explore the different types of experimentation most commonly used by entrepreneurs.

## 7.2 TYPES OF EXPERIMENTS

**>> LO 7.2    Identify the different types of experiments most commonly used.**

Entrepreneurs have many different types of experiments and tests available to them, and some require more effort than others. Overall, the amount of effort put in tends to correlate to the believability of the information coming out. Giff Constable, author of *Testing With Humans*, illustrates this concept on his truth curve (see Figure 7.2).

# Karima Mariama-Arthur, WordSmithRapport

**Karima Mariama-Arthur, founder, owner, and CEO of WordSmithRapport**

Karima Mariama-Arthur was a skilled lawyer and she loved the legal profession, but she lacked "a bona fide sense of fulfillment." Thinking about what was next for her, she considered her skillset and where she excelled. "I knew what I was good at, but knowing *only* that wasn't good enough. I had to research how my skills in law, business, and academia could prove valuable in a new context. I needed to understand how my professional wheelhouse was transferrable."

Eventually WordSmithRapport, a boutique consulting firm, was born! Karima is the founder, owner, and CEO—it's a one-woman show, and it's quite successful as she works with clients in Greece, Cuba, the United States, Russia, France, and Dubai. The firm specializes in helping clients solve performance and leadership challenges. For Karima, it's all about developing the talent that exists inside companies. The mission of WordSmithRapport lies in answering one fundamental question: *How can we help advance the human condition utilizing our passion and expertise?*

Before starting a business of her own, Karima had only ever worked for large firms, academic institutions, and policy-based organizations. "I had always been the talent, but never my own boss," she said. "I had no frame of reference for what might be required to start a business of my own." She just starting talking to people, then more people, and then more people. She prioritized educating herself on the administrative aspects of business as well, to ensure she would be operating legally and at full capacity. In addition, she committed to learning more about the consulting and professional development industries. A better understanding of the services industry (beyond legal services) was also necessary. "All of these efforts took a great deal of time, effort, and money," said Karima, "But the experiences were very illuminating and showed me gaps in my thinking and inspired me to confront any inexperience." Educating herself enabled her to avoid many pitfalls faced by entrepreneurs. She admits, "I made plenty of my own mistakes, but I could have made a ton more without taking the time to gather valuable insights from others."

Testing new service business ideas is difficult because you can't build a prototype for a service business like you can for a new app. The point of testing is to reduce risk and uncertainty and Karima did this through talking, asking, and listening to everyone she came into contact with. Karima consequently mitigated many of the tangible risks that come along with stepping away from a career to become an entrepreneur. "Any time you step outside of your comfort zone there is always the likelihood of doing poorly or simply doing worse than you thought you would. Those things I controlled as much as I could. I did good research. I was smart with money. I took my time, asked lots of questions, and followed sound advice."

## Critical Thinking Questions

1. How did Karima test the idea of her consulting firm?
2. Why is it so difficult to test a service concept? ●

**Source:** Karima Mariama-Arthur (interview with author, November 26, 2018).

---

**TABLE 7.2**

Checklist for Experimentation

| |
|---|
| Bring people through an experience and watch their behaviors and decisions. |
| Test your product and the value you create for customers before you've finished the product itself. Consider what aspect of the product or service you want to test before testing the whole thing. |
| Prioritize what you want to learn. You don't have time to run experiments on everything. Quick testing helps you prioritize and test the most important risks and assumptions. |
| Create a structured plan for your experiment before you start. A chaotic experiment leads to chaotic results. |
| Set up success metrics before you begin so you don't rationalize your results after the fact. |
| Weave customer interviews into experiments, when appropriate, to maximize learning and insights. |
| Keep an open mind about your results, good or bad, and use good judgment when interpreting what you learn. |

**Source:** Constable, G., & Rimalovski, F. (2018). *Testing with humans* (pp. 23–24). New York, NY: Author.

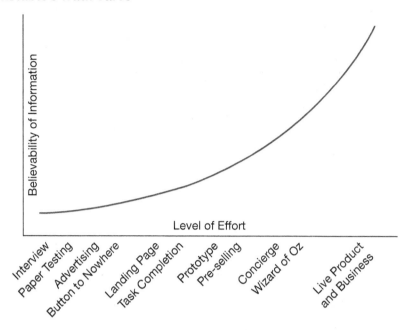

**FIGURE 7.2**

**Giff Constable's Truth Curve**

## Interview

Interviews are a fast and inexpensive way to get insights into your idea from your target customers before you begin the experiment.

## Paper Testing

Creating a paper test is a simple way to outline your vision and to spot any mistakes before the process goes any further. These tests can be carried out using a range of techniques, including wireframe (or blueprint), storyboarding, or drawing the product you envision.

San Francisco-based electric skateboard manufacturer Boosted used wireframes (see Figure 7.3) to illustrate how their users would navigate their new mobile app prototype. The technique helped them to troubleshoot any problems before rolling the app out to their customers.[3]

## Advertising

Advertising involves spreading the word about your business using brochures or social media directed to your relevant target market and assessing the level of response.

## Button to Nowhere

Say you want to add a new feature to your website or app, but first you want to find out if your customers will click on it. Instead of spending hours building it, you could use a test called "button to nowhere."[4] This just means that when your users click on the feature, nothing happens. They might receive an "under construction" pop-up message (see Figure 7.4), but essentially, they won't be able to access anything else. The button to nowhere test is a great way to measure user interest in a new feature—the more clicks, the higher the likelihood that your new feature will attract interest.

**FIGURE 7.3**

**Boosted Wireframe Example**

**Source:** https://www.justinmind.com/blog/20-inspiring-web-and-mobile-wireframe-and-prototype-examples/

**FIGURE 7.4**

**Button to Nowhere**

**Source:** Kishfy, N. (2013). Button to nowhere. *Medium.* Retrieved from https://medium.com/@kishfy/button-to-nowhere-77d911517318

## Landing Page

Another useful way to gauge the level of customer response to your business's website is to include a particular call to action such as "click here for more information."

Shyam Devnani, founder of online meal service India in a Box (featured in Supplement B: The Pitch Deck), created a landing page with three different meal options to see which options the customers clicked on most. Nothing was behind the button except "thank you for visiting . . . we are still building this site."

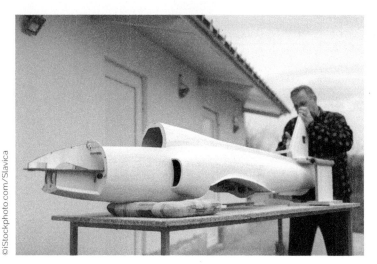

**Rapid prototyping**

## Task Completion

Task completion (also known as usability testing) involves watching someone using your product to understand what works and what doesn't. For instance, say you're creating a website to provide easier access to exam results for students. The user goal would be to look up grades, but the task would be to look up the results for a specific exam (e.g., midterms).[5]

## Prototype

A prototype is an early and often crude version of a product, but there are many different types of prototypes (that we discuss later). The crudest version is called rapid prototyping: You might build a model of a product out of foam, wood, boxes, plastic, or other scrap-like material with a view to finding potential customers to interact with the physical product.

Standly was a venture idea for a standing desk that Babson students could use with their laptops in class. The first rapid prototype was made of three pieces of wood and cardboard. Students were able to test the desks in class to see if they liked to stand while using their laptops during class. Though a good experiment, the venture didn't really take off as the desk didn't generate enough sales.

## Preselling

Preselling is a testing technique that involves booking orders for your product before it has been developed. This method is most commonly used on crowdfunding sites like Kickstarter. Monthly journal *Living a Great Story* used Kickstarter to launch its campaign, while Jim Poss, founder of solar-powered trash compactor company Big Belly, managed to sell one of his compactors to a ski resort in Vail, Colorado, before he had even finished the product.[6]

## Concierge and Wizard of Oz

During the concierge test, the customer interfaces with the product but the "technology" is going on behind the scenes, while during the Wizard of Oz test, customers think they are interfacing with the real product, but it is actually you behind the scenes manually providing the service.

For example, VentureBlocks (featured as a case study in Chapter 4 and the game bundled with this book) used a concierge model when it was testing early versions of the game. When a user chose a question to ask in the simulated game, a live person would let them know if they were correct or incorrect and award them points in the form of poker chips.

## Live Product and Business

You are up and running for real! Thanks to all the previous tests you have carried out, you have gathered enough insights and validation to launch your live product and business in the marketplace.

Some of the experiments in Constable's truth curve (Figure 7.2) also count as prototypes. For instance, a paper test or storyboard is a type of prototype. In the next section, we will explore prototypes in greater detail.

## 7.3 A DEEPER LOOK AT PROTOTYPES

>> **LO 7.3**   **Explore prototypes in greater depth.**

As we found in Chapter 4, prototyping is an essential part of the design process. Prototypes can be basic models or sketches that inform others and communicate what our ideas look like, behave like, and work like before the real product or service is launched.[7]

The prototype as depicted in Constable's truth curve (Figure 7.2) is really an **MVP (minimum viable product)**. An MVP is a version of a new product that allows a team to collect the maximum amount of validated learning about customers with the least effort.[8] In other words, entrepreneurs need to build products that have the most important features and benefits without overbuilding. Overbuilding a product wastes precious resources that entrepreneurs don't have in the startup stage. The MVP as prototype comes before preselling in the truth curve because it requires you to actually build the product that adds value and is meeting the needs of customers. You don't have to build a lot of them, but you do have to build it. You may even make money at the MVP stage. Barbara Baekgaard and Pat Miller, founders of luggage design company Vera Bradley, spent a couple of years at the MVP stage when they were running a small cottage operation from their hometown in Indiana and selling their bags at trade shows. In addition, search-and-discovery mobile app Foursquare began as a one-feature MVP offering their users check-ins and badges as rewards. After monitoring user responses, Foursquare enhanced the product to include recommendations and city guides. Today, Foursquare has more than 50 million monthly active users who have checked in more than 8 billion times. Finally, Instagram's MVP originally focused on photo filters only; users could use filters on their photo and save them in an album. Since then, Instagram has expanded to include videos, geolocation, and the ability to interact with other social networks.[9]

The concept of prototype covers a continuum from very rapid, low-cost early prototyping to MVP or even a pilot. Let's take a deeper look at different types of prototypes.

> **MVP (minimum viable product):** a version of a new product that allows a team to collect the maximum amount of validated learning about customers with the least effort.

## Different Types of Prototypes

### MVP

As described above, an MVP as prototype is the first functional and working version of your product ready for release to actual customers (see Figure 7.5).

### Rapid Prototypes

Rapid prototypes are quickly created models used to visualize a product or service. Rapid prototypes could be made out of crude paper models or storyboards.

---

**FIGURE 7.5**

---

**MVP**

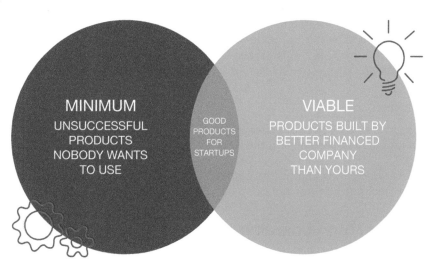

MINIMUM
UNSUCCESSFUL PRODUCTS NOBODY WANTS TO USE

GOOD PRODUCTS FOR STARTUPS

VIABLE
PRODUCTS BUILT BY BETTER FINANCED COMPANY THAN YOURS

---

*Source*: S-Pro. (2018). What is a minimum viable product? *Medium*. Retrieved from https://medium.com/@sprocompany/what-is-a-minimum-viable-product-and-how-to-build-an-mvp-for-your-startup-9a02c0d4a56a

**LEGO prototype**

## Mock-Up Prototype

A mock-up prototype is usually presented as a 2D or 3D model that looks like the finished product but lacks the right functionality. It may be used as a replica of the real product during experimentation.

## High Fidelity Prototype

A high fidelity prototype is a more sophisticated version of a mock-up that has enough functionality to allow users to really interact with the product or service. An app that includes customer functions and some animation is a good example of a high fidelity prototype.[10]

### LEGO Prototypes

LEGO is particularly useful for creating rough, simple prototypes of your ideas. Tim Brown, CEO of IDEO, used LEGO to build a prototype of a complex insulin injection device.

### Role-Playing

Role-playing (or experiential prototyping) is a method that helps you to step into the shoes of your user by capturing their emotional experience of testing a product or service.

### Wizard of Oz Prototypes

As mentioned earlier, Wizard of Oz testing can also be considered prototypes with faked functions. A common example of this type of prototype is a virtual assistant in which someone behind the scenes types out the responses to the user.

### User-Driven Prototypes

This method focuses on the user creating the prototype, which in turn enables you to better understand their thinking. For example, if you have an idea about how to improve the waiting experience at airports, you might ask users to draw their own version of what this might look like, or build a LEGO prototype.[11]

### Pilots and Prototypes

Although commonly used interchangeably, pilots and prototypes are not the same thing—in fact, a prototype, at least in its crude version, is often created before the pilot testing.

A **pilot experiment** is a small-scale study conducted to assess the feasibility of a product or service.

**Pilot experiment:** a small-scale study conducted to assess the feasibility of a product or service.

### Storyboards

A **storyboard** is an easy form of prototyping that provides a high-level view of thoughts and ideas arranged in sequence in the form of drawings, sketches, or illustrations (see Figure 7.6).

Storyboarding may sound simple, but it is such an important part of prototyping that we have devoted the following section to it.

**Storyboard:** an easy form of prototyping that provides a high-level view of thoughts and ideas arranged in sequence in the form of drawings, sketches, or illustrations.

## The Power of Storyboarding

Walt Disney animator Webb Smith developed storyboarding in the 1930s by pinning up sketches of scenes in order to visualize cartoons and spot any problems or inconsistencies before the animation went into production.[12] Since then, not only has storyboarding become standard for movies, commercials, documentaries, and advertising, but it is also

## FIGURE 7.6

### Storyboard

**Source:** Storyboards Help Visualize UX Ideas by Rachel Krause on July 15, 2018. https://www.nngroup.com/articles/storyboards-visualize-ideas/

becoming popular as a business and management tool for explaining projects or products to employees, clients, customers, stockholders, and others.[13]

What does storyboarding mean to the entrepreneur? A storyboard provides you with a better understanding of your own idea and how it interacts with customers. It is a way of compiling your thoughts and ideas into one visual, easy-to-understand, logical document or set of documents.[14] Often, it is helpful to draw a storyboard before interacting with customers or other stakeholders because it can bring clarity to the idea, better tell the story of the idea, and highlight the potential value it brings to customers. There are no hard and fast rules for storyboarding, but there must be a clear sense of what needs to be accomplished and an effort to maintain the flow or sequence of thoughts and ideas.

Remember the old adage, "A picture is worth a thousand words." Because of the visual element, a storyboard gets the main message across very quickly. It is also more likely than a lengthy, detailed, written document or speech to provoke reactions, discussion, and feedback from the people who are viewing it. As long as your storyboard flows well and is interesting and interactive, you can expect it to generate ideas and further questions.[15]

Storyboarding requires that the customer be at the center of the story. It is a way for you to draw the idea in action, which generates further questions for additional experimentation.

Basic storyboards are simple and inexpensive to create, and they do not require any artistic training or talent. They can be rough, hand-drawn sketches or simple PowerPoint slides. If you are sketching on a piece of paper, separate your page into quadrants, and then you can start to fill in each one. Your goal is not to create a work of art but to communicate: to use visual imagery to make your entrepreneurial idea more understandable.[16]

The problem-solution-benefit framework (see Figure 7.7) provides a basic structure for storyboarding. In this structure, there are three main questions to keep in mind:

- What is the problem your customer is experiencing?

- What are you offering as a solution to the problem?

- How will your customer benefit from your product/service offering?

**FIGURE 7.7**

### The Problem-Solution-Benefit Framework

| State the Problem | Show the Solution | Show the Benefit |
|---|---|---|
| • What is the problem your customer is experiencing? | • What are you offering as a solution to the problem? | • How will your customer benefit from your solution? |

Let's apply these questions to Rent the Runway, a business founded by entrepreneurs Jennifer Fleiss and Jennifer Hyman that rents designer dresses by online subscription.[17]

**The problem:** Many women (even those in well-paid jobs) cannot afford designer dresses to wear to special occasions. "I want to wear a designer dress, but they are very expensive, and I would probably wear it only once."

**The solution:** Give women access to designer dresses by creating an online business renting designer dresses for one-tenth of the original cost. "I get access to the latest dresses, but I get to rent for the night rather than buy!"

**The benefit:** The rental model gives many more women the opportunity to wear designer dresses, which they could have never afforded before. It provides designers with an opportunity to build their brand because their dresses are being showcased by a larger demographic of young, fashionable women. "This service would let me feel like a movie star for my fancy party that's coming up next month."

© Astrid Stawiarz/Getty Images Entertainment/Getty Images

Rent the Runway, founded by Jennifer Fleiss and Jennifer Hyman, makes designer dresses more affordable for everyone.

Another version of a storyboard (Figure 7.8) uses a four-quadrant framework. This storyboard illustrates an idea for a new entrepreneurship course. The idea is for faculty members to create an Introduction to Entrepreneurship course in which first-year college students create, develop, operate, and launch a new business.

This storyboard shows a before-and-after scenario. The upper left quadrant shows a traditional classroom setting, with a professor standing at the top of the class, lecturing students on the theory of entrepreneurship. One student is sleeping; another student is hoping a friend will text him to give him something else to do; a third student doesn't understand the theory that the professor is teaching. The *problem* is that students are not engaged during the entrepreneurship course.

The second part of the storyboard (the upper right quadrant) suggests a *solution* to boost student engagement by separating them into teams and loaning each team $3,000 (funded by the college) as startup money for their new ventures.

In the third (lower left) quadrant, the students, armed with the money, *organize* their businesses into different function units. While they are given the freedom to create their own ideas, they are encouraged to think about how their product or service satisfies a human need. They sell their product, but they also suffer from challenges, setbacks, and great victories—as depicted in the zigzag graph illustrated with happy and unhappy faces.

The final quadrant, on the lower right, shows the *outcome*. Students pay the startup money back to the college, and the remaining profits go to charity. What are the *benefits*

**FIGURE 7.8**

## Storyboard of an Idea to Boost Student Engagement

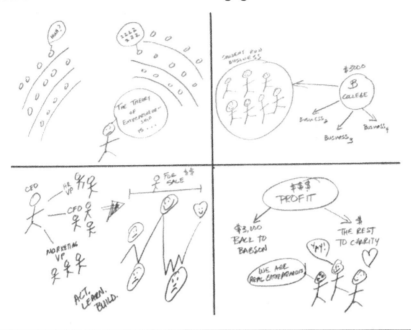

**Source:** Storyboards Help Visualize UX Ideas by Rachel Krause on July 15, 2018. https://www.nngroup.com/articles/storyboards-visualize-ideas/

of this idea? The students are much more engaged because they acted in order to learn. They were given the opportunity to build something real, practice entrepreneurship, and get a taste for the real entrepreneurial experience.

This storyboard generated lots of questions that needed to be answered before the course could be rolled out.

## Back of a Napkin

The simplest of all entrepreneurial plans is sketching out the idea on the back of a napkin. Although this type of plan would certainly get you kicked out of a formal meeting with investors, it can be a highly effective way to gain clarity on the business idea and how it will work. There is something about sketching and pictures that makes an idea come alive. According to Dan Roam, author of *The Back of the Napkin*, we can visually solve problems with pictures. "We can use the simplicity and immediacy of pictures to discover and clarify our own ideas, and use those same pictures to clarify our ideas for other people, helping them to discover something new for themselves along the way."[18]

## Sketches on a Page

Using sketches on a page to write your plan is a little more complicated than using the back of the napkin. While it is also informal, it requires a more focused approach based on how the product works or can work in the future. Sketches on a page help you think about the idea today and also what it could become in the future. You can sketch your idea by hand on blank paper, or you can do this electronically using PowerPoint, Prezi, or other software of your choosing.

A simple technique is to create a gallery sketch. With a large piece of white paper as your "canvas," use color, arrows, and labels to indicate all of the major components of the idea. Add clarifying notes as needed. Make an effort to sketch boldly, avoiding faint lines and small pictures. If the idea is for a service, try sketching a map of the events that take place when the service is provided.

## Create a Storyboard and Take Action

By this point in the book, we are sure you have at least one idea, if not hundreds, floating around in your mind. We hope you've developed a practice of writing down your ideas. Now it's time to take one of your ideas and draw it in action using a storyboard format. The simplest format is the four-quadrant version depicted in Figure 7.8—the storyboard to boost student engagement.

Artistic talent is not required. Simply focus on visually representing the four aspects of your idea: problem, solution, organization, and outcomes/benefits. As you create your sketches, questions will probably arise related to your idea. Once you've completed the storyboard, write a list of all the questions that you have, now that you have envisioned your idea in action. It's okay if you have a long list. As a matter of fact, the longer the better.

Identify the three questions you want to answer first, and go answer the questions. Remember, small actions lead to quick information. Be specific: What's the question? How will you answer the question? What did you learn? How will you build this learning into the next iteration?

### Critical Thinking Questions

1. At the outset of this exercise, how did you feel about being asked to create a storyboard? Do you think people with artistic training or talent have an advantage in storyboarding? Why or why not?

2. Is your list of questions longer or shorter than you expected? How easy or difficult was it to translate your top three questions into experiments?

3. What did you learn from this exercise that surprised you? ●

Taking the gallery sketch one step further, draw a "before and after" scenario. Scenarios are short stories that depict your business, or the product/service, in action. The "before" scenario shows what the lives of your customers are like today. The "after" scenario shows what their lives could be like after your venture is started. The "after" scenario represents what you dream the business could be and the impact it can have on customers in the near future.

## 7.4 HYPOTHESIS TESTING AND THE SCIENTIFIC METHOD APPLIED TO ENTREPRENEURSHIP

>> LO 7.4    **Demonstrate how to test hypotheses and explain the scientific method.**

Many types of prototypes, especially rough prototypes, are used to test hypotheses. Experiments are used to prove or disprove the validity of an idea or hypothesis. Getting out of the building and testing our hypotheses enables us to gain new insights into our target customers' wants and needs. However, testing a hypothesis is not just about gathering data—it also involves matching the results of our tests to the original hypothesis and potentially adapting our original assumptions to better understand our customer target base.[19]

When we hear the word *experiment,* we may think of scientists wearing white coats working with test tubes in laboratories or the extensive clinical trials and experiments undertaken by pharmaceutical companies when testing a new drug.[20,21] Yet the scientific method is not just limited to scientists with PhDs; it can be adapted to entrepreneurs starting new ventures. Experiments can, for example, involve observations of students studying in a library, or employees working on a group project, or consumers visiting a store. They can also involve constructing or formulating products and testing how they perform. In fact, continuous testing is an ongoing requirement for entrepreneurs.

Entrepreneurs are, by definition, experimenters, and that is why it is valuable to understand the process of experimentation—otherwise, the experiments could become disorganized and fruitless.

The scientific process of experimentation consists of the following six steps (see Figure 7.9):

1.  Ask a question. For example, can tattoos be used not only on humans but in different ways?

2.  Form a hypothesis. For example, tattoos are about individual expression; people are interested in "tattooing" their cars, bikes, or motorcycles.

3.  Conduct research. For example, study why people tattoo their bodies. Google "car tattoos" to see if they exist. Start talking to people to better understand their perception of car tattoos.

4.  Test the hypothesis. Develop a sketch of what you think a car with a tattoo could look like and share with others to get feedback.

5.  Analyze the results. For example, What did you learn? What changes should be made to the original concept? Is your original hypothesis supported? If yes, what's your next question or hypothesis?

6.  Communicate the results. For entrepreneurs this is really about communicating with your team and figuring out the next test![22]

## FIGURE 7.9

### The Scientific Method

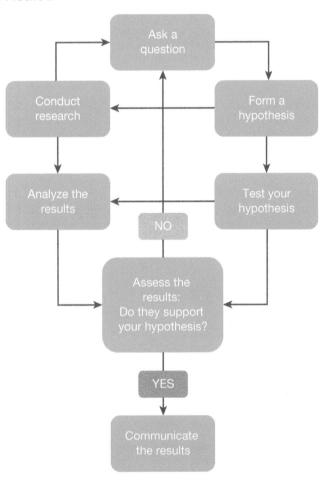

**Source:** Retrieved from http://generalchemistryfordson2013.weebly.com/scientific-method-flow-chart.html

## The Six Steps of Scientific Experimentation in Action

Let's apply the steps of the scientific method to the initial experimentation process undertaken by robotic surgical lighting company Sybo Technology, founded by University of Utah bioengineering student Brody King.[23] King was inspired to start his company when he found himself adjusting the light for a surgeon he was shadowing during a medical procedure.

1.  Ask lots of questions

It is important to ask lots of questions to define the most specific one. For instance, when developing SpaceX, Elon Musk started out by asking, "What would most affect the future of humanity?" The answer at the time was space exploration, which has led to an even more specific question, "How can we send people to Mars?"

2.  Carry out background research

The most successful entrepreneurs become experts in their industry. How? By talking with other experts. When King started Sybo Technology, the Sybo team sought advice from more than 80 industry professionals, each of whom provided his or her perspectives on the product. The team also consulted friends, family, and social networks such as LinkedIn. Thanks to all the advice, they received much greater clarity and validation around their idea.

3.  Develop a hypothesis

Without a clear hypothesis, it is almost impossible to abandon popular assumptions in favor of new solutions. The Sybo team came up with the following hypothesis: "By automating the light adjustment process, surgeons and staff would achieve greater efficiency and enhanced focus on the patient during procedures."

4.  Test the hypothesis by running experiments

King and his team's first experiment to test the hypothesis was in the form of a simple surgeon survey consisting of only 12 questions. The response showed that 87.5% of surgeons would benefit from an automated light. These results proved to the Sybo team that they had a viable product.

5.  Analyze the data

Analyzing data and recording results is an essential part of the experimentation process. Barclay Burns, a professor of Entrepreneurship and Strategy at the University of Utah, created a method called the "Five Types of Value" (see Table 7.3) to analyze both qualitative (nonnumerical data that can be observed and recorded) and quantitative data (data that can be measured).

**TABLE 7.3**

Five Types of Value

| |
|---|
| 1.   Value in use: Consumers enjoy using the product and will likely refer it to their friends. |
| 2.   Value in exchange: The service is offered at a competitive price. |
| 3.   Value in distribution: Focuses on the availability and accessibility of the product. |
| 4.   Value in finance: Assesses the financial health of the organization and its ability to provide a high value while maintaining healthy margin. |
| 5.   Value in fitness: Monitors the continuous process of gathering resources and innovating. |

**FIGURE 7.10**

Sybo Technology Survey

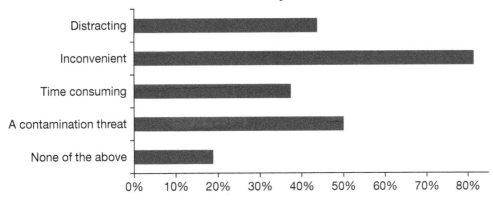

**The need to manually adjust my surgical lighting system is . . .**

**Source:** Anderson, M. (2016). *The scientific method of entrepreneurship.* Retrieved from https://lassonde.utah.edu/the-scientific-method-of-entrepreneurship/

6.  Assess the results

Once the accuracy of the data has been determined, it is time to draw conclusions. Figure 7.10 shows the results of a different survey sent by the Sybo team to surgeons. From these responses, the team identified "inconvenience" as the real pain point for manually adjusting lighting during surgery. Although the team's original hypothesis is still valid, it can now focus on aspects that provide a more comfortable and enjoyable experience for staff.

When you have followed the six steps, it is important to publish your results to get valuable feedback. Sybo Technology plans to do this by getting surgeons and staff to demonstrate the robotic surgical lighting product.

Although the scientific approach to experimentation is useful to entrepreneurship, keep in mind that you need to *think* like a scientist, not *act* like a scientist. Many scientific experiments take a huge amount of time, resources, and precision. As an entrepreneur, your goal is not to build the perfect experiment but to use low-cost, quick methods to shape ideas and to make them better through continual iteration. Entrepreneurial experimentation is about acting to learn, rather than getting bogged down in scientific rigor. By taking action and experimenting quickly and cheaply, you will have a better chance of refining your ideas into feasible and viable opportunities.

# 7.5 THE EXPERIMENTATION TEMPLATE

**>> LO 7.5   Describe the experimentation template.**

A good experiment is a well-planned experiment. Early, quick experimentation is design to support or reject a hypothesis, not necessarily to support or reject the entire idea. So, it's important to answer the following questions before designing an experiment:

## Experimentation Template

1.  What is the hypothesis?

2.  What is the pass/fail metric?

3.  Who are the participants in the experiment?

4.  How many participants are needed?

5.  How are you going to get participants?

6.  How will the experiment be run?

7.  How long is the experiment?

## Mockups

From the first Mindshift, you should have a storyboard. Now it's time to create a mockup—something more physical that potential customers can actually interact with. Once your mockup is complete, fill out the experimentation template, but make sure that the experiment can be conducted in 1 hour or less. Remember to start small so you can test and learn. If you are testing a service, the same rules apply. You need to simulate part of the service experience for customers.

### Critical Thinking Questions

1.  Was your hypothesis rejected or supported?

2.  Is user interaction important at this stage? Why or why not?

3.  What do you think your second experiment will be? ●

Take a group of students at Babson College, for instance. They had an early idea of creating software or some type of electronic gadget that students could use to "ping" other students when they were being distracting in the class. For example, if someone was speaking too long or spending too much time on Facebook or email, or just not staying engaged in the class, that person would be notified by his or her classmates through an app.

Rather than invest time and effort in developing the app or the software, the students obtained a professor's approval to conduct a quick, low-cost experiment. They used about $15 to buy fabric at a discount store and then purchased some wine corks. With these materials they created yellow flags similar to those used by referees in American football. Each student was given a few flags at the beginning of the class and was allowed to throw them at someone perceived to be distracting or unproductive in the class.

The hypothesis was that classmates "calling out" classmates would be a distraction. However, the exact opposite happened. Because the students knew they could be flagged, the flags actually served as a deterrent. In fact, the professor reflected at the end of the class that it had been one of the most engaging class discussions she had experienced in the entire semester. Not only was the experiment cheap, but it also generated an unexpected outcome, which led to many other interesting questions in need of testing to find answers.

### Low-Cost Customer Engagement

One of the most important parts of an experiment is customer engagement with your product or service. Involving real customers in your experiment is a great way to test hypotheses, as it provides you with immediate feedback on how your product or service is received. It is also an excellent way to make connections with people who may buy your product or service when it is fully launched.

The following entrepreneurs involved real customers to test their hypothesis. Joel Gascoigne, founder of social media management platform Buffer, decided to test customer demand for his product before it was even built by creating a simple landing page and sharing it with his Twitter followers. Positive response from his potential customers gave Gascoigne the encouragement he needed to build the product. Thanks to his quick, cheap experiment, Gascoigne was able to build a relationship with his customer base before even launching Buffer online. As of 2018, more than 3 million people use the Buffer platform to schedule posts to Facebook, Twitter, LinkedIn, Instagram, and more.[24]

Christina Sembel, founder of San Francisco–based Farmgirl Flowers, also used low-cost experimentation to establish a market for her product.[25] For a year, she delivered free bouquets to city coffee shops together with a pile of 50 business cards. Sembel said, "I'd go back every week and count how many business cards were left." If most of the cards were gone, she would conclude that she'd found the right place to fill with flowers. "All the initial chatter about the company, all the inquiries, was because of those coffee shops. It was the cheapest thing I could have done," Sembel said.

Low-cost experiments, such as Farmgirl Flowers making free deliveries to coffee shops, can create success for a startup.

We could say that Gascoigne, Sembel, and the students at Babson College used the "test and learn" approach to experimentation.[26] Test and learn is a quick, cheap way to generate knowledge about what works and what doesn't. It allows you to put your ideas and hypotheses to the test and generates results that help you to make tactical decisions. For example, because his Twitter followers gave a positive response to his Buffer product, Gascoigne was able to build and roll it out online; the students at Babson were encouraged to further test or modify their "flagging" idea after their experiment gleaned some surprising results; and the feedback Sembel gained from real customers and retailers through her low-cost experiment allowed her to grow her flower venture into a hugely successful business.

One of the major benefits of testing hypotheses is the real-time data it generates. Entrepreneurs operating a startup will be far more likely to gather evidence and data by conducting simple, low-cost experiments. Experimentation can be used to produce real and current data, as we will explore in the next section.

## Generating Data and the Rules of Experimentation

Organizations have traditionally relied on large amounts of historical data to gauge customer tastes and preferences. Direct mail, surveys, advertising, and catalogs are just a few of the methods that larger companies use to gather data about their customers.[27] Yet not all of these methods are reliable for entrepreneurs. Furthermore, they can be costly or they depend on feedback from existing customers that startups just don't have.

But what about when the data are lacking altogether? Often, when there are insufficient or nonexistent data, people tend to use either their intuition or their experience to make decisions. The problem with intuition is that it is often unreliable and doesn't provide the knowledge or evidence to support the feasibility of an idea.

Similarly, we can't rely wholly on experience and conventional wisdom—in fact, many innovations challenge what we thought we knew or what we thought we wanted. For example, when entrepreneur David Boehl founded his online advertising company, GraphicBomb, he defied all conventional wisdom warning him against mixing family and business by hiring two of his siblings to work for him full time.[28] Boehl has never regretted his decision, crediting his sisters with being honest, loyal, trustworthy, and forthcoming with valuable feedback. Fear of failure tends to discourage entrepreneurs from experimenting at all. Experiments can be perceived as risky and sometimes even scary, and nobody likes the idea of failing. But today's entrepreneurs are required to experiment. It's the only way they can prove a concept.

Entrepreneurial experiments are different from analytical experiments involving big data. Unlike major corporations like OfficeMax and Amazon, smaller organizations and especially startups usually do not have the resources to fund data systems analytics, nor may they even have existing data to rely on. In this case, how can entrepreneurs get the data they need if it doesn't exist?

Paul Lemley, founder of live broadcasting app Hivecast, discovered a powerful way of gathering his own data by asking at least one random person one question every day.[29] He said, "Don't stop asking people questions about your existing or future products. Even if they're hypothetical questions, people will always surprise you with their answers."

# When Links Break

Should values be the first item discussed among partners before fully embarking upon a business? Perhaps an entrepreneurial venture is in the incubation phase, and the first hints of self-consciousness begin to form. *Is this a good idea? Will the public even buy this product?* After all, some initial validation would save a significant amount of time and money, if the idea turns out to be a flop.

Startups have been testing their appeal in the digital age through the use of landing pages, or early websites that offer all of the proposed services, items, experiences, of the company, without having working links that will allow the consumer to purchase those products. Developers track the number of clicks each broken link receives and gauge the general interest before too much time or money is wasted.

The moral dilemma is made clear as advertisers will market the page as genuine, essentially duping consumers into going to the website and finding they're not able to purchase any of the seemingly real products. Too much of this practice will turn consumers distrustful of whichever advertising channel led them to the fake website.

With the advent of crowdfunding sites like Kickstarter and GoFundMe, there are different avenues for gathering statistics on public appeal, while at the same time receiving a round of funding. Whether companies wish to be upfront about whether the product they are selling is real or not is up to their own ethical code. Do they care about deceiving consumers into showing preferences for products?

**Critical Thinking Questions**

1. How much deception is allowable in the early marketing of a venture?

2. Will consumers shy away from an advertising channel if they have been led to a website with broken product links?

3. How early into an entrepreneurial idea must values be established? ●

**Sources:**

Dahl, D. (2011, Sept. 6). How to assess the market potential of your idea. *Inc.* Retrieved from https://www.inc.com/guides/201109/how-to-assess-the-market-potential-of-your-new-business-idea.html

McLeod, S. (2015, Jan. 27). How to setup a landing page for testing a business or product idea. *Medium.* Retrieved from https://medium.com/early-stage-startup-validation/how-to-setup-a-landing-page-for-validating-a-business-or-product-idea-d72c35fc012c

Wilmes, L. (2018, Sept. 27). Landing pages: One giant leap for marketing. *Abstract Marketing Group.* Retrieved from https://www.abstraktmg.com/inbound-lead-generation/landing-pages-one-giant-leap-for-your-marketing-strategy/

By using this low-cost experiment, Lemley was able to identify his customer needs, generate a group of potential customers, and build brand awareness. The point is that unlike larger organizations, entrepreneurs do not need expensive systems or large amounts of cash to generate the data they need to gauge customer needs and preferences. Small-scale experiments do not need to be risky or expensive. Entrepreneurs have more freedom to experiment, as they have a lot less to lose in the beginning than larger organizations do.

The essential thing to remember about experiments, large or small, is that all results must be taken into account, even if they fail to support the hypothesis and contradict original assumptions. Ignoring data just because they tell us what we don't want to hear is detrimental to the success of any venture.

The goal of experimentation is not to conduct the "perfect" experiment but to see it as an opportunity for further learning and better decision making. Failure is also important, for if you cannot fail, you cannot learn.[30]

Though there is no one best or perfect way to conduct an entrepreneurial experiment, there are a few "rules" based on the information we have provided in this chapter so far. Table 7.4 shows some rules key to learning through experimentation. You will notice that two of the rules focus on stakeholders: the different types of stakeholders and the importance of interacting with them. Jeffrey Brown, president and CEO of Brown's Super Stores, Inc., in Philadelphia, has grown his entire business based on stakeholder interaction.[31] For instance, every day, Brown walks down the aisles of his grocery store observing his shoppers: the products they choose, whether they read the ingredients on the labels, and whether they can find everything they need. Brown even takes his lunch at a table near the store deli to encourage dialogue with his customers. Brown's store is located in one of the most impoverished areas in Philadelphia. Most of his customers live in poverty and many of them have criminal records. Yet that hasn't prevented Brown from building a highly successful business, which has since expanded to 12 supermarkets across Philadelphia. So how did he do it?

First, he asked his customers what they wanted. Most responded that they wanted to be treated with respect and to shop in a store that was clean and equipped with helpful

**TABLE 7.4**

The Rules of Experimentation

| 1. | Focus on all types of stakeholders: customers, partners, suppliers, distributors, even real estate agents. |
|----|----|
| 2. | Ask lots of questions. Remember, every question you have about your idea is fertile ground for an experiment. |
| 3. | Think like a scientist, but don't act like a scientist. In other words, it's important to think through your hypothesis, what you want to test, and how you are going to test, but don't get bogged down in the rigor. |
| 4. | Build your learning into the next iteration. Don't ignore negative information, just as you don't want to ignore positive information. A general rule of thumb is that six pieces of information saying the same thing can be a fact! |
| 5. | Keep track of your data. You may think a piece of information is not important, but it is essential to keep track of everything. |
| 6. | Keep your experiments low cost and quick, and use them to shape and improve ideas. |
| 7. | Don't just talk with stakeholders—interact with them. |
| 8. | Don't ignore data just because you don't like what they're telling you. |

staff. Second, they wanted food they could eat; for instance, some customers were North African and wanted to buy food from their country, while others were Muslim and needed a halal option. Thanks to these continuous conversations, Brown was able to provide these products and much, much more. For instance, in one conversation with a customer, a woman asked him why he wasn't employing previously incarcerated people. The outcome of this suggestion led to Brown founding Uplift, a nonprofit that trains people with criminal records to work in the grocery business. Both Uplift and Brown's Super Store team work together to run low-cost experiments to trial different ideas, such as providing onsite dietitians, cooking classes, health clinics, and mini branches of credit unions. By listening to his stakeholders and testing their feedback through experimentation, Brown has built a thriving business in a location where many others would have failed.

# 7.6 INTERVIEWING FOR CUSTOMER FEEDBACK

**>> LO 7.6   Explore the interviewing process for customer feedback.**

In Chapter 4, we used interviewing to help us identify needs of users. We called those need-finding interviews. Now it's time to adapt some of those interviewing skills to a different type of interview called feedback interviews. Feedback interviews are used to get feedback on prototypes—any type of prototype that has been discussed in this chapter. Feedback interviews are useful when used in conjunction with experimentation because they help you get more information on the "why" people are interacting with your product or service in different ways.

In general, a feedback interview involves the following:

1. The use of some type of prototype

2. Asking users their opinion of the product or service

3. Determining whether there is value for the user in the use of the product or service

4. Identifying ways to make the product better

5. Determining whether you are targeting the correct customers

For example, say you are looking to start your own French gourmet food truck business with a goal of selling to wealthy customers, such as business executives, at exclusive business events such as conferences and office parties. As a startup, the first step is to think about whom you know. Whom do you know who works in the business world? Or, if you don't know anyone personally, whom do you know who might know someone in the business world who can provide you with an introduction? Go through your list of contacts, or try networking sites like Facebook, Twitter, and LinkedIn. Research the companies and experts who might be able to offer you some guidance, and try to establish contacts there, too.

Think about what you want the end result of the interview to be. What is the aim of the interview? Do you need to test assumptions or learn about preferences and attitudes? What is it you want to gain from the interview?

Second, draft an introduction to the interview (four or five sentences) that lays out your intentions and the purpose of the interview. For example, say your interviewee is an events manager at a large bank. Your goal is to find out what he thinks of your gourmet French food truck business and whether it is something that the bank staff and clients would be interested in for corporate events (see Figure 7.11).

Third, prepare your interview questions. In order to get the most information from the person you are interviewing, you need to minimize yes/no questions, such as, "Do you like food trucks?" Instead, ask open-ended questions:

- "What do you think of the explosion of the food truck industry?"

- "What would motivate you, your clients, and your employees to buy from a food truck?"

- "Do you have any frustrations concerning the food from food trucks or the service provided?"

If your interviewee expresses enthusiasm for your idea, you can ask, "What do you like best about this venture concept?" If the interviewee's reaction is less than enthusiastic, you might ask, "In what ways could this venture concept be improved to have greater appeal for people like you?"

Make sure you also record some basic facts about the person (gender, occupation, age, profession, industry, affluence). There is no need to ask these questions directly, as they can be offensive. Do your best to make some reasonable guesses.

**FIGURE 7.11**

### Sample Interview Introduction

Alex's Pictures–Moscow/Alamy Stock Photo.

*Hello—I am Antonia, founder of the Le Gourmet food truck, which offers organic French food based on the finest ingredients, located in Boston, Mass. I was referred to you by Gavin Jones, head chef at the restaurant Beaujolais. I am interested in your views on my plans to sell my product at office conferences and other business events. I have a few questions that will take approximately 30 minutes. Everything you say will be treated as strictly confidential.*

RESEARCH AT WORK

# Why Overconfident Entrepreneurs Fail

In a recent study on confidence and accuracy, psychologist Lewis Goldberg asked experienced neurologists and their administrative assistants to identify whether patients had organic (physiological) or non-organic (distressing experiences) brain damage. Although the neurologists were more confident in their diagnoses compared to their untrained administrative assistants, the results showed that the administrative assistants were as accurate as the neurologists. The lesson? Just because we feel confident doesn't mean we are always right.

Entrepreneurs face difficult, ambiguous problems every day, but they will be less able to handle them if they have an above-average measure of confidence. Overconfident entrepreneurs are less likely to listen, learn, and change. As serial entrepreneur Mike Cassidy says, "The thing that scares me most is someone who is convinced they are right because they will never change."

However, there is a difference between overconfidence and determination. Above all, entrepreneurs need to be determined enough to identify risks, overcome obstacles, and find creative ways to bring their product to the market. Unlike overconfident entrepreneurs, determined entrepreneurs really listen, make fewer mistakes, and seek out ways to solve problems.

### Critical Thinking Questions

1. Confidence is necessary, but how can you tell the difference between confidence and overconfidence?

2. Why are we talking about overconfidence in a chapter on testing and experimentation?

3. How can you be confident and curious at the same time? ●

**Source:** Fuur, N. (2012). Why confident entrepreneurs fail: The overconfidence death trap. *Forbes.* Retrieved from https://www.forbes.com/sites/nathanfurr/2012/11/13/why-confident-entrepreneurs-fail-the-overconfidence-death-trap/#6d68a232207c

Another useful interviewing technique is Peel the Onion, which is a way of delving into a problem one layer at a time (see Figure 7.12). Begin with the challenges the person faces, and then continue to dig deeper in order to understand the root of the problem. Simply asking, "Why?" or saying, "Tell me more about _____" will help you gain a deeper understanding.

**FIGURE 7.12**

### Peel the Onion for Deep Understanding

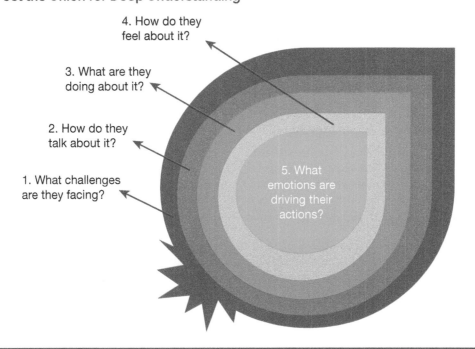

4. How do they feel about it?

3. What are they doing about it?

2. How do they talk about it?

1. What challenges are they facing?

5. What emotions are driving their actions?

**TABLE 7.5**

A Five-Dimensional Model of Curiosity

| |
|---|
| Deprivation Sensitivity |
| Recognizing a gap in knowledge, the frustration this brings, and the determination to fill it |
| Joyous Exploration |
| Delighting in the wonder of the world and the fascination it holds |
| Social Curiosity |
| Enjoying the process of learning about others by talking, listening, and observing |
| Stress Tolerance |
| Being able to handle the anxiety that comes with new experiences or uncertain situations |
| Thrill Seeking |
| Being open to taking certain social, financial, and physical risks to experience new adventures |

**Source:** Kashdan, T. B., Stiksma, M. C. Disabato, D. J., MdKnight, P. E., Bekier, J., Kaji, J. Lazarus, R. 2018. The five-dimensional curiosity scale: Capturing the bandwidth of curiosity and identifying four unique subgroups of curious people. *Journal of Personality Research, 73*: 130–149.

## The Case for Curiosity

Ask any successful entrepreneur about curiosity and they will say, "Yes, I'm a very curious person!" It's an important strength for many entrepreneurs. Experimenting, prototyping, hypothesizing, and interviewing would never come to fruition without a keen sense of curiosity. Opportunities would never be identified without curiosity. A growing body of research shows that curiosity increases perseverance and boosts performance. Todd B. Kashdan is a professor of psychology and senior scientist at the Center for the Advancement of Well-Being at George Mason University. Kashdan and his team, in conjunction with George Mason colleague Patrick McKnight, created a five-dimensional model of curiosity (see Table 7.5); the five dimensions are deprivation sensitivity, joyous exploration, social curiosity, stress tolerance, and thrill seeking. Each of these dimensions is essential to entrepreneurship.

## How to Stay Curious

You may relate to most of the five dimensions, but it still takes a lot of practice and discipline to maintain and nurture curiosity. Here are some tips to help you build your curiosity strength:

1. Connect with other curious people.

Naturally curious people are keen to trade questions, explore, and collaborate. Having these people in your life will encourage you to uncover new ideas and see things from a different perspective.

2. Be a curiosity ambassador.

By asking questions and listening carefully to responses, you will encourage the people around you to do the same. Similarly, staying curious, rather than judgmental, when approaching the unknown is a more productive way to tackle tough challenges. Try not to play the expert in any room you enter. It will hinder your ambassadorship here.

3. Focus on learning.

You can only stay curious when you make the commitment to continuous learning. Only through learning will you be able to ask the right questions, find the right answers, and recognize new opportunities. Entrepreneurs are notorious for being insatiable learners.

4. Broaden your networks.

Curious people tend to be comfortable asking questions, which can lead to all sorts of productive relationships with diverse groups (see Chapter 8 for more information on networking). Entrepreneurs understand that they may not be the smartest person in the room but they need to surround themselves with the smartest people they know.

5.  Ask "Why?" "What if . . . ?" and "How might we . . . ?"

Being naturally curious doesn't just mean asking questions; it also means learning to frame questions in the right way. When we were kids, asking questions was second nature, but as we grew older and more self-conscious, we tended to stop questioning in the same way. Yet by asking "Why?" "What if . . . ?" and "How might we . . . ?" we have an opportunity to challenge existing mindsets and create new ideas.

As the old saying goes, "Curiosity killed the cat, but satisfaction brought it back." In other words, without risk there is no reward. Entrepreneurs need to foster curiosity to reap the benefits of confronting new challenges and leaping into the unknown.

So, act to learn. Act to experiment. Act to test assumptions. Just be curious!

In the next chapter, we will explore the concept of evaluating opportunities through the medium of business models. ●

---

**$SAGE edge™**

Get the tools you need to sharpen your study skills. SAGE edge offers a robust online environment featuring an impressive array of free tools and resources.

- Access practice quizzes, eFlashcards, video, and multimedia at
  **edge.sagepub.com/neckentrepreneurship2e**

---

## SUMMARY

### 7.1  Define experiments and describe why we do them.

An experiment is a test designed to help you learn and answer questions related to the feasibility and viability of your venture. Experiments need to have a clear purpose, be achievable, and generate reliable results. Experiments guide us toward which customer opinions to listen to, what important product or service features should take priority, what might please or upset customers, and what should be worked on next. An experiment begins with a hypothesis, which is an assumption that is tested through research and experimentation.

### 7.2  Identify the different types of experiments most commonly used.

Entrepreneurs have many different types of experiments and tests available to them, and some require more effort than others. Overall, the amount of effort put in tends to correlate to the believability of the information coming out. Giff Constable's truth curve illustrates the many different types of experiments commonly used by entrepreneurs.

### 7.3  Explore prototypes in greater depth.

Prototypes are basic models or sketches that inform others and communicate what our ideas look like, behave like, and work like before the real product or service is launched. An MVP as prototype is "that version of a new product which allows a team to collect the maximum amount of validated learning about customer with the least effort."

### 7.4  Demonstrate how to test hypotheses and explain the scientific method.

When testing hypotheses, entrepreneurs need not actually develop elaborate, extremely robust experiments; the goal is to think like a scientist, not to emulate one perfectly. Experiments are used to prove or disprove the validity of an idea or hypothesis. Getting out of the building and testing our hypotheses enables us to gain new insights into our target customers' wants and needs. The scientific process of experimentation involves the following six steps: asking lots of questions, developing hypotheses, testing hypotheses by running experiments, analyzing the data, and assessing results.

### 7.5  Describe the experimentation template.

The experimentation template is seven key questions for entrepreneurs to ask themselves before designing an experiment.

### 7.6  Explore the interviewing process for customer feedback.

Feedback interviews are used to get feedback on prototypes. Feedback interviews are useful when used with experimentation because they help you get more information on the "why" people are interacting with your product or service in different ways. Experimenting, prototyping, hypothesizing, and interviewing would never come to fruition without a keen sense of curiosity. Opportunities would never be identified without curiosity. Entrepreneurs can follow five dimensions to strengthen and maintain their curiosity: deprivation sensitivity, joyous exploration, social curiosity, stress tolerance, and thrill seeking.

## CASE STUDY

### Katrina Lake, CEO, Stitch Fix

Katrina Lake, at age 35, was one of the youngest female CEOs to take a company public in 2017 and one of very few females leading a tech company. Katrina Lake is the founder of Stitch Fix, a fashion e-commerce site that provides personalized styling services. It is a subscription-based model that charges $20 a month for a personal stylist. Each month, Stitch Fix mails a box with five pieces of clothing chosen by personal stylists based on customer preferences. If the customer decides to buy anything, the $20 styling fee is credited against the total purchase bill. Today, the company is valued at more than $2.5 billion.

Katrina thought the traditional e-commerce experience was plagued with ongoing customer dissatisfaction. Stitch Fix resolves two pain points for customers. First, personalized styling services can be expensive. Second, companies are experiencing too many returns of unwanted clothes purchased online. Stitch Fix revolutionizes the e-commerce fashion space by using technology to provide tools and data on shopping preferences to stylists who make recommendations to customers on clothing that fits their preferences.

"In a lot of ways, I think our value proposition is almost the opposite to a company like Amazon. It's not endless choice," Katrina explained. "In fact, it's a very select group of things that we think are highly, highly relevant for you. I think that discovery element is actually some of the hardest parts of apparel. A lot of times you're not looking for jeans that are going to ship to you fastest; you want the jeans that are going to fit your body best. That is a very different value proposition than I think what Amazon has been historically amazing at."

Katrina Lake grew up in a multicultural home in San Francisco with a Japanese mother and American dad. She studied economics at Stanford University and joined a consulting firm after graduating in 2005. She wasn't thinking of being an entrepreneur but admitted that she always had lots of ideas on how the businesses she was consulting could work better. As Katrina recalled, "We were working with a large retailer—this was in 2006. I remember asking the CEO why does every single size need to be on the floor? The customer has to walk in and find the size and take it themselves to a fitting room. I told them—how about keeping half the store as a warehouse and distribution center and the other half is like a museum? You see what you like, select them, and when you go to the fitting room everything that you wanted would be there. There would also be a few recommendations. It would be a much better experience than weeding through racks and trying to find your size. The CEO and others looked at me like I had seven heads."

Katrina left consulting in 2007 and moved to a venture capital fund, Leader Ventures. She wanted to "meet the next crazy entrepreneur with a crazy idea in retail," and she felt she was most likely to meet that person while working for a venture capital fund. If she found a company that reflected how she felt about retail, she was hoping to join that company. She met hundreds of entrepreneurs over the course of 2 years. "I realized that all of these entrepreneurs were super-unqualified normal people with lots of ideas—just like I was. A more powerful realization from my time in venture capital was that I realized that if I have all of these ideas, then I shouldn't be in the peanut gallery lobbying my ideas to people and should just do it myself and that I *could* do it myself!"

Having not quite found her big idea, she applied and was accepted to Harvard Business School in 2009. During her time in business school, Katrina started to explore different industries. The idea for Stitch Fix was based on two trends that Katrina noticed. One was that more and more dollars were moving to e-commerce, and this trend would make it harder for physical stores to survive. She noticed how Netflix was quickly replacing the Blockbuster model. The second trend related to depersonalization. With the surge of online shopping, depersonalization would increase and customer satisfaction would likely decrease—especially with apparel because it's an emotional purchase for many. Katrina decided to create a solution that used data and technology to bring a high level of personalization to the shopping experience in a way that was scalable.

A self-proclaimed mediocre student, Katrina decided to focus on her idea while at Harvard. She wanted to use her time there to get to a point where she was able to fund her new company and start paying back her student loans by the time she graduated. It was a risky entrepreneurial journey she was willing to take, though the risk wasn't that great because she would have a Harvard MBA that she could fall back on.

Katrina's entire value proposition was about making the shopping experience better online. "You could sit on your computer the entire evening with 30 browser tabs open trying to compare and contrast different jeans you want to buy. If you had a box that could get sent to you that had two pairs of jeans, or even better, one pair of jeans, and they fit you great—that is an infinitely better experience than the other alternatives out there." Katrina started exploring the idea by asking 20 of her friends and family to fill out surveys to understand the brands people liked. She realized that to scale the business, it would be very difficult to source all the clothes that customers thought they wanted. Instead, she developed a model that would send clothes to her customers from existing inventory that she would create. She used personal credit cards and bought an inventory of clothes from various retailers, kept track of their return policy (e.g., 14-day return policy), and made up personalized boxes of clothes that were relevant based on what people shared on their survey profile. If people wanted to buy the clothes, they would write her a personal check. If not, she would return the clothes within the stipulated return window. This experiment tested Katrina's assumptions. She was able to understand people's preferences based on the information they shared and their mindset while buying and trying new clothes. She also confirmed that people found value in good clothes made by brands that were not as well known.

Katrina was convinced that she wanted to pursue this idea and started looking for seed capital. Steve Anderson of Baseline Ventures was the first investor; he gave her a seed of $500,000 and is now one of the largest shareholders in Stitch Fix. However, she did find it difficult to convince other investors based on an experiment conducted with only 20 people. Her business model required a lot of investment in inventory, which deters most investors. Further complicating operations, her business model focused on using actual human designers and stylists rather than bots to process the data and personalize the experience. There was potential for too much variability and inconsistency.

After earning her MBA in 2011, Katrina moved to San Francisco. New York may have been the more obvious location for a fashion company, but Stitch Fix is really a technology company that employs many data scientists, and Silicon Valley had that type of talent. She used the seed money to set up an office, get inventory, and set up the website. Once the Stitch Fix website was running, customers signed up to use the service through an online form. Katrina sent out PayPal invoices to people who signed up because she was afraid that bots might be signing up on her website. She felt that if someone was willing to pay $20 before receiving anything, it was likely that they were real customers. The $20 fee continues to be an integral part of Stitch Fix's operations today.

Immediately following her move to San Francisco, Katrina was a CEO and personal stylist. She sourced most of her inventory at trade shows where some brands would agree to sell her only six pieces of an item. Katrina would then pick the clothes based on customers' preferences, pack, and send boxes of five items. She quickly hired her first stylist in early 2012! Katrina hired Eric Colson, the then-VP of Data Science and Engineering at Netflix, to lead the data science aspect of Stitch Fix. Since both Netflix and Stitch Fix were based on making recommendations to the customer, she felt that Eric would be a natural fit.

Word about Stitch Fix soon started to spread, with people sharing their positive customer experience with others. Katrina leveraged the chatter and started reaching out to small and medium-size social media influencers (those with around 50,000 to 100,000 followers) to help drive more traffic to the site. However, while the business was growing, raising funds was still a challenge for Katrina. Venture capitalists at the time wanted businesses that weren't human resources–heavy and were scalable to reach $1 billion. It didn't help that the hybrid model that Stitch Fix was proposing integrated both humans and data to run a company in a way that was very new to the investors. It hadn't been done before, which made it a more difficult story to tell investors. "When you're doing something that nobody else is doing, you are either the smartest or the stupidest person in the room," said Katrina.

To date, Katrina Lake has raised more than $122.4 million in six rounds of financing. Stitch Fix turned profitable in 3 years and currently has more than 5,000 employees, most of whom are stylists, and approximately 100 data scientists, and is currently valued at more than $2.5 billion. Katrina emphasizes company culture and diversity. Almost 86% of her employees are women.

## Critical Thinking Questions

1.  What hypotheses did Katrina have about her business and target customers?

2.  How did she test those hypotheses and what did she learn?

3.  What other testing or experimentation could she have done?

4.  Who is the target customer for Stitch Fix? Do some research on your own!

**Sources:**

Crunchbase. (2019). Stitch Fix funding rounds. Retrieved from https://www.crunchbase.com/organization/stitch-fix/funding_rounds/funding_rounds_list#section-funding-rounds

Lake, K. (2017). Changing the game. *LinkedIn*. Retrieved from https://www.linkedin.com/pulse/changing-game-katrina-lake/

Recode. (2018). Full video and transcript: Stitch Fix CEO Katrina Lake at Code 2018. *Vox*. Retrieved from https://www.recode.net/2018/5/30/17397150/stitch-fix-katrina-lake-transcript-code-2018

Steinmetz, K. (2018). Stitch Fix has one of Silicon Valley's few female CEOs. *Time*. Retrieved from http://time.com/5264160/stitch-fix-has-one-of-silicon-valleys-few-female-ceos/

©iStockphoto.com/ipopba

# 8

# Developing Networks and Building Teams

"I believe your social capital, or your ability to build a network of authentic personal and professional relationships, not your financial capital, is the most important asset in your portfolio."

—Porter Gale, author of the bestselling book, *Your Network Is Your Net Worth: Unlock the Hidden Power of Connections for Wealth, Success, and Happiness in the Digital Age*[1]

# Chapter Outline

# Learning Objectives

8.1   Explain the role of networks in building social capital.

8.2   Demonstrate the value of networks for entrepreneurs.

8.3   Describe different ways of building networks.

8.4   Illustrate the benefits of virtual networking.

8.5   Explain how networking can help to build the founding team.

## 8.1 THE POWER OF NETWORKS

**>> LO 8.1   Explain the role of networks in building social capital.**

Entrepreneurship is about collaboration, creating together, taking action with limited resources, and courageously navigating uncertainty. A strong network helps us do these things. Studies show that by making connections with people who share our values, we are able to achieve more than if we had acted alone.[2] In general, we have two sources of personal differentiation. We have our human capital and our social capital. Our human capital is our talent, intellect, charisma; it is what we know and who we are. Social capital, on the other hand, is our source for ideas, support, reputation, new knowledge, and resources.

The best networks can provide entrepreneurs with access to external sources of information, financing, emotional support, and expertise, and they allow for mutual learning and information exchange. Network building is a dynamic process, which expands and evolves over time; continuously making purposeful and valuable connections is essential for business success.[3]

Network building helps develops our social capital, which refers to our personal social networks populated with people who willingly cooperate, exchange information, and build trusting relationships with each other. Like physical capital (materials) and human capital (skills and knowledge), social capital is a productive asset. In other words, it's valuable.[4]

Social capital is less tangible than physical or even human capital because it "exists in the relationships among persons,"[5] and the value of these relationships can be difficult to assess and measure. However, in spite of its intangible nature, using social capital is a valuable way of getting work done, acquiring information, and finding resources of all types.

Social capital works through a wide range of channels. When you exchange ideas or information with someone at college, you are building social capital. Social capital can be found everywhere—in your local community, faith-based organizations, schools, clubs, online social media groups, and more. Anywhere that provides the opportunity to interact socially will help you build social capital if you recognize the value in purposeful relationships. As Bill Nye, the famous Science Guy, says, "Everyone you meet knows something you don't!"

Social capital is divided into three dimensions: the structural dimension, the relational dimension, and the cognitive dimension (see Figure 8.1). The structural dimension describes the components of your network, such as the type of social ties you may or may not have (i.e., the contacts in your network) and the degree to which these ties may be formal or informal.[6]

The relational dimension is what your contacts represent, such as a trusting relationship. When trust is present between two people, the relationship is stronger and an

**Social capital:** personal social networks populated with people who willingly cooperate, exchange information, and build trusting relationships with each other.

SAGE edge™

Master the content at **edge.sagepub.com/ neckentrepreneurship2e**

# Markesia Akinbami, Ducere Construction Services

Photo courtesy of Markesia Akinbami

**Markesia Akinbami: owner of Ducere Construction Services**

Markesia Akinbami owns a holding company called Ducere Investment Group, based in Atlanta, Georgia. The holding company offers a unique set of services, the largest being its construction services and supplier diversity consultant firm called Ducere Construction Services. Markesia, with her husband, operates Ducere Construction in Atlanta, Georgia, and Gainesville, Florida. She also operates a government health care consulting service directly out of Ducere Investment Group. Both ventures came to be through the various working relationships that Markesia has developed over the course of her professional career.

Markesia operated a residential construction business that ceased operations when the U.S. economy tanked in 2008. She and her husband agreed that they did not have the commercial construction experience expected of them, but the opportunity seemed so excellent that they moved forward with it anyway. Soon after the business closed, she met the director of Supplier Diversity at the University of Florida and was invited to participate in a mentorship program at the university where she could hone her skills as a business leader in the construction

industry. The bridges that she built and the mentoring she received through this program paved the way for her future success. As Markesia recalled, "That is often the case with bridges, which are links that go further than sharing a sense of identity and are often built through schooling and careers."

The couple worked with their mentor on multiple projects and quickly found themselves better suited to thrive in the construction industry. They started Ducere Construction services 3 years later, but it was not simply a redo for them. This company had new elements that have proven to be instrumental in its success. Along with specializing in many aspects of commercial construction, Ducere Construction also offers a powerful supplier development program for minority-run businesses. As Ducere is a minority-run business, its management is committed to advancing the mission of other diverse firms. According to the Ducere website, "The program's primary objectives are to provide opportunities and train businesses on how to capitalize on the opportunity. The competency of small and diverse suppliers is crucial to creating long-term success and competitiveness in the marketplace." It does this by subcontracting work to these firms while also providing seminars and training sessions that provide action plans that owners can use to grow their companies.

The health care consulting arm of Markesia's business stemmed from her great desire to help people struggling with mental health, behavioral health, and substance abuse issues within her community. She found that many government programs openly welcome private industry partnerships to help advance public health initiatives. The health care practice is profitable primarily through the consulting revenues it gets from working with small medical practices on things like operations and audit compliance. Yet, that is not its primary focus. Ducere also collaborates with other companies, like the Salvation Army and state agencies, on providing outpatient care to discharged mental health patients. The problem with outpatient care is that many of these people go through rehab or receive medical care, but they fall back into old habits or fail to implement the self-care practices they were taught. "These situations prove to be deadly for many folks," she says, and her partnerships aim to prevent that. From a business standpoint, these partnerships are essential for the Ducere Investment Group. "Without them, there wouldn't be a definite place for Ducere in the unorganized space of health care," says Markesia. These partnerships provide some control and clarity amidst the chaos and allow Markesia and her team to identify and seize opportunities, not just for the success of the business, but often for the betterment of many people in her community.

Ducere, like many successful ventures, was founded by entrepreneurs who developed strong social capital—that is, networks populated with people who willingly cooperate, exchange information, and build trusting relationships with one another. For Markesia, taking on a mentor was one of the most effective means of building her network because it was a relationship that connected her not just to new knowledge but also new people. Markesia quotes, "Never underestimate the power of partnerships. Your big success could be one connection away."

**Critical Thinking Questions**

1.  Why is it important to maintain a close network?

2.  How much of Markesia's success can be attributed to social capital? ●

Sources:

Markesia Akinbami (interview with author, December 19, 2018). http://www.ducereinvestmentgroup.com/ http://ducereconstruction.com/partnership/

**FIGURE 8.1**

## Three Dimensions of Social Capital

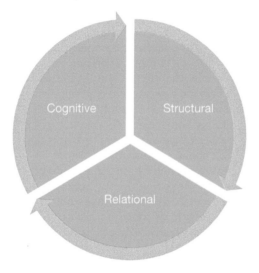

exchange of resources or overall support for your ideas or venture is greater.[7] You are more likely to convince people of your idea when they trust you. It may also be helpful to think of your social capital as an "emotional bank account."[8] You can "make conscious efforts to make meaningful deposits in your relationships"[9] by actions you take with those in your network; making these deposits builds your "balance" so that when a "withdrawal" is needed, the relationship has the necessary social capital to cover it.

The cognitive dimension describes the norms, visions, values, interpretations, and beliefs you may share with others, which provide a good foundation for working well together toward a common goal.[10]

Some observers argue that in the United States today, people are less likely to interact socially than they were in the past. Today, more time is spent at the workplace, commuting to work, and using devices like personal computers, smartphones, gaming consoles, and television, leaving less time for volunteering, joining community groups, and socializing with friends, family, and neighbors. Even spending time participating in online social networks is not as "real" as the face-to-face social interaction of the past. The decline of community networks that used to be so prevalent in the past has led to a loss of social capital.[11] However, the good news is that anyone can build social capital if they make an effort to actively and purposefully form connections with others.

The Organisation for Economic Co-operation and Development (OECD), a global organization promoting economies throughout the world, identifies three main varieties of social capital:[12]

**Bonds:** the connections with family, friends, and others who have a similar cultural background or ethnicity.

- **Bonds:** Connections with people who are just like us, such as family, friends, and others who have a similar cultural background or ethnicity.

- **Bridges:** Links that go further than simply sharing a sense of identity; for example, making connections with classmates or colleagues who may have different backgrounds, cultures, or other characteristics.

**Bridges:** the links that go further than simply sharing a sense of identity; for example, making connections with distant friends or colleagues who may have different backgrounds, cultures, and so on.

- **Linkages:** Connections to people or groups regardless of their position in an organization, society, or other community.

**Linkages:** the connections to people or groups regardless of their position in an organization, society, or other community.

There are many benefits to social capital. It creates a sense of shared value to the people who are connected in the network, especially when cooperation, trust, and mutual exchange are high. Our bonds with friends and family can be especially important when it comes to providing emotional, social, and economic support.

Famously, the most powerful contact in Bill Gates's network before Microsoft took off was his mother, Mary Gates. Mary Gates sat on the board of United Way with John Akers, a senior IBM executive. The relationship led to her son, Bill, pitching the Microsoft operating system to Akers, who awarded him the contract. Microsoft would eventually surpass IBM as the most powerful computer company in the world.[13] Personal bonds or "strong ties" to family and friends can be beneficial, but they can also be restrictive. Forming connections with people who are too similar to ourselves can prevent us from seeing the bigger picture, as they are less likely to challenge our ideas, which may deprive us of valuable feedback and information.[14] In addition, when bonds are too strong, social capital can have a negative impact on society. As an extreme example, members of drug cartels are often bound together by personal loyalties, and their actions go against the interests of society and inhibit social and economic progress.[15]

That's why it is important to expand beyond our range of strong ties and capitalize on the external relationships or "weak ties" in our network, such as people we meet at trade shows and exhibitions, as well as potential investors and banks, to capture a wider range of information. A combination of social bonds, bridges, and linkages is the best way to build a diverse and productive network. Let's explore why networks are so valuable in the entrepreneurship world.

## 8.2 THE VALUE OF NETWORKS

**>> LO 8.2**   **Demonstrate the value of networks for entrepreneurs.**

Building relationships and social interaction are key to starting a business. An entrepreneur is required to interact with investors, mentors, advisors, professors, potential employees, resource providers, and other stakeholders.[16] Keep in mind that in a networking group of 20 to 40 people, the number of possible referrals and leads that you could obtain is almost incalculable.

New research released by the Economist Intelligence Unit on the benefits of informal professional networks and communities, including online (Facebook, LinkedIn) and physical (parties, entrepreneurial events) networking, showed that informal networking (unstructured, free-flowing communication) was far more important to entrepreneurial success than formal networking (meeting in a formal setting).[17] Out of the 1,000 entrepreneurs surveyed across 10 cities—six cities in Asia, two in Europe, and two in the U.S.—the study found that 78% of startups benefited from active informal networking. In fact, the greater the number of networking activities, the higher the chance of greater profitability, revenue growth, and innovation.

### Advantages to Networks

There are three main advantages to networks: private information, access to diverse skillsets, and power.[18] *Private information* is the type of information that is not available to the general public. Gathering unique information from network contacts, such as the release date of a new product or what investors look for during a pitch, can give entrepreneurs the edge over the competition. The value of private information increases when trust is high in the network.

Second, networks provide *access to diverse skillsets.* A highly diverse network of contacts gives you a broader perspective of certain situations and enables you to trade information and skills with people who have different experiences and backgrounds from your own. By actively taking part in events and seeking out new contacts at meetings, you will be able to find people with complementary skills and experience to help you grow your venture. As the late Nobel Prize winner Linus Pauling said, "The best way to have a good idea is to have a lot of ideas."[19]

Finally, networks can give you access to *power*—people in senior or executive positions who can provide expert advice and introduce you to other powerful people in their network. Additionally, given the depth and breadth of your own network, you may actually have power.

Let's take a closer look at our personal networks and the different types of roles people play. First, people in your network can help you to progress by offering information and instruction, especially when you are trying to learn complex tasks. They can also refer you to others who might be able to assist you in achieving difficult tasks.[20] Second, people can help protect your venture by giving you advice when you are confronted with high-risk situations or are going through a rough patch. Third, people can provide personal and emotional support by listening to your concerns, empathizing, and offering advice when required. Finally, people become your role models. You can be inspired by their achievements, and in many cases, they represent what you would like to be when you progress as an entrepreneur. In sum, networks can provide three types of support: career support, psychosocial support, and role modeling (see Table 8.1).

## Impression Management and Self-Confidence

Despite the value of networking, other research has found that students in entrepreneurship classes often don't take advantage of networking opportunities provided to them in class. Students are given access to guest speakers, other entrepreneurs, and each other, yet often they do not use these opportunities to build their networks. What stops students from networking effectively? Poor impression management and lack of confidence were the two biggest inhibiting factors identified during the study.[21]

**Impression management** is paying conscious attention to the way people perceive you and taking steps to be perceived in the way you want others to see you. When people interact with you, they form opinions. More and more research shows that first impressions are formed in a tenth of a second, so it pays to be mindful of how you might be perceived by others.[22] For example, the social cues that venture capitalists notice are things like the following: How much does this person believe in this idea? How confident are they when speaking? How determined are they to make this work?[23]

**Impression management:** paying conscious attention to the way people perceive you and taking steps to be perceived in the way you want others to see you.

| TABLE 8.1 | | |
|---|---|---|

Types of Support

| CAREER SUPPORT | PSYCHOSOCIAL SUPPORT | ROLE MODELING |
|---|---|---|
| • Sponsorship<br>• Coaching<br>• Exposure and visibility<br>• Challenging assignments<br>• Protections and preservation | • Encouragement and emotional support<br>• Acceptance and confirmation<br>• Counseling<br>• Friendship<br>• Personal feedback | • Behavior to emulate<br>• Work ethic and values<br>• Inspiration and motivation |

**Source:** Murphy, W., & Kram, K. (2014). *Strategic relationships at work* (p. 23). New York, NY: McGraw-Hill.

**TABLE 8.2**

Gain Trust Without Saying a Word

| |
| --- |
| • Don't hunch over your phone just before you are due to meet other people. |
| • Make the handshake more personal by keeping your elbow by your side rather than greeting with a fully extended arm. |
| • Lean forward and make eye contact during the conversation to show interest. |
| • Stand straight with your shoulders squared and your weight balanced evenly on each foot. |
| • Reserve your smiles for the appropriate moments rather than smiling continuously throughout. |
| • Try to be sensitive to what others are thinking and feeling. |

**Source:** Shellenbarger, S. (2018). The mistakes you make in a meeting's first milliseconds. *Wall Street Journal.* Retrieved from https://www.wsj.com/articles/the-mistakes-you-make-in-a-meetings-first-milliseconds-1517322312

Research shows that entrepreneurs who display strong social competence are more likely to receive outside funding.[24]

You can manage the impressions others form of you by the way you dress, being aware of your body language, being polite and courteous, and being confident and open. Your attitude is also part of impression management; Making an effort to interact with and learn from others goes a long way toward making a positive impression. Table 8.2 lists a few ways in which you can gain trust without saying a word.

But there can be implicit bias present when forming impressions—both when we form impressions of others and when others form impressions of us. Implicit bias refers to the attitudes or stereotypes that affect our understanding, actions, and decisions in an unconscious way.[25] Implicit bias rears its head most often in issues related to gender and race; it has been referred to as stereotype confirming. "It sets people up to over-generalize, sometimes leading to discrimination even when people feel they are being fair."[26] Researchers in this area claim that everyone possesses implicit bias, even when they think they don't.[27] For example, a man may believe he and his female cofounder are equal, but he may still open the door for her when they walk into buildings. Though his intentions are good, his implicit bias is that "she needs help because I'm a man." Researchers also suggest that the implicit biases we have may not necessarily align with our declared beliefs.[28] For example, a venture capital firm led by three women claim they want to give women entrepreneurs greater access to capital. Yet when you look at their portfolio of investments, most of the deals were made with ventures led by white, male, tech entrepreneurs. The implicit bias is that men are more often successful high-growth entrepreneurs. The good news is that researchers have suggested that implicit biases are malleable and we can unlearn and de-bias ourselves. The first step is working to recognize the implicit biases we have.

Lack of confidence also plays a part in students' reluctance to make connections with others. Fear of failure, of not asking the "right" questions, and insecurity about themselves and what they want to achieve are factors that may prevent students from approaching guest speakers and asking questions. In some cases, networking is regarded negatively because some people may think of it as an insincere way of gaining a personal advantage.

While in college, or even in this course you are taking, it may not seem important to network with your classmates. However, never underestimate the value of networking with your peers. The students you sit next to in class might become your cofounders, your partners, your advisors, your employers, your stakeholders, and even your mentors one day. Interact with them, learn from shared experiences, make connections, and use them to expand your network. Keep in mind that many of the most successful ventures are built on relationships forged in college. Dropbox founders Drew Houston and Arash Ferdowsi met at MIT; Instagram founders Kevin Systrom and Mike Krieger met at Stanford; and Stacey Bendet and Rebecca Matchet,

# How Women "Can Play to Win" as Opposed to "Not to Lose"

Less than 3% of venture capital funding goes to women-led startups, suggesting a strong bias against women. Researchers Dana Kanze, Laura Huang, Mark Conley and E. Tory Higgins wanted to dig deeper into this phenomenon. They examined the questions asked by venture capitalists to male entrepreneurs and female entrepreneurs during pitch competitions. They analyzed six years of startup pitch competitions that included 189 pitching entrepreneurs and 140 potential investors. The researchers found that 67% of the questions posed to male entrepreneurs were *promotion-focused*—questions focused on the company's vision, its home-run potential, and anything that could maximize or accelerate financial gains. For example, questions might be how fast can you grow or what is your customer acquisition strategy? On the other hand, 66% of the questions asked to female entrepreneurs were *prevention-focused*—questions that focused on their ability to prevent a crisis or problem and reduce loss. Because the crux of prevention-focused questions related to mitigating loss, example questions might be when will you break-even or what percent of customers are repeat buyers? Interestingly, the gender of the venture capitalist did not make a difference. Women VC's asked male entrepreneurs promotion-focused questions and female entrepreneurs' prevention-focused questions, just as their male VC counterparts did.

Is this difference in the types of questions asked to female vs male entrepreneurs important? It is extremely important. The authors of this research conducted a second phase of the study and they simulated entrepreneur pitches and investor decisions. Kanze and colleagues found that startups raised $16.8 million on average when investors predominately asked promotion-focused questions. When they asked mostly prevention-focused questions, startups raised just $2.3 million.

The research suggest that female entrepreneurs may not be able to get prevention-focused questions, but they can control their response. Let's look at an example posted by Jeff Kauflin, a fintech writer for Forbes who interviewed lead researcher, Dana Kanze.

*Let's say a VC asks how you're going to defend your startup's market share. Kanze recommends this response: "We're playing in such a large and fast-growing market that's bound to attract new entrants. We plan to take increasing share by leveraging our assets. It's not about protecting or defending our little sliver of the pie . . . I'm shooting for the stars."*

*Or perhaps an investor asks when you plan to break even. Kanze suggests: "We're not managing the business to break even at all. We're managing to aggressively increase sales." She says investors in early-stage startups rarely care about profitability, and whenever she told VCs she was entirely focused on growth, she was never penalized.*

Rather than answering a prevention-focused question with a prevention-focused response, women entrepreneurs should respond with a promotion-focused answer.

## Critical Thinking Questions

1. How do you explain that female VCs and male VCs both ask prevention-focused questions to women entrepreneurs?

2. Have you ever paid attention to the types of questions asked to you (prevention-focused or promotion-focused) while presenting or pitching?

3. Think of a prevention-focused question asked to you during a recent interview or pitch? How could you have answered the question in a promotion-focused manner? Explain.

4. Do feel gender differences and bias will persist in entrepreneurship? ●

**Sources:**

Kanze, D., Huang, L., Conley, M. A., & Higgins, E. T. (2018). We ask men to win and women not to lose: Closing the gender gap in startup funding. *Academy of Management Journal, 61*(2): 586-614.

Kauflin, J. (2017, October 13). How females entrepreneurs can beat investors' gender bias. *Forbes.* Retrieved from https://www.forbes.com/sites/jeffkauflin/2017/10/13/how-female-entrepreneurs-can-beat-investors-gender-bias/?sh=1cffd7bd5b7e

founders of contemporary clothing company Alice and Olivia, met at the University of Pennsylvania.[29] Without being immediately conscious of it, these founders had become self-selected stakeholders before the venture had even existed. In the next section, we will explore the concept of self-selected stakeholders and their value to entrepreneurial ventures.

## Self-Selected Stakeholders

Usually, entrepreneurs do not think about stakeholders such as employees, contractors, suppliers, customers, and the like until after the business has started. However, entrepreneurs need to understand the importance of self-selected stakeholders.[30] These are the

**Self-selected stakeholders:** the people who "self-select" into a venture in order to connect entrepreneurs with resources in an effort to steer the venture in the right direction.

people who "self-select" into an entrepreneur's network in order to connect them with resources such as subject-matter expertise, funding, advice, introductions to others, new perspectives, feedback on concepts, mentors, and so on, in an effort to steer the venture in the right direction.

A stakeholder self-selects into your venture to offer some type of short-term or long-term commitment in an effort to steer your venture in the right direction. Unlike venture capitalists and other investors, your self-selected stakeholders do not need to be pitched to or sold to. They are helping you because they feel motivated to give you access to information and resources that you didn't otherwise have. When people self-select into your network without any hidden agenda or motive, there is a huge opportunity to collaborate with them to build a better business.

Stakeholders can provide valuable resources to entrepreneurs, helping cocreate and bring the venture to life. Cocreation is a strategy that focuses on bringing people together to initiate a constant flow of new ideas that help to create ventures and transform businesses for the better in an uncertain and unpredictable world. For example, Thorkil Sonne cocreated with a leading IT company and founded Denmark-based The Specialists, which focuses on finding work opportunities in technology for people with autism. Sonne has a goal to create 1 million jobs for people all over the world.[31]

Self-selection also ties in with the concept of enrolling others in your journey, as part of the Entrepreneurship Method discussed in Chapter 1. Key to building the network is the idea of enrolling people in your idea rather than selling them. You aren't asking for favors. You are sharing in hopes they want to be a part of your network. They have something to offer, and you have something of value to provide. Building your network is not a sales job. It's not about trying to convince someone to do something that he or she may not ordinarily do. Rather, people join your network because they want to. People enroll in your vision because they're moved by your enthusiasm or idea. They see something that they want to become part of.

Peter Senge, founding chairperson of the Society for Organizational Learning, offers the following three guidelines for enrollment:

1. Be enrolled yourself. If you're not buying the future vision, opportunity, or team, others won't, either.

2. Be truthful. Don't inflate the benefits beyond what they really are.

3. Let the other person choose. Don't try hard to "convince" them—that comes across as manipulative and ultimately hurts enrollment.[32]

The first step to finding self-selected stakeholders is to think about the people you already know: your family and friends, people you have met at work, and people you encounter in school and social activities. These stakeholders may not even be part of the eventual founding team, but they are a valuable source of information and, potentially, investment.

One of the best ways to form a range of diverse connections with self-selected stakeholders is through shared activities.[33] Sports teams, clubs, community service ventures, and voluntary and charitable associations bring together all sorts of people from different experiences and backgrounds. Remember that new ventures require a variety of talents, from marketing to technology to finance, and confining yourself to a particular group whose experience mirrors yours is unlikely to expand your skillset. Your goal is to learn more about the talents of acquaintances to find areas of mutual interest.

©iStockphoto.com/skynesher

**Activities such as running clubs can help you find connections with people from a variety of backgrounds.**

Participating in a shared activity builds trust and passion and allows people to be themselves outside a formal environment in the attainment of a common goal. Team members can build a loyal bond that may transfer to a working relationship. For example, Ahmed El-Sharkas and Ahmed Eshra, founders of Knowledge Officer, a platform that builds personalized learning paths, met while jogging on the same running track. As they ran together, they bounced ideas off each other before agreeing to meet again to explore next steps.[34]

# 8.3 BUILDING NETWORKS

>> **LO 8.3  Describe different ways of building networks.**

Forging connections goes beyond striking up conversations with friends and acquaintances; a really useful network expands to meeting other individuals in your geographic location. Entrepreneurs get support and networking opportunities from so many areas, including chambers of commerce, civic organizations, seminars, incubators, accelerators, and many other organizations dedicated to supporting entrepreneurs (see Table 8.3). Check online and in the local newspaper for public calendars of local events, including public lectures.

Many cities around the world have Meetup groups—local get-togethers of people who share a passion for interests ranging from hiking to sightseeing to biking to meditation to entrepreneurship. They provide a way to find people locally who share a common interest with you. Go to Meetup.com and enter your zip code to see a wide variety of Meetups near you. One group set up in Vancouver, Canada, is for the "Extremely Shy"

**TABLE 8.3**

Top Organizations for Entrepreneurs

| | |
|---|---|
| Entrepreneurs' Organization (EO) | Provides different programs aimed at specific needs and areas of focus that any entrepreneur could use |
| Ernst & Young Entrepreneur of the Year program | Program for entrepreneurs to compete for Entrepreneur of the Year award |
| Tugboat Institute | Brings purpose-driven leaders together to create businesses that have a positive impact on the world |
| Small Giants Community | Similar to Tugboat Institute, in that it attracts entrepreneurs who are more purpose driven than profit driven |
| Mastermind Talks | Invitation-only community for entrepreneurs, where members receive educational training and connections to past attendees |
| Kauffman Foundation | Offers entrepreneurs help ranging from educational opportunities to policy changes |
| Powderkeg | Growing community of more than 10,000 tech entrepreneurs and others who are building innovative companies across America |
| Young Entrepreneur Council (YEC) | Exclusive group of peers that offers entrepreneurs the chance to partake in monthly Q&As and join active social groups |
| Young Presidents' Organization (YPO) | Premier leadership organization composed of top executives from all over the world |
| Startup Grind | Global community of entrepreneurs that publishes helpful content and hosts conferences all over the world |
| Baby Bathwater Institute | Brings together a variety of entrepreneurs from across all kinds of industries and puts on unique events to keep members progressing |

**Sources:** Hall, J. (2018). 11 entrepreneur organizations with strong communities to support you. *Forbes.* Retrieved from https://www.forbes.com/sites/johnhall/2018/04/08/11-entrepreneur-organizations-with-strong-communities-to-support-you; Rampton, J. (2015, January 2). 12 organizations entrepreneurs need to join. *Entrepreneur.* Retrieved from http://www.entrepreneur.com/article/241192

## Analyzing My Network

Have you ever stopped to think about the network you already belong to?

Think about the people in your current network. First, list their names in a column on a piece of paper. Try to list 15 to 20 people that you know. Next, for each person, mark their name

- with an (A) if they help you get work done,
- with a (B) if they help advance your career or entrepreneurial ideas,
- with a (C) if they provide personal support, and
- with a (D) if they are a role model.

Now, count how many As, Bs, Cs, and Ds you have. What type of people are most plentiful in your network? What type

of people do you need more of and why? Keep in mind that entrepreneurs need all types in their network.

### Critical Thinking Questions

1. How easy or difficult was it to think of 15 to 20 people in your current network? Could you think of more than 20 people?
2. Do you think the A, B, C, and D categories are a helpful way to categorize the members of your network? Would you use other categories instead or in addition?
3. How do you think others would categorize you as a member of their networks? What qualities do you possess that would be valuable to others in their networks? ●

**Source:** Based on Murphy, W., & Kram, K. (2014). *Strategic relationships at work.* New York, NY: McGraw-Hill.

and is the most active Meetup group in Canada, as well as being one of the top five most active groups in the world.[35] Meetups typically run from 1 hour to all day, and they can feature formal presentations or simply be free-form networking events. Many Meetup groups focus on technology (such as the SaaS consortium) or skills (such as public speaking or podcasting). As Meetups have gained traction in entrepreneurship communities around the world, they have become a powerful tool for not only networking but also recruiting new talent, building trust group to share ideas, learning new content, and meeting prospective investors.[36]

### Incubators and Accelerators

**Incubator:** an organization that helps early stage entrepreneurs refine ideas, build out technology, and get access to resources.

Incubators and accelerators are among the best places for entrepreneurs to network and find mentors. Often the two terms are used interchangeably, but they do not mean the same thing. An **incubator** is an organization that helps early-stage entrepreneurs to refine an idea while also providing access to a whole network of other

---

**TABLE 8.4**

Top Five Incubators and Accelerators in the United States and Canada

| UNITED STATES | CANADA |
|---|---|
| 1.  Y Combinator | 1.  Le Camp |
| 2.  Tech Stars | 2.  Creative Destruction Lab |
| 3.  500 Startups | 3.  DMZ |
| 4.  AngelPad | 4.  Extreme Accelerator |
| 5.  Capital Factory | 5.  Ideaboost |

**Sources:** The ten best startup incubators in the world. (2018). *Tendercapital.* Retrieved from https://tendercapital.com/en/the-ten-best-startup-incubators-in-the-world/; Colwell, A. (2019). The top 40 startup accelerators and incubators in North America in 2019. *Salesflare Blog.* Retrieved from https://blog.salesflare.com/top-startup-accelerators-incubators-us-canada

startups, mentors, and other valuable resources. Leading incubator 500 Startups, based in Mountain View, California, offers entrepreneurs seed funds, expert guidance, and access to investors. Recently, 500 Startups expanded into Europe and has plans to set up in Israel and Turkey.[37]

In contrast, an **accelerator** is an organization that provides tailored support for existing startups that have already built a successful product or service (usually through an incubator) by helping to develop, scale, and grow their business. Typically, accelerators offer startups free office space, feedback, and access to investors. Y Combinator, also based in Mountain View, California, is considered to be the most successful accelerator for startups, having facilitated the growth of such companies as Airbnb, Dropbox, Stripe, Reddit, Twitch, Coinbase, and Weebly.[38] Table 8.4 lists the top five incubators and accelerators in the United States and Canada.

**Accelerator:** an organization that provides tailored support in order to help new ventures scale and grow.

## Learning How to Network

Networking is not just about collecting business cards. You may walk away from a networking event with a whole stack of business cards but with no meaningful relationships or connections forged. A business card isn't enough for someone to remember you by—you need to have meaningful conversations to maintain a relationship and provide value in a way that makes you memorable.

Networking is a two-way game. It's a targeted search, with a philosophy of contributing, giving value, sharing and exchanging information, and interacting with people.

### Networking Events

Before you attend a networking event, do your research. Think about who might be there, and decide whom you would like to meet. Think of what you are going to say before you arrive. Your list of topics does not have to be solely business related. You could talk about anything from business, to sports, to weekend plans, to industry events. Remember, relationships can be forged on mutual personal interests or hobbies and not just business interests. However, it is always best to steer clear of potentially incendiary topics like politics, religion, and other issues that might elicit a strong emotional reaction.

Walking into a room full of strangers can be daunting, but the good news is that like any other skill, the skill of networking can be learned. And in keeping with the theme of this book, it takes practice. Here are some networking tips:

- Read the room: How crowded or empty is it? Is there a focal point or an activity taking place that could be a conversation starter?

- Look for potential groups to join: Look at nonverbal cues such as body language and eye contact to identify whom to approach as a likely conversant and whom to avoid.

- Commit fully to the discussion: Don't look over the shoulder of the person you're talking to as if you're hoping someone more interesting will show up.

- Be careful not to dominate the conversation: Make sure you let the other person speak and offer thoughts and opinions.

- Keep questions brief: When approaching a desired contact with a question, briefly introduce yourself, keep your question short, and explain why you are asking.

- Disengage gracefully: Look them in the eye, shake hands and say their name followed by "it's been good talking with you," or words to that effect.

- Thank people for advice: Follow up with a short note or email within 24 hours and consider connecting on LinkedIn or other professional networking sites.

Even if you consider yourself to be a confident speaker, it is worth practicing your body language. Research shows that domineering people tend to take control of the conversation and avoid eye contact a lot of the time. People who are open to making new connections generally "adopt an open stance, shoulders apart and hands at their sides, turning slightly toward newcomers to welcome them," says networking expert Kelly Decker, of Decker Communications.[39] While influential people tend to lead conversations, good networkers will listen and show interest by nodding, leaning forward, raising their eyebrows, and mirroring the speaker's gestures—for example, tilting their heads in the same way.

### The Give and Take of Networking

Bear in mind that networking is a two-way street. The quid pro quo (something that is given or done in return for something) strategy is often used by networkers to initiate a business relationship.[40] The idea behind it is to first identify something your contact needs and then offer something of value. This could involve sharing some information, sending a link to an article about the subject in question, or offering your contact an introduction to someone who knows more about the subject.

Kare Anderson, author of *Mutuality Matters,* points out that when you do favors for somebody, they are more likely to repay them. Doing favors for others helps people with good ideas to find ways to capitalize on their opportunities. She provides a list of favors that may only take as little as 5 minutes and are a great way of quickly building trusting relationships:

- Use a product and offer concise, vivid, and helpful feedback.

- Introduce two people with a well-written email, citing a mutual interest.

- Read a summary and offer crisp and concrete feedback.

- Serve as a relevant reference for a person, product, or service.

- Share or comment on something on Facebook, Twitter, LinkedIn, Tumblr, Google+, or other social places.

- Write a short, specific, and laudatory note to recognize or recommend someone on LinkedIn, Yelp, or other social place.[41]

Remember that many people who are new to networking events will be as nervous as you are. If you see someone standing alone, why not approach him or her? He or she is likely to be more welcoming because you have made an effort to strike up a conversation. More important, don't assume "anyone standing alone is a loser and should be avoided."[42] This person might end up being one of your most valuable contacts. In fact, never assume that anyone—regardless of who they are or what they do—can't be a worthwhile acquaintance.

Ivan Misner, founder of business networking organization BNI, tells the story of a financial advisor friend who received a huge portion of business referred to him by a gardener on Cape Cod in Massachusetts. The gardener worked in the gardens of the grandest homes on Cape Cod and had built up good professional relationships with wealthy families living there. When the gardener heard the financial advisor was trying to get referrals in the area, he mentioned his name to his contacts in the wealthy families, and that is how the financial advisor ended up getting a huge chunk of business.[43] So the moral of the story is, never underestimate the power of the "loner" or the person with a "low wage" job, or the person sitting next to you at an entrepreneurship event. Pursue all networking opportunities—you never know where they may lead. Networking is simply about human connection and connecting with all types of people.

Finally, make a real effort to remember names (this could involve mentally writing a person's name on or above their face) and use names during conversation to fully assimilate them. Write down information soon after you meet someone.[44]

Guy Kaw4saki, author of *The Art of the Start,* provides some additional tips for networking:[45]

- Discover what you can do for someone else. Great networkers want to know what they can do for you, not what you can do for them.

- Ask good questions. The mark of a good conversationalist is to get others to talk a lot and then listen.

- Unveil your passions. Don't just talk about business—let the conversation expand into your hobbies as well.

- Read voraciously so that you have an array of information to draw on during conversations.

- Follow up with a short but personal note within 24 hours. Something like, "Nice to meet you. Hope your blog is doing well," is fine—but be sure to mention at least one personal item to show that you're not just sending a canned email.

- Prepare a self-introduction of 7 to 9 seconds (*not* a 30-second elevator speech). Tie it to why you're attending the event. This will help people figure out what to say to you.

## Networking to Find Mentors

Mentors can be an invaluable resource for entrepreneurs as they offer advice based on years of experience, help you progress with your venture, and warn you of known pitfalls. They can also provide valuable connections and industry contacts. For instance, health and wellness entrepreneur Amy Backlock acknowledges the pivotal role her mentor played when she was setting up her personal training business.[46] Amy's mentor was a doctor of physical therapy who owned many rehabilitation centers. Not only was he an expert in his field but he had the contacts Amy needed to get her venture off the ground. She said, "He was a source of endless information, important contacts, and a terrific sounding board for me, all contributing to my success."

Most well-known entrepreneurs credit their mentors for their success. Steve Jobs taught Mark Zuckerberg how to build a team; Bill Gates credits Warren Buffett for his ability to deal with complex problems; and Richard Branson references British airline entrepreneur Sir Freddie Laker for his advice and guidance when trying to get Virgin Atlantic off the ground.[47] Deborah Sweeney, founder of online legal and business filing service MyCorporation, says her mentors include "my mom (full-time career woman and amazing, supportive mom), a few of my female professors, a mentor in my law practice, and colleague-mentors with whom I graduated law school."[48]

Yet entrepreneurs typically don't just have one mentor; they may build up a network of mentors over time, which can be useful when you are seeking different perspectives or guidance during particular stages of your venture. Mentors can also play a very important role in larger companies. For example, at the multinational manufacturer W. L. Gore, instead of bosses new hires are assigned mentors—people who can guide them through Gore's famously unique nonhierarchical culture and address any questions, concerns, or issues the new hire may have.[49]

How do you go about finding your mentor? Look in your personal network—the ideal mentor might be right in front of you. Sometimes the person who knows you best can be the right fit for you.

Check out your college connections, too, as they can be a valuable resource for mentors. Anywhere you have the opportunity to form connections—networking events, Meetup groups, and so forth—may be the right step toward finding the right mentor for you.[50]

However, for some entrepreneurs, asking someone to be your mentor can be daunting. Why would a successful business person or seasoned entrepreneur want to take the time to help you grow your fledgling new venture? The answer is that many mentors gain personal pleasure in sharing their experience to help others succeed. Now a mentor himself, Richard Branson is a champion of young entrepreneurial talent; he has said he gets "a real sense of pleasure from seeing talented people realize their ambitions and grow professionally and personally." Branson also believes that mentors can learn a lot from their mentees: "As I've learned, in the process you can gain new insights and discover fresh approaches to doing business by simply discussing how things work."[51]

While face-to-face networking is essential for building valuable relationships, it is also possible to network from a remote location. In the next section, we will explore the benefits of virtual networking.

# Building My Network

In the first Mindshift, you analyzed your network and probably identified some gaps. Now it's time to work on filling in those gaps. For this Mindshift, you need to add three new and significant people to your network.

Step 1: Identify what types of people you want to add to your network. No names at this point, just types. For example, you may want to meet someone who has built an app or you may want to meet someone who understands commercial real estate. Write down the three types of people; you should have three *different* types written down.

Step 2: For each of the types of people, identify an event (physical and not virtual) where you could potentially meet people who fall into your category. For example, you may go to an entrepreneurship club meeting or attend a speaker event on campus.

Step 3: After you find them, send them a follow-up thank you email within 24 hours. Don't simply connect on social media; rather, email specifically why you enjoyed connecting with them, what you learned, and how you hope to stay connected. You may even want to try to set up a next meeting. Why not?

## Critical Thinking Questions

1. How did you approach people at the events you attended? Did some approaches work better than others?

2. What did you learn from each person you met?

3. How will you maintain your relationship with these new people? ●

# 8.4 VIRTUAL NETWORKING

>> **LO 8.4**   **Illustrate the benefits of virtual networking.**

With the proliferation of online social networks, networking has definitely evolved! One of the speediest and simplest ways to connect with others is through social media. Twitter, LinkedIn, Facebook, Instagram, and YouTube all provide ways to connect with people who are experts in the field, potential stakeholders, or fellow entrepreneurs—anyone who can potentially help you develop, build, and grow your entrepreneurial venture. Some of these people may become self-selected stakeholders and eventually become part of your founding team. Let's explore how you can use these social media sites to build your network.

## Networking Through Social Media

Twitter is one of the easiest platforms to use to find people who might become stakeholders. Signing on to Twitter is free (just choose a user name and a password) and easy (write a 280-character bio about yourself). You can upload a photo and you're ready to go.

To find others on Twitter who share your interests, you can do a keyword search (https://twitter.com/search-home) and see everyone who is using that keyword at that very instant. You can search for other people's Twitter bios and profiles at www.followerwonk.com. You can also compare users, even compare yourself to competitors, influencers, or friends. Followerwonk is also a good tool for analyzing impact, tracking followers, and retrieving "social graphs" based on Twitter statistics.

In addition to Twitter, you can interact with individuals or groups on LinkedIn (see Table 8.5). LinkedIn also has a section devoted specifically to questions and answers, which provides you with a view into the real-life challenges that business people face and the solutions that others offer. Anyone can post a question, and anyone can provide an answer. To reward helpful, quality answers, the question-asker can award a "good answer" tag. As an entrepreneur looking to build your knowledge, you can use these tags to identify the best answers from which to learn. Posting answers is a good way to show your own expertise and to demonstrate your willingness to be of help to others. When you share information with others, they will feel more inclined to reciprocate.

**TABLE 8.5**

LinkedIn Groups Dedicated to Entrepreneurs

| | |
|---|---|
| Executive Suite | This group is all about connecting executives so they can share advice on leadership, decision making, and more. Members will join more than 321,000 others and gain access to their web series, discussion boards, and practical advice. |
| A Startup Specialists Group | With more than 281,000 members, this group, catering to startups, mentors, founders, and investors, is a great resource for entrepreneurs. It provides support, tips for building your business, crowd funding, best business practices, networking, and more. |
| Band of Entrepreneurs | This "non-profit organization of, by, and for entrepreneurs" group has close to 27,000 members and provides support on topics like legal help, human resources, public relations, technology, and more. |
| Bright Ideas and Entrepreneurs | This group facilitates discussions between entrepreneurs all over the world. With more than 22,000 members, this group invites you to share ideas and connect with other like-minded professionals. |
| Digital Marketing | The 1.1 million members of this group discuss areas of the digital marketing landscape, including social media marketing, mobile marketing, search engine marketing, online advertising, and more. |
| Entrepreneurs Meet Investors | With almost 5,500 members, this group is great for entrepreneurs seeking startup funding or for more established businesses in need of capital for further growth. |
| Entrepreneur's Network | Founded in 2008, this group with nearly 46,000 members aims to connect current and aspiring entrepreneurs to find answers, ask questions, and connect with similar professionals. |
| Future Trends | This group consists of 500,000 members and connects fellow trend hunters and visionaries from a variety of industries, such as marketing, consumer insights, strategic planning, and trend tracking. |
| Leadership Think Tank | With more than 263,000 members, this group aims to identify the relationship between leaders and followers through open discussions about leadership concepts and practices. |
| On Startups | This group of more than 644,000 members gives entrepreneurs the chance to discuss marketing, sales, finance, operations, recruiting, and other startup-related topics. |

**Source:** Lopez, J. (2018). 20 LinkedIn groups every entrepreneur should belong to. *Business News Daily.* Retrieved from https://www.businessnewsdaily.com/7185-entrepreneur-linkedin-groups.html

Neena Dasgupta, CEO and director of Zirca Digital Solutions based in India, offers the following advice to entrepreneurs:

> Always remember to spend time making a list of people you would want to do business with in the future. These could be clients, investors, and potential partners. Next, create a highly-personalized note for each person and send them requests. When you're opening up this dialogue, don't forget to avoid hard-selling, and instead focus on how you can build a relationship.[52]

Table 8.5 lists a range of LinkedIn groups dedicated to entrepreneurs and small-business owners.

Facebook has grown from a social platform to a business platform—most businesses have a presence on Facebook. It is also useful for posting articles on Facebook pages and connecting with others who share mutual interests. Facebook groups are also beneficial for connecting with others and starting dialogues around shared interests. There

**TABLE 8.6**

Facebook Groups for Entrepreneurs

| | |
|---|---|
| The Startup Chat Mastermind Group | This group is an offshoot of The Startup Chat Podcast, hosted by Steli Efti and Hiten Shah. Network with other fans of the show and get advice on topics ranging from startup growth to getting yourself into an entrepreneurial mentality. |
| Women in Business | This group is the virtual clubhouse of the Women In Business Club. The goal is for people to share what they're working on and get honest answers to their biggest business questions. |
| Intrepid Entrepreneurs | Facebook page where entrepreneurs and aspiring entrepreneurs come together to ask and answer questions, as well as give feedback on projects, ideas, and other forms of content. |
| The Intentional Entrepreneur | Learn how to find more (and better) clients, ace sales calls, and other must-dos when starting an online business. |
| Freedom Hackers Mastermind | Thriving community where entrepreneurs can gather feedback, network, discover interesting content, and help other entrepreneurs on their journey. |
| Savvy Business Owners | Facebook group for self-employed businesswomen. |
| Entrepreneurs Hustle | Group consists of a mix of seasoned business owners and new entrepreneurs, which makes for a great balance of people who are both asking for help and offering knowledge. |
| Small Business Connections | Group where members connect with other business owners, share events, and participate in themed discussions based on each day of the week (like Tech Tuesday and Winning Wednesday). |

**Source:** Shah, K. (2018). 19 Facebook groups that will make you a better entrepreneur. *Gusto.* Retrieved from https://gusto.com/blog/growth/best-facebook-groups-entrepreneurs

are also specific Facebook groups for entrepreneurs (see Table 8.6) that provide a forum for entrepreneurs to meet and exchange ideas. Don't be wary of connecting with your competitors—they are a valuable source of learning and inspiration. Both Facebook and LinkedIn make it easy to find out which face-to-face conferences the people in your network are attending.

Unlike Twitter, LinkedIn, and Facebook, YouTube is not a social networking and interaction site. However, you can use YouTube as a resource for identifying experts and getting video tutorials on a specific topic. When you find an expert on YouTube, you can use other social media like Twitter and LinkedIn to establish first contact.

Instagram is also a useful networking tool. People can send short videos and photos to connect with others and showcase where they have been and what business activities they have been involved with. Lana Hopkins, founder of Mon Purse, an Australia-based leather bag and purse customization and personalization company, showcases her products during her global business travel.[53] Allowing people an insight into your professional life gives them the opportunity to get to know you and your business.

In other countries around the world, online startup support networks are becoming more popular as a means of funding early-stage ventures. VC4Africa is Africa's largest online entrepreneurship network, which brings together venture capitalists, angels, and entrepreneurs to support Africa's rapidly growing startup scene. Through its 90,000 members, the network connects entrepreneurs from 12,000 startups with the knowledge, contacts, and financing necessary to build their businesses.[54] To date, entrepreneurs have raised more than $27 million in funding through VC4Africa.[55]

## Maintaining Your Network

Once you've started to build your network, it's important to maintain it—something that's easy to forget when your network is mainly virtual and you are not interacting face-to-face on a regular basis. Maintaining your network involves staying in touch through occasional interaction. Research shows we can really manage up to only 25 relationships, but we can maintain up to 150.[56]

This interaction can take the form of tweeting a useful piece of information, replying to a request for information, answering a question, or attending an event. For example, if you see an interesting video on YouTube, send a link to people in your network who might be interested. If one of your stakeholders posts a question on LinkedIn to which you know the answer (or know someone who knows the answer), answer the question or recommend an expert. Figure 8.2 lists several skills important to maintaining relationships.

If you're a member of Meetup groups, then let your network know that you're attending an upcoming meeting. You can also tweet your attendance or announce it on LinkedIn and Facebook. After the event, you can tweet or email any people with whom you talked, by thanking them for the conversation. Another way to maintain your network is to provide value back to them by writing a blog post. As an entrepreneur, you can use a blog to showcase and share your thoughts and activities with your stakeholders.

Overall, the frequency of interactions you have with your stakeholders can vary over time. There will be times when you're actively seeking advice, which means you will have more interactions. Some stakeholders will want to be involved on a daily or weekly basis. Others are fine with less frequent interactions. Overall, maintaining relationships is a skill like any other, and it pays to learn it.

By participating in social networking sites, you build credibility, transparency, and trust. If people get an insight into your professional life, see the connections you have made, and what thoughts and information you share, they will get to know you and want to build a relationship with you. Whether you're networking in person or online, it is important to look for potential candidates for your founding team. The next section focuses on how you can network to build a founding team.

**Lana Hopkins, founder of Mon Purse**

## 8.5 NETWORKING TO BUILD THE FOUNDING TEAM

>> **LO 8.5**   **Explain how networking can help to build the founding team.**

A founding team is a group of people with complementary skills and a shared sense of commitment coming together in founding an enterprise to build and grow the company. The founding team usually consists of the founder and a few cofounders who possess complementary skills. There is no "right size" for the number of people on a founding team, but two to four seems to be the typical number.

**Founding team:** a group of people with complementary skills and a shared sense of commitment coming together in founding an enterprise to build and grow the company.

---

**FIGURE 8.2**

### Skills for Maintaining Relationships

| Skills for Maintaining Relationships | |
|---|---|
| • Curiosity | • Self-Management |
| • Questioning | • Accountability |
| • Deep Listening | • Intuition |

**Source:** Adapted from Murphy, W., & Kram, K. (2014). *Strategic relationships at work.* New York, NY: McGraw-Hill.

# When to Focus on Values

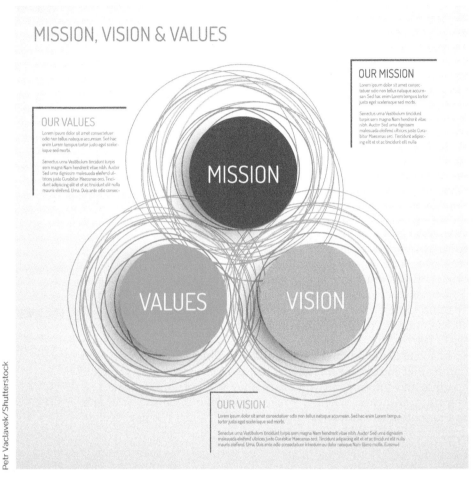

Petr Vaclavek/Shutterstock

**Mission, vision, and values statements**

Every well-established company has a value statement, which often goes along with a simple mission statement. For an entrepreneur in the early stages of launching a new business, time is one of the most valuable resources. An entrepreneur may be tempted to skip writing a values statement. After all, very few employees at any company would be able to recite their company's value or mission statement without pulling out the company handbook. Is it necessary to spend time on forming a values statement in the early stages of a startup? Is it even necessary to have a values statement at all?

Traditionally, a values statement allows employees to band together in their vision for how the company can change the world in a major and beneficial way. It often gives the workplace a sense of higher meaning, which can be a valuable motivational tool for employees. Additionally, having a values statement ensures that

every member of the team is on the same page, and there is a written confirmation as to the direction that the business is taking.

In today's business climate, a company's brand is inherently tied to the company's culture. Workers, especially those in highly skilled industries, will be more interested in a job if they can find a higher meaning than just a paycheck. Essentially, if the values of the company are readily apparent to the business of the company, employees and candidates could be more excited to work for the company, rather than having to turn to a vague values statement. All of this suggests that the right thing for an entrepreneur to do is to create a values statement in the startup phase of his or her company. An entrepreneur can "save time" by spending time creating a sufficient values statement up front. The end result is a purposeful company culture and better motivated employees.

## Critical Thinking Questions

1. Could a lack of a values statement lead a company astray?

2. Can a values statement be inherent to the operation of a company, without a need to write it down?

3. How does a values statement affect the morale of employees? ●

**Sources:**

Parker, M. (2016, October 18). Have company mission statements become outdated? *The Globe and Mail.* Retrieved from https://www.theglobeandmail.com/report-on-business/careers/leadership-lab/have-company-mission-statements-become-outdated/article32403376/

Smith, C. (n.d.). Can an organization have a successful strategic plan without effective mission & vision statements? *Chron.com.* Retrieved from https://smallbusiness.chron.com/can-organization-successful-strategic-plan-effective-mission-vision-statements-30779.html

The goal of the founding team is to build and grow the company and provide economic and social returns for themselves, employees, other owners, and potential investors. Research shows that more and more, new fast-growth ventures have been founded by entrepreneurial teams rather than sole entrepreneurs. In fact, overall, studies have shown that ventures started by teams typically perform better than those started by solo founders.[57] When researchers asked venture capitalists the most important factors to new venture success, their response was, "the lead entrepreneur and the quality of the team."[58]

When considering potential founding team members, it is helpful to ask yourself two questions: "Can I build the company without them?" and "Can I find someone else just like them?" If the answer to both questions is no, then you have most likely discovered a cofounder. However, if the answer to both questions is yes, then you can still keep them in your network, maintain the relationship, and potentially hire them at a later date as employees.[59]

Researchers have cited the most likely outlets where entrepreneurs find their founding teams: colleagues in organizations where they were previously employed; organizations similar to the founding firm; prior working relationships across organizations (e.g., buyers, suppliers, consultants); family members and friends; and deliberate search by the lead entrepreneur.[60]

Another way to find founding team members is through social networking sites, which enable you to find and interact with people you might otherwise never meet who share your passion and could ultimately be a resource. For example, selective networking site Cofounder's Lab (https://cofounderslab.com) provides a global forum for entrepreneurs to connect with like-minded entrepreneurs, cofounders, and advisors. Applications from entrepreneurs to join Cofounder's Lab are first screened for skillsets (50% of the members are engineers), and if the applicants are accepted, they are given access to the network for a $50 annual fee.

Overall, team members are generally found in the network of the lead entrepreneur. This means most founding teams have a lead entrepreneur (usually, but not always, the team CEO) who creates the vision; has full belief in the venture; and has the motivation and passion to persevere, inspire team members, and make judgments and decisions during difficult times.[61]

Google re:Work has done research on the importance of shared vision and good manager behaviors (https://rework.withgoogle.com/). Though founding teams are more about leadership and taking action, parts of Google's suggested group exercise are extremely important for founding teams. To create a vision, the team needs to answer three questions in the beginning, when the founding team is just forming:

Core Values: What do we believe in?

Purpose: Why do we exist?

Mission: What do we want to achieve?

During the early stages of a startup everything is constantly changing, so it's important for the group to continue to revisit these questions. As the venture gets more traction, two additional questions need to be asked:

Strategy: How will we realize our mission?

Goals: How do we plan to accomplish our strategies?

## Characteristics of a Great Founding Team

Finding the right cofounders to build and scale your venture can make all the difference between your business succeeding or failing. The most successful teams are composed of members who possess the experience, skills, and abilities to manage complex problems, cope with pressure, and overcome obstacles to achieve rapid growth. Table 8.7 outlines a list of useful questions to ask potential founding team members.

Positive social relations within the team are also key when it comes to providing social and emotional support.[62] Bernd Schoner, cofounder of RFID tech startup ThingMagic, started with friends from MIT he had worked with before. They thought they knew each other well enough to start a company, but they found that "outside pressure causes people to act differently," which caused "extreme turmoil." Schoner has learned from this experience and believes that founding teams must have the right balance of personalities and characteristics in order to achieve success.[63]

Jenn Houser, a serial entrepreneur and cofounder of Upstart Bootcamp, has outlined the following useful characteristics to look for when you are evaluating potential cofounders.[64]

### 1. Possess the right skills.

Houser recommends identifying the top three to five business operations you need to carry out well over the next 3 years; then ask yourself who has the skills and expertise to accomplish these operations. She points out the importance of examining the track record of each candidate. Whether or not the person is a friend, she or he should be considered only if she or he has demonstrated the ability to do the job.

### 2. Take a hands-on approach.

During the startup stage, you and your cofounders will be doing everything—from answering the phone to ordering office supplies. Make sure your chosen cofounders are not only willing but happy to do whatever it takes to achieve goals.

For example, in 2003, former chemist and lab director Ron Holt founded the cleaning company Two Maids & A Mop, headquartered in Birmingham, Alabama. In the beginning, Holt was one of the maids with a mop: "I put my hands onto surfaces that I never thought I would," Holt says. "As a former lab director, to find yourself on a bathroom floor, cleaning up somebody's [mess]—it's not where you thought you'd be in life."[65]

Although it wasn't a glamorous start, cleaning toilets was a valuable way for Holt to learn about the cleaning business and the people he would eventually employ.

---

**TABLE 8.7**

Early Questions to Ask Potential Team Members

| |
|---|
| Who needs to be on the team at the start? |
| What skills does each person bring to the table? |
| Are there any skill gaps? Can these gaps be outsourced? |
| What type of work experience is related to the idea? |
| What is the network of each member? |
| Do you have ways of attracting new team members? |
| What are the personal and business goals of each member? |
| What is the role of each member, and is each role distinct? |
| How are you dividing ownership? |

### 3. Use positive problem solving.

You want to choose entrepreneurial team members who are curious and driven—people who see problems not as obstacles but as challenges that must be overcome in a creative and innovative way. An entrepreneurial mindset is required for all team members.

### 4. Leave ego at the door.

Team success depends on collaboration and a collective willingness to work for the good of the enterprise. Cofounders with a big ego or a personal agenda are less likely to work well with others. One way to find out if potential cofounders have big egos is to ask them about a time when they achieved team success, and listen carefully to the number of times they say "I" or "we" in their response.

**The Microsoft founding team**

Entrepreneur John Rampton believes his ego was responsible for killing his new payments venture.[66] Rampton refused to ask for help when he needed it, missed opportunities to learn, set impossible goals, controlled all the decision making, and micromanaged his employees.

Having learned the hard way, Rampton concluded, "My business isn't about me. It's about my customers and how I can enhance their lives. If I'm not listening to their wants and needs, they won't continue to support me and my business. Focus on your customers."[67]

### 5. Share similar attitudes toward values, goals, and risk.

Jenn Houser advises that cofounders need to be aligned with the goals to be achieved, the values they share, and the risks they may need to take to get there. The best relationships are based on trust, and your team should feel comfortable about discussing potential ethical dilemmas and how they will be resolved. Before you commit, she recommends investing several days with your cofounders in hashing out every detail of the business and how the partnership arrangement will work.

### 6. Care deeply.

Although cofounders need to have the intelligence, skills, and experience to achieve goals, they also need to care deeply about the enterprise. Someone who doesn't care deeply about the success of the startup may be likely to become unavailable when things get tough, or even to jump ship at a crucial moment. Plenty of passion combined with a high degree of smarts can even compensate for limitations in experience. Finding a cofounder who has complementary skills and equal enthusiasm for your ideas can help minimize risk and increase the odds of startup success.[68]

Many startups fail because the cofounders came together too quickly rather than spending time together first. Spending time with your potential cofounders on a startup weekend or working together in a previous job allows for more bonding and building a relationship of trust and respect. The bottom line is connecting with your cofounders are like entering into a marriage on both an emotional and financial basis. Get to know each other first, before you commit, and make sure the others feel the same way about you as you do about them.

Atish Davda, founder of liquidity manager EquityZen, has created a list of attributes to look for in founding team members (see Figure 8.3).

## The Value of Team Diversity

Diversity comes in many forms. We often think of diversity as referring to demographic characteristics such as age, gender, race, and ethnicity, but diversity is also found in people's career paths and goals, viewpoints, educational backgrounds, and life experiences. Most of the diversity we have in the world is composed of what we don't see. So always look below the surface! (See Figure 8.4).

**FIGURE 8.3**

## Key Attributes of Founding Team Members

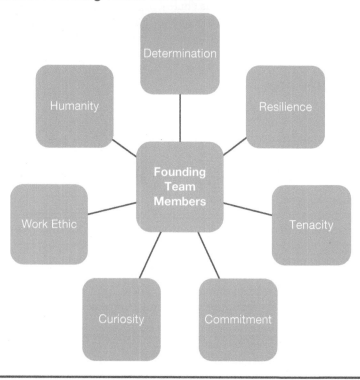

**Source:** Adapted from Davda, A. (2014). How you can build an incredible founding team. *Creator.* Retrieved from https://creator.wework.com/knowledge/can-build-incredible-founding-team/

**FIGURE 8.4**

## Dimensions of Diversity

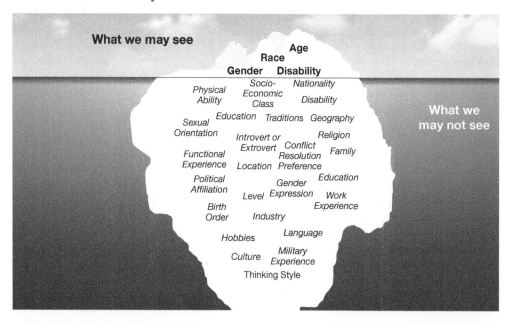

**Source:** Adapted by Susan Duffy, Babson College from "Turn Diversity to Your Advantage" by Salomon, Mary F and Schork, Joan M. Research Technology Management, Arlington, Vol. 46, Iss. 4. (Jul/Aug 2003): 37; http://www.brookgraham.com/WhatWeDo/Iceberg.aspx; https://spark4community.com/1043-2/

## Homogeneous and Heterogeneous Teams

Which do you think is more important: homogenous teams, whose members possess the same or similar characteristics such as age, gender, ethnicity, experience, and educational background; or heterogeneous teams, meaning a group of people with a mix of knowledge, skills, and experience? Although there is no conclusive research to suggest that homogenous is better than heterogeneous or vice versa, the results of studies argue the benefits and disadvantages of both.

In homogeneous teams, members are likely to feel included because of their shared backgrounds, cultures, languages, and experiences. This helps the team to communicate more effectively and avoid misunderstandings as well as prejudices. However, sharing similarities does not mean that personality conflicts do not exist—any team, whether homogeneous or heterogeneous, is liable to have conflicts at times. Further, studies have shown that lack of diversity in homogeneous teams can stifle creativity and information processing. Indeed, it is difficult to form a homogeneous team without others feeling excluded because they do not share the same characteristics as the team members.[69]

In a heterogeneous team, there is a greater mix of experiences, skills, ethnicities, and backgrounds. A diverse set of collective characteristics can aid decision making and expand a "group's set of possible solutions and allows the group to conceptualize problems in new ways."[70] Studies have found that this type of team tends to have a higher degree of creativity and innovativeness than homogeneous teams.[71]

Researchers have argued, however, that team diversity alone will not necessarily result in better performance. What matters more than demographic diversity (age, gender, race, etc.) is team commitment and cognitive comprehensiveness, a process in which team members examine critical issues with a wide lens and formulate strategies by considering diverse approaches, decision criteria, and courses of action. Team-level cognitive comprehensiveness is positively related to entrepreneurial team effectiveness. Effective teams also tend to have a high level of member commitment, encourage each other to use different approaches, offer different perspectives on problems, and use a range of potential solutions to solve problems.[72]

Finally, there are certain drawbacks to heterogeneous teams. Groups that have a greater mix can find it more difficult to communicate and understand each other, especially if they have to navigate across different languages and cultural backgrounds. This may lead to some members feeling misunderstood or isolated, which may produce conflicts and negative emotions among members of the entrepreneurial team, resulting in poor performance.[73]

## Groupthink and Healthy Conflict

A team whose members are from diverse backgrounds, hold complementary skills and experiences, and have commitment to the venture could be considered healthy. And even though conflict arising from personality difference can be destructive, there is such a thing as healthy conflict. Testing and challenging assumptions is a state that gets the team out of groupthink, a phenomenon in which people share too similar a mindset, which inhibits their ability to spot gaps or errors. Patrick Lencioni, author of *The Five Dysfunctions of a Team*, states that "productive debate over issues is good for a team." Disagreeing on issues makes things uncomfortable, but it builds clarity. "If you don't have conflict on a team, you don't get commitment," Lencioni said. "If people don't weigh in, they won't buy in."[74] Healthy conflict builds clarity; for example, if team members point out flaws in an idea, then they can work together to build it into a more robust idea.

The challenge is to ensure that constructive conflict over issues does not degenerate into dysfunctional interpersonal conflict.[75] In other words, team members need to be able to argue without taking it personally or impairing their ability to work together. In her study of teams, Stanford University professor Kathleen Eisenhardt found teams that engaged in healthy conflict shared six traits:

- developed multiple alternatives to enrich the level of debate;
- shared commonly agreed-upon goals;
- worked with more information rather than less;

**Homogenous team:** a group of people with the same or similar characteristics such as age, gender, ethnicity, experience, and educational background.

**Heterogeneous team:** a group of people with a mix of knowledge, skills, and experience.

**Cognitive comprehensiveness:** a process in which team members examine critical issues with a wide lens and formulate strategies by considering diverse approaches, decision criteria, and courses of action.

**Groupthink:** a phenomenon in which people share too similar a mindset, which inhibits their ability to spot gaps or errors.

- injected humor into the decision process;
- maintained a balanced power structure; and
- resolved issues without forcing consensus.[76]

Overall, the teams worked with more, rather than less, information and debated on the basis of facts, not emotions. When teams stay with the topic of the debate and argue their points productively, there is less chance of personal attack.

One way of preventing groupthink and promoting healthy conflict is the use of a devil's advocate to challenge assumptions and encourage different perspectives. Author and hospitality expert Paul Rutter believes that all teams should have a devil's advocate. He said, "Having an effective devil's advocate can be a guardian angel in disguise, helping your company avoid mistakes that cost time and money. This can ultimately improve employee engagement, customer loyalty, and create repeat business."[77]

Credit: Cartoon Resource/Alamy Stock Vector

"Emphasize our unique differences, pass it down."

**This cartoon describes the concept of groupthink.**

However, not all teams welcome the presence of a devil's advocate. In a classic study in decision making carried out in the early 1960s, several groups of managers were formed to solve a complex problem. The groups were identical in size and composition, except that half the groups included a devil's advocate, whose role was to challenge the group's conclusions and force the others to critically assess their assumptions and the logic of their arguments. The groups with the devil's advocate performed significantly better than the other groups by generating better-quality solutions to problems.

After a short break, the groups were told to eliminate one person from their group. In each group, it was the devil's advocate whom the group chose to ask to leave. Despite the fact that the devil's advocate was the reason for the team's high performance and competitive advantage, the members chose to eliminate that member because he or she made them feel uncomfortable. "I know it has positive outcomes for the performance of the organization as a whole, but I don't like how it makes me feel personally."[78] However, as we have learned, although we may think engaging in conflict is awkward and uncomfortable, it can be valuable and constructive if it is carried out in the right way.

In sum, healthy and constructive conflict is good, provided team members are clear on the organization's goals and free of hidden agendas. Steve Jobs said it best when he stated, "It's okay to spend a lot of time arguing about which route to take to San Francisco when everyone wants to end up there, but a lot of time gets wasted in such arguments if one person wants to go to San Francisco and another secretly wants to go to San Diego."[79] ●

---

**⑤SAGE** edge™

SUMMARY

**8.1    Explain the role of networks in building social capital.**

Networks provide social capital such as access to sources of financing, information, expertise, and support, and networks can be excellent sources for loyalty. They allow for learning and information exchange, and social capital enables access to a range of resources, including venture capitalists, angel investors, advisors, banks, and trade shows.

**8.2    Demonstrate the value of networks for entrepreneurs.**

Relationships are key to business success, and entrepreneurs in particular will need to skillfully interact with a vast array of stakeholders. Networks provide entrepreneurs with access to private information, diverse skillsets, and power. Networks can also be relied on for personal and emotional support.

**8.3    Describe different ways of building networks.**

Building a network extends beyond socializing with friends and acquaintances, and it often involves active participation in organized networking events. In a new relationship, it is better to give value to get value; value is a two-way game.

**8.4    Illustrate the benefits of virtual networking.**

Social media sites and other forms of virtual networking provide additional channels to meet or interact with stakeholders from the world over. Entrepreneurs have a number of different virtual communities in which they can participate, with many communities offering access to a specific subset of interests in entrepreneurship. Common social media platforms like Facebook also contain groups that are similar to online entrepreneurship communities.

**8.5    Explain how networking can help to build the founding team.**

One of the most valuable things an entrepreneur can do is connect with individuals who serve as great complements on a founding team. Research even suggests that team-started ventures are more successful than solo-founded ventures. Networking skills can often be relied on as the means to that end.

KEY TERMS

Bonds  182

Bridges  182

Cognitive
   comprehensiveness  201

Founding team  195

Groupthink  201

Heterogeneous team  201

Homogenous team  201

Impression management  183

Linkages  182

Self-selected stakeholders  185

Social capital  179

CASE STUDY

## Jeff Goudie, AmeriCan Packaging

Jeff Goudie, cites his network as his most important resource when he launched a manufacturing company in the Dominican Republic. It was also his network that came to his rescue when things got a little murky.

After graduating with an MBA from Babson College in 2014, Jeff wanted to buy a business. At first, he and one of his classmates from Babson, Mike Cassata, wanted to buy a wood recycling factory, given the boom of the recycling industry. When that plan fell through, both Jeff and Mike started to look for jobs. Jeff joined BizCorps, a strategy advisory firm specializing in emerging markets, as a consultant. As part of his job, he had the opportunity to work in Bogotá, Colombia, for 13 months. The experience was fulfilling, fun, and rewarding; however, Jeff still wanted to do something on his own. He reached out to a childhood friend's father, who was an investment banker also looking for business opportunities in manufacturing. Together they identified an attractive opportunity for metal packaging in the Dominican Republic.

He learned that the Dominican Republic was the heart of the cigar industry, with major players such as Cohiba, Macanudo, and Swisher in the same geographic area. The issue, however, was that there were no metal packaging manufacturers in the area to support the cigar producers. "The supply chain for tobacco manufacturing was wide open. Nobody in this hemisphere was doing it!" said Jeff.

Jeff reached out to his network in Miami, his hometown, to understand the cigar manufacturing and packaging industry better. He learned that the entire supply chain for the production of cigars existed in Latin America, except for the metal packaging components. The metal packaging was sourced from China and Switzerland. If metal packaging was sourced in the Dominican Republic, Jeff knew that he could compete with China on price, compete with Switzerland on lead time, and be able to fulfill emergency production requirements and just-in-time inventory needs. Jeff concluded that the market was big enough for him to enter. It also held opportunities to diversify into other industries, such as cosmetics and promotional packaging. With data supporting his analysis, Jeff began to look for a suitable warehouse to set up his metal packaging plant close to tobacco manufacturers in the Dominican Republic.

Setting up an entire plan from scratch would be a big investment, and Jeff was having serious doubts about taking the leap. However, when he went to visit one of the prospective warehouses, all of this changed. Jeff recalled when he visited the warehouse in 2015, "Something just felt right and I ended up signing a 5-year lease to the warehouse immediately without informing my investor!" He then wrote a makeshift business plan to present to his friend's father, who was his main investor, and went on to raise $2 million in capital to set up what was now called AmeriCan Packaging.

What Jeff did not anticipate, however, was the extremely high supplier bargaining power that was a function of the mature metal packaging industry. AmeriCan Packaging needed to have a strong enough offering for the neighboring tobacco companies to switch from their established suppliers to his product, but getting his COGS low enough was proving to be difficult. He had overestimated the willingness of the metal printing suppliers to supply a small player such as AmeriCan. Because they had much bigger scales of operations, they were reluctant to work with smaller quantities of products.

To get started, Jeff needed to get a test batch of metal cans printed. "The quality of printing on tin cans and the color is an important branding component of metal packaging. Cigar companies usually need a proof of color from suppliers like AmeriCan before placing an order," Jeff explained. He was unable to find a good local printer who could match the stringent color quality requirements of the industry. "We had a lot of potential customers interested, but all of them wanted to see printing proofs, and unfortunately none of my suppliers would do so. It was a complete conundrum. These companies were mature, vertically integrated companies owned by oligarchs; they made all the cans for their other companies (beer, canned foods, paint, etc.). They didn't care about printing qualities, and they really didn't care about new customers." Jeff stated. Jeff finally found a good printer in Costa Rica, but he ran into another issue: They wouldn't print samples. In order to get a sample on an offset lithograph line, the set up and clean up time was enormous, so his suppliers said no, no, and no again! He ended up having to gamble. He had to get 20,000 tins printed as samples, as that was the minimum order quantity, only to get the sample rejected again. He was stuck with a massive stock of 20,000 and no customers.

He started to attend industry trade shows, through which he hired a consultant from Barcelona. This consultant brought in a wealth of industry knowledge and soon became indispensable to the success of the company. He reached out to universities to create an internship program for his company and was able to recruit some good talent to build on his know-how. He also leveraged LinkedIn to look for people across the supply chain. He sent more than 100 LinkedIn messages to get some of the industry experts on board as a consultant. Only 10 out of 100 replied, and he was able to hire 1 out of those 10 people. He also reached out to friends, family, professors, and others in his personal network.

Having been unable to get that first order, Jeff realized that for the established cigar industry to accept him, he needed to win their trust, which wasn't easy. Just as all hope was getting lost, the customer who had rejected the 20,000 tins he printed came in, desperate for metal cans. Their Chinese supplier had cancelled their order at the last minute. The company bought every single one of the rejected tins, and they placed an order for 300,000 more, along with an $80,000 deposit. This situation made apparent the value of Jeff's offering to the cigar manufacturer: AmeriCan could fulfill just-in-time and emergency inventory because it was a local manufacturing plant.

Jeff needed to build his reputation in the Dominican Republic, and he decided bringing on a new partner could expedite this, so he sold the majority stock position of AmeriCan to a cigar manufacturer who had a good reputation. This immediately placed AmeriCan in good standing within the industry. AmeriCan was now positioned to take bigger orders and assure people that Jeff would be able to fulfill them. The cigar manufacturer also joined the board of the company as an advisor and mentor and was successful expanding their book of business.

Jeff understood that Latin America–based cigar companies did not like dealing with suppliers from China due to differences in quality and business culture. This meant that strong relationships could be a precursor to business with smaller companies. He realized that he had been making a mistake in trying to get through to bigger companies that were driven by product prices (which were hard to compete on with China). Instead, he focused on the smaller companies that were more relationship driven, something he was good at building.

Just as the business started to grow, Jeff's business partners saw the value of the opportunity in the metal packaging industry, they started asking for more, and the team started to break down. As Jeff recalled, "The relationship soon got messy, and in August 2018 I left the company without being paid my fair share. They also fired my consultant from Barcelona and stopped the internship programs. I didn't have the money or reputation to fight to stay."

However, all the customer relationships that Jeff established were now part of his personal network. Today, he is working for one of his biggest customers from AmeriCan, running a new business unit related to metal packaging! So, the journey continues for Jeff, and his advice is, "Just do it. Even if you don't know how to do something, you can figure it out; nothing is impossible."

## Critical Thinking Questions

1. Think about Jeff's journey and identify the opportunities he had to grow his network. Now think about all the opportunities he had to use his network.

2. Identify all the resources Jeff received from his network.

3. Assuming you wanted to, could you do what Jeff did with your current network?

**Source:** Jeff Goudie (interview with Babson MBA graduate assistant Gaurav Khemka. September 30, 2018)

# PART III

## Evaluating and Acting on Opportunities

# 9 Creating Revenue Models

"My goal was never to just create a company. A lot of people misinterpret that, as if I don't care about revenue or profit or any of those things. But what not being just a company means to me is not being just that—building something that actually makes a really big change in the world."

—Mark Zuckerberg

# Chapter Outline

# Learning Objectives

9.1    Define a revenue model and distinguish it from the business model.

9.2    Illustrate the 10 most popular revenue models being used by entrepreneurs.

9.3    Explain how companies generate revenue by profiting from "free."

9.4    Identify the drivers that affect revenue as well as cost.

9.5    Identify different strategies entrepreneurs use when pricing their product or service.

9.6    Explain different methods of calculating price.

## 9.1 WHAT IS A REVENUE MODEL?

>> LO 9.1    **Define a revenue model and distinguish it from the business model.**

Over the course of the previous chapters, we have described numerous enterprises founded by entrepreneurs from all sorts of industries and backgrounds. Diverse though the businesses may appear to be, they all have one very important thing in common: the ability to generate revenue, which is the income gained from sales of goods or services.

In Chapter 5, we presented several ways in which entrepreneurs use business models, but business models cannot be complete without an understanding of the underlying revenue model. In other words, how will the business earn revenue, manage costs, and produce profit?

While the terms are sometimes used interchangeably, a *business model* and a *revenue model* are not the same thing. Recall from Chapter 5 that business models fulfill three main purposes: they help entrepreneurs fulfill unmet needs in an existing market, deliver existing products and services to existing customers with unique differentiation, and serve customers in new markets. In other words, a business model describes how a venture will create, deliver, and capture value.

A revenue model is a key component of the business model; it identifies how the company will earn revenue and generate profits. In other words, it explains how entrepreneurs will make money and capture value from delivering on the customer value proposition (CVP) that is outlined as part of their business model. As an entrepreneur, if you have a clear strategy for generating revenue from your business, you will have a better chance of surviving. Part of this strategy is asking a few simple questions:

- How much are my customers willing to pay?

- How many customers do I need?

- How much revenue can be generated through sales?

- If I have more than one revenue stream, how much does each stream contribute to the total?

Over the course of her career, Kathey Porter, featured in Entrepreneurship in Action, used different types of revenue models for each of her businesses. In the next section, we will take a look at the different types of revenue models that are available to the startup entrepreneur.

**Revenue:** the income gained from sales of goods or services.

**Revenue model:** a key component of the business model that identifies how the company will earn income and make profits.

Master the content at
**edge.sagepub.com/ neckentrepreneurship2e**

# Kathey Porter, Porter Brown Associates

**Kathey Porter, president and founder of Porter Brown Associates**

Kathey Porter is a consultant, author, college educator, and podcaster who focuses on entrepreneurs and small-business owners. But she started in the corporate world as a marketing executive for Revlon. Using her corporate experience, she later began helping small businesses become suppliers for larger companies. She believes the key to small-business growth is to have large companies as customers, often called a B2B (business to business) model.

As president and founder of Porter Brown Associates, Kathey operates a profitable and growing consulting enterprise. She and her team service the U.S. federal government, corporations, and small businesses. They train vendors to work with the federal government, help corporations connect and partner with smaller businesses, and act as a strategy consultant to those small businesses so they can scale. According to Kathey, their mission is quite simple: "We provide tools for our clients to be successful."

Kathey's road to successfully founding and operating Porter Brown Associates included more than just a stint in corporate America. She always maintained some form of side business but held off plunging 100% into entrepreneurship until her daughter was in college. "Timing is just as important as money," says Kathey. "The fastest way to go out of business is to take on more than you can handle. Entrepreneurs tend to want to take on everything, but only say yes if it complements your skillset. You can ruin yourself, your name, and your reputation by taking on more than you can handle."

Kathey is keenly aware that skills gaps and mismanagement of priorities can drive entrepreneurs to failure. She recalls an early failure when she opened and ran a seasonal franchise retail business in a mall. Due to miscommunication with the franchisor over the allocation of revenues, the store ran into financial hardship and had to file for bankruptcy. Another time, she passed on an offer by an investor to start a hair care line and instead opted to launch a children's bedding line. After months of preparing and finding a manufacturer in China, Kathey realized the bedding market was tough, if not one of the toughest, to penetrate, and she ended up missing out on a lot of upside in the hair care market. With these setbacks, she says, "At that time, I was embarrassed and ashamed, but I see now that it set me up for success with the consultancy. The lessons I learned now help me counsel other small-business owners."

Kathey says her skillset in entrepreneurship has been developed and built over time. "Just like doctors, lawyers, and others, it takes practice."

## Critical Thinking Questions

1. Kathey was a franchise owner, created a bedding line, and is now a consultant. Can you identify the revenue model she used for each?

2. Describe Kathey's path to successful business ownership. Why was corporate experience useful to her?

3. If you started a business using a professional revenue model, what service would you offer? ●

**Source:** Kathey Porter (interview with the author, December 2018)

## 9.2 DIFFERENT TYPES OF REVENUE MODELS

>> **LO 9.2**   **Illustrate the 10 most popular revenue models being used by entrepreneurs.**

As we have discussed, different types of revenue models have different revenue streams. Some companies operate using one primary revenue model while others use a combination of models.[1] Each type determines different ways in which revenue is generated, which also affects who your customers will be. For example, a retailer that generates revenue through online sales tends to attract the type of customers who prefer shopping from their computers or mobile devices rather than traveling to the local mall. Let's take a look at 10 main types of revenue models. Remember: The customer is not always your end user!

## Unit Sales Revenue Model

The **unit sales revenue model** measures the amount of revenue generated by the number of items (units) sold by a company. Typically, retail businesses rely on the unit sales revenue model by selling products or service directly to consumers, whether face-to-face or online. The idea is that you earn revenue when you sell the product or service to the end user. There are two different types of unit sales: physical goods, which include clothing, food and beverages, housewares and hardware, furniture, cars, and so forth; and intangibles, which are often digital products such as music sold through iTunes or games and apps sold to smartphones and tablets. Software support may also be unit priced, meaning that customers pay by the minute or by the hour.

Another variation of the unit sales revenue model is called the razor-and-razor-blade model. This phrase was coined by Gillette, which generates huge revenue from offering a physical product like razors at no or low cost to encourage sales of the more expensive razor blades (see Figure 9.1). This has also become known as the printers-and-ink model, which most of us have encountered: The printer is sold at a low cost, but the ink or toner cartridges are priced much higher, generating ongoing revenue for the printer manufacturer. Similarly, Sony and Microsoft discount their video game consoles, but the losses incurred are more than covered by the sales of the games themselves.[2]

**Unit sales revenue model:** generating revenue by the number of items (units) sold by a company.

## Advertising Revenue Model

The **advertising revenue model** relies on the amount of revenue gained through advertising products and services. Advertising has been around for a long time, as has this revenue model: A century ago, magazines and newspapers accepted advertisements and charged by the space or by the word, and early radio and television charged by the minute or second to broadcast ads. Today the ad revenue model has evolved from its traditional format to encompass the digital world.

Meaningful advertising revenue generated in the digital world is dependent on attracting traffic or developing a dominant niche. For example, Google AdWords is not only Google's main advertising product but also its main source of revenue. The AdWords service is a type of advertising revenue model called cost-per-click (CPC), which charges

**Advertising revenue model:** generating revenue by advertising products and services.

---

**FIGURE 9.1**

### The Razor-and-Razor-Blade Model

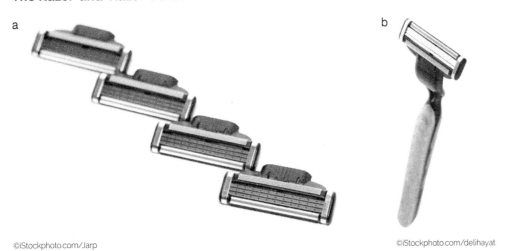

a

b

©iStockphoto.com/Jarp

©iStockphoto.com/delihayat

the advertiser a fee every time a user clicks on the ad. The model is intended to attract traffic to the advertiser's business while generating income for providing the AdWords service. AdWords also includes the cost-per-action (CPA) advertising model, whereby advertisers pay only when the click converts to an actual sale of a product or service. Google is an example of a business that has developed a niche by offering this form of advertising to people running businesses all over the world.

Another form of online advertising is called promoted content (also known as "sponsored" or "suggested" content), which works by having ads appear in the flow of the content that the users are reading. Often, these ads are blended in so neatly to the content that users may not even realize that they are ads. But Google isn't the only digital company with an advertising product. In 2018, Amazon became the third biggest online advertising platform behind Facebook and Google.[3] Many types of businesses use digital platforms such as Twitter, Facebook, Instagram, LinkedIn, Pinterest, Snapchat, and Yelp to publish paid ads to promote their services. For example, hand-dyed yarn startup Expression Fiber Arts uses Facebook to advertise by offering free products and downloads, discounts, and coupons. This advertising strategy has earned the company more than $1 million in annual sales over a 2-year period.[4]

## Data Revenue Model

**Data revenue model:** generating revenue by selling high-quality, exclusive, valuable information to other parties.

Companies use the data revenue model when they generate revenue by selling high-quality, exclusive, valuable information to other parties. There are more than 100 data brokers operating in the United States that buy and sell third-party data. Some of these data are sold to small organizations that help landlords research potential tenants, but a large portion of it is sold to people search organizations like Spokeo, Zoominfo, PeopleSmart, Intelius, and more.[5] Data brokers tend to collect third-party information from people with whom they have no relationship, while tech giants like Facebook, Google, and Amazon collect enormous amounts of detailed data directly from their users. In 2018, Facebook came under fire for allowing British political consulting firm Cambridge Analytica to harvest the personal data of millions of users without their consent and use it for political purposes.[6] As a consequence, the industry is under pressure to evolve and balance the value of data with the privacy of its users.

## Intermediation Revenue Model

**Intermediation revenue model:** the different methods by which third parties such as brokers (or "middlemen") can generate money.

**Brokers:** the people who organize transactions between buyers and sellers.

The intermediation revenue model describes the different methods by which third parties, such as brokers (or "middlemen"), can generate money. Brokers are people who organize transactions between buyers and sellers. These "middlemen" play important roles in connecting people to different services. For example, eBay acts as an auction broker as it manages the transaction between seller and buyer and generates revenue by charging a listing fee plus commission on a sale. Other common examples of intermediaries include real estate brokers who take a percentage commission each time they match a buyer and seller and credit card companies that earn revenue through the sales transaction process.

In recent years, various entrepreneurial ventures have emerged to put a new creative spin on the role of the middleman, in an effort to connect people with services in a more efficient and less expensive way. Well-known examples include Airbnb, which offers short-term accommodation that private homeowners rent out to visitors, usually tourists, at a fraction of the price of hotels, and Uber, which connects customers with drivers to provide a faster, more efficient ride-sharing service.

## Licensing Revenue Model

**Licensing revenue model:** earning revenue by giving permission to other parties to use protected intellectual property (patents, copyrights, trademarks) in exchange for fees.

The licensing revenue model is a way of earning revenue by giving permission to other parties to use protected intellectual property (copyrights, patents, and trademarks) in exchange for fees. We will explore intellectual property in more detail in Chapter 14. In the technology industry, technological innovations are licensed to other users. For example, when we use our personal computers, the software is under license from the developer of that software.

Technological innovations are often sold to larger companies that have the financial and technical expertise to maximize their potential. Take apps, for instance. Many people design iPhone apps and then license them to Apple, which has the capability to market them to a wider audience. However, licensing is not just limited to technology companies. Stephen Key, cofounder of licensing company inventRight, began by licensing his ideas for novelty gifts to specialty items companies, including bathtub toys, puppets, and a red plastic arrow emblazoned with the words, "Straight from my heart."[7]

Music-streaming app Spotify generates revenue from subscriptions, licensing, and on-screen advertising.

## Franchising Revenue Model

The franchising revenue model describes the process whereby the owner of an existing business (known as the franchisor) sells the rights to another party (known as a franchisee) to trade under the name of that business. The franchisor helps the franchisee by providing support in marketing, operations, and financing, and in return, the franchisee pays the franchisor royalties based on an agreed percentage of sales.

In Chapter 1, we explained the concept of franchising and how it can be a beneficial way for entrepreneurs to get a head start in launching their own businesses. By following an existing business model, entrepreneurs do not have to spend the same amount of time on marketing, building the brand, developing processes, and sourcing product.

Familiar franchises such as Anytime Fitness, Hampton Inns, Pizza Hut, Subway, KFC, and Supercuts regularly appear on lists of the top 500 franchises in the United States; however, some lesser-known (and somewhat quirky) franchises are also causing a bit of a stir. The Christmas Décor seasonal franchise is run by professional decorators who take the burden from homeowners by putting up Christmas decorations on their behalf. Or what about pooper scooper services franchise DoodyCalls? This franchise scoops 10 million poops from backyards and apartment complexes every year.[8]

**Franchising revenue model:** earning revenue by selling franchises of an existing business to allow another party to trade under the name of that business.

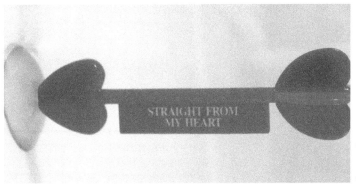

inventRight's novelty toy arrow

Source: https://www
.inventright.com/index
.php?option=com_
content&view=article&id=107

## Subscription Revenue Model

The subscription revenue model involves charging customers to gain continuous access to a product or service. This type of model has been traditionally applied to magazines and newspapers that charge customers a subscription fee to receive each issue of the publication. Today, a growing number of startup companies also use the subscription revenue model. For example, Blue Apron and Home Chef earn revenue by providing subscribers with a complete set of ingredients to make a meal at home; Birchbox delivers monthly beauty products to subscribers; and Barkbox charges a subscription fee to deliver a monthly box of doggy treats to dog lovers. Another type of subscription model is applied to user communities such as Angie's List, where members pay for access to a network of reviews on local businesses.

**Subscription revenue model:** charging customers to gain continuous access to a product or service.

## Professional Revenue Model

The professional revenue model provides professional services on a time and materials contract. For example, consultants, lawyers, and accountants often charge by the hour for their services. Websites like Get a Freelancer, PeoplePerHour, and Elance also use this model by allowing freelancers to charge a fixed fee for projects posted online by other companies.

**Professional revenue model:** earning revenue by providing professional services on a time and materials contract.

© DoodyCalls

**Dog waste service DoodyCalls uses a franchising revenue model.**

**Utility and usage revenue model:** a pay-as-you-go model that charges customers fees on the basis of how often goods or services are used.

**Freemium revenue model:** mixing free (mainly web-based) basic services with premium or upgraded services.

## Utility and Usage Revenue Model

The **utility and usage revenue model** charges customers fees on the basis of how often goods or services are used. This is also known as a pay-as-you-go model. Some mobile phone carriers use this model by charging users a fee for the number of minutes used on calls or for the volume of text messages.[9] The greater the number of minutes or volume of texts, the higher the payment. Hotels also use this model by charging customers by the night. Car rental companies also generate revenue through this model by charging per unit of time. For example, Avis and Hertz rent cars on a daily or weekly basis, while Zipcar rents cars by the hour, allowing multiple customers to use the same car at different times on the same day.[10]

## Freemium Revenue Model

The **freemium revenue model** involves mixing free (mainly web-based) basic services with premium or upgraded services. In this model, businesses create at least two versions or tiers of products or services. The company gives away the low-end version of the service for free. The free "basic" version usually comes with limits on usage and functionality. The company also creates and sells higher-end versions that offer more functionality and performance. The business networking site LinkedIn gives members free access to build a profile and maintain a professional network. It charges a fee for its premium service, which further benefits job seekers and recruiters with added functions such as search filtering, sending personalized messages, and tracking visits to one's profile. Similarly, online tool SurveyMonkey allows users to create free surveys with up to 10 questions, with an allowance of up to 100 responses. SurveyMonkey charges a fee to upgrade to its premium service, which provides users with the ability to customize their survey designs and receive unlimited responses.[11]

So far, we have explored the typical ways in which businesses generate revenue through different types of revenue models. These are summarized in Table 9.1.

**TABLE 9.1**

Ten Types of Revenue Models

| | |
|---|---|
| **Unit Sales** | The amount of revenue generated by the number of items (units) sold by a company |
| **Advertising** | The amount of revenue gained through advertising products and services |
| **Data** | The amount of revenue generated by selling high-quality, exclusive, valuable information to other parties |
| **Intermediation** | The amount of revenue generated by third parties |
| **Licensing** | The amount of revenue generated by giving permission to other parties to use protected intellectual property (patents, copyrights, trademarks) in exchange for fees |
| **Franchising** | The process whereby franchises are sold by an existing business to allow another party to trade under the name of that business |
| **Subscription** | The amount of revenue generated by charging customers payment to gain continuous access to a product or service |
| **Professional** | The amount of revenue generated by providing professional services on a time and materials contract |
| **Utility and Usage** | The amount of revenue generated by charging customers fees on the basis of how often goods or services are used |
| **Freemium** | The amount of revenue gained by mixing free (mainly web-based) basic services with premium or upgraded services |

# Revenue Model Pivot Practice

Your entire business can pivot if your revenue model changes. Not all revenue models fit for all business types, but it can be fun to experiment with different models just to see the possibilities. Refer to Table 9.1 and our discussion on the 10 types of revenue models. Let's say we had an idea for a new app that kept track of all the food in your house or apartment. At any given time, you could open the app and see the food inventory in your refrigerator, freezer, and pantry. The app would tell you when food was expired and could even offer recipes that use the food you have on hand. The "unit sales" revenue model would be to sell the app in the app store for $5.99. If we changed to an "advertising" revenue model, we would likely let people download the app for free and earn revenue through the sales of advertising. Potential advertisers could be grocery stores, food TV networks, publishers of food books or magazines, etc. If we then changed to a "professional" revenue model, our app may not exist at all. We may simply charge people to let us enter their homes on a weekly basis and do the inventory for them as well as cook meals. Now, the professional model may not make sense, but bringing a business through each revenue model may uncover new opportunities. What if we used a "subscription" revenue model for the food inventory app? What would this look like? Well, maybe the original concept of the inventory app would go away, but we could offer a delivery service that would deliver the ingredients for you to cook your own meal at home. No inventory and no waste! Sound familiar? Take a look at businesses that have been started on the concept of food kits: Blue Apron, Home Chef, HelloFresh, Sun Basket, and Purple Carrot, just to name a few.

For this Mindshift, take the product or service you are working on and apply the 10 revenue models in Table 9.1 to your idea. Yes, some of them may not make sense, but many of them will. Think creatively!

## Critical Thinking Questions

1. Did you notice that when you change the revenue model the customer often changes as well?

2. Did you find a revenue model that works better for your idea than your original model?

3. Did your idea change dramatically in some models versus others? Which ones and how? ●

In the next section, we take a closer look at how some companies have generated revenue by profiting from "free."

# 9.3 GENERATING REVENUE FROM "FREE"

**>> LO 9.3  Explain how companies generate revenue by profiting from "free."**

Many of us like getting a bargain, but most of us love the idea of getting something for free. But as an entrepreneur running your own business, how comfortable would you feel giving away your products and services for nothing? Unlikely as it may sound, the freemium revenue model, which offers a product or service for zero cost, is becoming more popular as a means of encouraging widespread customer adoption (see Figure 9.2).[12]

Skype is an example of a freemium model that provides the functionality to make free calls, which are fully routed through the Internet. Because of its lack of infrastructure, the costs of running Skype are minimal. It earns its revenue by charging for Skypeout, a premium service that charges users low rates for calling landlines and cell phones. In 2011, Skype was acquired by Microsoft for $8.5 billion.

The free newspaper *Metro* is another great example of a business that gives away a free product yet still makes huge profits. The *Metro* was first circulated in Stockholm, Sweden, before being made available in dozens of cities all over the world. In Britain in particular, the *Metro* has become the nation's most profitable newspaper.[13] But how does the *Metro* team make money from giving away free newspapers?

First, its readership is wealthy commuters, on average around 37 years old (described as "urbanites")—a demographic that attracts advertisers such as large supermarket chains and businesses that pay generously to reach this target audience. The *Metro* is also paid to feature major events such as Wimbledon tennis and other annual occasions. Second, the *Metro* keeps its editorial costs low by keeping its content short, punchy, and easy to read—just engaging enough for a quick 20-minute read on the train or bus to or from

# How to Make an Ad

Peter Horree/Alamy Stock Photo

**Red Bull paid $13 million to settle a false advertising lawsuit for its slogan, "Red Bull gives you wings."**

Even if an entrepreneur does not choose an ad-based revenue model, the world of entrepreneurship is riddled with advertisements. Every new venture needs a certain amount of marketing to bridge the gap between consumer and product or consumer and service. That marketing could be in the form of sales calls, in which some persuasion must be done to pique the interest of consumers.

The inevitable ethical issue of truthfulness comes as a natural result of advertisements. Can an advertisement stretch the truth? Could it be ethical to try to convince people to buy a product that they don't need?

The Federal Trade Commission has banned any advertising that is untruthful, misleading, and unfair. However, there is an ethical gray area, which stretches beyond the prosecution of

the law. A slight exaggeration will rarely draw the ire of the law but could bring the dissatisfaction of a customer.

For the most part, consumers demand a certain level of accountability in advertising, and there are official organizations in a number of countries that vet advertisements for truthfulness. Additionally, consumers, themselves, have a tendency to respond negatively to advertisements that feel misleading, and they have developed the ability to filter out traditionally seductive advertising.

Nonetheless, the question will inevitably arise of how to market a product or service to create revenue. Entrepreneurs could find a hazardous substance in their product and choose to market their product despite the public health issue. Eventually, though, the desire for accountability from consumers tends to bring those hazardous substances to light.

## Critical Thinking Questions

1. Could an advertisement be legal, yet unethical?

2. How much accountability is demanded of advertisements in the modern economy?

3. Does truthfulness matter in issues of business? ●

**Sources:**

Benge, V. A. (n.d.). The federal truth in advertising law. *AZCentral.* Retrieved from https://yourbusiness.azcentral.com/federal-truth-advertising-law-7108.html

Federal Trade Commission. (n.d.). Truth in advertising. *FTC.gov.* Retrieved from https://www.ftc.gov/news-events/media-resources/truth-advertising

LaMarco, N. (2018, December 3). Negative effects of false advertising. *Houston Chronicle.* Retrieved from https://smallbusiness.chron.com/negative-effects-false-advertising-25679.html

## FIGURE 9.2

### Freemium

©iStockphoto.com/venimo

work. Finally, it has developed its own distribution network by controlling news racks in train and bus stations where commuters can help themselves to the free publication. However, making "free" work financially is not without its risks. Obviously, if you are giving away something for nothing, you need to make sure you are still earning substantial revenues. The key to a sustainable revenue model involving "free" is earning enough money on some part of the business to pay for the costs of supporting the free side of the business.

Let's look at the two types of free financial models.

© wichayada suwanachun / Shutterstock

**Free communication and video chat service, Skype**

## Direct Cross-Subsidies

Direct cross-subsidies refers to pricing a product or service above its market value to pay for the loss of giving away a product or service for free or below its market value. For example, cell phone companies lose money by giving away the phone handsets for free, but then they cover the loss by charging monthly service fees.[14] Similarly, some airlines advertise amazingly low fares, but then add fees for amenities like checked bags, additional legroom, or the ability to choose one's seat. Hotels may offer a low nightly rate but then add a mandatory "resort fee"—even if the guest doesn't use any of the hotel's "resort" facilities.

Cross-subsidization attracts customers by eliminating, or reducing, the up-front cost of a product or service. It then makes up the loss with subsequent charges, which the company expects customers to be willing to pay because they are pleased with the product or service and don't want to go through the hassle of switching. The added business gained by attracting customers with the below-market price generates more revenues for the organization through the cross-subsidy fees. Table 9.2 lists several ways of implementing direct cross-subsidies.

**Direct cross-subsidies:** pricing a product or service above its market value to pay for the loss of giving away a product or service for free or below its market value.

---

**TABLE 9.2**

Ideas for Direct Cross-Subsidies

- Give away services, sell products
- Give away products, sell services
- Give away software, sell hardware
- Give away hardware, sell software
- Give away cell phones, sell minutes of talk time
- Give away talk time, sell cell phones
- Give away the show, sell the drinks
- Give away the drinks, sell the show

---

## Multiparty Markets

A multiparty business involves giving a product or service to one party for free, but charging the other party or parties (see Table 9.3). The classic example of a multiparty market is the ad-supported free content model so common on the Internet: Consumers get access to content for free while advertisers pay for access. Similarly, some online dating services allow women to enroll for free while men pay substantial charges to participate. Other examples include allowing job seekers to post résumés for free while charging employers for posting jobs, or giving children free admission while charging adults.

**Multiparty business:** giving one party a product or service free, but charging the other party (or parties).

**TABLE 9.3**

Ideas for Multiparty Markets

| IDEA | EXAMPLE |
|------|---------|
| Give away scientific articles, charge authors to publish them | Public Library of Science |
| Give away document readers, sell document writers | Adobe |
| Give away listings, sell premium search | Match.com |
| Sell listings, give away search | Craigslist New York Housing |
| Give away travel services, get a cut of rental car and hotel reservations | Travelocity |
| Give away house listings, sell mortgages | Zillow |
| Give away content, sell stuff | Slashdot/ThinkGeek |
| Give away résumé listings, charge for power search | LinkedIn |

**Source:** Anderson, C. (2009). *Free: The future of a radical price.* New York, NY: Hyperion.

The challenge for the multiparty market model is to prevent costly overuse by those who get the service for free, as well as making the business valuable enough to the party that does pay.

Financially, the freemium model is often a viable option for web-based companies because of the low marginal cost of providing the service for free users: Online storage and bandwidth are cheap. However, companies running freemium models need to be constantly focused on the average cost of running the service for free users, as well as the rates at which free users convert to paying users. If the costs of supporting free customers grows too high or the number of paying customers is too low, the freemium business model will not work. Table 9.4 gives examples of some freemium ideas.

**TABLE 9.4**

Freemium Ideas

| IDEA | EXAMPLE |
|------|---------|
| Give away basic information, sell richer information in easier-to-use form | BoxOfficeMojo |
| Give away federal income tax software, sell state income tax software | TurboTax |
| Give away online games, charge a subscription to do more in a game | Club Penguin |
| Give away computer-to-computer calls, sell computer-to-telephone calls | Skype |
| Give away free photo-sharing services, charge for additional storage space | Flickr |

**Source:** Anderson, C. (2009). *Free: The future of a radical price.* New York, NY: Hyperion.

## 9.4 REVENUE AND COST DRIVERS

**>> LO 9.4   Identify the drivers that affect revenue as well as cost.**

Now that we have explored the freemium model, let's take a look at how companies drive revenue.[15] Revenue models influence who your customers are and how you reach them. Although choosing and establishing your revenue model is an important step, it is equally important to have a deep understanding of what is driving both your revenue and your cost, in order to generate as much value (profit) as possible for your company.

## Revenue Drivers

It's tempting to believe that merely selling products or services will make you money, but more factors must be taken into consideration. Drawing from the information we have provided so far in this chapter, let's apply some key revenue drivers to the idea for a new funky coffee shop. The coffee shop provides unlimited coffee for free but charges a per-minute flat fee for the amount of time your customers spend in the café.[16]

As illustrated in Figure 9.3, the first key revenue driver is your *customers*. How many customers will come into your coffee shop? How much are they willing to pay to stay? How will you attract customers to your location?

The second key driver is *frequency*. How often will your customers come into your coffee shop? What incentives can you offer to keep them coming back?

The third driver is *selling process*. How much time will you be able to sell? What kind of upselling or cross-selling opportunities can you find? For example, you might add products such as snacks to sell alongside the unlimited free coffee to generate more revenue.

The fourth driver is *price*. If you think your price per minute should be higher than what your competitors charge, what are the factors that increase the value of your product? If you raise or lower prices, what will be the impact on your customer base?[17]

But how do you determine your revenue drivers when your business hasn't even begun yet? By getting out of the building! Actively testing your assumptions and hypotheses is the best way of figuring out the underlying factors that will drive revenue for your business.

For example, let's take a look at the first key revenue driver: your customers. You might be able to sketch a brief outline of the number of customers you think will come to your coffee shop, but how do you get a more accurate estimate? You may think that customers will be attracted to your coffee shop because it is unique and trendy, but no matter how great you think your coffee shop is, people won't come if it's in the wrong location. A coffee shop situated on the outskirts of town, with very little around it, is not conducive to attracting foot traffic. Ideally, you want your coffee shop to be in a location with a high density of shoppers, which means city centers and shopping malls. If your target customer base is students, then you would want to be close to a university campus.

---

**FIGURE 9.3**

**Four Key Revenue Drivers**

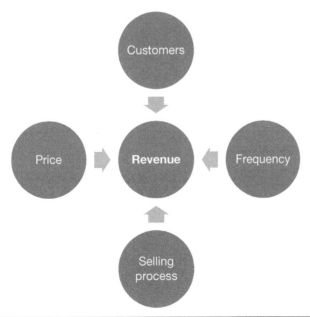

---

For more details about revenue drivers, see Supplement A: Financial Statements and Projections for Startups.

Renting a retail space in these shopping districts is expensive, so you need to be sure that enough people will be attracted to your coffee shop to walk in and pay to spend time there on a regular basis. How do you justify paying high rent before you even open for business?

One of the best ways to scout suitable locations for your coffee shop and determine the number of customers that might potentially buy from you is to go to your local shopping mall and watch customers as they go in and out of different coffee shops. Do this on different days, and at different times of day. Record the busy and slow periods. This will give you a better idea of the volume of customers you might expect to walk into your coffee shop and therefore the revenue you can expect to get. This, in turn, will enable you to determine whether the volume of traffic will justify the expense of the high rent you will need to pay for an advantageous location.

## Cost Drivers

Understanding the factors that drive costs are just as important as your key revenue drivers.

When it comes to cost drivers, two different types of costs should be taken into consideration: cost of goods sold (COGS) and operating expenses. COGS and operating expenses are both types of expenses, but there are some differences between them.

**Cost of goods sold (COGS):** the direct cost of producing a product.

### Cost of Goods Sold (COGS)

COGS occur when a sale takes place. For example, with regard to a T-shirt store, the cost is in how much money it takes to produce each T-shirt: the material, the design, the manufacturing, the packaging, and so on. Once you know how much goes into producing your T-shirts, you can think about ways to reduce costs, if you need to. For example, you might find a lower-cost manufacturer, or use less expensive material, or even negotiate with young artists to see if they can provide their designs at a lower cost. Lowering the COGS means you could potentially sell your T-shirts at a lower price to your customers.

However, there also needs to be a balance between reducing your costs and satisfying your customer. In other words, you would need to ensure that you are not devaluing your product to the extent that it would reduce your customers' willingness to buy it at all. For example, if your customers are attracted to your T-shirts because of their great quality, then it would be unwise to use cheaper material to save costs. If you can get the balance right, you can use the savings you make to invest in other areas, such as marketing or reducing debt.

### Operating Expenses

**Operating expenses:** the costs of running your business, including your rent, utilities, administration, marketing/advertising, employee salaries, and so on.

Operating expenses are the costs of running your business, including your rent, utilities, administration, marketing/advertising, employee salaries, and so forth (see Figure 9.4). These kinds of expenses are more difficult to reduce. Cutting operating expenses can yield beneficial short-term gains, but it does not always work in the long term—for reasons we explore next.

**FIGURE 9.4**

**Retail Operating Expenses**

| Operating Expenses | |
| --- | --- |
| • Rent | • Insurance |
| • Utilities | • Transportation |
| • Administration | • Taxes |
| • Marketing/Advertising | • Legal Fees |
| • Salaries | • Office Supplies |
| • Accounting | • Benefits |

Imagine that you have a retail store and wish to cut operating expenses. If you move your store to a cheaper but less popular location to save on rent, you will save more money. However, over time you might lose out on revenue because the new location might not attract as many customers—or the right kind of customers—compared to the more expensive location. Similarly, you will save costs if you cut out advertising and marketing expenses, but as sales depend on marketing, in the long term, you will lose customer awareness. When people don't know about your store, or start forgetting about it, your sales will suffer.

Another way to decrease operating costs is to reduce employee salaries or reduce the number of employees altogether, which has an immediate positive effect on the bottom line. However, it also might damage customer relationships if there aren't enough skilled, knowledgeable staff to help drive sales. Striking the right balance in the areas of COGS and operating expenses can be tricky, but if you know your business inside out, it becomes more manageable over time. Covering your expenses depends on sales of your product and service, and successful sales require a carefully constructed pricing strategy.

## Income Statement

When your company is finally up and running, you will need some financial tools to help you measure the revenue generated and your company's profitability. The income statement (or profit and loss statement) is a financial report that shows revenue, expenses, and profit for a period of time, typically a month, quarter, or year. It subtracts the COGS and expenses (administrative, marketing, research, and other operating expenses) from the total revenue to give you a net income figure, which will be either a profit or a loss. Furthermore, every entrepreneur needs to develop a pro-forma income statement to estimate the impact of revenue and expense on the profit of the venture. While the income statement is based on measuring financial activities on a monthly or annual basis, the pro forma income statement is a projection or estimate of what the company could potentially do (see Supplement A: Financial Statements and Projections for Startups).

The income statement also reflects depreciation and amortization of your company's assets. Depreciation really means the cost of wear and tear on your physical assets such as machinery, equipment, and the building in which you operate. When you purchase an asset that has a useful life of more than 1 year, you will not include the entire cost of that asset on the income statement in the year that it is purchased. Instead, you are able to spread the cost of that asset over a predetermined period of time; therefore, you record only a portion of the cost each year until the asset is fully depreciated. Amortization works similarly to depreciation; the main difference is that amortization relates to intangible assets such as patents, trademarks, copyrights, and business methodologies. Amortization matches the useful life of an intangible asset with the revenue it generates. A sample income statement is illustrated in Figure 9.5.

**Income statement (or profit and loss statement):** a financial report that shows revenue, expenses, and profit for a period of time, typically a month, quarter, or year.

**FIGURE 9.5**

**Sample Income Statement**

| | |
|---|---|
| **Revenue** | $200,000 |
| (-) Cost of Goods | $100,000 |
| **Gross Profit** | $100,000 |
| (-) Sales, General and Administrative | $50,000 |
| (-) Marketing | $5,000 |
| (-) Research and Development | $2,000 |
| (-) Depreciation and Amortization | $2,000 |
| **Operating Profit** | $41,000 |
| (-) Interest Expense | $1,230 |
| (-) Taxes | $8,500 |
| **Net Income** | $31,270 |

# The Dark Side of Entrepreneurship

Entrepreneurship can be both productive and unproductive in an economy. Productive motives are those that benefit society, while unproductive motives are those that can do more harm than good. Generally, entrepreneurship focuses on positive outcomes such as job creation, economic growth, and technological progress. However, there is a darker side of entrepreneurship that can be unproductive. Unproductive entrepreneurs have been referred to as parasites that can damage the economy.

Researchers Hmieleski and Lerner wanted to study dark personality characteristics of individuals *intending* to start a business and their *motives* (productive or unproductive) for doing so. They looked at what psychologists refer to as the dark triad: narcissism, psychopathy, and Machiavellianism. *Narcissim* relates to one's self-centeredness and the need for attention and admiration from others. Those that are high in narcissism "are superior and too important to be bothered by others' needs." *Psychopathic* people demonstrate little, if any, empathy. Interestingly, those high in psychopathy do very well under stressful and uncertain conditions. Yet, they have been described as "insensitive to the needs of others and lack remorse." *Machiavellianism* relates to the need for money, power, and competition, and these types are likely to engage in deviant behaviors.

Next, Hmieleski and Lerner identified potential productive and unproductive motives for wanting to start a business.

## Productive Entrepreneurial Motives

- Generate value for society
- Produce products/services that enrich the lives of people
- Develop a culture in which its employees value their work
- Be admired for the value that it adds to the community
- Attract employees who value the mission of the company as though it were their own

## Unproductive Entrepreneurial Motives

- Achieve financial success, even if it is a little destructive to society
- Maximize profits, even at the cost of employees' well-being
- Grow quickly, even if it means sacrificing quality
- Earn financial profit at all costs
- Outsource work to reduce costs as much as possible

The sample included 508 undergraduate and 234 graduate students at U.S. business schools because the researchers wanted to study individuals who *intended* to start a business rather than entrepreneurs who had already started a business. Hmieleski and Lerner had two questions they wanted to answer with their data:

1. Are narcissism, psychopathy, and Machiavellianism positively associated with a person's intention to start a business?

2. How do narcissism, psychopathy, and Machiavellianism relate to motives for starting a business? Are the motives productive or unproductive?

For Question 1, researchers found that for both undergraduate and graduate students, the higher the narcissism the more likely the student was intending to start a business. When it came to psychopathy and Machiavellianism, there were no significant conclusions. Those dark personality characteristics didn't impact intention to start a business. However, narcissism played a strong role in predicting who intended to become an entrepreneur.

When examining entrepreneurial motives (Question 2), it was found that students with strong intentions to start a business had unproductive motives if they scored high on psychopathy and Machiavellianism. Conversely, students with strong intentions to start a business had productive motives if they demonstrated lower levels of psychopathy and Machiavellianism. Unlike the MBA sample, narcissistic undergraduates were more likely to have productive entrepreneurial motives. The researchers concluded that undergraduates have a "desire for attention and admiration, considering the social appeal of productive value creation—particularly among idealistic undergraduates who are currently part of a generation that has grown up with models of prosocial-oriented startups being viewed as cool by their peers."

## Critical Thinking Questions

1. Can you identify examples of productive and unproductive entrepreneurship in society?

2. As you read this, you might have intentions to start a business someday. What are your motives for doing so?

3. What's your opinion on the researchers' conclusion that this generation of undergraduates wants to be a part of prosocial-oriented startups? ●

**Sources:**

Baumol, W. J. (1990). Productive, unproductive, and destructive. *Journal of Political Economy, 98*(5), 893–921.

Hmieleski, K. M., & Lerner, D. A. (2016). The dark triad and nascent entrepreneurship: An examination of unproductive versus productive entrepreneurial motives. *Journal of Small Business Management, 54*(S1), 7–32.

The operating profit represents the amount left over from revenue once all costs and expenses are subtracted. The interest expense is a good indicator of the company's debt, as it represents interest due in the period on any borrowed money. Taxes are the last expense item before net income. This line item includes all federal, state, and municipal taxes that are due for the period.

Net income is what is left after all costs, expenses, and taxes have been paid; it shows the company's real bottom line. Over time, you can begin to compare your company's income statements; this helps you chart trends in your company's financial performance. The trends will, in turn, help you to set financial goals and strategies.

## 9.5 PRICING STRATEGIES

>> **LO 9.5**  **Identify different strategies entrepreneurs use when pricing their product or service.**

Startup entrepreneurs often struggle with how much to charge for their products or services. If your price is too high, you might drive customers away, but if your price is too low, then you run the risk of making very little profit. So, where do you begin?[18]

Let's say you want to start an online luxury cupcake business. You plan to make the cupcakes from fresh, natural, organic ingredients, at home with some part-time help from a friend. A courier service will deliver the beautifully packaged and personalized cupcakes up to a distance of 200 miles from your location. Your cupcake business is designed to target events such as weddings, children's parties, and corporate gatherings. If the business takes off, you aim to open a retail space in your local area and hire a couple of employees to help you run the business.

To find out how much to charge, you need to find out the going rate of cupcakes. The best place to begin is to check out your competition. Visit cupcake stores and other online cupcake companies and see how much they charge. Don't be afraid to ask people in the cupcake business direct questions about pricing and running a cupcake business; most people want to help and will be happy to give advice. Besides, making connections in this way may lead to partnerships or collaborations in the future.

In addition, talk to your friends and family to see how much they would pay, or have paid for cupcakes in the past, and ask them to share their experiences of online cupcake companies if they have used them before. You could even send out a survey to all your contacts asking them what price they would be willing to pay for a single delicious cupcake or box of premium cupcakes.

The next step is to think about your customers. What can they afford to pay? For example, you may decide to charge a higher rate for catering corporate events versus providing cupcakes for children's parties.

The key to sustaining a new business is to create consistent revenue streams. Once you have acquired new customers, your goal is to hear from them again and again. For events like weddings and children's parties, this may be difficult as they are typically one-time events. However, these customers may tell their friends how pleased they were with your service, and guests at the events may be impressed with how delicious and beautifully decorated your cupcakes were. Thus, you will rely largely on referrals and word of mouth to get more business in those areas. For corporate events, on the other hand, there are ample opportunities for repeat business. You could approach a corporation and offer a contract agreeing to provide cupcakes for all their corporate events, or a certain number of events per year. This would bring you a steady stream of revenue from a regular client.

Gigi Butler built America's most successful cupcake business, with 93 outlets operating in 23 states.

ZUMA Press Inc/Alamy Stock Photo

In addition, it is helpful to compare yourself to others in the field. Do you have the right credentials to run an online cupcake business? What experience do you have in the bakery business? What sort of business experience do you have to operate as an online cupcake company? If you have less experience than others, then you might want to consider charging lower prices to win new clients and gain real experience. However, if you have a background in bakery and catering, already have a solid customer base, and have business qualifications to match, then you could feasibly charge higher rates.

Once you have a better idea of your competition, your target market, and how your qualifications measure up against others, it is time to plan your pricing strategy.

## Pricing Products and Services

There is no right way to determine your pricing strategy, nor is there any such thing as long-term fixed pricing. As your business evolves, your prices will adjust according to demand. The best way to set a price is to base it on the information you have already gathered.

Several factors might influence your pricing strategy. For example, the positioning and brand of your product or service will affect how much it sells for. Understanding your brand is also very important when defining your business. Start defining your brand by choosing a name, logo, and design for your website. A useful exercise is to think of three to five words to describe your business that sets it apart from other competitors; for example, if very few competitors offer home delivery, you could include this in your brand description: "Luxury cupcakes delivered at home." Once you have defined your brand, you can carry the theme through your packaging, website, marketing materials, and other communications with potential customers.[19]

Using the cupcake example, think about how you are positioning your online cupcake business in the market. As you are promoting your cupcakes as a luxury product, you need to aim for a price that isn't too low. A low price on a luxury product can cause customers to doubt the quality of the item being sold.

## Different Types of Pricing Strategies

There are many different pricing strategies used by different companies. Let's take a look at some common pricing strategies (see Figure 9.6).[20]

### Competition-Led Pricing

**Competition-led pricing:** a pricing strategy that matches prices to other businesses selling the same or very similar products and services.

In competition-led pricing, you copy the prices suggested by other businesses selling the same or very similar products and services. However, matching a price is not generally enough to encourage customers to buy from you, especially if you're not an

**FIGURE 9.6**

**Pricing Strategies**

**Source:** www.learnmarketing.net

established brand. You need to find other ways to differentiate your product from your competitors to attract more customers.

## Customer-Led Pricing

In **customer-led pricing**, you ask customers how much they are willing to pay and then offer your product at that price. This is a technique used by some airlines signed up to the commercial website Priceline, to offer passengers a chance to name their own price for flights. Passengers make bids—however, they don't ultimately control the fares; the airline accepts or rejects each bid depending on how acceptable it is and whether other customers are willing to pay more for the same flight. This "name your own price technique" is a useful way of attracting people to your company, and it still allows you a measure of control over your own pricing.

**Customer-led pricing:** a pricing strategy that asks customers how much they are willing to pay and then offers the product at that price.

## Loss Leader

A **loss leader** is the practice of offering a product or service at a below-cost price in an attempt to attract more customers. This involves giving special discounts and reducing prices. Loss leaders can be an effective way of competing with an established brand offering similar products and services.

Walmart and Amazon are two examples of major companies that adopt the loss leader pricing strategy to compete in the marketplace.

However, there has to be some kind of consistency to raising and lowering prices; for example, a customer who has just bought a product at full price the previous day will not be pleased if that same product is being sold at a deep discount the next day. Therefore, it is important to know how long the lower price can be sustained and to know when to readjust pricing before the business begins to lose money.

**Loss leader:** a pricing strategy whereby a business offers a product or service at a lower price in an attempt to attract more customers.

## Introductory Offer

The idea of the **introductory offer** is to encourage people to try your new product by offering it for free or at a heavily discounted price for a certain number of days or to the first 100 customers. Introductory pricing is generally used for new products or services on the market. For example, San Francisco–based ecommerce business Headsets.com, founded by CEO Mike Faith, offers new products at a lower price to attract a loyal customer base.[21]

**Introductory offer:** a pricing strategy to encourage people to try a new product by offering it for free or at a heavily discounted price.

## Skimming

**Skimming** is a form of high pricing, generally used for new products or services that face very little or even no competition. If your product is the first on the market, then you can sell it at a higher price and retain the maximum value upfront, until you are forced to gradually reduce your prices when competitors launch rival products. Innovative products like the iPad and Sony PlayStation 3, which were originally priced high when they were launched, are good examples of price skimming.[22]

**Skimming:** a high pricing strategy, generally used for new products or services that face very little or even no competition.

## Psychological Pricing

Customers' perceptions of price points are also important to the sale. **Psychological pricing** is intended to encourage customers to buy based on their belief that the product or service is cheaper than it really is. Flash sales, "buy one get one free," and bundled products are all methods of psychological pricing. In addition, specific prices, such as those ending in $0.99, are popular with customers, as $19.99 is a more appealing figure to most than $20. Odd though it may sound, pricing your product or service one cent lower can make a difference between selling and not selling. McDonald's, Chili's, and KFC are among dozens of fast-food restaurants that use psychological pricing to attract customers.

**Psychological pricing:** a pricing strategy intended to encourage customers to buy on the basis of their belief that the product or service is cheaper than it really is.

## Fair Pricing

**Fair pricing** is the degree to which both businesses and customers believe that the pricing is reasonable. Having done your financial homework as an entrepreneur, you might

**Fair pricing:** the degree to which both businesses and customers believe that the pricing is reasonable.

**FIGURE 9.7**

**Bundled Pricing**

think your product or service is priced fairly—but that doesn't mean your customers will. Regardless of how much benefit to the customer or how valuable you think your offering is, there are some customers who are simply unwilling to pay the asking price for items or services if they do not perceive it to be fair. This is where market testing can help to define what people perceive as a fair maximum price versus an unfair price.

### Bundled Pricing

A form of psychological pricing, **bundled pricing** is packaging a set of goods or services together; they are then sold for a lower price than if they were to be sold separately (see Figure 9.7). The customers feel they are getting a bargain, and the increased sales generate more profit for the company. Common examples of bundled pricing include fast-food value meals, *prix fixe* meals at restaurants, snack food combos at movie theaters, cell phone packages, and cable TV packages.

Once you have decided which type of pricing is the right one for your business, then it's time to start making some proper calculations.

**Bundled pricing:** a pricing strategy whereby companies package a set of goods or services together and then sell them for a lower price than if they were to be sold separately.

## 9.6 CALCULATING PRICE

>> **LO 9.6** **Explain different methods of calculating price.**

Number crunching is not an exact science, but there are a few ways to calculate prices that will help you decide which one is best for your business.[23] The key to pricing is to ensure you make a profit, as well as to create value for your customers.

Break-even analysis can also help set price. Break-even is that point when your revenue equals your costs. Then, anything sold beyond break-even is considered profit.

A quick break-even analysis can help entrepreneurs quickly determine what they need to sell monthly or yearly, and in some cases daily or weekly, to cover the costs of running the business—the cost drivers we have already discussed in this chapter.

Break-even is express both in units and in dollars. For example, you may hear an entrepreneur say that her monthly break-even is 1,000 units. If the selling price of each unit is $20, then the break-even can also be said to be $20,000 (1,000 units x $20 per unit) per month.

Let's start with calculating break-even units using the following formula:

Break-even units = Fixed costs/(sales price per unit – variable cost per unit)

Fixed costs are those costs that stay the same regardless of how much revenue you are generating or how much product you produce. These costs are typically those operating expenses that are incurred outside of actually producing the product, such as rent, salaries, and utilities. Though not always suggested in the accounting textbooks, entrepreneurs should use their total operating costs as their fixed costs because it's closer to reality for a startup.[24]

The sales price per unit is the selling price, such as the $20 in our brief example above. If you have multiple products, you can simply use an average sales price per unit. For example, if you were calculating the sales price per unit for a restaurant, you would use the average sale per person.

Variable cost per unit is the COGS plus any operating expenses that actually go up and down with production of the product. These may include shipping, inventory costs, or sales commissions.

Now let's look at a simple example involving a potential smoothie café. Here's what we know based on research:

- We want to sell smoothies at an average price of $6.50.

- Monthly fixed costs include rent, payroll, advertising, insurance, taxes. These total $6,000 per month.

- The variable expenses include the fruit, milk, yogurt, juice, vegetables, ice—everything that goes into making the smoothie. Here you have to determine the cost of one smoothie. For example:

Fruit: $0.75

Milk: $0.50

Juice: $0.25

Vegetable: $1.00

Cup: $1.00

Ice: $0.10

The total variable cost per one smoothie would be $3.60.

Now we have enough information to calculate break-even units:

BEU = $6000 / ($6.50 – $3.60)

BEU = 2,069

Our smoothie café would have to sell 2,069 smoothies on a monthly basis before we start to become profitable. Now, you have to ask yourself, "Is this possible?" Additionally, you can play with the variables. What if you increased the selling price to $8.00 per smoothie? This would certainly reduce the number of smoothies to break even, but what happens if your competition is selling their smoothies closer to $6.50? You could reduce the variable costs or not include as many ingredients in each smoothie. You could also look to lower some of your fixed costs. Can you find a better location in a lower-rent area? Do you need to hire so many people in the beginning? It's best to put all of these data in an Excel spreadsheet, and you can begin playing around with the numbers. There are also break-even calculators on the Internet that you can use, but we encourage making your own spreadsheet based on your own variable and fixed costs.

# Is Value the Same Thing as Price?

| PRODUCT | WHAT DO I PAY, OR WHAT WOULD I PAY? | ACTUAL PRICE FOUND ONLINE (OR PRICE RANGE) | PRICE DIFFERENCE |
|---|---|---|---|
| Extra-whitening toothpaste with mouthwash in the paste (average-size tube) | | | |
| Artisan, wood-fired pizza with local ingredients (large) | | | |
| 100% electric car, 4 door | | | |
| Bath soap (1 bar) | | | |

Using the chart on this page, identify what you think you pay, or would pay, for the listed items. Then, look up the actual price on the Internet.

## Critical Thinking Questions

1. What are the differences between your pricing estimates and the actual pricing? What do you believe is the source of the differences?

2. As a consumer, do you care more about the price of certain items than others? What influences your level of concern about price?

3. In this exercise, did you learn anything that surprised you? ●

## Cost-Led Pricing

**Cost-led pricing:** a pricing strategy that involves calculating all the costs of manufacturing or delivering the product or service, plus all other expenses, and adding an expected profit or margin by predicting your sales volume to get the approximate price.

Cost-led pricing involves calculating all the costs involved in manufacturing or delivering the product or service, plus all other expenses, and adding an expected profit or margin by predicting your sales volume to get the approximate price.

For example, say it costs you a total of $2 to make a cupcake. To cover your costs, you could add a 50% markup, which would mean selling each cupcake at $3, resulting in a profit of $1 per cupcake. However, you would need to make sure that this price was competitive—too low and it will put people off by giving an impression of poor quality; too high and you may be pricing your cupcakes out of the market. You also need to ensure that you will have enough people buying the cupcakes to generate profit for your business.

## Target-Return Pricing

**Target-return pricing:** a pricing method whereby the price is based on the amount of investment you have put into your business.

Target-return pricing involves setting your price based on the amount of investment you have put into your business. Using the cupcake business example again, you can save significant costs by working from home, but you still have expenses from investing in machinery, ingredients, paying a part-time worker, and utility and delivery costs.

Let's assume you have invested $3,000 in startup costs for your business. Your expected sales volume is 10,000 cupcakes per year. This means you need to cover your $3,000 investment from your cupcake sales as well as generate a profit. If your cupcakes sell for $3 each, that means 10,000 cupcakes sold per year will generate $30,000 in gross profit (profit before operating expenses).

However, remember that your cupcakes cost you $2 to produce, which amounts to $20,000 in production costs, leaving you with $10,000. Take away the $3,000 you have invested in the company, and you make a profit of $7,000. This means you make 70 cents profit on each $3 cupcake.

## Value-Based Pricing

Value-based pricing involves pricing your product based on how it benefits the customer. Your buyers have a major influence over your pricing strategy. Think about what your product means to your buyers. Is it going to save them money or make them money? Let's say you have created a water softener suitable for homeowners to install. Because hard water is full of minerals that build up in the water lines, forcing appliances to work harder, your water softener guarantees the customer a significant saving in energy bills. On this basis, you could build in a higher price because you can assure your customers that they will make back that money within, say, 2 years of purchasing your water softener.

But what if there is no monetary benefit to your buyers? Certainly your cupcake business will not help your customers save or make money, yet there is still a value in pleasure. What is it about your cupcakes, in particular, that could appeal to customers? You may price your cupcakes the same as your competitors in the beginning, but what makes them different enough for customers to pay more? Value-based pricing would reflect whatever added value your customers perceive in your cupcakes. You could also think about different ways of generating additional revenue: selling cupcake mix, decorations, and other accessories might be ways of bringing in extra money.

In addition to the factors associated with the various pricing calculations described so far, there are two more factors your pricing calculation needs to take into consideration: your livelihood and your mistakes. For example, are you taking a salary for yourself, or do you intend to live off the profit and use any additional income to reinvest in the company? Your price also has to cover the costs of any mistakes. Say your sales volume predictions are off. You might not sell 10,000 cupcakes in a year. How much leeway have you built into your pricing to cover the costs of inaccurate estimates and other errors? Typically, you need to account for being off by a factor of two or more and still be profitable—that is, if you plan to sell 10,000 cupcakes, you need to be able to make a profit even if you end up selling only half that many, or 5,000 cupcakes. ●

**Value-based pricing:** a pricing method that involves pricing a product based on how it benefits the customer.

---

## $SAGE edge™

Get the tools you need to sharpen your study skills. SAGE edge offers a robust online environment featuring an impressive array of free tools and resources.

- Access practice quizzes, eFlashcards, video, and multimedia at
  **edge.sagepub.com/neckentrepreneurship2e**

---

## SUMMARY

**9.1  Define a revenue model and distinguish it from the business model.**

The revenue model specifies exactly how income and earnings will be generated from the value proposition, whereas the business model is the framework established to create value for the consumer while preserving some of that value for the entrepreneur.

**9.2  Illustrate the 10 most popular revenue models being used by entrepreneurs.**

There are many effective revenue models. Commonly employed models are the unit sales revenue model, advertising revenue model, data revenue model, intermediation revenue model, licensing revenue model, franchising revenue model, subscription revenue model, professional revenue model, utility and usage revenue model, and freemium revenue model.

**9.3  Explain how companies generate revenue by profiting from "free."**

The freemium concept has exploded in popularity in recent times. Many companies are finding that small, experience-amplifying transactions can be profitable after introducing consumers to a limited version of their product or service for free.

**9.4  Identify the drivers that affect revenue as well as cost.**

Revenue drivers include the customer, purchase frequency, selling process, and price.

**9.5  Identify different strategies entrepreneurs use when pricing their product or service.**

Pricing is critical for a product or service. Common pricing strategies include competition-led pricing, customer-led pricing, loss leader, introductory offer, skimming, psychological pricing, fair pricing, and bundled pricing.

**9.6  Explain different methods of calculating price.**

There are several methods to help you calculate the best price for your product or service, such as cost-led pricing, target-return pricing, and value-based pricing. A break-even analysis can help entrepreneurs to quickly determine what they need to sell monthly or yearly, and in some cases daily or weekly, to cover the costs of running the business.

## CASE STUDY

## Balaji Viswanathan, founder, Invento Robotics

Assume that you're in the business for the long run. Building anything big and important takes a long time. Assume that 5 years of your life are going to be gone building this. Most people give up by then. (Balaji Viswanathan)

Balaji Viswanathan, the founder of Invento Robotics and the widely publicized Mitra Robot, has always seen himself as an entrepreneur. According to Balaji, "Even as a child, my goals weren't conventional. I always thought that a pushcart vendor seemed to have more freedom and liberty than someone working in an office." Balaji's father was the manager of a bank in a rural area of India and gave loans to entrepreneurs. Since there was little to do in his village, Balaji spent his early childhood with his father and among the many entrepreneurs. "The concept of creating something out of nothing fascinated me," Balaji recalled.

Balaji was an engineering student at Thiagarajar College of Engineering in Madurai, India, and, at 17 years old, caught the entrepreneurship bug during his first year. In 2000, he noticed that all professors gave handouts for students to study from. The campus had only one photocopying center, so there would always be this mad rush from students every time new material was distributed. Balaji's idea? He spoke to professors ahead of time, got their materials, and printed the handouts so that they were ready for use when the class started. The students didn't mind paying a little extra for the copies because they didn't have to waste their time getting them from the photocopying center. Balaji reached a point where he was copying close to 20,000 pages of study materials a day, and he even started helping the professors with proofreading and building content for classes. "My father was at the time making Rs. 8,000 (~$115) a month as a bank manager and I was making the same amount in college, spending just 2 hours a day. This business allowed me to pay my way through college."

Naturally curious, Balaji started researching various sectors including defense, nanotechnology, and data storage. He wrote research papers and gave many award-winning presentations that were recognized at the national level. Balaji even had the opportunity to work with then-president of India Dr. A. P. J. Abdul Kalam, a renowned aerospace scientist, and shared some of his early ideas and research. "I was quite sure that I wanted to get into academia and become a professor. I felt that as a professor, I would have the time to research and enough time otherwise to run my own company on the side."

Upon completing his undergraduate degree, Balaji left India in 2004 to earn a master's in engineering from the University of Maryland. There he started working extensively in the field of robotics. While working on his master's, he secured an internship with Cougaar Software, a robotics and AI company that now works directly with the U.S. Army. "Giving up a chance to join the company full-time right after the internship is one of my big regrets. At the time, I wanted to finish my master's and maybe even get a PhD. Now I realize that you don't necessarily need a degree." After his master's degree, Balaji worked at the Microsoft headquarters in Redmond, Washington, as a software design engineer for a little over 3 years. His passion for AI and robotics was only growing stronger. He bought a bunch of robotic kits and started building his own robots.

Balaji Viswanathan founded Invento Robotics, headquartered in Bengaluru, India, in 2016. Invento Robotics develops humanoid robots that use AI to interact with people. These robots have been piloted throughout India to handle customer interactions at banks, cinemas, hospitals, and retail outlets. Balaji recalled an early adopter, a senior executive at one of the largest public sector banks in India, Canara Bank. "The executive wanted to leave a legacy and was very excited about having robots going around the branch talking to customers. His legacy would be bringing those robots to the bank." Generally, Invento's robot prototypes were being used to help build a technology-oriented brand awareness for the companies that rented them. It helped them stand out from their competition. "We started selling the vision of the technology to these companies through our prototypes."

Balaji feels that other robotics companies, such as Honda Asimo and Boston Dynamics, have had failing business models. As Balaji explains, "These companies fail, not in terms of their technology but in terms of their value proposition to the customers. Having looked into the industry for a long time, I felt I intuitively understood how a profitable business model in this space could be created. Not just that, I felt that India as a country does not a have a visible product or a brand and that this might be a good way to help create that product! We want to make a trend-setting, cutting edge product that could be made in India for the world. That is our core vision."

Balaji cofounded Invento Robotics with his wife, Mahalakshmi, someone with complementary skillsets to his. While Balaji himself is quite technologically inclined, his wife is skilled in operations, management, and finance, something he feels has helped maintain a good balance. Not just that, Balaji tapped into his personal network of friends and family to get some initial funding to start the business. He also tapped into his very extensive network on Quora. His network on Quora is not comparable to anyone else's.

Quora is a question-and-answer website where questions are asked, answered, edited, and organized by its community of users (similar to Answers.com). Balaji is currently (and has been for a while) the most followed person on Quora, with more than 500,000 followers and close to 5,000 answers to questions that have been viewed approximately 320 million times. He was able to not only get feedback on his idea but also hired most of his team through this platform. "Finding the right people to build a hardware company was quite a challenge."

Having learned from some of his earlier startup experiences, Balaji wanted Invento to focus, from day 1, on revenue generation and building a scalable business model. He had a novel way to generate revenue in what is otherwise a highly capital- and research-intensive industry. He focused on big events because he observed that corporate clients and event organizers want something unique—a wow factor—at each event. He rented each one of his humanoid prototypes to events. Mitra (meaning "friend" in Hindi) is one of the better known of Invento's humanoids. Mitra was featured at the large, heavily attended Global Entrepreneurship Summit in 2017, in Hyderabad, India. The robot briefly interacted with Prime Minister Narendra Modi and Ivanka Trump.

Overall, the prototype rental model generated regular revenues that were used for further product development. Invento Robotics has made more than 20 prototypes and has created a revenue model that has helped fund their ongoing research. "These robot prototypes were hot off the press," noted Balaji. "As these robots were representative of what the future would look like, the incomplete functionality was not a deal breaker but a signal to competitors and customers that we are looking into the future."

Balaji warns that being a capital-intensive business with a longer-term payout than other industries creates a few challenges. "Investors were skeptical of a hardware robotics company that was operating out of India." But today the 30-member company is generating regular revenue streams and is also profitable, which has started to attract the attention of investors. Their customers include GM, Suzuki, and Accenture. In addition to funding challenges, there have also been "human" challenges because it's hard to create patience in both customers and employees—results take time. "We can't expect an iPhone to be developed on Day 1. A product like this takes time and since the industry is fairly new, it is going to take some time. We are at the same level as cars were in the 1980s." A third challenge is cash flow, given that Invento requires capital-intensive research and top talent. To keep the company nimble and forward looking, every time the company begins to get cash flow positive, they invest money to bring themselves back down to almost negative cash flow. Balaji explains, "If the company remains only cash flow positive, it would flat line and not grow. With this structure in place, the company is constantly chasing positive cash flows, helping it guide the operational and investment decisions."

Regardless of the challenges, Balaji is very strategic when attracting customers. "One of the ways we manage the risk in our business is by getting the right kind of customers. Our customers understand that they are not buying today, but buying tomorrow." Such strategic focus has created an impressive list of customers for Invento Robotics: HDFC Bank, PVR Cinemas, and Accenture—all companies invested in a vision for the future. Invento Robotics's long-term goal is to be the Apple of the robotics industry. "We are thinking about how we can put a million of our robots in business spaces over the next few years. After that, we would love to expand into homes and reach a point where every house can own a robot—our robot."

## Critical Thinking Questions

1. What is unique about renting "prototypes" of robots that don't have complete functionality?

2. Look up Balaji Viswanathan on Quora. What types of questions does he answer and is there something new you can learn from him about robotics and artificial intelligence?

3. Can you identify other ways that Invento Robotics can generate revenue while they are still perfecting the product?

**Sources:**

Balaji Viswanathan (interview with Babson MBA graduate assistant Gaurav Khemka. April 20, 2019)

Invento website (http://www.mitrarobot.com/)

©iStockphoto.com/PeopleImages

# 10 Planning for Entrepreneurs

"Plans are of little importance, but planning is essential."

—Winston Churchill, former British prime minister

# Chapter Outline

# Learning Objectives

10.1    Examine "planning" from an entrepreneurial perspective.

10.2    Explain vision as an important part of planning.

10.3    Explain the different types of plans used by entrepreneurs.

10.4    Describe the questions to ask during planning.

10.5    Debate the value of writing business plans.

10.6    Implement the tips for writing business plans.

## 10.1 WHAT IS PLANNING?

>> LO 10.1   **Examine "planning" from an entrepreneurial perspective.**

Over the course of this book, we have emphasized the importance of learning by doing and acting in order to learn. Taking action in the real world, collecting data, gathering feedback, and testing business models are the most beneficial ways to develop a product or service that people actually want as well as to build a scalable business.

As we have learned, when you are first starting out as an entrepreneur, it is important to think about whom you know, what you know, and how you're going to implement your idea. This is why it is important to have a plan that helps you take the first steps on your journey to building a new venture and proving it is viable and feasible before you go any further. From an entrepreneurial perspective, planning is a process of envisioning the future for your business, including what you plan to do and how you plan to do it.[1]

Every business needs to start with some type of plan. Plans help you to get out of your head and see your idea for what it really is—the good, the bad, and even the ugly! They help crystalize your thoughts, allow you to clearly articulate where you want your business to go, and can be the foundation for an overall business strategy. In short, planning pushes you to move forward.

Planning is different from a plan. Planning is a verb and therefore implies action. If planning pushes you to move forward and take action, then a plan helps you organize those actions in some way. Planning is about answering the most important questions we have posed throughout the book. Dr. Emmet (Tom) Thompson, founder of AFC Management, believes that planning is the key to success.

**Planning:** a process of envisioning the future for a business, including what one plans to do and how one plans to do it.

## 10.2 PLANNING STARTS WITH A VISION

>> LO 10.2   **Explain vision as an important part of planning.**

All planning starts with a vision. Cameron Herold, a business coach and mentor, presented the concept of vivid vision in his book *Double Double*. Vivid vision challenges the entrepreneur to imagine what a business could be 3 years into the future. Three years is a reasonable amount of time to "nail down" specific, measurable goals; vivid vision is not just fantasizing so far into the future that it becomes pure speculation. Three years makes you stretch just enough to think about how to get from today to your idea of success in Year 3.

Master the content at
**edge.sagepub.com/
neckentrepreneurship2e**

# Dr. Emmet C. (Tom) Thompson II, AFC Management

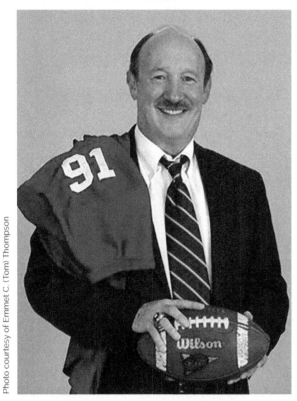

Photo courtesy of Emmet C. (Tom) Thompson

**Dr. Emmet C. (Tom) Thompson, founder and president of AFC Management**

Dr. Emmet "Tom" Thompson is the oldest collegiate football player in NCAA history. At the age of 61 he kicked an extra point for the 2009 Austin College football team. Though he was told being on the team would be impossible, he said, "I did all the hard work, all the running, all the things that the team did to earn my spot." For Tom, his football experience was not that much different from his entrepreneurial pursuits. "The harder things are in the beginning, the more victory you enjoy in the end."

Tom is the founder and president of AFC Management, a company founded in 1996 that serves as an umbrella for his business interests in corporate fitness management, real estate, and book production. Tom's newest business under the AFC Management umbrella is a movie development company, 91 Kick Entertainment, and he is producing a movie based on his own life. It's clear that he is an entrepreneur in many forms—a business leader, football coach, author, motivational speaker, educator, and now movie producer!

As he reflects on his successful career, he admits there is a trend that he doesn't like. He laments that too many young entrepreneurs plan for short-term gains, rather than long-term payoffs. Tom says, "More and more, young people are more concerned with how something works than with how something lasts, in relationships and in business. Delayed gratification and patience will pay off over time." However, he also acknowledges that patience and waiting for the longer-term payoff requires planning. In fact, one of Tom's favorite quotes is by Ben Franklin, "If you fail to plan, you are planning to fail." Tom emphasizes that his secret to his success has been his long-term vision for AFE Management, including a plan for how to achieve it.

Tom reminds aspiring entrepreneurs not to wallow too much in short-term setbacks because they need to keep their eye on the big picture. "Short-term chaos can often keep people from remembering the long-term outcome they envisioned at the start, so don't lose sight of the dream," he says, "If you start thinking of all the things you need to be and do, you'll get caught up in that instead of thinking of your own vision. Planning too many things keeps you from planning the most important things."

## Critical Thinking Questions

1. What is the significance of planning to the success of Tom's entrepreneurial career?

2. Do you think younger entrepreneurs only think in the short term? Do you agree with Tom's view of young people?

3. Do some research on Tom Thompson. How did he get the point where he was a 61-year-old kicker for a college football team? What is the entrepreneurial lesson from this experience? ●

**Source:** Emmet Thompson (interview with author, January 23, 2019).

The best way to begin the vivid vision exercise is to get out of your usual working environment (your class or your office) and go to a spot that, for you, is relaxing and peaceful—it could be a nearby park or someplace farther away such as the ocean, mountains, or a lake. Start sketching (see Chapter 7 for more on sketching) or writing and aim to create a document no more than three pages long.

TABLE 10.1

## Cameron Herold's Vivid Vision

The following is an example of vivid vision elements from Cameron Herold. Herold believes that "Creating a vivid vision brings the future into the present, so we can have clarity on what we are building now. It is a detailed overview of what my business will look like, feel like, and act like 3 years out."

| What I Do | Why I "do what I do" is simple and clear: I love helping CEOs turn their dreams into reality. |
|---|---|
| My Programs | My content is about my leadership and growth expertise and is designed specifically for CEOs and entrepreneurial minds. I am frequently invited to present at conferences and keynote talks at large-scale events. I set a firm limit for the number of annual speaking events I do, which increases the demand for my services, and my fees increase each year. This allows me more time with my family. |
| Live Programs | While on the road speaking, I book half-day and full-day workshops for groups or companies, in the same city, to teach their employees the systems to become more entrepreneurial. I run 2-day growth camps and leadership team retreats in my home city that attract companies and employees from around the globe. |
| Remote Programs | I leverage webinar technology, and companies book me to do remote training for their employees. Prior webinars I've done are available online for thousands of companies around the world to use—and for their employees to learn from as well. |
| Coaching/ Mentoring | My clients stay with me for an average of 24 months. Those who leave do so only because they've learned enough to no longer need me to guide them. I am coaching 24 clients per month by reducing the number of lower-leverage speaking events I do. My fees increase each year for new clients. |
| Leadership | Clients say that I hold them accountable for doing the things they need to do in order to successfully grow their company. Clients I coach love setting goals with me because our efforts directly correlate to an increase in their company's productivity. CEOs value having me on their team as a senior leader who they normally couldn't afford. Clients consistently say I've made (or saved) them millions of dollars. |
| Communication | People trust me because I say what's on my mind. I am respected for that. People say I'm a breath of fresh air and that I say what other people are thinking but won't say. My inner voice helps me filter my decisions. |
| Customer Service | My clients are very clear about what I promise them and say that I overdeliver with every interaction. My client companies feel grateful to have me helping them, as I feel grateful to play a role in their growth. I deliver incredible value. They are thrilled they have time with me consistently. |
| My Mentors | I connect and learn from those who have already "figured it out." I study fiercely—what the great companies do and how they do it—so I don't have to reinvent the wheel. I'm known as a "connector" because of how many people I know and regularly call on, leveraging social networks and the CEOs I meet globally. My track record of hyper-growth with my clients and honesty in my relationships is what accelerates and grows my network. |
| Profitability | I continue to be extremely profitable doing exactly what I love. My revenues have grown 100% in 3 years. |
| Balance | I choose international engagements where I'm able to add days of personal time to enjoy the country with my wife, and as our four children get older, we include them more as well. |
| Core Values | I live the core values that I have set for my company—and I ask people to call me on any deviation. • Do What You Love • Be Authentic • Deliver What You Promise • Balance Is Key |

**Source:** Adapted from Herold, C. (2011). *Double double: How to double your revenue and profit in three years.* Austin, TX: Greenleaf Book Group.

# The Vivid Vision Checklist

Using the vivid vision checklist, try to imagine your business or some new idea in action 3 years from now.

When you finish your own vivid vision, share it with your friends, family, and anyone else you feel would be interested in seeing it. The act of publicly sharing your picture makes your vision more real and compels you to take action in order to achieve your goals. Besides, as Herold says, "the more people who know with clarity what my company looks and feels like, the better chance there is that people will be able to help me to make it happen."[2]

Pretend you have traveled in a time machine into the future. The date is December 31, 3 years from now. You are walking around your company's offices (the startup you founded 3 years before) with a clipboard in hand.

- What do you see?
- What do you hear?
- What are clients saying?
- What do the media write about you?
- What kinds of comments are your employees making at the water cooler?
- What is the buzz about you in your community?
- What is your marketing like? Are you marketing your goods/services globally now? Are you launching new online and TV ads? What is being said on social media?

- How is the company running day to day? Is it organized and running like a clock?
- What's in the office space? Are people sitting, standing, talking? When they move from their workspace, where do they go?
- What kind of stuff do you do every day? Are you focused on strategy, team building, or customer relationships?
- What do the company's financials reveal?
- How are you funded now?
- How are your core values being realized among your employees?

## Critical Thinking Questions

1. Is 3 years a useful and reasonable length of time to look ahead and envision your business? If you think 3 years is too long or too short, explain why.

2. In the vivid vision checklist, which questions did you find the most useful? The most challenging? Explain your answers.

3. Is there anything in your plans for your business that is not covered in the vivid vision checklist? Anything that is not relevant to your business? ●

**Source:** Herold, C. (2011). *Double double: How to double your revenue and profit in three years.* Austin, TX: Greenleaf Book Group.

©iStockphoto.com/RawpixelLtd

**An example of a gallery sketch**

Once you have visualized your goals, then you can write a three-page description or draw a large sketch of these thoughts, detailing what your company will look and feel like in 3 years' time. Remember that this exercise does not involve how you are going to build the business or the steps you need to take to get there. It is simply a description of how your business might look in the future—specifically, just 3 years down the road.

Cameron Herold created his own vivid vision (see Table 10.1). Keep in mind that although Herold presented his vision in writing, the vision can also be shown as a visual such as a gallery sketch, a photo montage, or a video.

Your own vivid vision should describe what the future looks like rather than detailing how you're going to get there.

Envisioning the future is just a start. Generally the plan is the document that records the answers to questions. As this chapter will illustrate, there are many types of plans available to entrepreneurs today, including simplified plans, plans that emphasize planning with preparation, and those that flow from planning with imagination. What is most important, regardless of the type of document created, is that the questions get answered.

# 10.3 PLANS TAKE MANY FORMS

>> LO 10.3 **Explain the different types of plans used by entrepreneurs.**

As we discussed, plans are an important way to develop a vision, gain clarity, answer important questions, estimate timelines, and set goals. Many entrepreneurs are initially resistant to the idea of sitting down and writing a plan, or they feel that they lack the time for this task. However, this section demonstrates that there are several alternatives to choose from to help you take action and envision a future for your business—or decide, based on solid information, whether your business idea even *has* a future.

What type of plan to use when is often determined by the stage of the business. We will discuss six alternative planning tools. These include the Business Model Canvas, the business brief, the feasibility study, the pitch deck, and the business plan.

## Business Model Canvas

The Business Model Canvas (BMC), introduced in Chapter 5, is a type of visual plan. It is especially useful for identifying any gaps in the business idea and integrating the various components. We say it's visual because the entire business is depicted on one page by filling in the nine blocks of the business model:

- Key partners
- Key activities
- Value proposition
- Customer relationships
- Customer segments
- Key resources
- Channels
- Cost structure
- Revenue streams

The sample BMC in Figure 10.1 illustrates the nine components using an idea for a new T-shirt store that sells trendy T-shirts emblazoned with original designs by young, emerging artists.

By thinking through all nine components of your business model, you will be able to visualize how all the various parts work together: the value created for customers, the processes you must have to deliver value, the resources you need, and the way you'll make money.

## The Business Brief

The business brief is less visual than the two previous types of plans, and it requires a bit more detail and writing. Typically, a business brief is a two- to three-page document outlining the company overview, value proposition, customers, and milestones. It's something you can easily send to stakeholders that will give them an at-a-glance understanding of who you are, the business, and its potential. Creating a business brief is not too time intensive, and it indicates that you're doing your homework and thinking critically

FIGURE 10.1

## Sample Business Model Canvas

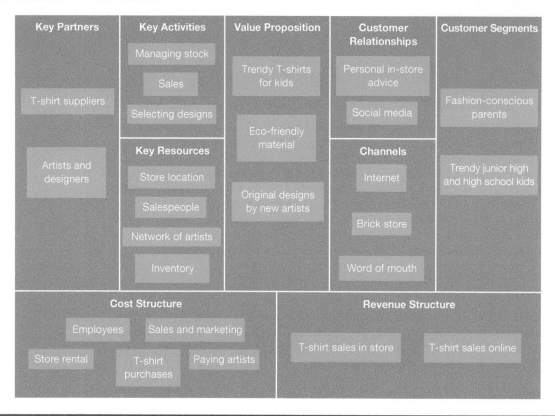

TABLE 10.2

Points to Include in a Business Brief

| |
| --- |
| • Description of the business idea (company overview) |
| • Value proposition that highlights the problem being solved or need being met |
| • Customer profile and market size |
| • Proof of market demand and future growth |
| • Description of the entrepreneur/team |
| • Actions taken to date and future actions planned |
| • Simple pro forma income statement (up to 3 years) |

about the business. Table 10.2 lists the points to include in a business brief. Figure 10.2 is a sample business brief for an online meal service called India in a Box.

## Feasibility Study

**Feasibility study:** a planning tool that enables entrepreneurs to test the possibilities of an initial idea to see if it is worth pursuing.

A **feasibility study** is an essential planning tool that enables entrepreneurs to test the possibilities of an initial idea to see if it is worth pursuing. It serves as a solid foundation for developing a business plan when the time comes. The feasibility study focuses on the size of the market, the suppliers, distributors, and the skills of the entrepreneur.

**FIGURE 10.2**

### Sample Business Brief: India in a Box

#### COMPANY OVERVIEW

India in a Box is an online meal service (subscription and on-demand) delivering authentic Indian food that is healthy and can be prepared in 5 to 10 minutes. We are on a simple mission to bring a taste of India to every home in the U.S.

Through the India in a Box online store, customers receive their choice of curry and can add rice or naan. Curries are easily prepared by adding water, stirring, and heating.

#### VALUE PROPOSITION

Cooking a traditional Indian meal requires time, knowledge, and passion. We captured and simplified the essence of this process. By using a specialized dehydration process, we ensure that 95% of nutrients are preserved during packaging compared to 50% in our competitors' products. Each dish has a simple ingredient list, is 100% vegetarian and gluten-free, and contains no added preservatives, sodium, or sugar. We start with whole, fresh ingredients and slowly simmer to develop complex sauces and then naturally condense through dehydration to lock in flavor and nutrition. The shelf life of our products is nine months.

#### MARKET

Key trends supporting the startup and scale up of India in a Box:

- Ethnic food industry is $11 billion and growing at 15% Year on Year (YOY).
- Indian cuisine is the second fastest growing cuisine with a 20% YOY growth rate projected until 2018.
- Eighty-eight percent of people are willing to pay more for healthful, great-quality food (Nielson 2015 report).
- Over $750 million has been invested in just the first half of 2015 in food technology companies, including meal kits and subscriptions.

#### CUSTOMERS

Our target consumers are Indian food lovers and enthusiasts. There are over 5 million Indians and 130,000 Indian students in the U.S. Indians are now the largest international cohort of students residing in the U.S. Specifically, our customers are the following:

- **Urban Food Explorers:** Whole Foods shoppers (health conscious), time constrained, looking for convenience
- **Indian Americans:** Highly influential group who will be our brand evangelists, helping build brand credibility
- **Millennials:** Young yet particular about food consumption and their current and future wellness

#### ACTIONS TAKEN

**We have product.** With the help of a professional chef and our head of nutrition, Sucheta Gehani, we have created five delicious recipes from scratch. We partnered with Spicebox, a state-of-the-art commercial kitchen in India, to create, iterate, and finalize our recipes.

**We have co-packers.** We have developed strategic partnerships for co-packing our products. Our food is created in a commercial kitchen and then dehydrated by a separate manufacturer—both in Mumbai, India. Both of these companies have the necessary FDA approvals and meet the production standards required.

**We have a supply chain.** Product is shipped by air freight from Mumbai, India, and warehoused by Ship Bob, which has two United States warehouses (New Jersey and Chicago).

**We have sales.** In May, India in a Box launched its first batch of five products and completely sold out, earning $1,200 in one day. After we launched our online platform www.indiainabox .us, we took in $6,000 in three months, fulfilling orders from eight different states.

*(Continued)*

**FIGURE 10.2**    (Continued)

## OUR TEAM

**Shyam Devnani**, Founder and CEO:

Shyam is a Babson MBA 2015 alumni with an undergraduate degree in computer engineering. He has three years of experience as CEO of a startup garment textile manufacturing firm.

**Sucheta Gehani**, Head of Nutrition and Wellness:

Sucheta is a registered dietitian and brings to bear her expertise as a nutrition and health expert. Sucheta is passionate about health and wellness and is also a certified Yoga instructor.

**Meet Kouchar**, Operations Partner:

Meet is a serial food entrepreneur with companies such as SpiceBox (www.spicebox.in), Oye Kiddan, and the Bohri Kitchen in India. He is our new operations partner for food production and will help us set up our own kitchen and dehydration unit in India.

**Vinayak Agarwal**, Marketing Intern:

Vinayak is studying for his master's degree in international marketing from Hult University. He is a foodie and a passionate photographer who will bring to the company his digital marketing expertise to help us execute our social media strategies.

We are also looking at bringing on board a full time marketing/sales person and forming a board of advisors with industry experts.

## FINANCIAL PROJECTIONS

Our revenue model is selling our meal boxes online at a price of $24 for 3 curries and 3 portions of rice or naan. Our second product line will be curated regional experience boxes, which will be priced at $35. We project our Year 1 revenue at $261,000. Our gross profit margin is 61%, and we project a net profit of $1 million in Year 3.

| | YEAR 1 | YEAR 2 | YEAR 3 |
|---|---|---|---|
| **REVENUE** | $261,000 | $820,000 | $2,540,000 |
| **EXPENSES** | $132,000 | $343,000 | $980,000 |
| **GROSS PROFIT** | $129,000 | $477,000 | $1,560,000 |
| **SG&A** | $84,000 | $225,000 | $530,000 |
| **NET PROFIT** | $45,000 | $252,000 | $1,030,000 |

## FUTURE MILESTONES

We are currently looking to raise a $250K round of seed funding. This will enable us to bring the dehydration unit in house and also help expand our marketing and sales efforts to the west coast. With the addition of the new capital, we will grow our physical and online presence in highly Indian-populated regions with a demand for Indian food, such as New York, New Jersey, San Francisco, and Austin.

### Spring 2016

- Bring operations of manufacturing in-house with partner in India.
- Raise a round of seed funding.
- Bring on board an experienced marketing person to push online sales strategies.
- Target sales in Boston and the Bay Area.

### Summer 2016

- Launch curated regional subscription boxes.
- Increase product offerings to 15 with help of operations partner.
- Invest in our web platform and improve warehousing/fulfillment.

**Source:** Reprinted with permission from Shyam Devnani.

Every entrepreneur should conduct a feasibility study because it determines whether your idea is workable and profitable. It is typically created to assess the viability of a business concept.

The information you gather for your feasibility study will help you identify the essentials you need to make the business work: any problems or obstacles to your business, the customers you hope to sell to, marketing strategies, the logistics of delivering your product or service, your competition, and the resources you need to start your business and keep it running until it is established.

From the entrepreneur's perspective, the feasibility study is a useful way to assess whether you have the time, energy, abilities, and resources to get the venture off the ground. The conclusions you draw from the study will determine whether your venture is viable or not. Ultimately, the feasibility study is a valuable exercise in answering the question, Will my venture work? This feasibility study is for your eyes only, which means you need to be as honest as possible with the conclusions you draw from the study. If there are constraints, describe them and be realistic about whether your idea is worth further investigation.

The feasibility study is a written document of no more than 10 pages. It takes all of the action components we've been talking about in the book and places the learnings from the actions into a structure that can be used for decision making, such as "I do or do not want to move forward with this venture"—or, in short, a "Go/No Go" decision.

The feasibility study addresses the most critical elements entrepreneurs need to consider during the initial conceptualization of the venture (see Table 10.3). The key to the feasibility study is speed. It is a quick way to prompt you to zero in on what you need to know. It requires you to pursue answers to your questions and to gather real data from your interactions with potential customers, suppliers, distributors, and others. The feasibility study template (see Table 10.4) also prompts you to quickly find out the rules and regulations surrounding your startup, which could save you time and money.

To produce a feasibility study, there must be action, testing, information gathering, and analysis in order to reduce uncertainty and gain greater confidence about the opportunity and your approach. For example, if you haven't talked to at least 50 potential customers, *you are not ready to decide whether the business idea is viable.* "Talking" can include contacts by phone, social networking, and other electronic "conversations," but don't overlook the value of interviewing prospective customers face-to-face.

Though there is no one best format for a feasibility study, Table 10.4 gives a sample

**Talking to people face-to-face is a valuable way to test the viability of your business idea.**

template that can be used to organize all the data you have collected from the idea generation and business model stage, allowing you to clearly articulate where you are and where you want to go.

## TABLE 10.3

Critical Elements of Feasibility Study

| |
|---|
| • Does the idea fulfill a need or solve a big problem? |
| • Is there both short- and long-term market potential? |
| • Who are the customers, and what are they willing to pay? |
| • Does the opportunity provide competitive uniqueness? |
| • Is the business model feasible (can it be done) and viable (can it be sustainable)? |

**Source:** Kelley, D., Ceru, D., George, B., & Neck, H. (2014). *Feasibility blueprint guidelines.* Wellesley, MA: Babson College.

**TABLE 10.4**

Sample Feasibility Study Template

| | |
|---|---|
| Need Identification | Describe why there is a need for your business to exist |
| Venture Concept | Have a clear, concise description in 2–3 sentences. |
| Value Propositions | What makes you unique and why is this valuable for the customer? Prove that the customer wants what you are providing. |
| Market | Discuss the market size, potential market size, and target market size. Is the market large enough to meet your goals? Discuss trends and growth estimates. |
| Competitive Environment | Identify and compare your venture against the competition. By understanding the competition, you will have a better understanding of the dynamics of the industry in which you are competing and how you are differentiated. Are there specific laws or regulations you should be aware of? |
| Revenue Model | Describe your revenue model in terms of the revenue streams and the key factors that will influence those streams. You will also need to examine your cost model and determine the key drivers of your costs. Overall, you are assessing your potential profitability. Provide a simple income statement. |
| Startup Requirements | Identify the resources needed to start the business. What is absolutely essential before a sale can be made? What don't you have, but need? |
| Team | Critically assess your current team, its fit with the venture, and your ability to act (or not). |
| Decision | Based on the analysis laid out in the feasibility study, do you want to move forward? Why or why not? |

**Source:** D. Kelley, B. George, D. Ceru, H. Neck. Babson's Feasibility Blueprint Assignment for MBA students. Babson College. 2013.

Using a gourmet food cart venture as an example, suppose you want to offer mayonnaise as a condiment and grated cheese as a topping for your featured menu items. If you conduct a proper feasibility study before you progress with your plan, you will find that most health departments do not allow food carts to sell dairy-based or edible-oil-based condiments. This is useful information to know before you go out and buy dozens of bottles of mayonnaise and packets of cheese.

One of the main aims of the feasibility study is to establish whether your idea is a "go" or a "no go." Is your idea feasible and worthwhile, or should you just draw a line through it and move on?

Whether your decision is a "go" or "no go," you will need to state the reasons why. For example, if it's a "go," then you will need to develop and test prototypes, carry out due diligence, find a management team, try to get some early customers, seek funding if necessary, and prepare a launch plan.

While a "no go" may feel disappointing, remember that a decision not to go ahead is also a valid and valuable result of a feasibility study. It has saved you the time, effort, and expense that you may have spent on a concept that does not have the potential to succeed in the market.

Knowing your constraints can also lead to doors opening in other areas you might not have imagined. Take Jorge Heraud and Lee Redden, the founders of Blue River

*Photo courtesy of Blue River Technology*

**Robotic mower by Blue River Technology**

Technology, for instance.[3] They had an idea to build robotic mowers for commercial spaces. Having spoken to 100 customers over a period of 10 weeks, they learned that their original target market—golf courses—did not think their solution was viable.

However, during their market research, the two entrepreneurs discovered a huge demand from farmers for an automated way to kill weeds without chemicals. This gave the two entrepreneurs the "go" they were looking for. They built and tested the prototype and received $3 million in venture funding less than a year later. In 2017, agricultural equipment manufacturer John Deere acquired Blue River Technology for $305 million.[4]

The more data you gather during the feasibility study, the more evidence you will have to show investors when the time comes to develop your pitch deck or write a business plan.

## The Pitch Deck

The pitch deck is a presentation of varying lengths highlighting many of the essential elements found in a feasibility study and a business plan. Some call this the launch plan. Let's briefly discuss the specifics of the deck here. (An example pitch deck can be found in Supplement B.)

The pitch deck has replaced the formal business plan in most venues. A pitch deck is needed for collegiate competitions, applications to accelerators and incubators, and for angel and venture capital funding. There are many variations on the "ideal" pitch deck depending on your audience, so we encourage you to do your own research before preparing. The purpose of the pitch is to describe your product and get interest. In the case of using your pitch deck in front of professional investors, the goal is to get to the next meeting!

A pitch deck is essential for an investor meeting.

©iStockphoto.com/PeopleImages

There are no strict rules for the length or style of pitch decks. Author and entrepreneur Guy Kawasaki advises keeping pitch deck slides to a maximum of 10, while Mathilde Collin, founder of email app Front, used a 25-slide presentation that earned her $66 million from investors after only 5 days of pitching.[5]

## The Business Plan

The business plan is considered the most formal of planning tools. It is typically a lengthy written document discussing the business concept, product mix, marketing plan, operations plan, development plan, and financial forecast.

As stated earlier, the business plan has been replaced by the pitch deck in most venues, but traditional investors and bankers are likely to require a traditional business plan. The business plan needs to show that you are serious and that you've done your homework, given the level of detail that is necessary to complete a strong business plan. However, there is an ironic angle to this: When a business plan is created, it must be thought of as a work in progress because nothing goes according to plan. It is important to realize this ahead of time, as some entrepreneurs struggle when things don't go according to plan because so much energy has been put into creating the actual business plan.

A traditional business plan usually consists of 20 to 40 pages, plus additional pages for appendices. It also includes the organization's mission, strategy, tactics, goals, financials, and objectives, together with a 5-year forecast for income, profits, and cash flow.[6] This information is divided into three main parts.[7]

The first part is the business concept, where you discuss the industry, business structure, products and services, and how you plan to make your business a success. The second part is the market section, where you describe potential customers and the competitors in

**Business plan:** the most formal of planning tools. It is typically a lengthy written document discussing the business concept, product mix, marketing plan, operations plan, development plan, and financial forecast.

your market. The third part describes how you intend to design, develop, and implement the plan and provides some detail on operations and management. Finally, the financial section includes details of income and cash flow, balance sheets, financial projections, and the like. In addition to these components, a business plan also has a cover, title page, and table of contents (see Table 10.5).

It can be a complex task to start writing a business plan too early, especially for a startup when there are still so many questions to be answered. Business plans are useful for established companies with a history of data and operations because this data will help the business to plan and forecast more accurately, but startups have no such history. Startups are not just smaller versions of bigger companies—a startup begins with guesswork and untested assumptions. Nevertheless, in order to get later-stage funding, a business plan will likely be needed.

In the order of entrepreneurial activities, business plans come after idea generation, business model canvas, feasibility study, and pitch deck. Figure 10.3 illustrates the path from idea generation to business plan.

By following the steps of the Entrepreneurship Method, which we introduced in Chapter 1, you have a better chance of creating a solid, evidence-based business plan to present to potential investors when the time comes. By gathering, testing, and analyzing

---

**TABLE 10.5**

Components of a Business Plan

**BUSINESS PLAN OUTLINE**

1. **Cover**
2. *Table of Contents*
3. *Executive Summary* (2–3 pages)
   - Brief introduction and description of the opportunity
   - Company overview
   - Product or service description
   - Industry overview
   - Marketplace and target market
   - Competitive advantage
   - Business model (with summary of financials)
   - Management team
   - Offering
4. *Company Overview* (1–2 pages)
   - Company description
   - History and current status (stage of development)
   - Products and service description
   - Competitive advantages
   - Entry, growth, and exit strategies
5. *Industry, Marketplace, and Competitor Analyses* (3–6 pages)
   - Industry analysis
   - Marketplace analysis
   - Competitor analysis
6. *Marketing Plan* (1–4 pages)
   - Target market strategy
   - Product/service strategy
   - Pricing strategy
   - Distribution strategy
   - Advertising and promotion strategy
   - Sales strategy
   - Marketing and sales forecasts
   - Marketing expenses

7. *Operations Plan* (2 pages)
   - Operations strategy
   - Scope of operations
   - Ongoing operations
   - Operations expenses
8. *Development Plan* (1–2 pages)
   - Development strategy
   - Development timeline (milestones)
   - Development expenses
9. *Management* (1–2 pages)
   - Company organization
   - Management team
   - Ownership and compensation
   - Administrative expenses
10. *Critical Risks* (1–2 pages)
    - Market, customer, financial risks
    - Competitor retaliation
    - Contingency plans
11. *Offering* (up to 1 page)
    - Investment requirements
    - Offer
12. *Financial Plan* (up to 2 text pages, including financial statements)
    - Detailed financial assumptions
    - Pro forma financial statements
    - Breakeven analysis and other calculations
    - Do include statement within this section; do not place statements in the appendix.
13. *Appendices* (no maximum)
    - Customer survey and results
    - Other items to include may be menus, product specifications, team résumés, sample promotions, product pictures.

## FIGURE 10.3

### Path From Idea Generation to Business Plan

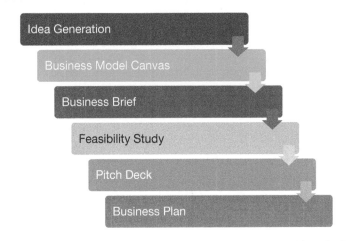

real data, you will be more able to illustrate your passion to create, the resources you have used, the actions you have taken to get your business on the move, the risks you have taken (and the ones you are prepared not to take), the people who have been enrolled in your journey, the experiments you have carried out to test what works and what doesn't, and where you would like the business to go next. In short, you will be able to prove that your product works, a real market exists, and your financials are not based just on guesswork.

## Summary of Different Types of Plans

Although we are not advocating one type of plan over another, we believe it's important that entrepreneurs understand what is available to them and for what purposes. Table 10.6 summarizes the different types of plans we have outlined for entrepreneurs.

## TABLE 10.6

Summary of Different Types of Plans

| TYPE OF PLAN | PRIMARY AUDIENCE | PURPOSE | OUTPUT |
|---|---|---|---|
| Business Model Canvas | Team members, advisors | Identify gaps and critically evaluate each part of the business and how the components integrate | Completed and tested business model canvas |
| Business Brief | Friends and family, investors, advisors, other interested stakeholders | To have something in writing to show anybody interested in the business; also good practice for describing the business in a concise way | 2- to 3-page typed document that is well formatted and professional looking |
| Feasibility Study | Team members, maybe early investors | Assess the potential of a new concept; can act as proof that the venture has market potential | 10-page typed document that is well formatted and professional looking |
| Pitch Deck | Early investors, judges of venture competitions, incubators, accelerators | To get the next meeting with a potential investor; to apply to an incubator program; win a competition; get funding | 10 to 20 slides, depending on length and purpose of the presentation |
| Business Plan | Banks, investors | Get funding | 25+ page document plus appendices |

# When to Be Transparent With Investors

In the process of creating a concise, well-thought-out business plan, entrepreneurs can learn quite a bit about their own business. Planning helps to maintain focus on a project and get all people working on the venture on the same page.

A business plan or extensive pitch deck must highlight the projected financials of the venture, including projected revenue and profit over a three to five year period. Investors will require financial projections because this is one way they analyze the potential success of the venture.

With such reliance on the projected and planned financials, it might be tempting for an entrepreneur to exaggerate some numbers or hide some information that may harm the chances of receiving funding. However, for the most part, investors will discover this eventually, and transparency leads to trust. If the entrepreneur is not transparent from the start, then future funding will be scarce.

In the book *Discovering Phi: Motivation as the Hidden Variable of Performance,* a thorough study of investment management leaders and other investment professionals concluded that about 28% of investors are in the industry to help clients. A further 36% of investors said that career risk comes from acting in the clients' best interest. If a good chunk of investors are not necessarily in the industry to help entrepreneurs, then how much does an entrepreneur owe an investor? If the entrepreneur cannot be certain that the investor has her best interests at heart, then that raises the question about how transparent she should be with the investor. This also suggests that the entrepreneur should work hard to ascertain the motives and strategies of the investor.

## Critical Thinking Questions

1. Are there certain "white lies" that entrepreneurs can tell to potential investors?

2. Is transparency the same thing as truthfulness in business?

3. What if an investor does not have the right intentions? Should an entrepreneur maintain her principles in dealing with this investor? ●

**Sources:**

Guardian Sustainable Business. (2014, August 4). Corporate transparency: Why honesty is the best policy. *The Guardian.* Retrieved from https://www.theguardian.com/sustainable-business/corporate-transparency-honesty-best-policy

McSwain, P. (2017, March 20). Transparency: Do we protest it too much? *Enterprising Investor.* Retrieved from https://blogs.cfainstitute.org/investor/2017/03/20/transparency-do-we-protest-it-too-much/

---

In addition to the plans we've outlined here, there are other options used by entrepreneurs to showcase their businesses. Among them are the following:

- LeanLaunchLab, which allows you to test hypotheses and refine your business model;

- Lean Stack, a paid service that compresses the essential parts of your business down to one page to send to investors who have little time to read through a large document; and

- Plan Cruncher is a free tool that, like Lean Stack, allows you to summarize your idea in one page.

How do you know what plan to create? Depending on your business, you may use a different type of plan in the beginning from other entrepreneurs. The best plan for you is the one that helps give you the clarity and direction to take action to create your future venture. Use the Entrepreneurship Method to take action and get out of the building, just as our featured entrepreneurs have done: test your ideas, get market feedback, generate momentum, revise assumptions, make continuous iterations, use your social network, make contacts, and get potential customers interested in your product or service.

Most of the successful entrepreneurs featured throughout this book started out by testing their ideas in the real world to see if they really had wings and if they could make them into a business, long before they sat down to write their formal business plan—and many never wrote a formal business plan at all. They also used the time to equip themselves with the basic skills required for a successful venture—financial management, production capabilities, and marketing and sales—either by learning the skills themselves or partnering with other people. When you, too, have proved your concept, and gathered the data to go with it, then you will be able to produce a solid, credible business plan.

# 10.4 QUESTIONS TO ASK DURING PLANNING

>> **LO 10.4**   **Describe the questions to ask during planning.**

Regardless of what type of plan you are working on, you must ask the following questions. Not all plans require lengthy, complex answers, but it is important to ask the right questions before you put your plan into action.

## What Is Your Business and How Does It Add Value?

A useful way to gain clarity on the type of business you are setting up, and the value it brings to your customer base, is to write a concept statement, which is a one sentence to one paragraph description of your vision for your product or service. The statement should include all the features of your product or service, potential problems that it solves, and the target market. It doesn't have to be long, but it does need to be clear and easy to understand. Here is a brief example of a concept statement for a tea company that is introducing a new in-cup tea brewing system:

> While there are lots of tea-drinkers in the world, not all of them are happy about the environmental impact of discarding teabags (many of which are made from nonbiodegradable materials). Although there are loose-leaf tea options, some people are put off with the time it takes to brew, and the special equipment it requires.
>
> The Tea-in-One product combines the tea mug and the strainer into one. The product addresses environmental concerns as it is partly ceramic (the mug) and silicone (the strainer). It is dishwasher safe and designed to keep the tea warm through extra insulation. The mug comes in 12 different colors and is marketed primarily toward women who often drink tea at home or at work.[8]

**Concept statement:** a written representation of your vision for your product or service.

## Who Is Your Customer?

In Chapter 6, we explored the different types of customers and how to find your target market. Write down who your target customers are (end users, distributors, retailers), their defining characteristics, and why they will buy your product or service. Remember to include all this information in the plan you are writing as it will help you gain clarity on the right customer segments for your business.

## How Big Is the Market?

Once you have a clear idea of your target customers, you will be able to conduct market sizing analyses to establish the size of your market and the share of the market you intend to capture. Chapter 6 includes more information about market sizing.

## How Will You Enter the Market?

Write down your strategy for entering the market. This involves describing the needs your product or service fulfills for your customer, the problems you are solving for them, and any evidence you have to show that your potential customers will want to buy your offering.

## What Do You Know About the Industry?

The more knowledge you have about your industry, the more likely you will be able to find ways to differentiate your ideas. Write down any research you have carried out that supports your ideas and make sure it is correct and up to date.

# What Do You Know About Your Competition?

Entrepreneurs make lots of mistakes and they learn from just about all of them. But there is one mistake that is too often made and is a clear indication that you haven't done your homework. The mistake? When an entrepreneur says, "We have no competition." *Every* venture has competition. Even Uber had competition from taxis, and now it has competition from Lyft. The iPhone had competition from BlackBerry. There is always competition. Sometimes it's direct (when businesses are selling the same products and services) and sometimes

it's indirect (when businesses are selling different products but solve the same problem or meet the same need), but it's always there.

For this Mindshift, you must complete a competitive analysis chart comparing your venture to *at least* one direct competitor and one indirect competitor. Use the competitive analysis template below as your guide, but feel free to change categories, especially in the "other information" category.

| | | COMPETITIVE ANALYSIS TEMPLATE | |
|---|---|---|---|
| | | YOUR COMPANY | COMPETITOR 1 NAME | COMPETITOR 2 NAME |
| | | | DIRECT COMPETITOR | INDIRECT COMPETITOR |
| Company Highlights | Company Offering | | | |
| | Age of Company | | | |
| | Competitive Advantage | | | |
| Market Information | Target Market | | | |
| | Market Share | | | |
| | Marketing Strategy | | | |
| | Online Reviews/ Influencers | | | |
| Product Information | Products and Services | | | |
| | Benefits and Features | | | |
| | Pricing | | | |
| | Distribution Channels | | | |
| Other Information | Company Strengths | | | |
| | Company Weakness | | | |
| | Online Presence | | | |
| | Media Mentions | | | |
| | Future Opportunities | | | |

## Critical Thinking Questions

1. What did you learn about your competition that you did not already know?

2. Are you positioning yourself in a unique way relative to the competition?

3. Can you effectively compete in the market(s) you have chosen? Do you need to shape your idea further? ●

## Who Is Your Competition? Why Are You Better?

Every startup has competition, and yours will be no exception. Preparing a competitive analysis is the best way to find out more about your competition and establish the reasons why your business is better.[9, 10] The "What Do You Know About Your Competition?" Mindshift provides a competitive analysis template that enables you to compare your venture with other competitors.

## Who Is on Your Team and What Do They Bring to the Table?

Note down the different members of your team, their key duties and responsibilities, and the unique skills they bring to the venture. If you are planning to add people to your team, write those down too, and add any details of when they will start work.

## What Are Your Financial Projections?

Include in your plan a concise forecast of your future revenues and expenses. This is a good exercise for taking stock of where your company is right now, the targets and milestones you hope to achieve, and any obstacles that you may need to overcome. Supplement A: Financial Statements and Projections for Startups provides more information on how to work out your company's financial projections.

# 10.5 THE BUSINESS PLAN DEBATE

>> **LO 10.5** **Debate the value of writing business plans.**

Of all the types of plans presented in this chapter, the business plan is the most complex and time-consuming document to create. There is considerable debate on the value of spending the time writing a business plan. Proponents of writing a business plan say it helps you gain clarity, keeps you organized, establishes the core message, and creates alignment among team members.[11] It also helps establish legitimacy because, if nothing else, you have a business plan.

Some entrepreneurs in the very early stages find the practice of writing a simple business plan *just for themselves* a great exercise in thinking about things they may not have thought of before. It ensures that you truly understand the components of the plan and the best way to communicate these details to your team and investors. Practicing your plan also helps you to question the validity of your ideas, the markets you intend to target, and the customers you would like to attract.

Others point out that many ideas are pursued but may not be opportunities. The process of writing a business plan helps you vet the idea and shape it into an opportunity. As a result, spending time writing a business plan could help save the entrepreneur a lot of time and money down the road. For example, it can take up to 200 hours to write a comprehensive business plan. That's about a $10,000 investment, assuming you might get $50 per hour for writing a plan ($50 x 200). However, launching a poor idea and unproven concept could cost you millions.[12]

A business plan can be useful at the stage when you have partners or team members on board. It allows everyone to articulate a vision and strategy and ensures that everyone is aligned with current and future plans for the business. It is also a valuable benchmarking tool, as it forces you to be honest about your company's performance by showing not only areas where your business exceeded expectations but also those instances when your strategies didn't work out and the lessons you learned.

Nevertheless, there is growing support for *not* writing a business plan.[13] Those against writing a business plan say that the plan is old as soon as it comes off the printer, it's based on untested assumptions, financial projections are too far out to have validity, and the actual writing and compiling discourages action and gathering real data.[14] As just mentioned, it can take 200 hours to write a comprehensive business plan. Opponents of the business plan feel these hours could be spent on actual activities that can help shape the business idea, get customer input, make early sales, and so on.

# Can We Think Ourselves Into (and out of) Planning?

Planning helps entrepreneurs face uncertainty and also helps them deal with the fact that they do not have all information they need to make decisions. According to researchers Brinckman and Kim, business planning is "an activity that is directed to predict the future and develop an appropriate course of action." They also suggest that given the future orientation of planning, new entrepreneurs may not want to engage in planning activities because the lack of information leads to fears, doubts, and decisions not to push forward. The researchers suggest that entrepreneurs tend to avoid planning for two main reasons: they prefer to focus on the present or the task of planning seems too time-consuming and daunting. This suggests that entrepreneurs feel they can use their time better on things other than planning.

Brinckman and Kim hypothesized that first-time entrepreneurs trying to get new ventures started would be more likely to undertake more business planning activities if they had entrepreneurial self-efficacy and entrepreneurial perseverance. Entrepreneurial self-efficacy (ESE) is one's belief in one's ability to perform entrepreneurial roles and tasks. ESE consists of five skills needed to be successful entrepreneurs: marketing, innovation, management, risk-taking, and financial control. Entrepreneurial perseverance (EP) refers to one's ability to continue entrepreneurial efforts regardless of setback, hurdles, and uncertainty. It's really the entrepreneur's ability to push through despite the highs and lows of starting a new business.

The researchers looked at 479 single-owner ventures to test their hypothesis. In other words, they only looked at ventures that were started by one person instead of a team. Additionally, all of the entrepreneurs in the sample were nascent entrepreneurs—those who are in the process of starting a new venture.

The researchers found the following:

- Founders with very high ESE developed more formal business plans than founders with low levels.
- Founders with high EP were more likely to engage in business planning activities, but they were not necessarily formal business plans.

- Founders with low EP were less likely to engage in business planning because it may be perceived as an overly challenging activity and takes too much time.
- Entrepreneurs with a bachelor's degree were more likely to have a formal, written plan.

This was the first study that used cognitive factors, ESE and EP, as variables to determine who does and who does not write formal business plans and why.

In sum, although formal business plans have their place, they may not necessarily be relevant to the new entrepreneur. Entrepreneurs are explorers—they take action to find answers, rather than basing their assumptions on speculation. They are also experts in using social capital—the people and connections you need to make your business a success. No entrepreneur is an island.

So, what should come before the business plan? As we have pointed out many times, at the early stages it is essential to follow the Entrepreneurship Method, to take action, and get out of the building. And make sure you have mastered the basic skills required for a successful venture—financial management, production capabilities, and marketing and sales. When you have proved your concept and gathered the data to go with it, then you will be able to produce a solid, credible business plan.

## Critical Thinking Questions

1. Think about your own ESE and EP. What does your self-analysis say about your propensity for writing a formal business plan?

2. Given the findings from this research, why are business plans less popular today than they were 20 years ago?

3. Explain the difference between "planning" and "the plan" as it relates to this research. ●

**Sources:**

Brinckmann, J., & Kim, S. M. (2015). Why we plan: The impact of nascent entrepreneurs; Cognitive characteristics and human capital on business planning. *Strategic Entrepreneurship Journal, 9,* 153–166.

Chen, C. C., Greene, P. G., & Crick, A. (1998). Does entrepreneurial self-efficacy distinguish entrepreneurs from managers? *Journal of Business Venturing, 13*(4), 295–316.

The idea that the business plan—the most formal and complex of plans—is the first step for an entrepreneur is an outdated view. The business plan is more often used for bank loans and professional investment, but many other types of plans should be generated prior to the formal business plan.

Eric Ries, author of *The Lean Startup*, argues that one reason startups fail is due to "the allure of a good plan, a solid strategy, and thorough market research." Ries hints that corporate strategic planning led us to the conundrum that if a business plan works for the greatest corporations in the world, then it must be good for startups too! Ries notes, "Planning and forecasting are only accurate when based on a long, stable operating history and a relatively static environment. Startups have neither."[15]

# 10.6 TIPS FOR WRITING ANY TYPE OF PLAN

>> **LO 10.6** **Implement the tips for writing business plans.**

When you feel you need some type of plan on paper, whether a feasibility study, pitch deck, or even a formal business plan, keep in mind what you put on paper represents *you*.

Remember, different audiences require different plans, and each plan should be tailored accordingly. For example, potential investors will be keen to know more about the financials because they will want to know details of the return on their investment, as well as a time frame for when there is an exit event.

The key to any written plan is knowledge—showing that you have done your homework through exploration, experimentation, and market research is one of the best ways to impress your audience. If your plan does not have a solid basis in fact and research, then do not waste time writing one. Following are some tips for writing formal business plans.[16] Keep in mind, though, that these tips are good for all types of plans we have discussed!

## Remove the Fluff

Decorative language can sound nice, but do not be tempted to use it in a business plan. Too much wordiness or jargon can detract from the main message. For example, opening with "In our current environment of fast food, hot dogs are still a much sought-after food enjoyed by people all over the U.S." is purely a waste of space. Most people will know that hot dogs are a popular fast food, and they don't need to be reminded of this.

A better introduction to your business is to describe what it is, its current location, and the target market. For example, "Harry's Gourmet Hot Dogs is a food truck located in southwest Washington that offers 25 different hot dog varieties to satisfy the discerning tastes of local office workers, residents, and seasonal tourists." Here, instead of fillers and unnecessary detail, you have used direct language to quickly and clearly convey a description of your company without taking up too much space.

## Define Your Target Audience

It might sound obvious, but many people neglect to properly define their target audience. Remember, there is no business in the world that will appeal to everyone. This is why it is so important to specify your target market, present how and why you have drawn these conclusions, and explain how you intend to target that particular customer segment.

## Be Realistic

Outline the challenges ahead, potential risks, lessons you have learned, and opportunities to progress. A strong idea will stand on its merit when you are realistic about it. Everything you write or present must be based in fact or well-researched assumptions.

## Focus on Your Competition

There is no such thing as no competition, regardless of how unique you think your business is. Focus on what your business does, but explain what differentiates your product or service from the competition and how you plan to compete now and in the future.

## Understand Your Distribution Channels

Make sure you know how your product or service will be delivered to your target customers. Any vagueness around your distribution channels will cause investors to second guess you and your business.

**You should always proofread, accuracy-check, and spell-check materials before showing your business plan to investors.**

## Avoid the Hockey Stick Projection

Ask any entrepreneur about "hockey stick projections" and they will smile and roll their eyes at the same time! A hockey stick projection is one that shows very few sales in Year 1, then suddenly, perhaps in Year 3 or 4, sales skyrocket. When you graph the growth in sales from Year 1 to Year 5, the line looks like a hockey stick, and it's typically unrealistic. Even though it can be difficult to establish solid financial projections, be conservative in your approach to financials. You may feel certain that your business will capture 50% of the market next year, but it is better to present a more plausible percentage, for example 10%. There is no use presenting figures based on guesswork or blown wildly out of proportion. If possible, back up your projections with examples to show investors that you are at least in the right ballpark. Remember, investors want a realistic picture of where your business is now and where you hope it will end up in the future. Overly optimistic projections are sure to put your investors off.

## Avoid Typos, Grammatical Mistakes, and Inconsistencies

Revise your plan thoroughly for any mistakes and inconsistencies before you show it to investors. For example, if your plan's summary includes the requirement for $60,000 in investment but your projection shows that you plan to have $70,000 in cash flow in the first year, you have clearly made a mistake. Careless mistakes like these will not impress investors. Ask other people to review your plan for you; a second pair of eyes is invaluable for picking up errors. Furthermore, avoid exaggerated language like "hottest" and "greatest"—these words will not validate your product or service and will certainly not endear you to investors.

## Be Honest About Your Weaknesses

Every business has its weaknesses, but it's better to be upfront about them rather than hide them. You don't need to go into too much detail about weaknesses, but you do need to include a well-thought-out strategy explaining how you plan to address these issues.

**TABLE 10.7**

Business Plan Resources

| WEBSITE ADDRESS | DESCRIPTION |
| --- | --- |
| https://www.sba.gov/writing-business-plan | The U.S. Small Business Administration guide to writing a business plan |
| http://www.entrepreneur.com/landing/224842 | *Entrepreneur* magazine's "How to Write a Business Plan" |
| http://www.entrepreneur.com/formnet/form/561 | A free template for writing a business plan from *Entrepreneur* magazine's Business Form Template Gallery |
| http://www.caycon.com/resources.php?s=4 | A collection of business plan resources in the Entrepreneur's Library—Startup Resources From Cayenne Consulting |
| http://www.businessnewsdaily.com/5680-simple-business-plan-templates.html | Eight simple business plan templates for entrepreneurs from *Business News Daily* |

## Use Visuals

Visuals are a good way to break up the text, help the plan flow better, and bring your idea to life. However, be careful not to crowd the plan with too many graphs, charts, and images. Use adequate white space for optimal legibility and a clean, uncluttered look.

The right time to write a business plan is when your business is more established, you have a fully functioning team involved, and you have the data to prove your concept. If you are considering expanding the business and seeking funding, now would be a good time to write a business plan. Table 10.7 lists some useful resources for writing a business plan when the time comes. ●

**$SAGE edge™**

Get the tools you need to sharpen your study skills. SAGE edge offers a robust online environment featuring an impressive array of free tools and resources.

- Access practice quizzes, eFlashcards, video, and multimedia at
  **edge.sagepub.com/neckentrepreneurship2e**

**10.1  Examine "planning" from an entrepreneurial perspective.**

From an entrepreneurial perspective, planning helps clarify the entrepreneurial vision and helps the entrepreneur articulate where the business is going and how it can succeed. Entrepreneurs can use alternative planning methods, including simplified plans, planning with preparation, and planning with imagination.

**10.2  Explain vision as an important part of planning.**

All planning starts with a vision. The vivid vision exercise is a good way to present your vison in writing or as sketch or video. It should describe what the future looks like rather than detailing how you're going to get there.

**10.3  Explain the different types of plans used by entrepreneurs.**

Different types of plans include the Business Model Canvas, the business brief, the feasibility study, the pitch deck, and the business plan.

**10.4  Describe the questions to ask during planning.**

Regardless of what type of plan you are working on, you must ask the following questions: What is your business and how does it add value? Who is your customer? How big is the market? How will you enter the market? What do you know about the industry? Who is your competition and why are you better? Who is on your team and what do they bring to the table? And, what are your financial projections?

**10. 5  Debate the value of writing business plans.**

Experts disagree on the value of spending the time writing a business plan. Some see a business plan as complex, time-consuming, and based on untested assumptions, while others believe it is a useful way to crystallize and organize ideas. Formal business plans have their place, but they may not necessarily be relevant to the new entrepreneur.

**10.6  Implement the tips for writing business plans.**

Tips for writing business plans include use visuals; remove any fluff; define your target audience; understand your distribution; focus on your competition; avoid typos, grammatical mistakes, and inconsistencies; avoid the exaggerated hockey stick; be honest about weaknesses; and be realistic.

Business plan   243

Concept statement   247

Feasibility study   238

Planning   233

## Boyd Cohen, cofounder, IoMob

Boyd Cohen is the cofounder of IoMob, a decentralized mobility network and platform built on blockchain technology. IoMob democratizes access to the mobility marketplace, both public and private. "In other words, if you are a user and want to get from point A to point B, then we'll give you a solution for the most optimal route, keeping in mind all mobility solutions available like public transport, bike shares, or taxi cabs. Any mobility service, even an individual provider, could be accessible by users through IoMob. We are not trying to be Uber. We are the anti-Uber," Boyd explains.

Boyd Cohen, an expert in smart cities and shared mobility, got his PhD in Entrepreneurship, Internet, and Sustainability from the University of Colorado in 2001. It was around this time that he read a book on profitable, environmentally responsible business practices called *Natural Capitalism,* by Amory Lovins, Hunter Lovins, and Paul Hawken. Being a die-hard capitalist at the time who worked for a big multinational consulting firm, Accenture, Boyd also enjoyed being in nature—mountain biking in the summers and snowboarding in the winters. *Natural Capitalism* inspired Boyd to view and use entrepreneurship as a medium to propagate positive change and bring these two worlds of capitalism and nature together. He dedicated his career both as an academic and an entrepreneur to this cause. Since then, Boyd has had a plethora of experiences, from starting companies, to consulting, to academia.

In 2011, Boyd wrote his first book, *Climate Capitalism,* as a sequel to *Natural Capitalism* along with one of the original authors, Hunter Lovins. At the time, the world was optimistic about Barack Obama's administration making real progress on climate change at the 2011 UN Climate Change Conference in Durban, South Africa. Frustrated with lack of action at both the national and international levels, Boyd started to view cities as potential agents for change. However, Boyd has been involved with making cities smarter since long before 2011. "Technically, I would say I've been in smart cities for over 12 years now. My first startup (2006), was a SaaS (Software as a Service) solution for cities to transparently track, monitor, and report their sustainability performance. Maybe we would've called them a smart cities project now, but in 2006 nobody was calling it that!"

In 2014, he and his colleague Jan Kietzmann wrote one of the most frequently cited peer-reviewed academic papers on shared mobility. Shared mobility refers to transportation services and resources that are shared among users, either concurrently or consecutively. This includes public transit; taxis and limos; bike sharing; car sharing (round-trip, one-way, and peer-to-peer); ride sharing (i.e., noncommercial services like carpooling and vanpooling); ride sourcing or ride hailing; shuttle services and "micro transit"; and more. Boyd believes that he has come full circle in his worldviews. Funnily enough, after writing a book (*Climate Capitalism*) that propagates using capitalism to tackle climate change and another book *(The Emergence of the Urban Entrepreneur,* 2016) that focused on innovation, entrepreneurship, and smart cities, his third book, *Post-Capitalist Entrepreneurship: Start-Ups for the 99%* (2017), was geared toward what steps can be taken beyond capitalism to make the economy more inclusive. For the book, he interviewed an entrepreneur, Jamie Burke, cofounder and CEO of Outlier Ventures, a venture fund well known for investing in blockchain. As they started to talk, Jamie told Boyd that if he were to start a blockchain company, Jamie would help him incubate the company. "At first I wasn't so sure. I mean, I was getting close to 50 and I've done several startups. I was sort of, kind of, enjoying my life as an academic. It's not so easy being an entrepreneur. But the blockchain bug got me."

Boyd knew that blockchain technology was a disruptive technology. As Boyd notes, "Digital currencies created through blockchain remove nation states and dilute the power of lobbyists and banks that are too big to fail. An alternative currency enables peer-to-peer transaction without involving its national governments. Similarly, blockchain can mediate peer-to-peer economies without the Ubers and the Airbnb's in the middle." Boyd feels that companies like Airbnb and Uber are platform companies that are not really sharing their "platform capitalism." This prompted Boyd to research and think about business models that support a truer, peer-to-peer sharing economy.

Burke told Boyd that they were doing a lot of work on a newer type of peer-to-peer model called *platform cooperativism*, a cooperative ownership of the platform. For instance, Airbnb would not be owned by Airbnb but by the homeowners and users. Boyd started to look into creating a blockchain-enabled platform for the few taxi cooperatives in Boulder and Denver, Colorado, his hometown. These taxi co-ops were not big enough to compete with the likes of Uber and therefore could not expect the customer to download three (or more) different apps for each taxi service. So Boyd created an app called Coopify that focused on building tech stacks for these co-op businesses that did not have the expertise or confidence to invest in technology. However, Boyd noticed a bigger opportunity, which had the potential to disrupt the market. Every city has its own bike sharing, car sharing, and public transport services that use closed networks to compete with each other. Boyd saw a powerful opportunity to use blockchain to connect them all. He pivoted the business idea in November 2017 and started reaching out to advisors. IoMob was born.

Boyd leveraged his extensive network to find the best people to invite to be IoMob advisors. The first one to join was Susan Shaheen from UC Berkeley, one of the world's leading experts on shared mobility and also sometimes called the "mother of shared mobility." Knowing that he did not have the ability to do blockchain computing, Boyd started looking for a cofounder/CTO for the company. "To me, one of the most important success factors for an entrepreneur is to identify where you're weak, where your team is weak, and convincing really good people who can fill that gap to join your team." He soon found Josep Sanjuas, a PhD in computer science, for the role of the CTO and got Victor Lopez, another computer science PhD, to join as the third cofounder. In late 2018, he resigned from his role as the dean of research at EADA Business School in Barcelona, Spain, to pursue IoMob full time. The company now has eight full-time people and two part-time people working on IoMob.

IoMob, as Boyd explains it, "is a decentralized mobility aggregation platform. IoMob stands for Internet of Mobility (inspired by IoT, or Internet of Things). Just like IoT, where different devices connected to the Internet can also be seamlessly connected together, IoMob does the same for mobility services through a digital layer. We connect every mobility service, public and private, into an open marketplace so that the end user has seamless access to discover, get multimodal routing, book, and pay for any mobility service you want through one open application connected to our marketplace." A mobility startup that wants to enter a market crowded with players that already have big private network effects can use IoMob's platform to reach out to customers.

IoMob leverages the blockchain ecosystem to create smart contracts between users, a function unique to blockchain. A smart contract allows any service provider to connect with customers (in this case, connected to the IoMob protocol) and charge whatever fees they deem fit, without the hassle of negotiating with the platform. Likewise, the customer can choose to accept the offer or not. This way, companies that offer their own mobility solutions can link to the IoMob platform to provide alternative modes of transport in case their services are unavailable. This might retain an existing customer base and help the other service provider monetize a customer he or she could not have had before. For example, if a bike sharing company has run out of bikes, it can link to the IoMob platform, which will then provide alternative transport solutions to the bike sharing company's customers. Today, IoMob's primary customers are governments and private operators. Boyd believes that mobility services such as Uber and Lyft would be the last ones to join IoMob's platform, and even if they did, they would be providing the service of fulfilling the requests of customers who could not find another mobility option.

Instead of writing a business plan in the beginning stage of the company, Boyd and his colleagues wrote three white papers explaining the concept behind Coopify and, later, IoMob. Because the company is in the pre-revenue stage, Boyd and his team are now focusing efforts on testing the proof of concept in real-world settings. Apart from being a semi-finalist in the City of Tomorrow, Ford Motor Company Pilot Competition in Pittsburgh, IoMob has scheduled test sprints with the Public Transit Authority in Portland, Oregon, and is in talks with the Netherlands, Singapore, and big brands such as Hyundai.

Boyd feels that one of the challenges they might face relates to the mindsets of business providers. "Capitalists are likely to take more time to come to terms with a completely open marketplace where your competitors could potentially know your inventory. On the other hand, smaller players love this openness. It is a way for them to feel like they've overcome the barrier to entry in a market," he says.

Boyd believes that mobility could either become monopolized by the likes of Uber or become a completely open mobility marketplace. A few multibillion-dollar OEMs, and car manufacturers who "see the writing on the wall," want to partner with IoMob for the future that depends less on private vehicle ownership. Another challenge that Boyd has faced with IoMob is communicating the vision of the company to potential stakeholders like public transit authorities. Because both the technology and concept are new, governments sometimes have a hard time grasping the context and IoMob's potential impact. However, over time, Boyd has tweaked the messaging to focus on the value proposition of IoMob as opposed to making it sound overly technical. "It's been an evolution of our own understanding of how to tell the narrative and how to share it with different audiences," says Boyd.

Boyd hopes to be able to leverage the billions of dollars being invested into blockchain technology to be able to scale up his operations successfully. To date, he has raised $700,000. And it's not just about immediate scale, but also about preparing for the future. The mobility market is changing every day. Boyd believes that he has a strong team that can tackle these changes and adapt accordingly.

Early in March 2019, Boyd and his IoMob team were one of 10 startups selected out of 360 to join the Techstars Accelerator Program in Amsterdam. "Techstars has taught us we have not been disciplined enough with ourselves as founders and as a team to ensure that everyone knows what their priorities are and is tracking their progress on a weekly basis. After going through this process the past few weeks, we are going to do a similar exercise every week with our own team." Additionally, Techstars introduced Boyd to a group of almost 90 mentors during the first 3 weeks of the Techstar program—it's referred to as the "Mentor Madness" phase. Mentor Madness forced Boyd and his team to be more open than ever to tough, constructive feedback. "This type of tough feedback is essential to achieving our global ambitions," said Boyd.

Boyd says that he has learned a lot of lessons through all his startup experiences. He reflects, "Don't fall in love with your cofounder. Dedicate less time to fundraising and more time to create a quality product or a service. Do not outsource competitive advantage. Media attention is great, but it is very difficult to convert this attention into monetary sales."

## Critical Thinking Questions

1. How do you begin planning for a venture when the technology is so new?

2. What evidence in the case did you see of Boyd Cohen planning?

3. IoMob is in its beginning. What do you think its future holds? Would you invest today?

**Sources:**

Boyd Cohen (interview with Babson MBA graduate assistant Gaurav Khemka, November 7, 2018)

Cohen, B., & Kietzmann, J. (2014). Ride on! Mobility business models for the sharing economy. *Organization & Environment, 27*(3), 279–296. Retrieved from https://www.researchgate.net/publication/267757539_Ride_On_Mobility_Business_Models_for_the_Sharing_Economy

Maxwell, L. (2018). An interview with Susan Shaheen. *UC Berkeley Institute of Transportation Studies.* Retrieved from https://tsrc.berkeley.edu/news/interview-susan-shaheen-%E2%80%9Cmother%E2%80%9D-shared-mobility

What is shared mobility? (2019). *Shared Use Mobility Center.* Retrieved from https://sharedusemobilitycenter.org/what-is-shared-mobility/

©iStockphoto.com/Gearstd

# 11 Anticipating Failure

"Failure is fuel. Fuel is power."

—Abby Wambach, retired soccer star

# Chapter Outline

# Learning Objectives

11.1 Describe failure and its effect on entrepreneurs.

11.2 Identify several reasons for failure.

11.3 Describe the consequences of fear of failure for entrepreneurs.

11.4 Explain the different ways entrepreneurs can learn from failure.

11.5 Describe the significance of "grit" and its role in building tolerance for failure.

## 11.1 FAILURE AND ENTREPRENEURSHIP

>> **LO 11.1 Describe failure and its effect on entrepreneurs.**

In Chapter 1, we explained the ill-defined, unstructured, unpredictable, chaotic, and complex nature of entrepreneurship. We also presented some daunting statistics showing that not all attempts to grow a business will be successful, especially when many of the attempts end in bankruptcy. The reality is that many startups fail; therefore, it is important to include the topic of failure when discussing entrepreneurship.

A business failure is generally conceived as the termination of a commercial organization that has missed its goals and failed to achieve investors' expectations, preventing the venture from continuing to operate and resulting in bankruptcy or liquidation. Any type of failure, however, can intensify the cognitive processes involved in learning, resulting in improvements in future performance and increasing the probability of future success. For this reason, many entrepreneurs see failure as part of the journey. In the case of business failures, having learned from failure, entrepreneurs often feel more confident, prepared, and motivated to attempt another startup venture.

Despite these perceived benefits, the failure of a venture can be not only financially costly but also emotionally painful, even traumatic. The experience is not that different from ending a long relationship or losing a loved one, resulting in feelings of grief and loss, leaving the entrepreneur feeling guilty and even ashamed while wondering what exactly went wrong and how it could have been avoided.

Big failures in business are the ones we hear about the most. Bankruptcy or forced sale is probably the biggest failure for a startup. California-based peer-to-peer used car startup Beepi is a good example of an epic fail.[1] Beepi had raised more than $150 million from investors, but it burned through the money too quickly—reports showed that the founders were overspending on their own salaries and expensive office furniture—and ended up laying off almost 200 employees before closing its doors for good in 2017. Or take Juicero, the home juice maker that had received almost $120 million in funding from Google Ventures, Kleiner Perkins, and Campbell Soup Company.[2] Although the device seemed like an efficient way to make juice at home, the startup folded after a Bloomberg article reported that the pre-packed packets of juice and vegetables to be transformed into juice by the machine generated the same amount of liquid as if the packets had been squeezed by hand. The company was shut down shortly after the negative marketing exposure.

Poor money management caused the downfall of Beepi and a badly researched product was to blame for Juicero's closure. We can usually find many reasons behind the closure of a startup. Contributing factors often include lack of market need, poor marketing, and loss of focus. Figure 11.1 lists the most common reasons behind the failure of startups.

**SAGE** edge™

Master the content at
**edge.sagepub.com/
neckentrepreneurship2e**

# David James, K12 Landing

Photo courtesy of David James

**David James, founder of K12 Landing**

David James holds the record at his high school for most magazines sold during a fundraiser. He found out the record was 74 so he sold 75! What does this have to do with entrepreneurship? Keep reading.

David earned an MBA from Babson College and a bachelor's in business administration from Bucknell University. During college, he interned with a large investment bank in New York City, and upon graduation transitioned into education as a corps member with Teach for America (TFA). There he was a founding member of the Boston region of TFA and taught 8th-grade science.

After completing his 2-year commitment with TFA, he helped restart a low-performing middle school in South Boston. Later he cofounded UP Academy Oliver, a public school for 6th–8th graders in Lawrence, Massachusetts, as part of a state-led district reform effort. During his time in education, he noticed that teachers didn't have enough high-quality training and development programs to choose from. He knew that teachers were required to participate in training every year, but the teachers didn't have a way to find something relevant and worthwhile. As a result, he

started to think about a new venture. He wanted to start a service to connect K–12 teachers to relevant training and development programs across the country. David called the service K12 Landing.

During his MBA program, David refined the idea for K12 Landing, raised a small amount of startup capital, hired a web development firm to build out a website, and even hired an employee to lead marketing. But by the time David finished his MBA, K12 Landing had not met expectations; the business model wasn't working and revenue wasn't generated. K12 Landing failed. Reflecting on his K12 Landing experience, he explained, "While I had strong knowledge of the K–12 education landscape, my lack of experience working with technology developers and sales led me to underestimate the barriers of starting the business." He added, "I was often frustrated by the slow rate of progress and lack of communication with developers. I fired my first developer and had to find a new one to rebuild the entire website.

Rather than looking at the experience of K12 Landing as a failure, David took away valuable lessons that led him to "pivot" his business and focus on higher education. "I now recognize the importance of leaning on your network and relying on people you know well, especially when starting a new venture." As David closed K12 Landing, he simultaneously began building a new venture called Beacon Instructional Partners that is focused on providing personalized instructional coaching to college professors. He recognized that he needed to pursue a venture that more closely aligned with his instructional background and would allow him to better leverage his network in the world of education.

His experience with K12 Landing and learning the nuances of starting a business paid off when he secured his first paying client soon after completing his MBA program. "With Beacon Instructional Partners I have more realistic expectations," said David, "and I am more intentional about how I manage things so that we set ourselves up for incremental growth." He also admits that after the K12 Landing failure he is more accustomed to the pressures of entrepreneurship as well as the need for sales skills and a keen understanding of the customer.

Beacon Instructional Partners has quickly expanded to four team members. After this initial success, David says that entrepreneurship in professional services often comes down to "being able to define exactly what you do and what value you can provide in language that clients understand and resonate with." But he's not all in just yet. David still has a full-time job with a national education consulting firm. "I will go full time when I have the confidence that it can support me and my family. This is the type of personal decision that varies for everyone." Ultimately, David provides great evidence that entrepreneurship is about learning as you go. With this mentality, failure doesn't exist. It's just part of the Entrepreneurship Method.

## Critical Thinking Questions

1. What is a pivot? How did pivoting positively affect David's career?

2. What can you learn about lack of ability from David's ventures with K12 Landing?

3. How would you handle the failure of a business venture? ●

**Source:** David James (interview with the author, December 15, 2018)

---

**FIGURE 11.1**

## The Top 20 Reasons Startups Fail

### Based on an Analysis of 101 Startup Post-Mortems

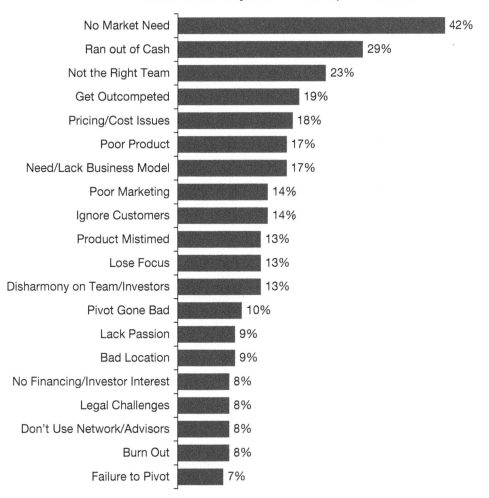

| Reason | Percentage |
|---|---|
| No Market Need | 42% |
| Ran out of Cash | 29% |
| Not the Right Team | 23% |
| Get Outcompeted | 19% |
| Pricing/Cost Issues | 18% |
| Poor Product | 17% |
| Need/Lack Business Model | 17% |
| Poor Marketing | 14% |
| Ignore Customers | 14% |
| Product Mistimed | 13% |
| Lose Focus | 13% |
| Disharmony on Team/Investors | 13% |
| Pivot Gone Bad | 10% |
| Lack Passion | 9% |
| Bad Location | 9% |
| No Financing/Investor Interest | 8% |
| Legal Challenges | 8% |
| Don't Use Network/Advisors | 8% |
| Burn Out | 8% |
| Failure to Pivot | 7% |

**Source:** CB Insights https://www.cbinsights.com/blog/startup-failure-reasons-top/

| **TABLE 11.1** |
|---|

Entrepreneurs Share Their Reasons for Failure

| **PSYCHE "MISTAKES"** |
|---|
| "Fear." —Philip Rosedale, founder, *High Fidelity, Inc.,* and *Second Life* |
| "Letting opinions cloud your purpose." —Scott Lewallen, founder, *Grindr* |
| "Trusting by default." —Jay Adelson, chair and founder, *Opsmatic* |
| "Not believing in myself was the biggest mistake I made as an entrepreneur." —Sam Shank, cofounder/CEO, *HotelTonight* |
| "Spending too much time worrying about competition and not enough time making what I'm building amazing." —Brenden Mulligan, founder/CEO, *Cluster Labs* |
| "Thinking that entrepreneurship was the most meaningful part of my life." —Mick Hagen, founder, *Zinch.com, Spatch, Undrip.com,* and *Mainframe* |
| **WAITING TOO LONG MISTAKES** |
| "My biggest mistake as an entrepreneur was waiting too long to start." —Jason Nazar, founder, *Docstoc.com* |
| "Not pivoting soon enough." —Peter Kazanjy, founder, *TalentBin* |
| "Waiting to see if a problem would resolve itself." —Joshua Forman, cofounder, *Inkling* |
| **HIRING MISTAKES** |
| "Hiring too fast and firing too slow." —Dan Yates, cofounder/CEO, *OPOWER* |
| "Hiring bad fits." —John Battelle, cofounder/CEO, *NewCo, Federated Media, Web 2.0 Summit, Wired* |
| "Getting the wrong people on the bus was the biggest mistake I made as an entrepreneur." —Hooman Radfar, partner, *Expa,* and founder, *AddThis* |

**Source:** Carman, E. R. (2015, June 25). Successful entrepreneurs reveal their biggest mistakes. *FounderDating.* Retrieved from http://founderdating.com/successful-entrepreneurs-reveal-biggest-mistakes/

It is also useful to hear how entrepreneurs themselves articulate the underlying reasons as to why their startups failed. Table 11.1 provides examples of entrepreneurs who attribute their failures to three main causes: their psyche, people mistakes, and market mistakes.

However, there is an important difference between the epic fail and the types of failure entrepreneurs should actually expect, embrace, and leverage. No one wants or even expects catastrophic failure such as bankruptcy, but all entrepreneurs experience countless small "fails" that require a quick reaction and sometimes a change in direction, often known as the **pivot**. Pivots for entrepreneurs include changing directions on such things as the product, customer segment, revenue model, or distribution channel.[3] A small fail is an event—an obstacle to overcome to get through the other side—whereas a big fail like the collapse of a business is a process that unfolds over time; it is more personal and can be more difficult to recover from.

**Pivot:** a change in business direction.

The most successful entrepreneurs embrace and leverage failure and pivot when they need to—a key component of the Entrepreneurship Method that we presented in Chapter 1 and have built on throughout this book. David James, featured in Entrepreneurship in Action, made a successful pivot from his education marketplace K12 Landing to setting up his own instructional consulting practice.

Small failures are considered the "valleys" in the entrepreneurial journey that include the setbacks, the missteps, the ill-planned experiments, the misplaced decisions—all manageable events that can help you build on what you learn. Small, reversible, informative failures along the way can highlight key issues and set you on a better path to success. The point is that if we can expect and embrace the learning from the small failures, then perhaps we can mitigate the risks of the big failures.

# 11.2 THE FAILURE SPECTRUM

>> **LO 11.2**  **Identify several reasons for failure.**

Amy Edmondson, a professor of leadership and management at Harvard Business School, believes that failures range from big to small along a failure spectrum (see Figure 11.2). Although many of us link the admission of failure with taking the blame, Edmondson believes that not all failures are blameworthy; her spectrum of failures runs from blameworthy to praiseworthy. Some of the reasons for failure on the spectrum are indeed blameworthy. For example, entrepreneurs who intentionally violate certain rules and regulations ("Deviance," at the top of the spectrum) are more likely to have failed businesses as well as a tarnished reputation. However, not all of the failures in the spectrum are bad—in fact, many of them are at least preventable or even praiseworthy. Someone who doesn't have the skills to do a job can receive more training; processes can be monitored and refined; and "failed" hypotheses and exploratory testing can be opportunities to expand knowledge, iterate, and set the scene for different, better approaches.[4]

Despite our misgivings about failure, it is not always bad. The failure spectrum describes situations that may be perceived as failures, yet can sometimes have positive rather than negative outcomes. Let's look at the failure spectrum in greater depth.

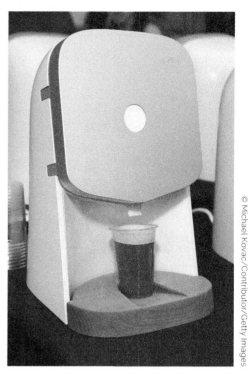

© Michael Kovac/Contributor/Getty Images

**Startup company Juicero collapsed due to poor product research.**

## FIGURE 11.2

### The Failure Spectrum

| | |
|---|---|
| **Deviance** | • The entrepreneur defies legal and ethical boundaries leading to mismanagement of the venture. |
| **Inattention** | • The entrepreneur gets sidetracked from the core business—either in a new business direction or by delegating too much too soon without following up. |
| **Lack of Ability** | • The entrepreneur is overextended and lacks the skillset to get the job done. |
| **Process Inadequacy** | • The wrong (or lack of) processes are set up in the organization such that communication breaks down among employees and things begin to fall through the cracks. |
| **Uncertainty** | • The entrepreneur takes unreasonable actions due to a lack of clarity about future events. |
| **Exploratory Experimentation** | • The entrepreneur conducts market tests to get early feedback and acquire important learning and information. |

**Source:** Adapted from Amy C. Edmondson. Strategies for learning from failure. *Harvard Business Review*, April 2011. https://hbr .org/2011/04/strategies-for-learning-from-failure

©iStockphoto.com/JasonDoiy

**Blood-testing startup Theranos collapsed under the weight of false claims and fraudulent charges.**

**Deviance:** when an entrepreneur defies legal and ethical boundaries, leading to mismanagement of the venture.

**Inattention:** when an entrepreneur becomes sidetracked from the core business.

## Deviance

**Deviance** occurs when an entrepreneur defies legal and ethical boundaries, leading to mismanagement of the venture. Blood-testing startup Theranos is a good example of a company that demonstrated deviance from social norms, as well as defiance of legal and ethical boundaries. Founded in 2003 by then-19-year-old Stanford drop-out Elizabeth Holmes, this startup promised to take the trauma out of blood testing by using just a single drop of blood that would run through the Theranos machine called the Edison. The company claimed that the Edison could run 240 different blood tests, but in fact, only a few could actually be done on the Edison.[5] The remaining tests were done on machines that were competitors of Theranos. The deviance was that customers, board members, and investors thought the Edison was actually running 240 tests using a single drop of blood. In 2018, Elizabeth Holmes and former company president Ramesh Balwani were charged with fraud for making false claims about the effectiveness of the blood-testing product.[6]

## Inattention

An entrepreneur gets sidetracked from the core business by **inattention**—either by moving in a new business direction or by delegating too much too soon without following up. Entrepreneur Siouxsie Downs became sidetracked from her main business, STEM education accelerator IQ Co-Op, by trying to manage too many different projects at once.[7] When her colleagues called her out for her lack of follow-through, Downs stepped back from some of the projects and appointed a trusted colleague to help her manage her deadlines. While she admits that letting go can be difficult, this incident made her realize that "If you don't, you will be done with the startup world," she says. "You will stretch yourself thin and give 0% to 15% effort on 20 things instead of 100% on three things. Know what you value the most and give that your all."

## Lack of Ability

**Lack of ability:** the lack of skillset to get the job done.

With **lack of ability**, the entrepreneur is overextended and lacks the skillset to get the job done. He or she may have been good at the start, but as the business grew, more skills were needed. It is very common for companies to outgrow their founders because the founders lack the skills and abilities to get the company to the next level. In some cases, the founders either can't or won't develop the necessary skills to develop the organization, and they may have to step aside as a result.[8]

For example, Eddie Lou, founder of workforce technology company Shiftgig, stepped down as CEO in favor of new CEO Wade Burgess.[9] Although Lou had the most suitable skills to set up the company, raise capital, and bring it to market, Burgess had a better skillset for growing the company to its next stage.

## Process Inadequacy

**Process inadequacy:** wrong (or missing) processes set up in the organization, causing communication breakdown.

**Process inadequacy** means the wrong processes are set up in the organization, so communication breaks down among employees and things begin to fall through the cracks. Paul Biggar and Nathan Chong are the founders of NewsTilt, a news website for independent, professional journalists. Biggar believes lack of communication was one of the reasons why the startup lasted only 2 months: "When Nathan and I signed up together, we had not spent any time working together, and that was a big mistake.[10] Nathan is certainly a great coder, but when we didn't share a vision, and we found it so difficult to communicate, there was no way we were going to get this built. You need a cofounder who gets you and whom you work together well with."

## Uncertainty

Uncertainty or lack of clarity about future events can cause entrepreneurs to take unreasonable actions. Keith B. Nowak, founder of social media instant messaging company Imercive, believes that company failed because it stuck to the wrong strategy for far too long. Nowak said, "If we had been honest with ourselves earlier on, we may have been able to pivot sooner and have enough capital left to properly execute the new strategy.[11] I believe the biggest mistake I made as CEO of Imercive was failing to pivot sooner."

**Uncertainty:** the lack of clarity about future events that can cause entrepreneurs to take unreasonable actions.

## Exploratory Experimentation

Market tests are conducted to get early feedback and acquire important learning and information. Some of these tests may fail miserably, but exploratory experimentation is crucial for learning. Joelle Mertzel, founder of countertop butter dish Butterie, tested the market for her prototype by interviewing more than 1,000 people waiting to board flights in airports all over the United States.[12] The results showed that 67% of the respondents agreed they would use the butter dish, which was enough proof for Mertzel to develop it into a viable product. Butterie now sells in Bed Bath & Beyond and is profiled on the shopping channel QVC.

**Exploratory experimentation:** a method whereby market tests are conducted to get early feedback and acquire important learning and information.

As Figure 11.2 illustrates, there are different kinds of failures. Some failures are small, adjustable, informative, linked to bigger goals, and designed to highlight key issues. Others involve rigid thinking, discouragement, and may result in reputational damage.[13] Although the reasons behind failed businesses are varied, it might surprise you that none of these count as the number one reason for startup failure. A study carried out by CBI Insights analyzing 101 startup postmortems found that 42% of startups failed because they didn't solve a big enough problem.[14] For instance, visual configurator platform company Treehouse Logic failed because its customers didn't have the time, desire, and patience to use its customization tools. Being able to customize just wasn't a big enough pain point for Treehouse Logic's target market.

Whatever the type of or reason for the failure, the most important thing for entrepreneurs is the lessons they learn.

# 11.3 FEAR OF FAILURE

>> **LO 11.3**  Describe the consequences of fear of failure for entrepreneurs.

Despite the learning and opportunities that may arise from perceived failures, many of us view failure in a negative way and try our best to avoid it. This is because the concept of failure provokes an emotional reaction or antifailure bias that inhibits us from learning from the experience. This causes us to put the failure out of our minds rather than tackling the reasons behind it.[15]

It is not surprising that we never hear much about the emotions of failure (pain, humiliation, shame, guilt, self-blame, and anger—often associated with grief) that entrepreneurs experience when their businesses go under. As serial entrepreneur Meggen Taylor said, "Your ego will be crushed. Your faith will be tested. And if work is your identity you will feel completely lost and soulless."[16] Expressing these emotions is often too much to bear, as admitting our failures can be emotionally unpleasant and can damage our self-esteem.

However, it is only by managing these emotions that entrepreneurs can begin the process of learning from failure. But this is not an easy process; sometimes we would rather blame others or external events for failures in order to maintain our self-esteem and sense of control.

**Meggen and Peter Taylor, co-founders of FindEverythingHistoric .com**

# From Tech Hero to Zero Net Worth

A company's ultimate failure may come at any time, before a first round of seed funding or as the company holds a billion-dollar valuation. Elizabeth Holmes, American entrepreneur and founder of medical testing company Theranos, learned that lesson the hard way, losing her $9 billion–valued company as lies and deception caught up with her. In the course of 1 year, Holmes went from being a billionaire to being valued by *Forbes* as having a net worth of "nothing."

Holmes dropped out of Stanford University at the age of 19 to start Theranos, a company that claimed to revolutionize the blood-testing process by using a finger prick instead of the more traditional needle-based method. Holmes claimed that a single drop of blood could be used to run more than 200 different health tests on their proprietary machine called Edison—a claim that was set to revolutionize health care. A pair of angel investors helped Holmes kickstart her company, raising an initial $6 million in 2004. Theranos grew exponentially, striking lucrative deals with Walgreens and Safeway to run blood-testing clinics.

As Theranos and the Edison technology began to gain widespread recognition in the startup world, with Holmes appearing on the cover of *Fortune* magazine (among other public achievements), *Wall Street Journal* reporter John Carreyrou took a deep dive into the company's practices and testing in 2015. He interviewed several former employees, including a former lab director, who exposed the company's severely exaggerated product marketing. Theranos claimed to be able to perform 204 tests with the finger prick, but in reality, only a handful worked.

The technology clearly did nowhere near what it advertised. Theranos was actually using competitors' equipment to perform the tests behind the scenes.

The company quickly spiraled downward after the report, losing the deals with Walgreens and Safeway. Holmes was banned from the lab-testing industry for 2 years by the Center for Medicare and Medicaid Services. She is (at the time of this writing) awaiting a 2020 trial, which will decide whether she will land in prison for up to 20 years and possibly pay millions of dollars in fines. Theranos ceased operations in 2018, and it has since been liquidated.

## Critical Thinking Questions

1. How much can a company exaggerate its product, yet still remain ethical?

2. Should advertisements be made for a product before that product is fully ready? When is the proper time to declare a product to the world?

3. What would you do if you were an employee of Theranos and knew what was happening? ●

**Sources:**

Carreyrou, J. (2015, October 16). Hot startup Theranos has struggled with its blood-test technology. *Wall Street Journal.* Retrieved from https://www.wsj.com/articles/theranos-has-struggled-with-blood-tests-1444881901

Clark, K. (2019, June 28). Theranos founder Elizabeth Holmes to stand trial in 2020. *Tech Crunch.* Retrieved from https://techcrunch.com/2019/06/28/theranos-founder-elizabeth-holmes-to-stand-trial-in-2020/

Herper, M. (2016, June 21). From $4.5 billion to nothing. Forbes revises estimated net worth of Theranos founder Elizabeth Holmes. *Forbes.* Retrieved from https://www.forbes.com/sites/matthewherper/2016/06/01/from-4-5-billion-to-nothing-forbes-revises-estimated-net-worth-of-theranos-founder-elizabeth-holmes/#2c1e97943633

For entrepreneurs, failure is especially difficult because it is hard to separate personal failure from professional failure, given how closely associated the identity of the business is tied to the identity of the entrepreneur.

What many successful entrepreneurs have realized is that it is acceptable and human to try and then fail. Feelings of doubt, uncertainty, frustration, and a yearning for help are all perfectly normal. Yet before entrepreneurs are able to move forward or even start their businesses, they need to first overcome their fear of failure.

## Signs of Fear of Failure

As we have learned, fear of failure can be a major impediment to seizing opportunities and transforming entrepreneurial objectives into real action.[17] Although many of us have a degree of fear of failure, some have a higher level than others. Researchers have suggested that the origins of fear of failure may lie in parent–child relations. For example, a child is likely to have a higher fear of failure if he or she is punished for failures and receives little or neutral praise for successful achievements. Studies also suggest that there is a connection between high parental expectations and a child's fear of failure, as well as other factors such as maternal irritability and paternal absence.[18]

# Overcoming the Stigma of Failure

As much as entrepreneurs should learn from and even embrace failure, the impact of failure can be harsh. In many areas around the world, in families, in communities, business failure can be a stigma. A stigma is "a quality of social dishonor: a market of degradation, loss of esteem, or loss of reputation."[19] Researcher Grace Walsh looked at how entrepreneurs who have failed can reenter entrepreneurship and avoid stigma. Recognizing the negative impact of stigma such as humiliation, guilt, pain, embarrassment, and shame, Walsh wanted to better understand how entrepreneurs avoided or overcame stigma and decided to engage in entrepreneurship again.[20]

Her sample included 15 first-time entrepreneurs in Ireland who started a business between 1997 and 2007 but ceased to exist within 5 years of starting. Additionally, these same entrepreneurs reentered entrepreneurship after their failure experience. Walsh found that entrepreneurs use detachment, acknowledgment, and deflection to overcome negative social repercussions associated with stigma. Detachment relates to the entrepreneur separating himself from the venture and subsequent failure, as well as limiting the importance of the failure. In other words, making it sound like the failure wasn't that big of a deal or rationalizing the failure. Acknowledgment relates to the entrepreneur's ability to openly discuss the failure with various stakeholders—owning up to the failure. Deflection is more like quieting a bully. The entrepreneurs would simply dismiss the naysayers or ignore the overly judgmental. By overcoming or avoiding stigma through methods such as detachment, acknowledgment, and deflection, these entrepreneurs were able to move on and engage in entrepreneurship once again.

## Critical Thinking Questions

1. Have you ever practiced one of the methods of overcoming stigma? What was the outcome?

2. Why do you think detachment, acknowledgment, or deflection could help a failed entrepreneur want to try to start a business again?

3. Does the stigma of failure look or feel different around the world? Why or why not? ●

Overall, studies show that individuals who are raised to believe that failure is unacceptable and has negative consequences will go out of their way to avoid failure. This means that rather than seeing mistakes as opportunities to learn and improve skills, or to compete against others, they will view them as threatening and judgment-oriented experiences. Here, failure is associated with shame—a painful emotion that many of us will avoid, even if it means losing out on lucrative opportunities. Avoiding the potential to make mistakes stunts the growth and maturity of individuals with a high fear of failure, which leads only to more mistakes and failures over time.[21] Understanding that failure is an important part of growth and learning is a vital lesson for entrepreneurs who want to succeed in their personal and professional lives.

People with a strong fear of failure tend to be anxious, lack self-esteem, and demonstrate reluctance to try new things. Table 11.2 illustrates some symptoms of fear of failure.

Once you establish the extent of your fear of failure, you can begin to develop some coping strategies to deal with it.[22] First, you can reframe specific goals so they become more achievable; for example, rather than setting a goal of earning $100,000 from a new product launch, you can expand the goal to focus also on what you learn from launching a new product. That way, even if the product does not meets its monetary target, you will not feel you have failed, as you have already committed to learning something of value from the experience. This ties in with the concept of acceptable loss outlined in the Entrepreneurship Method.

Second, if the product failed to generate as much revenue as you would like, it is helpful to separate your personal feelings from facts. Instead of thinking, "I feel terrible because I have failed," you can ask yourself, "What did I learn from this experience?" and "What are the positive things about what happened?"

Third, many of us try to suppress the emotions associated with fear, but by deliberately allowing yourself to feel the fear, you are more likely to diminish the fear of failure. Taking deep breaths for 2 minutes is a useful exercise to shift negative feelings and trigger a calm response.

**TABLE 11.2**

10 Signs You Might Have a Fear of Failure

| | |
|---|---|
| 1. | Failing makes you worry about what other people think about you. |
| 2. | Failing makes you worry about your ability to pursue the future you desire. |
| 3. | Failing makes you worry that people will lose interest in you. |
| 4. | Failing makes you worry about how smart or capable you are. |
| 5. | Failing makes you worry about disappointing people whose opinion you value. |
| 6. | You tend to tell people beforehand that you don't expect to succeed in order to lower their expectations. |
| 7. | Once you fail at something, you have trouble imagining what you could have done differently to succeed. |
| 8. | You often get last-minute headaches, stomach aches, or other physical symptoms that prevent you from completing your preparation. |
| 9. | You often get distracted by tasks that prevent you from completing your preparation, which, in hindsight, were not as urgent as they seemed at the time. |
| 10. | You tend to procrastinate and "run out of time" to complete your preparation adequately. |

**Source:** Adapted from Winch, G. (2013, June 18). 10 signs that you might have fear of failure. *Psychology Today.* Retrieved from https://www.psychologytoday.com/blog/the-squeaky-wheel/201306/10-signs-you-might-have-fear-failure

Credit: Forbes.com

**Entrepreneur Neil Patel (left) claims that living with his parents taught him to be careful with his money.**

Finally, a good way to deal with your fear is to seek support from the role models in your life. For example, serial entrepreneur Neil Patel believes that living with his parents until the age of 23 gave him the emotional support he needed to recover from a series of failed business ventures.[23]

## Global Fear of Failure

A strong fear of failure is often rooted in one's national culture. The Global Entrepreneurship Monitor report (GEM) measures fear of failure by country.[24] When you look at this on a map, you can also recognize regional differences (see Figure 11.3). The GEM failure rate is based on those who admit to perceiving opportunities to start a business but feel prevented from acting on those opportunities due to fear of failure. The lower the percentage shown on the map, the lower the fear.

Overall, different countries and the cultures associated with countries had different tolerances for failure, but perhaps not as much difference as you would think. In particular, fear of failure was lowest in Angola (16%) followed by Colombia at 23%. The highest is Morocco at 64%, Greece at 57%, and India at 50%. The United States is 35%.

How does fear of failure influence our ability to spot opportunities and act on them? To find the answer, GEM also assessed the personal perceptions about entrepreneurship experienced by people between the ages of 18 and 64 (see Figure 11.4).

**FIGURE 11.3**

### Fear of Failure Rates Around the World, 2018

Percentage of 18–64 population perceiving good opportunities to start a business who indicate that fear of failure would prevent them from setting up a business

Highest       Lowest    No data

**Source:** Global Entrepreneurship Monitor Adult Population Survey 2018/2019

The GEM study focused on how people's personal perceptions in these three economies have influenced their decision to start a business. These perceptions include the extent to which people see opportunities around them to start a business (perceived opportunities); how capable they think they are of starting a business (perceived capabilities); how many people would feel constrained by their own fear of failing (fear of failure); and the degree to which those capable of starting a business may intend to do so over the next 3 years (entrepreneurial intentions).

As Figure 11.4 illustrates, people in Africa have the highest percentage of perceived opportunities, perceived capabilities, and entrepreneurial intentions. In contrast, while perceived capabilities rank high in Latin America and the Caribbean, the same countries (along with Asia and Oceania) score the highest for fear of failure. Finally, Europe and North America score the lowest for entrepreneurial intentions. People in these economies may perceive opportunities and score relatively high in perceived capabilities, but very few intend to take the next step into entrepreneurship. The reasons for this may lie in lack of confidence, cultural differences, types of skills, the level of entrepreneurship education, and different types of businesses that exist in the economy. For example, many businesses are started in Africa for sustenance and survival, whereas many businesses in the United States are high-tech. These different businesses require different levels of skills, which may account for differences in perceived capabilities.

Yet despite the differences between the economic regions, Figure 11.4 shows similar fear of failure rates across the different types of economies. The question then becomes, What makes some people act when others don't, even if their fear of failure is almost the same? The answer lies in how we manage failure and our ability and willingness to learn from it.

**FIGURE 11.4**

## Self-Perceptions About Entrepreneurship

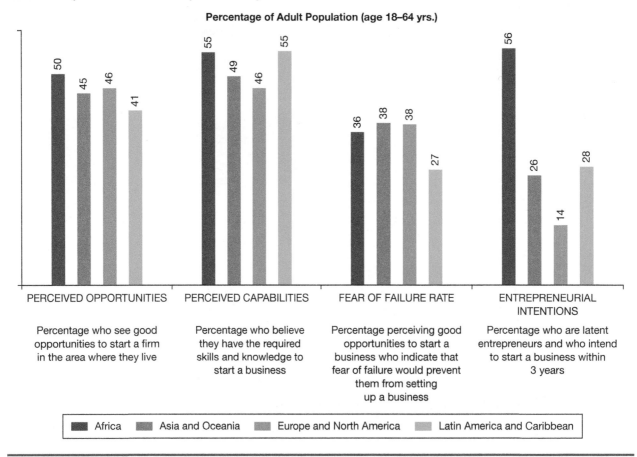

Percentage of Adult Population (age 18–64 yrs.)

| PERCEIVED OPPORTUNITIES | PERCEIVED CAPABILITIES | FEAR OF FAILURE RATE | ENTREPRENEURIAL INTENTIONS |
|---|---|---|---|
| Percentage who see good opportunities to start a firm in the area where they live | Percentage who believe they have the required skills and knowledge to start a business | Percentage perceiving good opportunities to start a business who indicate that fear of failure would prevent them from setting up a business | Percentage who are latent entrepreneurs and who intend to start a business within 3 years |

Legend: ■ Africa  ■ Asia and Oceania  ■ Europe and North America  ■ Latin America and Caribbean

**Source:** GEM 2018/2019 global report. Figure 5. Retrieved from http://gemconsortium.org/report

## 11.4 LEARNING FROM FAILURE

>> **LO 11.4**   **Explain the different ways entrepreneurs can learn from failure.**

As shown by the statistics we presented in Chapter 1, the reality of entrepreneurship is that businesses do fail, which is why it is important for aspiring entrepreneurs to learn from others who have experienced failed businesses. Learning from others can help them take steps to prevent it from happening to them and also to understand how to take valuable lessons from failure. As we have explored, the use of the term *failure* evokes fear that discourages entrepreneurs from trying again or attempting new approaches.

In Chapter 7, we introduced experimentation and described how each "failed" experiment is an opportunity to build our knowledge and increase evidence.

Jeff Bezos, founder of Amazon.com, is a big believer in experimentation, especially when it comes to learning from failures. "I've made billions of dollars of failures at Amazon.com," he said. "Literally billions. . . . Companies that don't embrace failure and continue to experiment eventually get in the desperate position where the only thing they can do is make a Hail Mary bet at the end of their corporate existence."[25]

Experimentation is about trying something, seeing what happens, learning from it, and then moving forward, adapting or pivoting based on those findings. The goal of experimentation is not to conduct the "perfect" experiment, but to see it as an opportunity for further learning and better decision making, rather than a series of failed tests.

**FIGURE 11.5**

### Intelligent Failure

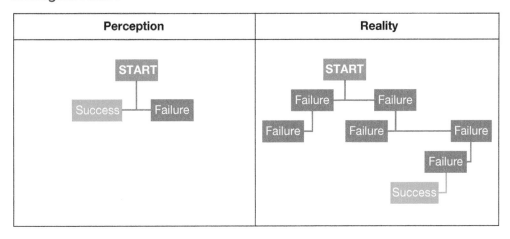

**Source:** https://sujanpatel.com/business/failing-fast-2/

In this context, perhaps it would be better to reframe the term *failure* as *intentional iteration*—a process that involves prototyping, testing, analyzing, and refinement. This may encourage entrepreneurs to perceive failure as simply a process of experimenting and learning from the setbacks, false starts, wrong turns, and mistakes, which will in turn help them develop the skills they need to tackle potential obstacles that may lie ahead.

This process of intentional iteration involves making intelligent failures—good failures that provide valuable new knowledge that can help a startup overcome hurdles and roadblocks (see Figure 11.5). Intelligent failures take place when experimentation is deemed necessary in order to find answers in situations that have never been explored before. Designing a new, innovative product or testing consumer reactions in an untapped market are tasks that may result in intelligent failures. With the right kind of experimentation, entrepreneurs can produce quick failures with positive results.[26]

For example, Sujan Patel, cofounder of marketing agency Web Profits, benefited from intelligent failure when he introduced his first marketing company, ContentMarketer.io. Patel said, "We tried to do way too much—both in terms of what the software did, and the work we had to put in to sustain it. We eventually ditched the bulk of the software, pivoted to providing only email outreach software (the part of ContentMarketer.io our customers used most), and rebranded as Mailshake. We're now making more money and putting in less hours doing it."[27]

Rather than giving up on his idea completely, Patel took the time to learn lessons from the failure and figure out what went wrong. This example shows how an entrepreneur can use failure in more productive ways.

**Intelligent failures:** good failures that provide valuable new knowledge that can help a startup overcome hurdles and roadblocks.

## Lessons Learned by Successful Entrepreneurs

Kurt Theobald is the cofounder and CEO of the e-commerce firm Classy Llama—his 11th startup over the course of 5 years. Despite 10 failures behind him, Theobald learned valuable lessons and persevered until he achieved success. Table 11.3 lists some of the lessons he learned along the way.

Theobald learned some valuable lessons from his 10 failed businesses that helped him to finally succeed with his 11th new venture, a growing business that earns more than $8 million in annual revenue.[28]

## Building a Blame-Free Environment

Many of us are guilty of playing the "blame game" when things don't go our way. After all, it's only human to blame other people or bad luck for our mistakes. However, a blame culture isn't healthy for you or your company, simply because you won't learn from the failure.

**TABLE 11.3**

Lessons Learned by Kurt Theobald

| | |
|---|---|
| Beware of "shiny object syndrome" | Theobald admits he was guilty of pursuing multiple opportunities that came his way but failed to be strategic about it, which led to many failures. He suggests that all entrepreneurs need to be strategic about pursuing opportunities and understand how to identify the right opportunity at the right time. |
| Fail fast . . . but not too fast | Although failing fast is useful to reduce the likelihood of really big failures, Theobald advises against giving up to soon. He admits that he was sometimes too quick to let go and move on to the next opportunity. Perhaps if he was a bit more patient and tried things from different angles it would have worked out. |
| Find your formula | One of Theobald's businesses failed because he hadn't worked out the exact formula—the fundamental underlying method of why a business is viable. In the end, there wasn't enough revenue coming in to sustain the startup, and Theobald was forced to file for bankruptcy. |
| Know who you are | Theobald believes that entrepreneurs who know who they really are have a better chance at success as they are better equipped to deal with failure. He explains, "I wrote two things in my journal: One, when I fall, I am getting up. Every single time. And two, I get up because it's who I am as an entrepreneur. Therefore, to not get up is to betray who I am. And so that's what kept me going through all the failure. You can't stop. You don't really have a choice because if you choose that then you might as well sacrifice your whole life." |
| Find your deeper purpose | Theobald believes that entrepreneurs must have a deeper purpose to cope with failure—a deeper reason for starting and growing a business other than potential wealth and the freedom of working for themselves. He cites Steve Jobs's return to Apple (Jobs demanded only a $1 salary) as an example of an entrepreneur with a deeper purpose who prioritized changing the world with his products over money. |
| Focus on others | Being an entrepreneur is not about you, but about focusing on others—your customer, team members, suppliers, stakeholders—and helping them succeed. This is not about giving up control, but rather sharing it with others. Remember, the more value you give, the more you get back. By shifting your thinking to others, the people around you will be more likely to help you resolve problems and overcome obstacles. |
| Recognize when your approach is wrong | Many of Theobald's businesses failed because he was using the same approach every time. He quotes a mentor who advised, "Nothing's going to give if you keep doing the same thing you've been doing. If you keep banging your head against the concrete wall, the wall doesn't suddenly give way. Instead, you end up knocking yourself out. You need to pick a different approach." |

**Source:** Wagner, E. (2013, October 22). 9 lessons from a 10-time startup failure. *Forbes*. Excerpted From Forbes.com. ©2013 Forbes. All rights reserved. Used under license.

Similarly, important lessons could be learned from failures that led to the demise of many startups by building blame-free cultures that encourage people to share, accept, learn from, and recover from failure. To do this, employees in a startup would also need to feel assured that they will not receive a negative reaction when they admit mistakes. When people feel comfortable enough to report failures, there is an opportunity for the team to work together toward understanding and analyzing what went wrong and to explore new approaches in order to prevent the same thing from happening again.

The key to building a blame-free culture is to communicate clearly what sorts of failures are acceptable and unacceptable. For example, lack of commitment, reckless conduct, violation of laws or standards, negligence, or wasting resources would be deemed unacceptable, whereas small fails that tend to occur through experimentation would be regarded as acceptable.

## Your Failure Résumé

In this Mindshift exercise, your assignment is to craft a "failure résumé" that includes all of your biggest fails![29] These can be from school, work, or even in social relationships. For every failure you list, you must then describe what you learned from each fail (and, if appropriate, what others learned). By creating a failure résumé, you are forced to spend time reflecting on what you learned from those experiences. As tough as this sounds, it's also a very rewarding experience.

Want to go a step further? Share your résumé with a classmate and compare. Don't focus on comparing the failures; rather, focus on comparing and contrasting the learning that resulted from each failure experience.

### Critical Thinking Questions

1. Was it easier than you expected, or more difficult, to list your biggest failures?

2. What emotions did you experience as you wrote your "failure résumé"?

3. How do you think you'll be able to take the lessons learned from your failures and use them to attain more success in the future? ●

Entrepreneurs also need to be open about their own knowledge limitations and admit the mistakes they have made in the past. This degree of openness encourages the rest of the team to be just as open and more willing to admit mistakes when they happen. Neha Motwani, founder of Fritternity, a fitness discovery and booking platform based in Mumbai, India, believes that accepting responsibility for failures is an essential part of being an entrepreneur: "As an entrepreneur you cannot find excuses or blame anyone else for any failure; you are in the driver's seat, whether you enjoy being there or not," she says.[30]

In essence, founders must give careful thought to making demands, giving orders, overruling thoughtful decisions, shooting the messenger, and assigning blame in order to build a culture in which people feel comfortable enough to share bad news and make the right choices.[31]

John Danner is an author and senior fellow at the Institute for Business Innovation in the Haas School of Business of the University of California, Berkeley. Like Motwani and others we have described earlier, Danner believes that failure in organizations should not be treated as a "regrettable reality," but rather as "a strategic resource—one that can help you make better decisions, create a more trusting and higher-performing culture, and accelerate your company's growth and innovation."[32]

Photo: Abhijit Bhatlekar/Mint

**Neha Motwani, founder of Fritternity**

## 11.5 GETTING GRITTY: BUILDING A TOLERANCE FOR FAILURE

>> **LO 11.5**  **Describe the significance of "grit" and its role in building tolerance for failure.**

Angela Lee Duckworth is a psychologist at the University of Pennsylvania who has spent more than a decade researching how character relates to achievement. Traditional wisdom leads us to believe that talent—as measured by things like IQ, SAT, and GMAT scores—is a predictor of achievement. Yet Duckworth found something different. She identified "grit" as a trait that supersedes traditional methods of measuring talent.

**Grit:** the quality that enables people to work hard and sustain interest in their long-term goals.

According to Duckworth, **grit** is the quality that enables people to work hard and sustain interest in their long-term goals. Grit is also related to resilience, not just in the face of failure, but in perseverance to stick to long-term commitments and goals.[33]

One of the first studies Duckworth carried out to show the relationship between grit and high achievement took place at the United States Military Academy at West Point—one of the most selective and rigorous military training facilities in the United States and one with an infamously high dropout rate. Duckworth received permission to have incoming cadets complete a short "grit questionnaire," along with all the other evaluative methods employed by West Point such as The Whole Candidate Score (which includes SAT scores, class rank, etc.). Her intent was to find out what qualities would predict whether a cadet would remain at West Point through the "beast" summer program or would drop out.

Examples of the questions on Duckworth's grit questionnaire: "I have overcome setbacks to conquer an important challenge," "Setbacks don't discourage me," "I have been obsessed with a certain idea or project for a short time but later lost interest," "I have difficulty maintaining my focus on projects that take more than a few months to complete," and "I finish whatever I begin." Participants were asked to rate themselves on a five-point scale ranging from "very much like me" to "not like me at all."[34]

The findings showed that the cadets with higher levels of grit were more likely to stay until the end of the summer, and grit proved to be a better predictor than The Whole Candidate Score. Since the West Point study, Duckworth has found that grit predicts the effectiveness of sales agents, the survival of first-year teachers in tough schools, and even the identity of the finalists of U.S. National Spelling Bee contests.[35]

Duckworth's research on grit is also related to Stanford psychologist Carol Dweck's research on mindset, which we explored in Chapter 2. Dweck believes that people with a fixed mindset tend to believe that intelligence and talent are something we're born with, and they avoid failure at all costs, whereas people with growth mindset develop their abilities through dedication, effort, and hard work. They think brains and talent are not the key to lifelong success, but merely the starting point. They see failure as an opportunity to improve their performance and to learn from their mistakes. Despite setbacks, they tend to persevere rather than give up. Over the course of her research, Duckworth has found that children who have more of a growth mindset tend to have more grit.

Like Dweck, Duckworth also believes in the concept of deliberate practice, which is the conscious effort to practice things that we can't yet do. However, this type of practice does not involve doing the same thing over and over again; deliberate practice is a highly structured activity that must have a purpose and be carried out with an eye on long-term achievement. Deliberate practice can be frustrating, confusing, and even boring; but the fact is that we are supposed to feel confused when we are tackling the unknown—feeling frustrated can be a sign that we are on the right track.[36] In sum, deliberate practice allows us to refine our skills by making and accepting our mistakes in order to help us progress toward the achievement of long-term goals. This ties in with one of the key messages of this text—that entrepreneurship is a method that demands practice.

## Building Grit

As defined in psychological studies by Duckworth and others, grit incorporates several different attributes. Let's examine each of these.

### Courage

In the context of grit, people are courageous when they are not afraid to fail. They understand that failure is an important part of the learning process if they want to succeed. For example, Amy Freeman, founder of The Spice and Tea Exchange, overcame homelessness and lack of education by creating her own franchise business.[37] "Facing adversity

## Go Get Rejected

Author, blogger, and entrepreneur Jia Jiang has a TEDx talk that has been viewed by more than 5 million people. The topic? Rejection. And not just one rejection but 100 rejections. Jia Jang went on a 100-day journey to overcome his fear of failure and figure out a better way to handle the pain and shame that rejection brings. He talks about a game called "Rejection Therapy" that was invented by Canadian entrepreneur Jason Comely. The game requires you to look for rejection for 30 straight days. Jia Jang decided to take the game further and look for rejection for 100 days. Day 1 was "borrow $100 from a stranger." Day 2 was "request a burger refill." Another day was asking to plant a flower in a stranger's yard. The stranger said no, but suggested that he go to another person's house down the street. The flower was planted! His journey produced some great life lessons. He learned that sometimes with rejection come other gifts. The trick is not to run when first rejected, but rather ask why. You may learn something you didn't know and get something you didn't expect.

For this Mindshift, look for rejection for 3 days! You can do it . . . it's just 3 days. View Jia Jiang's TEDx talk, "What I Learned From 100 Days of Rejection", for inspiration (https://www.ted.com/talks/jia_jiang_what_i_learned_from_100_days_of_rejection).

### Critical Thinking Questions

1. What did you learn about yourself during the 3-day challenge?

2. Did your feelings about rejection change from Day 1 to Day 3?

3. Do you think these types of challenges can really help people overcome their fear of rejection and failure?

early on taught me that while it's okay to get mad or feel hurt, you need to resolve and move on before negativity and isolation take hold," she says.

## Conscientiousness

Often, when we hear of someone being conscientious, we picture a person being meticulous in carrying out painstaking tasks. However, in the context of grit, being conscientious means working tirelessly in the face of challenges and toward the achievement of long-term goals.

## Perseverance

Perseverance is the commitment to long-term goals through purposeful, deliberate practice. Serial entrepreneur Com Mirza, founder of multimillion-dollar company Mirza Holdings based in Dubai, Saudi Arabia, is a big believer in perseverance. The first eight companies he set up failed to take off, but he persevered nonetheless by writing down his goals and practicing his entrepreneurial skills. Mirza advises, "Start writing and continue practicing. You'll soon feel your brain rewiring to be equipped for real success. You'll feel more confident in your ability to carry through on what you tell yourself."[38]

## Resilience

Resilience means the strength to recover from failure and overcome obstacles in order to persevere toward the achievement of long-term goals. Gritty people believe "everything will be all right in the end, and if it is not all right, it is not the end."[39]

## Excellence

In the context of grit, striving for excellence means committing to activities that enhance skills, as well as prioritizing improvement over perfection. In other words, striving for excellence is an ongoing process, as each activity highlights new opportunities.

## Removing the Stigma of Failure

Failure is still a topic that many of us would like to avoid, but that is changing. Initiatives are springing up to remove the stigma (feelings of shame and embarrassment) traditionally associated with failure.

Mobile technology nonprofit MobilActive runs an annual event called FAILFaire, which provides a forum for nonprofits all over the world to "openly, honestly, and humorously discuss [their] own failures." FAILFaire gives the opportunity for the participants to share their mistakes so others may understand and learn from them, in order to make better decisions in the future.

One failure that was openly discussed during the FAILFaire held in Bangalore, India, involved an initiative undertaken by Fiona Vaz, alumna of Amani Institute and Teach for India. Vaz attempted to set up a school with three other teachers as cofounders that failed because they couldn't all agree on important issues.

"It is tough for leaders to follow each other. We could not come to a consensus on key issues and did not know how to let go," she explained. "I realized that teachers help students overcome failure and pass exams—teacher-entrepreneurs should do the same for themselves as well," Fiona said.[40]

Similar to FAILFaire, the colorfully named F***up Nights is a global movement that holds events worldwide, giving entrepreneurs the opportunities to share their failure stories in front of a room full of strangers.[41]

DoSomething.org, a nonprofit set up to encourage people to take action on social change initiatives, holds a Pink Boa FailFest twice a year. The presenters wear a pink feather boa during a 10-minute presentation in which they discuss the history of their failure, what went wrong, and the lessons learned. Presenters allow 2 minutes of Q&A from the group at the end of the talk. They also employ fun, silly metaphors in discussing the lessons learned, such as a photo of a celebrity or a song lyric that takes the sting out of the failure.[42] If you are still unsure about sharing your failures in public, how about adjusting your physiology to better cope with failure? Improvisation teacher Matt Smith developed the "failure bow," which consists of raising your hands in the air, saying "I failed," grinning submissively, and moving on. Smith reports that athletes who use the failure bow find it helps them get over the fear of making a mistake. When they adjust their physiology, it helps them to change their mindset from embarrassment and shame to a more positive state that welcomes learning opportunities.[43] ●

---

**$SAGE edge**™

Get the tools you need to sharpen your study skills. SAGE edge offers a robust online environment featuring an impressive array of free tools and resources.

- Access practice quizzes, eFlashcards, video, and multimedia at
  **edge.sagepub.com/neckentrepreneurship2e**

---

## SUMMARY

### 11.1   Describe failure and its effect on entrepreneurs.

Learning and further opportunities often come with failure. Failure does, however, come with extreme costs (financial and emotional) that need to be well managed to enable success down the road. If failure is seen as an acceptable step on the path to success, it is much more likely that failure may serve to hone the business and the entrepreneurs behind it.

### 11.2   Identify several reasons for failure.

Failures come in all shapes and sizes. Common types of failure include deviance, inattention, lack of ability, process inadequacy, poor business process flow, communication uncertainty, and exploratory experimentation.

### 11.3   Describe the consequences of fear of failure for entrepreneurs.

Fear of failure makes the entrepreneur less likely to pursue and achieve the transformative power of learning from failure.

**11.4**    **Explain the different ways entrepreneurs can learn from failure.**

Failure often goes hand-in-hand with experimentation, with each iteration bringing a product or service nearer to the state necessary for market success. Something can be learned from any failure, and it's important that the firm and its founders establish a blame-free climate in which learning can be maximized.

**11.5**    **Describe the significance of "grit" and its role in building tolerance for failure.**

Grit is that "special something" that enables people to persevere though prolonged hardship to maintain commitment and achieve long-term goals.

---

### KEY TERMS

| | | |
|---|---|---|
| Deviance  262 | Inattention  262 | Pivot  260 |
| Exploratory experimentation  263 | Intelligent failures  269 | Process inadequacy  262 |
| Grit  272 | Lack of ability  262 | Uncertainty  263 |

---

### CASE STUDY

## Emily Lagasse, founder, Petwell Supply Co.

Emily Lagasse was working with the U.S. Peace Corps as a small-business development volunteer in a rural village in West Africa in 2008, and that is where she met her dog, Fenway. As soon as she and her new best friend came back to the United States, Fenway got very sick from eating traditional, U.S. dog food. This prompted Emily to cook for Fenway and her all-natural, homemade dog food worked! Fenway quickly got better! Emily concluded that the low-quality dog food available in pet stores was contributing to Fenway's poor health. "Traditional dog food had over 50 ingredients. Most of these were synthetic, most I couldn't pronounce, most of these I would not even eat myself." She realized that there must be other pet owners struggling with the same issue of having low-quality pet food. This prompted her to start her own pet food company, Fedwell Pet Foods, in early 2014 while pursuing her MBA at Babson College.

Fedwell was the first pet food on the market that did not have synthetic vitamins. Most dog food is extruded—made under high heat and pressure. This allows dog food producers to make product fast, but the downside is that food is then stripped of important nutrients. Emily was emulating the recipes she was using to cook at home for her dog—fresh wholesome ingredients that were friendly to a dog's natural diet. Her first product was oven-baked lamb kibble that had only meat, fruits, and vegetables and no synthetic vitamins. "We used the highest quality ingredients that you and I can eat. You can even pronounce everything that's on the label. Moreover, our food is baked, like crackers. This allows all the nutrients to be retained in the food." She started to sell in local pet stores and farmers markets in New England and online, but 80% of her revenue came from online sales. Some early national press coverage helped her direct traffic directly to her website.

"I had a lot of bumps in the road with getting the product made and distributed. It is a very competitive market," recalls Emily. "Things with my manufacturer got quite bad. I was trying to make a product that was better than existing ones, but manufacturers wanted to keep doing what they always did and were only interested in volume." Without scale Emily did not have leverage with the manufacturer to demand the quality levels she wanted. "After a lot of back and forth, I found out that the manufacturer broke the contract and was making the product differently than agreed upon. The manufacturer then got acquired by a bigger company who really didn't want to work with me. Being someone who did not expect to go back on their word, this caught me by surprise." It took Emily a year to find another manufacturer, and in 2016, she found a more supportive and willing manufacturer, but eventually this arrangement fell through as well.

The pet food industry was getting increasingly competitive given that it is a $30 billion market and growing rapidly. The opportunity for Emily was there but she was stuck in a hard cycle of not being able to sell through the product fast enough. Every time she almost got a deal for national distribution, it would fall through because of the intense competition. Even though the product was differentiated, it had a higher price point and distributors were not willing to take a risk. Even smaller distributors sold around 1,000 SKUs so there was little incentive to add a new brand. This meant that most of Fedwell's cash was tied up in inventory. Therefore, she didn't have the resources to spend on marketing, branding, and product development—the activities that could build her customer base and attract stronger distribution. Overall, she found it difficult to stand out in a crowded marketplace where most pet owners don't like switching food.

Emily, however, understood that most of her customers had pets with health issues. Additionally, she felt that veterinarians were diagnosing health issues and providing medications but not offering any type of holistic solution for preventative and long-term health. She started to experiment with health supplement bundles for dogs, such as a hip and joint bundle and a senior dog bundle. Through testing she learned that there was a market for local stores where pet parents could get medication and holistic products for their pets that were not easily available with other retailers. This prompted Emily to pivot away from Fedwell Pet Food products to Petwell Supply in 2018. Petwell Supply is a boutique pet store that sells food, treats, and medical remedies for pets in Somerville, Massachusetts. As Emily describes, "The store is set up in a way to help support different issues that dogs and cats face. You can find products that support your pet's allergies, kidney issues, cancer and we run education programs based around these issues as well!"

The idea of Petwell Supply was happening at about the same time that the relationship with her current dog food manufacturer was going sour. Emily decided to stop the manufacturing of Fedwell products and focus on getting the store up and running. "Most of my customers' pets are usually seeing the vet for some health issue or the other and thus Petwell aims to work in tandem with these vets to help provide a more well-rounded approach for the well-being of the pet," notes Emily. Petwell provides supplements like fish oil or probiotics that the vets prescribe but usually don't carry. Most of the remedies that Emily offers at Petwell are actually made by vets she met at trade shows, reflective of her focus on creating a great product.

Emily is working on engaging in conversations with local vets in the community to ensure that Petwell carries the products that they recommend. For example, instead of potential customers ordering a probiotic from a national marketplace like Chewy.com and waiting to get the product, Emily is working with vets so that they will recommend her store instead, where owners can walk in and get what they need on the same day. "There is a movement to support local neighborhood businesses in my area, so this approach is working for me." She is also in the process of connecting with social media influencers and bloggers to drive traffic and have online conversations with dog and cat owners all over the country to understand the different problems that these pet parents face regarding the health of their pets. Emily is taking a community-based approach to marketing her store. She was featured by the local press and has participated in community events, tagged sidewalks (spraying the sidewalk with chalk in the shape of PetWell's logo during the summer), and reached out to local dog walkers to help spread the word to the dog owners.

Emily is most concerned by not knowing what drives customer behavior. "Some days at the store are crazy busy and sometimes the store is empty, but this behavior cannot be traced back to anything." However, in order to help steady the demand and steady the revenue stream, Emily has added a lot of "regular" pet store services to her store, such as dog walking and grooming. She also conducts regular social events at the store as a way to engage with the local community. "I believe that customers do not necessarily react well to something completely new. They want the comfort of familiarity and this is one reason I offer the usual products such as pet food and treats along with supplements and prescription medication. That way customers will remember my store and come when the need arises. I can actually see some of that happening now!"

As Emily notes, "The store is an amazing touchpoint to directly interact with the customer and get real-time feedback and market trends on a regular basis." The store also gives Emily a sense of control over how she would like to react to this information and make changes if needed, almost immediately. This was in contrast with her experience with Fedwell, where she was heavily dependent on the manufacturers for her operations.

Her longer-term plan is to franchise the store nationally and also reformulate the food she used to produce at Fedwell to act as the natural alternative to a prescription diet. Because Emily is somewhat of an expert in pet food through her experience, she is looking forward to leveraging that expertise and getting back into reformulating food. However, Emily says that she now knows how exactly she wants her products manufactured and that all her not-so-positive experiences have been great lessons in themselves. She feels like she would be wasting an opportunity if she doesn't get back to reformulating the food and setting up a distribution channel for her products. Emily would like to leverage her knowledge on running an e-commerce company to grow her distribution channel once she introduces a reformulated product into the market. Although she believes that both distributors and online sales are important, she personally likes playing around with the data that online sales can generate. For instance, one insight that she learned through Fedwell sales was that her customers were usually married, with both partners working but without children. These were people who would travel with their pets everywhere. This love for data also prompted her choice of location for the store. She chose Somerville because it has the highest per capita millennial population in the United States.

The journey for Emily has not been easy. At the early stages of the business, she spent all of her time and effort growing the business. She missed social occasions like parties, birthdays, weddings, and even compromised on health and sleep at an unsustainable pace to help get her company off the ground. Now, however, she believes in the importance of having a well-rounded lifestyle and makes a point to take a little time off to do other things that make her happy, like hitting the gym. She feels she is the best version of herself when she is the healthiest. "It may sound cheesy, but I believe that the level of stress is directly related to your level of self-care."

When asked about what she would do differently with Fedwell, Emily said that she would find buyers and distributors for her product *before* manufacturing it. Emily credits her success to the strength of her network of seasoned entrepreneurs, professors, and investors who became advisors, especially when she was starting her first company. "When I was new to entrepreneurship, I lacked the confidence to get things going, and my mentors really helped me focus." However, she feels like she has grown as an entrepreneur. Today she is a lot more confident and relies on her network only for certain specific areas of guidance. If an expert is not available in her network, she starts asking around until she is connected to someone who can help. "My advice to young entrepreneurs is: Fail fast. That's a big one. And if you fail in one model, doesn't mean it's over. My story is an example of just that!"

## Critical Thinking Questions

1. How did Emily Lagasse learn from and rebound from failure?

2. Do you believe Petwell will be an ongoing success given the setbacks she had with Fedwell?

3. How can you fail fast with your own venture?

**Sources:**

Emily Lagasse (interview with Babson MBA graduate assistant Gaurav Khemka, December 7, 2018)

Petwell Supply. (2014). The FedWell pet foods story [Video file]. *YouTube*. Retrieved from https://youtu.be/JhZRGUReSZk - T

Petwell Supply (2019). Retrieved from https://www.petwellsupply.com/

Radio Entrepreneurs. (2017). Emily Lagasse July 2017 [Video file]. YouTube. Retrieved from https://www.youtube.com/watch?v=ZuU7xUZ4lPc

# PART IV

## Supporting New Opportunities

# 12 Bootstrapping and Crowdfunding for Resources

"What's a bootstrapper to do? You have to go where the other guys can't. Take advantage of what you have so that you can beat the competition with what they don't."

—Seth Godin, author of *The Bootstrapper's Bible: How to Start and Build a Business with a Great Idea and (Almost) No Money*

# Chapter Outline

# Learning Objectives

**12.1** Define bootstrapping and illustrate how it applies to entrepreneurs.

**12.2** Identify common bootstrapping strategies used by entrepreneurs.

**12.3** Explain the difference between crowdsourcing and crowdfunding.

**12.4** Describe the effects of crowdfunding on entrepreneurship.

**12.5** Define the four contexts for crowdfunding.

**12.6** Describe 10 ways in which entrepreneurs can conduct a successful crowdfunding campaign.

## 12.1 WHAT IS BOOTSTRAPPING?

>> **LO 12.1** **Define bootstrapping and illustrate how it applies to entrepreneurs.**

One of the most common beliefs held by prospective entrepreneurs is that vast amounts of money are needed to start a business: "I can't start a business because I don't have any money—how do I get money?" Looking at entrepreneurship from the outside, it's common to believe that the key to success is to raise as much capital as possible in the beginning, but this is simply not the case. Very few entrepreneurs manage to get formal funding for their new ventures, especially in the early stages—bank loans are notoriously difficult for newly emerging businesses to access, and investments from "angels" or other investors aren't as common as people would like to believe because entrepreneurs often have difficulty proving to potential investors the value of a business that hasn't gotten off the ground yet. It can be incredibly risky to bet on the unproven and the unknown.

Almost 8,500 new companies in the United States received formal equity investment in 2018.[1] Considering that an average of 627,000 businesses are started every year, the likelihood of a new business getting formal investment is very, very small.[2] Some research has reported that a third of small businesses have begun with less than $5,000.[3] This method of starting a business is so well established that its name is borrowed from the old expression "pull yourself up by your bootstraps" (the small fingerholds used to pull on the entire boot), meaning to lift yourself by your own efforts. In entrepreneurship, bootstrapping is the process of building or starting a business with no outside investment, funding, or support.[4]

Bootstrapping is all about finding creative ways to access every resource you have available to launch your venture while minimizing the amount of cash you spend.[6] This means applying the eight components of the Entrepreneurship Method, as described in Chapter 1. Here is a quick reminder:

1. Identify your desired impact on the world.

2. Start with the means at hand.

3. Describe the idea today.

4. Calculate affordable loss.

5. Take small action.

**Bootstrapping:** the process of building or starting a business with no outside investment, funding, or support.

**⑥SAGE edge™**

Master the content at
**edge.sagepub.com/
neckentrepreneurship2e**

# Bryanne Leeming, Unruly Studios

Photo courtesy of Bryanne Leeming

**Bryanne Leeming, founder of Unruly Studios**

Bryanne Leeming bootstrapped her business, Unruly Studios, by raising $42,000 through Kickstarter and winning startup competitions. Many of the world's most successful businesses began as bootstrapped ventures, such as Coca-Cola, Apple, and Microsoft. It took only $1,000 for Michael Dell to start Dell Computers.[5]

Bryanne's career background is in marketing, with degrees in cognitive science and art history from McGill. After college, she began pursuing an MBA at Babson College in Massachusetts. At the time, Bryanne wasn't totally set on starting her own business, stating that "starting a company is a pretty crazy thing to do." In the end, though, Bryanne saw a problem that needed solving and she had an idea how to solve it.

Bryanne started her company, Unruly Studios, while she was pursuing her MBA at Babson College. The goal of her company is to combine physical activity and STEM education in order to expose children aged 6–12 to coding in a fun and playful way. Children learn how to code by using a series of floor tiles called "Unruly Splats," each of which contains lights resembling "spilled milk." The tiles light up and make sounds when kids jump on each one. The Unruly Splats are programmable floor tiles that pair with a tablet preloaded with lots of recess-style games. Kids first play the preloaded games, then they change the code, ultimately learning how to code their own games.

To get to this point has required plenty of iteration, attention to detail, and bootstrapping. She built a successful Kickstarter campaign, raising more than $42,000 with an average pledge of $140. She received awards from Amazon's Alexa fund and has quality advisors hailing from Disney, Mattel, and the MIT Media Lab.

Additionally, winning venture competitions has helped her get early startup funding.

Although the current iteration of the Unruly Splat looks very impressive, it didn't start this way. Bryanne points out that "ideas are ugly when they start out, and the prototypes are especially ugly." She emphasizes that the first iteration doesn't have to be pretty, and it shouldn't be. The current iteration of the Unruly Splat is a sleek data collection marvel, whereas the first iteration was a 4' × 4' wood surface with integrated electronics that she could barely fit inside the back of her car. Bryanne stresses this point as an important principle behind entrepreneurship: to not stress about the first version of an idea. Starting a business is hard enough; worrying about how an idea/prototype looks, in the beginning, is adding an unnecessary level of worry.

Even before launching her Kickstarter campaign, Bryanne had to engage her users—the kids. She watched kids make their own games, and they gave her feedback on what they liked or didn't like about the product or system. This required a lot of testing, something that she and Unruly Studios put a lot of emphasis on. Thousands have tested Unruly Splats in schools and have made many of the recommendations in design and function for the product. This enabled the product to get better faster. Then, once she achieved the best product, the Kickstarter campaign was launched so she could get resources for greater production.

The key for Bryanne and her Splats has been a focus on making the product as good as it can be through constant testing and refining so that funding finds them as often as they seek it. They have had great support from many different sources because they are so focused on that 6-year-old's experience with the product. As Bryanne notes, "As long as we continue to do this, we will have something that people want, something that makes a positive impact on future generations of kids."

## Critical Thinking Questions

1. Why does Bryanne advocate for ugly prototypes?

2. How does Bryanne iterate so frequently?

3. What draws investors' attention to Unruly Studios, in Bryanne's eyes? ●

**Source:** Bryanne Leeming (interview with the author, December 11, 2018) https://www.unrulysplats.com/

6. Network and enroll others in your journey.

7. Build on what you learn.

8. Reflect and be honest with yourself.

The Entrepreneurship Method, as reflected in the components above, will enable you to think creatively about starting a business with little or no money. Take Sophia Amoruso, founder of American retailer Nasty Gal.[7] Amoruso started off buying vintage clothing in second-hand stores and selling them on eBay. She then used her profits to secure a warehouse for her stock and hire some staff. Thanks to some clever marketing over social media, Amoruso was able to build a loyal following and attract millions in investment.

Amoruso used a small amount of her own money to get her business off the ground, but other entrepreneurs go down different paths to find the money they need. For example, rather than seeking formal investment, it is more likely that entrepreneurs will turn to friends, family, and fools (sometimes called "the 3 Fs") for financial assistance. Many entrepreneurs have borrowed money from friends and family or people who are just simply won over by an idea and are willing to invest some cash in the business. Although borrowing from these sources can be an easier and quicker way to get the cash you need, it is better to treat the arrangement as a formal loan or investment with terms agreed by both parties. Many families have fallen out over arrangements like this due to lack of understanding or broken promises. You do not want this to happen to you.

## Bootstrapping or External Financing?

Bootstrapping is fundamentally an entrepreneurial approach to acquiring resources without accessing long-term external financing sources such as raising equity from venture capitalists or borrowing from banks. Reasons for bootstrapping can include complementing current traditional financing sources, reducing reliance on them, or eliminating them entirely. More often than not, entrepreneurs just can't get or don't have access to traditional forms of financing because they don't have a business history, proven track record, or simply don't have enough customers. Additionally, entrepreneurs may voluntarily choose self-funding or funding from family and friends for all or most of the venture's financing to maintain most or complete control and autonomy over business decisions. Not every business needs a lot of capital, and not every investor wants to invest in you! Bootstrapping is a way of getting started with very little.

Although it is more difficult to acquire funding from more formal channels such as venture capital firms or angel investors, there are some real benefits to the formal route. Not only do you get the money you need, but you also gain advice and guidance from people who are far more experienced than you, as well as their contacts and connections that will, ultimately, help your business become more profitable. However, most entrepreneurs choose not to seek out, or can't get access to, angel investors or other external investors—at least not in the beginning. The truth is that most entrepreneurs appreciate the degree of independence and control they acquire by funding the business themselves. It keeps them focused and determined and allows them to grow the business the way they want to—on their own terms. They have the freedom to test their products and services and make decisions without having to explain themselves to outside investors. By not relying on outside investors, the business does not share ownership by giving away equity. There is also no pressure to repay bank loans or any other debt. In addition, any cash flow or income from the business goes straight to the entrepreneur or back into the business rather than to the investors.[8]

Marketing information platform Mailchimp has been heralded as one of the most successful bootstrapped startups of all time. Mailchimp founder Ben Chestnut explained how seeking investment just didn't seem like the right thing for the company: "Every time we sat down with potential investors, they never seemed to understand small business. Something in our gut always said that didn't feel right."[9] So how did Chestnut bootstrap one of the most successful email marketing service companies in the world? First, he used his severance check when he was laid off from a media company in 2000; Chestnut's wife was a pediatric nurse, and her steady income gave him the support he needed to build the business; and finally, he saved money by hiring low-cost artists and creatives who learned on the job rather than expensive programmers and coders.[10]

The hard reality, however, is that in the beginning most new ventures are simply not ready for investment. Outside investors are more likely to invest in a business that has been bootstrapped from the beginning, as it showcases the entrepreneur's level of commitment and resourcefulness as well as the market reaction to and demand for the product or service. Conversely, an entrepreneur who bootstraps a business with a good product–market fit, a committed team, and a decent customer base is in a much better negotiating position with investors should they express an interest in the business.

## The Bootstrapped Startup

Most new ventures begin as marathon, not a race. This means that you are better off starting off at a steady pace and achieving desired milestones than trying to launch your dream business as quickly as possible. Beginning a business on a shoestring is the norm. By spending the time to build up the business piece by piece, you are more likely to generate a larger customer base as well as a steady stream of income. Once these building blocks are in place, there is a better chance of rapid growth and scalability.

As law firm president and author Jack Garson says, "You don't need to open your dream business on the first day. It's better to start with a successful hot dog stand than to get halfway through the construction of a full-service restaurant and run out of money."[11]

Furthermore, you don't need to quit your day job to start bootstrapping. In fact, many entrepreneurs use their own salaries to fund their startups until they feel secure enough to leave their full-time jobs. For example, Aytekin Tank, founder of online form builder Jotform, juggled both his full-time job and his startup for several years: "I'd wake up at 6 am, answer customer questions, and then go to work. It took me another 5 years to quit my job and start my own company—even though I already had a successful product."[12] Table 12.1 showcases some quotes from more entrepreneurs who bootstrapped themselves to success.

There are several different ways to bootstrap your new venture. You can use cash from your savings, carefully use certain credit cards, fund your startup out of your salary from your existing job (like Jotform founder Aytekin Tank), or take equity out of your home if you are a homeowner. However, all these methods require careful thought—you need to consider how far you are willing to risk your own personal finances before getting yourself into debt.

Once you have a cutoff point in mind, then you will be able to gauge whether you need to move beyond bootstrapping to additional financial resources or to end the business altogether. This ties in with the concept of affordable loss discussed in Chapter 1—how much are you willing to lose to take the next step to bring your venture to life?

**Sweat equity:** a non-monetary investment that increases the value or ownership interest created by the investment of hard work for no compensation.

Whatever your chosen bootstrapping strategy (discussed next), it is certain that you will put in a huge amount of effort to get your business up and running. In the entrepreneurial context, this is called sweat equity: a non-monetary investment that increases the value or ownership interest created by the investment of hard work for no compensation. For example, if you have decided to renovate houses for a living, you might save on the cost of hiring laborers by doing some of the work yourself and adding value to the properties at the same time. Or you might build your own prototype of a product, again creating value while saving the cost of hiring a designer or manufacturer. Even Bryanne, founder of Unruly Studios (see Entrepreneurship in Action, above), spent countless hours developing her crowdfunding campaign. This is also a type of sweat equity. But beyond sweat equity, let's take a look at a range of strategies entrepreneurs can use to bootstrap their businesses.

| TABLE 12.1 |
| --- |

Entrepreneurs Share Their Views on Bootstrapping

| |
| --- |
| *Bootstrapping is a force function for creativity and breakthrough. It'll challenge you to think outside the box and to do things differently.* Bryan Johnson, founder of Braintree, OS Fund, and Kernel |
| *Bootstrapping is the best guarantee that you can run your business the way you want.* Laura Roeder, founder and CEO of MeetEdgar |
| *By self-funding you have the ability to control your own destiny.* Nathan Chan, CEO of Foundr Magazine |
| *When you bootstrap, you have to care about every potential customer, client, and fan.* John Lee Dumas of EOFire |
| *Having limited resources means you won't survive unless you only focus on what brings the most value.* Oleg Shchegolev, CEO and cofounder of SEMrush |
| *Hire people that are on board with your vision, share similar values, and are prepared to work hard.* Steve Shelley, chair and cofounder of Deputy |
| *Will spending this money help me acquire or keep a customer? If the answer is no, don't spend it.* Kate Morris, CEO and founder, Adore Beauty |
| *Bootstrapping for as long as I did set me up for success down the road.* Chris Strode, founder of Invoice2go |
| *Bootstrapping forces you to relentlessly prioritize things that are actually going to move the needle.* Christopher Gimmer, cofounder at Snappa |
| *When you're bootstrapping, make sure to think about your customers, revenues, and profitability first.* Greg Smith, CEO and cofounder at Thinkific |

**Source:** Chan, J. (2019). 11 bootstrapping entrepreneurs share how they found business success without funding. *Foundr.* Retrieved from https://foundr.com/bootstrapping-entrepreneur

# 12.2 BOOTSTRAPPING STRATEGIES

>> **LO 12.2** Identify common bootstrapping strategies used by entrepreneurs.

The key to successfully bootstrapping your business is to look for creative ways and use whatever resources you have to save money while you are getting your business off the ground.[13] These "penny pinching strategies," illustrated in Table 12.2, will not only help minimize the costs of running your business but will also delay or alleviate the need for external funding through investments or bank loans.

Above all, remember the old saying, "cash is king." Rather than spending too much time fretting over balance sheets, forecasts, and profit and loss, focus on the amount of cash you have to keep your business operative. How long can you keep your business afloat with the cash you have? Weeks? Months? It's important to be mindful of your cash flow: cash in, cash out, and overall cash needs.

# 12.3 CROWDFUNDING VERSUS CROWDSOURCING

>> **LO 12.3** Explain the difference between crowdsourcing and crowdfunding.

As new entrepreneurs quickly learn, formal investment is very difficult to get, and traditional bootstrapping methods can take you only so far. The emergence of

**TABLE 12.2**

Common Bootstrapping Strategies

| |
|---|
| • Work from home to save on renting an office; or if you need an office, use coworking spaces instead. |
| • Never buy new what you can borrow, lease, or get for free; for example, borrow or lease office equipment such as computers, printers, and so on. |
| • Take as little salary for yourself for as long as possible. |
| • Use your network of friends and family to get what you need at a reduced rate or for free. |
| • Educate yourself on basic legal and accountancy matters before paying high fees to a lawyer or accountant. |
| • Reimburse advisors and consultants with equity and goodwill where possible. |
| • Be frugal with your travel—drive rather than fly, and choose cheap accommodation. |
| • Hire help if you need it, but keep in mind that some employees may agree to work temporarily for an equity share in the business rather than a cash payment. |
| • Attend every possible networking event to make connections and get introductions to people who may be able to contribute to or enhance your business. |
| • Offer discounts to early customers to ensure a consistent cash flow. Not only will this help to cover overhead, but it will also help you build a loyal customer base. |
| • Negotiate payment terms with suppliers (if you have them), and explain how they will benefit when your business takes off. |
| • Outsource some tasks if you are struggling to keep up with the workload. For example, 99designs and Elance are good examples of websites that can provide you with the services you need, allowing you more time to focus on the parts of the business that generate the most income. |
| • Don't give up your day job until the business is being productive and making proper money. |

**Source:** Based on information from Sharp, G., (2014). *The ultimate guide to bootstrapping: How you can build a profitable company from day one* [Kindle ed.]. Real. Cool. Media; Victor, A. (2018). Bootstrapping strategies for building successful business. *Medium.* Retrieved from https://medium.com/@agvictorsblog/bootstrapping-strategies-for-building-successful-business-8fc0b1f65513

**Crowdfunding:** the process of raising funding for a new venture from a large audience (the "crowd"), typically through the Internet.

crowdfunding—the process of raising cash for a new venture from a large audience (the "crowd"), typically through the Internet—has been a new pathway for many entrepreneurs. People who use crowdfunding to raise money are known as "crowdfunders," and people who contribute financial support to crowdfunding ventures are known as "backers."[14] Usually, crowdfunding works by drawing on small contributions from a large number of people to fund entrepreneurial ventures.[15]

MINDSHIFT

# Bootstrapping for Your Business

By now you should have a pretty good understanding of the different ways to bootstrap a business, from working out of your home, to using free resources from your network, using personal credit cards, crowdsourcing, and crowdfunding. Think about the idea or venture concept you are working on and identify at least 10 strategies you can use to bootstrap your venture idea. If you can't think of 10, then ask people, "How can I start this ["this" being your idea] with virtually nothing?" You will be surprised what others will say!

**Critical Thinking Questions**

1. Do you think you can really start a business with little to no formal outside help from investors or bankers?

2. Can you describe the mindset of a bootstrapper?

3. Did anything surprise you in your list of 10 strategies? What and why? ●

Crowdfunding is often confused with crowdsourcing, but the two are not the same. Crowdfunding focuses on raising cash for new projects and businesses, whereas crowdsourcing involves using the Internet to attract, aggregate, and manage ostensibly inexpensive or even free labor from enthusiastic customers and like-minded people. Thus, crowdfunding is a resource for money, and crowdsourcing is a resource for talent and labor. Like crowdfunding, crowdsourcing is a form of bootstrapping because it is a valuable method of saving money by utilizing the expertise and knowledge of the crowd to bring your ideas to life.

Throughout this text we have emphasized the importance of information as a critical and valuable resource, and finding ways to access this information is key to the success of your business. However, sometimes it can be difficult or even costly to acquire information. Crowdsourcing is a means of obtaining information that is contributed and shared by the members of a given crowdsourcing platform. Companies have capitalized on information resources by tapping into crowdsourcing social media platforms and social networking sites. Let's take a look at three different ways in which crowdsourcing has been used to gain knowledge and information.

> **Crowdsourcing:** the process of using the Internet to attract, aggregate, and manage ostensibly inexpensive or even free labor from enthusiastic customers and like-minded people.

### Crowdsourcing to Improve Medical Treatment

In 2011, the University of Washington's department of biochemistry challenged a group of gamers to produce an accurate model of a retrovirus enzyme (that came from an AIDS-like virus) by playing an online science game called Foldit.[16] The players managed to produce an accurate model in just 3 weeks, beating the experts who had been struggling to find the solution for more than a decade. Since that event, the WHO Special

---

ENTREPRENEURSHIP MEETS ETHICS

## When to Proclaim a Product Is Ready

With the advent of crowdfunding websites, the process of investing in startups has become democratized. No longer are entrepreneurs needing the help of bigger investors; they can amass small investments from a vast number of individuals. The newness of this style of investment system means that there is still a significant amount of uncertainty on both sides of the venture.

Because it can be easier to gain small amounts of funding from a large number of individuals, instead of a large amount of money from one or a few sources, the constraints on entrepreneurs to provide a conclusive and realistic business plan are lessened.

This raises the questions of whether or not it is right to look for investments when the product is not finished and whether the entrepreneur can say the product is finished when they know they just need the additional crowdfunding to get the product ready for market.

Business sense says that it is helpful to market a product before it is fully finished, as it will make the process significantly easier. For example, software companies have used this strategy for some years now—what many refer to as "vaporware." They hold significant marketing campaigns before the software is completely finished.

This is obviously the best route for an entrepreneur, as money will come more swiftly and allow for the completion of an idea. But, is this strategy fair to the consumer?

If a consumer feels cheated by an entrepreneur's lack of fulfillment on a desired product, that negative feeling could have a rippling effect. It may seem that it is just one customer or small investor lost, but bad reviews and a troublesome reputation are sure to follow in any future ventures.

### Critical Thinking Questions

1. Can an entrepreneur lie about the readiness of a product to consumers or investors?

2. Does crowdfunding require enough accountability from investors?

3. Should an entrepreneur be absolutely certain a product will appear as marketed before looking for funding? ●

**Sources:**
Burkus, D. (2013, December 25). Sell your product before it exists. *Harvard Business Review.* Retrieved from https://hbr.org/2013/12/sell-your-product-before-it-exists
Fuld, H. (2018, February 23). How to hype up your product before it's ready for the market. *Inc.* Retrieved from https://www.inc.com/hillel-fuld/if-your-marketing-activity-begins-when-product-is-ready-you-missed-boat.html
Katai, R. (2016, April 11). How to launch a product before it's ready. *Bannersnack.* Retrieved from https://blog.bannersnack.com/launch-product-before-ready/

Programme for Research and Training in Tropical Diseases has set up a crowdsourcing initiative that involves groups of experts and nonexperts who solve health problems and then share the solution with the public. For example, WHO launched a contest to design a video to encourage HIV testing in China. The winner of the contest was not a professional videographer, but he won a cash prize for his educational and engaging video detailing the benefits of testing for gay men and their partners. Thanks to these crowdsourcing initiatives, WHO is achieving a number of medical breakthroughs worldwide.

## Crowdsourcing to Reduce Labor Costs

Many companies use crowdsourcing to save on labor costs. For instance, say you wanted to find a designer to create a new logo for your startup. This might cost you $400 if you were hiring a traditional designer, but by harnessing creative talent through crowdsourcing or websites like Upwork, you will likely pay half that figure.[17]

On a much larger scale, consider the benefits of crowdsourcing to the XPRIZE Foundation. The foundation focuses on finding solutions to complex problems such as air and ocean pollution and adult illiteracy. XPRIZE launched a competition to challenge teams from all over the world to build a spaceship for a $10 million reward. Although this seems like a lot of money, it would likely have cost the foundation much more, as it would have had to fund research and development teams to generate the idea and pay enormous labor costs to build the spaceship. By using crowdsourcing, XPRIZE succeeded in saving on labor costs as well as inventing creative ways to build a new type of spaceship.

## Crowdsourcing Through Technology

Technological advances are greatly reducing the costs of design, manufacturing, and sales. What's especially exciting for entrepreneurs with product companies is the low cost of 3D printing and other tools that enable small companies to become microfactories. For example, free software tools like Google's Sketchup enable users to create a sketch of a 3D model of their own invention; this can then be turned into a 3D physical prototype using a specialized desktop printer like the MakerBot, which costs less than $1,000.

One of the XPRIZE contenders for the $10 million prize, SpaceShipOne

Once you're happy with your prototype, you can have it manufactured in China or similar countries. Chinese manufacturers have become efficient enough to manufacture in small batches (as small as a batch of one) while maintaining low costs—something that was previously impossible. Now small companies and even individuals have access to manufacturing lines that had been previously reserved for large factories.

Websites like Alibaba.com list China's manufacturers, products, and capabilities.[18] You can search the site to find companies that make items similar to yours. When you've selected your top choices, you can instant-message the factory using Alibaba's real-time English–Chinese instant-messaging system. Within two decades, Alibaba has earned revenue of $40 billion.

Where does crowdsourcing come in to 3D printing? Plastic is not the only material used by 3D printers—other materials like wood can be used. Wikihouse, for example, designs and builds houses through a form of 3D printing without involving a construction team.[19] Thanks to crowdsourcing, Wikihouse blueprints are submitted by the crowd that has created plans and designs of any type of house imaginable. These blueprints are freely available online for anyone who fancies building an affordable custom-built home. Aspiring homeowners can get the parts digitally printed before assembling the parts themselves, much in the manner of an IKEA furniture pack kit.

# 12.4 CROWDFUNDING STARTUPS AND ENTREPRENEURSHIPS

>> **LO 12.4**  **Describe the effects of crowdfunding on entrepreneurship.**

Just as crowdsourcing is a useful way to acquire valuable feedback and information, crowdfunding can be an effective way of getting the funds needed to start a business or, at least, show proof of concept. Crowdfunding is rapidly gaining momentum and shows no signs of slowing down. Crowdfunding has helped raise billions for all types of businesses: art, theater, photography, charity, retail, fashion, gaming, real estate, and much more.

Crowdfunding makes all types of entrepreneurship accessible to those who want to start their own business. In a time when banks have become more nervous about lending money and investors are more cautious than ever before, crowdfunding has become a democratized method of raising money for many budding entrepreneurs.

An estimated market value of $34 billion was raised globally through crowdfunding campaigns in 2017, with North America and Europe dominating the industry. Table 12.3 provides some additional statistics on the crowdfunding industry.

Many crowdfunding projects seek small amounts of money (often under $1,000) to fund one-off occasions like community or arts events, with family and friends being the main contributors. However, more and more projects are becoming a valuable source of funding for entrepreneurial ventures.[20] California-based Pebble Time, which makes smart watches, holds the record for the largest amount of money raised on a crowdfunding platform. Since the Pebble Time launch in 2012, backers have given more than $20 million through crowdfunding platform Kickstarter.[21] In 2016, digital health platform Fitbit acquired Pebble, but it phased out the watches in June 2018.[22] Similarly, strategic card game Exploding Kittens was heralded as Kickstarter's most-backed project of all time, with almost 220,000 people supporting the campaign.

What kind of people tend to back crowdfunding campaigns? According to the 2012 American Dream Composite Index,[23] crowdfunding backers tend to be between the ages

View Pictures/Luke Hayes/VIEW/Newscom

**Wikihouse designs and digitally prints the parts of a house for later assembly.**

## TABLE 12.3

Key Crowdfunding Statistics

| | |
|---|---|
| Number of U.S. crowdfunding platforms | 191 |
| Number of jobs created by crowdfunding | 270,000 |
| Amount that crowdfunding has added to the global economy | $65 billion |
| Average global success rate for crowdfunding campaigns | 50% |
| Amount raised by average successful crowdfunding campaign | $7,000 |
| Length of time it takes to prepare a successful campaign | 11 days |
| Duration of average campaign | 9 weeks |
| Average campaign donation | $88 |

**Source:** Fundly. (n.d.). *Crowdfunding statistics.* Retrieved from https://blog.fundly.com/crowdfunding-statistics

of 24 and 35, are more likely to be men, and have an income of more than $100,000 per year. This is a basic demographic snapshot of people who are most likely to invest in your startup through crowdfunding. Let's explore the different types of crowdfunding sites used by entrepreneurs and participants today.

## Types of Crowdfunding Sites

Launched in 2009, U.S.-based Kickstarter is the most established crowdfunding site, as well as the largest platform for creative projects in the world. Kickstarter makes its money by charging a percentage of the funds collected from each successful project, in addition to payment processing fees.[24] It does not accept projects associated with charitable donations, loans, or general business expenses.[25] The expectation is that the money raised will be used to further develop or complete a project and that backers will receive some reward for contributing. As of April 2019, more than $4 billion had been pledged to more than 160,000 projects by more than 16 million backers on Kickstarter.[26]

North American entrepreneurs can join the Kickstarter community for free and start their own campaign by pitching ideas directly to a huge worldwide audience of potential online backers. There are three basic rules:

- Projects must create something to share with others.

- Projects must be honest and clearly presented.

- Projects can't fundraise for charity, offer financial incentives, or involve prohibited items.[27]

Each Kickstarter project is set up to run during a set period of time with a set fundraising goal. Project creators can build web pages that describe the projects they are looking to fund and the specific goals they would like to reach and broadcast their ideas through promotional videos, photos, and other information. Kickstarter also includes a facility to get feedback before the page is launched, notifies you of funds donated, allows you to track funds and the number of backers, includes a way to notify backers of progress, and includes a mechanism to reward backers for their support. Although campaigns are allowed to last from 1 to 60 days, it is worth keeping in mind that the most successful campaigns tend to last 30 days or less, with the most contributions coming in during the first and the last week.[28]

When setting a funding goal, Kickstarter crowdfunders must be aware that a project must be fully funded by the time the period of the campaign ends, or they get nothing. For example, if you decide to set a funding goal of $10,000 and receive pledges of only $5,000 within your specified funding period, then you will not receive anything. In contrast, if you surpass your funding goal early on, you will still be able to receive contributions right up until the campaign comes to an end. Yet in most cases, potential backers are less likely to fund a project once it has reached its original goal.[29]

Rewards tend to come in many different forms; for example, if you are looking to put on a play, you might offer potential backers free tickets on opening night, front row seats, or the chance to meet the actors backstage after the event. Similarly, in the case of a clothing line, you might give away some items of clothing for free or for a discounted price to your early backers. However, as noted in the basic rules, Kickstarter does not allow monetary rewards or equity in a company. Recent studies have shown that backers who are promised to be first to receive a certain product when it is launched, alongside the reward, tend to give larger amounts of money.[30]

Coolest Cooler

**The Coolest Cooler, which broke Kickstarter's funding record.**

Not all Kickstarter projects are successful, of course—and some have had unexpected twists and turns. One of the most infamous Kickstarter campaigns is the Coolest Cooler, a modern take on the ice cooler, which not only keeps drinks and food cool but also features a USB charger, a battery-powered blender, Bluetooth speakers, cutting board, and easy rolling tires. Oregon-based entrepreneur Ryan Grepper was initially looking for $50,000 in donations from the online community and ended up receiving more than $13 million from more than 60,000 backers. However, despite the huge amount of money raised, the Coolest Cooler suffered from a range of setbacks, including delayed production and selling the cooler on Amazon before fulfilling its promise to deliver to its backers first. These "growing pains" led some of its supporters to lose faith in the product.[31] As of June 2018, 40,000 coolers have been delivered to 60,000 backers, with 20,000 still waiting for their product.[32]

There are several alternatives to Kickstarter. Another crowdfunding platform, Indiegogo, is the largest global fundraising site in the world. Anybody on Earth, regardless of their geographic location, can use Indiegogo. Although it has a smaller community of backers than Kickstarter, it has a larger international presence. Unlike the Kickstarter model, on Indiegogo almost anything goes. For example, a male couple who wanted to become parents requested more than $75,000 from backers to pay for gestational surrogacy.[33]

Other crowdfunding sites that are popular with entrepreneurs include RocketHub, which focuses on science-related projects; Peerbackers, which funds creative, civic, and entrepreneurial projects; and Quirky, which helps inventors raise funds. Quirky might be considered both a crowdfunding and crowdsourcing platform as it involves collaboration with backers on the development of a product or prototype. Also worth examining are iFundWomen, a platform designed for female entrepreneurs, , and GoFundMe, which focuses solely on fundraising for nonprofits. Table 12.4 lists a number of crowdfunding platforms relevant to entrepreneurs. It is important to note that depending on the crowdfunding site, startups will be charged a transaction processing fee between 3% and 5%.

## TABLE 12.4

Crowdfunding Sites for Startups and New Projects

| SITE | CAMPAIGN TYPE | INDUSTRY FOCUS | CAMPAIGN/FUNDING FEES |
|---|---|---|---|
| CircleUp | Equity and credit | Early-stage consumer goods | Not available |
| GoFundMe | Reward, donation | People, charity, causes | 0% of personal campaigns, 5% of charity campaigns |
| iFundWomen | Reward | Women-led businesses | 5% of the total funds raised |
| Indiegogo | Reward, equity | Tech and innovation, creative works, community projects | 5% of all funds raised |
| Kickstarter | Reward | Creative arts | 5% of the total funds raised |
| Patreon | Reward, subscription | Artists and creators | 5% of successfully processed payments |
| Peerbackers | Reward | Entrepreneurs and businesses | 5% of successful campaigns |
| Republic | Reward, equity | Nonaccredited investing for startups with a focus on diversity | 6% of the total cash funds + 2% "Crowd Safe" security |
| RocketHub | Reward | Science, arts, education, business, social good | 4% of fully funded campaigns, 8% of partially funded campaigns |
| SeedInvest | Equity | Accredited investing for new startups | 7.5% of the total amount raised in a successful round |

**Source:** Adamson-Pickett, J. (2018). Best crowdfunding for startups: How to fund your small business. *Business.org.* Retrieved from https://www.business.org/finance/loans/best-crowdfunding-sites-for-startups

## Equity Crowdfunding

For startups that are seeking investment in return for shares or equity, there is a new form of crowdfunding called equity crowdfunding—a form of crowdfunding that gives backers the opportunity to become shareholders in a company. In 2012, President Obama showed his support for this type of funding by signing the JOBS Act, which legalizes equity crowdfunding in the United States.[34] U.S. sites like Crowdfunder, AngelList, Fundable, and Circle Up provide investors with the opportunity to invest in companies in exchange for ownership or the promise of future returns.

The equity crowdfunding model is also gaining popularity all over the world. Crowdcube, a leading equity crowdfunding platform based in Britain, attracted almost $66 million from investors in 2017. Or what about OurCrowd, which exclusively focuses on investment in Israeli startups? It recently announced that it has reached $1 billion in funding commitment in just 6 years.[35] These are only two examples of many international equity crowdfunding sites that are changing the way people invest.

# 12.5 THE FOUR CONTEXTS FOR CROWDFUNDING

**>> LO 12.5   Define the four contexts for crowdfunding.**

As we have explored, different crowdfunding sites offer different things to both crowdfunders and backers. We have already taken a look at some entrepreneurs who have raised funds through crowdfunding, but what about the backers themselves? What sort of reasons do people have for donating, lending, or investing in a startup? To answer this question, we need to explore four different contexts or circumstances in which people fund a project through crowdfunding: patronage model, lending model, reward-based crowdfunding, and investor model (see Figure 12.1).[36]

## Patronage Model

The patronage model describes the financial support given by backers without any expectation of a direct return for their donations. Crowdfunding platform Patreon allows its patrons to fund illustrators, authors, podcasters, musicians, and other independent

**FIGURE 12.1**

**Four Types of Crowdfunding**

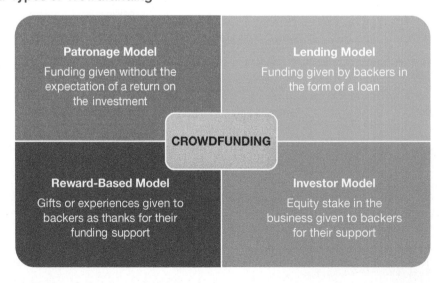

## The Informational Value of Crowdfunding to Music Entrepreneurs

It's well known that crowdfunding brings much-needed financial resources to startup entrepreneurs. Now that crowdfunding is part of mainstream entrepreneurship, research has uncovered additional advantages for entrepreneurs. Researcher Jordana Viotto da Cruz wanted to know how entrepreneurs respond to information obtained from backers gathered during a crowdfunding campaign. Specifically, will entrepreneurs release their products to the market even if the crowdfunding campaign was not successful?

Crowdfunding protocol is very clear. If you reach your funding goals, the funds are released to you. If you do not reach the goal and even if you have a significant number of backers, you still do not get the funds. The only way to get funds is to reach your stated campaign goal. An entrepreneur is faced with an important decision when she has a significant number of backers, positive feedback, but did not reach her goal. Does she continue? Does she still try to bring her product to market?

Viotto da Cruz evaluated 1,505 U.S.-based projects on Kickstarter that aimed to produce a music album. Then she selected those whose albums were being sold elsewhere (such as Amazon or iTunes) after the campaign end date. This resulted in a final sample of 707 music entrepreneurs. Interesting results emerged regarding those music entrepreneurs with failed campaigns. First, contributions made by backers signal a possible market.

If the contributions were significant, and even though the goal wasn't reached, the musician could conclude there is a potential market. Second, the musicians gave increased attention to the feedback from backers and they were able to adapt their product (album) before release. Finally, many musicians used the failed campaign as a rationale for not continuing with the project. In other words, the market had spoken and it said "no"!

Viotto da Cruz summarized, "We empirically show that when not successful on crowdfunding, thus not accessing capital, project owners may decide to release the product in the market if contributions suggest positive valuation from the 'crowd.'"

### Critical Thinking Questions

1. This research focused on music entrepreneurs. What type of information do you think other entrepreneurial types are seeking to gather from crowdfunding? Give examples.

2. What is crowdfunding protocol? Do you agree with the approach?

3. Are music entrepreneurs a good research sample? Why or why not? ●

**Source:** Viotto da Cruz, J. (2018). Beyond financing: Crowdfunding as an informational mechanism. *Journal of Business Venturing, 33*(3), 371–393.

---

creators. As of January 2019, Patreon has more than 3 million patrons supporting artists from many different fields.[37]

## Lending Model

In the lending model, funds are offered as loans with the expectation that the money will be repaid. Lending models can take different forms; for example, some backers will expect interest to be paid on the loan, while other backers might expect to be reimbursed only if and when the project starts generating revenue, or if it begins to make a profit. There can also be elements of the patronage model within the lending process; for example, in the case of microfinanced loans, where small amounts of money are loaned to impoverished people in developing countries, backers might waive any expectation of repayment because the loans are promoting the social good.

**Lending model:** a crowdfunding model where funds are offered as loans with the expectation that the money will be repaid.

## Reward-Based Crowdfunding

Reward-based crowdfunding involves rewarding backers for supporting a project. As in the example of Kickstarter, this is the most popular form of crowdfunding today. Rather than giving away precious equity or a large share in the profits, entrepreneurs give

**Reward-based crowdfunding:** a crowdfunding model that involves rewarding backers for supporting a project.

rewards to their backers, which can often take the form of more unique offerings such as product samples or experiences.

For example, Mamu Thai Noodle Truck rewarded its backers by hosting a cooking class featuring all their favorite recipes from the food truck menu.[38]

## The Investor Model

The **investor model** involves giving backers an equity stake in the business in return for their funding. This model takes a few different forms; for example, investors can either buy shares in the company, which means they would be given a degree of ownership or certain rights in a project, or investors can take a share of the future revenue or profits of a company without taking ownership. In 2014, veteran-owned Bottle Breacher, which sells custom-engraved bottle openers made from .50-caliber bullets, gave away a 20% stake in their business to *Shark Tank* investors in exchange for $150,000 in order to grow their bottle-opening enterprise. By 2018, the company had generated more than $17 million in sales.[39]

## The Advantages of Crowdfunding for Global Entrepreneurs

There are many benefits to crowdfunding for entrepreneurs all over the world. Not only will crowdfunding provide the money you need to get your business off the ground, but it also provides you with an idea of the level of enthusiasm and interest in your product or service before launch. This saves you money on expensive marketing as well as enabling you to gather valuable customer feedback and to test ideas at very little cost.

Crowdfunding also enables you to build early relationships with customers who have a keen interest in your product and who will most likely purchase it when it is launched. When backers choose to fund a project, they become emotionally invested—not only in the development process but in the product itself when it comes to fruition. The point is that committed, emotionally invested customers are more likely to spread the word about your offering and help to promote it through their own social networks.

Another major advantage to crowdfunding is that there are different options to choose from. Just because you have a backer does not mean you have to give away ownership or an equity stake in your venture. In many cases, you will be able to keep your equity and your independence. Most types of crowdfunding websites offer different things, and an entrepreneur is in the fortunate position of being able to choose which crowdfunding method to use.

Finally, crowdfunding is an exciting process. It is an excellent way for you to make new contacts, build your brand, attract customers, raise awareness for your products, and create a buzz before your product even hits the market. However, do not be fooled into thinking that crowdfunding is a quick and easy process. By setting up a crowdfunding campaign, you are exposing your business idea to the world, so it is important to ensure that it's ready for that level of scrutiny. To succeed in crowdfunding, you need to plan ahead; think deeply about the type of customers you would like to attract, consider how to reach them, clearly communicate your vision, and convince your online audience that your product or service is worth investing in. You must also gather support from your friends, family, and other contacts, not only to donate or invest in it through your chosen crowdfunding model, but also to help promote your product with *their* friends, family, and other contacts.

## 12.6 A QUICK GUIDE TO SUCCESSFUL CROWDFUNDING

>> **LO 12.6**   **Describe 10 ways in which entrepreneurs can conduct a successful crowdfunding campaign.**

Crowdfunding may seem like a temptingly easy way to get your hands on the funds you need for your new venture. However, like anything worthwhile, it involves a lot of thought,

## Kickstarter Assessment

Kickstarter has projects in 15 different categories—from games to music to food. For this Mindshift exercise, go to the Stats area of Kickstarter (https://www.kickstarter.com/help/stats) and choose a project category that interests you. Then, identify what you believe to be the top five reasons for successful *and* unsuccessful campaigns in that category.

### Critical Thinking Questions

1. What conclusions can you draw about the project category you chose? In what ways is it typical or atypical of Kickstarter projects?

2. Of the top five reasons for success, which do you think are most attainable for your entrepreneurial idea?

3. Of the top five reasons for failure, which do you think your entrepreneurial idea is most vulnerable to? ●

commitment, and hard work. The following tips have been provided by entrepreneurs who have successfully raised funds through crowdfunding sites such as Kickstarter and Indiegogo.[40]

## 1. Make Sure Your Product or Service Solves a Real Problem

Many of the entrepreneurs described in this text have become successful through their ability to solve a problem—they have managed to create something that people want to buy. If you think you have identified a product that provides a solution to a problem, then you will need to convey this message to your prospective backers. See if you can communicate your idea to your audience in no more than two sentences—if you can't, then spend time getting a clearer sense of the essence of your product.

## 2. Test and Refine Your Idea

Don't waste your time setting up a crowdfunding campaign and presenting an idea that is half-baked. The most successful crowdfunding efforts are a result of testing, refining, and planning. For example, the first time Ryan Grepper, inventor of the Coolest Cooler, launched his product on Kickstarter, he failed to get the funding he was looking for.[41] In response, Grepper went back to the drawing board and refined the cooler to produce a much sleeker model with additional features. Eight months later, Grepper put his product on Kickstarter for a second time, only to earn more than $13 million in pledges from enthusiastic backers. Grepper's crowdfunding campaign success shows the merit in refining and testing your idea until it is ready for launch.

## 3. Be Prepared

You launch your product on a crowdfunding site, and hopefully the pledges start pouring in. Suddenly, thousands of people want your product! Exciting though this is, many entrepreneurs make the mistake of failing to plan for how they will deliver their product to such a large group of consumers. Successful entrepreneurs prepare for this possibility in advance by setting up links with their suppliers, distributors, and warehouses before launching their products on a crowdfunding site, to ensure they are able to deliver as promised.

Industry watchers have noted a number of common crowdfunding mistakes (see Table 12.5). Review those so that you are clear on what *not* to do; then read the rest of this section for more tips on what you *should* do to achieve success in crowdfunding.

**TABLE 12.5**

Common Crowdfunding Mistakes

| |
| --- |
| • Choosing the wrong crowdfunding platform |
| • Setting an unrealistic funding goal |
| • Not having enough presence on social media |
| • Lack of updates or communication with your backers |
| • Failure to get feedback and advice from the "crowd" and other crowdfunders |
| • Insufficient media coverage |
| • Failure to deliver product or rewards post-campaign |

## 4. Seek and Accept Advice

It is always useful to seek guidance from other entrepreneurs who have been through the crowdfunding process and have either succeeded or failed. You can ask the successful entrepreneurs for advice about how they did it, as well as requesting feedback on your idea. It is also very important to talk to entrepreneurs who have failed at crowdfunding, so you can learn about the type of things to avoid. Not all advice you get will be useful, of course, but listen with an open mind and think critically about how you can constructively apply the lessons others have shared.

## 5. Get Your Campaign Started—Now!

Don't rely on crowdfunding sites alone to broadcast your product and attract an audience. Successful entrepreneurs have already started to build their customer base by spreading the word through social media and other outlets, before they even sign up to crowdfunding. For example, Danish entrepreneur Jonas Gyalokay, founder of wireless dongle Airtame, and his team each sent out 100 personal emails to their respective contacts explaining the importance of their idea and how meaningful it was to them. They ended the note by asking for support.

Even if your product isn't ready before your crowdfunding launch, you can release drawings or post a photo of the prototype on sites like Facebook or Twitter so your audience can provide feedback. People who are already familiar with your product will be more likely to pledge when it is officially launched on a crowdfunding site.

## 6. Money Matters

There are very few successful crowdfunding entrepreneurs who have launched a product without some kind of financing beforehand. Whether you use your own money, max out credit cards, or seek an investor, you will need some cash not only to manufacture your product but to cover delivery costs should your product be a hit.

When you are setting a funding goal, be aware of how much money you will actually *need* rather than how much you would *like*. Many projects fail because of crowdfunders setting unreasonable funding targets. If your goal is perceived by potential backers to be "too high," then they will not support you. By the same token, setting a target that is too low might attract backers but leave you with insufficient funds to deliver your product. It is important to do your financial homework to make sure the amount you set is realistic and conservative enough to attract backers, while also high enough to cover all your manufacturing and delivery costs.

## 7. Focus on the Pitch

In a crowdfunding campaign the video pitch is everything (see Figure 12.2). Remember, you are launching a product to people from all over the world, most of whom you've never met and who don't know you. Your job is not to just sell them your vision but also to earn their trust. The way to do this is to be totally transparent about your idea. Why do you truly believe your product will change/improve their lives? How are you solving a problem? If you have competitors, why is your product better than theirs? One of the best ways to get your message across is to make a video. Although 33% of Kickstarter projects have been successfully funded without videos, that figure increases to 66% when a video is included; this means that you are 50% more likely to achieve funding if you include a video as part of your launch.[42] You can even shoot on your phone if you have a tight budget. The goal is to let your potential backers see who you are.

In many cases, backers invest in a project based on their impression of the person as well as the product. If you are making a video, make sure your video is high quality and free of sound and signal problems. Also, when you are writing the description of your project, it is important that it be free of grammatical and spelling errors. As recent studies have shown, projects with spelling mistakes are 13% less likely to be successful than projects without.[43]

## 8. Make the Most of Crowdfunding Opportunities

Crowdfunding isn't just a money-making operation—it comes with additional perks. You get important feedback from backers, which can lead to more ideas and opportunities, and if you're successful, you also get the added benefit of press coverage, which can open lots of doors into other industries. For example, within a few days of launching its Kickstarter campaign, smart video doorbell startup SkyBell was featured on Engadget and TechCrunch, which led to an increase in exposure and a lucrative deal with companies like American multinational conglomerate Honeywell.

## 9. Commit to Your Campaign

Successful crowdfunders commit to managing the campaign.[44] If your idea proves to be popular with backers, you will need to reply to a lot of emails and potentially send out surveys to gain valuable feedback.

**FIGURE 12.2**

**Example of a Kickstarter Campaign Site**

In the first week of launching his product on Indiegogo, Canary home security device founder Adam Sager replied to 3,000 emails. Overwhelming as this may sound, never underestimate the importance of engaging with your audience. Once you have made this connection, then you can continue the dialogue after the campaign is over, which can lead to all sorts of exciting opportunities. For example, smart kitchen company Anova Culinary originally raised more than $2 million through Kickstarter, only to be later purchased by Electrolux for $250 million.[45]

## 10. Avoid the Crowdfunding Curse!

Delays and setbacks in product delivery, and failure to deliver the promised rewards, are the biggest problems experienced by successful crowdfunders, who are often unprepared for the extent of the demand. Research has shown that more than 75% of products are delivered later than expected.[46] In addition, funded projects sometimes fail altogether to deliver what they promised, which causes bad feeling among those who have been generous enough to donate.

If your product is not ready to be shipped and you know you are going to miss your initial deadline, then be honest about it. Make sure you update your backers via email and through the crowdfunding site. The worst thing you can do is to not communicate with your backers. Frustrated, impatient backers can destroy an entrepreneur's reputation and a product. They have put their faith in you by pledging to fund your idea, and they deserve to know what is happening. Don't let them down. If you are honest with them about the situation, and they are enthusiastic about your product, then many of them will cut you some slack. The lesson is to make a good-faith effort at all times to fulfill your promises.

Figure 12.3 summarizes the 10 tips we have presented in this section in the form of a checklist; you can track your stage of completion in carrying out the advice given in each tip.

If your first crowdfunding campaign does not succeed, it doesn't mean that all is lost. Small changes can go a long way to ensuring your chances of success next time around. ●

**FIGURE 12.3**

**Crowdfunding Checklist**

| 1. | Make sure your product or service solves a real problem. |
|----|----------------------------------------------------------|
| 2. | Test and refine your idea. |
| 3. | Be prepared. |
| 4. | Seek and accept advice. |
| 5. | Get your campaign started—now! |
| 6. | Money matters. |
| 7. | Focus on the pitch. |
| 8. | Make the most of crowdfunding opportunities. |
| 9. | Commit to your campaign. |
| 10. | Avoid the crowdfunding curse! |

**$SAGE edge™**

Get the tools you need to sharpen your study skills. SAGE edge offers a robust online environment featuring an impressive array of free tools and resources.

- Access practice quizzes, eFlashcards, video, and multimedia at
  **edge.sagepub.com/neckentrepreneurship2e**

SUMMARY

**12.1   Define bootstrapping and illustrate how it applies to entrepreneurs.**

Entrepreneurs use their own sweat equity in combination with other bootstrapping strategies to make enough progress to get in a better position to attract more formal types of funding.

**12.2   Identify common bootstrapping strategies used by entrepreneurs.**

The list of common bootstrapping techniques is extensive. It includes ideas like using the home as the office, renting or leasing before buying, minimizing personal salary initially, developing and reaching out to contacts, offering equity reimbursement, and maintaining low operating inventories.

**12.3   Explain the difference between crowdsourcing and crowdfunding.**

Crowdfunding involves raising funds from a large audience, typically through the Internet. Crowdsourcing involves using the Internet to attract and manage low-cost or free labor generated by enthusiasm for the product or service.

**12.4   Describe the effects of crowdfunding on entrepreneurship.**

The crowdfunding movement has provided a democratic means of funding that has never before existed on the scale it exists today. Equity crowdfunding has emerged as a popular crowdfunding alternative, where ownership stakes (stock) are issued in exchange for funding.

**12.5   Define the four contexts for crowdfunding.**

Crowdfunding largely falls into one of four types: patronage model, lending model, reward-based model, and investor model. There are many benefits to crowdfunding for entrepreneurs: It provides you with the money you need to get your business off the ground, enables you to attract early customers, and allows you to test your ideas at very little cost.

**12.6   Describe 10 ways in which entrepreneurs can conduct a successful crowdfunding campaign.**

Crowdfunding is flexible and exciting but not without its challenges; it's not free money. Entrepreneurs still need to make sure their product/service addresses a real business need, a benefit to customers that is being under-addressed or unaddressed. Successful campaigns start as early as is feasible, maintain commitments, and do not overpromise.

KEY TERMS

Bootstrapping   281

Crowdfunding   286

Crowdsourcing   287

Equity crowdfunding   292

Investor model   294

Lending model   293

Patronage model   292

Reward-based
 crowdfunding   293

Sweat equity   284

CASE STUDY

## Daymond John, founder, FUBU

FUBU is an American hip-hop apparel company started in 1992 by Daymond John, a current investor on *Shark Tank*, along with Keith Perrin, J. Alexander Martin, and Carl Brown. FUBU currently sells T-shirts, rugby shirts, hockey and football jerseys, baseball caps, and accessories, all embroidered with the now-popular FUBU logo.

Daymond John grew up in the heart of a thriving hip-hop culture in an area of Queens, New York, called Hollis. Also out of the Hollis neighborhood came hip-hop legends such as Russell Simmons, LL Cool J, and all three members of Run-DMC. Daymond had a love for hip-hop and the culture that surrounded it, especially the clothes. Daymond explained how the idea for FUBU was sparked. "We started to hear rumors that clothing companies, apparel companies did not want rappers, African Americans, inner-city kids, anybody wearing their clothes. I started to get fed up hearing about all these types of brands and I wanted to create a brand that loved and respected the people that loved and respected hip-hop, and I called it FUBU: For us by us!"

Daymond tested and experimented with his concept from 1989–1992. He printed a few "FUBU" labels and attached them to Champion-branded T-shirts that he bought off the rack from local retailers. He wore the T-shirts himself to see if people noticed. He also tested a hat concept. He noticed that many rappers were wearing a particular kind of hat. It was a type of ski cap with a small piece of shoestring on top. These hats were mostly sold by street vendors for $20. He thought he could do better, so he bought $40 worth of fabric. He stitched 80 hats together, added the FUBU labels, and tried to sell them for $10 on a street corner outside a local mall. He sold out in 3 hours and made $800.

He was the consummate bootstrapper, and the word about FUBU started to spread around town. He started selling more and more hats and soon added T-shirts to his product line. He approached retail booths outside the malls whose street corners he would stand on and asked them to sell his goods on "consignment" for him. "I was trying to figure any and every way out that I can to increase my sales!" He was sourcing his T-shirts from companies that would provide high-quality T-shirts with no brand name. He would then sew or screen print or even embroider his logo on the T-shirt and sell it. While continuously improving the product, he was also testing the market to see what customer preferences were in terms of pricing, colors, and styles.

Daymond was working at Red Lobster in the early days of FUBU, so he would spend early mornings visiting potential printers and embroiderers and make the T-shirts at night. He even closed FUBU three times because he ran out of cash. "I would be walking around the blocks when someone would say, Hey! Aren't you that little kid that sells FUBU? I need some more; I've been looking for you! I had to keep opening the business back up because the business started to call me instead of me calling the business." Fortunately, a friend of Daymond's, J. Alexander, saw FUBU's potential and invested, but he brought more to the table than money.

J. Alexander came up with a very interesting marketing plan. "The big black guys in the neighborhood had little options on what they could have to be very stylish. They had to go to Rochester Big & Tall and get a big white shirt or a black shirt or they had to pay a lot of money to get this stuff custom made for them because nobody was really making them. We just found a place that made 4X, 5X, 6X shirts and we made around 20 of these shirts. We made 20 of those shirts because we knew that these guys are normally bodyguards. Not all of them, but the ones we gave T-shirts were bouncers and something like that. They would not just wear it once—not like some of the stylish kids who don't want to be seen wearing something twice. We knew that these guys would wear it forever." These early adopters were walking billboards for FUBU!

Soon hip-hop artists who visited the clubs noticed FUBU on bouncers and bodyguards and demand started to increase. FUBU T-shirts were also being worn by video music director Ralph McDaniels's bodyguards. Between 1985 and 1998, Ralph was well-known for bringing hip-hop music artists into the spotlight, and Daymond wanted a meeting with Ralph. Since his bodyguards were wearing FUBU, Ralph was familiar with the brand and agreed to the meeting. Daymond recollected, "We were scared to death but he was very sweet and told everybody that FUBU was the next best thing. I really owe Ralph so much as he was one of my mentors and he was also mentor to the community. He really put us out there and after that all the rappers, all of them, were ready to wear our stuff because Ralph gave us the thumbs-up!"

Daymond John brought in business partners to help get the work done. While the partners together had accumulated around $50,000 in credit card debt at the time, they decided to go to the 1995 MAGIC fashion trade show in Las Vegas. They couldn't afford a booth at the time, but Daymond made the best use of his limited resources. He and his partners wore their FUBU-branded apparel and approached like-minded brands, such as Timberland. "I would stand outside their booth and say, 'Hey! How are you doing? I got this new brand, FUBU' and people would say, FUBU? the For Us By Us stuff? Where is your booth? I'll walk over to your booth. I would say, Instead of walking into my booth, you want to hop into a cab and head to the Mirage Hotel. I have my booth in one of the rooms there and we worked it out. We wrote $300,000 in orders and that's when I realized how much capital I actually needed."

To fulfill the Las Vegas orders, Daymond approached banks for a loan but none would work with him. As a result, Daymond's mother gave FUBU a $100,000 loan to cover operating expenses. Daymond set up manufacturing inside the house. He and his partners brought in sewing machines and hired seamstresses, all with the objective of completing the Las Vegas order by hand. Since he was paying all salaries on time, and paying for raw materials in advance, and having stores take credit for 30, 60, or 90 days, Daymond ran out of money within 4 months after having completed only $75,000 of the $300,000 orders promised.

The stores were starting to lose trust in Daymond, and Daymond was worried about losing his mother's house. Daymond's mother knew he needed a strategic investor and placed a classified advertisement in a local newspaper asking people to fund the company. Thirty of the 33 people who answered the ad were loan sharks charging extremely high interest rates, but one legitimate inquiry emerged. It was Norman Weisfeld, the president of Samsung's textiles division. Samsung agreed to finance the operations of the brand but asked Daymond to commit to selling $5 million within the next 3 years. Daymond said yes and the deal with Samsung was done.

With Samsung's backing, FUBU reached $30 million in revenue in 3 months, and the big retailers started to show renewed interest. Daymond recalled the resistance and discrimination of some buyers. "Many of the big retailers wanted to jump in on the highly profitable hip-hop bandwagon. Some of them were scared because they didn't want 'those' type of people in the store or were afraid of shootouts or shoplifting. One large retailer also asked me to take off the picture of myself and my three partners because we apparently looked like a gang." Undeterred, FUBU reached $350 million after 2 years and today has sales in the billions thanks to product line expansion, licensing, and partnering.

Today, Daymond John is semi-retired from FUBU and is now a Shark on *Shark Tank*. He's invested more than $8M in *Shark Tank* entrepreneurs.

## Critical Thinking Questions

1. Identify and evaluate all of Daymond John's bootstrapping methods.

2. If FUBU was being started today, would it be a good candidate for crowdfunding?

3. How does discrimination impact entrepreneurs? What evidence of discrimination was presented in the case? How did he handle the discrimination? What would you do?

**Sources:**

Feloni, R. (2018). Shark Tank investor Daymond John landed a deal that helped him make $30 million by taking out a newspaper ad. *Business Insider.* Retrieved from https://www.businessinsider.com/shark-tank-daymond-john-newspaper-ad-samsung-deal-2018-2

FUBU. (2019). Retrieved from https://fubu.com/

Raz, G. (2018, April 8). FUBU: Daymond John [Podcast]. *Stitcher.* Retrieved from https://www.stitcher.com/podcast/national-public-radio/how-i-built-this/e/54019004

Shark Tank cast: Daymond John. (n.d.). Retrieved from https://abc.go.com/shows/shark-tank/cast/daymond-john

# 13 Financing for Startups

"There are two times for a young company to raise money: when there is lots of hope, or lots of results, but never in between."

—George Doriot, American Venture Capitalist

# Chapter Outline

# Learning Objectives

## 13.1 WHAT IS EQUITY FINANCING?

>> LO 13.1   **Define equity financing for entrepreneurs and outline its main stages.**

In Chapter 12, we explored bootstrapping, the different ways in which entrepreneurs can get ventures started without formal external funding. We also explained how many entrepreneurs sometimes use bootstrapping to retain control, grow their business the way they want to, and keep hold of the company's equity.

Although bootstrapping may be ideal, if not necessary, in the beginning, as the company gains traction and shows evidence of potential, many entrepreneurs begin to look at the possibility of equity financing, which is the sale of shares of stock in exchange for cash. It gives entrepreneurs capital, which are financial resources to run the business including producing and selling the product. In other words, equity financing is a way to get capital from investors to start or grow a business. Most student entrepreneurs are not in a position to seek investment just yet; still, it is important to at least be familiar with the language of entrepreneurial finance for the future.

It's important to recognize that not all opportunities are investment worthy, but those that are face significant challenges. Sometimes it seems that entrepreneurs spend more time trying to raise money than actually working on the business. It becomes another full-time job for the founders. Additionally, balancing growth while preserving equity is a challenge, and entrepreneurs need to give serious thought as to whether—or at what point in time—they really need outside investment to grow. The general rule of thumb is to avoid seeking investment for as long as possible, to give your enterprise time to grow and build value so that you can secure a better deal with investors later on. However, sometimes competition will drive you to seek investment as early as you can, and some businesses are more capital-intensive than others. For example, if you have proprietary technology that has a proven market but you need additional funds to get the next version of the technology produced to reach a larger market, then equity financing is a logical next step.

**Equity financing:** the sale of shares of stock in exchange for cash.

### Splitting the Ownership Pie

The idea behind equity is similar to splitting a pie. When you are the only owner of the company, you own 100% of a small pie. When someone invests in your company to enhance growth, then your pie becomes bigger. As you need to give away equity in exchange for the investment, the company is no longer fully yours. However, if the company does well, then your smaller slice of the bigger pie will be much larger than the original smaller pie.

There is no magic formula telling you how much equity to keep or give away. Google gave up the majority of its ownership, so cofounders Larry Page and Sergey Brin

Master the content at
**edge.sagepub.com/
neckentrepreneurship2e**

# Joel Barthelemy, GlobalMed

Virtual health care platform GlobalMed has provided health solutions for the U.S. Department of Veterans Affairs.

For Joel Barthelemy of GlobalMed, entrepreneurship started at "5 years old selling vegetables and flowers out of the back of a wagon." If he didn't have something one of his customers wanted, he would do everything he could to get it. This same commitment to customer needs has enabled him to build multiple successful companies. Joel says, "You have to make an impact." And he feels impact is about looking ahead and seeing the shifts before they happen.

Joel serves as the founder and CEO of GlobalMed Telemedicine, a health care technology company that is "the platform of platforms for virtual health" and provides hardware and software for virtual health solutions. He and his team developed the first lightweight, true HD video examination camera and the first cloud-based Image Management Exchange for Telemedicine. GlobalMed has been recognized as one of *Inc. Magazine*'s and Deloitte Technology's 500 fastest-growing private companies as well as one of the best places to work in Arizona. GlobalMed is the outcome of Barthelemy's 25 years in high-tech health care and his 14 years specifically in visual collaboration and connected health care.

GlobalMed has clients worldwide. For example, GlobalMed is helping U.S. military veterans access health care by providing the company's telehealth solutions to the U.S. Department of Veterans Affairs (VA). The VA operates the largest telehealth program in the United States, with 700,000 veterans receiving telehealth services for 50 different specialties. This allows providers to treat patients in remote locations via online, visual technology. Further, GlobalMed's Transportable Exam

Station that provides a mobile, tablet-based telemedicine platform is used by health providers around the world. All in all, GlobalMed has delivered more than 15 million consults across 55 countries.

Joel's goal is to change the way people receive health care worldwide and to make sure it is available to all. There is a race to do this worldwide as populations age and more and more people need affordable, available health care. Joel leads this race with an innovative, future-focused platform aimed to help people globally in all types of environments. Barthelemy explains, "I'm focused on changing the way health care is delivered so that anyone can have access to health care anywhere."

Joel was a victim of the "dot com crash" of 2001 and lost a lot of money in the process. As he began GlobalMed, he "took on additional debt and reinvested himself." Now that the business is established, Joel has used an acquisition strategy to fund his later-stage growth. GlobalMed recently bought a competing, Miami-based company called TreatMD, which has expanded the functionality of GlobalMed's existing platform. Additionally, they bought an Oregon-based R&D company that has unique behavior modification software that has potential to help patients with chronic conditions.

As Barthelemy explains, "We're a debt-free company, we haven't taken outside investment, and we're profitable. . . . With all countries experiencing an aging population, there are few safer bets." For Joel, it's about building a profitable business related to something you love. He also believes in helping others do the same. One of Joel's favorite sayings is, "Ask me for money and I'll give you advice; ask for advice and I'll give you money." He spends a significant amount of his time nowadays "investing in companies that are run by people who love what they do." Joel's success has allowed him to be an angel investor and fund projects that he believes in.

## Critical Thinking Questions

1.  Has Joel ever experienced failure? If so, how did he react to the failure?

2.  How does Joel remain a leader in his industry? ●

**Sources:**

Joel Barthelemy (interview with author, January 24, 2019).

AZBIO Board of Directors. Retrieved from https://www.azbio.org/az-bio-board-of-directors/joel-e-barthelemy

Robeznieks, A. (2017). Here's why GlobalMed acquired telemedicine startup TreatMD. Retrieved from https://medcitynews.com/2017/03/her-es-globalmed-acquired-telemedicine-startup-treatmd/

collectively own just 16% of Google stock. Though 16% for the founders may not sound like very much, think about it: 16% of an enormous Google-size pie is pretty lucrative.[1] At the time of this writing, Google was worth more than $800 billion, so 16% works out to almost $128 billion.

However, splitting the pie starts before investment, if there is a team involved. And splitting the pie in an early-stage company represents a unique challenge because what you are splitting is rather worthless.[2] The founders agree to a percentage of ownership of something that doesn't really exist, and the question becomes, How do you determine who should get what percentage of the pie in the beginning? Does everyone get an equal share? Entrepreneur Mike Moyer, who wrote the book *Slicing the Pie*, uses a common example of four students working on a venture in an entrepreneurship course. They split the "equity" four ways and each gets 25%. They even incorporate the business. The class ends and one student really takes the idea forward and the other three are slackers, yet they all want to keep their 25% stake in the company. What do you do? Legally, they may have a right to that 25%, but it's not really the right thing. Moyer says new entrepreneurs make two mistakes: "The first is to divide the pie *before* you build the company. This is quite common, and founders often wind up where my hapless student did. The other mistake is dividing up the pie *after* you build the company, which often leads to internal battles that can cripple a startup team."[3] Moyer suggests creating a process for allocating equity based on contribution, including time, money, intellectual property, and other resources. This will help later when formal financing, such as what we talk about next, is warranted.

## Stages of Equity Financing

There are several stages of investment,[4] but for the purposes of this chapter we focus on the initial stages of equity financing usually provided to young companies: seed-stage financing, startup financing, and early-stage financing. Seed-stage financing usually consists of small or modest amounts of capital provided to entrepreneurs to prove a concept. Startup financing is the money provided to entrepreneurs to enable them to implement their idea by funding product research and development; and early-stage financing consists of larger amounts of funds provided for companies that have a team in place and a product or service tested or piloted, but as yet show little or no revenue. Florida-based augmented reality (AR) startup Magic Leap is a good example of an early-stage company that managed to raise more than $2 billion in funding before releasing its Magic Leap One AR headset.[5]

One of the most important factors to consider when you are seeking investment is to find investors who are most suitable for your stage of the company. Timing is also a factor. There is no use trying to raise funds when the venture is down to its last dollar. For one thing, it can take at least 6 months to raise money; in addition, a desperate early venture may give away far too much equity to investors, which can seriously dilute the position of its founders.

As the business grows and starts to take in more revenue, entrepreneurs may seek second-stage or later-stage financing. Even further down the road, a profitable company looking to expand and go public through an initial public offering (IPO) may seek investment through the third or mezzanine stage of financing. Finally, entrepreneurs may need bridge financing to cover the expenses associated with the IPO. These stages are displayed graphically in Figure 13.1.

## Forms of Equity Financing

Depending on the stage of their venture, entrepreneurs have several equity financing options available to them. As we discussed in Chapter 12, entrepreneurs looking to raise initial funds tend to turn to friends, family, and fools (the 3 Fs). Typically, the 3 Fs either invest cash in exchange for equity in the business, provide a loan, or lend money in the form of a loan that can later be converted to equity (called convertible debt). Entrepreneurs may also use crowdfunding to raise money from their immediate network, as well as reaching out to a wider market. In general, entrepreneurs may raise from $1,000 to $100,000 through the 3 Fs.

However, entrepreneurs seeking more formal financial capital to fund a growing business may choose to seek an angel investor. They are investors who use their own money to provide funds to young startup private businesses run by entrepreneurs who are neither friends nor family.[6] Entrepreneurs may choose to seek a

**Seed-stage financing:** a stage of financing in which small or modest amounts of capital are provided to entrepreneurs to prove a concept.

**Startup financing:** a stage of financing in which the money is provided to entrepreneurs to enable them to implement the idea by funding product research and development.

**Early-stage financing:** a stage of financing that involves larger funds provided for companies that have a team in place and a product or service tested or piloted, but have little or no revenue.

**Angel investor:** a type of investor who uses his or her own money to provide funds to young startup private businesses run by entrepreneurs who are neither friends nor family.

### FIGURE 13.1

## Stages of Equity Financing

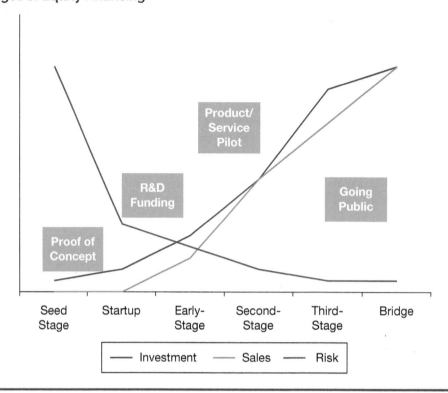

**Source:** https://www.marsdd.com/mars-library/angel-investors-seed-or-venture-capital-investors-that-depends-on-your-stage-of-company-development/

**Venture capitalist (VC):** a type of professional investor who generally invests in early-stage and emerging companies because of perceived long-term growth potential.

venture capitalist (VC) who is a professional investor who generally invests in early-stage and emerging companies because of perceived long-term growth potential.

Angel investors and VCs tend to be looking for the same types of opportunities, but there are differences between them, as illustrated in Table 13.1.

Seed-stage and startup entrepreneurs tend to seek out angel investors when they are initially trying to grow and scale the organization. VCs also invest in startups, but they are more likely to invest in companies in the early to third stage of business.

### TABLE 13.1

The Differences Between Angels and VCs

| ANGELS | VCS |
|---|---|
| Individuals worth more than $1 million | Funds consisting of limited partnerships |
| Invest from $25k to $100k in personal funds | Invest from $500,000 upwards in VC funding |
| Fund seed or early-stage companies | Fund from early- to late-stage companies |
| Carry out informal due diligence | Conduct formal due diligence |
| Responsible for own decisions | Decisions made with committee |
| Exit with returns on personal investment | Exit with returns to fund's partners |

**Source:** Adapted from Adams, P. (2014, January 12). How do angel investors differ from venture capitalists? Retrieved from http://www.rockiesventureclub.org/colorado-capital-conference/how-do-angel-investors-differ-from-venture-capitalists/

Table 13.2 lists some other factors and key questions that investors take into account when making the decision to invest.

TABLE 13.2

**TABLE 13.2**

Factors That Investors Take Into Account

| FACTOR | KEY QUESTIONS |
|---|---|
| Market conditions | Is the market ready for your product/service? Is the market size big enough? Is the market reachable? |
| Competition | Who are the competitors in your industry? How does your product compare with similar items in the market? Is there a unique and compelling competitive advantage? |
| Market opportunity | What is the opportunity for your product? How many customers? What is the proof that there is a market? |
| Founders | Are they experienced in the industry? Have they done startups before? Can the investor work with them? Are they coachable? |
| Social proof | Is there evidence that others believe in the founders' vision as much as they do? Does the company have a board of advisors? What are their customers saying about the business? |
| Value add | How much value can investors bring to your business through their expert advice and guidance? |
| Potential for return | If an investor puts in $1 today, what will they get in 5 years? 10 years? Does the potential return match the potential risk? |

**Sources:** What investors look for before investing in a small business. (n.d.). *Accion*. Retrieved from https://us.accion.org/resource/7-things-investors-look-investing/; Newlands, M. (2014). 5 things investors want to know before signing a check. *Entrepreneur*. Retrieved from https://www.entrepreneur.com/article/234536; What investors look for. (n.d.). *Fundable*. Retrieved from https://www.fundable.com/learn/resources/guides/investor/what-investors-look-for; Harroch, R. (2015). 20 things all entrepreneurs should know about angel investors. *Forbes*. Retrieved from http://www.forbes.com/sites/allbusiness/2015/02/05/20-things-all-entrepreneurs-should-know-about-angel-investors

# 13.2 THE BASICS OF VALUATION

>> **LO 13.2** **Illustrate the basics of business valuation.**

Before entrepreneurs seek equity investment, it is essential for them to know the value of their company so that when the time comes to raise funds, they will understand how much of the business they will need to sell and at what price. That's what investment is: Entrepreneurs are selling part of their business in exchange for investment in the form of cash to operate and grow the business. Putting a value on a company that has very little or no financial history is not an exact science. However, when it comes to fundraising, most investors will expect to see an approximate valuation of your business. This is needed so both the entrepreneur and investor can negotiate the equity percentage and division of ownership. But how do you value a business without any financial history?

The valuation of a seed-stage, startup, or early-stage company is based on the anticipation of future growth. How much time will it take for the business to become profitable? What potential does it have to grow? How can you prove to investors that your business is worth investing in? What is the exit strategy so investors can see how they might realize a return on their investment?

## How Can Entrepreneurs Value Their Companies?

As we have learned, there are very few overnight successes; entrepreneurs need to use the tools available to them to determine just how much their company is actually worth.

Typically entrepreneurs value their companies based on the firm's potential in their chosen market. The easiest way to do this is to check out similar companies operating in the same industry to see how they are being valued.

Sites such as BizBuySell and BizQuest will help you to find out how much businesses are worth in your industry and how much they have been valued at when they have reached profitability. For example, a company that's currently valued at $10 million after 5 years could mean that it was valued at a fraction of that price at the startup stage. You can also seek advice from lawyers and accountants who can help to determine the market rates for companies like yours.

However, be careful not to get too carried away by other valuations. Just because a similar company is worth millions doesn't mean your company is worth the same. Overvaluing your startup is dangerous—not only does it put investors off, but it puts the company and the entrepreneur's reputation at risk. Entrepreneurs typically have their valuation calculation and investors have their own. The true valuation falls somewhere in the middle!

## How Do Investors Value Startups?

Expert investors do deals all the time, so they will have a very good idea of what your business is worth. There are a number of reasons investors fund startups, and their decisions are not necessarily just based on the numbers. By knowing the criteria that matter to them, you can better position your company to attract investors.

First, investors will want to know your experience and your team's past successes. Second, they will want to see how many people use your product or service. Even if your business is not currently profitable, showing that you have 100,000 users, for example, proves to the investor that you have a potentially scalable business if provided with the appropriate amount of funding.

Second, having a distribution channel already set up is also attractive to investors. In fact, distribution is so important that PayPal cofounder Peter Thiel believes that "Poor distribution—not product—is the number one cause of failure." For example, the founders of Morphcostumes, spandex costume manufacturer of the "morphsuit,"[7] attracted investment because they had already spent months perfecting their product, and they set up a website and a Facebook page that became distribution channels to customers all over the world.[8]

Third, the industry in which you are operating might just be very popular at the moment. VCs are typically interested in investing in technology, as it usually means big business. For example, the top three industries invested in by VCs in 2018 were the Internet industry, health care, and mobile and telecommunications.[9] However, it often takes quite a bit of negotiation before entrepreneurs and investors agree on what they both consider a fair valuation of the company. Take the show *Shark Tank* in the United States (called *Dragon's Den* in the UK and Canada), where budding entrepreneurs get to pitch their ideas to angel investors in the hope of receiving investment. On any given episode, you will hear something like the following:

**People wearing Morphsuits**

Entrepreneur:    "We are asking for $150,000 for 10% of the company."

Shark:    "Your pre-money valuation is too high at $1.35 million. I'll give you $150,000 for 30% of the company."

What does all of this mean? First, let's talk about two important definitions: pre-money valuation and post-money valuation. Pre-money valuation is the company's value before it receives outside investment, while post-money valuation is the company's value after it receives a round of financing. In the *Shark Tank* exchange above, what is the entrepreneur's valuation of the company before receiving funding?

The entrepreneur is asking for $150,000 for 10% of the company, which means that the post-money valuation is $1.5 million ($150,000 ÷ .10 = $1.5M). The pre-money valuation is simply the post-money valuation less the investment—in this case, $1.35M ($1.5M – $150K = $1.35M). The Shark, however, thinks that a $1.35 million valuation is far too high, so she counters with the new offer of $150,000 for 30% of the company. With this offer, the Shark believes the pre-money valuation of the company is really only $350,000.

It is with certainty that entrepreneurs and investors will always disagree on the valuation! The answers to the key questions will help investors determine an approximate value for your business before giving you an idea of how much they are willing to invest. This is why it is important to do your own homework in order to prove that your business is worth investing in. By providing an estimated valuation of your business before you meet with investors, you can display business savvy and commitment to growth.

TV show *Shark Tank*, where budding entrepreneurs get to pitch their ideas in the hope of receiving investment.

© Tyler Golden / Disney ABC Television Group / Getty Images

## The Age of the Unicorn

A popular term in the venture capital industry is *unicorn*, originally coined by Aileen Lee, founder of Cowboy Ventures. A unicorn is a tech startup company that has received a $1 billion valuation, as determined by private or public investment.[10] Although unicorn startups are rare (there is a less than 1% chance of startups becoming one after raising venture capital), they are becoming more common. So far there are 35 unicorn companies in the United States. Table 13.3 lists the top 10. Though Epic Games was founded in 1991, the popularity of its Fortnite Battle Royale game, the company received substantial investment for growth in 2017.

**Unicorn:** a tech startup company that has received a $1 billion valuation, as determined by private or public investment.

## TABLE 13.3

The Top 10 Unicorns in the U.S. (2018)[11]

| COMPANY | WHAT IT DOES | VALUATION | YEAR FOUNDED |
|---|---|---|---|
| Juul Labs | Electronic cigarettes | $16 billion | 2017 |
| Epic Games | Video game developers | $15 billion | 1991 |
| DoorDash | Food delivery | $4 billion | 2013 |
| Snowflake | Cloud computing | $3.95 billion | 2012 |
| UiPath | Business task automation | $3 billion | 2005 |
| Circle | Cryptocurrency investment platform | $3 billion | 2013 |
| Roblox | Online game creation platform | $2.4 billion | 2005 |
| Bird | Electronic scooters | $2 billion | 2017 |
| Automation Anywhere | Robotic process automation (RPA) | $1.8 billion | 2003 |
| Discord | Voice, video, text app for gamers | $1.65 billion | 2012 |

**Source:** Baston, N. (2018). 35 U.S. tech startups that reached unicorn status in 2018. *Inc.* Adapted from https://www.inc.com/business-insider/35-us-tech-startups-that-reached-unicorn-status-in-2018.html

## Convertible Debt

**Convertible debt:** (also known as convertible bond or a convertible note)—a short-term loan that can be turned into equity when future financing is issued.

Because valuation can be complicated when a business is new, entrepreneurs and investors often opt for **convertible debt** (also known as a *convertible bond* or *convertible note*), which is a short-term loan that can be turned into equity when future financing is acquired. Convertible debt is a middle ground between debt and equity financing.

For example, say you are running a startup and you fully believe that you need to attract a significant amount of venture capital to make your business succeed. However, you are aware that VC investment doesn't happen overnight, so you still need to raise money in the immediate future to get your business off the ground. In this early stage of business, you might first ask potential lenders such as friends, family, and angel investors to invest, but you will need to think about the terms to offer them in exchange for their investment.

In the context of seed financing, these early lenders will loan you the money to help you attract venture capital. But rather than get the money back with interest when you do receive investment from a VC, these lenders receive stock, instead. In other words, the initial debt converts to shares of stock after an agreed certain point, which is called a *conversion event*—for example, entrepreneurs and investors may agree to set the conversion after a product reaches $100,000 in profit or achieves $1 million in revenue.

### Benefits and Advantages

One of the main advantages of issuing convertible debt is that it removes the need for valuation—in other words, you don't have to spend lots of time trying to figure out how much your company is worth to establish a stock share price. In fact, valuation becomes much easier after the first round of financing when there is a lot more data and information to work with.

Another benefit of convertible debt is that if your company succeeds, your investors may be entitled to a discount off the share price or bonus when converting the debt into equity, which can provide an incentive for your investors to commit. However, caution must be used when setting a discount—if the discount is too low, investors may not want to commit, and if the discount is too high, the investor may take this into account when pricing the stock, which may end up coming out of your own shares.

Finally, by issuing convertible debt, you the entrepreneur will remain the majority stockholder, with no interference from your lenders. Depending on the terms, they will have no control, no voting rights, nor any say over how you run your company.

### Cautions and Disadvantages

However, there are also some disadvantages to convertible debt: Early lenders may not want to take the risk of having their money tied up until the debt is converted into equity. They may also be wary of losing money if the conversion event doesn't happen (i.e., if profits don't reach $100,000 or revenue does not reach $1 million) or if the company ends up filing for bankruptcy. However, a clause can be added to address the possibility of the conversion event not occurring. For example, the initial investment could remain as a debt (which the entrepreneur must repay).

For entrepreneurs, convertible debt can be a daunting prospect: Accumulating debt before the company takes off can be significantly risky. Similarly, if entrepreneurs fail to pay back the loan, they could be sued by the lenders. In addition, convertible debt requires a lawyer to draft the terms, which can be an expensive bill to pay early on in the life of a startup.

To summarize, entrepreneurs using convertible debt to gain financial support from early lenders such as friends, family, and angels can be condensed into the following: "I need money, and you have it. But I don't know how much my company is worth, so let's see if professional investors or the passage of time will set the value for us while giving you an upside that's more in keeping with the risk."[12]

In the following sections, we will explore how angel investors and VCs can help entrepreneurs grow their businesses.

# 13.3 ANGEL INVESTORS

>> **LO 13.3** Describe angel investors and how they finance entrepreneurs.

In the past, an "angel" in the context of investment was used to describe wealthy people who invested in Broadway theatrical productions.[13] Over the years, the term *angel* has evolved to mean anyone who uses personal capital to invest in an entrepreneurial venture. Angels are eligible to invest as long as they are **accredited investors**, which means they earn an annual income of more than $200,000 or have a net worth of more than $1 million. Research shows that startups that have received angel backing are more likely to survive. With angel investment, entrepreneurs are able to scale sooner, hire employees, and generate greater revenue, which all leads to great potential for later-stage investment. Apple, Google, and Netscape are just a few well-known companies that have benefited from angel funding in the early stages.[14]

**Accredited investors:** investors who earn an annual income of more than $200,000 or have a net worth of more than $1 million.

We may tend to think of angels as motivated by a pure spirit of goodness—so it's important to remember that the primary reason why an angel (or anyone else, for that matter) chooses to invest is to earn money. However, angel investment is not just about the money. Often experienced self-made entrepreneurs themselves, angel investors can add significant value by providing advice, skills, and expertise, as well as lucrative contacts. They typically enjoy the experience of mentoring others and the personal fulfillment of nurturing a new business and watching it grow. It is generally thought that the typical amount invested by angels can range from $25,000 to $100,000.[15] Angel investors usually look for opportunities in young startups that can be expected to return 10 times their investment in 5 years.[16]

## Finding an Angel Investor

Angels used to be a notoriously elusive group, but thanks to sites like AngelList, today it is much easier to find a business angel. There are still some angels who will accept only referrals, but most angels will consider unsolicited submissions of ideas. Even so, when looking for an angel, it's always best to start with whom you know. Tap your network and think about who could provide you with an introduction to an angel. For example, Steve Jobs was introduced to his business angel through another investor, and Google's Sergey Brin and Larry Page found their angel through a faculty member at Stanford University.[17] Among those who can provide you with referrals to angels are attorneys, other entrepreneurs, work colleagues, university faculty, VCs, and investment bankers. Angels receive many unsolicited ideas every day, but having a professional vouch for you is always a good start.

Angels originally were wealthy patrons who supported theatrical productions.

© David M. Benett / Getty Images Entertainment

Table 13.4 outlines some reasons why angels and entrepreneurs can sometimes be a good match. The most successful working relationships are based on finding the right match for your business. The perfect match very much depends on the type of angel you are looking for.

## Types of Angel Investors

Business angels have many different objectives and styles of operating.[18] They range from silent investors to those who want full involvement in the operations of the company, either as a consultant or as a full-time partner in the business.

As angels have gotten more sophisticated, different types of angels have emerged. There are five main types of business angels: entrepreneurial, corporate, professional, enthusiast, and micromanagement. Let's take a look at each of these.

**TABLE 13.4**

Why Angels and Entrepreneurs Are Good for Each Other

| |
|---|
| • After friends and family, angel investors provide up to 90% of outside equity raised by startups. |
| • Angels invested an estimated $25 billion in startups in 2018. |
| • Angels funded almost 70,000 early-stage ventures in 2018. |
| • Angel-invested early companies (less than 5 years old) over a 25-year period accounted for all of the net new jobs in the United States. |
| • Economic research shows that the largest growth comes from innovative startups, the kind angels fund. |
| • Angels provide entrepreneurs with mentoring, monitoring, and guidance. |
| • Angels provide entrepreneurs with connections and introductions to their widespread network. |
| • Angels teach entrepreneurs valuable business strategies that go beyond funding. |

**Source:** Angel Capital Association. (n.d.). Angels and the entrepreneurial ecosystem. Retrieved from http://www.angelcapital association.org/about-aca/

## Entrepreneurial Angels

*Entrepreneurial angels* are entrepreneurs who have already successfully started and operated their own businesses, which they may or may not still be running. Either way, they generally have a steady flow of income that allows them to take higher investment risks. Entrepreneurial angels are the most valuable to early ventures—not only are they knowledgeable about the industries in which they invest, but because of their personal experience, they are in a great position to advise and mentor entrepreneurs.

## Corporate Angels

*Corporate angels* are individuals who are usually former business executives, often from big multinationals, looking to use their savings or current income to invest. Although they primarily seek profit, many corporate angels want to play a larger part in the company, often seeking a paid position in the venture. Because of their experience managing bigger corporations, corporate angels can often become frustrated with working in a small company with limited resources. As a result, corporate angels may be very controlling; in some cases, this can result in a clash of cultures, even leading ultimately to a breakdown of the investor–entrepreneurial relationship.

## Professional Angels

*Professional angels* are doctors, lawyers, dentists, accountants, consultants, and the like, who use their savings and income to invest in entrepreneurial ventures. For the most part, they are silent investors, but some of them (the consultants, for example) may wish to be taken on by the company as paid advisors.

## Enthusiast Angels

*Enthusiast angels* are independently wealthy retired or semiretired entrepreneurs or executives who often invest their personal capital in startups as a hobby. They tend to invest in several different companies and rarely take a role in active management.

## Micromanagement Angels

*Micromanagement angels* are entrepreneurs who have achieved success through their own companies and want to be involved in the ventures they invest in. Many micromanagement angels demand directorship or a position on the board of advisors and expect regular updates on the running of the company. They will intervene in the running of the business if it does not perform to their expectations.

There are many types of angels, including the five principal types described above and summarized in Figure 13.2. The majority of them will be looking to invest in an entrepreneurial venture that meets the criteria outlined in Table 13.2. They will want to know your level of expertise in your chosen area of business, the extent of the market opportunity for your product or service, the estimated valuation of your business, the current state of your finances, and your expenses and projections for the future.

There are several reasons business angels will reject a pitch, some of which will be beyond your control. For example, sometimes business angels will reject a pitch for geographical reasons—in fact, most angels like to invest locally. Unless you are willing to move your company to their locale, then there's not much you can do in this instance. Another reason for rejection is that the angel does not operate in the same sector as you do—this is why researching the most appropriate angel for your business is paramount before you get in touch. Angels might also reject approaches that do not come via a trusted referral, so make sure to use your resources to find the right way to connect.

Angels will also reject entrepreneurs who do not come across as knowledgeable or passionate; they may decline to invest in a project because they believe the market is too small, the financial projections exaggerated/not believable, or there is very little need for your product or service at all. It is useful to review these reasons for rejection when you are preparing to meet with an angel investor, so that you can come prepared with excellent arguments that will convince him or her that your business is worth a shot.

**FIGURE 13.2**

## Types of Angel Investors

**Entrepreneurial Angels**

- Experienced entrepreneurs
- Willing to take bigger risks
- Provide mentorship

**Corporate Angels**

- Commonly former business executives
- Looking for ROI or a paid position in the new venture
- May clash with startup culture

**Professional Angels**

- Professionals from other fields (doctors, lawyers, etc.)
- Commonly silent investors
- May want to become paid advisors

**Enthusiast Angels**

- Independently wealthy
- Retired entrepreneurs or executives
- Investing is a hobby

**Micromanagement Angels**

- Experienced entrepreneurs
- Looking for hands-on involvement in new ventures

## Angel Groups

In recent years, angel investors have begun to form groups to evaluate and invest in startups. It's not uncommon for angels to pool funds to invest in a venture, and they work together to conduct due diligence, analyze financials, and learn more about the opportunity. Typically, angel groups meet regularly to hear pitches, ask the entrepreneurs questions, and decide if there is enough interest to hear more. Table 13.5 lists the top 10 angel groups in the United States, ranked by number of deals. These angel groups are spread all over the country and tend to specialize in specific areas. For example, Golden Seeds focuses solely on women-led startups, while Arizona-based Desert Angels looks for opportunities to invest in Southwest regional startups.

Yet the formation of angel groups has not been the only way angels have evolved over the last few years. Angel investing in entrepreneurs is also breaking barriers for women. There has been a major increase in the percentage of angel investors (many of whom are more likely to invest in women-led companies). In 2017, almost one in four angel-backed companies were led by women.[19]

Research also suggests that women are better investors than men, as they take more time researching potential entrepreneurial ventures, spot more market opportunities than men, and take on less risk.[20] Women-led angel funds such as Belle Capital, Golden Seeds, and the Texas Women Ventures fund are doing much to increase the visibility of women angels by showing the amount of value they can add to entrepreneurial ventures.

In stark contrast to the rise in women angels, there are very few minority business angels (defined as African American, Hispanic, Asian, or Native American), accounting for less than 13% of the angel population.[21] In an effort to address this imbalance, groups like TiE Angels, a South Asian funding community, have been set up for entrepreneurs seeking minority investors.[22]

The Angel Capital Association lists the following as the best time to seek angel investment:[23]

Most Active Angels Groups in the United States, 2017

| Top Angel Groups Ranked by Number of Deals |
| --- |
| 1.  Keiretsu Forum |
| 2.  Houston Angel Network |
| 3.  Y Combinator[1] |
| 4.  Central Texas Angel Network |
| 5.  New York Angels |
| 6.  St. Louis Arch Angels |
| 7.  Desert Angels |
| 8.  Golden Seeds |
| 9.  Ben Franklin Technology Partner, Launchpad Venture Group[2] |
| 10.  500 Startups, Pasadena Angels[3] |

**Source:** Angel Resource Institute, https://angelresourceinstitute.org/reports/halo-report-full-version-ye-2017.pdf

1   Unique as an incubator, but very actively funding deals
2   Tied for 9th place
3   Tied for 10th place

- Your product is developed or near completion.

- You have existing customers or potential customers who will confirm they will buy from you.

- You've invested your own dollars and exhausted other alternatives, including friends and family.

- You can demonstrate that the business is likely to grow rapidly and reach at least $10 million in annual revenues in the next 3–7 years.

- Your business model is in top shape.

Angel investors get you over the hurdle that is referred to as the "valley of death," that stage when there is no steady stream of revenue and the company may be burning through cash (see Figure 13.3). There is a high probability that the "startup will die off before a steady stream of revenues is established."[24] Once you successfully navigate through the valley and your business is at a later stage, venture capital may be needed.

---

**FIGURE 13.3**

**The Valley of Death**

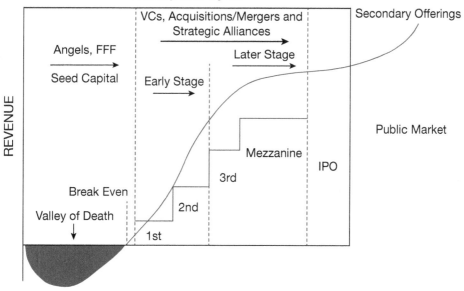

Startup Life Cycle

**Source:** http://www.eban.org/about-angel-investment/early-stage-investing-explained

---

## 13.4 VENTURE CAPITALISTS

>> **LO 13.4**   **Explain the role of venture capitalists and how they finance entrepreneurs.**

Like angel investors, VCs are often former or current entrepreneurs, but unlike angels, they are mostly professional money managers. Like angel investors, VCs look for opportunities that are likely to return 10 times their investment in 5 years.[25]

Typically, these venture capital money managers form a venture capital limited partnership fund that earns money through ownership of equity in different companies. The fund usually goes through a 10-year cycle before it dissolves and the assets are distributed to each of the partners. In terms of investment in early-stage to late-stage ventures, VCs investment generally starts at $1M, but in 2018, there were a number of "megadeals"

**FIGURE 13.4**

### Venture Capital Investments by Stage

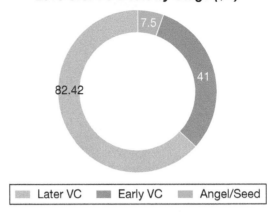

*2018 U.S. VC Deals by Stage ($B)*

7.5

41

82.42

Later VC    Early VC    Angel/Seed

**Source:** 2018 U.S. VC Deals by Stage chart—"NVCA 2019 Yearbook. Data Provided by PitchBook."

in excess of $100M.[26] Unlike angel investors, VCs are not really interested in smaller, seed-stage investments because it takes as much effort to monitor a small investment as it does a large one.[27]

The majority of VCs invest in businesses that have proved there is a significant market for their product and service. It is extremely rare for VCs to invest in the seed stage of business. In fact, it is commonly believed that seed-stage entrepreneurs have a better chance of winning $1 million or more in the lottery than getting venture capital investment.[28] As Figure 13.4 illustrates, VCs invested in only 7.5% of seed-stage companies in 2018.[29]

However, when considering an investment in a business, many VCs actually look for entrepreneurial ventures that have received seed funding in the early stages because it legitimizes the entrepreneur, helps to validate the idea, and shows an ability to stimulate belief among the entrepreneur's personal network.[30] Investors attract other investors.

Even if VCs do invest in young companies, their investment often comes at a price, as they tend to take more equity, more control, and may even take over the running of the company. However, although it is rare for seed-stage entrepreneurs to receive venture capital, it is not impossible. For example, online mobile photo-sharing, video-sharing, and social networking service Instagram received $250,000 VC seed investment that returned $78 million to the VC fund. It is widely regarded to be one of the most successful seed investments in history.[31]

Despite many success stories, the history of venture capital has been rocky, to say the least. Let's take a brief historical look at the highs and lows during the evolution of the venture capital industry.

## A Brief History of Venture Capital

One of the most useful ways for entrepreneurs and VCs to succeed in the future is to reflect on, and learn from, mistakes made in the past. Venture capital traces its roots back to the early 20th century. Wealthy families such as the Rockefellers, Bessemers, and Whitneys were looking for ways to earn profits by investing in promising young companies.

Although venture capital was largely disorganized and somewhat informal at this stage, a more professional structure called American Research and Development (ARD) was created in 1946 by cofounder and Harvard Business School professor General George F. Doriot (considered the "father of venture capital"). Today, ARD is mostly recognized for its enormously successful investment in Digital Equipment Company (DEC) in 1957 when its initial investment of $70,000 was valued at more than $355 million when DEC went public in 1968.

The introduction of the Small Business Investment Act of 1958 furthered the progress of the venture capital industry, as it officially allowed small-business investment companies (SBICs) to finance entrepreneurial ventures seeking startup capital. During the 1960s, the United States experienced a mild boom in the number of young companies that went public, but a recession in the early 1970s hit the SBICs, and many ended up in liquidation and sank into obscurity.

However, the venture capital industry began to experience a new high thanks to a 1979 rule that allowed pension funds to invest in venture capital for the first time. This opened the door to pension fund managers who rapidly invested huge amounts of money into new venture capital funds with the expectation of enormous returns. Huge successes of DEC, Apple, Genentech, and many more spurred more and more investment as each venture capital firm vied for the next success story. However, despite billions of investment in startups by multiple venture capital firms during the 1980s, the returns declined. The firms had risked too much by overinvesting and had failed to nurture or monitor the companies properly. Because of these problems, VCs became more cautious and limited investment in early-stage companies. As a result, growth in the venture capital industry slowed down from the late 1980s to the first half of the 1990s.

---

## RESEARCH AT WORK

# Why Most Entrepreneurs Can't Access Capital

The Kauffman Foundation, a leading nonprofit organization supporting entrepreneurship, says that at least 81% of entrepreneurs do not access a bank loan or venture capital. Additionally, their research suggests that startups are at a generational low and much of this is due to lack of access to needed startup capital. By talking with thousands of entrepreneurs, Kauffman has identified three trends that prevent entrepreneurs from accessing capital.

The first trend relates to banks. Banks have become so large and the community bank is disappearing. On average, it takes $30,000 to start a business, but the large banks don't earn money when the loan is less than $100,000. If an entrepreneur gets a loan greater than $100,000 it's very difficult to pay back on a monthly basis.

The second trend relates to the types of businesses being started today. More and more businesses are service businesses that do not have physical assets that can be used for collateral, so banks are not interested.

The third trend relates to venture capital. Venture capital only serves a very tiny percentage of new businesses. Less than 1% of businesses ever raise venture capital, and it's very geographically focused, with much of the VC money concentrated in California, New York, and Massachusetts. According to Kauffman, less than 1% of VC funding touches rural areas, only 1% goes to minority-owned businesses, and less than 2% goes to female entrepreneurs.

The Kauffman Foundation concluded:

> Very little of the total capital flow to entrepreneurs is geared toward women and people of color. With 81 percent of funding coming through personal net worth, family wealth, or connections to networks, it's not a mystery why today's make-up of entrepreneurs is overwhelmingly white, older, and male.

> Going forward, we know communities need to build the mechanisms and networks that help more people start new businesses. With the nation's changing demographics, it is both a moral and strategic imperative to ensure inclusion and equity as communities seek to grow local economies.

### Critical Thinking Questions

1. Why is there so much talk about venture capital in entrepreneurship when it's so difficult to access venture capital money?

2. Think about the examples discussed in this chapter that have received venture capital or angel financing. Do you see any patterns?

3. How can we create inclusion and equity for nontraditional entrepreneurs? ●

**Source:** https://www.kauffman.org/currents/2018/07/3-trends-that-prevent-entrepreneurs-from-accessing-capital

After this slow period, another boom was just around corner (known in retrospect as the dotcom bubble) as the Internet began to thrive and innovative Silicon Valley firms began to pop up. During the late 1990s, Amazon.com, America Online, eBay, Yahoo!, and Netscape were among the first tech firms that received venture capital funding. Blinded by the race to find the "next best thing," investors poured money into startup Internet companies without giving too much thought to how these companies would turn a profit, if ever.

The early dotcom businesses themselves made big mistakes. They had attracted venture capital because of the potential of the Internet—their whole theory relied on attracting huge numbers of people to their sites, without any clear strategies about how they could translate site visits into sales and sales into profits. These companies failed to plan properly, neglected research and development, and carried out limited promotion and advertising. As a result, hundreds folded.

When Internet stocks collapsed on the NASDAQ in 2000 (called the "dotcom crash"), so did the startups, leaving investors to deal with huge losses. Investors had overvalued the companies and had based their investments only on ideas without proving they had market potential. As a result, VCs lost large portions of their investments.

Since the crash, VCs have become a lot more cautious when investing in new ventures, and new ventures today have to do a lot more to prove themselves worthy of investment. But the momentum seems to be shifting in favor of VCs (see Figure 13.5): 2018 was a record year when VCs invested more than $130 billion in the U.S. compared to $82 billion in 2017, and 2019 numbers are expected to be similar to those in 2018. Interestingly, the number of deals done by VCs is down but investment is up, as depicted in Figure 13.6.

However, due to the gradual rise in venture capital investment in the years after recovery from the 2008 worldwide financial crisis, some experts predicted that another dotcom boom might be on the horizon. The rise of smartphones and tablets spawned the growth of a whole new generation of venture capitalist companies hoping to capitalize on this new market.[32] For example, messaging firm Snapchat received more than $500 million in venture capital in its first 5 years. But it's not just technology that has

**FIGURE 13.5**

### Venture Capitalist Investment Over 20 Years

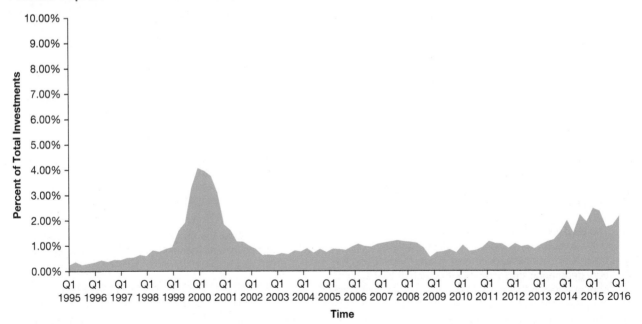

**Source:** Based on data from PricewaterhouseCoopers (2016) historical trend data. Retrieved from https://www.pwcmoneytree.com/HistoricTrends/CustomQueryHistoricTrend

FIGURE 13.6

### The Rise of Capital Investment

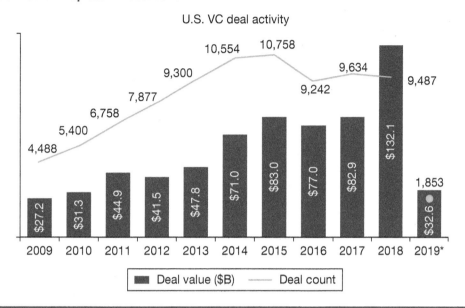

U.S. VC deal activity

Deal value ($B) ——— Deal count

**Source:** National Venture Capital Association. (2019). *1Q 2019 Pitchbook–NVCA Venture Monitor* (p. 4). Retrieved from https://nvca.org/research/venture-monitor/

attracted VCs: The growing demand for healthier food has given rise to food companies like meatless plant-based burger maker Impossible Foods, which has raised $750 million in investment to date.[33]

## How Venture Capital Works

There are many types of venture capital firms investing in businesses at different stages and across many sectors. Though there are about 1,000 active venture capital firms in the United States, they all operate very similarly.[34] So, let's take a look at how venture capital generally works. Today's VCs do not readily invest in seed-stage ventures as they once did, given the higher risk level. Yet there are many types of VCs out there, and the lines between informal and professional investors are blurring. It remains true, however, that professional VCs have the ability to catapult your venture from seed to high growth, so it's important to know how they operate.

Venture capital firms work within a specific investment portfolio, which means they have a defined list of the types of businesses in which they would like to invest. By narrowing these options, investors are often able to become experts in specific industries, which makes them better able to identify ventures that they think have the greatest potential.

VCs have very specific criteria for investing in an entrepreneurial venture, and these factors will very much influence the amount of investment made. Unlike banks, which seek return on capital through interest payments, VCs look for ventures that will earn them five to 10 times their original investment. They place a high value on quality management teams with excellent business skills who can deliver on their commitments.

One of the most important criteria for assessment is you, the entrepreneur, and your management team.[35] The VC will base its decision on how well you work together, the complementary skills you have, and your shared commitment to growing the business. VCs take an interest in entrepreneurs who surround themselves with smart, talented, well-respected people who support their ideas.

In relation to the industry, your company will be assessed for industry-market fit, its anticipated growth rate, the value-added potential, and the age and stage of development of your enterprise. The VC will also ensure that your goals for growth, control, and harvest (the stage at which they will cash in their investment) are aligned with their goals and strategies. The decision regarding the amount of investment will be based on these criteria.

In short, investors look for three main things: great teams, big markets, and unique and innovative ideas. However, they do not give them equal weight: The team trumps everything else. Most investors would rather have an "A" Team with a "B" idea than a "B" Team with an "A" idea.

## Finding the Right VC for Your Venture

We've discussed how VCs decide whether a given venture is right for their investment; now let's explore how you, as an entrepreneur, can find a VC that is right for you. First, recognize that venture capital is a long-term investment. Typically, a venture will not see an exit event until 5 to 10 years after launch.[36] All going well, additional funding will be provided by the VC every year or two as the company grows. Because you're going to be dealing with one another over a number of years, it is important to make the right match between the VC and the entrepreneur. If a good choice is made, you will have a mutually rewarding working relationship both financially and personally. It's also not uncommon to have more than one VC firm as an investor.

The process of choosing a suitable VC is going to involve in-depth research on your part, and the first step is to find ways to get in touch with them. VCs are an elusive bunch, just as angels are; they prefer to be contacted through referrals from other VCs, angels, founders in their portfolio, or lawyers. It's not likely that you will reach a VC through an email! Investors rely on a trusted network, a tight circle, to send them deals. Once you have names and contact information, what information should you research and what kinds of questions should you ask? Table 13.6 lists some guidelines for this process.[37]

---

**TABLE 13.6**

Guidelines for Finding the Right VC for Your Startup

| |
|---|
| 1. Look for a reputable brand of VC; securing investment from a credible company will encourage other investors to fund your startup. |
| 2. Identify whether they are a good fit for your industry and have the connections to help grow your business. |
| 3. Check their track record by taking three things into account: (1) their history of providing follow-up funding; (2) how they manage exits; and (3) how they treat their founders. |
| 4. Find a VC partner that really believes in you and your business; getting mental and emotional buy-in is essential for a successful working relationship. |
| 5. Make sure your goals are aligned with theirs in terms of building a brand, scaling a company, and planning a timeline. |
| 6. Establish the levels of autonomy and availability; although you may value your independence, you will also need to check whether the VC will invest time in you when you need it. |
| 7. Make sure the VC partner is someone you get along with who personally believes in what you are trying to achieve. |
| 8. Carefully assess the agreement for fair terms; more VCs are tweaking agreements to benefit startups, so it pays to shop around for the best terms. |
| 9. Check the location of your VC; keep in mind that a far-flung location can mean spending lots of time and money on travel to attend important meetings. |

---

**Source:** Timmons, J., & Spinelli, S. (2008). *New venture creation* (8th ed.). Boston, MA: McGraw-Hill Irwin; Cremades, A. (2018). How to find the right VC for your startup. *Forbes.* Retrieved from https://www.forbes.com/sites/alejandrocremades/2018/12/11/how-to-find-the-right-vc-for-your-startup/#ca0ed188f24d

When you, as an entrepreneur, get the opportunity to meet with a VC, it is important to be prepared. You will be expected to explain clearly and concisely the market opportunity your business presents; the size and potential growth of your market; why customers will be attracted to your product/service; how your business makes money, or will make money in the future; how soon it is anticipated to reach profit; why you and your team are the right people for the job; and how your investor can exit the investment. By providing this information to the VC, you are displaying your confidence, knowledge, and commitment in your business, as well as reassuring the VC that you are in it for the long haul.

If the first meeting goes well, you will be invited for a second meeting that involves a formal presentation to several of the VC partners. This is the meeting that can either break or seal the deal, so it is crucial to allow yourself sufficient time to prepare. Following the second meeting, the VC partners will discuss whether they wish to invest in your company.

## Why VCs Might Say No

VCs typically review more than 100 plans and proposals a month, but usually thoroughly read and review one or two of these. On average, a partner in VC firms will do only one to three deals per year. This means a couple of things: Your venture really has to stand out from the crowd, and you should not take it personally if your firm is turned down. However, you can boost your chances of success by knowing why a VC may be likely to say no.

One of the most common reasons why VCs do not choose certain companies for investment is that the opportunity presented does not fit in with the fund's criteria. For example, the fund might invest only in companies within a specific geographic location or industry sector, the deal might be considered too small/too big, or the business might not be quite mature enough for them to invest. As with angels and their criteria, some of these factors are beyond your control, but you can avoid wasting your time and the time of potential investors if you research their criteria ahead of time.

Another reason funds reject some applications is that they have a policy to review opportunities only via a referral. With such specific criteria, you need to carry out some

---

**TABLE 13.7**

Reasons VCs Might Say No to Your Business

| |
|---|
| Negative founder or team dynamics |
| The team is missing a key skillset |
| The founders don't have a clear mission |
| The team demonstrates a lack of focus (trying to do too many things at once) |
| Founders display negative behavior (racism, sexism) |
| Dishonesty |
| The founding team works in different locations |
| The VC receives negative references about the founding team |
| Investment needed is too much for the VCs |
| Poor-quality presentation or pitch |
| Licensing or IP issues |
| Unclear value proposition |

**Sources:** Bamberger, B. (2018). 5 common reasons why VCs decide not to invest. *Fast Company.* Retrieved from https://www.fast company.com/40523247/5-common-reasons-why-vcs-decide-not-to-invest; Downey, S. (2018). The real reasons why a VC passed on your startup. Retrieved from https://entrepreneurshandbook.co/the-real-reasons-why-a-vc-passed-on-your-startup-917c30103ecb

careful research to find the most appropriate VC for your business and go through the proper channels in order to reach VCs. Table 13.7 lists some more reasons why VCs might say no to your business.

## What About a Bank Loan?

**Debt financing:** borrowing money to start a business that is expected to be paid back with interest at a designated point in the future.

When equity financing is not an option, which for the majority of entrepreneurs it is not, then debt financing might be possible. **Debt financing** means borrowing money to start a business that is expected to be paid back with interest at a designated point in the future. Earlier we talked about convertible notes, a form of debt financing, but for many small businesses, bank loans are the "go to." However, only 18% of businesses (startups and beyond) ever access a bank loan.[38] The U.S. Small Business Association gives microloans to women, minorities, and veterans and the loans range from $500 to $50,0000 and carry interest rates between 8% and 13%.[39] Unfortunately, the demand is high and the process is long.

If an entrepreneur can't attract friends and family, angels, or VCs, then going to a bank may be a good option, but is it? Let's say you are starting a new business and you need a $300,000 loan to get the business operational. The bank say yes, but the loan is for a 5-year term at 12% interest. You may be thinking, "Yes! Where do I sign? At least the interest rate is lower than my credit card!" Well, you might want to think again. For a $300,000 loan at 12% interest for 5 years, your monthly loan payment would be $6,700 . . . starting just about now! Can you afford to make monthly loan payments of $6,700? Even if the loan was for 10 years, you would still have to pay $4,300 per month.

New business loans are very risky for banks, so they are not as common as you may think. Banks expect entrepreneurs to have the following:[40]

Capital: assets that can be used to create product that can then be sold and converted to cash to pay back the loan.

Collateral: personal assets (such as a home) to borrow against, so if the entrepreneur cannot pay back the loan, the bank can take the home and sell it in order to recoup the loan.

Capacity: a track record in business to prove the entrepreneur has the capacity to generate income to make loan payments.

Credit Rating: a poor credit rating will get you turned down immediately, but even a good credit rating is no guarantee you will get a loan.

The point is whether you approach an angel, a VC, or go directly to a bank, there is no easy way for you to acquire the money you need. The best way to secure funding is to build something that inspires people to invest in you in the long term.

Investors of all types, banks, and entrepreneurs go through a process to build a trusting relationship that will last a long time. Decisions and deals are not made overnight. If anyone is considering investing or loaning you money, the next stage is an intensive due diligence process.

## 13.5 DUE DILIGENCE

>> **LO 13.5** Describe how investors carry out due diligence processes.

**Due diligence:** a rigorous process that involves evaluating an investment opportunity prior to the contract being signed.

**Due diligence** is a rigorous process carried out to evaluate an investment opportunity prior to a deal being finalized. When considering an investment opportunity, both angel investors and VCs conduct a due diligence process, but typically, angel investors and groups do not carry out as much due diligence as VCs due to time, resource constraints, and a general lack of information given the early stage of the venture.

An angel or angel group generally conducts a proper analysis of the market opportunity to ensure it fits with investment goals and carries out background checks, legal checks, and financial analysis. Angels will also consider any personal conflicts that may

# Find an Investor–Entrepreneur Pair

Investors and entrepreneurs usually have different perspectives. Sources of these differences include the size of the opportunity, the future growth potential of the business, appropriate business model, scalability, and company valuation, just to name a few. We often hear about the entrepreneur's side *or* the investor's side, but a lot can be learned from comparing the two perspectives.

Your Mindshift is to find an investor–entrepreneur pair. In other words, find an entrepreneur who had angel or venture capital financing and talk to the entrepreneur. Then talk to his or her investor. The order can be reversed; it doesn't matter whether you first talk to the investor or the entrepreneur.

Begin your conversation with a broad, open-ended question such as, "Tell me about the process of receiving funding from Investor X." Conversely, when talking to the investor, ask, "Tell me about the process of funding Company Y." Probe a lot, take notes, and then compare notes. What similarities and differences did you find?

## Critical Thinking Questions

1. Was it easier than you expected to find an entrepreneur and investor to interview, or harder?

2. What obstacles or challenges did you encounter in your conversations?

3. Did you learn anything that surprised you or that ran counter to your expectations? ●

get in the way of the deal; different ways in which they can add value; and ultimately whether they want to establish a long-term working relationship with the entrepreneur.[41]

## The Due Diligence Process for VCs

Like angels, VCs are very careful when it comes to due diligence, particularly because of their history of making impulsive, wild investments in young companies. In general, investing in early-stage companies is risky, especially when millions of dollars are at stake, and VCs need to identify any potential red flags to ensure they are making a sound investment. During this process, entrepreneurs, their teams, and the company itself will undergo a vigorous appraisal, which generally lasts several weeks or even months. During this period, the backgrounds of the entrepreneurial team will be verified; references thoroughly checked; and corporate compliance, employment and labor, intellectual property rights, and legal issues reviewed. Table 13.8 lists the steps taken by VCs when creating a due diligence plan.

During this time, it is important for the founding team to carry out its own due diligence on the VC. It is perfectly appropriate to ask VCs for the contact details of companies in their portfolio with whom they have achieved success, as well as those with whom the deals did not work out. Talking to others who have been involved with the VC is an invaluable way of garnering information that will help you decide whether or not you will be able to build a long-term successful relationship with them.

## Exits/Harvesting

Part of the due diligence process involves the discussion of exit options. When VCs and business angels invest in a business, there is an expectation that they will receive a return on their investment when the firm exits the investment, within a certain time period, usually in around 5–10 years. Typically, this money is repaid through one of three types of exit strategies: an IPO, mergers and acquisitions, or buyback.

An **initial public offering (IPO)** is a company's first opportunity to sell stocks on the stock market to be purchased by members of the general public. Smaller companies are often bought by larger companies through *acquisitions,* which are ways for bigger companies to increase their profitability and, in some cases, swallow the competition.

**Initial public offering (IPO):** a company's first opportunity to sell stocks on the stock market to be purchased by members of the general public.

**TABLE 13.8**

Due Diligence Process for VCs

| Founders | VCs need to like and trust the entrepreneurial team before proceeding with the investment. They tend to look for high-energy, mission-driven founders who are committed to building a successful organization. Given the changing business landscape, VCs need to know that the founders have the ability to react to customer demands, competitive threats, changing and new regulations, and more. VCs find out more by asking the following questions: <ul><li>Who are the founders and what are their backgrounds?</li><li>Do they have relevant experience?</li><li>How well do the individuals function as a team?</li><li>Do they have a track record of success?</li><li>What critical resources do they have access to?</li><li>How well do they evaluate risk?</li><li>Are they detail oriented?</li><li>Do they exhibit a capacity for a sustained effort?</li></ul> |
|---|---|
| Market | VCs may conduct rigorous market analysis to establish the existence and size of the market for the product: <ul><li>Who are the users of the product and how many of them are there?</li><li>What are the drivers that are fueling the growth?</li><li>How is the company positioned against competitive threats?</li><li>Describe the competition.</li><li>Is the customer, the supplier, and/or the competition fragmented?</li><li>Are there attractive substitutes?</li><li>What regulations govern this market space?</li><li>What are the barriers to entry?</li><li>What is the distribution channel and who controls it?</li><li>What are the market boundaries?</li></ul> |
| Product/Service | VCs will analyze the product or service by asking a number of key questions: <ul><li>What customer problem is being solved?</li><li>What unique technology and/or knowledge does the company have?</li><li>How does this technology and/or knowledge create value for the customer?</li><li>Why is this product or service superior to the competition?</li><li>Are there any strategic relationships?</li><li>Does this product exhibit scalability?</li><li>What are the barriers to enter? IP protection?</li></ul> |
| Finance | VCs assess how a startup is going to make money by investigating key financial drivers: <ul><li>How will the company sell its product or services?</li><li>How will the customer perceive value?</li><li>Are there comparable companies to benchmark?</li><li>Who are the key market influencers that the company needs to target?</li><li>What are the financial requirements, e.g., capital investment, cash?</li><li>Is the business model scalable?</li><li>What is the potential for recurring revenue?</li><li>What are the anticipated margins?</li><li>What is the exit strategy? Is it feasible?</li></ul> |

For example, one of the biggest acquisitions of 2018 was when Amazon purchased doorbell-camera startup Ring for $1 billion.[42] Ring was founded by Jamie Siminoff, who had pitched his idea to *Shark Tank* investors in 2013 but walked away without a deal. Ring has grown to be the largest company ever to appear on *Shark Tank*. As Siminoff said about the reluctant *Shark Tank* business moguls, "Obviously, I think they wish they had invested."

A less common exit strategy is a *buyback*, which gives the entrepreneur an opportunity to buy back a venture capital firm's stock at cost plus a certain premium. However, buybacks are rare because the young company usually does not have the cash to buy out its investors, unless it has reached a highly profitable state.

BrandonKleinVideo / Shutterstock

Doorbell camera company, Ring.

The due diligence process is complete when all the issues have been resolved to the satisfaction of both parties. Getting through the due diligence process is the final step before contracts are signed and you finally receive capital. It is also an essential part of building a foundation of trust and commitment with your investor—and remember how important that foundation is because you will be in the newly forged relationship for years to come.

## Rich or King/Queen? The Trade-Off Entrepreneurs Make

Very few entrepreneurs manage to make money and maintain full control of their businesses. Entrepreneurs who give up a bigger slice of equity to investors tend to build more valuable companies than those who give up less equity or none at all. Any investment comes with a price, and before you sign on the dotted line, you need to have a very clear idea of how you want to run your business and what matters to you most.

By giving away equity, you will have less control over your decisions and may even be at risk of losing your position of CEO. Why? Because once you give up equity, directors will join the board and will take over much of the decision making, including the decision to either keep you as CEO or move you to a different position, or even push you out of the company altogether.

For example, a study of 212 U.S. startups from the late 1990s and early 2000s showed that 50% of the founders were no longer the CEO after 3 years. In fact, the same research shows that four out of five entrepreneurs are forced by investors to relinquish their CEO roles.[43] One of the most famous examples of an entrepreneur pushed out of his own company was the late Steve Jobs, who was fired by Apple's board of directors less than 10 years after he cofounded Apple Computers with Steve Wozniak. More recently, Rob Kalin, the founder of the online crafts marketplace Etsy; Travis Kalanick, founder of Uber; and Jack Dorsey, founder of Twitter, have all been fired from their own companies. Being pushed out or moved to a "lesser" position can come as a real shock to entrepreneurs who have worked tirelessly on building their ventures from the ground up, as well as to employees who have worked alongside them. In fact, the way this leadership transition is handled by both the investor and the entrepreneur can make or break a company.

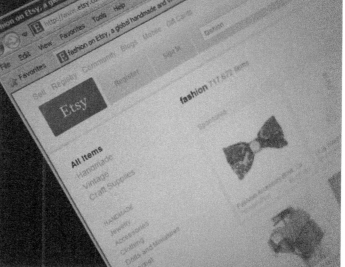

Credit Etsy

Online crafts marketplace Etsy, originally founded by Rob Kalin

# Replacing the Founder CEO

It isn't uncommon for founder CEOs to be ousted from their own startups, but it is important that their investors have made this move for the right, ethical reasons. Silicon Valley startup lawyer Jose Ancer believes that there are usually two main motives behind the investors' decision to push out a CEO when a company is struggling: performance or power.

When VCs have good intentions, they will replace the CEO to improve the performance of the company to benefit all stockholders. However, if the reason is more focused on power, the VC will likely push out the CEO in favor of someone they can easily control and influence, which does not always benefit stockholders.

So, how can founders ensure that the VC has their best interests at heart? By holding frank discussions with the VC partners before a formal agreement has been signed. This involves the founder asking the VC about their philosophy on founder management and how they would manage the transition process if the CEO needed to be replaced. After the discussion, the founder should verify the VC's responses by talking to other teams that have worked with those particular partners before.

Once these facts have been confirmed, then the terms can be committed to paper to ensure that everybody is in agreement. These terms may include involving the CEO and other executive members to suggest suitable candidates as the replacement CEO, being part of the interview process, and making sure the process is as transparent as possible.

Although founders may never visualize being ousted from their own company, the reality is that it does happen. This is why it's important to make sure you choose the right VC with the best intentions for your company. As Ancer said,

> Save for the very, very small number of unicorns in which founders can keep strict control (think Facebook), reputable VCs will never tell a founder CEO that she/he will stay CEO as long as they want to. The job of a Board of Directors is to do what's best for all of the Company's stockholders as a whole, even if that means making a founder CEO unhappy.

### Critical Thinking Questions

1. What would you do if you were forced to leave your own company?

2. How would go about choosing the right VC for your startup?

3. Can an entrepreneur really be picky when choosing investors? ●

**Source:** https://siliconhillslawyer.com/2018/03/26/replacing-founder-ceo/

One of the most common mistakes founders make is believing they can grow the business through inspiration, passion, and perspiration. Although these three key elements are helpful in getting a business off the ground, entrepreneurs need better resources to fully capitalize on future opportunities. As a company evolves, it needs different skills to grow into a more valuable business.

For example, a startup that has developed a product may not have the expertise or financial resources to market and sell it to customers or the know-how to set up after-sales service. This means relying on people with different skills, like financial executives, accountants, lawyers, and so on. More employees may need to be hired and a new organizational structure put in place. All these elements can be overwhelming for a founder and team who lack these skills.

Of course, it is entirely possible to remain in full of control of your business by keeping as much equity as you can. You may have less financial investment to increase the value of your business, but if you have more interest in being in control (i.e., being the "King/Queen"), then this is a viable option for you.

Thinking about what matters most to you—to be rich or to be all-powerful—is a useful exercise in how you define business success and what it means to you. As Figure 13.7 illustrates, maximizing control over wealth and vice versa can negatively impact success. Although the ideal would be to make tons of money and be completely in control, history shows that few entrepreneurs have managed to do both. ●

## FIGURE 13.7

**The Trade-Off Entrepreneurs Make**

**FINANCIAL GAINS**

|  | WELL BELOW POTENTIAL | CLOSE TO POTENTIAL |
|---|---|---|
| **LITTLE** | Failure | Rich |
| **COMPLETE** | King/Queen | Exception |

*(vertical axis: CONTROL OVER COMPANY)*

**Source:** Wasserman, N, The founder's dilemma, *HBR*, February 2008 issue. https://hbr.org/2008/02/the-founders-dilemma

---

MINDSHIFT

# Watch *Shark Tank* as an Investor

Google "Shark Tank Episodes" and watch one full episode of your choice. What is interesting about students who watch *Shark Tank* is that they are always more focused on the entrepreneur than the actual "Sharks." For this Mindshift, you need to practice the Shark mindset. In other words, focus more on the Sharks than the entrepreneurs. For each pitch, identify the following:

1. Body language of the Sharks

2. Questions they ask the entrepreneurs

3. How they respond to the answers given by entrepreneurs

4. What was the original ask by the entrepreneurs?

5. What were the offers made by the Sharks (if any)?

6. What was the final deal offered and accepted (if any)?

## Critical Thinking Questions

1. Do you recognize patterns when a deal was successfully negotiated?

2. How different were the asks from the entrepreneurs and the offers from the Sharks?

3. Would you characterize the Sharks as angel investors or venture capitalists? Why? ●

---

Get the tools you need to sharpen your study skills. SAGE edge offers a robust online environment featuring an impressive array of free tools and resources.

- Access practice quizzes, eFlashcards, video, and multimedia at
  **edge.sagepub.com/neckentrepreneurship2e**

## SUMMARY

**13.1 Define equity financing for entrepreneurs and outline its main stages.**

Equity financing is the sale of ownership stake within the company in exchange for funding. Seed-stage financing, startup financing, and early-stage financing describe funds in support of different early-business objectives. As the organization grows, it may then seek out second- or later-stage financing through subsequent rounds of financing. Businesses may also choose to undergo an IPO, opening the firm to general market funding and offering an exit to early investors.

**13.2 Illustrate the basics of business valuation.**

Investors use a variety of factors to come to valuation proposals, including market conditions, opportunities, competition, comparables, and how much value a given venture can add to the mix.

**13.3 Describe angel investors and how they finance entrepreneurs.**

Angel investors are typically high-net-worth individuals who are accredited investors investing their own money in startup ventures. Other types of angels include corporate angels, professional angels, enthusiast angels, and micromanagement angels, each characterized by distinct goals and value-added capabilities.

**13.4 Explain the role of venture capitalists and how they finance entrepreneurs.**

Venture capitalists differ from angels in the sense that they are professional money managers. Entrepreneurs should also exhibit at least as much caution as venture capitalists when seeking VC funding; the owners are likely to concede a significant ownership stake in the venture, and need to be certain of both why venture capital is absolutely necessary and which firm would provide the best guidance.

**13.5 Describe how investors carry out due diligence processes.**

To ascertain the prospects of any potential investment, angel investors and venture capitalists alike conduct due diligence processes of the firm under consideration. Essential to this process is identifying a method and timing for the investors to recoup their capital at exit, such as completing an IPO.

## KEY TERMS

| | | |
|---|---|---|
| Accredited investors 311 | Due diligence 322 | Seed-stage financing 305 |
| Angel investor 305 | Early-stage financing 305 | Startup financing 305 |
| Convertible debt 310 | Equity financing 303 | Unicorn 309 |
| Debt financing 322 | Initial public offering (IPO) 323 | Venture capitalist (VC) 306 |

## CASE STUDY

### Rich Palmer, founder, Gravyty

Rich Palmer's venture, Gravyty, uses artificial intelligence (AI) to help make the process of fundraising a lot more effective. His startup journey is full of many twists and turns.

Rich worked with a company called Capital IQ in 2007, after earning his undergraduate degree in IT, computer science, and economics from Rensselaer Polytechnic Institute. At Capital IQ, he ran the portfolio analytics division and analyzed portfolios of stocks, options, and derivatives to help hedge fund managers decide whether to buy, sell, or over/underweight certain sectors the next day. He used data analytics to predict what factors in the economy or in a particular business sector might make the stock price rise or fall. Rich noted, "However, working on Wall Street didn't really fit with who I am or how I worked. So after about 4 years, I decided to quit and start my own company (not Gravyty)."

He pitched a business idea called OvenAlly to Y Combinator, a prestigious accelerator. OvenAlly was an online platform that Rich describes as "an Etsy for homemade food." The Y Combinator pitch was an enriching experience for Rich as he got to sit across the table from people like Paul Buchheit (founder of Gmail), Paul Graham (founder of Viaweb and Y Combinator), and Sarah Livingstone (author of the book *Founders at Work* and cofounder of Y Combinator). He recalls vividly, "I'm sitting across from these awesome, wonderful people. They looked at me and said, very poignantly, well, have you ever started or tried to sell your own food from your own kitchen? And I went [expletive deleted] . . . no! They said if you're going to start a company that does X, shouldn't you also try to do Y as well to understand all the issues around X? They ended up not funding it because they didn't think we could surpass some of the legal and operational hurdles!"

Being a self-proclaimed "scrappy guy," getting through Y Combinator rounds was enough validation for Rich Palmer to quit his Wall Street job and start OvenAlly with a friend in 2011. "The company failed fantastically,"! Rich exclaimed. "While I and my software engineer and cofounder sat in a room and coded for 3 months to come up with a beautiful website, things went south from Day 1. The chefs had questions on liability if the food was poisoned or had razors in it, and we weren't able to answer them." While Rich was trying to figure out the legal side of the business, his cofounder's father passed away, prompting the cofounders to shut down the company. Today, a quick look at ovenally.com leads you to a beautiful page that says, "The Kitchen is closed. OvenAlly was a marketplace for homemade food that allowed buyers and sellers to interact across the country. Unfortunately, we have shut our doors in pursuit of new opportunities."

Rich took a little time off to think about the advice he got at Y Combinator "about doing X" to solve a "first-person problem" and reflecting on his next entrepreneurship move. It was around this time an old friend from Capital IQ offered him a role in a company called Relationship Science, a New York City company dedicated to figuring out the route for one person to connect with someone they wanted to connect with. As Rich explained, "For example, if one wanted to connect with someone like Elon Musk, how would they do that? We raised $120 million, sourced data from 15,000 different public sources, and mapped out connections." Rich joined Relationship Science as a senior product manager and software engineer in October 2011. Although the pay was good, Rich again felt like he was solving a problem that he didn't have nor had experience with.

During this time, he met his wife, who got a job in Washington, D.C. Rich was able to follow her and work remotely for Relationship Science. Then, everything changed in an instant.

"I was down in D.C. for about a year, and I was working out in the gym that was in my building. I'm a relatively healthy guy. I drink socially. I don't smoke. I don't do drugs. None of that stuff! I ended up on one of the stationary bikes and had a brain aneurysm. Basically, a blood vessel burst in my brain and nearly f@#*ing killed me! I went from being this high-power dude to not being able to really walk or talk or think anymore. It was a pivotal moment for my entire world, my entire universe, and entire way of thinking!" After this incident and during his recovery, Rich decided his life needed a "reset." He took the GMAT to pursue an MBA at Babson College in order to start a company with meaning.

At Babson, Rich met Adam Martel (MBA alum from Babson) who was working in the development and fundraising office of the college. Adam developed relationships with donors of the college who would financially support such things as academic scholarships, new buildings, faculty chairs, and general college operations. Adam and Rich developed a great friendship and started exploring the prospect of starting a business together. After going through the process of coming up with some of their "worst business ideas" that included a hair gel company and a wine-based company, Rich reflected back on his experience at Y Combinator and how he should focus on the "X where he or his cofounder had experience." Soon enough, Adam and Rich were looking for things that they were good at and trying to find an overlap. Gravyty surfaced as their meaningful idea that fit with their life experience.

Rich had significant experience in predictive analytics, modeling, and AI while Adam had deep domain expertise related to fundraising and donations in the nonprofit world. Although Rich could predict who to talk to, Adam was able to give insight on how to talk to a potential donor. After a little brainstorming, the two came up with an MVP (minimum viable product) that used predictive modeling offered by AI to reach out to, create, and develop relations with potential donors. Services included drafting communications, developing donor guides, and recommending travel based on locations of donors. They pitched the idea to a few hospitals, colleges, and other nonprofit organizations. The initial response was good so they dove deeper into the idea to start Gravyty.

The startup process began in August 2015, and they had a working prototype used by early adopters by January 2016. Rich and Adam needed startup financing, and an early potential investor offered Gravyty $100,000, but the terms were not quite what Rich and Adam were looking for. Rich recalled, "We turned down the $100,000. It was one of the hardest decisions we ever had to make." A couple of months later, in March 2016, the founders pitched Gravyty during a competition at South by Southwest (SXSW), a large popular tech and music festival in Austin, Texas. They placed second in the pitch competition and that same investor reengaged with them. This time the group agreed on terms and Gravyty had its first investment of $100,000. Adam quit his job at Babson and they hired another developer. Gravyty then applied to and was accepted into Mass Challenge, a global, zero-equity startup accelerator based in Boston, Massachusetts.

After the initial $100,000, Gravyty raised additional funding from 29 investors, mostly angel investors. "We could go to one VC and raise the same amount, but each one of our investors donates to organizations or is on the board of a nonprofit or a school and so that helps us create a network effect." Rich's number one rule when looking for investment is to do your due diligence on the audience. "We had a chance to attend a board meeting of Babson trustees. Aware that a good percentage of the members on this board were potential investors or connected to prospects, we went to the Babson website, took everybody's name, their pictures, the list of boards they sit on, the things they've done, and created a bunch of note cards. One side had the picture and the other side had all the relevant information about that person." Rich familiarized himself so he could weave the person on the other side into the conversation. As Rich recalled, "One of the people we spoke to ended up being connected to a big nonprofit tech company (not on the postcard) and wanted to introduce them to the founder, who had started six prior nonprofit tech companies and was basically the Steve Jobs of the space." That person now sits on the board of Gravyty and his experience and expertise have helped shape the business.

Rich always wanted the funding at Gravyty to be done in a way that did not dilute equity too much and too quickly. Their first round of funding was only $300,000. After growing a little, and onboarding clients from top universities and hospitals, Gravyty raised another modest round of $300,000 that allowed the team to expand from three to eight. Over the summer of 2018, they raised $3 million, which has allowed them to grow strategically into a 20-member team and focus next-level efforts on sales and marketing. Today Gravyty works with some of the largest hospitals and schools in the United States (including Babson), and nonprofits such as the Cure Alzheimer's Fund, AARP, WGBH, Yale, City of Hope, and more.

Raising capital is a challenge for all entrepreneurs, and Rich learned that not all investors are the same. He explains:

> West Coast investors tend to accept more risk and look for certain types of companies and entrepreneurs. They are willing to let valuations go a little high as well. Conversely, those on the East invest in hardware and biotech companies, usually less risky propositions because they've had bad experiences with high valuations in the past. West Coast investors are more likely than East Coast investors to accept a convertible note. Look out for the "terms" of the deal. Understanding the terms will help ensure that money is not taken off the table in the event of a liquidation event. Also, entrepreneurs need to understand how dilution of their stake in the company will affect future payouts to investors and themselves. The investor–entrepreneur relationship is like a marriage; it will likely last many years and cover some heavy topics, so it is important to negotiate in good faith and with the right people. We entrepreneurs also need to remember that investors need us as much as we need them! If they're controlling the entire conversation or pushing lopsided terms, they're likely going to be bad partners.

Rich has two pieces of advice for aspiring entrepreneurs: "First, always look at problems on a first-person basis. How can your experience and understanding directly influence the solution to a problem you know about? Those problems are easier to iterate on since you already know many of the details. And second, I see my cofounder and my employees more often than I see my family, and picking the right people for these roles is very important. If you can work together in the hardest of circumstances there will be many points where you're going to love each other or you're going to fight with each other, but the only way you get through that is by talking to and understanding that person and getting to know that person better."

## Critical Thinking Questions

1. Why was Gravyty a success for Rich when his other ventures failed?

2. Explain what Rich means by looking at problems on a first-person basis.

3. Not all companies need financing or are investor worthy. Why is Gravyty attractive to investors when OvenAlly was not?

**Sources**

Rich Palmer (interview with Babson MBA graduate assistant Gaurav Khemka, November 15, 2018)

Godfrey, R. L., Pulsipher, G. L., & Smith, H. W. (2011). *The 7 laws of learning: Why great leaders are also great teachers.* Springville, UT: Bonneville Books.

Godfrey, R. L., & Smith, H. W. (2009). *Home of the brave: Confronting and conquering challenging times.* New York, NY: Hachette.

Smith, H. W. (1994). *The 10 natural laws of successful time and life management.* New York, NY: Warner Books.

Smith, H. W. (2000). *What matters most: The power of living your values.* New York, NY: Fireside.

Smith, H. W. (2001). *The modern gladiator: Increasing productivity in the global age* [Audiobook]. FranklinCovey.

Smith, H. W. (2013). *The power of perception: 6 Steps to behavior change.* Juxtabook Digital Marketing.

# SUPPLEMENT A
# FINANCIAL STATEMENTS AND PROJECTIONS FOR STARTUPS

## Angelo Santinelli

## Chapter Outline

## Learning Objectives

A.1    Explain the purpose of financial projections for startups.

A.2    Describe financial statements as an essential part of financial projections.

A.3    Clarify the relationship between the three financial statements.

A.4    Describe the journey of cash through the cash conversion cycle.

A.5    Discuss how to build a pro forma financial statement.

A.6    Explain how to apply assumptions when building pro forma statements.

## A.1 FINANCIAL PROJECTIONS FOR STARTUPS

>> **LO A.1**    **Explain the purpose of financial projections for startups.**

As we have explained in this textbook, developing an entrepreneurial mindset, testing and experimenting, building business models, and planning are all elements of the Entrepreneurship Method, and now it's time to discuss another key element: financial projections. Through the iterative process discussed so far, entrepreneurs learn how to assess the problem–solution fit, product–market fit, competitive and industry fit, and now we will look at financial fit. Through action entrepreneurs develop assumptions, opinions, and a market perspective based on objective data and analysis. This primary data enables entrepreneurs to make a convincing case for financial projections, and prove that their startup is worth investment.

In Chapter 13: Financing for Startups, we touched on the topic of financial projections. Potential investors (angels, VCs) sometimes decline to invest in a project because they feel the financial projections are exaggerated or not believable. This is because financial projections are often built on a foundation of untested assumptions and third party data sources that are interpreted to portray market size and growth that exaggerates or distorts the revenue projections.

In many cases, entrepreneurs first develop pitch decks or other similar planning tools before testing the feasibility of their ideas to confirm whether or not the idea is indeed an opportunity. As result, they lack the necessary data to support their financial projections, which means the exercise is nothing more than guesswork.

Presenting carefully thought-out financial projections to investors is an exercise in lowering perceived risk in both you as an entrepreneur and your idea. When you are able to frame the opportunity from the perspective of the target market(s), understand

**$SAGE edge™**

Master the content at
**edge.sagepub.com/
neckentrepreneurship2e**

the resources required to capitalize on the opportunity, and know how to allocate those resources under varying market conditions, investors will be more inclined to have serious investment discussions. Similarly, the confidence and knowledge that you have developed from building realistic projections should make the process of convincing others, employees and investors alike, a little easier.

# A.2 THREE ESSENTIAL FINANCIAL STATEMENTS

>> **LO A.2**   **Describe financial statements as an essential part of financial projections.**

**Income statement:** a financial report that measures the financial performance of your business on a monthly or annual basis.

**Balance sheet:** a financial statement that shows what the company owes, what it owns, including the shareholder's stake, at a particular point in time.

**Cash flow statement:** a financial report that details the inflows and outflows of cash for a company over a set period of time.

Financial statements provide a window into the financial health and performance of a company. Every entrepreneur needs to understand the three essential financial statements: an income statement, a balance sheet, and a cash flow statement. The income statement (or profit and loss statement) is a financial report that measures the financial performance of your business on a monthly or annual basis. It shows sales and expense-related activities that result in profit or loss over a set period of time. The balance sheet is a financial report that shows what the company owes, and what it owns, including the shareholders' stake, at a particular point in time. The cash flow statement is a financial report that details the inflows and outflows of cash for a company over a set period of time. Each statement examines the company from a slightly different perspective, yet together they provide a holistic economic view of the company.

In the following sections, we will take a closer look at each of these three financial statements.

## The Income Statement

The income statement measures the financial performance of your business on a monthly or annual basis. It subtracts the COGS (cost of goods sold) and expenses (administrative, marketing, research, and other operating expenses) from the total revenue to give you a net income figure, which will be either a profit or a loss. Using Table A.1 as a guide and assuming revenue of $10,000 as an example, let's explore the different line items of the income statement in further detail.

**TABLE A.1**

Income Statement

| Revenue | $10,000 |
|---|---|
| (-) Cost of Goods Sold | $4,000 |
| Gross Profit | $6,000 |
| (-) Sales, General and Administrative | $2,000 |
| (-) Marketing | $1,000 |
| (-) Research and Development | $500 |
| (-) Depreciation and Amortization | $250 |
| Operating Profit | $2,250 |
| (-) Interest Expense | $100 |
| (-) Taxes | $675 |
| Net Income | $1,475 |

First, revenue is recorded on the income statement when the company makes a sale of a product or service and then delivers to the customer, thereby creating an obligation for the customer to issue payment to the company. It is important to note that there is a difference between a sale (revenue) and an order (bookings). An order may or may not become a sale. Orders become sales only when the product is shipped to and accepted by the customer. A sale is recorded on the income statement, while an order might only show up in a backlog—orders that have been received but not delivered to the customer. Also, the revenue number should be expressed net of any discounts offered. Table A.2 explains the distinctions between revenue, bookings, and backlogs.

**Backlog:** orders that have been received but not delivered to the customer.

COGS represents the total cost to manufacture a product. Costs are expenditures of raw materials, labor, and manufacturing overhead used to produce a product. For a service business, COGS may include the cost of service staff and associated overhead.

Subtracting COGS from revenue leaves you with three types of profit margins: gross margins, operating profit, and net income. A high gross margin percentage that remains consistently high over time can be an indicator of the company's long-term competitiveness.[1] It also shows that the company has sufficient funds for sales, marketing, product development, and other expenses.

Operating expenses are the expenditures that the company makes to generate income. These expenditures generally include sales, general, and administrative (SG&A); research and development (R&D); and marketing expenses. These expenses directly lower income.

As we explored in Chapter 9, the income statement also reflects depreciation and amortization of your company's assets. Recall that depreciation really means the cost of wear and tear of your physical assets such as machinery, equipment, and the building in which you operate. Amortization works similarly to depreciation; the main difference is that amortization relates to intangible assets such as patents, trademarks, copyrights, and business methodologies. Amortization matches the useful life of an intangible asset with the revenue it generates.

If you have studied accounting in the past, you might hear depreciation referred to as a "noncash" expense that is usually ignored when calculating free cash flow or EBITDA (Earnings Before Interest, Taxes, Depreciation, and Amortization). This is an accepted practice, but it avoids the obvious, which is that equipment and buildings eventually need to be replaced. From a short-term perspective, depreciation is a noncash charge to earnings, but in the long term, someone has to write a check for replacement. It is best to ask your accountant about the various rules for depreciating assets.

The second most important profit margin to monitor is operating profit, which is the amount left over from revenue once all costs and expenses are subtracted.

**Operating profit:** the amount left over from revenue once all costs and expenses are subtracted.

Another component of EBITDA is interest expense, which shows the extent of the company's debt burden as well as representing any interest owed on borrowed money. Taxes are the last expense item before net income. This line item captures federal, state, and sometimes municipal taxes due for the period. Sales taxes are not recorded here.

**Interest expense:** the extent of the company's debt burden as well as representing any interest owed on borrowed money.

The third profit margin item is net income, which indicates what is left after all costs, expenses, and taxes have been paid. It is important to note that there is a difference between income and cash; for instance, it is quite possible for a company to have positive net income, but have a negative cash flow, which causes it to struggle to pay its bills. We will explore this concept in more detail later.

**Net income:** indicates what is left after all costs, expenses, and taxes have been paid.

## TABLE A.2

Revenue, Bookings, and Backlog

| Revenue = Sale | Shown on the income statement net of any discounts when a customer receives and accepts an order |
|---|---|
| Bookings = Order | An order is a promise to purchase, which does not show up on the income statement until the customer receives and accepts the product or service |
| Backlog = Orders − Revenue | Orders that have been received but not delivered to the customer |

The income statement alone does not reveal much about a company's long-term viability or financial health. It tells you little about how and when the company receives cash or how much it has on hand. For an accurate picture of financial health, the balance sheet and cash flow statements need to be analyzed.

## The Balance Sheet

The balance sheet (see Table A.3) is a statement that shows a "snapshot" at a particular point in time of what the company has today (assets), how much it owes (liabilities), and what it is currently worth (shareholder equity). Numbers in Table A.3 are for illustrative purposes only.

As explained in Table A.4, the Balance Sheet gets its name from a basic equation, which must be equally balanced.[2]

Assets include cash, machines, inventory, buildings, and what you are owed and what you have the right to collect. **Current assets** include cash and other assets such as inventory, accounts receivable, and prepaid expenses that can be converted into cash within a year. Cash usually includes both cash and cash equivalents, or short-term, low-risk investments. Inventory represents what the company has to sell, as well as materials that are to be made into products. There are three basic types of inventory: raw materials, which include any goods or components used in the manufacturing process; work-in-process

**Current assets:** cash and other assets that can be converted into cash within a year.

Balance Sheet

| ASSETS (WHAT THE BUSINESS OWNS) | | LIABILITIES (WHAT THE BUSINESS OWES) | |
|---|---|---|---|
| **Current Assets** | | **Current Liabilities** | |
| Cash | $36,000 | Accounts Payable | $68,000 |
| Inventory | $128,000 | Accrued Expenses | $88,000 |
| Accounts Receivable | $43,000 | Short-Term Debt | $25,000 |
| Prepaid Expenses | $16,000 | Other Current Liabilities | $0 |
| **Fixed Assets** | | **Long-Term Debt** | $200,000 |
| Property, Plant, and Equipment | $601,000 | **Shareholder Equity** (what the business is worth) | |
| Accumulated Depreciation | ($8,000) | Retained Earnings | $335,000 |
| | | Capital Stock | $100,000 |
| **Total Assets** | $816,000 | **Total Liabilities and Shareholder Equity** | $816,000 |

TABLE A.4

The Balance Sheet Equation

| What You Own | = | What You Owe + What You Are Worth |
|---|---|---|
| **Assets** | = | **Liabilities + Shareholder Equity** |
| *Both sides of this equation must always balance.* | | |

(WIP) or semi-finished products, which are partially assembled items awaiting completion; and finished goods, which are ready to be sold (see Figure A.1).

Accounts receivable refers to money owed to the company for goods or services provided and billed to a customer. When the company ships a good or provides a service to a customer on credit and sends a bill, the company has the right to collect this money. Prepaid expenses represent payments the company has already made for services not yet received. These are usually things like insurance, deposits, and prepayment of rent. Prepaid expenses are considered current assets because the company has already paid for these services and will not have to use cash to pay for them in the near future.

Fixed assets might also appear on the balance sheet as property, plant, and equipment (PP&E). These are productive assets that are not intended for sale and are used over time to produce goods, store them, ship them, and so on. This commonly includes land, buildings, equipment, machines, furniture, trucks, autos, and other goods that have a useful life of 3 to 5 years, although the life of some assets, such as land and buildings, could be much longer. These assets are reported at cost less accumulated depreciation. Recall that depreciation is an accounting convention that appears on the income statement and represents the decline in value of the asset, due to age, wear, and the passage of time. Accumulated depreciation is the sum of all the depreciation charges taken since the asset was acquired.

## Other Types of Assets

"Other assets" is a catchall category that includes items such as the value of patents, goodwill, and intangible assets. Goodwill represents the price paid for an asset in excess of its book value. You will see this on the balance sheet when the company has made one or more large acquisitions. Intangible assets represent the value of patents, software programs, copyrights, trademarks, franchises, brand names, or assets that cannot be physically touched. One important note is that only items that have been purchased can appear here. For instance, companies are not allowed to create a value for things like a brand name and place it on the balance sheet.

Another type of asset includes long-term investments, which refers to assets that are more than 1 year old and are carried on the balance sheet at cost or book value with no appreciation. Examples of long-term investments include cash, stock, bonds, and real

**Accounts receivable:** money owed to the company for goods or services provided and billed to a customer.

**Prepaid expenses:** the payments the company has already made for services not yet received.

**Goodwill:** the price paid for an asset in excess of its book value. You will see this on the balance sheet when the company has made one or more large acquisitions.

**Intangible assets:** the value of patents, software programs, copyrights, trademarks, franchises, brand names, or assets that cannot be physically touched.

**Long-term investments:** assets that are more than 1 year old and are carried on the balance sheet at cost or book value with no appreciation.

---

**FIGURE A.1**

**Manufacturing Inventory**

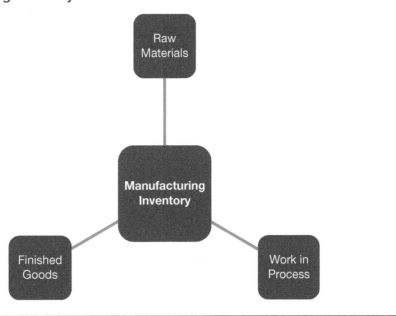

**Liabilities:** economic obligations of the company, such as money owed to lenders, suppliers, and employees.

**Current liabilities:** bills that must be paid within 1 year of the date of the balance sheet.

**Accounts payable:** money owed by a business to its suppliers.

**Accrued expenses:** costs incurred by the company for which no payment has been made.

**Short-term debt:** the portion of long-term debt that must be paid within a year.

**Other current liabilities:** short-term liabilities that do not fall into a specific category, such as sales tax, income tax, and so forth.

**Long-term debt:** obligation for debt that is due to be repaid in more than 12 months.

**Shareholder equity:** the money that has been invested in the business plus the cumulative net profits and losses the company has generated.

estate. It is possible that the assets are worth much more, or much less, than the original cost, but the convention is to carry them at cost.

## Liabilities and Shareholder Equity

Let's turn our attention to the other side of the balance sheet: liabilities and shareholder equity. Liabilities are economic obligations of the company, such as money it owes to lenders, suppliers, and employees.

Current liabilities are bills that must be paid within 1 year of the date of the balance sheet. They are organized based on who is owed the money. Accounts payable is money owed by a business to its suppliers. Accrued expenses are costs incurred by the company for which no payment has been made. For example, wages and taxes may be indicated on the balance sheet to be paid at a future date, but that payment hasn't occurred just yet. Short-term debt is the portion of long-term debt that must be paid within a year. A common example of short-term debt is money owed to lenders such as bank loans. Other current liabilities are short-term liabilities that do not fall into a specific category; these will include sales tax, income tax, and so forth.

Long-term debt is an obligation for debt that is due to be repaid in more than 12 months. Bank loans, finance and leasing obligations are all examples of long-term debt.

Shareholder equity represents the money that has been invested in the business plus the cumulative net profits and losses the company has generated (see Figure A.2). This is a liability that is not usually repaid over the normal course of business. Subtracting

### FIGURE A.2

**Total Shareholder Equity**

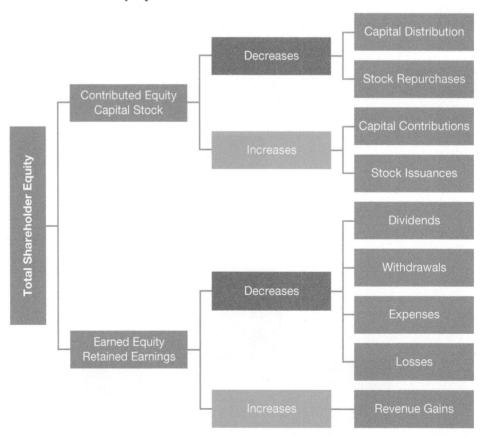

what the company owns (total assets) from what it owes (total liabilities) provides the percentage of its value to the owners, or its shareholders' equity.

There are two main components of shareholder equity. One component is retained earnings, the cumulative amount of profit retained by the company and not paid out in the form of dividends (a sum of money paid to shareholders from company profits) to owners. The other component is capital stock, which represents the original amount the owners paid into the company plus any additional paid-in capital to purchase stock in the company.

Shareholder equity increases when the company makes a profit (increase in retained earnings) or sells new stock to increase the capital stock. If the company has a loss, which lowers retained earnings, or pays a dividend, which also lowers retained earnings, these actions will result in a decrease in shareholder equity.

## The Cash Flow Statement

The cash flow statement tracks the movement of cash into (cash inflows) and out of (cash outflows) the company over a period of time. Cash inflows include loans, sales, interest, and shares; while outflows include payment to suppliers, wages and salaries, and dividends to shareholders (see Table A.5).

The cash flow statement is like a cash register for the company. It shows the cash that is available at the beginning of the period—in other words, cash that is already in the register. It also shows cash received during the period such as cash from the sale of a product or service, or cash received from investments, borrowing, or the sale of assets and stock, less the cash paid out in the period. This is cash actually paid out to support operations necessary to make and sell a product or service, or cash used to pay down loans, taxes, or the purchase of assets. This then leaves you with cash at the end of the period. Only cash transactions affect cash flow and are considered on the cash flow statement.

Cash flow statements are generally divided into two basic parts: cash generated from operations or profit-making activities, and cash generated from investment and financing activities. The first examines the profit-making inflows and expense outflows, while the second examines inflows and outflows of cash related to the purchase and sale of assets, and financing activities such as bank borrowing and stock sales. Together they form the full picture of cash moving through the company (see Table A.6).

The first line of the cash flow statement is net income. The first thing to do when examining cash flow is to add back depreciation and amortization that appear on the income statement. As you may recall, these are considered "noncash" charges related to the declining value of tangible and intangible assets. So, even though a write-down, or charge, may appear on the income statement, no cash actually left the company. Because we want to determine only cash in this statement, we add back both depreciation and amortization expenses.

**Retained earnings:** the cumulative amount of profit retained by the company and not paid out in the form of dividends to owners.

**Capital stock:** the original amount the owners paid into the company plus any additional paid-in capital to purchase stock in the company.

## TABLE A.5

Examples of Cash Inflows and Outflows

| CASH INFLOWS | CASH OUTFLOWS |
|---|---|
| Loans | Payments to Suppliers |
| Sales | Wages and Salaries |
| Interest | Dividends to Shareholders |
| Shares | Taxes on Profits |
| Receipts from Debtors | Loan Payments |

The next step is to examine the changes in the balances of current assets and current liabilities on the balance sheet. If a current asset balance increases, we are using cash. If a current asset balance decreases, we are adding cash. Conversely, an increase in a current liability balance adds cash, while a decrease in a current liability balance uses cash (see Table A.7).

Initially, it is best to understand the inflows and outflows of cash related to the operating activities of the company by determining the sources (inflows) and uses (outflows) associated with current assets and current liabilities to arrive at the degree of cash flow from operations.

Next, we shift our focus to cash changes stemming from investment and financing activities. One option might be to simply stockpile cash on the balance sheet, but this isn't the most productive use of cash. Another option might be to return cash to shareholders in the form of dividends, or to pay down any debt that the company may have amassed. And still another option might be to invest in productive assets such as machinery and equipment, or to acquire all or part of another business. This may show up as a separate line item in the cash flow as "Investments in Fixed Assets" or something similar.

## TABLE A.6

Cash Flow Statement

| | |
|---|---|
| **Net Income** | **$50,000** |
| (+) Depreciation and Amortization | $1,000 |
| (+) Sources: Decrease in Assets or Increase in Liabilities | $12,000 |
| (-) Uses: Increase in Assets or Decrease in Liabilities | ($15,000) |
| **Increase/(Decrease) Cash from Operations** | **$48,000** |
| (-) Net Property Plant and Equipment | ($8,000) |
| **Increase/(Decrease) Cash from Investments** | **$40,000** |
| (+) Increase in Net Borrowing | $0 |
| (+) Sale of Stock | $0 |
| (-) Paying of Dividends | $0 |
| **Increase/(Decrease) Cash from Financing** | **($4,000)** |
| **Increase/(Decrease) in Cash** *(Should be equal to cash on the Balance Sheet)* | **$36,000** |

## TABLE A.7

Inflows and Outflows of Cash

| SOURCES (INFLOWS) OF CASH | USES (OUTFLOWS) OF CASH |
|---|---|
| • Decrease in Assets | • Increase in Assets |
| • Increase in Liability | • Decrease in Liability |
| • Increase in Shareholder Equity | • Decrease in Shareholder Equity |
| • Profit from Operations | • Loss from Operations |

Finally, you must examine cash inflows and outflows from financing activities such as selling stock, borrowing, or paying dividends. Borrowing money increases the amount of cash on hand. Conversely, paying down your debt lowers the amount of cash on hand, while the sale of stock by a company increases the amount of cash coming into the company.

Adding the cash flow from operations to the cash flow from investing and financing leaves us with either a cash increase or decrease for the period. If a company has either cash in the bank or access to additional cash, it can withstand negative cash flow for several periods. It is good business practice for entrepreneurial managers to strive to achieve profits and convert those profits into cash.

### Net Income Versus Cash Flow

Although net income (or profit) and cash flow are both crucial to the success of the business, there are important differences between the two.

Net income, as it appears on the income statement, is determined by accounting principles and includes accruals and noncash items such as depreciation and amortization. In other words, there are items on the income statement that determine net income for a period that do not represent actual cash coming in or going out of the company for that period. For instance, in respect of how revenue is recorded on the income statement, the credit sales are captured as an obligation to pay (asset) in the balance sheet as an account receivable. Even though no cash has changed hands, the revenue on the income statement still reflects the sale. This treatment also applies to expenses and capital expenditures on the income statement.

Cash flow, in contrast, deals only with actual cash transactions. A company's operating policies, production techniques, and inventory and credit-control systems will influence the timing of cash moving through the business; and this is what the entrepreneurial manager must master in order to convert profit into cash.

# A.3 LINKAGES BETWEEN THE THREE FINANCIAL STATEMENTS

>> **LO A.3**   **Clarify the relationship between the three financial statements.**

The power of financial statements lies in the linkages. It is important to understand how the three financial statements are linked to one another and how decisions with regard to the operations of a company will impact its financial performance. A company's pricing and credit policies will have a direct impact on revenue, an income statement item; and accounts receivable, a balance sheet item. Although each financial statement provides a different view of the company, each statement is also related to the other.

For instance, net income on the income statement is added to retained earnings on the balance sheet. The ending cash balance on the cash flow statement is equal to the cash on the balance sheet. Every entrepreneur needs to understand how cash and goods and services flow into and out of the company.

Figure A.3 shows what happens when a sale is made, the product or service is delivered, and the cash is collected. When a sale is made and the product or service is accepted by the customer, revenue on the income statement increases. Assuming that credit is extended for the sale, accounts receivable on the balance sheet also increases. Once the obligation to pay is met by the customer, accounts receivable decreases and the amount paid becomes a cash inflow on the cash flow statement. Additionally, when a sale is made, the value of the product is moved from inventory (a balance sheet item) to cost of goods (an income statement item).[3]

As with the *sales* cycle explained above, these types of connections between the various statements can be charted in similar fashion for the *expense* cycle, the purchase of fixed assets, and investments. When you understand how cash moves through the company, you begin to understand how policies related to credit, inventory, and payables can affect the time it takes for cash to be converted into products and returned back to the company at a profit.

**FIGURE A.3**

## Income Statement/Balance Sheet/Cash Flow Statement

### Income Statement

| | |
|---|---|
| Revenue | $$$$ |
| (-) Cost of Goods | $$ |
| Gross Profit | $$ |
| (-) Sales, General and Administrative | $ |
| (-) Marketing | $ |
| (-) Research and Development | $ |
| (-) Depreciation and Amortization | $ |
| Operating Profit | $$ |
| (-) Interest Expense | $ |
| (-) Taxes | $ |
| Net Income | $$ |

> When a sale is made, Revenue increases on the Income Statement and an obligation to pay is incurred by the customer, which increases Accounts Receivable on the Balance Sheet.

> When a sale is made, the value of the product is moved from Inventory on the Balance Sheet to Cost of Goods on the Income Statement.

### Balance Sheet

| Assets (What You Own) | | Liabilities (What You Owe) | |
|---|---|---|---|
| **Current Assets** | | Current Liabilities | |
| Cash | $$ | Accounts Payable | $$ |
| Inventory | $$ | Accrued Expenses | $$ |
| Accounts Receivable | $$ | Short-Term Debt | $$ |
| Prepaid Expenses | $$ | Other Current Liabilities | $$ |
| **Fixed Assets** | | **Long-Term Debt** | $$ |
| Property, Plant and Equipment | $$ | **Shareholders' Equity (What You Are Worth)** | |
| Accumulated Depreciation | $$$ | Retained Earnings | $$ |
| | | Capital Stock | $$ |
| **Total Assets** | **$$$$** | **Total Liabilities and Shareholders' Equity** | **$$$$** |

> When Net Income on the Income Statement increases, Retained Earnings on the Balance Sheet increases. The opposite is also true. A decrease in Net Income will decrease Retained Earnings.

### Cash Flow Statement

| | |
|---|---|
| **Net Income** | $$$ |
| (+) Depreciation and Amortization | $ |
| (+) Sources: Decrease in Assets or Increase in Liabilities | $ |
| (-) Uses: Increase in Assets or Decrease in Liabilities | $ |
| **Increase/(Decrease) Cash from Operations** | $$$ |
| (-) Net PP&E | $ |
| **Increase/(Decrease) Cash from Investments** | $$ |
| (+) Increase in Net Borrowing | $ |
| (+) Sale of Stock | $ |
| (-) Paying of Dividends | $ |
| **Increase/(Decrease) Cash from Financing** | $$ |
| **Increase/(Decrease) in Cash** | $$ |
| **(Should be equal to cash on the Balance Sheet)** | |

> When the customer pays for the product or service, Accounts Receivable on the Balance Sheet decreases while a receipt of cash in recorded on the Cash Flow Statement.

# A.4 THE JOURNEY OF CASH: THE CASH CONVERSION CYCLE

**>> LO A.4  Describe the journey of cash through the cash conversion cycle.**

Cash is used to purchase materials, which are then made into products. This creates obligations to make payments to certain suppliers of those materials, which is captured on the balance sheet in accounts payable. These products are stored, which appears on the balance sheet in inventory, and are eventually sold and delivered to customers. Then the company has the right to collect cash for the selling price of the products, which appears on the balance sheet in accounts receivable. Once collected, this cash has now returned to the company. You hope that this journey produces more cash that is returned to the hands of the company. This journey is called the cash conversion cycle (CCC), and it refers to the number of days a company's cash is tied up in the production and sales process. CCC can be calculated using the equation shown in Figure A.4.

**Cash conversion cycle (CCC):** the number of days a company's cash is tied up in the production and sales process.

**FIGURE A.4**

**Cash Conversion Cycle**

Calculated in days, this equation shows how long the journey is for cash from the point of leaving the company to the point of return.

Days sales outstanding (DSO) is a measure of the number of days that it takes to collect on accounts receivable. Remember, if you do business in cash then your DSO is zero, but if you sell on credit, then this will be a positive number. DSO is calculated using the following equation:

**Days sales outstanding (DSO):** a measure of the number of days that it takes to collect on accounts receivable.

DSO = Average Accounts Receivable/Revenue per day

Average Accounts Receivable = (Beginning Accounts Receivable + Ending Accounts Receivable)/2

Revenue per day = Revenue/365

Days of inventory (DOI) is a measure of the average number of days it takes to sell the entire inventory of a company. DOI is calculated using the following equation:

**Days of inventory (DOI):** a measure of the average number of days it takes to sell the entire inventory of a company.

DOI = (Average Inventory)/COGS per day

Average Inventory = (Beginning inventory + Ending inventory)/2

COGS per day = COGS/365

Days payable outstanding (DPO) is a measure of the number of days it takes you to pay your bills. DPO is calculated using the following equation:

**Days payable outstanding (DPO):** a measure of the number of days it takes you to pay your bills.

DPO = Average Accounts Payable/COGS per day

Average Accounts Payable = (Beginning Accounts Payable + Ending Accounts Payable)/2

COGS per day = COGS/365

To calculate CCC, you need to include several items from the financial statements:

- ▸ Income statement
- ▸ Revenue and COGS
- ▸ Balance sheet
  - Beginning and ending inventory
  - Beginning and ending accounts receivable
  - Beginning and ending accounts payable

Note that because balance sheet items capture a snapshot in time, you want to use an average over the period of time that you are investigating. So if you are looking at 1 year, then you need to look at the ending period for the current year and the same ending period for the previous year.

Let's use an example to explore this equation in more detail. Suppose you are making men's shirts and selling them through a retail channel. The DOI is 80 days. You purchase enough cotton material to make a shirt. This purchase creates an obligation for the shirt maker to pay (account payable) for this material in 30 days (DPO). The raw material arrives (inventory) and the manufacturing process begins.

At the end of 80 days, the completed shirt is sold to the retailer (DOI). The retailer now has an obligation to pay the shirt maker (account receivable) and takes 40 days to pay for the completed shirt. This means that from the time cash left the shirt maker 30 days after the purchase of raw material, it took 90 days for cash to make its way back to the shirt maker. In this case the formula would be:

$$CCC = DSO + DOI - DPO$$
$$= 80 + 40 - 30$$
$$= 90$$

Figure A.5 illustrates this process.

The CCC, or days that it takes for cash to return to the business, must be funded. Any increase in sales usually results in an increase in working capital necessary to support this higher level of sales. Therefore, you must be able to fund the growth of the company.

**FIGURE A.5**

## Cash Conversion Cycle

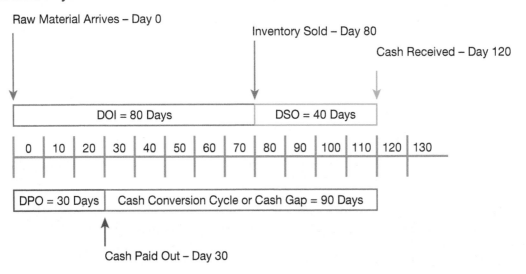

As a stand-alone number the CCC doesn't tell you much. Like many other metrics and ratios it must be compared over time and to other competitors in the industry. In general, a decreasing CCC is a good thing, while a rising CCC should motivate you to look a little more deeply into the management policies of the business to try and find the cash necessary to fund the company.

# A.5 BUILDING PRO FORMA FINANCIAL STATEMENTS

>> LO A.5   **Discuss how to build a pro forma financial statement.**

Now that you have a better understanding of the three financial statements, it's time to turn our attention to developing projections or forecasted financial statements. When entrepreneurs are assessing the long-term viability of a business it's important to make projections and develop pro forma financial statements. Rather than looking at financial statements from what has happened, as we have been discussing, we must now look at how to project what could happen. Pro forma financial statements give an idea of how the actual statement will look if the underlying assumptions hold true.[4]

The pro forma financial statement should include at least three scenarios of your financial forecast—each containing an income statement, the balance sheet, and the all-important cash flow statement. Each of these three scenarios should manipulate the various revenue and cost drivers in an attempt to determine where there is leverage in the business model to deal with what may go right and what may go wrong. All of your assumptions and estimates should be carefully documented and built into the model so that you can dynamically change them to conduct "what if" analyses in real time.

Although there are many preexisting, dynamic, pro forma models on the Internet,[5] be mindful not merely to insert estimates randomly without corresponding backup for every assumption. Anyone who has been through this process knows that the numbers are estimates that will change over time. Nevertheless, you must be able to defend every assumption, and the components must logically support one another. In the end, the pro forma financial plans must be strategically compelling and operationally achievable, and they must convey both confidence and realism to investors.

Your goal is to determine how much absolute cash is required to get to cash flow break-even and how this cash might be logically staged so that you can achieve a step-up in valuation at each stage. It is worth noting that items will emerge that you have not considered and that items that you have considered will be magnified to either the positive or negative.

Creating pro forma statements can be a time-consuming process, but there are major benefits to doing so. First, it gives investors a degree of comfort that you understand how to build a business and execute the business model. Second, it shows that you have a good understanding of how the market may evolve and how to respond to these changes. Finally, it is a useful way of providing structure and discipline as operating decision points arise.

## The Mechanics and Research

All too often, entrepreneurs begin the process with an existing model or business planning software and, before long, find themselves tweaking elements of the model to "make the numbers work." Instead, it is best to set the spreadsheet models aside and thoroughly research various business model elements that drive revenue and costs. This process requires both primary and secondary research. Figure A.6 outlines the overall process, or mechanics.

## Research

Much of your research should focus on the customer and market size and growth potential. A common beginner mistake is to assume that an exceedingly large population is your market and all you will need to do is get 1% of that market to be successful.

**FIGURE A.6**

## The Mechanics

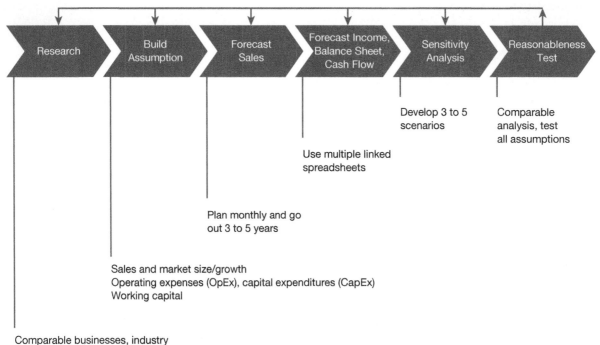

Although understanding the aggregate market size is useful, it is recommended that you segment your market in greater detail to better understand the various subgroupings and their respective buying habits and behaviors. Understand how they differ and how they are similar in terms of needs, expectations, price sensitivity, amount, and frequency of purchase, to name a few.

For the purpose of forecasting, it is also useful to understand how each subgroup is growing and changing over time. In general, the more you know about your primary and secondary target markets, the more reliable your forecasts will be.

**Primary research** refers to data gathered by yourself through sources such as focus groups, interviews, and surveys. **Secondary research** refers to data gathered from external sources: industry publications, company websites, government agencies, and the like. Secondary source articles and research reports can be useful as a means to get smart about an industry but, given the pace with which markets develop today, the data can get stale rather quickly. It is more beneficial to use primary data gathered in real time through observation, conversation, and rapid prototyping.

One useful approach is to first determine the questions that need to be answered about your target market, channels of distribution, required resources, cost drivers, and revenue drivers. Next, consider the data required to answer these questions. When you have gathered that data, then think about the primary and secondary sources of the data.

Remember to document the source of every assumption so that you can reference it if asked. Let's say that you want to start a pizzeria restaurant. Let's call it Town Pizza. Table A.8 lists some of the critical questions that you will want to answer before even opening a spreadsheet.

In addition to fundamental market research, it is also useful to find some yardsticks, or generally accepted rules of thumb for your industry. The best source of this information can usually be found by examining businesses that are comparable to yours in terms

**Primary research:** refers to data gathered by yourself through sources such as focus groups, interviews, and surveys.

**Secondary research:** refers to data gathered from external sources such as industry publications, websites, government agencies, and so on.

## TABLE A.8

Key Spreadsheet Questions

| KEY QUESTIONS | SOURCES | | |
| --- | --- | --- | --- |
| | DATA REQUIRED | PRIMARY | SECONDARY |
| **Customer and Market**<br><br>• What is pizza consumption in the U.S.? Is it growing?<br>• Who eats pizza, how much and when?<br>• When is pizza consumed most? What days of the week? Time of year?<br>• What is the population and composition of households in the area? What is the college population? What is the working population?<br>• What percentage of these people will be likely diners? (lunch, dinner)<br>• How can you estimate the traffic to the pizzeria and typical purchase order?<br><br>**Revenue Drivers**<br><br>• What else is sold at the typical pizzeria restaurant? (sandwiches, salads, pasta, beverages)<br>• What is the consumption of these items relative to pizzas?<br>• What is the average order? What are the average prices for each item?<br>• What is the contribution margin?<br>• What are breakeven points?<br><br>**Cost Drivers**<br><br>• What does it cost to make a pizza? A sandwich? A salad? etc.?<br>• What is the average size of a pizzeria?<br>• What does build out cost?<br>• What are the typical operating expenses? (monthly, yearly)<br>• What costs are fixed? Which are variable?<br>• What fixed assets are needed? (equipment) What does it cost? Should you buy new or used?<br>• What are the working capital requirements? | • U.S. pizza consumption data<br>• Census data<br>• Traffic patterns<br>• Demographics<br>• Typical pizza restaurant menu and pricing<br>• Average pizzeria statistics<br>• Ingredients cost<br>• Real estate data<br>• Construction estimates<br>• OpEx and CapEx for typical pizzeria | • Pizzeria owners, managers, and employees<br>• Various customer segments of the pizzeria dining market<br>• Associations<br>• Consultants and experts<br>• Accountants, lawyers, real estate agents<br>• Suppliers<br>• Contractors | • Industry research reports<br>• Association research<br>• Town census<br>• Periodicals<br>• News articles<br>• Websites/blogs<br>• New and used equipment sites<br>• Annual reports |

of industry and business model. There are numerous approaches to finding this information. Secondary sources are readily available on the Internet and include everything from historical data from public companies to industry associations and publications.[6] Similarly, primary data can be gathered through interviews with experts, business owners, potential customers, and observation. The comparable data will be extremely useful in both forming and validating your assumptions. In other words, everything covered in this text so far will help you build your assumptions.

## Building Assumptions: Forecasting Sales

Forecasting sales can be a complex process. One useful way to estimate sales is the bottom-up (or build-up) method, a technique that involves first estimating revenue and costs from the smallest unit of sales and building up from there.

Let's apply this method to the Town Pizza example. As you can see from the revenue worksheet (Table A.9), Town Pizza sells pizza, sandwiches, salads, and drinks. By using the build up method you can present the assumptions gathered from your research to estimate revenue for a typical day, and then extrapolate what that revenue might be for a typical month and year.

**Bottom-up (or build-up) method:** estimating revenues and costs from the smallest unit of sales, such as a day.

## TABLE A.9

Revenue Worksheet

| PRODUCT DESCRIPTION | SUGGESTED PRICE | EST. UNITS PER DAY | AVERAGE DAILY REVENUE |
|---|---|---|---|
| Pizza | $13.00 | 42 | $546.00 |
| Sandwich | $8.00 | 21 | $168.00 |
| Salad | $8.00 | 11 | $88.00 |
| Beverage | $2.00 | 37 | $74.00 |
| **Total Average Daily Revenue** | | | $876.00 |
| **Total Average Monthly Revenue @ 30 days/month**<br>**\* Does not account for seasonality spikes** | | | **$26,280.00** |

**Assumptions:**

U.S. Pizza Market

- Average traffic: 370 customers per month
- Average daily pizza sales = 42
- Sandwich sales are 50% of pizza sales
- Salad sales are 50% sandwich sales
- Beverages are 100% of pizza and sandwich sales
- Seasonal spikes: Super Bowl (Feb), Halloween (Oct), Thanksgiving (Nov), Christmas (Dec)
- Typical pizzeria average annual sales = $396,594.00
- 94% of Americans eat pizza; Average = 46 slices or 5.75 pizzas per year
- Pizza market is growing approximately 2% annually

Market Size/Growth

- Population = 27,982 (Households = 8,594), College Students = 5,974, Business employees = 1,050 (Total Pop 35,006)
- 62% of households < 45 years old (does not include college students and business employees)
- Growth 1% per year
- Currently 5 pizza restaurants in town

As Table A.9 shows, the monthly revenue has been estimated at $26,280 or $315,360 per year before accounting for seasonal spikes. This fits pretty closely to the national average of $396,594, which does include seasonal spikes, so our bottom-up approach appears to be feasible.

Furthermore, you can examine the market data to see if there will be sufficient demand for our pizzeria by using a top down approach. As you can see in the assumptions, the town comprises 8,594 households, of which 62% are age 45 and younger. Just to be conservative, let's assume that your primary target market is people aged 45 and younger, and likely to be either college students or families. That would leave 16,517 people in town under the age of 45. Add to that the college students and workers who come into town each day and the figure becomes 23,541. So, if 94% of these people eat pizza and the average person eats 5.75 pizzas in a year, that means approximately 127,000 pizzas are eaten by this population yearly. If the average pizzeria serves 14,400 pizzas per year and there are currently only five pizzerias in town, then there should be room in the market for our Town Pizza.

The process of gathering the data and formulating the assumptions helps you better understand the business model and the levers that might be used to generate more revenue. For instance, will spending more on advertising and promotions bring more people to the store? This type of scenario or sensitivity analysis can be explored in more detail once you have completed building the integrated pro forma financial statements.

Now that you have this baseline to work with, you can plot out what the first 2 or 3 years of revenue might look like on a monthly, quarterly, and yearly basis. This would also allow you to make estimates for seasonal spikes or lows.

## Building Assumptions: Cost of Goods and Operating Expenses

With a firm estimate on top line revenue, you can now turn your focus to estimating costs. The first cost item on the income statement is COGS (Table A.10). Recall that COGS includes the cost of raw materials and direct labor in the production of the product. Here you can once more use the buildup method to estimate the exact costs for each product, or as a first cut, you might want to use comparable data from a typical pizzeria.

Say you have found that the average raw materials and labor cost for a typical independent pizzeria is 30%. Given your estimated monthly revenue of $26,280, COGS would be $7,884, leaving you with a gross margin of $18,396 or 65%. Once again, our estimates are close to the average.

Businesses also incur operating expenses (see Table A.11), such as salaries, rent, advertising, marketing, and possibly research and development. These costs can also be estimated and validated through primary and secondary research. Reliable estimates can be accomplished through Internet research and validated through conversations with pizzeria owners, associations, accountants, lawyers, real estate brokers, and government officials, to name a few. It is worth sweating the details to get these estimates as close to the actual expenses as you possibly can. Once again, the buildup method is employed to round these numbers up to the monthly or yearly costs.

As you can see from the worksheet, the estimated operating profit is $6,022.00. This is not to be confused with net profit, which is profit after interest, depreciation, and taxes have been paid.

## Labor Estimates

A more complex business that might involve research and development of a product and a greater number of employees would require a more detailed approach to structuring new hires. In many types of business people can account for 75% to 85% of operating costs. Therefore, the schedule of new hires must be carefully thought out and matched to product development and sales requirements and milestones.

Given the time and cost involved in screening, hiring, and onboarding new employees, a plan that takes these items into consideration should be constructed for each department. A common mistake is to hire people too quickly and terminate poor performers too slowly. However, regardless of the size or complexity of your business, it is good practice to build a simple table to estimate this expense separately (Table A.12).

**TABLE A.10**

Cost of Goods Worksheet

| PRODUCT DESCRIPTION | SUGGESTED PRICE | EST. COGS (%) | EST. UNITS PER DAY | COGS ($) |
|---|---|---|---|---|
| Pizza | $13.00 | 30% | 42 | $163.80 |
| Sandwich | $8.00 | 31% | 21 | $52.08 |
| Salad | $8.00 | 25% | 11 | $22.00 |
| Beverage | $2.00 | 13% | 37 | $9.62 |
| **Total Daily COGS** | | | | $247.50 |
| **Total Monthly COGS** | | | | $7,425.00 |
| **Total Monthly Gross Margin (Total Monthly Revenue – Total Monthly COGS)** | | | | $18,855.00 |

**TABLE A.11**

Operating Expense Worksheet

| OPERATING EXPENSE TYPE | ESTIMATED MONTHLY EXPENSE |
|---|---|
| Rent | $2,333.00 |
| Labor | $7,925.00 |
| Outside Services | $275.00 |
| Credit Card Processing (1.9% of Sales) | $500.00 |
| Utilities | $525.00 |
| Advertising and Coupons | $100.00 |
| Maintenance and Contingency | $500.00 |
| Repair and Maintenance | $100.00 |
| Insurance | $250.00 |
| Office Supplies | $75.00 |
| Equipment Rental | $250.00 |
| **Total Monthly Expenses** | $12,833.00 |
| **Total Monthly Operating Profit** <br> **(Gross Margin – Operating Expense)** | **$6,022.00** |

Assumptions:

Rent: 1,000 ft$^2$ at $28/year = $62,500.00

Labor: 1 Mgr, plus 3 hires

Fringe Rate: 15%

CC Processing: 1.9% of sales

**TABLE A.12**

Labor Estimates

| POSITION | EST. ANNUAL/HOURLY WAGES | MARCH | APRIL | MAY |
|---|---|---|---|---|
| Manager | $31,200.00 | $2,650.00 | $2,650.00 | $2,650.00 |
| **Hourly Employees** | | | | |
| Kitchen Staff | 1 @ $13 per hr. | $2,297.00 | $2,297.00 | $2,297.00 |
| Counter/Wait Staff | 2 @ $11 per hr. | $1,944.00 | $1,944.00 | $1,944.00 |
| Benefits | 15% | $1,033.00 | $1,033.00 | $1,033.00 |
| **Total Monthly Cost** | | $7,924.00 | $7,924.00 | $7,924.00 |

**Assumptions:**
- 1 Manager
- 1 Kitchen Staff
- 2 Counter Staff

**TABLE A.13**

Capital Equipment and Other Expenditures Worksheet

| EXPENDITURES | ESTIMATED COST |
|---|---|
| Pizza Ovens | $21,995.00 |
| Walk-in Refrigerator | $10,500.00 |
| Pizza Table/Work Tables | $13,000.00 |
| Mixer | $3,500.00 |
| Prep Sink/Dishwasher | $1,350.00 |
| Pots and Pans | $500.00 |
| Phone, POS, Coolers, CC Machine, Misc. | $1,000.00 |
| Restaurant Build Out | $33,500.00 |
| Signage | $1,250.00 |
| **Total Expenditures** | **$95,595.00** |

**Assumptions:**

- All prices assume new purchases; best efforts will be made to purchase used equipment in good repair.
- Build out estimate provided by contractor for 1,000 sq. ft. including restroom. (Carpentry, electrical, plumbing labor included. Fixtures broken out separately.)

With your top line revenue and operating expense worksheets completed, you can now turn your attention to expenditures necessary to build out and run the business (see Table A.13). These expenditures, or capital expenses, will not appear as a line item on your income statement. Because the expenditures will be used over a period of time, usually more than a year, they will appear on your balance sheet as an asset and on your cash flow statement as an outflow. What will appear on your income statement is depreciation, which reflects the annual decrease in value of these assets over their useful lives.

## A.6 BUILDING ASSUMPTIONS: OPERATING POLICIES AND OTHER KEY ASSUMPTIONS

>> LO A.6   **Explain how to apply assumptions when building pro forma statements.**

As we saw earlier when describing the CCC, operating policies can greatly affect the speed at which cash makes its journey back to the company. In constructing pro forma financial statements, these policies need to be carefully considered and enforced by the company. Some of the more critical policies are as follows.[7]

- **Purchasing Policy:** the price and timing of raw materials, and other goods and services necessary to build, sell, and support products

- **Pricing Policy:** how pricing will be determined for your products and services

- **Compensation Policy:** the level of compensation and benefits for each type of position in the business

**Purchasing policy:** the price and timing of raw materials and other goods and services necessary to build, sell, and support products.

**Pricing policy:** how pricing will be determined for your products and services.

**Compensation policy:** the level of compensation and benefits for each type of position in the business.

**Credit policy:** the process and timing in which obligations to pay for products and services sold will be billed and collected.

**Payables policy:** the process and timing in which obligations to pay for goods and services received by the business will be paid.

**Inventory policy:** the level of various types of inventory (e.g., raw materials, work-in-process, finished goods) maintained and the speed with which inventory moves from the business to the customer.

- **Credit Policy:** the process and timing in which obligations to pay for products and services sold will be billed and collected

- **Payables Policy:** the process and timing in which obligations to pay for goods and services received by the business will be paid

- **Inventory Policy:** the level of various types of inventory (e.g., raw materials, work-in-process, finished goods) maintained and the speed with which inventory moves from the business to the customer

Other critical assumptions can affect the timing of cash flows both into and out of the business. For instance, when do you expect to make the first sale, and how long will it take for the business to ramp up to full capacity? In our pizzeria example, it may take several months to obtain permits and complete a build out of the restaurant before the grand opening. Then it may take several more months before advertising efforts begin to bring in the traffic that you anticipated would be necessary to achieve peak sales. This logic can also be extended to the productivity of new hires. Be sure to take into account the time and training it may take before new hires hit their stride and begin achieving the established sales quota.

Assumptions must also be considered for local, state, and federal taxes; interest; and inflation. Understand how your various expense-related items might increase over time as well. It is important to carefully document the source of every assumption made because it may be necessary to revisit it, or to defend it during due diligence.

## Building Integrated Pro Forma Financial Statements

With your research and analysis completed and assumptions made, you are now ready to build integrated pro forma financial statements. The logical place to begin is with the income statement. Using the validated assumptions from the revenue worksheet, build out a monthly pro forma income statement, balance sheet, and cash flow statement for a minimum of 2 years, followed by Years 3 through 5 on an annual basis. This time horizon will give you a good sense for the value-producing ability of the business.

When building your pro forma statements, remember the linkages between the three financial statements described earlier. Also ensure you understand how changes on one statement can affect the other statements. Understanding these linkages and especially how cash makes its journey through the business can mean the difference between success and failure. It is essential that you understand how the growth in your business will be funded and the amount of funding you will need until your business is producing enough cash to survive without constant external funding.

The cash flow statement is used to determine when and how much funding is required to get the business off the ground and support growth in the earlier years. This can be achieved by leaving the third section, financing activities, blank to determine the cumulative amount of cash needed. View a set of sample financial statements on the companion site for this text.

## Sensitivity Analysis

With the first full set of pro forma financial statements completed, you can now begin to address critical assumptions related to the revenue and cost drivers to test what your business might look like in different scenarios relating to customer traffic and seasonality, or cost of raw materials. For instance, if the restaurant were to open in the summer, might customer traffic be lighter due to vacationing college and high school students? If so, how might that affect revenue? Alternatively, what costs might need to be adjusted during peak selling months, and how might that affect cash flow and profitability?

During this analysis, a minimum of three scenarios is recommended: best case, worst case, and likely case. Thinking through the drivers and operating policies and understanding what can go right, what can go wrong, and what you would do to mitigate any controllable circumstances is probably the greatest benefit to building pro forma financial statements.

## Reasonableness Test

Using comparable data that you gathered during your research, compare your statements to those of similar businesses. Unless you have an entirely new and disruptive business model, your numbers should not be too different from businesses of similar size and scope.

Specifically, take a look at your top line revenue and determine whether sales ramp too quickly or too slowly. Have you accounted for seasonal changes in demand? Does the rate of sales growth level off at some point in time? Do expenses continue to rise in lockstep with sales, or should you expect to achieve scale effects that allow COGS and other operating expenses to grow at a slower rate as sales increase? Are there other efficiencies to your business model that are reflected in your operating policies?

Consider all of the questions that a potential investor may have about your business model and its effects on your financial model, and be prepared to answer those using data from your research and comparable analysis. If certain numbers do not pass the reasonableness test, revisit your assumptions until you are comfortable and confident that you can defend the model. ●

---

---

SUMMARY

**A.1 Explain the purpose of financial projections for startups.**

Financial projections enable the entrepreneur to frame the opportunity from the perspective of the target market(s), understand the resources required to capitalize on the opportunity, and know how to allocate those resources under varying market conditions.

**A.2 Describe financial statements as an essential part of financial projections.**

The three essential financial statements are the income statement, the balance sheet, and the cash flow statement. The income statement measures performance on a monthly or annual basis. The balance sheet shows what the company owns and what it owes at a given point in time. The cash flow statement assesses the inflows and outflows of money over a period of time.

**A.3 Clarify the relationship between the three financial statements.**

Although each financial statement provides a different view of the company, they are all needed to provide a complete picture. For example, a company's pricing and credit policies will have a direct impact on revenue, an income statement item; and on accounts receivable, a balance sheet item.

**A.4 Describe the journey of cash through the cash conversion cycle.**

The cash conversion cycle is the number of days a company's cash is tied up in the production and sales process. The number of days in the cycle is calculated by adding the days sales outstanding (DSO) to days of inventory (DOI), then subtracting days payable outstanding (DPO).

**A.5 Discuss how to build a pro forma financial statement.**

The pro forma financial statement should include at least three scenarios of your financial forecast, each containing all three types of financial statements. Each scenario should manipulate revenue and cost drivers to show how the business can deal with what may go right and what may go wrong. It should show a best case, a worst case, and a likely case.

**A.6**  **Explain how to apply assumptions when building pro forma statements.**

Assumptions include operating policies, which determine the speed of the cash conversion cycle, as well as taxes, interest, inflation, and the time it will take to ramp up the business. When assumptions are applied, integrated financial statements can be created and sensitivity analysis and reasonableness test applied.

## KEY TERMS

Accounts payable  336

Accounts receivable  335

Accrued expenses  336

Backlog  333

Balance sheet  332

Bottom-up (or build-up)
method  345

Capital stock  337

Cash conversion cycle (CCC)  341

Cash flow statement  332

Compensation policy  349

Credit policy  350

Current assets  334

Current liabilities  336

Days of inventory (DOI)  341

Days payable
outstanding (DPO)  341

Days sales outstanding (DSO)  341

Goodwill  335

Income statement  332

Intangible assets  335

Interest expense  333

Inventory policy  350

Liabilities  336

Long-term debt  336

Long-term investments  335

Net income  333

Operating profit  333

Other current liabilities  336

Payables policy  350

Prepaid expenses  335

Pricing policy  349

Primary research  344

Purchasing policy  349

Retained earnings  337

Secondary research  344

Shareholder equity  336

Short-term debt  336

# Introducing...

# $SAGE vantage™

## Course tools done right.

## Built to support teaching. Designed to ignite learning.

**SAGE vantage** is an intuitive digital platform that blends trusted SAGE content with auto-graded assignments, all carefully designed to ignite student engagement and drive critical thinking. Built with you and your students in mind, it offers easy course set-up and enables students to better prepare for class.

**SAGE vantage** enables students to engage with the material you choose, learn by applying knowledge, and soar with confidence by performing better in your course.

| PEDAGOGICAL SCAFFOLDING | CONFIDENCE BUILDER | TIME-SAVING FLEXIBILITY | QUALITY CONTENT | HONEST VALUE |
|---|---|---|---|---|
| Builds on core concepts, moving students from basic understanding to mastery. | Offers frequent knowledge checks, applied-learning multimedia tools, and chapter tests with focused feedback. | Feeds auto-graded assignments to your gradebook, with real-time insight into student and class performance. | Written by expert authors and teachers, content is not sacrificed for technical features. | Affordable access to easy-to-use, quality learning tools students will appreciate. |

To learn more about **SAGE vantage**, hover over this QR code with your smartphone camera or visit **sagepub.com/vantage**

# 14

# Navigating Legal and IP Issues

With Contributions From Richard Mandel, JD

"The law serves many purposes and functions in society. Four principal purposes and functions are establishing standards, maintaining order, resolving disputes, and protecting liberties and rights. The law is a guidepost for minimally acceptable behavior in society."

—Judy Kanarek, Quora contributor and YouTuber

# Chapter Outline

# Learning Objectives

## 14.1 LEGAL CONSIDERATIONS

>> **LO 14.1  Discuss how legal considerations can add value to entrepreneurial ventures.**

Typically, when entrepreneurs start a company, they tend to focus on building and developing the product or service, attracting a customer base, and finding the right people to help with the launch. All these activities are essential to get early startup ventures off the ground, but focusing on the legal side should also take priority. John Suh, CEO of online legal solutions company LegalZoom, calls these "the necessary evils."

"When you think of law and tax, they're the necessary evils," Suh said. "Entrepreneurs just want them to be taken care of as quickly and efficiently as possible, so they can get back to the real business of building the company."[1]

It may not sound as exciting as building a new product, but dealing with the law is an essential part of the process. Seeking expert legal advice is essential. Most entrepreneurs either lack the skills to understand the legalities of setting up a business or neglect the legal side altogether. Facebook cofounder Mark Zuckerberg made several big legal mistakes in the early startup stage, including setting up Facebook as the wrong business structure. Zuckerberg may excel at anticipating user needs, but he was certainly no expert in legal matters.[2]

Before you meet with a legal expert, it is important to be prepared by knowing a certain amount of information in order to ask the right questions and make the best decisions for your new venture. Legal experts are in a great position to add value to your business if they are the right fit. And that "if" is important: Although some lawyers may be great at drawing up contracts and preparing documentation, not all can work with startups and small businesses. Because startup companies face a variety of unique legal issues and funding challenges that are simply not experienced by more established companies, one of the most important things to look for in a lawyer is familiarity with and comfort in working with startups. You will also want to look for one who understands the industry you are in. For example, if you are in the fashion industry, you will need a lawyer who has some experience in the many areas that are likely to affect your business, including textile production, international trade, manufacturing law, and e-commerce.

How much does it cost to hire a lawyer? Startup legal costs vary widely, depending on the type of business you are setting up. A simple, home-based cupcake-baking business may cost only a few hundred dollars in legal fees, whereas a larger, more complex enterprise is likely to cost a good deal more. In general, a business attorney will charge

# Cameron Herold, 1-800-GOT JUNK? and COO Alliance

Photo courtesy of Cameron Herold

**Cameron Herold, 1-800-GOT JUNK? and COO Alliance**

"It has less to do with the idea and much more to do with execution and focus." This is Cameron Herold's motto that brought him great entrepreneurial success, built a consulting business, and enabled him to publish five books. Currently based in Scottsdale, Arizona, Cameron moves between the U.S. and Canada, and is a graduate of Carleton University in Ottawa, the capital city of Canada. He operates three businesses. First, Cameron runs the COO Alliance—a network for leading Chief Operating Officers. Second, for the past 12 years, Cameron has coached entrepreneurs and executives globally, which has led to his third business as a paid speaker, having given lectures and talks at events in 28 countries on six continents. Cameron has an expertise in "simplifying business problems and guiding business leaders to previously unimagined success." He consults with businesses that have at least $2 million in revenue and the intention of growing to $200 million. He estimates that he has actively consulted for more than 120 companies, and many of them have raised hundreds of millions of dollars to continue scaling.

Cameron worked on a number of projects while he built, tested, and proved valuable core beliefs about entrepreneurism. Like many founders, Cameron got his entrepreneurial bug in college when he had a house painting business and 12 employees. This business was a learning laboratory for him because he could practice in the real world what he was learning in the classroom. "For example, it is one thing to learn concepts and theories about the hiring process, and it is another to hold your own interview for a new employee; doing both at once creates excellent business leaders," according to Cameron. "Start something. This allows you to practice doing something. You can learn how to run a company regardless of its product or service."

For Cameron, being an entrepreneur is about creating your own value and creating something from nothing. In one of his larger successes, Cameron joined 1-800-GOT-JUNK?, a massive Canadian franchisor and full-service junk removal company, as its 14th employee and COO. In that entrepreneurial environment, he oversaw growth from 14 employees to thousands, alongside massive increases in revenue. Once he helped 1-800-GOT-JUNK? scale, he left the company because his passion is in growing entrepreneurial companies. However, even today, Cameron coaches the CEO of 1-800-GOT-JUNK?

Business law addresses the challenges that all businesses face regarding legal matters such as intellectual property (IP) and hiring and firing employees. Cameron is an expert in growing revenue, so naturally he confronts these issues from a revenue perspective. For example, he advises some clients to "spend most of your money in the early days on sales and marketing instead of operations and legal issues because revenue solves many problems. In your early days, you should beg and borrow in order to scale." There are products and services that require serious IP protection for profitability, but Cameron believes that should never detract from a focus on sales.

Yet Cameron has not underestimated the importance of hiring the right people. He has developed tried-and-true knowledge on employee hiring. He says, "The old phrase, 'hire for attitude; train for skill,' is outdated. You can find people with both—people with an attitude for growth, but with some relevant practical experience and a skillset." In consulting with clients, Cameron expounds, "Always raise the bar. Any time you bring on a new employee, make sure they are better than the average of your group!"

Cameron offers key advice for aspiring entrepreneurs in a few areas. Primarily, he has a simple formula that he shares with every client and leader: "Focus multiplied by Faith multiplied by Effort equals Success." Faith is the confidence in your abilities and vision. "So someone who is only 50% dedicated in all three categories, focus, faith and effort, has a 12.5% chance of success. Even someone who is 80% dedicated in all categories has only a 51.2% chance of success," according to Cameron. He uses this to remind entrepreneurs that success is much more dependent on the process than the idea. He says, "The people who really make it eat, sleep, and breathe their product and employees. Most people think that it's because there is a great idea, but it is much more about the formula."

## Critical Thinking Questions

1.  Have you worked for a company or started your own? If so, what did you learn about running a company?

2.  Do you agree with Cameron's claim that success depends more heavily on the work put in than it does the business idea?

3.  What is the formula for success Cameron shares with business leaders? ●

**Source:** Cameron Herold (interview with author, January 2, 2019)

at least $200 per hour, but a simple startup may only need 1 or 2 hours of work to draw up the required documents. Some legal practices provide a free 1-hour consultation for new clients and/or payment plans for startups. Before you decide on a lawyer, do some research and compile a list of four or five possible candidates, their qualifications, and their rates. Like anything else worthwhile that you need to buy for your business, it pays to shop around.

Of course, there are a wide range of free resources regarding legal issues and documents available through the Internet to entrepreneurs looking for advice. However, be careful using these resources as they may not be strictly accurate or relevant to the type of business you are trying to set up. Using certain sites online (see Table 14.1) is a good way to gather research and identify the type of legal counsel you might need. Although legal advice can be expensive, the expense far outweighs the risk of attempting to do it all yourself with the help of free, potentially inaccurate information online.

Entrepreneurs can also receive legal support from clinics operated at law schools all over the United States. For example, second- and third-year law students at Santa Clara University in California provide affordable legal services to entrepreneurs looking to set up a business or for advice on the legal issues that may arise from running a business.[3] Apart from clinics, law school websites can also be useful for legal information, as they may provide certain forms or documentation for no charge. Washburn University of Law, in particular, provides a wide range of forms and information, which can be accessed for free.[4]

The United States government also provides resources for entrepreneurs. One such resource is the United States Patent and Trademark Office (USPTO), which provides a pro bono legal program to support entrepreneurs. The Small Business Administration also sponsors the SCORE association, a network of volunteer business counselors throughout the United States and its territories who are trained to serve as counselors, advisors, and

**TABLE 14.1**

Useful Online Legal Resources

| | |
|---|---|
| **United States Patent and Trademark Office** | You can learn about patent and trademark basics, search existing patents, and register trademarks. https://www.uspto.gov/ |
| **Quora** | A question-and-answer website on thousands of topics but also a good place to ask legal questions. There is an area devoted to startup law. https://www.quora.com/topic/Startup-Law-1 |
| **Docracy** | Free, open-sourced site for contracts and other legal documents. Documents are free to download and edit. https://www.docracy.com/ |
| **U.S. Small Business Administration** | A comprehensive site for entrepreneurs that offers free guides for legal compliance in starting and running a business. https://www.sba.gov/ |
| **Startup Company Lawyer** | Good sources for answers to frequently asked legal questions such as "When do I need to incorporate a company?" and "What state should I incorporate in?" and "What type of entity should I form?" http://www.startupcompanylawyer.com/ |
| **LegalZoom\*** | Provides legal services to help start and run a business as well as file trademark applications. https://www.legalzoom.com/ |
| **NOLO\*** | Offers low-cost DIY kits for setting up business entities. https://www.nolo.com/ |
| **Rocket Lawyer\*** | Helps you draft legal documents to start a business, manage employees, or rent property. https://www.rocketlawyer.com/ |

**\*Note:** The authors are not advocating or promoting any paid services. We have no relationship with any site promoting products for a fee.

mentors to aspiring entrepreneurs and business owners. These resources can be incredibly useful in finding out the different legal requirements for your venture. Armed with this information, you will have a better chance of finding the right legal help when the time comes.

The best lawyers not only will be able to provide legal counsel but will also add value for many years as your business grows.[5] They will have experience with early-stage startups, know the industry, and be up front with their fee structure. They may also have an impressive list of contacts, which can be very useful in connecting you with investors and advising you on fundraising. What's more, a good lawyer will be a person you can actually relate to. The best way to hire legal experts is the same way you would hire an employee. When the time comes, ask yourself, "Is this the right person to advise and represent my company?"

## 14.2 TYPES OF LEGAL STRUCTURES

**>> LO 14.2**   **Explain the most common types of legal structures available to startups.**

One of the most important choices entrepreneurs make when starting a business is choosing the right type of legal structure for their company. The type of structure affects the authorities you need to notify regarding your business, tax and other contributions you may have to pay, the records and documentation you will need to maintain, and how decisions are made about the business.

As legal structures vary from state to state (and country to country), it is essential that entrepreneurs do as much research as possible before deciding on a particular form of organization. Depending on your situation, there are several structures to choose from, and it is important to understand the differences among them. If, after researching the question, you are still not sure which one best suits your business, then paying a few hundred dollars for a legal consultation can be a worthwhile investment. Let's examine some of the most common legal structures used in the United States.

### Sole Proprietorship

**Sole proprietorship:** a business owned by one person who has full exposure to its liabilities.

A **sole proprietorship** is a business owned by one person who has not formed a separate entity to run it. This is the simplest and most inexpensive form of legal structure for startups, but it is rarely the correct choice. It means the business is completely managed and controlled by you, the owner, and that you are entitled to all the profits your business makes. However, it also means you are personally exposed to all the risks and legal responsibilities or liabilities of the business. But many large organizations began as sole proprietorships; for example, eBay was a sole proprietorship owned by founder Pierre Omidyar for 3 years before he joined with other partners.[6]

The main reason sole proprietorship is the most common choice of business structures is that forming a sole proprietorship is quite simple. In many jurisdictions and industries, there is no legal filing at all to set yourself up as a business owner.[7] If your business is in an industry and/or a location where licenses or permits are necessary, you may just need to pay a nominal fee to obtain the right license or permit. For example, for a painting business you might need a home improvement contractor license; for any retail business you will likely need a sales tax permit. Because you and your business are treated as one entity, you have to file only one personal tax return outlining your income and expenses. (You do, however, have to use a separate form, Schedule C, to report your business income.)[8] The business's income is added to whatever other income you (and your spouse) may have and is taxed at your personal income tax rate after a 20% deduction is allowed.

However, as previously mentioned, you are also held personally liable for any debts the business incurs (see Figure 14.1). There can be quite a lot of pressure to running a sole proprietorship, especially when it comes to fulfilling all your financial obligations. For example, say you have borrowed money to run your business, but you lose a major customer, which leaves you unable to repay the loan. Or say an employee of yours is

**FIGURE 14.1**

## The Sole Proprietor

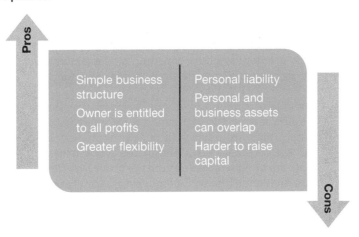

Pros

Simple business structure

Owner is entitled to all profits

Greater flexibility

Personal liability

Personal and business assets can overlap

Harder to raise capital

Cons

involved in an automobile accident while on the job and injures another driver; you, as sole proprietor, are fully responsible for dealing with the injured person's claims. Either of these scenarios could potentially mean having to sell personal assets such as your car, your investments, or even your house to raise the money. You could even be driven to personal bankruptcy. Some of the other business structures we will discuss provide at least a minimal level of protection against such personal losses.

## General Partnership

A general partnership involves two or more people who have made a decision to comanage and share in the profits and losses of a business. Like a sole proprietorship, setting up a general partnership is relatively low cost and straightforward. As each partner reports profits and losses on individual tax returns rather than corporate returns, a process called pass-through taxation, taxes are also paid at your personal income tax rates (after the previously mentioned 20% deduction).

**General partnership:** a business owned by two or more people who have made a decision to comanage and share in the profits and losses.

For example, say you and your business partner decide to open a café. To qualify for general partnership legal status, you and your partner must be involved in the business and contribute toward setting up and paying the costs of running the café. You and your partner will split the profits and losses between you.

Although partnership arrangements can be quite flexible, it is wise to have a formal agreement drafted by a legal expert to lay out the terms of the partnership. Typically, this agreement will cover the percentage of shares you are each entitled to, your individual rights and duties, and the consequences of one of you leaving the business for any reason.

Sharing the burden of running the business with someone else can be a great asset to a startup. However, like the sole proprietorship legal structure, in a general partnership each partner is still personally liable for the company's financial obligations. In a worst-case scenario, this means that if one partner is responsible for running the company into the ground, the other partner will still be liable. And if the offending partner cannot pay, the other partner would be liable for the full amount. Therefore, before entering into a general partnership it is essential that the partners know each other well and establish a high degree of trust.

## C Corporation

A C corporation (sometimes known as a "C-corp") is a separate legal entity created by the state government and owned by an unlimited number of shareholders. This means that the corporation, not the shareholders, is legally liable for its actions. The most money that shareholders can lose is their personal investment—the value of their stock.

**C corporation:** (sometimes known as a "C-corp")—a separate legal and taxable entity created by the state government and owned by an unlimited number of shareholders.

Another advantage to the C corporation is transferable ownership, which means it can issue shares of stock to investors in exchange for capital. In addition, because the corporation is a separate entity, it benefits from continuous existence, which means that it will still survive after the demise of its owners. This allows the corporation to plan for the future.

Many people believe that corporations are so complex that they are reserved for larger, more established businesses with numerous employees. In reality, however, corporations normally are not very time-consuming or expensive to set up. Many corporations are owned by only one or a few stockholders who elect themselves as directors and officers.

An alleged disadvantage is double taxation: The corporate profit is taxed twice—first on the profit it makes, and second, the shareholders are taxed on the dividends. However, in a startup, corporate profits are often paid out to the owners as additional compensation (which means that corporate tax is eliminated on nonexistent corporate profits). Otherwise these profits are often retained to fund the growth of the startup, thus eliminating any current tax on dividends (the sum of money paid to shareholders from company profits) and leaving only the corporate tax at a rate calculated without adding the income of stockholders and their spouses.

## S Corporation

**S corporation:** (sometimes known as an "S-corp")—a type of corporation that is eligible for, and elects, special taxation status.

An S corporation (sometimes known as an "S-corp") is a corporation whose stockholders elect special treatment for income tax purposes. For all other purposes, it is identical to a C corporation. In order to qualify as an S-corp, the corporation must be a U.S. domestic corporation. In addition, it must have no more than 100 shareholders, who in most cases must be individual U.S. citizens or legal immigrants (not corporations, partnerships, or trusts), and all of whom must own only one class of common stock (ordinary shares).

Unlike the C-corp, the S-corp does not have to deal with double taxation, as there is only one level of tax to pay. Similar to a partnership, the income and losses are passed through to the company's shareholders' tax returns and taxed at the individual rates, after a 20% deduction. This is especially attractive for corporations expecting to lose money in the short term, as such losses will offset other income earned by shareholders, acting as a so-called "tax shelter." S-corps often consider a later switch to C-corp status because their growth may be limited by the restricted number and types of shareholders permitted. Another reason for switching to C-corp status is the fact that an S-corp's future retained earnings would be taxed to stockholders as so-called "phantom income"— earnings are taxed but not received by the individual.

## Limited Liability Company

**Limited liability company (LLC):** a business structure that combines the taxation advantages of a partnership with the limited liability benefits of a corporation without being subject to the eligibility requirements of an S-corp.

A limited liability company (LLC) is a business structure that combines the pass-through taxation aspects of a partnership with the limited liability benefits of a corporation without being subject to the eligibility requirements of an S corporation.

This means that profits and losses are reported on individual tax returns in the same manner as other pass-through entities; therefore, double taxation does not apply, and there is potential tax sheltering from losses while personal assets are protected. Modern limited liability company statutes allow LLCs to have continuous existence, similar to corporations. And just as with partnerships and corporations, it is advisable for the LLC's owners (called "members") to enter into ownership agreements, often contained within an operating agreement that serves the combined purposes of bylaws and stockholder agreements in corporations. LLCs are rapidly replacing S corporations as the entity of choice for many startup businesses.

## Limited Partnership and Limited Liability Partnership

There are a variety of other forms of business entity that may be used in certain circumstances. One example is the limited partnership (LP), a pass-through tax entity made up of two kinds of partners: general partners who manage the business but have personal exposure for its liabilities, and limited partners who are essentially silent investors but are protected from liability.

Recently, however, the LP has been largely replaced by the LLC. It acts as a pass-through entity, grants limited liability to *all* members, and does not prohibit any member from getting involved in management.

Another example is the limited liability partnership (LLP). This is essentially a general partnership that, in exchange for registering with the state and paying an annual fee, gets a form of limited liability for its partners. However, the partners are still not protected from the consequences of wrongful acts committed by themselves and, in some cases, by their employees. Generally, this form is popular only among firms of licensed professionals, such as lawyers and accountants, who want to avoid classifying their partners as employees of the business. This means that these employers do not have to comply with employment laws and regulations (such as mandatory or enforced retirement) with regard to their partners.

The principal types of legal structures we have described are summarized in Table 14.2.

## Benefit Corporation

In Chapter 1, we mentioned a benefit corporation (or B-corp) as a form of organization certified by the nonprofit B Lab, which ensures that strict standards of social and environmental performance, accountability, and transparency are met. B Lab certification ensures that the for-profit company fulfills its social mission. It is available to businesses operating as any one of the business entities mentioned above (not just corporations).

In addition to the B Lab certification, many states have enacted statutes creating a new form of business entity also called a B or Benefit corporation that is not subject to the fiduciary obligations of other business corporations. Most business corporations must justify all their actions as contributing ultimately to increased shareholder wealth.[9]

On the contrary, a statutory B corporation declares in its charter one or more social benefit goals. This protects it and its managers from lawsuits from shareholders claiming that the company is spending more time or resources on social issues than on maximizing profit.

**TABLE 14.2**

Types of Legal Structures

| BUSINESS ENTITY | STRUCTURE | LIABILITY | TAXATION | NOTES |
|---|---|---|---|---|
| Sole Proprietorship | One owner | Unlimited | Pass-through | |
| General Partnership | Two or more partners | Unlimited Joint and Several | Pass-through | |
| C Corporation | Stockholders, directors, officers | Limited | Taxable entity | Potential double tax on dividends |
| S Corporation | Stockholders, directors, officers | Limited | Pass-through | Subject to eligibility requirements |
| Limited Liability Company (LLC) | Members, optional board of managers | Limited | Pass-through | May elect to be taxable entity |
| Limited Partnership | General partners, limited partners | General partners: Unlimited  Limited partners: Limited | Pass-through to all partners | Limited partners largely prohibited from management |
| Limited Liability Partnership (LLP) | Two or more partners | Limited with some restrictions | Pass-through | Generally used only for professional practices |
| Benefit Corporation (under corporate law) | Stockholders, directors, officers | Limited | May be either C-corp or S-corp, if eligible | Charter sets forth social purpose(s) |

A statutory B corporation is similar to a corporation as it also has shareholders and employees. However, the main difference lies in the fact that managers in a statutory B corporation are held responsible for ensuring the right balance is met between pure profit and its declared social benefit goals.

## Not-for-Profit Entities

**Not-for-profit:** a tax status granted to companies performing functions deemed by Congress to be socially desirable that exempts them from income tax and, in some cases, allows them to receive tax-deductible donations.

Not-for-profits are not technically a different form of business entity. Not-for-profit is a tax status available to corporations, LLCs, trusts, and other structures that meet specific criteria set out in the Internal Revenue Code.

All not-for-profits are exempt from income tax on their profits (so-called "surplus"), and some are also eligible to receive donations that are tax deductible to their donors. Only those companies described in Section 501(c) of the tax code are eligible; these include charitable organizations, business leagues, civic leagues, labor organizations, chambers of commerce, social clubs, fraternal organizations, cemetery companies, and the like.

Those also eligible to receive tax-deductible contributions are the smaller list of organizations in Section 501(c)(3), including religious, educational, scientific, and charitable institutions. One important condition applicable to all not-for-profits, however, is that none of the organization's earnings are permitted to benefit individuals. In other words, although not-for-profits can pay reasonable compensation to employees, they cannot have shareholders; all profit must be reinvested in the business and used for the organization's exempt purpose.

## 14.3 LEGAL MISTAKES MADE BY STARTUPS

>> **LO 14.3**   **Outline the most common legal errors made by startups.**

It is very common for entrepreneurs to make mistakes at the very beginning of their ventures.[10] Even the most successful entrepreneurs have fallen into legal traps in the early stages of setting up. As we mentioned, one of the best ways to avoid costly mistakes is by hiring the right legal counsel. Some entrepreneurs rely on friends and family who offer free advice or steep discounts. Although it is always useful to get input from people you know or through contacts, never let that be a substitute for seeking professional guidance from a lawyer experienced in startups and expert in the legal areas that are most relevant to your business.

As mentioned in the previous section, it is vital to choose the right business structure for your company. Choosing the wrong entity could incur higher taxes than necessary or expose you to significant personal liabilities. It is also important to be aware that business structures differ from state to state; setting up the wrong structure puts you at risk for financial penalties. In California and Nevada, for example, licensed professionals such as doctors, lawyers, architects, and accountants are legally permitted to form an LLP but are not allowed to operate as an LLC.

Keep in mind that experienced investors generally invest only in C corporations, so if you want to seek immediate external funding, you might be better off forming a C corporation rather than an LLC or an S-corp. However, if you don't plan to seek external financing until sometime down the road, be aware that it is normally relatively easy and inexpensive to convert to a C corporation from any of the pass-through entities.

It is essential that you enter into a formal written agreement with your cofounders early on that formalizes the terms of the business. This is necessary regardless of the form of entity you have chosen. It may be a partnership agreement in a general or limited partnership, a stockholder agreement in an S or C corporation, or an operating agreement in an LLC, but the purpose of the agreement is the same. Failing to enter into this agreement is almost certain to cause problems later on.

## The Founders' Agreement

**Founders' agreement:** a clear agreement between founders on a number of key issues that their business might face.

In addition to formal agreements, entrepreneurs may also sign a shorter, less technical contract call a founders' agreement, which is a clear agreement between founders

**TABLE 14.3**

What Goes in a Founders' Agreement?

| The Basics | • Name of cofounders<br>• Name of the business<br>• How long the agreement is valid for |
|---|---|
| The Business | • What business are you in?<br>• What products do you offer?<br>• What are your goals?<br>• What are the company's values? |
| Roles and Responsibilities | • What is each founder responsible for?<br>• What is the unique contribution of each?<br>• What is each called (his or her title)?<br>• How do decisions get made? |
| Ownership Breakdown | • How are you splitting the equity?<br>• Is there a vesting schedule? |
| Salary and Compensation | • What's the baseline for all involved?<br>• How can founders use company money?<br>• Who approves investments or debts? |
| Termination | • What happens when a cofounder underperforms?<br>• What happens when one wants to leave the business?<br>• What happens if one of the founders dies? |

**Source:** Prakash, P. (2019). Why a founders' agreement is important for every small business. *Fundera.* Retrieved from https://www.fundera.com/blog/founders-agreement

on a number of key issues that their business might face.[11] The founders' agreement usually comes before the formal written agreements and helps founders answer the tough questions before entering into legal contracts. Although the founders' agreement may not be legally binding, it provides a useful overview of how your cofounder relationships will work, how the business will be structured, and how you and your cofounders intend to tackle problems in the future. Table 14.3 summarizes the type of information that is commonly included in a founders' agreement. You can also check out https://www.pandadoc.com/founders-agreement-template/ for an example of a founders' agreement template.

It is also important to ensure you have the right vesting schedule in place to protect the other cofounders. **Vesting** is the concept of imposing equity forfeitures on cofounders over a certain period of time on a piecemeal basis should they not stay with the company. Without a formal vesting schedule in place, it is possible for a cofounder to walk away from the company at any time with a chunk of the equity, leaving the remaining cofounders working to increase the wealth of a noncontributing owner. A similar concern arises when including equity in a compensation package for an employee. Vesting is discussed in more depth later in this chapter.

In the next section, we explore the issue of intellectual property ownership, which can also cause legal complications if not handled correctly from the outset.

**Vesting:** the concept of imposing equity forfeitures on cofounders over a certain period of time on a piecemeal basis should they not stay with the company.

# 14.4 INTELLECTUAL PROPERTY (IP)

**>> LO 14.4** Define IP and how it affects entrepreneurs.

**Intellectual property (IP)** is intangible personal property created by human intelligence, such as ideas, inventions, slogans, logos, and processes. IP law includes the copyright, trademark, trade secret, and patent protections for physical and nonphysical property that is the product of original thought and that can, in some sense, be owned. IP is a valuable asset for which entrepreneurs need to create an IP strategy that supports

**Intellectual property (IP):** intangible personal property created by human intelligence, such as ideas, inventions, slogans, logos, and processes.

**Companies that depend on intellectual property**

and evolves with the business. Intellectual property rights legally protect inventions.[12] IP is the backbone of innovation all over the world because it plays a significant role in economic growth and development.

Many startups are dependent on IP protection, regardless of industry or line of business; from manufacturing to tech enterprises to restaurants, IP protection is essential to the survival of small businesses. Without it, powerful companies like Amazon, Google, eBay, or Staples would never have gotten off the ground.[13]

Entrepreneurs and small businesses are becoming increasingly dependent on protecting their IP in order to bring their products and services to market. In fact, protecting IP has become more important to entrepreneurs than ever before.[14] The late Steve Jobs realized the importance of protecting IP early on: "From the earliest days at Apple, I realized that we thrived when we created intellectual property. If people copied or stole our software, we'd be out of business."[15]

IP is one of the most valuable assets for startups when it comes to transforming ideas and innovations into real market value. It is also one of the major assets that investors look for in a startup. A 2018 article in *Forbes* magazine asserted that out of 100 questions investors ask startups, 10 of them will relate to IP.[16] If the IP is usable and owned by the startup, investors will be more comfortable in investing, and it can increase the valuation of the new venture. Protecting your IP also prevents competitors from trying to copy your products and services.

However, IP law can be complex, confusing, and entirely misunderstood. In the flurry of setting up new ventures, many entrepreneurs neglect the issue of IP protection and fail to seek advice from experts. Yet, if the IP protection isn't in place, the whole venture can collapse.

Determining IP ownership is not straightforward. For instance, say you create IP for a venture while still employed at another company, or when you have just left a job. In many employment contracts and under the law of most jurisdictions, the rights to inventions that substantially relate to the employee's old job description belong to the company.[17] This means that your IP is owned by your former employer—not you. It is fundamental in the early stage of a startup that you seek legal advice from an IP attorney and review employee contracts and applicable law to determine whether there is anything that might prevent you from obtaining IP ownership.

Furthermore, a startup may use an independent contractor or a third party to help develop an innovation or trademark. Without a formal agreement in place, that third party may have a right to a portion of any IP that results from her contribution, even though she may have been paid to create it. Table 14.4 outlines some more resources for IP information.

Finally, be aware of the relationship between IP and hackathons—events where software and hardware developers intensively collaborate to generate new ideas and inventions. A number of popular innovations, such as the ideas for Twitter and GroupMe, arose from hackathons.

When organizations hold internal hackathons whose participants are their own employees, they automatically own the IP of whatever creative innovations arise. However, taking part in an external hackathon is not so clear-cut, especially if you are already an employee at a tech organization. Developing a proof-of-concept prototype product at a hackathon and then disclosing it could destroy any chance of patenting it in the future. Even worse, with so many people involved, it is not clear who can claim IP ownership of the innovation.[18] Similar issues can arise in the context of group projects in college classwork. In summary, it behooves you as an entrepreneur to educate yourself about IP and to seek legal guidance whenever appropriate.

**TABLE 14.4**

Resources for IP Information

| U.S. Patent and Trademark Office | The site offers a wealth of information about patents, trademarks, and IP law and policy. https://www.uspto.gov/ |
|---|---|
| U.S. Copyright Office | The authoritative source for information about copyright. https://www.copyright.gov/ |
| World Intellectual Property Organization (WIPO) | An all-encompassing site to help navigate the world of copyright, patent, trademarks, and industrial designs. https://www.wipo.int/about-ip/en/ |
| Managing Intellectual Property | A source of the latest news and updates on IP-related issues around the globe. https://www.managingip.com |
| LegalTemplates | Download free nondisclosure agreement template. https://legaltemplates.net |
| Pat2PDF | A web-based tool that finds patents and downloads them as PDFs. https://www.pat2pdf.org/ |
| Inventors Digest | An online hub loaded with inventor and IP developer news, as well as IP trends and tips. Referred to as the magazine for "idea people." https://www.inventorsdigest.com/ |
| PatentWizard | Designed by a patent attorney, the site helps you take the critical first steps toward filing an early provisional patent. https://www.neustel software.com/patentwizard/ |

## The Four Types of Intellectual Property

IP is an essential asset to a company as it provides opportunities for others to invest or collaborate and allows the founders to license, exchange, or even franchise their IP. In order to protect their IP, entrepreneurs need to be very knowledgeable about the different types during the early days of their business. There are four types of IP that fall under the protection of U.S. law: copyright, trademark, trade secrets, and patent.[19]

Many types of innovations have arisen from hackathons

epa european pressphoto agency b.v. / Alamy Stock Photo

### Copyright

**Copyright** is a form of protection provided to the creators of original works in the areas of literature, music, drama, choreography, art, motion pictures, sound recordings, and architecture. It is important for tech entrepreneurs to be aware that computer code is classified as a literary work for purposes of copyright protection.[20] Another crucial thing to remember is that copyright does not protect ideas; it protects the tangible expression of the idea, such as written materials or recordings. Generally, U.S. copyright lasts for the duration of the author's life plus 70 years.

Copyright infringement cases can prove costly. For example, in 2018, music publisher Wixen brought a $1.6 billion lawsuit against Swedish music streaming platform Spotify for copyright infringement. Wixen alleged that Spotify had used thousands of songs from its artists without a proper license.[21] In the end, the parties agreed to settle the case for an undisclosed amount.

**Copyright:** a form of protection provided to the creators of original works in the areas of literature, music, drama, choreography, art, motion pictures, sound recordings, and architecture.

Some limited uses of copyrighted material are allowed without the permission of the copyright owner; this is called "fair use." Generally, it must be shown that the work is of a type meant to be copied, the use is for a noncommercial purpose, it constitutes only a small portion of the work, and/or it won't have a negative effect on the market for the work. Fair use is a "gray area" in U.S. law; there are no absolute rules or boundaries around what is and is not fair use.

## Trademark and Service Mark

**Trademark:** any word, name, symbol, or device used in business to identify and promote a product. Its counterpart for service industries is the service mark.

Any word, name, symbol, or device used in business to identify and promote a product is a **trademark**; its counterpart for service industries is the service mark. Although the law affords some limited protection to trademarks without registration, a federally registered trademark generally lasts 10 years and, if still in use, can be renewed every 10 years thereafter. Trademarks and service marks are the legal basis of most branding campaigns.

Under Armour, the third-largest sports apparel company in the United States, has sued apparel company Armor & Glory, fishing apparel firm Salt Armour, shock-absorbing shorts retailer Ass Armor, and sports drink company Bodyarmor Superdrink for trademark infringement due to the use of "armour" or "armor" in their company names. In the case of Armor & Glory, the lawsuit stated, "Armor & Glory's name is likely to cause confusion, mistake and deception as to the two companies' connection, which would dilute the distinctiveness and further damage and irreparably injure Under Armour's brand." Armor & Glory has since changed its name to AG365.[22]

## Trade Secret

**Trade secret:** confidential information that provides companies with a competitive edge and is not in the public domain, such as formulas, patterns, compilations, programs, devices, methods, techniques, or processes.

A **trade secret** is any confidential information that provides companies with a competitive edge and is not publicly known or accessible, such as formulas, patterns, customer lists, compilations, programs, devices, methods, techniques, or processes. Trade secrets last for as long as they remain secret; they are protected from theft under federal and state law. Companies can protect their trade secrets by having their employees and contractors sign nondisclosure, work-for-hire, and noncompete agreements or clauses. Famous examples of trade secrets allegedly include the recipe for Coca-Cola's beverages, KFC's ingredients, and the formula for WD-40.[23]

## Patent

**Patent:** a grant of exclusive property rights on inventions through the U.S. and other governments.

A **patent** is a grant of property rights on inventions through the U.S. government. It excludes others from making, using, selling, or importing the invention without the patent owner's consent. In order to be granted a patent, the product or process must present a new or novel way of doing something, be nonobvious, or provide some sort of solution to a problem.

In the United States, the invention must not have been made public in any way before 1 year prior to the filing application date (the 1-year grace period does not exist in most other countries). Laws of nature, physical phenomena, mathematical equations, scientific theories, the human body or human genes, and abstract ideas cannot be patented. However, it is possible for a mobile app to be patented if it meets the criteria of the USPTO.

The duration of a patent is generally 20 years from the filing date of application, and it can be costly to file a patent. The Dog Umbrella and Leash (Patent No. 6,871,616) is an example of a novel and arguably useful invention, which is designed to keep a dog dry on a wet day.[24] It may not be a scientific breakthrough, but it qualifies for patenting.

It is important to note that although copyright protects artistic expression and trademark protects brand, there is no way to protect or patent an idea. Of course, the whole innovation must begin with an idea, but an idea must be turned into an invention before it can qualify for patenting.[25] This does not necessarily mean creating a prototype, but you must be able to meaningfully describe the invention, how it is made, and how others could use it. For example, the dog umbrella would have started out as an idea, but the inventors would have needed to flesh out the concept and create a sketch of it in order to explain its intended use.

# Patent Search

What is the coolest product that you own or would like to own? This can be anything from the stylus you may use on a tablet computer to a Frisbee you would play with in a park.

Your Mindshift task is to find the patent for this item. Use the "quick search" function on the United States Patent and Trademark Office website (http://patft.uspto.gov/). While you are searching, pay attention to the sections and content you see in patents: the abstract, the description, the patent's claim, and so on.

Once you have a good idea of what a patent looks like, try to find a patent that pertains to one of your own ideas.

## Critical Thinking Questions

1. How easy or difficult was it to think of a cool product for your patent search? What factors came into play?

2. Did you find many other patents for products related to the one you were searching for?

3. What did you learn that surprised you or contradicted your expectations? ●

In summary, IP rights are the basis for every single business; without them, entrepreneurs would be less likely to risk bringing new innovations to the marketplace; investors would not invest; and customers would end up with less choice. Fewer businesses means more unemployment and less economic growth.[26] The importance of IP protection cannot be overestimated—this is why it can be so devastating to businesses of any size when IP is compromised.

## Nondisclosure Agreement

One way for a startup to protect its IP is through a nondisclosure agreement (NDA) or confidentiality agreement, which is a legal contract that outlines confidential information shared by two or more parties.[27] This means that neither party has the right to share this information with competitors, the general public, or anyone else outside those involved in the agreement.

Adam Bornstein, founder of marketing and branding agency Pen Name Consulting, learned about the importance of a comprehensive NDA during the early stages of his business. Rather than spending the money on a lawyer to create a detailed NDA, Bornstein used a basic file he found online—which, as he was to find out, didn't cover the right information about his company, nor did it prevent people from sharing it. Bornstein said, "I discovered my error after a business meeting, where I mentioned a potential client and what they needed help with.[28] The person I was meeting with (who signed my weak NDA) then went after that client themselves—ultimately stealing work from me. There was nothing I could legally do. It probably cost me $30,000 in potential revenue."

Bornstein advises that all entrepreneurs should invest in a strong NDA for their business. As he found out, the cost associated with paying for an NDA that protects your company and ideas far outweighs the price of someone else poaching business from you.

As an entrepreneur, you will come across several situations where you will be required to share confidential information with another person or company. When should you ask them to sign an NDA? Usually, when you have something of value to share about your business and you want to make sure the other party does not steal it. Table 14.5 outlines some guidelines for when an NDA is required.

However, NDAs should not be used when you just have a half-baked idea with no resources. If you place an NDA in front of someone, especially an early investor, she may not sign it. As seasoned entrepreneur Gary Bizzo notes,

Investors are shrewd people, and many I work with won't sign an NDA for any reason.[31] One told me that by signing an NDA with one entrepreneur, it could

**Nondisclosure agreement (NDA):** a legal contract that outlines confidential information shared by two or more parties.

force him to abandon or severely limit him from accepting a really good idea down the road from another source. A couple of investors have actually told me they were already involved in ventures similar to the one presented to them and were surprised the entrepreneur had not done their due diligence.

Although you may not need an NDA in the very early stages of your business when you haven't really cemented your idea yet, when the right time comes, NDAs are essential to entrepreneurs, especially to protect against the growing threat of IP theft.

**TABLE 14.5**

Guidelines for When to Use an NDA

| 1. When talking to your competitors | In some situations, you will likely find yourself in conversation with your competitors. Without an NDA in place, they could copy your business and you could copy theirs. Signing a mutual nondisclosure agreement is the best way protect both parties. |
| --- | --- |
| 2. When disclosing patent information | If you have invented something and patented the information, never disclose the patent information to outsiders until after the NDA has been signed by all parties involved. |
| 3. When discussing trade secrets | Always use an NDA to protect your trade secrets, and even then, make sure that you only disclose them on a need-to-know basis with people you trust the most.[29] |
| 4. When taking on a partner or an investor | When you're considering taking on a new partner or investor, make sure the information you share, such as business financials, personal information, and so on, is protected by an NDA. Bear in mind, however, that most investors will refuse to sign NDAs for startups in the very early stages. |
| 5. When discussing the sale or licensing of a product or technology | When in discussions about licensing or selling your product, you need to make sure that the potential buyer does not disclose the details of your product or, indeed, any information about your company to a competitor. A signed NDA will protect all sensitive company information. |
| 6. When employees have access to confidential and proprietary information | Without a strong NDA in place, there is nothing to stop your employees from accessing valuable information (client lists, supplier agreements) and using these data to set up a competing business after they have left your company. Make sure that every employee signs an NDA at the time of hire. |
| 7. When sharing business information with a prospective buyer | If you are considering selling your business, then you will need to disclose every single detail of your financial and operations information to that acquiring company. An NDA will ensure all your information stays protected.[30] |

## 14.5 GLOBAL IP THEFT

>> **LO 14.5**   **Assess the global impact of IP theft.**

Any business that has a trademark, trade secret, patent, or copyright is dependent on IP protections. Consider this scenario: You have just launched your T-shirt business with a trademarked brand, and sales are really taking off. A few months later, you come across another website set up in a different country that is selling counterfeit versions of your T-shirts for a fraction of the price. You start losing sales, your brand becomes tainted, investors think twice about investing in your company, and your reputation becomes damaged—and all because someone has stolen your unique trademark and copied it for financial gain.

Millions of people all over the world violate IP laws every day. Recent statistics show that global online piracy is rife in the area of digital content such as movies, music, software, games, and e-books. More than half of global Internet users aged 16 to 24 have streamed music illegally, with the number highest in Spain and Brazil.[32] Ignoring copyright by downloading your favorite song from a peer-to-peer website without paying for it is similar to going into a music store and stealing a CD, yet people who would otherwise characterize themselves as law-abiding do it all the time. IP theft costs the United States between $225 and $600 billion every year, and it has a huge negative impact on legitimate businesses.[33]

Why does IP protection sometimes fail? IP rights are territorial, which means that although your rights may be protected in the United States, they are not necessarily protected in other countries. Countries such as the United States impose strict IP laws, but countries like China and India have a rich history of IP rights violations. However, according to the U.S. Chamber of Commerce's 2018 International IP Index, out of the 50 countries assessed for their commitment toward protecting IP, China ranks 25th—a marked improvement from where it ranked just a few years ago.[34]

## RESEARCH AT WORK

# Patent Trolls

U.S. patents have encouraged innovation, but they have also become subject to patent trolls—individuals or firms who own patents but have never actually produced useful products of their own.[35] Patent trolls issue legal complaints against alleged patent infringers in an effort to extract a licensing fee for the life of the patent. AT&T, Google, Verizon, Apple, and BlackBerry are only a few of the thousands of companies being sued every year by patent trolls. Yet, the biggest impact of patent trolls is on small startups. One survey of software startups reported that because of this issue, 41% were forced to either exit the business or change strategy.

According to a study by Santa Clara University professor Collen Chien, 50% of these patent trolls target companies that make an annual revenue of less than $10 million. They do this because they know that startups have limited resources and are more than likely to settle out of court, rather than risk a lengthy, costly suit.

Needless to say, the endless patent litigation has led to significant damage to innovation. Research findings have shown that it reduces VC investment in startups; it also decreases research and development, as the more research firms carry out, the more likely they are to be sued for patent infringement. Although the impact of patent trolls on startups may not look good, positive change is happening. The Patent Trial and Appeal Board, set up as a result of the America Invents Act of 2011, has rejected a number of bad patent claims. The process has been gradual, but it is certainly a step in the right direction.

"It probably hasn't made patent trolls go away, but it's changed their demands," noted Mark Lemley, a law professor at Stanford University. "Now they sue and ask for $50,000 rather than sue and ask for $1 million."

Even for startups with limited resources, there are protections against patent trolls. First, it is necessary to leverage a network. A good example of this is the LOT Network (www.lotnet.com), which is free for any company that makes less than $25 million per year. The mission of the LOT Network is to fight patent trolls. Companies that join LOT pledge that if they sell a patent to a company that's in the business of patent trolling, all LOT members will automatically get a free license to that patent. This ensures that patent licenses cannot solely fall into the hands of the patent troll. The LOT Network is growing in popularity, as evidenced by its membership of more than 300 companies, including Amazon, Slack, Canon, and Tesla.

### Critical Thinking Questions

1. How would you protect your startup against patent trolls?

2. Do you think individuals or firms have the right to hold patents without producing any useful products of their own? Why or why not?

3. What are the effects of patent trolls on startups? ●

**Sources:**

Borenstein, N. (2018, April 10). More patent trolls are targeting startups. Here's what you can do. *Entrepreneur.* Retrieved from https://www.entrepreneur.com/article/310648

Chien, C. (2012, September 13). Startups and patent trolls. *Santa Clara Law Digital Commons.* Retrieved from https://digitalcommons.law.scu.edu/cgi/viewcontent.cgi?article=1554&context=facpubs

AP Photo/Nati Harnik

**Thousands of counterfeit Rolex watches seized during an investigation in Philadelphia, PA**

Nevertheless, there is still a strong market for counterfeit goods in the United States. In 2017, U.S. Customs and Border Protection officials seized almost 35,000 shipments containing counterfeit goods. Nike, Rolex, and Louis Vuitton are among the most counterfeited items.[36]

Major corporations can afford to wage massive legal battles and get compensation for IP theft, but how can a startup or a small business protect its IP in different territories? Entrepreneurs who are seeking to sell their innovations abroad must first conduct a search to ensure their company's name and brand can be used in the foreign country. Then, they must register for local IP ownership in that country or extend U.S. registrations to foreign countries at the beginning of the process. Also, it would be wise to seek proper IP counsel to protect IP rights abroad.

Finally, don't depend wholly on your patent for your business strategy. Building customer relationships, promoting your trademarked brand, providing quality products and services, and implementing rapid innovation will also help you defend your business against the effects of IP theft.

## 14.6 COMMON IP TRAPS

>> **LO 14.6**   **Describe the common IP traps experienced by entrepreneurs.**

IP can be a minefield, and many inventors fall into common traps that hamper the potential of exciting innovations.[37] Patenting can cost thousands of dollars, and some inventors find that they earn less than the cost of registering the patent. In a classic example, Robert Kearns, the inventor of the intermittent windshield wiper, sued car manufacturers Chrysler and Ford for copying the technology he had patented. Following a court battle that spanned decades, Kearns was finally granted a total of $40 million in compensation, which may sound like a lot, but it is nothing in comparison to what Kearns would have made if he had been credited with his invention from the beginning. Let's explore the common IP pitfalls and how entrepreneurs can avoid them.

### Publicly Disclosing Your Innovation

You might be bursting to tell the world about your discoveries, but don't. Disclosing your new product or service in public before you have filed a patent application means that in most countries you will not be permitted to patent it at all. (We've mentioned

MINDSHIFT

## Patent Battle

A patent battle started between Apple and Samsung in 2011. After many years of countless court appearances, settlements, and appeals, the battle finally ended in 2018. At issue was the claim from Apple that Samsung copied the iPhone and infringed on many of Apple's patents.

For this Mindshift, play the role of a law student, dig into the Apple and Samsung dispute, and apply your learning from this chapter to answer the Critical Thinking Questions.

### Critical Thinking Questions

1.  What are the central IP issues associated with this case?

2.  What, specifically, did Apple claim that Samsung copied?

3.  What was Samsung's response?

4.  How was the dispute finally resolved in 2018? ●

the 1-year grace period in the United States.) For example, a professor at Imperial College London, Robert Perneczky, discovered a protein that had the potential to significantly improve the chances of spotting the onset of Alzheimer's disease. However, Perneczky failed to qualify for a patent because of a detailed article he had written about his discovery that had been published in an academic journal. Because Perneczky's idea had been disclosed to the public, he was prevented from patenting it.

It is impractical to avoid disclosing anything at all about your discoveries, but try to refrain from revealing every single step. One way of protecting your IP that works in the United States is to file a provisional patent application before you make your idea public. This secures your rights as the inventor and gives you 12 months to complete the research and develop your idea into a working prototype. However, you will have to file a full patent application as soon as the 12 months are up; otherwise, the knowledge it holds will become publicly available. Also, your invention cannot have changed substantially from the date of the initial filing. Bear in mind that the United States has changed from being a "first to invent" to a "first to file" country, which means that if an inventor waits too long to file a patent application, he or she may lose out to someone else who is working on a similar innovation.

The intermittent windshield wiper, invented by Robert Kearns, who sued Chrysler and Ford for copying the idea

## Failure to Protect Product and Processes

As Robert Kearns learned, it is easy for innovations to be copied by others. This is why it is important for entrepreneurs to ensure their products and processes are fully protected. Some inventors and other scientists protect their products by building unique markers into them; for example, a unique chemical "thumbprint" can reveal through a simple test whether someone else has copied their product. Another option some entrepreneurs use is to license their innovation to a larger organization that has all the tools already in place to protect and commercialize the invention. The inventor then profits through a stream of royalties.

## Inability to Determine Originality

Entrepreneurs often build on existing products, tools, and techniques to create their innovations. However, the outcome must be considered both novel and useful if it is to qualify for IP protection. This means ensuring that products and services contain enough features to significantly improve the way they are used by others, with the intention of solving a problem. For example, when Jeffrey Percival and his research team developed the Star Tracker 5000—a low-cost device that determines a space rocket's altitude and tracks stars—the concern was it was not original enough, as it was mostly formed of standard components. To make his product more original, Percival added an algorithm that rapidly transmits digitized images. By enhancing the features of the product, Percival was able to license it to NASA for its space missions.

## Failure to Assign Ownership

In the early stages of a startup, a number of people may be formally involved in contributing to the innovation process. This is why it is best to make formal agreements regarding IP ownership prior to any further development, in order to decide who owns and controls the innovation and who doesn't. Ownership can even vest in people you haven't paid, people you have paid but who haven't signed a formal assignment of ownership, or people who have otherwise made a valuable contribution to the innovation.

For example, InBae Yoon invented a medical device called the trocar, used to withdraw fluid from a body cavity, which he subsequently licensed to a larger organization.

However, Yoon had originally collaborated with electronics technician Young Jae Choi to create the product. Yoon failed to pay Choi for his work or obtain an assignment of his rights. Some years later, a competitor discovered the technician's involvement, amended the patent to assign him partial ownership, and won a court case to secure a separate licensing agreement with Choi to allow them to use the product. The same kinds of problems can arise with people who may have coauthored copyrighted material or helped to design a logo for a company's trademark.

### Failure to Protect IP in Global Markets

As we mentioned earlier, IP rights are territorial, which means that although your rights may be protected in the United States, they are not necessarily protected in other countries. For example, in China, Apple Inc. lost a court battle with Chinese technology firm Proview International Holdings, which claimed it owned the iPad trademark in the Chinese market.[38] The case seriously threatened Apple's ability to sell the iPad in China. Apple finally agreed to pay $60 million in 2012 to settle the 2-year dispute.

Entrepreneurs hoping to sell in other territories need to get the right legal advice and carry out due diligence before even starting their business, in order to understand how to navigate any obstacles up front. Otherwise, they risk running into some major difficulties along the way.

## 14.7 HIRING EMPLOYEES

>> **LO 14.7** **Explain the legal requirements of hiring employees.**

There may come a time when you need to hire some help when your business takes off. Yet there's more to the hiring process than interviewing and selecting the best person for the job. As an employer, you need to understand federal and state labor laws in order to protect both your business and your employees. In this section, we describe some of the regulatory steps you need to consider when hiring your first employee.[39]

### Equal Employment Opportunity

Employers in the United States need to be aware that federal laws prohibit discriminating against employees on the basis of race, sex, creed, religion, color, national origin, or age. Workers with disabilities are also protected, though employers can refuse to hire on the basis of a disability if it prevents the worker from fulfilling job tasks. Some states forbid discrimination on the basis of sexual orientation.

Globally, the rules are not the same. For example, the global rights index provided by the International Trade Union Confederation (ITUC) shows that Austria, Finland, the Netherlands, Norway, and Uruguay score the highest for equality at work; however, the level of inequality in other countries is rising. The report showed that China, Belarus, Egypt, Colombia, and Saudi Arabia are among the worst in the world for equal opportunities and workers' rights.[40]

### Employer Identification Number

Before you hire your first employee, make sure you get an employer identification number (EIN). You will need to use this on documents and tax returns for the IRS. It is also necessary when reporting employee information to state agencies. There is also a regulatory requirement to register your newly hired employee with your state directory within 20 days of the hire date. You can apply for the EIN online.

### Unemployment and Workers' Compensation

Register with your state's labor department to pay state unemployment compensation taxes, which provide temporary relief to employees who lose their jobs. Depending on the size of your business, most states will require you to register for workers' compensation insurance to protect against any work-related injuries. (Some states make exceptions for very small businesses.)

## The Danger of Going on *Shark Tank*

Since 2009, a whole host of budding entrepreneurs have pitched to the business moguls on *Shark Tank* in the hope of receiving investment. Many of the contestants benefit from the exposure they receive from showcasing their ideas on such a popular show, but others have not fared so well. For instance, just 6 months after Nicki Radzley, cofounder of Doddle & Co., appeared on *Shark Tank* to introduce her colorful Pop pacifiers (the pacifiers pop closed when they hit the ground), she noticed several imitation products online. Radzley managed to persuade Amazon to take down some of the products, but she has not sought legal action against the imitators, as it would be a costly process for a new startup with only one full-time employee. Another *Shark Tank* contestant, Lani Lazzari, founder of skin-care line Simple Sugars, also discovered that someone online was mimicking her brand and even thanking customers for watching the show. Finally, entrepreneur Lori Cheek, who created online dating social network Cheek'd Inc., was accused of stealing the idea by a man who claimed that he had passed on information to his social worker, who had then told Cheek. During the lawsuit, Lori Cheek said that she had never met the man or his social worker before.[41]

It may not be illegal to steal an idea off a TV show, but is it ethical? One point of view is that the entrepreneurs have waived their rights to confidentiality by showcasing their ideas on a show that attracts millions of viewers. But is it fair that everyone who appears in public with a new idea is at risk of their idea being copied or stolen?

Many contestants have had many positive experiences on *Shark Tank*, but there is clearly a downside to being in the public eye. As Simple Sugars entrepreneur Lazzari said, "*Shark Tank* has been such a positive thing for us . . . but any time you get that much visibility for something, people see it and there are negative things that happen."

### Critical Thinking Questions

1. Do you think it is ethical to steal or copy an idea from a TV show like *Shark Tank*? Why or why not?

2. How would you feel if you shared an idea on *Shark Tank* and someone else exploited that idea?

3. Do you think there should be laws to prevent people from stealing or copying ideas from TV shows? Why or why not? ●

## Withholding Taxes

To comply with IRS regulations, you will need to withhold part of your employees' income and keep records of employment taxes for at least the most recent 4 years. You will need to report these wages and taxes every year. There may also be a requirement to withhold state income taxes, depending on the state in which your employees are located.

## Employee Forms

Make sure you set up personnel files containing important documents for each employee that you hire. Each employee must fill out a W-4 form that lets you, as the employer, know how much money to withhold from their paychecks for federal tax purposes. You can ask employees to fill out this form every year if they wish to change the withholding amount. This form does not have to be filed with the IRS. The Form 1-9 is another form you need to complete within 3 days of hiring your new employee; this requires employers to verify the new employee's eligibility to work in the United States. In addition, you must file IRS Form 940 every year to report federal unemployment tax, which provides payment of unemployment compensation to employees who have lost their jobs.

## Benefits

As an employer, you will need to decide what sorts of benefits you will provide your employees. The law requires you to pay and withhold Social Security taxes and an additional rate for Medicare and to pay for unemployment insurance. Businesses with more than 50 employees must also provide family and medical leave and health insurance. In a few states, employers must provide a certain number of paid sick days. You are not required by law to provide life insurance, retirement plans, or paid vacation leave, but by offering a competitive benefits package, you will have a better chance of attracting high-caliber employees. If you choose to provide these optional benefits, be aware that they are subject to many regulations; consultation with an accountant experienced in such benefits is a worthwhile investment.

## Safety Measures

All employers have a responsibility to their employees to maintain a safe and healthy workplace environment. This means training employees to do their jobs safely, ensuring the workplace is free from hazards, maintaining safety records, and reporting any serious accidents at work to government administrators. You should also have provisions in place such as medical treatment and rehabilitation services to support employees who are injured on the job.

The key to complying with legal requirements is being organized. Maintaining payroll records, filing tax returns on time, keeping your employees informed, and ensuring you are up to speed with federal reporting requirements go a long way toward running an efficient business. Table 14.6 outlines 10 steps to setting up a payroll.

## Hiring a Contractor or an Employee?

When hiring people, it is important to distinguish between contractors and employees.[42] Many startups and small businesses use independent contractors because of the advantages they bring. For example, it generally saves money to hire contractors because they don't require contributions toward health care, compensation insurance, or any other benefits. In addition, there can be cost-saving benefits when it comes to office space and equipment, as contractors will usually provide their own.

Furthermore, working with independent contractors gives employers greater flexibility in hiring and letting go of workers. For example, you could hire contractors for a specific project, and then let them go when the job is finished. Equally, if you do not like their work, you never have to see them again. There can also be valuable cost savings in hiring contractors who are experts in their field and are ready to hit the ground running, which means saving time and money on training.

| TABLE 14.6 | |
|---|---|

Ten Steps to Setting up a Payroll

| 1. | Get an Employer Identification Number (EIN) |
|---|---|
| 2. | Find out whether you need state or local tax IDs |
| 3. | Decide if you want an independent contractor or an employee |
| 4. | Ensure new employees return a completed W-4 form |
| 5. | Schedule pay periods to coordinate tax withholding for IRS |
| 6. | Create a compensation plan for holiday, vacation, and leave |
| 7. | Choose an in-house or external service for administering payroll |
| 8. | Decide who will manage your payroll system |
| 9. | Know which records must stay on file and for how long |
| 10. | Report payroll taxes as needed on a quarterly and annual basis |

**Source:** U.S. Small Business Administration. (n.d.). *Hire and manage employees.* Retrieved from https://www.sba.gov/business-guide/manage-your-business/hire-manage-employees

Independent contractors are not protected by the same laws as employees, which means there is less chance of dealing with the same legal claims that could be brought by employees. However, there are some disadvantages to hiring independent contractors. Because contractors have autonomy in what, when, and how they perform their job duties, you may feel you have less control over them. Also, independent contractors may be present for only a short period of time before leaving again, which might be disruptive to the other employees.

Finally, it is important to be aware that the classification of workers as independent contractors or employees is not your choice. The classification is dictated by the facts of the relationship. State and federal agencies are very strict on workers who are classified as contractors versus employees, and you may risk facing government audits as a result.

Misclassifying independent contractors and employees could have costly legal consequences. For example, if the individual you thought you were hiring as an independent contractor actually meets the legal definition of an employee, you may need to pay back wages, taxes, benefits, and anything else an employee would receive in your company—health insurance, retirement, and so on. Table 14.7 outlines some of the main differences between employees and contractors.

Whether the person you hire is a contractor or an employee depends on all of the factors listed above, but the most significant factor is the amount of control the employer has over the work being carried out.[43] For example, if you expect the person to show up at the same time every day and work a set period of hours, and you expect to closely oversee her duties, then you will have hired an employee rather than retained a contractor.

## Compensating Employees

It is often the case that a startup's need for additional employees outstrips the company's ability to pay in cash. When faced with this resource constraint, entrepreneurs often come up with alternative ways to compensate employees, such as giving them flexible hours, additional days off, and small perks such as gift cards or a lunch paid for by the company.

### TABLE 14.7

Differences Between Employees and Contractors

| EMPLOYEE | CONTRACTOR |
| --- | --- |
| Duties are dictated or controlled by others | Decides what, when, and how duties are performed |
| Works solely for employer | Provides services to other clients |
| Uses tools or materials provided by employer | Supplies own tools or materials |
| Working hours set by employer | Sets own working hours |
| Tax, benefits, and pension paid by employer | Pays own tax, benefits, and pension |
| Expenses paid for by employer | Pays own expenses |
| Tasks must be performed by the employee | Can subcontract work to others |
| Employer provides annual and personal leave | Not provided with annual and personal leave |
| Paid regularly (weekly, monthly, etc.) as per employee contract | Provides an invoice when work is performed and the task is completed |
| Provided with training | Does not receive training |

**Source:** "Hire a Contractor or an Employee." US Small Business Association https://www.sba.gov/content/hire-contractor-or-employee retrieved on August 2, 2015.

## Compensation in the Form of Equity

Entrepreneurs often attempt to obtain services from employees and contractors in exchange for a share of the business. This raises two legal issues.

First, in the context of issuing shares to friends and family, issuance of shares to employees and contractors risks noncompliance with securities laws. Although the workers are not investing cash in the business, their time and labor is considered an investment under the law, triggering the protection of securities regulation. Therefore, just as much care must be paid to having the right processes in place when issuing shares to employees and contractors as when issuing shares to traditional investors.

Second, it is important to note that income tax is triggered any time an individual receives any form of property in exchange for performing services, not just when he or she is paid in cash. Therefore, the receipt of shares as compensation for work can result in an unexpected tax bill. This may not seem much of a problem in the early days of a startup when the shares may not be worth very much, but it could become an issue later on.

However, if the shares are subject to a vesting schedule, the problem becomes magnified as the tax may not apply until the shares have vested (when, it is hoped, they will have greatly increased in value). This same problem exists when founders' stock is made subject to a vesting schedule, since by doing so, you are tying the retention of stock to the performance of services. There are tax techniques available to mitigate, and in some cases eliminate, this unwelcome tax issue, so be sure to consult competent tax professionals before agreeing to pay compensation in the form of equity.

## Unpaid Internships

The thought of receiving the services of enthusiastic young interns looking for work experience rather than financial compensation can be very attractive to the resource-constrained startup. However, bear in mind that such arrangements may be illegal. The Fair Labor Standards Act provides a minimum wage, overtime pay, and other protections to most workers. Putting an intern to work in your business might require compliance with these requirements. In 2018, the U.S. Department of Labor addressed the issue of unpaid interns and adopted a "primary beneficiary" test, allowing this practice if the benefits of the internship flow primarily to the intern and not to the employer. The Department of Labor has published a list of seven factors it will consider in determining the "primary beneficiary," including whether the internship is tied to the intern's formal education program and the extent to which the intern's work complements, rather than displaces, the work of paid employees.[44] ●

---

**⑤SAGE edge™**

Get the tools you need to sharpen your study skills. SAGE edge offers a robust online environment featuring an impressive array of free tools and resources.

- Access practice quizzes, eFlashcards, video, and multimedia at
  **edge.sagepub.com/neckentrepreneurship2e**

---

## SUMMARY

**14.1  Discuss how legal considerations can add value to entrepreneurial ventures.**

Understanding the legal considerations applicable to the business is as important as understanding user needs. Taking legal considerations into account may add value to the firm. Whether it is a lawyer, free website content, or some form of legal expert, obtaining competent legal advice will certainly help improve the performance of the venture.

**14.2  Explain the most common types of legal structures available to startups.**

The most common types of legal structures are sole proprietorship, general partnership, C corporation, S corporation, limited liability company (LLC), limited partnership, limited liability partnership (LLP), and benefit corporation. In addition, most of these business structures can be run as a not-for-profit provided the company complies with IRS section 501(c).

**14.3  Outline the most common legal errors made by startups.**

Startups may make some common mistakes that could be expensive. The most common mistakes they make are in choosing the legal structure of the venture, not having a written agreement defining the many parameters of their relationship, and not paying close enough attention to drafting the right vesting schedules. To protect their business ideas, entrepreneurs can also sign a founders' agreement, which is a clear agreement between founders on a number of key issues that their business might face.

**14.4  Define IP and how it affects entrepreneurs.**

IP is intangible personal property created by human intelligence, as a result of creativity such as inventions, trade secrets, slogans, logos, and processes. The four main types of IP are copyright, trademark/service mark, trade secret, and patent. It behooves entrepreneurs to understand IP because startups are, by definition, innovative and likely to involve the creation of IP. One way for a startup to protect its IP is through a nondisclosure agreement (NDA) or confidentiality agreement, which is a legal contract that outlines confidential information shared by two or more parties.

**14.5  Assess the global impact of IP theft.**

Millions of people all over the world violate IP laws every day by ignoring copyright. IP theft costs the United States between $250 and $600 billion every year.

**14.6  Describe the common IP traps experienced by entrepreneurs.**

Entrepreneurs often make mistakes in the following areas:

- Public disclosure of an invention or innovation;
- Failure to protect products, processes, brands, and so on;
- Inability to determine originality;
- Failure to allocate ownership; and
- Failure to protect IP in global markets.

**14.7  Explain the legal requirements of hiring employees.**

Legal requirements related to hiring employees include registering employees with the state labor department, keeping records of employee tax history, preparing the appropriate legal documentation, and complying with safety regulations.

CASE STUDY

## Matthew Vega-Sanz, cofounder, Lula

When he came to Babson College in early 2016, Matthew Vega-Sanz did not want to start his own company; he wanted to go to Wall Street instead. He started a student consulting firm with his brother and two of his best friends. It was a branch of one of the biggest student consultancy organizations in the world, 180 Degrees Consulting. Through this consulting experience, Matthew got the chance to work with tech companies and started to think to himself, "Wow! Startups are cool." Two years later, Matthew found himself dropping out of Babson because his own startup, Lula, was growing and he couldn't do college and entrepreneurship at the same time. The business was getting too big.

During a crisp spring evening in 2016, Matthew and his brother were craving pizza. "We didn't want Domino's; we were sick of it already and none of the Papa John's around would deliver. I tried calling them and bribing them but none of them would deliver to Babson," Matthew laughed. When he realized that Uber would charge him $30 to deliver an $8 pizza, he decided to stick with Domino's. While waiting for his pizza to be delivered, Matthew walked outside and saw the parking lot filled to capacity and thought, "Wouldn't it be cool if I could take one of these cars and go pick up the food?" The idea of Lula was born.

Lula is a first of its kind peer-to-peer car sharing platform where college students can rent out cars from their peers and others registered on the platform. While companies like Turo focus on drivers above the age of 25, Lula targets college students. When the brothers look back, the story of its origins is quite entertaining.

After the infamous pizza spark, Matthew mentioned the idea to friends, who liked it but didn't inspire him to take action. A few months later, Matthew's brother, Michael, was hanging out in his dorm and told Matthew about Babson's BETA Challenge. BETA stands for Babson Entrepreneurial Thought and Action. It is an action-based challenge in which new ideas are judged on actions taken and milestones achieved between the semi-final stage and final stage of the competition.[45] Even though the application deadline had passed, the link was still live and the brothers decided to apply. Matthew recalls, "I go to Michael's room and we draft up probably the world's worst executive summary and submitted it. I had forgotten about it and was already planning to do an internship in a company like J. P. Morgan. Around the first week of April 2016, I'm walking out of the library and one of my friends comes up to congratulate me on getting through to the semi-finals."

The brother duo had the only business idea in the competition that had not generated any revenue. They lost the competition that year; however, they received a lot of positive feedback and concluded they "were on to something." Michael asked Matthew if he was interested in working on the concept of Lula over the summer break. That summer they raised some seed money, started developing the app, and ultimately launched a pilot in early 2018. The pilot was 8 weeks long and targeted Babson and a few other campuses around Babson. The conclusion? Users liked the app! There was customer validation.

The positive feedback and early traction from the pilot helped the brothers raise $620,000 to develop a newer version of the Lula app. They launched the app in September 2018 and were aiming to be in 30 campuses in five states and have about 90 registered on the platform. However, within the first week of the launch, they were in 200 campuses and surpassed all projections that they had for Year 1. Within the first 2 weeks of the launch, they were listed in the top 100 apps in the iOS App Store and even getting ahead of Zipcar in the ranking. As Matthew explained, "The only marketing we were doing was a couple of $100-a-day on Instagram. It was mostly word of mouth. We realized that kids need cars and there was not really much competition since car rental companies prefer people aged 25 and up." Today Lula is in more than 400 campuses across all 50 states in the United States.

Matthew credits a lot to his advisors in the extended Babson network. Lula won the SoFi Entrepreneur Pitch Competition at Babson and went to California to be part of the program. There they developed a relationship with the founder of SoFi, the leading provider of student loan refinancing, who then came on board as an advisor and, later on, an investor in the company. Matthew and his brother were also able to leverage the services of the law firm that visited the Babson campus on a regular basis, and this free legal advice saved the brothers and the company "a bunch of money."

Lula, as a company, had to resolve significant challenges if the business was going to truly start. Their greatest challenge was insurance. The brothers were at a legal crossroad: The app was ready to launch, but they couldn't launch the app because they didn't have insurance. If they didn't have insurance, they could not legally operate.

Initially, Matthew and Michael thought that they would just need regular car insurance, but they quickly realized that companies like Geico or Progressive did not want to insure a startup—especially one that caters to young, high-risk drivers. Insurance experts suggest they speak to brokers that focus on specialty insurance lines.[46] "We were rejected by over 40 insurance brokers over 16 months because nobody wanted to listen to a company that wanted to provide rental services to people below the age of 25," said Matthew. Although some companies provided rentals to people ages 21 to 24 at a premium, asking for insurance for students 3 years younger than 21 sounded "crazy" to insurance companies. Insurance experts advised the brothers to stop working on Lula because it was not possible.

It was a frustrating period for the startup. As Matthew recollected, "Even the companies that were willing to listen to us were only providing us insurance in case the *company* got sued and not insurance on physical damage to the car. We were in legal battles because insurance companies would try to use confusing language, hoping we would not catch onto the fact that they weren't going to give us physical protection. We had to call our lawyers because what they were stating in the email was completely different than what was offered in the policy. Not just that, they were pushing us to sign, saying they wouldn't accept the deal otherwise. Luckily, we were able to catch them." In other words, Matthew quickly learned that the insurance they were being sold only protected Lula in the case of a lawsuit.

To resolve the ongoing insurance battle, Matthew decided to treat the insurance companies as their investors and made a pitch deck for them. He sent out emails saying that if they would invest in and work with Lula, they could potentially generate $55 million in revenue over the next 5 years. Within 2 weeks, they got positive responses from insurance companies and three firm offers. "The first insurance company to bite gave us probably the worst insurance coverage. If I was a student and knew what the insurance policy covered, I would not rent a car. We basically had no protection. Thankfully, we didn't have any crashes and we took this data to other insurance companies showing that 18-year-olds aren't as bad they thought." Lula is now partnering with the same insurance company that works with Lyft and Airbnb, with a multimillion-dollar protection policy. They now have 20 times the coverage for half the price. The major hurdle to the successful startup of Lula was overcome.

Other issues arose. One of Lula's competitors, Getaround, had filed for a patent on the peer-to-peer car-sharing model. The patent was loosely based on renting a car through a mobile device, and if that patent had been granted, it would have killed Lula as a business. Because Getaround was a heavily funded company, potential investors in Lula were scared of the potential patent being a huge roadblock. The Getaround patent was rejected because it was too general, which opened up investment doors for Lula.

Lula encountered pushback by college campus administrators who wanted Lula to operate on college campuses only after getting official permission from the university. Matthew believes that this was because of their previous interactions with companies like Zipcar that needed to rent a parking spot at the college. Matt explained, "Lula, unlike Zipcar, was a peer-to-peer model that allowed anybody to download and rent the car. When the college administrators asked us how they got parking spots on campus, we explained that the students that already had a parking space were renting their cars out. We also explained that the Lula service was similar to Uber or Lyft and they didn't need permission to operate on campus."

Matthew learned that raising money isn't as easy and glamorous as it seems on shows like *Shark Tank*. "Only 3–5% of startups ever get funding. There are hundreds of companies trying to get funding, and getting funding on an average takes around 6 months. What is not portrayed in movies (or on *Shark Tank*) is how it is a full-time job in itself and how much time it takes away from running the business." The journey so far has also taken a toll on Matthew's personal life. His parents hate that he and his brother are barely home, and he has lost a bunch of friends because of not having the time to spend with them. However, Matthew is excited about where Lula can go as a company.

Matthew's advice to aspiring entrepreneurs is that "When you're starting a company, listen to who your customer is going to be. When we started, we thought investors such as venture capitalists knew all this stuff, but at the end of the day they don't know nearly as much as you think they do. We had parents, professors, and investors telling us that there wasn't a need for this or that this wasn't a very good idea. So many people, who we thought were credible, gave us what we can call, in hindsight, bad advice. But every time we spoke to our target demographic, college students, they told us, 'Yes, there is a need for this!' So, my advice is don't launch a business unless you have random people across the target demographic telling you they need this."

## Critical Thinking Questions

1. With the early legal challenges faced by Lula, what do you think kept the founders pushing forward?

2. Where do you think Lula will be 5 years from now? It's early in the life of the startup; would you invest today?

3. Look up the status of the company today. Are you surprised? Why or why not?

**Source:** Matthew Vega-Sanz (interview with Babson MBA graduate assistant Gaurav Khemka, November 30, 2018)

# 15 Engaging Customers Through Marketing

"The best marketing doesn't feel like marketing."

—Tom Fishburne

# Chapter Outline

# Learning Objectives

15.1    Discuss entrepreneurial marketing and explain how it is different from traditional marketing.

15.2    Explain the principles of marketing and how they apply to new ventures.

15.3    Describe branding and the importance of building a brand.

15.4    Discuss the different types of marketing tools available to entrepreneurs.

15.5    Practice marketing yourself.

## 15.1 WHAT IS ENTREPRENEURIAL MARKETING?

>> **LO 15.1  Discuss entrepreneurial marketing and explain how it is different from traditional marketing.**

Not too long ago, there were only three main ways to draw attention to your product or service: Invest in expensive advertising, persuade the mainstream media to tell everyone about you and your company, or hire dozens of salespeople to try and attract new customers. But times have changed and the old rules no longer apply. Thanks to technology, there is a new form of marketing on the scene that is available to any entrepreneur. Entrepreneurial marketing is a set of processes adopted by entrepreneurs based on new and unconventional marketing practices to gain traction and attention in competitive markets.[1]

Most entrepreneurs suffer constraints associated with money, people, and time, but the good news is that entrepreneurial marketing actually requires fewer resources. Just a few years ago, traditional marketers suggested that depending on word-of-mouth was a risky strategy and that you needed to spend lots of money to control and manage the message. Today, word-of-mouth is called "social media marketing," and if one person says something about your business or product, thousands, if not millions, hear about it almost instantaneously. If you want traditional marketing, take a marketing class. If you want to learn more about entrepreneurial marketing, stay right here!

Entrepreneurial marketing today is not about chasing sales; it's about chasing reputation, credibility, and buzz. The sales then follow. Methods for building reputation, credibility, and buzz have moved mostly online. The Internet has changed the rules of marketing.

**Entrepreneurial marketing:** a set of processes adopted by entrepreneurs based on new and unconventional marketing practices in order to gain traction in competitive markets.

### How Entrepreneurial Marketing Is Different

Marketing today is really about proving to customers that you can solve their problem or fulfill a need they have. It's about delivering a clear message in a very noisy marketplace. It's about storytelling, building community through social media, content, and interactivity.[2] Furthermore, with so much information available through websites, reviews, and social channels, the buyer is in more control than ever. Marketing is more challenging for all businesses, so you can imagine it's even a bigger challenge for a startup that no one has ever heard of. This is why entrepreneurial marketing is not traditional marketing. Table 15.1 explains the differences between traditional marketing and entrepreneurial marketing.

Innovation, risk taking, resourcefulness, value creation, and proactivity are some of the main features of entrepreneurial marketing. For the entrepreneur, marketing and sales are not separate units. Until there is enough traction and enough customers, marketing and sales are very much about finding, acquiring, and keeping customers. Entrepreneurial marketing focuses on building trust, finding out customer preferences,

**⑤SAGE** edge™

Master the content at
**edge.sagepub.com/
neckentrepreneurship2e**

**TABLE 15.1**

Traditional Marketing Versus Entrepreneurial Marketing

| TRADITIONAL MARKETING | ENTREPRENEURIAL MARKETING |
|---|---|
| • Big cash investment<br>• Main focus is on the product<br>• Goal is to maximize profit<br>• Short-term relationship with customer<br>• Delivers marketing message as a monologue<br>• Sales focus through interruption and coercion<br>• Reaches the masses<br>• Intermittent communication<br>• Uses advertising to communicate to customers | • Investment of time, energy, creativity, commitment<br>• Main focus is on the customer<br>• Goal is to meet and satisfy customer needs<br>• Long-term interactive relationship with customer<br>• Delivers marketing message as a dialogue<br>• Relationship-focused through content and participation<br>• Reaches underserved, niche markets<br>• 24/7 communications<br>• Communicates directly with customers |

and creating ongoing value. It also provides the entrepreneur with the opportunity to highlight the company's strengths while showcasing the different ways the product adds value.

Unlike traditional marketing, which is mostly centered on the product and how it can make money, entrepreneurial marketing requires an interactive approach. Entrepreneurs create a dialogue and build long-term relationships, adapting the business to meet their customers' needs. To paraphrase Seth Godin, the goal is not to find customers for your products, but to find products for your customers.[3]

To illustrate this point further, think of the Internet as a city and social media as a cocktail party. If you were at a cocktail party, would you do any of the following?

- March into the party filled with a mix of people you do and do not know, and shout "BUY MY PRODUCT!"

- Ask people for a business card before you agree to speak with them

- Try to get around to everyone in the room, rather than having fewer but higher-quality conversations

- Talk over people rather than listening to what they have to say

- Provide valuable information solely on the basis of getting something tangible in return

- Avoid cocktail parties altogether because this type of social interaction makes you feel uncomfortable

The point is that people tend to do business with people they like, and when someone likes you, he or she is keen to introduce you to others. The same concept applies to social media. It is the place where people gather to exchange information and discuss things they are interested in. Making yourself likeable by interacting with your customers directly and providing them with important information takes you one step closer to building lasting relationships and making valuable business connections.

Maine-based surfboard manufacturer Grain Surfboards is an excellent example of a company that does a great job engaging its customers. It applies boatbuilding techniques to make hollow, wooden, eco-friendly boards. Not only does the website share the history of wooden board building, but it provides details of how the boards are made—something that most companies are wary of for fear competitors will steal their ideas. However, sharing information to educate is one of the best ways to build customer loyalty and grow your business. In addition to selling surfboards, the company offers workshops where you can build your own surfboard and regularly shares content and images on Facebook and Instagram. Equally delighted with the high level of engagement, Grain Surfboards'

| ENTREPRENEURSHIP IN ACTION |
| --- |

## Charlie Regan, Nerds on Site

Photo courtesy of Charlie Regan

**Charlie Regan, CEO of Nerds on Site**

Charlie Regan is an owner and the CEO (capability expansion orchestrator) of Nerds on Site, a technology solutions company headquartered in London, Ontario. Established in 1995 by a pair of self-proclaimed "nerds" (John and David), Nerds on Site expanded rapidly in the local London, Ontario region. Initially, the problem to solve was a simple one: Computers were too bulky for it to make sense for people to shuttle them into a repair shop, yet people did it because they didn't have other choices. Large companies can afford to have departments devoted to remedying issues, but what about a small to medium-sized company? Making the repair person mobile was the idea that led to Nerds on Site. Today, Nerds on Site has franchise locations in more than 10 countries, including South Africa, UK, Australia, Bolivia, and Mexico, and has serviced more than 100,000 clients. Furthermore, it has a client satisfaction rating of 96.5%.

Nerds on Site is a global brand, but they operate the entire company with fewer than 15 full-time employees. They manage this thanks to their constantly improving franchise tools and back-end support for each of their "Nerds." Nerds on Site corporate headquarters functions as a partner to each of their Nerds on Site franchisees. Each Nerd is supported by the corporate infrastructure but is empowered to grow and build at their own pace.

This strategy is part of Charlie's vision to support and grow as many small and medium-sized enterprises (SMEs) as he can. Charlie wants Nerds on Site to be the best franchise partner possible in order for the brand to grow and the SME model to spread.

All Nerds are private franchisees, which allows individual franchise owners to sell and market services on their own, with their own creative capital behind it. "They are marketing themselves and their talents," Charlie says, "and when clients ask where the corporate office is, our Nerds can point to their cars and say 'that is my world headquarters right there.'" The franchise model allows Nerds to maximize their creativity as they are only responsible to themselves and their own local client base. "You need to market your business better than anyone else and to do that, you have to believe in it more than anyone else."

Nerds on Site operates a bit differently from most franchises. Charlie believes in letting Nerds control their own marketing, whereas most franchisors are all about consistency—consistency in messaging, consistency in approach, consistency in design, and consistency in types of advertising used—because franchisors are trying to create a brand, and strong brands are built on repetitive and consistent messaging. But, perhaps Charlie has cracked the code by allowing his franchisees a bit more freedom. The Nerds are more likely to be able to tell a personal story, build authentic relationships with clients, and think and act more entrepreneurially.

Charlie wants there to be more startups, with people taking more risks creating more impactful organizations worldwide: "Just try. You didn't learn how to walk by understanding the locomotion of muscles . . . you fell, bumped into sharp objects, and you learned how to walk by doing." He wants as many people as possible to be entrepreneurs, and he thinks everyone can own small businesses that serve specific needs.

### Critical Thinking Questions

1. What was the "problem" that small and medium-sized companies faced that led to the creation of Nerds on Site?

2. What is unique about Nerds on Site's marketing strategy at both the corporate and franchisee level?

3. Why does Charlie want more SMEs? ●

**Source:** Charlie Regan (interview with the author, August 30, 2018)

©iStockphoto.com/kongxinzhu

**Wooden surfboard**

fans also help spread the company's ideas through their own social media, which has helped to cement its number one position in the marketplace. Thanks to its innovative and entrepreneurial approach to marketing, Grain Surfboards has achieved something that would have been considered impossible in the past: a way to reach its buyers directly without investing in expensive ads, hiring teams of salespeople, or begging the media to showcase the company.

Entrepreneurial marketing tools are not just reserved for entrepreneurs; more and more large, established companies are using the same tools in different ways to draw attention to their products. Although these industry giants may have a bigger budget and enormous resources, that should not stop new entrepreneurs from waging their own successful campaigns. Entrepreneurial marketing tools level the playing field: With a bit of knowledge, imagination, and ingenuity, entrepreneurs can make their products and services be heard and seen in very noisy marketplaces.

## 15.2 THE BASIC PRINCIPLES OF MARKETING

>> **LO 15.2**   **Explain the principles of marketing and how they apply to new ventures.**

The rules may have changed, but the traditional principles of marketing still hold some value, and it's important to know them.[4] **Marketing** for entrepreneurs still involves showing how a product meets customer needs, pricing the products in a way that accurately represents the value perceived by the customer, promoting products in innovative ways to reach customers, implementing delivery of the products, and maintaining the relationship with the customer even after the sale is made.[5]

Getting all these elements to balance is tricky. It requires a lot of research and commitment to ensure your product is in line with your marketing vision. This is why it helps to use an established marketing framework to help develop your marketing strategy.

The basic principles of marketing are grounded in the **marketing mix**, a framework that helps define the brand and differentiate it from the competition. This framework helps companies crystalize their offering and how they intend to take it to market.

The marketing mix is made up of four main elements, known as the 4 Ps: product, price, promotion, and place (see Figure 15.1). It is important to be familiar with the 4 Ps, as they are still relevant to entrepreneurs with limited resources, but do bear in mind that they don't apply as well to entrepreneurial marketing as they do to traditional marketing. Each of the 4 Ps should be considered in relation to the others, in order to build the best overall marketing strategy for your offering.

The **product** is anything tangible or intangible (such as a service) offered by the company. This includes the features, the brand, how it meets customer needs, how and where it will be used, and how it stands out from competitors. A good way of assessing your product is to look at it objectively—as if you were someone seeing it for the first time. Then ask yourself some critical questions, such as, "Is this product or service suitable for my target market?" and "Is this something today's customers will want or need?" and "How can I market this product better than my competitors?" By repeatedly asking these questions, you will have a better understanding of your product or service and how it fits into the marketplace.

The **price** covers the amount that the customer is expected to pay for the product, its perceived value, and the degree to which the price can be raised or lowered depending on market demand and how competitors price rival products. Again, get into the habit of continually examining the pricing structure of your products and services to ensure it is appropriate for your target market. Depending on changes in the market, you may need

**Marketing:** a method of putting the right product in the right place, at the right price, at the right time.

**Marketing mix:** the combination of product, price, promotion, and placement of what a company is offereing.

**Product:** anything tangible or intangible (such as a service) offered by the company.

**Price:** the amount that the customer is expected to pay for the product.

**FIGURE 15.1**

## Elements of the Marketing Mix

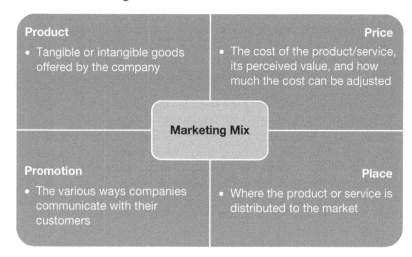

to raise or lower your price. Make a point of frequently examining competitors' pricing in order to price your products accordingly.

The third element of the marketing mix is **promotion**: all the ways in which companies tell their customers about their offering. This may involve advertising online, through social networking, direct mail, in the press, or even on TV if you have the budget. It also includes public relations such as being featured in blogs, newspapers, magazines—all free aspects of promotion. Both large and small companies need to continually experiment with finding ways to promote their products and services in order to find out what works and what doesn't. A promotional tactic that works one day may not work the next, so continuous development of new strategies is essential to retaining and increasing your target customer base.

Finally, **place** is where the product is actually distributed to your target market: trade fairs, retail stores, catalogs, mail order, online, and so forth. You can always revisit where you sell your product. For example, if you're selling retail products, you might start off selling online and then also decide to rent a retail space in order to make your company more visible to your target market. Ask yourself where else you could sell your products and what changes you need to make in order to reach your target market. Wherever you choose to sell, it is essential that your customers receive the best buying information on your product or service to help them make a buying decision.

Any type of marketing requires a discussion of who the customer is and how you are going to reach them; therefore, it is a good idea to use the 4 Ps framework to evaluate the strength and completeness of your marketing approach. Important questions can be answered using the 4 Ps framework:

- What are the benefits and features of my product? (Product)

- What is the value of my offering, and what are customers willing to pay? (Price)

- How will they know my business exists? (Promotion)

- How will the customers be reached? Where will they buy my product or service? (Place)

The marketing mix is constantly changing; you don't simply develop it and move on. By continually reviewing and tweaking your marketing mix, you will be better able to adjust to an ever-changing competitive environment.

Although the 4 Ps model is arguably the most recognized, newer marketing models have been developed to enhance the traditional model. Some of them extend

**Promotion:** all the ways in which companies tell their customers about their offering.

**Place:** where the product is actually distributed to your target market; for example, trade fairs, retail stores, catalogs, mail order, online.

**People:** the people who are responsible for every aspect of sales and marketing.

**Packaging:** every single visual element of the external appearance of an offering, as viewed through the eyes of your customer.

**Positioning:** a marketing strategy that focuses on how your customers think or talk about your product and company relative to your competitors.

the 4 Ps to 7 Ps, including **people**, which refers to the people responsible for every aspect of sales and marketing; **packaging**, which is a process that explores every single visual element of the external appearance of an offering through the eyes of your customer; and **positioning**, which is a marketing strategy that focuses on how customers think or talk about your product and company relative to your competitors.[6]

Your people are an important part of the marketing mix and the marketing strategy. They are responsible for enforcing every aspect of your sales and marketing activities. Hiring the right people with the right skills and abilities to market your products effectively is at the core of any marketing strategy. Often, in the early days of a startup the entrepreneur is wearing many hats and is playing the role of chief marketing officer and salesperson.

It is also important to objectively assess the visual element of the packaging of your product or service. Remember, your packaging represents you and your company, and first impressions count. Always be prepared to adjust elements of your packaging to encourage potential buyers to buy your product. Packaging is also an important part of branding, which we will discuss in the next section.

Positioning is something that should be at the forefront of every entrepreneur's mind. What are people saying about you, your company, and your product when you're not present? What are the words that people use about you to describe you and your offerings to other people? Knowing what other people think of you and your product determines the extent to which they will buy from you and how much they are willing to pay. Be vigilant in monitoring what other people think about you, especially on social media, and be sure to make the changes you need to enhance interaction with your target customer because positioning is at the heart of branding.

## 15.3 BUILDING A BRAND

>> **LO 15.3**    **Describe branding and the importance of building a brand.**

**Branding:** the process of creating a name, term, design, symbol, or any other feature that identifies a product or service and differentiates it from others.

**Branding** is the process of creating a name, term, design, symbol, or any other feature that identifies a product or service and differentiates it from others. Your brand is a promise to your customers, letting them know what they can expect from your offering and how it differentiates you from among your competitors. The face of your brand is your logo, which should also be integrated into your website, packaging, and promotional materials to communicate your brand message. People are more likely to invest in brands that are trustworthy, are worth spending money on, are fashionable, are adept at meeting their needs, and that they have an emotional connection to.

**Brand strategy:** a long-term plan to develop a successful brand; it involves how you plan to communicate your brand messages to your target customers.

A **brand strategy** is a long-term plan to develop a successful brand. It involves how you plan to communicate your brand messages to your target customers. This brand message can be channeled through your advertising, distribution, and packaging.

Two of the most classic and powerful brands are Coca-Cola, which has managed to differentiate itself from other sodas through its consistent strategic branding, and Nike, which involves famous athletes as part of its branding strategy, encouraging people to buy its products through the transfer of the emotional attachment they may feel for these star athletes. Over the years, both of these brands have evolved their branding strategies to appeal to generations of customers. See Figure 15.2 for the world's 10 most powerful brands.

While there isn't one "right" way to guarantee brand success, you can start defining the brand you would like for your company by answering the following questions:

- What is the primary goal of your company?
- What are the best features and benefits of your products or services?
- What are your customers and prospective clients already saying about you and your company?
- What sorts of qualities do you want them to associate with your company?

Your responses will help you to create a brand name that resonates with your target customers.

**FIGURE 15.2**

## Top 10 Most Powerful Brands in the World

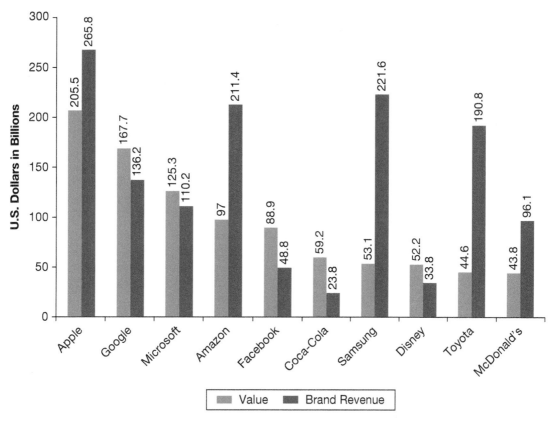

**Source:** The world's most valuable brands. (2019). *Forbes.* Retrieved from http://www.forbes.com/powerful-brands/list/#tab:rank

## How to Build a Brand

Building a brand helps your customers understand what your product is in the simplest way possible and helps build an emotional connection to your product. Follow the steps below to build a successful brand.[7]

- *Choose a name.* A successful brand starts with a name. It could be a family name, which can add credibility to the business, or an obscure name that has nothing to do with the actual product. For example, the Starbucks name and logo have incredible brand recognition around the world, but they have no relationship to coffee whatsoever. Or you could go with an edgy name that carries shock value, such as UK-based clothing retailer FCUK (which actually stands for French Connection UK). Whatever name you choose, make sure it passes the SMILE test first (see Table 15.2).[8]

  Some experts believe that a strong brand can be created by just using one word—a concept first introduced by marketing professional and author Al Ries, who believed it made the brand easier for consumers to remember. Many top companies, such as Google, Salesforce, Uber, and Hubspot, have adopted this approach.[9] In fact, as Figure 15.2 shows, most of the world's most powerful brands consist of only one word. The key to defining your brand is knowing what your customers think of you and acting on that knowledge to build a successful brand. Alexandra Watkins, founder of San Francisco–based Eat My Words, a company that specializes in creating catchy brand names, believes that brand names should make people smile rather than scratch their heads. On this basis, she devised the Eat My Words® SMILE and SCRATCH Test™ (see Table 15.2)—a fun way to test your company or product name to see if you should keep it or scratch it off the list. Some of the names Watkins claims have passed the test include SPOON ME for a chain of frozen yogurt stores; BLOOM, a natural energy drink for women; and NEATO for a home-cleaning robot.

- *Design a logo.* Your logo is the gateway to your overall brand image. It triggers people's emotions and perception of the brand and answers questions such as, Who are you? What do you do? and What's in it for me? When designing a logo, make sure it shows up well in different types of media, its design and message are clear, and it is instantly recognizable. Put your logo everywhere you can—on your company website, social media, packaging, email signature, and all written communication.

- *Spread the word.* Get your brand out into the world. Social media is a great way for cash-strapped entrepreneurs to spread the word about their brand. Keep track of your online followers, and listen to what they have to say about your brand. Engage with your followers, be responsive to their needs, and reward them for following your brand.

- *Know your customer.* Knowing what your customer wants is key to building a successful brand. In order to achieve brand success, you need to know how your brand is perceived—who loves it, who hates it, and who would recommend it—what would make it stronger, how customers feel about competitor brands, and the extent to which customers will emotionally connect with your brand. You can find out this information through surveys and by keeping an eye on your followers and observing how they behave over a certain time period.

- *Become your brand.* Incorporate your brand into every aspect of your business. In an office environment, this includes how you greet people over the phone and what you and your employees wear. For example, if your aim is to promote sophistication through your brand, then you may want your employees to choose a polite yet formal manner over the phone and to dress smartly.

## TABLE 15.2

Eat My Words® SMILE and SCRATCH Test™

| **SMILE**, the qualities of a powerful name: |
| --- |
| Simple—one, easy-to-understand concept |
| Meaningful—your customers instantly "get it" |
| Imagery—visually evocative, creates a mental picture |
| Legs—carries the brand, lends itself to wordplay |
| Emotional—empowers, entertains, engages, enlightens |
| **SCRATCH** it off the list if it has any of these deal-breakers: |
| Spelling-challenged—you have to tell people how to spell it |
| Copycat—similar to competitors' names |
| Random—disconnected from the brand |
| Annoying—hidden meaning, forced |
| Tame—flat, uninspired, boring, nonemotional |
| Curse of knowledge—only insiders get it |
| Hard-to-pronounce—not obvious, relies on punctuation |

# One Sentence, Clear Message

Because entrepreneurs are so close to their ideas, you can easily fall into the trap of assuming everyone else understands what you are saying about what you are doing! Entrepreneurs have to develop a habit of quickly communicating their core offering—the essence of the business—so people want to hear more. What you believe is very clear in your head may not reach the same level of clarity for the listener, whether in person, on your website, or on social media. If we want our product or service or business to be shared by word of mouth, then we really need to get it down to one compelling sentence. That sentence should lead with the most important benefit or the need you are fulfilling.

For example, in 2011 Uber's slogan was "You push a button and in five minutes a Mercedes picks you up and takes you where you want to go." Later this was shortened to "Tap a button, get a ride."

For this Mindshift you must do two things: First, write your one sentence that describes your business idea. Second, share that sentence with at least five people and see if they get it. Of course, if they don't get it, you should rewrite it and try again!

## Critical Thinking Questions

1. How difficult was it to create one sentence that clearly communicates your idea?

2. When you shared your sentence with others, did they get it? Why or why not?

3. Can you identify any other business that has been able to get their description down to one sentence? ●

**Source:** Bailey, D. (2017). The art of describing a product in one sentence. *Inc.* Retrieved from https://www.inc.com/dave-bailey/the-art-of-describing-a-product-in-one-sentence.html

- *Write a tagline.* Although it can be difficult to capture the essence of a brand in one succinct statement, a tagline is important for communicating your brand message. Keep your tagline short, simple, clear, and memorable. (See Table 15.3 for some approaches.)

- *Always deliver on your brand promise.* Customers are more likely to buy into your brand if it consistently meets and exceeds their expectations.

- *Be consistent with your brand.* It is possible to tweak a logo or a tagline, but make sure you always retain the brand voice and deliver on your brand promise.

## Marketing Trends

Successful brands only stay successful when they stay on top of their marketing. This involves keeping a close eye on the current and future marketing trends, such as virtual

## TABLE 15.3

Slogan or Tagline Approaches

| APPROACH | EXAMPLE |
|---|---|
| Stake your claim | Death Wish Coffee: "The World's Strongest Coffee" |
| Make it a metaphor | Red Bull: "Red Bull gives you wings." |
| Adopt your customer's attitude | Nike: "Just do it." |
| Leverage labels | Cards Against Humanity: "A party game for horrible people" |
| Describe it literally | Aritzia: "Women's Fashion Boutique" |

**Source:** Kumar, B. (2017). How to build a brand. *Shopify.* Retrieved from https://www.shopify.com/blog/how-to-build-a-brand

reality, artificial intelligence (AI), influencer marketing, experiential marketing, marketing through education, and honesty.[10]

1.  Virtual Reality

    Integrating virtual reality (VR) into marketing strategies is becoming more and more popular; in fact, 75% of the world's biggest brands have launched VR campaigns. One of these brands is California-based for-profit shoe company TOMS Shoes, which gives away a pair of shoes for every pair purchased. Thanks to a VR tool set up in stores, customers can experience what it is like to gift the shoes to someone in Peru. Offering an immersive, exciting experience is a powerful way to build an emotional connection with their customers.

2.  Artificial Intelligence (AI)

    The demand for more AI tools, such as voice-enabled devices like Amazon Echo with Alexa, is growing.[11] Many companies are using AI technology as a "live" chat tool (Chatbots) on their websites, to enable their customers to receive faster responses and save the cost of hiring customer support staff.

ChameleonsEye/Shutterstock

**Realistic image of Domino's pizza**

3.  Honesty

    This low-tech approach may look a little out of place among all the latest technological advances, but honesty is more than just a passing craze. Being honest about your products and services by addressing any flaws or areas for improvement adds integrity to your brand, which may also translate into loyalty and sales. For example, pizza restaurant chain Domino's is on track to overtake its rivals by adopting a marketing strategy based on transparency.[12] Rather than posting "artistic," well-lit photos of its food online, it publishes realistic images of food—what you see is what you get. As Dennis Maloney, Domino's chief digital officer, says, "A lot of customers are out photographing their food. They know, depending on where you take it and the light you're under, food looks different. It feels much more honest and transparent when the images are imperfect."

4.  Influencer Marketing

    Many brands are seeking the help of influencers on Instagram, Facebook, Snapchat, Twitter, YouTube, and Pinterest. For instance, pet foods company Pedigree used a group of influencers to promote its "Buy a Bag, Give a Bowl" campaign to showcase their mission to give a bowl of food to a dog in need in exchange for each bag of dog food bought at the store.[13] These influencers spread the word over blogs, posts, and video content, leading to a huge surge in media value. Celebrities are strong influencers. Singer and actress Selena Gomez is one of the most-followed people on Instagram, with more than 135 million followers. As a paid influencer for companies, she gets $550,000 per post.[14]

5.  Experiential Marketing (Engagement Marketing)

    Experiential marketing, or engagement marketing, is a marketing strategy that provides people with a hands-on experience of what the company stands for. Whiskey company Glenfiddich has used experiential marketing to turn the concept of tasting sessions on its head.[15] To market their new Glenfiddich Experimental Series, the whiskey company set up a tasting event that invites customers to log into an app and answer questions about themselves. They are then matched with a drink that corresponds to their personality profile.

**Sarah Ingle's partnership with Pedigree in their "buy a bag, give a bowl" campaign.**

6.  Marketing Through Education

    The explosion of data has left many consumers a little world-weary and harder to engage. This means that marketers must also be educators and must offer easy-to-understand, engaging content to provide the information consumers are looking for. Exploring new ideas, sharing information, and providing value are key to building your brand and fostering customer engagement. As salesperson and motivational speaker Zig Ziglar once said, "You can have everything in life you want, if you will just help enough other people get what they want."[16]

These are just a few examples of marketing trends that brands need to pay attention to, especially in this era of social media, when savvy consumers tend to hold all the cards.

## Reframing the 4 Ps

A 5-year study conducted by Harvard Business School, involving 500 managers and customers across numerous countries, presented the argument that because of the new relationships businesses have with customers, the traditional 4 Ps model is narrow and outdated and is not strictly relevant in a modern business environment.[17]

According to this research, the 4 Ps model overemphasizes product technology and quality, understates the necessity of explaining the value of the product and why customers need it, and distracts businesses from promoting themselves as important sources of information and problem solving. Researchers believe that a solutions-focused approach is needed when it comes to marketing products. Today's customers have far

**FlowDog physical therapy for dogs**

more input into the business–customer relationship, which necessitates a new framework that better reflects what the customer wants and cares about.

**FIGURE 15.3**

The S.A.V.E. Framework

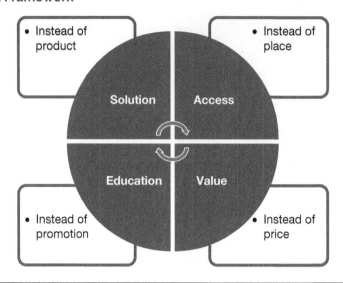

The study inspired the S.A.V.E framework—Solution, Access, Value, Education—which reinterprets the 4 Ps model by transferring the emphasis from products to *solutions*, place to *access*, price to *value*, and promotion to *education* (see Figure 15.3). Let's examine these factors one by one.

*Solution rather than product*: Researchers argue that businesses tend to get caught up in the features and functions of their product, when all customers really want to know is how the product solves their problems. S.A.V.E. advocates marketing a product based on how it meets customer needs, rather than emphasizing its features.

*Access rather than place*: Here, the focus is on how accessible your company is to your target customer. The exact location where someone can purchase your product is not so important. This approach considers the customer's journey from when they first hear of your company to when they actually make the purchase. Customers want to see that businesses care about customer feedback and are available if they need advice and support.

*Value over price*: Customers are drawn to value more than to price. This means that entrepreneurs need to build a strong case for showing customers why their product offers superior value to the competition, rather than focusing on the actual price tag.

*Education rather than promotion:* Today's businesses are in a good position to educate customers by providing information that they want to read that is up to date and relevant. This helps to build a relationship of familiarity and trust before a purchase is even made.

Figure 15.4 compares the message of FlowDog, a Boston-based physical therapy facility for dogs, with the 4 Ps on one hand and the S.A.V.E. model on the other.

Regardless of how many marketing models there are out there, the lesson is to take a broad approach to encompass all the elements that are relevant to your business. Then, test them, tweak them, and adjust them where needed.

## 15.4 ENTREPRENEURIAL MARKETING

**>> LO 15.4   Discuss the different types of marketing tools available to entrepreneurs.**

Entrepreneurs who are just getting started always have one eye on the budget. It can be difficult to reach your chosen audience at the right time without compromising the quality of your marketing efforts. However, there is a wide range of entrepreneurial marketing

FIGURE 15.4

**FlowDog: The 4 Ps Versus S.A.V.E.**

| 4 Ps | S.A.V.E. |
|---|---|
| **Product**<br><br>FlowDog provides the following:<br><br>• Physical therapy for orthopedic and neurological conditions<br>• Hydrotherapy for therapeutic swimming in a pool heated 84–89 degrees Fahrenheit<br>• Fitness swimming for weight loss, weight management, and cross training<br>• Massage to increase blood flow and relieve muscle tension<br>• Reiki for stress reduction<br>• Acupuncture for pain and tension relief<br>• Physical therapy products to supplement service (e.g., special harnesses, toys to improve cognition) | **Solution**<br><br>FlowDog brings peace of mind to the dog owner by providing an array of therapeutic services for a complete solution that increases the quality of life of postsurgical, injured, and aging dogs. By providing hands-on treatment, owner education, and products to use at home, FlowDog gives dogs every opportunity to fully recover, prevent injury, and even prolong life. |
| **Place**<br><br>FlowDog is located in Waltham, MA. The facility is located in an office park area and is zoned for a dog-related business. There is ample parking. | **Access**<br><br>FlowDog is conveniently located to dog owners in both Boston and the surrounding area for suburbs. With strong relationships with Boston-area vets, customers are often referred to FlowDog by their primary veterinarian or specialty/surgical hospital. |
| **Price**<br><br>An initial evaluation for physical therapy is $185/hour and follow-up appointments are $110. Other treatments (massage, reiki, acupuncture) range in price from $40 to $80. FlowDog rates are competitive with other facilities in the Boston area. | **Value**<br><br>Physical therapy reduces recovery time after surgery and reduces prolonged medication usage. It is often used as an alternative to surgery or as a way of preventing surgery. On average, dog owners can expect to pay $2,500 to $3,500 for a common knee surgery such as an ACL tear. Overall, FlowDog's focus is on prolonging the dog's life. |
| **Promotion**<br><br>FlowDog advertises in local dog newsletters, vet offices, and online. The company uses Facebook to communicate with customers about upcoming events. | **Education**<br><br>The FlowDog website offers case studies of dogs who have recovered from or better managed various medical conditions such as arthritis, cruciate tears, and spinal injuries. Because each dog is unique, a special treatment plan is created after the initial evaluation that meets the needs of both dog and owner. |

tools that don't have to cost the Earth, such as guerrilla marketing, social media marketing, designing a website, and building a fan base. But success does depend on patience, consistency, and ingenuity.

## Guerrilla Marketing

One form of entrepreneurial marketing is guerrilla marketing, which is a low-budget strategy that focuses on personally interacting with a target group by promoting products and services through surprise or other unconventional means. A successful guerrilla marketing campaign enhances the customer's perception of value, inspires word of mouth, and increases sales.

**Guerrilla marketing:** a low-budget strategy that focuses on personally interacting with a target group by promoting products and services through surprise or other unconventional means.

RICHARD B. LEVINE/Newscom

**Snapple's World's Largest Popsicle campaign**

Guerrilla marketing strategies are almost limitless: email, interactive poster campaigns, advertisements on cars, T-shirts, street branding (writing marketing messages with paint or chalk on pavements or walls), characters in costume, flash mobs (a large group of people that seemingly comes out of nowhere to perform an act in a public place), projecting images/videos/messages in public areas, and even YouTube videos that can go viral in minutes.

When guerrilla campaigns go viral, they can reach a huge audience. For example, to heighten awareness of its company and prove its blending expertise, global blender provider, Blendtec, posted a video on YouTube called "Will It Blend?" where viewers were asked for suggestions for items to blend.[18] The campaign was an instant hit, gathering 6 million views in 6 days. Since its launch, Blendtec has uploaded more than 150 videos blending everything from marbles, glow sticks, and Bic lighters, to Apple products, golf balls, and magnets. Thanks to the success of the Blendtec campaign, its founder, Tom Dickson, has been propelled into the media spotlight, making several TV appearances, including on the *Today Show* and Discovery Channel.

There is even a guerrilla marketing technique called snow branding, which involves making imprints of the product's name and brand during the night on snow-covered pavements, walls, cars, and the like.[19] When people emerge the next morning, they are surprised by these novel images that are aimed to create a good feeling, a sense of awareness, and a positive memory of the company's brand.

Guerrilla marketing strategies are also used by major companies. In an effort to promote the new Colgate Max Night toothpaste, Colgate partnered with various local pizzerias, which were supplied with special Colgate-branded boxes for pizza deliveries.[20] When customers opened the box, they were greeted with a design of the inside of a mouth. The message? To remind people to use Colgate to brush their teeth at night, so that their "dinner breath" doesn't turn into "morning breath."

Guerrilla marketing can be a creative and affordable way to reach your desired target market, but it has its limitations. In order to conduct a successful guerrilla campaign, you need to have a good understanding of your target market and where the high traffic exists; for example, subway, mall, university campus, and so on. You also need to get the timing right: Should you conduct the campaign during business hours, at weekends, or morning, or night?

Guerrilla marketing success can be difficult to measure: How do you know the good feeling or memory you're giving your customer is going to translate into sales? Monitoring the media (newspapers, radio) for mentions of your campaign and taking the time to scout blogs, forums, and social networks to see who is talking about your company and your product is a good start in measuring the campaign's impact on sales.

Finally, you need to have a good sense of the community and any legal, social, or moral restrictions that may cause a negative reaction to a campaign. In a classic example of guerrilla marketing going wrong, fruit drinks company Snapple came under fire when it attempted to create the world's largest popsicle in the middle of Manhattan—on a sunny day in June.[21] Inevitably, the 25-foot-tall popsicle began to melt, flooding the surrounding streets. Streets were closed off as firefighters were called in to clean the streets of the sticky goo. Snapple learned a valuable lesson that day: Always prepare for the unexpected!

Planning a guerrilla marketing campaign requires commitment, creativity, consistency, patience, and a true understanding of your target market. Getting it right could have big payoffs. Guerilla marketing can be considered a bootstrapping technique because many guerrilla efforts can be done quite inexpensively, so what do you have to lose? Take action, test, and see what works with your customer base.

# Marketing Through Social Media

Social media has become an essential business tool for entrepreneurs to market their products and services and themselves. When used properly, social media can launch businesses to new levels of success. For example, fine artist Iris Scott is on track to exceed $1 million in revenue thanks to her creative use of social media to market her art.[22] From early on, Scott engaged in two-way communication with her followers by sharing her art on Facebook and Instagram, taking on board their suggestions, and offering her works for prices as low as $50. Through the support of her followers, Scott decided to try finger painting, which created a real spike in interest and more demand for her works. Several years after she started to market her art on social media, some of Scott's paintings now hang in the Filo Sofi Arts Gallery in New York, one of which has a price tag of $45,000.

Artist Iris Scott used Facebook and Instagram to promote her finger painting artwork, which is now worth up to $45,000.

As the Iris Scott example shows, social media is the most powerful way of spreading word of mouth about your products and services. Social media is also a valuable way of following market trends, finding new employees, and building and maintaining relationships with customers. It is also a useful way to find potential stakeholders. Social media sites like Twitter, LinkedIn, Facebook, Instagram, and YouTube all provide ways to connect with people who are experts in the field or fellow entrepreneurs—anyone who can potentially help you develop, build, and grow your venture. Some of these people may become self-selected stakeholders or may even become part of your founding team.

This is why it is so important for entrepreneurs to create their own social media strategy. Figure 15.5 lists some of the most popular forms of social media.

## Getting the Most From Social Media

Anyone can engage in social media, but it takes a smart, dedicated entrepreneur to use social media wisely and productively. Here are some tips:

### Start With Research

The most successful social media strategies start with solid research. Take a look at how your competitors use social media. What kind of content do they share with their customers and followers? What sort of language do they use to engage their followers? It also helps to read blogs and join discussions about subjects that are relevant to your business. Contributing to conversations helps you learn more about what is important to your customers, and it helps to boost your profile and showcase your knowledge about a particular area.

### Think About Your Goals

After conducting your research, think about the goals you would like to achieve. Do you want your social media presence to attract customers, increase recognition of your brand, or both? Many companies use social media to provide efficient customer service; for example, online food ordering company Seamless provides round-the-clock customer service on Twitter, and American Airlines tweets if there are airline delays and responds quickly to tweets from frustrated passengers. Considering that more than 70% of Twitter users surveyed expect a response from a brand within an hour, it is very much worthwhile for companies to make the effort to provide excellent customer service over social media, especially as it could increase customer satisfaction by almost 20%.[23]

**FIGURE 15.5**

### Popular Forms of Social Media

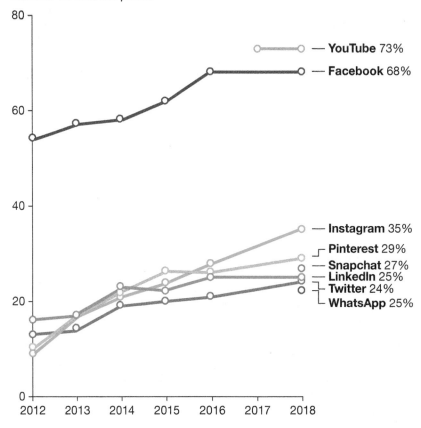

**Majority of Americans now use Facebook, YouTube**

*% of U.S. adults who say they use the following social media sites online or on their cell phone*

**Source:** Survey conducted Jan. 3–10, 2018. Trend data from previous Pew Research Center surveys.

## Design Your Strategy

Next, think about ways in which you can measure your online presence. For example, you can catalog the number of visits to your site, the number of followers, the types of comments people make about your business, and who they share them with. It also helps to design your strategy around your target audience—how do you engage them? What media platforms do they use the most? Choose one or two social media sites to begin with that fit in with your industry and your target market.

## Post Regular Updates

Once you have launched your social media campaign, make sure you post regular updates. Followers will expect to see quick messages on Twitter several times a day and longer blog posts or articles on Facebook at least a couple of times a week. New York City shop Squish Marshmallows posts images on Instagram twice per day, which owner Katherine Sprung credits for the increase in foot traffic into the shop.[24]

## Monitor Your Social Media

Be vigilant about monitoring your social media—every day, check for new followers, any feedback, questions, or complaints. Then make sure you address them all. In addition, check out who your new followers are and how many of them have retweeted your posts.

Who has viewed your LinkedIn profile? How many people have viewed or subscribed to your YouTube channel? Also, keep a close watch on your competitor's sites—what are people saying about them? Is your business mentioned in customer reviews on their site?

Posting interesting content online on a regular basis is one of the best ways to get feedback from your followers and grow your online community. If you are a confident public speaker, then videos are also a powerful way to build trust with potential customers by letting them get to know you before they buy from you. You can choose to share videos or images on sites such as YouTube, Vimeo, Flickr, Slide Share, and Instagram.

## Creating Content That Drives Sales

As we have learned, marketers must also be educators—ready to provide easy-to-understand, engaging content that appeals to their target audience. Whether you are using up-to-the-minute social media or traditional media such as magazines, newsletters, and other print collateral, the content matters. Let's take a closer look at how you can create interesting, engaging content online that ultimately translates into sales.

For many of us, the word *sales* evokes images of the pushy salesperson using hard-sell tactics to pressure us into buying stuff we don't need. So, it's time to let go of that outdated image and realize that today, most of us spend 40% of our time at work "selling" in one way or another: persuading, influencing, and convincing others in ways that don't necessarily translate into an immediate purchase.[25] In this sense, we are all salespeople, whether we realize it or not.

Sales has evolved from using hard-core sales techniques to a soft sell through engaging content that is genuine and creative, adds value, and builds relationships. Creating content is not about advertising your business or self-promotion. Instead, it aims to educate, inspire, and entertain people enough that they will grow to trust you and your brand. It is a way for your customers to get to know the human side of your business by injecting personality and authenticity into everything you produce. Here are some more tips to help engage your consumers:[26]

1. **Make your content about them, not you.**
   Most people, including your customers, don't like it when other people talk about themselves. When presenting content, make sure it is relevant to your audience: 90% about them and 10% (or less) about you.

2. **Develop a fresh point of view.**
   Rather than just talking about the industry in which you operate, try and broaden your scope to other areas. For instance, Trulia, the real estate search service, expands its content beyond the real estate market to provide novel geographic data based on social trends and demographics.[27]

3. **Pick your battles.**
   It is important to share your own point of view, but make sure you still come across as being likeable. Using inflammatory language, becoming overly political, or taking divisive standpoints may put off some of your customers. In 2017, an activism-themed ad from Pepsi featuring model Kendall Jenner triggered a massive backlash on social media. As a result, the ad was pulled and an apology was made by Pepsi for "missing the mark."[28]

4. **Be authentic.**
   Social media is about building long-lasting relationships, which means being authentic from the get-go. This involves participating in your customers' conversations, commenting on their content, and sharing your own thoughts and opinions. As *Unmarketing* author Scott Stratten says, "Setting up an automated Twitter program to tweet for you and automatically add followers is a great way to say to people 'We don't actually care what you're saying, just buy from us.' It would be like sending a mannequin to a networking event with your company logo on it. Yeah, creepy."[29]

**♀trulia**

MENU +

TRULIA RESEARCH   LIVABILITY

### Best Places to Live to Avoid Natural Disasters

By Jed Kolko, Former Chief Economist | Aug 15, 2013 5:00AM

Today, Trulia added three new hazard maps – for wildfires, hurricanes, and tornadoes – to the two hazard maps we introduced earlier this summer, featuring earthquakes and floods. As part of your home search, you can now check Trulia to find whether the neighborhood of your dreams puts you in the eye, at the epicenter, or in the path of a natural disaster. You'll see that California is high risk for wildfires, Florida for hurricanes, Oklahoma for tornadoes, and more.

**Trulia's website showing the best places to live to avoid natural disasters.**

Credit: Screenshot from Trulia Trends

5. **Use your gut.**

When reading over your content, ask yourself who it best serves, you and your company or the reader? If the answer isn't "the reader" then have another go. The effort will pay off in additional business and loyalty from your customer.

The key to good content is quality. If you can create content that is meaningful to your audience, they will share it through their own social networks—think tweets, retweets, likes, comments, reviews. It also helps to get in touch with people in a similar market who already have a large number of followers, and build a relationship with them. For example, if you have a product designed for mothers of young children, then you could get a list of the top mommy bloggers, send them the product, and get them talking about it. All going well, the product will be picked up by a company that will have heard of it through your more high-profile mommy bloggers. Over time, they may even share some of your content with their audiences, which gives your business an even larger platform to promote itself. In return, you can share some of their content in order to develop a mutually beneficial relationship.

It is important to be available to your online community. Publishing content regularly through blogs, infographics, videos, tweets, and taking part in conversations is essential if you want to maintain a loyal following. Getting your users involved is an even better way of spreading the word about your company.

Philadelphia-based mobile app and web development company Chop Dawg has discovered a unique way to engage its 500,000 followers over social media.[30] Currently writing a book, company founder Joshua Davidson live-streams his meetings with his publisher on Twitter to provide his Chop Dawg audience with an inside view of the book-writing process. Thanks to live-streaming, Davidson has gained an average of more than 1,000 people watching him create his book as it happens.

## Building Your Website

However you choose to market your content, it is always important to build a decent platform that showcases you, your company, and your content. This is where a good-quality website can make a real difference in attracting customers.

Websites with crisp, clean designs and a clear description of your product or service, together with simple, uncluttered pages that flow well in relation to each other, tend to be the most successful. It is particularly important that your website be quick and easy to navigate on both a large computer screen and a mobile device. Recent studies show that smartphones are the most popular way to browse the Internet in the UK.[31] Remember, it's all about participation and content, not coercion and persuasion!

Site builder tools like Wix, Duda, and Squarespace and content management systems like WordPress have made it easier for entrepreneurs on a tight budget to build their own sites. Whatever method you choose, do seek guidance to ensure you are using the best possible search engine optimization. This is what enables people to find you online via Google or other search engines, so it is worth the investment. Because Google search results also take into account the number of times websites are shared on social media, it is also important that your site includes links to your social media pages and vice versa, in order to boost Google search rankings.

Remember that the act of building a website will not encourage visitors to flock immediately to your site. Attracting an audience takes time and patience. It won't be perfect from the very start, but it will evolve over time in line with industry fluctuations and the response you get from your audience. Table 15.4 contains 10 tips to help you avoid mistakes in building your first website.

## Building a Fan Base

**True fans:** people who will buy anything you produce; they will wait in line for your products, drive for hours to attend one of your events, and preorder your next product without even knowing what it looks like.

Regardless of which marketing technique you use, it all comes down to one main goal: to attract enough people to your company to make what you are doing financially worthwhile. But how many people do you really need for your business to thrive? According to cofounder of *Wired* magazine Kevin Kelly, building a lasting, sustainable business is based on 1,000 true fans.[33] True fans are people who will buy anything you produce; they will wait in line for your products, drive for hours to attend one of your events, and

# What "About Us"?

Did you know that the "About Us" page is one of the most visited pages for any new business website? This section of a website helps you build trust, legitimacy, and connection with your customers. Follow these basic steps to create your own "About Us" page. Keep in mind that the content created in this Mindshift can be used anywhere at any time! Create your own "About Us" story using the steps below. Our example is based on www.yellowleafhammocks.com.

**Start with a quick introduction that explains the concept of your business.**

Example: Yellow Leaf Hammocks offers ridiculously comfy hammocks with impeccable craftsmanship and transformative impact.

**Describe what you stand for as a business. Communicate your why.**

Example: Our motto is "Do Good. Relax." In addition to sustainable social change, we believe passionately in travel, naps, good food, great friends, long talks, broadened horizons, and a spirit of adventure. We are also 100% positive the world would be a better place if everyone spent 15 minutes a day in a hammock.

**Describe what you specialize in or talk about the work you love doing.**

Example: Each perfectly engineered Yellow Leaf Hammock directly empowers our artisan weavers and their families. We train mothers to weave the world's best hammocks, then spread good times and relaxation around the world, then break the cycles of poverty and build a brighter future.

**Tell a quick story about why you started your business.**

Example: Our artisan weavers and their families were previously trapped in extreme poverty and debt slavery. Now they are empowered to earn a stable, healthy income through dignified work. We call this a "prosperity wage." This is the basis for a brighter future, built on a hand up, not a handout.

**Give a glimpse into your goals.**

Example: Yellow Leaf Hammocks is breaking the cycle of extreme poverty through sustainable job creation.

**Make it easy for the customer to take action.**

Example: Join the community, live the lifestyle, and spread "Do Good. Relax."!

Now create a one-paragraph "About Us" description or a web page. Share it with 10 people and see if you can get some fans! Take a look at www.yellowleafhammocks.com/pages/about-us to see their engaging design.

## Critical Thinking Questions

1. What was the most difficult part of your "About Us" to develop? Why?

2. What did you learn from those you shared your "About Us" with?

3. What other places can use your "About Us" content?

**Source:** Adapted from https://www.beamlocal.com/how-to-write-a-powerful-business-description-for-your-website/

---

preorder your next product without even knowing what it looks like. For instance, more than 400,000 Tesla fans have signed up for the much-anticipated Model 3 electric car, most of whom ordered it sight unseen.[34]

But of course, you don't need half a million fans to make a living when you first start your business; besides, 1,000 seems like a more realistic number. If you added only one true fan a day, it might only take a few years to reach 1,000. You might calculate the value of a true fan by assessing the amount their support generates; for instance, 1,000 fans paying $100 for your product or service on an annual basis amounts to $100,000. With 1,000 fans in tow, the possibilities are endless. Imagine being able to persuade 1,000 people to come and dine at the restaurant you just opened, or holding a seminar for which 1,000 people have signed up and paid $200 to hear you speak.[35] Given that there are more than 7 billion people in the world, doesn't capturing 1,000 of them seem achievable?

But like everything worthwhile, the path to gaining your true fan base is not easy. It requires patience, consistency, and a keen focus on building long-term relationships. Entrepreneur and blogger Yaro Starak is a good example of someone who successfully garnered 1,000 true fans. He started his blog Entrepreneurs-Journey.com in 2005, with the intention of using it as a platform to share his own experiences of being an Internet

**TABLE 15.4**

Top 10 Mistakes to Avoid When Building Your First Website

| | |
|---|---|
| **Inaccessibility** | Make sure your website is available to everyone, including those with a disability. Can the size of the text be easily changed to cater to the visually impaired? Does your color scheme provide the right contrast between text and background design so the content can be easily viewed? |
| **Difficult-to-find contact information** | Some sites bury their contact information, which can be frustrating for people trying to get in touch. Easy-to-find contact information including a phone number and address is essential to new businesses, as it gives your site visitors the confidence that they are dealing with a genuine business, rather than a fraudulent one. |
| **Overusing the "wow" factor** | Flash can add pizzazz to your site but don't overdo it—not everyone has flash or even has enough bandwidth to support it. The same goes for graphics—use them sparingly as too many will slow down the functionality of your site. Similarly, don't go to town on audio and never let it play automatically—always let your visitors choose if they want to hear it or not. |
| **Slow load times** | We are an impatient bunch. A recent study by Akamai Technologies showed that on average, online shoppers will wait only 4 seconds for a website to load before doing their shopping elsewhere.[32] If your website is not loading within 4 seconds, then identify the elements that are slowing it down (Flash, large images, etc.) and remove them. |
| **Not getting picked up by search engines** | If you want to achieve higher rankings, you need to do at least the basics. These include a site map, concise and relevant content, use of standard mark-up tags that are recognized by search engines as well as meta tags such as keywords. Seek professional advice on this if you have the budget. |
| **Long sections of text** | A wall of text is difficult and frustrating to read online. Visitors want to see text in digestible chunks that they can scan quickly. To break up the text and to make it more user friendly, include subheads, bulleted lists, **highlighted keywords,** and short paragraphs—all written in jargon-free simple language. |
| **Poor navigation** | There is nothing more off-putting for online visitors than a disorganized, poorly structured site. The user experience should be as smooth as possible and populated by links and menus, all of which should work and should be frequently tested. Ask yourself how many clicks a visitor will need to access a piece of information on your site. Make their journey as easy and speedy as you can. |
| **Not monitoring your site** | There is no excuse for not keeping an eye on your site. There are many free tools available. They provide valuable insights into the type of visitors that your site attracts, including factors such as where they come from, what content they read the most, and what links are the most popular. |
| **Not updating your content** | Don't be one of those people whose site displays outdated information or creates blogs once in a blue moon. Frequently published fresh, new content is a way of building credibility with your audience. |
| **Failing to link to social platforms** | Your business will most likely have its own Facebook page, a Twitter and LinkedIn account, and maybe a Pinterest board. Visitors to your website should be able to move from your site to your social media presence as smoothly as possible, and vice versa. Connecting your social media to your website is essential to drive traffic to your site. |

**Source:** Scocco, D. (2007). 43 web design mistakes you should avoid. Retrieved from www.dailyblogtips.com

entrepreneur (Starak used to run a proofreading business and a card game website). Yet, more than a decade later, it has become his main source of income, generating more than a million dollars. Because of his commitment to sharing information, thousands of people have learned how to make a living out of blogging part time, and they have become loyal followers as a result. Table 15.5 outlines Starak's tips for building a fan base.

The point is that it's not only giants like Apple and Tesla than can generate a diehard fan base. In fact, many of the classic megabrands such as Levi, Gap, and Lee Jeans have either slowed down or are on the decline.[36] This phenomenon is known as the long tail theory, first introduced by journalist Chris Anderson (see Figure 15.6). The theory holds that the focus is shifting from mainstream products and services offered by big brands, positioned on the vertical axis at the head of the tail, toward a wide variety of smaller niche markets at the horizontal axis at the bottom of the tail. Why is this happening? Because the Internet has given rise to unlimited numbers of retail sites offering easily accessible, cheaper products. Fewer than a few decades ago, the big brands operating in all sorts of industries needed to create bestsellers and blockbusters mainly because the cost of distribution was high and the shelf space limited. But in today's economy, the

**TABLE 15.5**

How to Build Your Fan Base

| | |
|---|---|
| 1. | From the day you start your business, always have an email and newsletter opt-in form; the more people who join your newsletter, the more chance you will have of converting them into true fans. |
| 2. | Make sure you have the right mindset about the business you're going into; prepare to live and breathe your subject area every day and be confident about the content you are creating. |
| 3. | Watch other people in your industry and study the types of information they are sharing to keep up to date with your competition. |
| 4. | Maintain an ongoing dialogue with your audience; don't give them a reason to stray elsewhere. |
| 5. | Share your own unique stories and use those messages to build a community of followers. |
| 6. | Build relationships with other people who are willing to promote whatever you're selling. They could be journalists, bloggers, and other influencers. |
| 7. | When you're writing blogs, make sure you have an engaging headline. Also make sure to check out Facebook to find the most popular shared blogs. |
| 8. | Remember that people learn in different ways, so be prepared to use different types of social media such as Podcasts, imagery, and videos to promote your message and build a strong personal connection. |
| 9. | Stay in control of your content; your blog and your email list are two things that you own—they are the best ways to generate a buzz and garner your true fans. |
| 10. | When things don't work out, learn from your mistakes and keep moving forward. Perseverance is key to finding and maintaining your true fan base. |

**Source:** https://www.easyspace.com/blog/2014/10/01/interview-with-yaro-starak-founder-of-entrepreneurs-journey-com/

**FIGURE 15.6**

## The Long Tail Chart

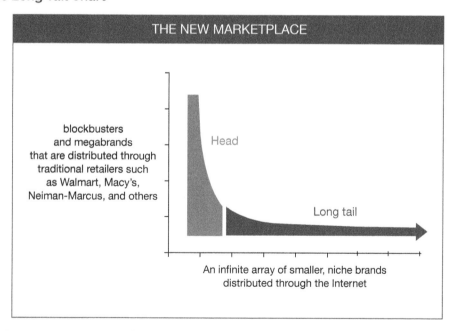

THE NEW MARKETPLACE

blockbusters and megabrands that are distributed through traditional retailers such as Walmart, Macy's, Neiman-Marcus, and others

Head

Long tail

An infinite array of smaller, niche brands distributed through the Internet

**Source:** https://www.forbes.com/sites/robinlewis/2016/05/31/the-long-tail-theory-can-be-reality-for-traditional-megabrands/#7fe46b4f6372>

Internet solves both problems, providing small businesses with a chance to take some market share away from the megabrands. Examples of today's most successful businesses that took advantage of the long tail include Amazon, which makes thousands of books available that otherwise wouldn't be found in bookstores; iTunes, which provides

# How Social Media Can Provide Marketing Headaches

As social media has only been around since the turn of the millennium, and new platforms pop up every year, the field of social media marketing is relatively new. Although it is easier than ever for companies to communicate with current and potential customers, social media marketing has also given rise to a number of horror stories. If a company's social media account becomes overly political, suggestive, or ill-humored, the repercussions can destabilize that company's credibility and hurt customer relations.

Social media is a new way for companies to market, and as such, it carries with it a number of ethical quandaries. First, is marketing to consumers healthy for them? According to a study from the journal *Psychological Reports: Disability and Trauma*, addictions to technology and social media share similar traits with substance and gambling addiction. Social media marketing, especially in a very engaging manner, can cause some harm to those who have difficulty controlling their relationship with social media.

However, there is a line to be drawn, and social media is quite often too valuable a tool to pass up. Creating an enticing social media presence can stray away from traditional marketing tactics, but how far can you take your marketing? Different brands like to stay conservative in the online, social sphere, while others attempt more intimate interactions. The decision on what path to take is up to the entrepreneur, and riskier campaigns can be pulled off. For example, Eggo teamed up with Netflix's *Stranger Things* to promote waffles and the show, tapping into audience interests. But, the pitfalls of taking a chance on social media campaigns can be dire. Playing politics in advertisements can be a dangerous game, and that only highlights the fact that all social media posts must be carefully considered.

## Critical Thinking Questions

1.  Is it fine to play politics with social media marketing, even if you know it caters to the target audience?

2.  How do companies create social media disasters? How much does a mistake impact the brand?

3.  Should a company have a strict review process in place before any social media posts are made live? ●

**Sources:**

Bergstrom, B. (2018, February 1). 24 creative social media campaign examples to boost your inspiration. *CoSchedule*. Retrieved from https://coschedule.com/blog/social-media-campaign-examples/

Conick, H. (2017, April 6). Marketing's ethical line between social media habit and addiction. *American Marketing Association*. Retrieved from https://www.ama.org/publications/MarketingNews/Pages/marketings-ethical-line-between-social-media-habit-addiction.aspx

niche music to people who prefer not to follow the mainstream; and Netflix, which has expanded the world of movies beyond the restrictions of a bricks-and-mortar retailer.[37] What does all this mean for entrepreneurs? That regardless of your product or service, there is a market for it, and if you can get 1,000 true fans to buy it from you, then you're well on your way to making a decent living.

## 15.5 CREATING YOUR PERSONAL BRAND

**>> LO 15.5  Practice marketing yourself.**

So far, we have focused on the role of marketing in entrepreneurship and the marketing tools available to entrepreneurs, the different ways of marketing new ventures through social media, and the importance of building your fan base. In this section, we will explore one of the most fundamental parts of marketing your business: marketing you, the entrepreneur.

At the early stages of a new venture, you are marketing yourself just as much as you are marketing a product, service, or company. This is why it is important for you to recognize that, from the beginning, you and your business are one. Most investors will invest in you first and foremost and not just in your idea. Investors will want to see that they can build a long-term relationship with you over a period of years and that you are capable of collaborating to build the business. This is why it is worth spending time figuring out how you're going to market yourself, and not just your company, before you pitch anything. Remember that when the time comes, pitching is a huge part of marketing yourself. In fact, the pitch is so important to "marketing the idea" that we've created an entire supplement on it! (See Supplement B: The Pitch Deck.)

As we learned in Chapter 8, research shows that people will unconsciously decide whether they like you or not within one-tenth of a second. People decide in fewer than 90 seconds whether they want to hear more about an idea or not, and it takes between 7 and 20 seconds to create a first impression.[38] So we have fewer than 20 seconds to make a good first impression and fewer than 90 seconds to engage our audience in our ideas. How you market yourself really matters.

Research shows that we have fewer than 20 seconds to make a good first impression.

Researchers conducted an experiment that compared first impressions with assessments built over a period of months. They compared the ratings given to college professors by students at the end of the semester with ratings of the same professors given by another group of students based on three 10-second video clips, which they were shown before the lectures. The results showed that both groups of students had pretty much the same opinions of the professors. This experiment indicates that a 10-second first impression gleaned from the second group of students was almost as powerful as the impressions the other students had derived while interacting with professors over the course of an entire semester. Such is the power of first impressions.[39]

Although we can train ourselves in what to say, we are often ill-prepared for how to say it. It is essential that you focus on other factors that could get in the way of conveying a positive first impression. For example, slouching while standing or sitting, avoiding eye contact, frowning, relying on technical jargon, reading slides, speaking too fast or too slowly, untidy physical appearance, and gesturing too much are all actions that can put off your audience. Research has shown that 93% of our communication is nonverbal:

- 55% of the message is conveyed through facial expression

- 38% of the message is conveyed through tone of voice

- 7% of the message is conveyed through words[40]

Another factor in nonverbal communication is the nonvisual dimension. We all see the world differently, so it pays to be aware of the different sensory learning styles of your audience in order to build a rapport. Numerous studies have shown that people learn information in different ways. For example, some are visual learners, while others are auditory or kinesthetic learners.[41] You can use these learning preferences to your advantage by using various kinds of media. For example, you might present a slide show with images. Ensuring that you describe your ideas and concepts clearly and confidently will appeal to auditory learners. If available, bring a prototype of your product along to give your audience something to touch and feel.

## How to Build Your Personal Brand

Creating a strong first impression is essential to building a sustainable personal brand (see Table 15.6). More and more often, we look at the people behind the companies rather than the companies themselves. For example, we associate Jeff Bezos with Amazon, Microsoft with Bill Gates, and Arianna Huffington with *The Huffington Post*. We know so much about them because they have such strong personal brands, which they leverage to attract more customers to buy their products and services. The point is that personal branding is always a part of a company's success. As growth marketer Kevin Payne said, "As an entrepreneur, by now you should know that business isn't conducted based solely on the products and services you provide, but by your character, integrity, and personal relationships you build with others. Remember people don't buy from businesses, they buy from people that they like."[42]

# How a Pitch Can Help Build Your Brand

What is the relationship between trust and early-stage investors' interest in investment during an entrepreneurial pitch? Is trust really a factor when it comes to investing, or do investors focus primarily on economic gains?

These are the questions Lakshmi Balachandra, a professor at Babson College, sought to answer. Balachandra carried out an experiment by studying 101 videos of entrepreneurs pitching to a network of angel investors from the Tech Coast Angels (TCA) in California—the largest angel group in the country. The results showed that trustworthiness displayed by entrepreneurs during the pitch had a direct impact on whether the angels would invest or not. In fact, angels who perceived trustworthiness were 10% more likely to invest. Angels were also more likely to rate "coachability" three times more important than competence during the trustworthiness assessments. For instance, investors will have more confidence that they can help "coach"—or make up any skills that are lacking—if the entrepreneur comes across as being trustworthy.

Other factors that led to an assessment of trustworthiness included the number of meaningful social network connections; the ability for entrepreneurs to accept suggestions, critique, and feedback; and commonalities between the angels and the entrepreneurs, such as background and expertise. It is clear from this research that entrepreneurs need to demonstrate trustworthiness while pitching.

## Critical Thinking Questions

1. Give some reasons why trustworthiness is so important to potential investors.

2. Explain the relationship between trustworthiness and coachability. How can an entrepreneur demonstrate coachability during the pitch?

3. What are some ways you can demonstrate trustworthiness during a pitch? ●

**Sources:**

Balachandra, L. (2011). *Pitching trustworthiness: Cues for trust in early-stage investment decision making* (Unpublished doctoral dissertation). Carroll School of Management, Chestnut Hill, MA.
How venture capitalists really assess a pitch. (2017). *Harvard Business Review*, May-June, 25–28.

---

**TABLE 15.6**

Tips for Building Your Personal Brand

| |
|---|
| • Be authentic: Be honest about your attributes and qualities. Think about your strengths, passions, values, and beliefs and use them to promote a strong brand foundation. |
| • Be visible: Focus on increasing your visibility internally and externally. In addition to publishing content on your own online platform, increase your exposure to more people by guest speaking on podcasts, guest blogging, and applying to speak at conferences. |
| • Build a brand vision: Think about what you want to be an expert on; what you want to be known for. |
| • Write down your brand mission: Note why you want to build a personal brand, the people you want to influence, and what you want to accomplish. |
| • Consider your brand personality: Think about the personal characteristics you can draw on to build your brand. For instance, do you want to be seen as quirky and humorous or more formal and businesslike? |
| • Learn to influence: Draw on whatever personal power or network you have and use your influence in a positive way to promote your personal brand. |
| • Be unique: Don't be tempted to copy someone else's personal brand, even if it is someone you admire. Remember, it is your uniqueness that will differentiate you from your competitors. |

**Sources:** Basu, T. (n.d.). How to build a personal brand (complete guide to personal branding). *Thinkific*. Retrieved from https://www.thinkific.com/blog/personal-branding-guide/; Payne, K. (n.d.). *Personal branding for entrepreneurs*. Retrieved from https://kevintpayne.com/personal-branding-for-entrepreneurs/

Successful entrepreneurs build a personal brand based on trust and authority, attract more customers, gain more media exposure and attention, and create a lasting platform that secures a loyal following of people they want to impact most. ●

**$SAGE edge™**

Get the tools you need to sharpen your study skills. SAGE edge offers a robust online environment featuring an impressive array of free tools and resources.

- Access practice quizzes, eFlashcards, video, and multimedia at
  **edge.sagepub.com/neckentrepreneurship2e**

**15.1   Discuss entrepreneurial marketing and explain how it is different from traditional marketing.**

Entrepreneurial marketing is a set of processes adopted by entrepreneurs based on new and unconventional marketing practices to gain traction and attention in competitive markets.

In the past, marketing was largely based on interruption and coercion. Today's marketing is really about building relationships, engaging with people, and creating a community. The new marketing rules focus on participation and content to build a successful business.

**15.2   Explain the principles of marketing and how they apply to new ventures.**

The right product, in the right place, at the right price, at the right time. For entrepreneurs, this extends to identifying needs, serving those needs, communicating the value proposition, supplying the product or service, and supporting the customer relationship from then on.

**15.3   Describe branding and the importance of building a brand.**

Branding is the process of creating a name, term, design, symbol, or any other feature that identifies a product or service and differentiates it from others. Branding is important because people are more likely to invest in brands that they have an emotional connection to, are trustworthy, are worth spending money on, are fashionable, and are adept at meeting their needs.

**15.4   Discuss the different types of marketing tools available to entrepreneurs.**

There is a wide range of entrepreneurial marketing tools available to budget-conscious entrepreneurs. Some of these tools include: building a brand, guerrilla marketing, social media marketing, designing a website, and building a fan base.

**15.5   Practice marketing yourself.**

Creating a strong first impression is essential to building a sustainable personal brand. Successful entrepreneurs build a personal brand based on trust and authority, attract more customers, gain more media exposure and attention, and create a lasting platform that secures a loyal following of people that they want to impact most.

| | | |
|---|---|---|
| Brand strategy   386 | Marketing mix   384 | Price   384 |
| Branding   386 | Packaging   386 | Product   384 |
| Entrepreneurial marketing   381 | People   386 | Promotion   385 |
| Guerrilla marketing   393 | Place   385 | True fans   398 |
| Marketing   384 | Positioning   386 | |

## Justin Real, founder, Realplay

The Realplay story is evidence that an entrepreneur markets himself before marketing his company. Realplay is a LinkedIn-style platform for amateur baseball and softball players that connects players, coaches, and recruiters through automatically generated video and statistics. The platform, consisting of on-field cameras and an image-recognition system, is designed as an easy-to-use amateur sports solution that edits a game and uploads every at-bat video to a player's profile page through a machine learning algorithm. Players have access to their own videos, coaches use videos to help players improve, and recruiters have a larger pool of prospects.

Every kid wants to make it to the majors and Justin Real was no different. As Justin explained, "I played college baseball, been playing baseball my whole life. My first job was working at a batting cage for 3 years teaching kids how to play baseball. *This* is my life." And so Realplay was born in 2016 out of a deep love for baseball, past experiences, a fascination with the possibilities of AI, a rock-solid financial model, and a problem that wasn't being solved very well. Players liked watching themselves play; parents wanted to preserve memories; coaches wanted to develop the best players; and recruiters wanted to find those players. The solution before Realplay? Low-quality video, unconnected video, no data, and video storage issues. Realplay became a high-quality, user-friendly solution for different stakeholders with different needs who all wanted access to the same information—the information that Justin could automate, tag, and post.

Justin Real thought he was going to be a successful consultant. He liked working on different projects and different companies in different industries. "The idea of dedicating your life to one job, one product was not something I saw myself doing," said Justin. One consulting project he worked on involved the potential development of a brainwave scanner helmet for baseball players that could measure the neurological effects of the "chess match" between a pitcher and a batter. Justin was hired to test the market, see how customers would react to the product, and what go-to-market strategies would be effective. As Justin recalled, "I kept getting the 'why are you doing this?' questions. I learned that why and how pitchers and batters react was not as important as the data and the visualization. I also learned a lot about how it was currently being done." What players and coaches wanted were statistics based on pitches and at-bats, but more than anything, the most important thing was literally *seeing* how they react and the patterns in those reactions. "How much they could see mattered," noted Justin. The helmet never went anywhere, but Justin identified an opportunity to do something that was sort of being done, but do it better, faster, and using innovative business structures that hadn't been tried yet.

Realplay installs proprietary camera systems at high school fields and multifield sport complexes. Baseball and softball combined are the most popular sport being played in the United States. Additionally, as Justin recalls, "High school and summer travel ball were the markets that were the least served by other video companies and seemed like the right market to be in for Realplay." The camera systems are installed at the beginning of the season so video can be captured at every home game. Unlike other camera solutions, Realplay cameras provide video footage from three different angles of specific players, tailored to the time they spend on the field. Using AI and machine learning, the cameras track a player by his or her jersey number, which makes the process of video editing more efficient. "What used to take 9 hours of human labor per game, we can do in 15 minutes."

Justin's experience in baseball outweighed his experience in technology. However, he had several jobs in technology where he learned the invaluable skill of taking a high-tech product and "dumbing it down so that I could explain it to people who needed to use it but didn't want to hear the technical jargon behind it. I was also then able to communicate what their needs were to the people who were actually designing the technology." While earning his MBA at Babson, he took technology courses and also enrolled in online courses at MIT to better understand computer vision, machine learning, and AI. Through networking, Justin eventually found his CTO, Andreas Randow, an ex-pat German who could bring the technology from Justin's whiteboard to the real world. According to Justin, "He is an expert in data visualization and machine learning the way that I am an expert in baseball. He has never played a day of baseball in his life. But the two of us came up with a solution that is unmatched by any technology company or baseball company!"

As Justin worked to raise capital to develop the platform and camera systems, he also learned the importance of developing the perfect pitch. He knew in the early stages that he was working to sell himself as a trustworthy and committed entrepreneur just as much as he was trying to sell his solution and vision. "The easiest pitch in the world is to describe an existing business. The more far away from reality the description of the business is, the lesser it will be believed and less you can back that pitch up as an entrepreneur."

Justin gives the example of running a bagel business to elaborate on the need to build reality into your pitch. "Let's say your business claims to sell the best bagels in the world. Someone will ask you how you do it. That question really means 'what is your business?' The answer to this question needs to be unflinchingly based in reality because any deviation from that will make it sound exponentially worse. If someone answers that question saying, 'We put the most love into our bagels, and we care deeply about our customers' that only answers *why* the business is good but *not* how it operates. That does not answer *why* the business works. So, taking that approach, what I've been doing is cutting off what we want to do and replacing it with what we actually do and why it works." For Justin, this recipe has impressed all those he meets because he is believable, authentic, and very much understands and is able to communicate what makes Realplay work.

Justin stresses that it is not the job of the pitcher to sell what the business is trying to do, but rather what it can do now. "Any information that focuses on the opportunity of a business should be based on fact and not conviction," says Justin. The pitch should clearly articulate operations and in a way that helps investors envision the bigger picture and potential impact of the business. If they understand the traction you have now, they can understand the potential in the future.

The focus of the pitch should also be on why the entrepreneur is so excited about the opportunity because it's difficult to separate the opportunity from the entrepreneur in the beginning. For Justin, it was important to build a story of what he has done, the customers he has acquired, the testing that was done, the feedback received. What work is still needed to do? All of this ties back to the facts of the business as well as the reality of who is running the business. "No one is going to back your idea if you don't have a business. It's really simple: If you can't answer how do you make your money, how much money do you need, and how much money the investor will get in 5 years, all in one sentence each, you don't have a business; you might have an idea, but you don't have a business."

Testing the pitch led Justin to create numerous iterations of the pitch. With each iteration, he added more clarity, more facts, more evidence, more realistic financial projections. With each new day of operational experience came stronger evidence of how the business operates. "When people poke holes in your pitch, they are probably right. Acknowledge that and the only way one can overcome that is by irrefutable evidence that you are right in what you're saying." Over time, his pitch became very comprehensive, so much so that he didn't feel the need to keep changing the pitch for different audiences. According to Justin, "The only time the pitch actually changes is if the ask of the pitch changes."

The following anecdote illustrates how effective Justin is in marketing himself before his business. He held a meeting for a group of investors so they could all be together in the same room while he made a formal pitch to all of them at the same time. He did this because he felt that people are likely to poke holes in the argument and question the execution of the project. He wanted to have a formal event that would allow him to get through a full pitch. Not just that, he wanted prospective investors to meet people who had already invested in Realplay. This would create an opportunity for current investors to be more candid with potential investors and tell them why they had already invested. After a lot of coordination and communication over LinkedIn, Justin organized the event in downtown Boston for this group of investors in the fall of 2018. As Justin recalled, "One thing that the event was able to showcase was that I have the capability to get a group of very qualified people in a room to listen to what I have to say. I also believe that pitching in a setting like this where the social effect, the business side of things, and the full story come together is more effective."

In May 2019, after 4 years of bootstrapping, Justin received $750k investment in a round led by LaunchPad Ventures and is using that money for operations and scaling. Time will tell whether Realplay succeeds in the long term. It's still early. But one thing is for certain: Justin Real is a success because he focused on building a business that reflects who he is, what he values, and what he loves. That makes selling Realplay very easy.

## Critical Thinking Questions

1. Why is selling yourself just as important as selling your concept, in the early stages of a venture?

2. How is a pitch part of marketing your venture?

3. What is the difference between a good pitch and a good idea?

4. Would you invest in Realplay today? Why or why not?

**Sources:**

Justin Real (interview with Babson MBA graduate assistant Gaurav Khemka, January 18, 2019)

Realplay. (2019). *Crunchbase.* Retrieved from https://www.crunchbase.com/organization/realplay

# SUPPLEMENT B
# THE PITCH DECK

## Chapter Outline

## Learning Objectives

## B.1 TYPES OF PITCHES

>> **LO B.1**  **Describe the pitch process and different types of pitches.**

Every entrepreneur must have a pitch, and it can take many forms. However, what's common across all forms are two outcomes: (1) the receiver of the pitch understands your business and (2) the receiver is compelled to learn more. Whether you have 30 seconds or 30 minutes to pitch, these two outcomes are essential. Some pitches are more informal, without any presentation material besides yourself, while others are formal and require a pitch deck. A pitch deck is a presentation in PowerPoint (or a similar presentation software) that describes in detail the nature of the business, the need, the customer, the business model, profit potential, team, and call to action. But before getting to the pitch deck, let's look at the different types of pitches.

Dan Pink, in his book *To Sell Is Human,* gives a description of the first elevator pitch ever! He shares the story of Elisha Otis, who founded Otis Elevator Company in 1853. Contrary to popular belief, Otis didn't invent the elevator, but he did invent a much safer elevator. Before Otis, elevators were used to move materials from one floor to another, rather than people. The problem was that elevators were unreliable because the ropes would break, the platform would fall, and all contents would be destroyed. During the World's Fair in New York in 1854, Otis was looking to spread the word and get interest in his invention. So he gathered attendees and gave them a demonstration. With Otis standing on a platform common to most elevators at the time, his team hoisted him three stories into the air. Otis then abruptly took an axe and cut the ropes that were holding the platform in place. The platform started to fall, but Otis's invention, the safety brake, engaged and prevented the platform from falling to the ground. This demonstration of how his product worked is the most important take away from the concept of an elevator pitch. According to Dan Pink, "It was a simple, succinct, and effective way to convey a complex message in an effort to move others."[1]

Since the days of Otis, "elevator pitch" has evolved into a metaphor for a short pitch. For the past few decades, the elevator pitch was the standard way to pitch an idea. This meant that if you happened to find yourself in an elevator with someone important, you would be able to pitch your idea from the time of the doors closing to when they opened again. The idea was to use this short amount of time (less than 1 minute) to explain why your business was exciting and unique. Today, thanks to a more democratic working

**Master the content at**
**edge.sagepub.com/**
**neckentrepreneurship2e**

structure that allows us easier access to influential people, and new technology that provides us with a whole set of tools to get in touch with others, the elevator pitch has evolved into several different forms. What's interesting now is that speed and brevity are even more important than ever. Table B.1 identifies pitch approaches that are even shorter than an elevator ride.[2]

Spend some time trying to apply the approaches in Table B.1 to your own business idea. The work done here will only help you when it's time to create your full pitch deck. For each of these approaches, and really any type of pitch you do, you need to answer three questions in advance:

What do you want the receiver of the pitch to know?

What do you want the receiver of the pitch to feel?

What do you want the receiver of the pitch to do?

Most of the pitch types described in Table B.1 are self-explanatory, but the Pixar pitch deserves a bit more explanation because it's a "storytelling" approach and the ability to tell a story is an essential skill of all entrepreneurs.

## The Storytelling Approach

Regardless of your audience, it is essential that you articulate your idea clearly and tell a compelling story. Indeed, storytelling is part of our nature, and it is a powerful way of engaging and connecting with people.[4] Many of us make decisions based on stories that move or inspire us. Opening a pitch with "I have a story to tell" immediately alerts the audience that you have something to say that is interesting, personal, compelling, dramatic, and complete.

### TABLE B.1

Pitch Types Shorter Than an Elevator Ride!

| TYPE | DESCRIPTION | EXAMPLES |
|------|-------------|----------|
| The one-word pitch | Identify the one word that describes the business | Google: Search<br>Obama U.S. presidential campaign: Hope |
| The question pitch | Ask one question that can evoke emotion and compel people to respond | Uber: Are you tired of filthy taxis that you have to flag down in the middle of a rainstorm? |
| The rhyming pitch | Rhymes help the message stick | Five Guys: Five Guys burgers and fries |
| The subject-line pitch | The email subject line that is useful, specific, and evokes curiosity | Venture Blocks: Your students can learn how to interview customers in 30 minutes |
| The Twitter pitch | A message that is 140 characters or less | Babson College: Come join the only college that educates entrepreneurial leaders who generate economic and social value—EVERYWHERE |
| The Pixar pitch | Tell a complete story in six sentences | Toy Story: *Once upon a time,* there was a boy named Andy who loved to play with his toys. *Every day* when Andy wasn't around, the toys would come to life. *One day,* Andy got a new toy, Buzz Lightyear, that became his and all the other toys' favorite. *Because of that,* Woody became jealous and tried to get rid of Buzz Lightyear. *Because of that,* Buzz ended up at Sid's house and was almost destroyed. *But then,* Woody and the other toys rescued Buzz, and they all became friends.[3] |

Most stories are based on a three-part narrative arc, which can be traced back to ancient Greece and the stories of the philosopher Aristotle. Aristotle's arc still applies to storytelling today: an introduction that presents the characters and ideas; the climax that outlines the problem at its height and how your solution can overcome the most complex of issues; and the resolution that explains how you expect things to work out.[5]

A story will be successful only if it is authentic and is told with genuine enthusiasm and energy. Starbucks founder Howard Schultz is known as an excellent storyteller who has used examples drawn from his personal life to ignite passion in others. According to Schultz, the philosophy behind Starbucks was based on his father's failure to find any meaning or fulfillment in his work. When his father ended up with a work injury and no compensation or health insurance, Schultz vowed that he would create the type of company that he could feel passionate about—one that both inspires and takes care of its staff.[6]

The Pixar pitch can be useful for explaining business ventures, even though this approach was designed to tell the story of a movie in six sentences.[7] Every movie made by Disney Pixar follows a narrative structure that can be summed up by the six chronological sentences outlined in Table B.2.

Let's now apply the Pixar pitch to a business called Attack! Marketing. Attack! is a marketing agency that provides experiential strategy and activation to lifestyle brands.[8] In other words, it takes the human approach to marketing by offering opportunities for people to taste, touch, and smell the products to inspire brand loyalty.

- Once upon a time, advertising agencies and brands in the United States were focusing solely on the concept of the campaign.

- Every day, millions of dollars would be spent on data collection, giveaways, and logistics, which neglected to engage the customer in a meaningful way, resulting in low trial rates and conversion numbers.

- One day, we developed a business called Attack! that revolutionized the consumer experience by introducing the human element, allowing consumers to taste, touch, and smell the products during live marketing events.

- Because of that, more consumers fell in love with the brand.

- Because of that, agencies saw a significant increase in the number of people who tried out the products and services and more conversions.

- Until finally, the Attack! philosophy became so widely accepted we were labelled as the pioneers in this approach.

The longer the pitch, the more important it is to tell a good story. The key to telling a good story is to tell the right story to the right audience. This involves understanding what type of people they are. Do your research. Who are they? What are their wants and needs? What is the best way of moving them? Don't be afraid to make your pitch

**TABLE B.2**

Six-Sentence Pitch Structure

| 1. Once upon a time, . . . |
| --- |
| 2. Every day, . . . |
| 3. One day, . . . |
| 4. Because of that, . . . |
| 5. Because of that, . . . |
| 6. Until finally, . . . |

interactive by asking your audience for input—this makes them feel part of the story, and it will encourage them to become more engaged with your idea.[9]

In fact, successful pitches all have to do with drawing people in and moving them in some way. A study of the Hollywood pitch process conducted by Kimberly Elsbach of the University of California and Roderick Kramer of Stanford University showed that when pitchers invited studio executives to collaborate on an idea, there was a better chance of the project being green lit.[10] However, pitches were unsuccessful when the pitcher didn't listen or was unwilling to accept feedback or constructive criticism. Bringing people into your story and allowing them to participate is a powerful way of getting the buy-in you need. Everybody wants to be a part of something new and exciting, and everybody wants to feel like they had a part in its creation. That is why entrepreneurship is so enticing for so many—entrepreneurs, advisors, investors, employees, and even customers.

# B.2 OVERVIEW OF THE PITCH DECK

>> **LO B.2**   **Describe the pitch deck and its importance to potential investors.**

As mentioned above, a pitch deck is a presentation in PowerPoint (or a similar presentation software) that describes in detail the nature of the business, the need or problem it solves, industry characteristics, the customer, the market size, the business model, profit potential, team, and call to action. Keep in mind that it's usually impossible to get everything into a pitch, so your goal is to make sure the receiver is intrigued and interested enough to want to know more—to want to meet again. As highlighted in Chapter 10, there are many types of plans, and a pitch deck has become a visual and oral plan. In the past decade, the pitch deck has become one of the most valuable tools an entrepreneur can have when trying to raise startup capital or find other types of resources. A pitch deck is a good way to describe your business to a potential investor; it can also be used for meetings with potential partners, advisors, employees, or even a reporter who might be doing a story on your startup! Any stakeholder who has a vested interest in your business could be an audience for your pitch.

There are no strict rules for pitch deck length or style. For example, some people suggest that the pitch deck should have only 5 slides while others recommend 6, 10, 11, 12, 15, or even 30 slides.[11] Regardless of the slide count or style, all pitch decks need to answer the same fundamental questions:

- What is the problem/need?
- How will you solve the problem or meet the need in a unique way?
- Who is the customer, and are there enough customers to build a viable venture?
- What is the size/extent of the market for this product/service idea now and in the future?
- How will you reach, acquire, and keep the customer?
- Whom will you compete with, and how are you different?
- What is the revenue/expense model?
- What capabilities does your team have to execute the venture?
- What have you done so far?
- What is your call to action?

Typically, an initial meeting with a possible investor will be 30 minutes to 1 hour, but you should not use all of this time to present. Generally your pitch should not exceed 20 minutes, but different situations call for different pitch lengths. For this reason, we suggest being prepared to give a 1-, 3-, 10-, 15-, and 20-minute version. Whatever time is allotted for your pitch, it's important to leave room for questions. One of the biggest mistakes entrepreneurs make during a pitch is failing to leave time for questions at the end of the pitch.[12] If you can anticipate the questions in advance, it is also smart to create some backup slides with the answers to show that you have done your homework.

# B.3 THE PITCH DECK

While there is no one "right" pitch deck format, we have provided you with a basic template to follow that will help answer the essential questions. We use the company India in a Box, introduced in Chapter 10, as a pitch deck example. If you recall, India in a Box uses a subscription model to deliver authentic Indian meals that can be prepared by customers in minutes.

## Slide 1: Title

The title slide should include the name of the company, logo, your name, and contact information (see Figure B.1). This is the first slide your audience will see and will likely be on screen the longest while they wait for you to present. Don't be boring here. Pay attention to slide design. In addition, consider putting your name and company on every slide so your audience will remember you and your company.

## Slide 2: Company Purpose/Description

The purpose or vision slide is a quick overview of your company (see Figure B.2). Why does your company exist? Develop one sentence that describes what your company does. For example, it is a useful exercise to fill in the following blanks:

_____ [company] is _____ [product/service] for

_____ [target market] that _____ [problem].

For example: FlowDog *is* an aquatic and rehabilitation center *for* dogs *that* suffer from physical injuries.

_____ [company] sells _____ [product/

service] to _____ [target market] in order to _____ [solution].

For example: VentureBlocks *sells* computer-based simulations *to* educators *in order to* help teach core topics related to entrepreneurship.

---

**FIGURE B.1**

**Example Title Slide**

---

**Source:** Shyam Devnani (Contact information has been removed for publication.)

**FIGURE B.2**

### Example Company Purpose/Description Slide

**Source:** Shyam Devnani

You could also include a comparison with a widely known brand, which will help the listener to immediately grasp the concept. For example, "We are the Uber for pets" or "we are the Netflix for video games."[13] Remember from Table B.1, these short pitches could come in handy as you prepare the opening for your pitch deck.

## Slide 3: The Problem/Need

Describe the problem that your company is solving or how you are addressing a customer need (Figure B.3). Additionally, you should describe how the problem is currently being solved by other companies, and point out any inefficiencies in how it is being solved, or why the existing solutions are insufficient. Keep in mind that you need to prove to your audience that the problem is a big one. As venture capitalist Skylar Fernandes says, you need to solve the customer's #1 problem—not the #10 problem![14]

## Slide 4: The Solution

The solution is really your value proposition, because if you can solve the customer's problem or fulfill their need in a unique way, then you are already creating value. Don't just type the solution on a slide, as in Figure B.4. If possible, offer a live demonstration. If the product or service is not yet fully developed, show a prototype or a picture of a prototype. If the solution is web-based, a mockup landing page is a must.

Another option is to show a **use case**—a methodology used in the software industry to illustrate how a user will interact with a specific piece of software.[15] Figure B.5 illustrates a use case to show how easy it is to prepare a meal from India in a Box. For entrepreneurs, use cases are also a good way of showing an audience how customers will interact with their products or services and how their lives are made easier through the interaction.

**Use case:** a methodology used in the software industry to illustrate how a user will interact with a specific piece of software.

## Slide 5: Why Now?

There is a window of opportunity for many new ventures. You need to convince your audience that the time is now for your new product or service. This means pointing out trends or changes that prove that your company is timely (see sample slide in Figure B.6).

**FIGURE B.3**

## Example Problem/Need Slide

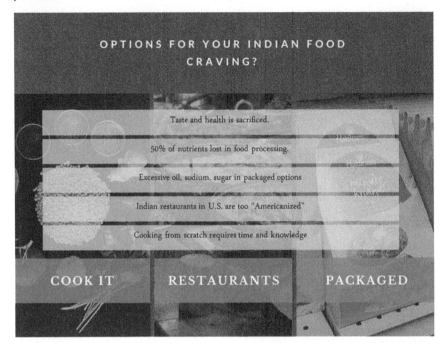

**Source:** Shyam Devnani

**FIGURE B.4**

## Example Solution Slides

**Source:** Shyam Devnani

**FIGURE B.5**

## Use Case Highlighting Cooking Instructions

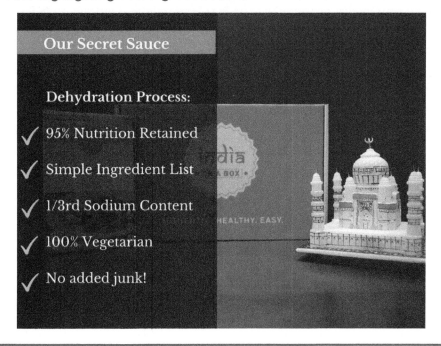

**Source:** Shyam Devnani

**FIGURE B.6**

## Example Why Now? Slide

**Source:** Shyam Devnani

## Slide 6: Market Opportunity

As we discussed in Chapter 6: Developing Your Customers, the solution is powerful only if there is a market of customers willing to pay for the product or service. When it comes to creating your market opportunity slide, it is important to think about the three sub-groups of the market: TAM, SAM, and SOM (see 6.7: Market Sizing in Chapter 6). As a brief reminder:

- **TAM**, or total available market, refers to the total market demand for a product or service.

- **SAM**, or serviceable available market, is the section of the TAM that your product or service intends to target.

- **SOM**, or share of market, is the portion of SAM that your company is realistically likely to reach.

It is important for investors to see that you have thought through TAM, SAM, and SOM, so they have a better idea of the fraction of the market you intend to target. If you cannot prove that you have a good chance of penetrating the local market, then they will be unable to see the growth potential of your business.

## Slide 7: Getting Customers

After depicting the market size and showing the target market, it is essential that you demonstrate an understanding of your customers—who they are and how you will reach them (see Chapter 6). This is where you talk about your interactions with customers and what you have learned about them during the planning process.

Using the café and donut example above, it's not enough to simply describe that your target market consists of 125,000 people living in a particular geographic area within the city of Baton Rouge. You also need to show that you have done your homework to better understand what kinds of people are likely to go to a café that serves high-end coffee and funky, gourmet donuts!

**FIGURE B.7**

**Example Getting Customers Slide**

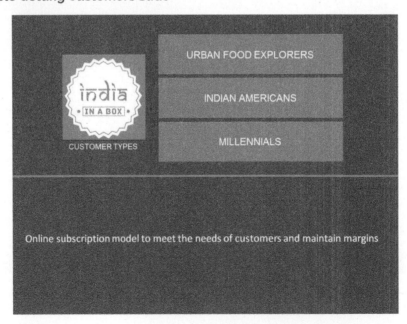

**Source:** Shyam Devnani

Additionally, you need to articulate how you will reach those customers, what they are willing to pay, and how you intend to keep them coming back (Figure B.7). Here you can begin to really build a market size number in terms of dollars using a simple calculation:

number of customers × price × frequency of purchase = market size $

You can do this calculation for a day, week, month, or year, and it should connect to your overall financials. Let's think about this for a single day. On an average day you may anticipate that 300 customers will enter the café and the average receipt based on 1 coffee and 1 donut is $7.50. Three hundred customers x $7.50 x 1 purchase = $2,250 total receipts for an average day. If there are 30 days in a month, then total monthly receipts could be $67,500. As a result the annual revenue could be $810,000.

## Slide 8: Competitor Analysis and Differentiation

The competitor analysis shows how your company differentiates itself from others providing similar solutions, or how it has carved out a unique space that fulfills unmet needs. Competition is a good thing because it shows that there is a market for products and services. The key is to show how you are doing something better, different, and more compelling. A strong analysis will show the audience your competitive advantage—the source of why or how you will outperform others.

The competitive grid analysis compares your company to your most significant competitors and details their strengths and weaknesses relative to your own business. Figure B.8 illustrates an example of a competitive grid analysis for a new business called Best Cuts, comparing it to two different competing hair salons in terms of pricing, capacity, location, and other attributes.

---

**FIGURE B.8**

---

**Example of Competitive Grid Analysis**

### Competitive Grid

| Competitor | Bobo Salon and Styling | Johnny's Hair | BEST CUTS |
|---|---|---|---|
| Offerings | Men's/women's cut/styles/color perms | Men's cuts only | Men's/ women's cut/ style/ color/ perms |
| Service Prices | Starts at $38 | Starts at $50 | Starts at $30 |
| Retail Prices | 100% markup | 100% markup | 75% markup |
| Location | High traffic, highly visible | Moderate traffic, highly visible | High traffic, not visible |
| Expertise | 20+years, up-to-date trends | 15+ years, young hairstylists | 13+ years, up-to-date trends |
| Service | Set hours, little schedule flexibility | Manager never there | Custom hours to suit clients needs |
| Turnover | Low | High | Sole stylist |
| Capacity | 11 active chairs | 8 active chairs | 1 active chair |
| Client Base | Over 4000 | ? | Over 300 |

---

**Source:** http://www.slideshare.net/smarty23b/sample-business-plan-presentation2)

Another way to compare your company with the competition is to use a positioning matrix illustrating how you intend to position your business relative to the competition. Figure B.9 illustrates this concept with the Gourmet Donut Co. example.

The competitive matrix positions your company relative to the competition on selected variables. In Figure B.9, we look at the competition for the Gourmet Donut Co. based on price and flavors. Other possible variables could be price and quality or flavors and healthfulness of ingredients such as processed versus all natural. But in the example here, we will stick with price and flavors. After analyzing the competition in the Baton Rouge market, you can see that there are five donut shops that offer basic flavors of donuts at a low price, such as Dunkin' Donuts and Krispy Kreme. Their coffee is priced low as well. Starbucks and CC's offer expensive donuts, though basic flavors, and high-end coffee. You can see from the matrix that Gourmet Donut Co. is positioning itself very differently with its gourmet flavors.

Showing that you have done your homework on the competition is essential. One of the worst mistakes entrepreneurs can make in a pitch is claiming they have no competition. You will always have competition, and how you define that competition is important (see Figure B.10). Remember when you acquire customers you are taking them away from someone or something else. Who is that someone or something else? For example, before there was iTunes, there were music stores. Though iTunes was a great innovation, it still had competition.

## Slide 9: Traction

Traction describes all the work you've done to date to build your venture. Your audience, especially investors, want to see the actions you have taken to construct your venture and the milestones you have achieved. Examples of traction include the following:

- Early customer adoption and showing you have revenue
- Completion of customer research
- Working website
- Working prototype or minimum viable product

**FIGURE B.9**

**Gourmet Donut Co. Competitive Positioning**

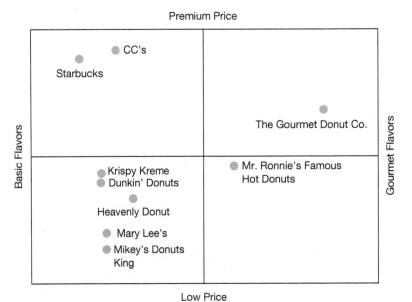

**FIGURE B.10**

**Example Competitor Analysis and Differentiation Slide**

**Source:** Shyam Devnani

- Submission of patent application

- Formation of team

- Product testing

- Contracting of suppliers

- Creation of first batch of product

- Successful crowdfunding campaign (where relevant)

- Securing of space (in the case of retail)

- Securing of investment or loans

Other evidence of traction includes recognition and press. For example, if you have won pitch competitions or been mentioned in blogs, magazines, TV shows, or other media, then you can talk about it here.

You could also include your future milestones or planned next steps. These could include expansion into new locations or overseas, the number of customers you intend to reach, or hiring more staff and employees. See Figure B.11 for an example of a traction slide.

## Slide 10: Financials

In Chapter 13: Financing for Startups, we explored some options for financing. Your financials need to demonstrate that you have a clear understanding of potential profit and loss. It's important to highlight the key drivers of revenue and expenses, but keep it at the highest levels for now. In other words, you should not present a detailed income statement, cash-flow statement, and balance sheet (see Supplement A for further explanation), but you do need to show at least 3 years of revenue projections. Be realistic with these projections, and explain the assumptions underlying the projections. Have backup slides of detailed financials in case you are asked about them during the question and answer period.

In Figure B.12, Shyam shows 3-year profit potential for India in a Box. You may also want to consider showing three different scenarios, such as best case, worst case, and likely case. This shows investors and others that you are trying to be as realistic as possible with your projections.

### FIGURE B.11

#### Example Traction Slide

**Source:** Shyam Devnani

### FIGURE B.12

#### Example Financials Slide

| | YEAR 1 | YEAR 2 | YEAR 3 |
|---|---|---|---|
| REVENUE | $261,000 | $ 820,000 | $ 2,540,000 |
| EXPENSES | $ 132,000 | $ 343,000 | $ 980,000 |
| GROSS PROFIT | $ 129,000 | $ 477,000 | $ 1,560,000 |
| SG&A | $ 84,000 | $ 225,000 | $ 530,000 |
| NET PROFIT | $45,000 | $252,000 | $1,030,000 |

61% GROSS PROFIT MARGIN | $1 Million PROFIT YEAR 3

**Source:** Shyam Devnani

## Slide 11: Team

Showing you have a strong team with the right skillsets is more important than you might think. Your audience may not be convinced that the opportunity is there, but if the team is strong, then it's more likely that the team will be able to pivot as necessary to give the business the best possible chance for success.[16] The team slide should include a list of all team members, providing photos, their experience and education, and their role in the company (see Figure B.13). It's important that the team slide makes the audience think to themselves, "Yes, the team can actually do this. And, if they can't, they have the ability to pivot if necessary." If you have an advisory board, then include those names as well. Talent attracts other talent. So if you have an amazing team, you might even consider moving this slide to the beginning of your presentation. See Chapter 8 for more on building quality teams.

## Slide 12: Call to Action

The call to action is the most often-forgotten slide! It doesn't matter if you are pitching to a venture capitalist, an angel investor, an audience in a pitch competition, your professor, a friend, your class, or your grandmother, you must always have a call to action (Figure B.14). By this point, you've likely spent about 15 minutes presenting your idea. So now it's time to ask for something.

What you ask for depends on your audience. If you are presenting to an investor, you are probably asking for money. If this is the case, then you need to say how you plan to use the money. For example: "I'm asking for $200,000 for 20% of the company. The money invested will primarily be used for . . . (e.g., building out the sales channel, customer acquisition through marketing, packaging, redesign, hiring)." If you are pitching to your classmates, you might be asking for feedback on the idea. If you are pitching to your professor, you might be asking him or her to act as an advisor. If so, then tell your professor what you are looking for in an advisor. If you need team members, ask for them, but be specific in the skillsets you are looking for. The bottom line is, don't ever pitch without asking for something at the end because you could be missing a major opportunity.

**FIGURE B.13**

**Example Team Slide**

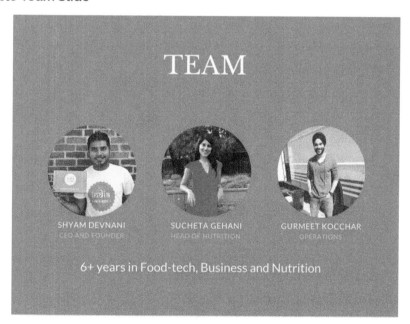

**Source:** Shyam Devnani

**FIGURE B.14**

**Example Call to Action Slides**

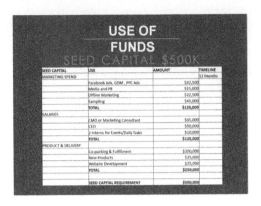

**Source:** Shyam Devnani

# B.4 THE QUESTION AND ANSWER PERIOD

>> **LO B.4**   **Anticipate and prepare for the types of questions that may be asked during the question and answer period.**

During the question and answer period (Q&A) at the end of your presentation, the title slide should be showing. As we mentioned earlier, it is also useful to have a series of backup slides that can help you answer the most anticipated questions. In addition, you will likely pitch to more than one audience, so remember to incorporate answers to new questions that may have arisen in previous meetings.

For pitches in front of investors, or applications to incubators, or pitch competitions, you can be sure that some of the following questions will be asked.[17]

## Team Questions

- Why is the team capable of executing what you have proposed today?
- How do you divide up responsibilities among the team members?
- What is the equity split among team members?
- How are decisions made among the team members?
- Who is the boss?
- Who came up with the original idea?
- Who else do you need to add to your team in the short term?
- What obstacles have you faced, and how did you overcome them?
- Are you open to changing your idea?

## Product/Customer Questions

- What makes customers try your product/service?
- What is the technology behind your product?
- How does your product work in more detail?

- What are the risks?
- What is the next step in your product evolution?
- Where do most of your customers come from today?
- How many customers do you have today?
- Who is going to be your first paying customer?
- How are you understanding customer needs?
- How do you really know people want this?

## Competition Questions

- Which competitor do you fear the most?
- Are the barriers to entry high or low? In other words, is it easy for competitors to enter the same market?
- How much money have your competitors made?
- Why do you think you are unique among your competitors?
- Can the competition do what you are doing if they want to?
- Why hasn't this already been done?

## Financial Questions

- How did you calculate your market size?
- What are the assumptions behind your revenue projections?
- Are your numbers comparable to those of your competitors?
- What happens if you don't achieve your projected revenue?
- If I invest, what exactly are you going to do with the cash and what impact will it have on your business?
- What is the typical cycle between making initial customer contact and closing the sale?
- How much does it cost to acquire one customer?

## Growth Questions

- If your startup succeeds, what additional areas might you be able to expand into?
- Are there other applications for your product/service/technology?
- How are you defining success?
- How big do you want to grow?
- What is a likely exit strategy for this business?
- What competition do you fear most?
- Where do your growth projections come from?

Regardless of how prepared you are, there may be some questions that still take you by surprise. Two-time technology entrepreneur Caroline Cummings, who raised $1 million for her startup, wrote a blog post on the 10 most unexpected questions she was asked during her pitch to a venture capitalist (see Table B.3). These questions show that investors are interested in who you are as a person and how you think, just as much as they are interested in the opportunity you present to them!

**TABLE B.3**

Ten Most Unexpected Questions

| |
|---|
| Who believes in you, and how can I get in touch with them? |
| What entrepreneurs do you admire and why? |
| How do you track trends in your market? |
| Can you tell me a story about a customer using your product? |
| How do you know how much money you need, and could you scale your business with less? |
| How can I connect with five customers who have used your product? |
| What will your market look like in 5 years as a result of using your product or service? |
| What mistakes have you made thus far in this business, and what have you learned? |
| What if 3 to 5 years down the road we think you are not the right person to continue running this company—how will you address that? |
| Have you ever been fired from a job? Tell us about it. |

**Source:** Cummings, C. (2013, February 22). The 10 questions I didn't expect to be asked by investors. *Bplans Blog.* Retrieved from http://articles.bplans.com/the-10-questions-i-didnt-expect-to-be-asked-by-investors/

The pitch deck process is essential to engaging an audience in order to generate interest, and to secure commitment and, where appropriate, investment. The key to a good presentation is preparation. By creating the number of slides that succinctly outline the nature of your company, presenting with passion and knowledge, and taking the time to prepare the responses to questions you might be asked, you will have a better chance of engaging the right people to join you on your journey to entrepreneurial success.

# B.5 PUBLIC SPEAKING TIPS

**>> LO B.5   Illustrate the importance of public speaking skills to entrepreneurs.**

With all this talk about the pitch, we still need to address pitching! You can have the greatest slide deck in the world with amazing content and beautiful design, but none of it matters if *you* can't *deliver* the message. How are your presentation skills? Do you fear or embrace public speaking? Here are some tips to help you overcome nerves and anxiety.

- **Practice but don't memorize.** If you memorize your pitch, it becomes more evident when you go off script. Practice enough that your pitch sounds more conversational than overly rehearsed. Know the flow of your pitch, outline the essentials, but don't script out every single word. Did we say practice? Practice, practice, practice until it becomes no natural that it becomes virtually impossible to mess up!

- **Pay attention to time restrictions.** If you are given 3 minutes, do not go over. Don't assume that if you are given 3 minutes, that the receivers will give you an additional minute. Usually they will not even give you an additional 10 seconds, especially if you are pitching in some type of competition.

- **Don't hold anything in your hands.** Don't hold notes, a tablet, your phone, or anything because if you are nervous, it will be obvious. An entrepreneur pitching with index cards that are shaking in his or her hands does not scream, "Hey, invest in me!"

- **Don't read slides.** Slides are there to complement the entrepreneur, not replace the entrepreneur. Looking back at your slides or, in some cases, to the back of the room at a confidence monitor, prevents you from engaging with your audience. Reading slides is not much different than reading those index cards shaking in your hands. Furthermore, if you have to read your slides then there is too much text on your slides. The focus needs to be on you, not your slides. If your story can be told without you and with the slides alone, you do not have a good pitch.

- **Dress the part.** Use your best judgment here. A business suit is not always required and the world of entrepreneurship is less formal. If you are pitching in a competition, see what others are likely to wear. Also consider *what* you are pitching. If you are pitching a clothing line, you should be wearing your product. If you are pitching a new golf product, you would likely wear a golf shirt with your company logo. Though Mark Zuckerberg's hoodie is not necessarily good judgment, the point that a business suit is not always required should be clear.

- **Drink water.** TED speaker coach Gina Barnett suggests you start drinking water 15 minutes before your pitch to avoid dry mouth.[18] Dry mouth leads to pronunciation errors, which increases nervousness, which will increase the likelihood of you messing up even more!

- **Eye contact cannot be faked.** Nervous speakers look above their audience, to the back of the room, or as just mentioned, at their slides. They may think the audience doesn't notice, but they do. Take time to look audience members in the eye as you pitch. This will increase your connection with the audience as well as give you immediate feedback. Eye contact will tell you if your message is resonating, if they are confused, or if you are boring them to tears!

- **Learn to improvise.** Stage actors are trained in theatrical improvisation so the audience would never be able to tell when the actor forgot their lines. The actor was so skilled that she or he could create new lines on the spot that would not disrupt the flow or change the direction of the story. Public speakers need to do the same. Improvisation is needed when you forget where you want to go next and when that eye contact just talked about reveals that your audience is just not with you for one reason or another.

- **Move but don't pace.** Don't stand behind a podium. Stand boldly in front of your audience but don't move too much around the room and certainly don't pace. Your body movement can be your greatest asset as a speaker or your worst liability. Movement is bad when it's annoyingly repetitive such as playing with change in your pocket, putting your weight on one foot forcing you to lean or move from side to side, or using the same hand movements over and over. Using your body movements, however, can help you tell your story and also encourage people to focus on you rather than your slides. To emphasize points, use a hand gesture or step forward. Wherever you begin your presentation, think about an imaginary box around you that extends 3 feet in each direction. Move inside that box with intention and purpose!

- **Practice crisp articulation.** Poor diction can destroy a first impression, but poor diction typically results from inappropriate stretching prior to your talk! Usually before a presentation we are a bit nervous and tight. Public speaking coach Gary Genard offers a few warmup exercises in Table B.4.

- **Vary your voice to avoid the monotone trap.** It's important to vary the pitch of your voice to keep the attention of your audience. In general, the average speaker has a high voice, middle voice, and low voice. Unless you are actor James Earl Jones, we generally speak in our high or middle voice. The high voice comes from the head and our middle voice comes from our gut area. The high voice is best used to show enthusiasm but can be a bit annoying if an entire pitch is in a high voice. The middle voice is where you get the most resonance, forces you to slow down, and to articulate. Always start in your middle voice. To get there take a deep breath and begin speaking from your diaphragm area between your chest and abdomen.

### TABLE B.4

Exercises to Improve Diction

| EXERCISE | HOW TO DO IT |
|---|---|
| The Lion | Make a "lion face": widen your eyes, open up your mouth fully, and stick out your tongue. |
| Scrunch-Face | Now do the opposite, scrunching your face up into a tight little ball. Go back and forth between The Lion and Scrunch-Face. |
| Invisible Gum | Chew a gigantic imaginary wad of bubble gum. Keep your teeth apart but lips together. Really move that thing around in your mouth. Blow imaginary bubbles if you like! |
| Rubber Face | Imagine that your face is made of rubber, and manipulate it with your hands. Move it all around. Danger: this might make you yawn (which is good). |
| Jaw Relaxer | With the balls of both hands, apply medium pressure to the sides of your face just below the temples. Move slowly downward, allowing your hands to pull your face downward until you're making a "horror comic" face. |
| Exaggerated Diction | Recite aloud any passage you know by heart. Over-articulate each sound, working your mouth into exaggerated shapes. |

**Source:** Genard, G. (2018). *Speak for success! How to dramatically improve your voice for public speaking.* Retrieved from. https://www.genardmethod.com/blog/how-to-dramatically-improve-your-voice-for-public-speaking

- **Choreograph your rhythm**. Practice in advance where you will have pauses, what words or sentences you really want to emphasize, where you will slow down, and where you will speed up. Even think about when you want to smile or when you want to be serious. Think about when and how you should move in the imaginary box talked about above.

- **Embrace your nervousness**. That nervous feeling, those butterflies in your stomach, and shaking knees will not likely go away even with practice. The nerves will actually keep you focused and help you. The trick is not to let the nerves overpower and paralyze you. By employing some of the techniques above, you will control the nerves! ●

---

## ⑤SAGE edge™

Get the tools you need to sharpen your study skills. SAGE edge offers a robust online environment featuring an impressive array of free tools and resources.

- Access practice quizzes, eFlashcards, video, and multimedia at
  **edge.sagepub.com/neckentrepreneurship2e**

---

## SUMMARY

**B.1   Describe the pitch process and different types of pitches.**

Preparing a pitch involves thorough understanding of the audience, deliberate framing of the problem and solution, the resources required (the "ask"), and the method by which all of this will be communicated. Some popular pitches include the elevator pitch, the storytelling pitch, the Pixar pitch, the question pitch, the one-word pitch, the rhyming pitch, the subject-line pitch, and the Twitter pitch.

**B.2   Describe the pitch deck and its importance to potential investors.**

A pitch deck is a presentation in PowerPoint (or equivalent) that describes in detail the nature of the business, the need or problem it solves, industry characteristics, the customer, the market size, the business model, profit potential, team, and call to action.

**B.3 Explain the content of pitch deck slides.**

While there are no strict rules for length or style, your slides should include the following information: title, company purpose/description, the problem/need, the solution, why now?, market opportunity, getting customers, competitor advantages and differences, traction, financials, team, and call to action.

**B.4 Anticipate and prepare for the types of questions that may be asked during the question and answer period.**

When it comes to the question and answer period, expect the unexpected. In this regard, it is useful to prepare a series of backup slides that can help you answer the most anticipated questions.

**B.5 Illustrate the importance of public speaking to entrepreneurs.**

Public speaking is an essential part of pitching. Tips include practice, but don't memorize, pay attention to time restrictions, dress the part, learn to improvise, and drink water.

KEY TERM

**Use case**   413

©iStockphoto.com/South_agency

# Supporting Social Entrepreneurship

"Social entrepreneurs are not content just to give a fish or teach how to fish. They will not rest until they have revolutionized the fishing industry."

—Bill Drayton, *Leading Social Entrepreneurs Changing the World*

# Chapter Outline

# Learning Objectives

16.1    Describe the role social entrepreneurship plays in society.

16.2    Explain how social entrepreneurship can help resolve wicked problems around the world that are connected to the United Nations Sustainable Development Goals.

16.3    Identify the different types of social entrepreneurship.

16.4    Explain how social entrepreneurs can use capital markets to fund their ventures.

16.5    Identify the primary attributes of stakeholders and how stakeholders can help or hinder a social entrepreneur.

16.6    Distinguish between corporate social responsibility and social entrepreneurship.

16.7    Explore audacious ideas being pursued by social entrepreneurs today.

16.8    Illustrate the global diversity of entrepreneurship.

# 16.1 THE ROLE OF SOCIAL ENTREPRENEURSHIP

>> **LO 16.1**  **Describe the role social entrepreneurship plays in society.**

In Chapter 1, we introduced social entrepreneurship as the process of sourcing innovative solutions to social and environmental problems. What's the difference between social entrepreneurs and traditional entrepreneurs? Social entrepreneurs and business entrepreneurs share some similarities: Both types found new organizations, identify opportunities, create and implement innovation solutions or services, find information and resources, form connections, and create marketing initiatives to promote offerings.[1]

However, the main difference between traditional and social entrepreneurship lies in its intended mission. Traditional entrepreneurs create ventures with a goal of making a profit, and they measure performance by the profits they generate. In contrast, social entrepreneurs create ventures to tackle social problems and bring about social change; they measure performance by advancing social and environmental goals. Some also desire profit, in the case of for-profit ventures, while others are less concerned about profit. The great number of new nonprofit and nongovernmental organizations (NGOs) being started around the globe attests to this second category. In this chapter, we celebrate all types of social entrepreneurs—those who are mission-based and solving social problems—regardless of the nature of their profit motives. Organic Valley is a good example of a for-profit organization that does good by supporting family farmers and providing healthy organic food for consumers.

In this chapter, we discuss the different types of social entrepreneurship, explore the global social and environmental challenges facing us today, and share some stories of social entrepreneurs who have acted on opportunities to build scalable businesses. With the right entrepreneurial skills and a strong sense of empathy, compassion, and commitment, entrepreneurs are preserving and protecting future generations.

Master the content at
**edge.sagepub.com/
neckentrepreneurship2e**

# Organic Valley

*Picture Source: Organic Valley (with permission)*

**The Organic Valley Team**

*Picture Source: Organic Valley (with permission)*

**Organic Valley's organizational culture framework, Gibb's Triangle**

In 1988, seven Wisconsin farmers set out to change the way that organic farmers in the United States would be rewarded economically for their stewardship of the land, animals, and earth. It was a revolutionary idea. Historically and to this day, American agriculture operates predominantly as a commodity market with heavy government subsidies fueling what was grown where, and at what scale. The seven farmers decided that they had had enough. They wanted out of the commodity game.

They organized themselves into the Coulee Region Organic Produce Pool (CROPP), parent to the now nationally recognized billion-dollar brand Organic Valley. Thirty years later, CROPP is the largest fully organic, fully farmer-owned dairy cooperative in North America, selling milk, cheese, butter, yogurt, cream, eggs, and both fresh and processed meats. The cooperative has grown from seven entrepreneurs to more than 2,000 family farmers across 35 states. No small potatoes: CROPP represents more than 14% of all organic farmland in the United States and in 2017, it pulled in $1.1 billion in revenue.

From day one, Organic Valley's mission has been to keep family farmers on the land and to give consumers better food without chemicals. The cooperative is committed to many social and environmental issues, yet it is structured as a for-profit enterprise.

"I'd never been a very profit-oriented person," reflected founding farmer and recent CEO George Siemon. "But I realized that a profitable company allows a mission to flourish. You may start out with noble values, but if you don't have a viable business plan, the values don't carry the water."

As a cooperative, Organic Valley is owned by its farmers, and the farmers make the decisions. With so many owners, this means a lot of meetings, and a somewhat chaotic process that can move very slowly. But "None of us are as smart as all of us" is a foundational tenet for them, and they adhere to it.

Gibb's Triangle is a framework they use to defend their organizational culture. "It compares two potential paths," explained Siemon. "The first is built on prioritization that

begins with trust in human goodness, then sharing common goals and communicating them effectively. This path minimizes rules and controls. In contrast, the other path relies heavily on rules and controls, while minimizing trust. Over the years, the Gibb's Triangle has kept our cooperative viable. We must choose Gibb's first path and avoid the kind of tempting rigidity that wants to control everything that's human."

As a successful business with a nationally recognized brand, CROPP is sometimes accused of being yet another corporation profiting off the organic movement. But its missions remain front and center: saving family farms; providing meaningful work; proving that partnership is better; providing consumers with delicious organic food that is good for them, their families, the farmers, and the land.

Any time the question of "Are we getting too big?" comes up, the next question is always: "What is more important: size or mission?" Mission always wins. When it stops winning, CROPP is committed to stopping growth until the cooperative can regain its footing and its focus.

Logistically, Organic Valley is structured around regional pool points. So if you are standing in the dairy aisle in a grocery store in Boston, for instance, the Organic Valley products in that case came from family farmers living, working, and stewarding the land right around you in New England.

## Critical Thinking Questions

1. Should entrepreneurs exist to make money? Solve social and/or environmental problems? Or both? Explain your answer.

2. Explain how trust plays a central role in the longevity of Organic Valley.

3. What social or environmental problem would you like to solve? ●

**Source:** This feature was written by Rachel Greenberger, Director of Food Sol at Babson College. Material was sourced from CROPP Cooperative (2013). Roots: The first 25 years. LaFarge, WI: Organic Valley.

# 16.2 SOCIAL ENTREPRENEURSHIP AND WICKED PROBLEMS

>> **LO 16.2**   **Explain how social entrepreneurship can help resolve wicked problems around the world that are connected to the United Nations Sustainable Development Goals.**

In the 1960s, scholars coined the term **wicked problems**—large, complex social problems where there is no clear solution; where there is limited, confusing, or contradictory information available; and where a whole range of people with conflicting values engage in debate. More recently, Jeffrey Conklin, director of the Cognexus Institute, provided broader and more practical applications of the term (see Table 16.1).[2]

Issues relating to the environment, poverty, sustainability, equality, education, child mortality, sanitation, terrorism, and health and wellness are all examples of wicked problems, whether on a global, national, or local scale (see Figure 16.1).

The dramatic increase in life expectancy—an issue affecting many countries, particularly in the Western world—is an example of a wicked problem to which there are no easy answers. An aging population is likely to result in rising health care costs, an increase in the number of people claiming pensions, and potentially higher taxes for those supporting the nonworking retirees.

**Wicked problems:** large, complex social problems where there is no clear solution; where there is limited, confusing, or contradictory information available; and where a whole range of people with conflicting values engage in debate.

---

## TABLE 16.1

Conklin's Defining Characteristics of Wicked Problems

| 1. | The problem is not understood until after the formulation of a solution. |
|----|--------------------------------------------------------------------------|
| 2. | Wicked problems have no stopping rule. |
| 3. | Solutions to wicked problems are not right or wrong. |
| 4. | Every wicked problem is essentially novel and unique. |
| 5. | Every solution to a wicked problem is a "one shot operation." |
| 6. | Wicked problems have no given alternative solutions. |

**Credit:** Conklin, J. (2006). *Dialogue mapping: Building shared understanding of wicked problems.* Chichester, UK: Wiley Publishing. Reprinted with permission from John Wiley & Sons.

---

## FIGURE 16.1

**Global Wicked Problems**

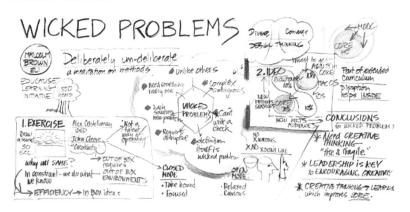

**Source:** David Sibbet, CEO of The Grove. Retrieved from http://redarchive.nmc.org/news/communique-2013-future-education-summit. Reprinted with permission of David Sibbet.

# United Nations Sustainable Development Goals

**Sustainable Development Goals**

**Source:** United Nations Sustainable Development Goals website: https://www.un.org/sustainabledevelopment/ The content of this publication has not been approved by the United Nations and does not reflect the views of the United Nations or its officials or Member States.

In 2012, world leaders came together at a UN conference to adopt the Sustainable Development Goals (SDGs), a set of universal goals to tackle environmental, political, and economic challenges. The SDGs have been called the strategic plan for the planet given the importance of protecting the future of the planet and its inhabitants—us! The SDGs were a replacement for the Millennium Development Goals (MDGs), which made great strides in reducing poverty, increasing access to water and sanitation, improving child mortality rates, and providing greater opportunities for free primary education. Although there were many impressive achievements made by the MDGs, there is still much to be done. The SDGs continue the objectives of the MDGs while incorporating some new goals—17 in total. Each goal is interconnected; for instance, tackling climate change leads to better management of our natural resources; promoting health and well-being helps eliminate poverty; and campaigning for peace and inclusiveness reduces gender inequality and cultivates economic prosperity. Based on the principle "of leaving no-one behind," the SDGs cover issues that impact us all, encouraging us to work together toward building a safer, more sustainable, better future for generations to come. Entrepreneurs around the world are creating new businesses to tackle one or more of the goals. Further evidence that the lines between social entrepreneurship and other forms of entrepreneurship are blurring, which suggests that all entrepreneurship is social.

## Critical Thinking Questions

1. Which SDG do you most resonate with personally, and why?

2. Why do you think the SDGs are labeled as the "strategic plan for the planet"?

3. How can the SDGs be used to create economic and social value at the same time?

4. Do you agree or disagree that "all entrepreneurship is social"? ●

---

**The International campaign End Water Poverty (EWP)**

Problems such as these are usually managed by policymakers who are responsible for creating ways to find solutions, but the path is fraught with obstacles. These problems are so complex that traditional linear problem-solving methods do not generally work. The nature of wicked problems poses significant challenges to social entrepreneurs, but also provides huge opportunities to make a real difference in their own countries and around the world.

The global water crisis is a good example of a wicked problem. According to the international campaign End Water Poverty (EWP), more than 600 million people worldwide have no access to clean, safe water. In addition, for at least 1 month a year, two-thirds of the world's population suffer from water scarcity. U.S.-based Planet Water Foundation is one of many nonprofit organizations addressing this problem by setting up water filtration systems, called Aqua Towers, in the world's most impoverished communities.[3] These systems kill harmful bacteria and provide thousands of people with clean water every day.

# How Entrepreneurship Is Saving the Planet

The UN Sustainable Development Goals (SDGs) can be considered the strategic plan for the planet! Irina Bokava, former director-general of UNESCO, summarized the UN Sustainable Development goals with the following powerful quote:

> There is no more powerful transformative force than education—to promote human rights and dignity, to eradicate poverty and deepen sustainability, to build a better future for all, founded on equal rights and social justice, respect for cultural diversity, and international solidarity and shared responsibility, all of which are fundamental aspects of our common humanity.

Pick one of the 17 SDGs that you feel personally connected to in some way, and find four startups or entrepreneurial companies that are working in the space related to your chosen goal. Two of your examples must be for-profit businesses and two must be nonprofit organizations. For each example, answer the following questions:

- What is the business or organization?
- How is your example connected to your chosen SDG?
- What is the mission of the business or organization?
- Who are the most important stakeholders?
- Who is the customer?
- Assess impact. How are success and value measured?

## Critical Thinking Questions

1. Compare and contrast your four examples. Do you see patterns?

2. Do you see differences or similarities between for-profit and nonprofit examples?

3. What do you now know that you didn't know before completing this Mindshift? ●

**Source:** #TeachSDGs (http://www.teachsdgs.org)

Whereas many of us avoid wicked problems because of their complex nature, these companies see wicked problems as a challenge to think differently or as an opportunity to break through constraints and develop creative solutions. Their focus lies in using their social entrepreneurs to generate the best alternative ideas.

Let's take a look at how two surfers, Alex Schulze and Andrew Cooper, created their own solution to a complex social problem. In 2015, college graduates Schulze and Cooper flew to Bali, Indonesia, for a surfing vacation. But instead of crystal-clear waters and pure white sand, they found piles and piles of plastic. When they made a few enquiries, they found that the local fishermen were catching more plastic in their nets than fish—something that threatened the fishermen's livelihood and the environment itself. This gave Schulze and Cooper an idea: What if the fishermen could be paid to collect the plastic as well as the fish? Determined to see their idea through, the two friends created 4ocean—a for-profit business that pays fishermen all over the world to catch plastic. The fishermen are funded by the sale of 4ocean bracelets made from recycled materials. To date, 4ocean has removed almost 4 million pounds of trash from the ocean and coastlines all over the world.

Companies like 4ocean are even more important when it comes to tackling the growing threat of climate change. A recent study conducted by the University of Hawaii shows that plastic releases greenhouse gases—gases that contribute to global warming—when exposed to direct sunlight.[4] In 2018, the Intergovernmental Panel on Climate Change warned that the world has less than a decade to reduce greenhouse gas emissions to prevent harmful droughts, floods, and other extreme weather events.[5]

This climate crisis has given rise to many other entrepreneurial ventures set up to find the solution to different aspects of climate change. For example, California-based Impossible Foods was set up to address the issue of animal farming—one of the biggest contributors to climate change—by creating a meatless burger made from plant-based products.[6] Fast-food chain White Castle was among the first to introduce the burger in 2018.

**Koe Koe Tech, the app that helps mothers track their pregnancies and learn how to care for their children, is an example of a social purpose venture.**

**Social purpose ventures:** businesses created by social entrepreneurs to resolve a social problem and make a profit.

**Social consequence entrepreneurship:** a for-profit venture whose primary market impact is social.

# 16.3 TYPES OF SOCIAL ENTREPRENEURSHIP

>> **LO 16.3**   **Identify the different types of social entrepreneurship.**

There are different models of social entrepreneurship. Figure 16.2 illustrates the territory of social entrepreneurship.[7] As we have described the differences between traditional and social entrepreneurship, let's take a look at (1) social purpose ventures, (2) social consequence ventures, and (3) enterprising nonprofits and their relationship to social entrepreneurship.

## Social Purpose Ventures

The aim of social purpose ventures is to resolve a social problem and make a profit. Koe Koe Tech is a good example of a social purpose venture: It was founded by Michael Lwin, a Myanmar American lawyer, in response to the shockingly high infant mortality rate in Myanmar. Lwin created the Koe Koe Tech app to help mothers track their pregnancies and learn how to take care of their children for the first 2 years of life. Within 3 months of launching, 40,000 people in Myanmar had signed up to the app.

## Social Consequence Entrepreneurship

Social consequence entrepreneurship describes a for-profit venture whose primary market impact is social. A good example of a for-profit venture with a social impact is Sword & Plough, a startup founded by sisters Emily and Betsy Núñez. Sword & Plough hires army veterans to recycle surplus military materials such as parachutes, sleeping bags, and tents into fashionable bags and accessories. The company was launched in 2013, benefiting from $312,000 in funding, thanks to a powerful Kickstarter campaign. It donates 10% of its profits to veterans' organizations.

---

**FIGURE 16.2**

**Typology of Ventures**

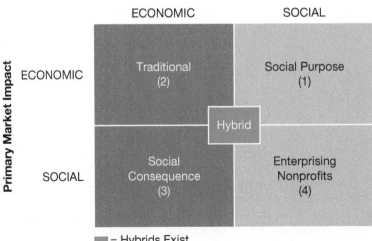

**Source:** Neck, H. M., Brush, C., & Allen, E. (2009). The landscape of social entrepreneurship. *Business Horizons, 52,* 13–19.

Since its founding, Sword & Plough has created almost 65 jobs for U.S. veterans and has recycled more than 30,000 pounds of discarded military material into thousands of products.[8] Through their innovative products, the founders aim to bridge the gap between civilians and the military by raising public awareness of veterans and the challenges facing servicemembers every day. Sword & Plough is just one of many for-profit companies in existence today that "does well [i.e., makes money] by doing good."

## Enterprising Nonprofits

**Enterprising nonprofits** are a form of social entrepreneurship in which both the venture mission and the market impact are for social purposes. This means that any profits made must be channeled back into the organization. Unlike social purpose ventures, profit may not be distributed to the owners of the enterprising nonprofit. There are more than 1.5 million nonprofit organizations in operation in the United States today, including charities, foundations, and others (see Table 16.2).

Compared to traditional nonprofit startups, enterprising nonprofits are more likely to survive in business after the first 5 years. This may have to do with revenue resources: Typically, enterprising nonprofits have better access to revenue streams from universities, hospitals, and foundations. Table 16.3 illustrates the differences between traditional nonprofit entrepreneurs and enterprising nonprofits.

Credit: AP Photo/Bartley Young

**Emily and Betsy Núñez, founders of Sword & Plough**

**Enterprising nonprofits:** a form of social entrepreneurship in which both the venture mission and the market impact are for social purposes.

---

**TABLE 16.2**

Quick Facts About Nonprofit Organizations in the United States

| | |
|---|---|
| 1,571,056 | tax-exempt organizations |
| 1,097,689 | public charities |
| 105,030 | private foundations |
| 368,337 | other types of nonprofit organizations, including chambers of commerce, fraternal organizations, and civic leagues |

**Source:** NCCS Business Master File 12/2015. Retrieved from http://nccs.urban.org/statistics/quickfacts.cfm

---

**TABLE 16.3**

Differences Between Traditional Nonprofit Entrepreneurs and Enterprising Nonprofits

| | TRADITIONAL NONPROFIT ENTREPRENEURS | ENTERPRISING NONPROFIT ENTREPRENEURS |
|---|---|---|
| Survival rate of business for the first 5 years | 50% | 84% |
| Gender breakdown | 41% women/59% men | 60% women/41% men |
| Average age of founders | 40 | 53 |
| Education level | 31% have a college degree | 89% have a college degree |
| Previous experience | 55% of founders start nonprofits in industries other than those they have been working in | 67% of nonprofit founders had more than 10 years' experience working in the private sector |

**Source:** http://www.kauffman.org/blogs/growthology/2015/03/six-ways-non-profit-entrepreneurs-are-distinct-from-traditional-entrepreneurs

Although there may be some differences between nonprofit entrepreneurs and traditional for-profit (also called enterprising) entrepreneurs, both types create their own ventures out of a desire to fill a gap and meet a need. There are two types of enterprising nonprofits: earned-income activities and venture philanthropy.

**Earned-income activities** involve the sale of products or services that are used as a source of revenue generation. For example, American retailer nonprofit ABLE sells women's clothing and accessories manufactured by women living in impoverished conditions in deprived countries.[9] By empowering women with new skills, ABLE provides a new opportunity to break the cycle of poverty in their communities.

In contrast to the earned-income model, venture philanthropy funding combines financial assistance such as grants with a high level of engagement by the funder. Venture philanthropists share their experience with nonprofit entrepreneurs to help grow and scale the company to drive social change. This might take the form of marketing and communications, executive coaching, human resources, or providing access to other contacts and potential funders. Typically, financial support is provided for 3 to 5 years, with the goal of enabling the nonprofit to become financially independent by the end of this period (see Table 16.4).

The poverty-fighting nonprofit Robin Hood foundation is a good example of a venture philanthropy fund.[10] Every year, the foundation funds more than 200 programs across New York City to help feed and offer job opportunities to more than 200,000 New Yorkers. Over the last 30 years, it has raised $2.5 billion for impoverished, neglected communities.[11]

Like many venture capital (VC) firms, venture philanthropists look for nonprofits whose social impact can be definitively measured and that demonstrate the potential to develop and grow. Venture philanthropy organizations include BonVenture in Germany, Impetus Trust and CAN-Breakthrough in the United Kingdom, d.o.b. Foundation in

**Earned-income activities:** the sale of products or services that are used as a source of revenue generation.

**Venture philanthropy funding:** a combination of financial assistance such as grants with a high level of engagement by the funder.

## TABLE 16.4

### Features of Venture Philanthropy

| CHARACTERISTIC | DESCRIPTION |
|---|---|
| High Engagement | Venture philanthropists have a close, hands-on relationship with the social entrepreneurs and ventures they support, driving innovative and scalable models of social change. Some may take board places on these organizations, and all are far more intimately involved at strategic and operational levels than are traditional nonprofit funders. |
| Multiyear Support | Venture philanthropists provide substantial and sustained financial support to a limited number of organizations. Support typically lasts at least 3–5 years, with an objective of helping the organization to become financially self-sustaining by the end of the funding period. |
| Tailored Financing | As in venture capital, venture philanthropists take an investment approach to determine the most appropriate financing for each organization. Depending on their own missions and the ventures they choose to support, venture philanthropists can operate across the spectrum of investment returns. |
| Organizational Capacity Building | Venture philanthropists focus on building the operational capacity and long-term viability of the organizations in their portfolios, rather than funding individual projects or programs. They recognize the importance of funding core operating costs to help these organizations achieve greater social impact and operational efficiency. |
| Nonfinancial Support | In addition to financial support, venture philanthropists provide value-added services such as strategic planning, marketing and communications, executive coaching, human resource advice, and access to other networks and potential funders. |
| Performance Measurement | Venture philanthropy investment is performance based, placing emphasis on good business planning, measurable outcomes, achievement of milestones, and high levels of financial accountability and management competence. |

**Source:** John, R. (2006). *Venture philanthropy: The evolution of high engagement philanthropy in Europe*. Skoll Centre for Social Entrepreneurship Working Paper. Oxford, UK: Oxford Said Business School.

the Netherlands, Good Deed Foundation in Estonia, Invest for Children in Spain, Oltre Venture in Italy, and NewSchools Venture Fund, Social Venture Partners, and Venture Philanthropy Partners in the United States.

It is possible for enterprising nonprofits to use both earned-income activities and venture philanthropy. For example, Embrace is a nonprofit set up by Stanford graduate Jane Chen in an effort to improve the survival of low-birthweight babies, particularly in developing countries where incubators are too expensive to purchase. The organization originated with a class project in which students were tasked with designing a device to prevent neonatal hypothermia that cost less than 1% of a standard incubator.

The result was the Embrace Warmer—a miniature sleeping bag that maintains the baby's body temperature without the need for electricity. It costs just $25, in stark contrast to the $20,000 cost of a typical hospital incubator. So far, the Embrace Warmer has saved the lives of 200,000 premature babies. To support its humanitarian effort, Embrace has created Little Lotus, a brand that sells temperature-adjusting blankets and swaddles in the United States.[12] Drawing on the one-to-one giving model popularized by TOMS shoes, Bombas Socks, and Warby Parker glasses, an Embrace Warmer is shipped to every premature baby in need abroad for every sale of a Little Lotus item.

Another enterprising nonprofit is Goodwill, which operates more than 3,000 donation clothing stores across the United States. Funds from the sale of these donations are used to empower people from diverse backgrounds, such as youth, seniors, and people with disabilities or criminal histories, to become economically self-sufficient by providing job training programs in a variety of different areas. In 2017, Goodwill provided almost 300,000 people with the training they need to find employment. According to the 2018 Brand World Value Index, Goodwill is considered to be one of the top five most inspirational brands for consumers.[13]

## Hybrid Models of Social Entrepreneurship

Through the typology of ventures illustrated in Figure 16.2, we have described several types of social entrepreneurship, but there are emerging forms of social entrepreneurship that do not fit as neatly into this four-part typology. A hybrid model of social entrepreneurship describes an organization with a purpose that equally emphasizes economic and social goals.

To further explain the hybrid model, let's take a look at two organizations with the same goal: to solve the problem of poor eyesight in developing countries. The first organization is the Centre for Vision in the Developing World, a traditional nonprofit that channels donations toward self-refraction glasses that enable the wearer to make simple adjustments at a low cost to increase vision quality. The product eliminates the need for an optometrist or prescriptions.

The second organization, VisionSpring, aims to solve the same problem but has a network of more than 20,000 salespeople to sell glasses to people in their local communities who have limited access to eye care. Unlike the Centre for Vision in the Developing World, the VisionSpring model sustains itself financially through the sales of the glasses, rather than through donations.

As a result, VisionSpring is classified as a hybrid social venture model because it combines a nonprofit's concern for social issues with the for-profit goal to make money. Although hybrid models can be an excellent way of exploiting the advantages of both for-profit and nonprofit models, they are less likely to receive VC funding or philanthropic donations because they sit in a gray zone between business and charity. As Harvard doctoral candidate Matthew Lee, who is studying hybrid organizations, explains, "It's much harder to get started and be successful if you don't fit into a well-defined form that people understand." Lee adds, "Creating a new

**Hybrid model of social entrepreneurship:** an organization with a purpose that equally emphasizes economic and social goals.

**Better World Books drop box, where people can drop off unwanted books**

**TOMS Shoes is an example of a for-profit social entrepreneurial company doing good in the world.**

hybrid is difficult to explain as a rational choice taking this limitation into account."[14]

However, if entrepreneurs can get it right, the hybrid model could have big social and economic payoffs. Better World Books is another example of a hybrid model, which earns money by taking donations of new and unwanted books and selling them online. The venture was originally begun in 2002 by three students at the University of Notre Dame who wanted to sell their textbooks online to earn extra money. The students then decided to donate a portion of the sales from each book they sold to literacy campaigns.

Since then, Better World Books has set up relationships with almost 4,000 libraries to collect unwanted books of many different types and genres. It has also launched an initiative that provides drop boxes in certain locations, allowing people to drop off unwanted books. The collection bins even come with sensory technology that tells Better World staff when the bins are full, so they can empty them quickly.[15]

In its book-for-book program, Better World Books has learned from other organizations. One example is TOMS Shoes, a for-profit company based in California that operates a "buy a pair of shoes, give away a pair of shoes" initiative (often shortened to Buy One Give One, or BOGO). Since it was set up, Better World Books has donated more than 26 million unwanted books and raised more than $28 million in funds for literacy and libraries.[16]

# 16.4 CAPITAL MARKETS FOR SOCIAL ENTREPRENEURS

>> **LO 16.4    Explain how social entrepreneurs can use capital markets to fund their ventures.**

Traditional entrepreneurial ventures need capital in order to survive, and so do social entrepreneurs running for-profit, nonprofit, or hybrid operations. For example, social entrepreneur Genny Ghanimeh, founder and CEO of Pi Slice, a Dubai-based online microfinance social platform for entrepreneurs across MENA (Middle East and North Africa), sought capital from all different types of funding channels, including angel investment and philanthropists, to help get her startup off the ground.[17] Ghanimeh and her team also took part in different entrepreneurship competitions and partnered with other businesses to improve her chances of funding. Since setting up in 2013, Pi Slice has funded microloans to hundreds of micro-entrepreneurs across MENA, starting from as low as $20.[18]

For-profits can also seek investment from social venture capitalists (SVC), also known as impact-investment funds. These funds look both for a return on investment and to make a specific social/environmental impact. For example, thanks to SVC, clean energy provider BBOXX has transformed lives by developing technology to provide pay-as-you-go solar power to hundreds of people living in remote areas in Africa and Asia.[19]

In fact, the SVC market has increased over the last few years, with some estimating that it could grow to $3 trillion in the future, mainly because of the rise of more socially conscious entrepreneurs looking for impact investment opportunities.[20] Table 16.5 lists a few examples of impact-investment funds.[21]

Another type of fund is the "community" fund, and its goal is to invest in economic development and job creation in impoverished areas.[22] Venture Philanthropy Partners (VPP), for example, is based in Washington, D.C., and focuses on helping youths and children from low-income families in the national capital region. Since its inception in 2000, VPP has raised more than $100 million to help children and youths in the greater Washington area.[23] SJF Ventures operates as a traditional VC fund but also allocates a percentage of the fund to companies seeking investment to make a positive social or environmental impact across areas such as waste reduction, heath advancement, education, and natural resource conservation. One of these social enterprises is Living Earth,

# How Social Entrepreneurs Can Be Unethical

Although social entrepreneurs are generally a big-hearted breed, and should be supported as much as possible, they do not have complete ethical immunity in going about their business. There are ways that a sincere effort to do good in the world could be skewed the other way around.

First, if a social entrepreneur does not have a realistic business plan, he or she could end up doing more harm than good. If a socially geared company does not focus on raising some amount of money and growing the business, then they could very well be a failure story, among the many in the world of entrepreneurship. A failure by a company could produce a stronger negative effect on society, rather than positive. Not only are employees out of work, but the goodness intended at the outset of launching the company will remain unfulfilled.

Furthermore, there is a preconceived notion that a social entrepreneurial venture must be a nonprofit in order to work properly. However, a for-profit social entrepreneurial company could do just as much good, as it ensures the company has the finances to continue moving forward with ease.

Then, there is the issue of running the company in an ethical manner. A company must have an ethical framework, and if money is tight at a social entrepreneurial company, then employees could bear the cost. Although companies can have a valiant purpose, it would do no good to have disgruntled employees who are severely underpaid and without enough benefits. Also, serious questions must be asked in business dealings, as aspects like raw material could be acquired in an unethical manner.

## Critical Thinking Questions

1. Could a social entrepreneurial venture be unethical in its business practices? Can the end justify the means?

2. Is it fair to pay employees of a nonprofit less money than they could be making elsewhere?

3. How important should finances be to a social entrepreneur? ●

**Sources:**

Chell, E., et al. (2014, November 20). Social entrepreneurship and business ethics: Does social equal ethical? *Journal of Business Ethics*. Retrieved from https://link.springer.com/article/10.1007/s10551-014-2439-6

Fitzgerald, P. (2011, December 27). The social entrepreneur's dilemma. *Huffington Post*. Retrieved from https://www.huffingtonpost.com/patrick-fitzgerald/the-social-entrepreneurs-dilemma_b_1171080.html

a leading composting and organic material products company that provides a more sustainable solution to Texas landfills by collecting yard waste, tree trimmings, and other organic materials and mixing them to provide a range of high-quality composts, which are then sold to landscapers, retailers, and residents.[24]

In the area of health care, SJF also invests in digital diabetes coaching platform Fit4D, which uses a combination of technology and diabetes experts to empower people with diabetes to live healthy and fulfilling lives.

Finally, SJF raises funding for Jopwell, a career advancement platform, which connects leading companies with black, Latino, and Native American professionals to help those companies fulfill their diversity recruitment objectives.

In fact, a whole range of clean energy startups are emerging, offering products and services that challenge how we use power. For instance, California-based veteran-owned company Constructis builds kinetic energy systems for roads that harvest electricity every time cars drive over a hidden road device (similar to a small speed bump). The excess electrical power is sent to power poles, a nearby building, or a car charging system. Startup Breezi also promotes clean energy through its audio sensors for air conditioning systems. The sensors troubleshoot errors in the system to make it more energy efficient.[25]

## Microfinance as a Source of Social Financing

*Microfinance* is a term used to describe financial services (such as loans, insurance, savings) to people considered ineligible to receive traditional banking services. One of the earliest pioneers of microfinance is Nobel Peace Prize winner Muhammad Yunus. Yunus founded

TABLE 16.5

Examples of Impact Investment Funds

| **Sustainable Trade Financing** |
| --- |
| A UK-based $65 million fund invests in sustainable trade and targets high-impact, submarket rate returns for investors. The fund has provided more than $200 million in loans to 300 small and growing businesses is across Latin American and Asia, with borrower repayment rates surpassing 98%. |
| ***Example investment:*** The fund has invested in a fair trade and certified organic coffee cooperative in Ecuador. The cooperative's 300 active members are smallholder farmers who cultivate shade-grown coffee. The trade finance loan allowed the cooperative to cover operating costs and invest in new processing equipment. Additional revenue gained from fair trade coffee sales are used to sponsor projects in reforestation, education, and community-based health clinics in the community where smallholder farmers live. |
| **Low-Income Housing** |
| A private equity fund based in Brazil closed with $75 million in assets. Investments target market-rate financial returns and social benefits to rural communities in South America. The fund's investors include large financial institutions, private family offices, development organizations, and large-scale foundations. |
| ***Example investment:*** The fund has made an investment of $4 million to a provider of affordable homes designed for low-income families in rural settings. More than 10,000 homes have been constructed in three South American countries, focusing particularly in areas affected by natural disaster. |
| **Clean Energy Access** |
| A EUR 150 million European private equity fund invests between EUR 2–10 million in companies that provide clean electricity to rural communities in developing countries with limited access to energy. The fund targets competitive private equity returns and has made five investments in Asia and Africa. |
| ***Example investment:*** The fund made a EUR 2 million equity investment in a company that provides solar energy for lighting and refrigeration in rural Indian households, schools, and hospitals that have limited access to the main electricity grid. Enabled by this investment, the company has installed more than 40,000 systems and currently offsets 25,000 tons of carbon dioxide emissions. |
| **Clean Drinking Water** |
| An India-based impact investing fund manager started investing in microfinance institutions more than 10 years ago. After delivering 14% returns to investors, the fund manager decided to raise a second fund to target businesses across a broader set of sectors, including renewable energy, agriculture, health, and education. The fund provides risk capital and support to early-stage ventures, with investments averaging $50,000. |
| ***Example investment:*** The second fund invested in a company that sets up water purification plants in rural villages. The plants are owned by the local community and operated by the installation company, which sells the purified water to the village at affordable rates. The installation company also trains local entrepreneurs to develop businesses that deliver water to neighboring villages. |

**Source:** http://www.impactbase.org/info/examples-impact-investment-funds

**Microloan:** a very small, short-term loan often associated with entrepreneurs in developing countries.

the Grameen Bank in Bangladesh in the 1970s, offering microloans, or small short-term loans, to impoverished villagers to enable them to start their own businesses. He placed borrowers, mostly women, into small groups but not all group members could borrow at once. One borrower may receive a loan for $40, but the other members only become eligible for their own loans when the original borrower begins to pay back her loan. Such a process created motivation, accountability, and empowerment. Yunus made his first loan of $27 in 1976 to a group of women who wanted to expand their bamboo business.

To date, the Grameen bank has extended credit to more than 7 million people, mostly in Bangladesh, who were in the past at the mercy of local money lenders who charged cripplingly high interest rates.[26] Through his revolutionary ideas, Yunus has not only proved that the poor are credit-worthy, but he has crossed social boundaries to give the people of Bangladesh an opportunity to be entrepreneurs themselves.

Since the founding of the Grameen Bank, other microlending providers have sprung up to extend Yunus's mission of eliminating exploitation of the poor by moneylenders and create self-employment opportunities for the disadvantaged.

For example, nonprofit organization Kiva has enhanced the microfinance concept even further by enabling anyone to loan as little as $25 to entrepreneurs in developing countries who lack access to traditional banking systems. The hundreds of entrepreneurs are profiled on the Kiva website, and people can choose whom they would like to fund based on this information. Kiva does not charge interest or take a cut of the loan—the entire amount goes to the entrepreneur. When the entrepreneur repays the loan, the individual can decide if he or she wants to use it to make another loan to support a different entrepreneur.

Social enterprises like the Grameen Bank and Kiva have revolutionized many lives and businesses in developing countries. Nevertheless, Shivani Soroya, founder of Tala, spotted a gap. Although the informal microloans certainly helped people to start their own businesses, when it came to growing those businesses, they still had no access to formal banking institutions. Because they had no credit score, they were perceived as too risky for formal loans. Soroya's aim was to break down these barriers by providing mobile and web tools so that entrepreneurs could save business data in order to build up a credit score, to prove to formal institutions that the business is growing and worth the risk of small-business loans. Tala operates in markets where millions of people have no credit score, such as Tanzania, Kenya, and the Philippines. Soroya said, "It made me realize that there are billions of people around the world who are not even seen and don't even have an identity. That felt really wrong."[27] However, none of the social entrepreneurs profiled in this chapter carried out their mission all by themselves. They had a number of people to help them. In the next section, we will take a look at how people can help or hinder a social venture.

# 16.5 SOCIAL ENTREPRENEURS AND THEIR STAKEHOLDERS

>> **LO 16.5**   **Identify the primary attributes of stakeholders and how stakeholders can help or hinder a social entrepreneur.**

As we have learned, social entrepreneurs cannot resolve wicked problems in isolation. To gain support for their mission, social entrepreneurs need to think about how their actions affect their stakeholders, who are the people or groups affected by or involved with the achievements of the social enterprise's objectives.

**Stakeholders:** the people or groups affected by or involved with the achievements of the social enterprise's objectives.

Stakeholders include employees, volunteers, investors, customers, suppliers, and manufacturers, leaders in nonprofit organizations, community leaders, the government, sponsors, board members, and other entrepreneurs. By identifying your stakeholders, you will be able to better understand the impact of your enterprise's activities on others; give your stakeholders a platform to provide feedback, information, advice, and direction; and allow them to raise any concerns or obstacles that may stand in the way of achieving your objectives.

Linking all these stakeholders will help you get the best out of your social enterprise. A good way to identify your key stakeholders is to draw your own stakeholder map, as illustrated in Figure 16.3.

Building relationships with key stakeholders is an important way to gain support, but you must also prove to your key stakeholders how you intend to generate value for them. Although "doing good deeds" is a worthy objective, your stakeholders will want to understand the value of being involved with the venture.

When you create a social innovation, it is unlikely that all your stakeholders will be in immediate agreement. So it is your responsibility to communicate to stakeholders not only the value to be derived but also the potential for loss or consequences of your activities and suggest alternative solutions. There are two questions you need to ask yourself: (1) What is at stake for your stakeholders? This question will enable you to assess the level of risk for your stakeholders and force you to think about how you can reduce their risks. (2) How are you creating value for each stakeholder? Every stakeholder will see value in a different way.

With the potential for so many stakeholders, how do you decide which ones are the most important? Whom do you need to prioritize, and what level of attention should you give? The salience model helps social entrepreneurs select the most suitable communication approach for each group of stakeholders by classifying stakeholders based on their salience (or significance) in the social enterprise. There are three primary attributes

**FIGURE 16.3**

### Example of Stakeholder Map

of stakeholders to consider when you are trying to achieve your objectives: power, legitimacy, and urgency.[28]

A stakeholder in a position of power has the ability to either help or hinder your social objectives. For example, labor unions have the power to prevent or hinder organizational objectives, particularly when certain initiatives may lead to job loss and unemployment. Legitimate stakeholders are those whose actions are appropriate, proper, and desired in the context of the company, organization, or community.[29] For example, if you have a problem or need some advice, you may consult with the stakeholders you feel have the most legitimacy.

The third attribute is urgency, which describes the extent to which stakeholders demand your attention. For example, in a case where there are last-minute questions that need to be answered by your investors during the due diligence process, you would need to prioritize the needs of your investors over other stakeholders until the situation has been resolved.

These three attributes are not necessarily independent of one another; in fact, a stakeholder may have both power and legitimacy, or a combination of all three. However, by identifying the different types of stakeholders, you will be better able to assess which ones are the most salient in a particular context.

## Types of Stakeholders

In the 1990s, Ronald K. Mitchell and colleagues proposed a model of seven different types of stakeholders (see Figure 16.4). The model is based on the three factors of power, legitimacy, and urgency; note that each type of stakeholder occupies a position relative to these three overlapping circles. Let's examine each of these seven types using the

**FIGURE 16.4**

## Mitchell Stakeholder Typology

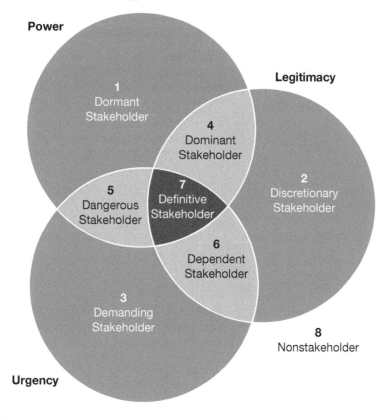

**Source:** Mitchell, R., Agle, B., & Wood, D. (1997). Toward a theory of stakeholder identification and salience: Defining the principle of who and what really counts. *Academy of Management Review, 22,* 853–866.

example of nonprofit organization familiar to many young entrepreneurs—the Collegiate Entrepreneurs Organization (CEO). CEO has chapters across 200 colleges and universities in North America. Its mission is "to inform, support and inspire college students to be entrepreneurial and seek opportunity through enterprise creation."[30]

### Dormant Stakeholders

Dormant stakeholders are "sleepers"—they hold power but do not tend to use that power unless they are given a reason to do so. However, dormant stakeholders may become significant when they begin to utilize their power; for example, a disgruntled member may complain about CEO on social media. The key to ensuring these stakeholders are satisfied is to be transparent and keep them informed at all times. Just because they are "sleeping" doesn't mean they will never wake up.

### Discretionary Stakeholders

Discretionary stakeholders have no power to influence and no urgent claims, but they have legitimacy. They may come in the form of philanthropists who donate to your organization and are willing to support social causes. For example, CEO provides visitors with the opportunity to donate money on its website to support the organization.

### Demanding Stakeholders

Demanding stakeholders possess the urgency attribute. They have no power or legitimacy and may be the only dissenting voice in the room. For example, persons protesting

# Practice Being "Other-Centered"

In this Mindshift, your challenge is to practice being "other-centered" for 1 week. Many of us live in a "me-centered" world, where events and relationships are measured by how much, and in what ways, they affect us. Being "other-centered" means stepping outside ourselves and shifting the focus onto serving others for the good of the greater community.[31]

For example, instead of getting frustrated at an older adult taking forever to put away her change at the checkout line, give her a reassuring smile, and maybe offer to help her with her bags of groceries. Think about different ways in which you can cheer up others. Make someone else's day.

## Critical Thinking Questions

1.  To what extent do you feel you are already "other-centered" in your life? Give some examples of your actions and decisions in this regard.

2.  Was it easier than you expected, or more difficult, to focus for an entire day on being other-centered? Would you want to continue this focus for a second day running?

3.  What did you learn from this Mindshift that surprised you? ●

outside the CEO national conference because they believe entrepreneurs create income inequality in the economy, but they do not have the power to enforce their claims. These stakeholders don't really impact CEO, and not a lot of time and energy should be devoted to them.

## Dominant Stakeholders

Dominant stakeholders have both power and legitimacy, which gives them strong influence in your organization. Dominant stakeholders of CEO include college presidents or deans of business schools where CEO chapters are located. Communicating with them regularly and responding to queries efficiently and accurately will help you maintain a good relationship with these stakeholders and keep the chapter on campus!

## Dependent Stakeholders

Dependent stakeholders have both urgency and legitimacy but lack the power to influence. These stakeholders are the most passionate, and their passion is likely to attract dominant stakeholders. For example, the student members of CEO are the most enthusiastic and passionate stakeholders connected to the organization, but they may not have the power necessary to effect change with the leaders of the national organization.

## Dangerous Stakeholders

Dangerous stakeholders possess both power and urgency but may use this power to coerce or even resort to violence. Social issues can be emotive, and power and urgency exercised against your objectives can be a significant hindrance. For example, a competing organization may emerge that could use false advertising or slander to get members from CEO to move their membership to the new organization.

## Definitive Stakeholders

Definitive stakeholders are the only ones who possess all three attributes of power, legitimacy, and urgency. These stakeholders have a significant role to play in your organization and must be given priority when it comes to handling their claims. In the case of CEO, the most definitive stakeholders are the foundations that fund CEO—the Kauffman and Coleman foundations.

## Conclusions From the Mitchell Stakeholder Typology

Remember that stakeholders are not static—they can evolve, and through that evolution, they may either gain or lose attributes. Social entrepreneurs must continuously monitor the internal and external stakeholder environment to maintain relationships with stakeholders and ensure support for their social mission.

Stakeholders are vital to social entrepreneurship, and communities of stakeholders are emerging all over the world to share knowledge, collaborate on ideas, and build and grow social ventures. Ashoka, Social Venture Network, Investors Circle, Echoing Green, Net Impact, and Social Enterprise provide forums to connect with and learn about other stakeholders. Connecting and collaborating with others is the key to resolving wicked problems.

## 16.6 DIFFERENCES BETWEEN SOCIAL ENTREPRENEURSHIP AND CORPORATE SOCIAL RESPONSIBILITY

>> **LO 16.6**  **Distinguish between corporate social responsibility and social entrepreneurship.**

Corporate social responsibility (CSR) describes the efforts made by corporations to address the company's effects on environmental and social well-being in order to promote positive change. Although social entrepreneurship may sound similar to the CSR model, they are not the same (see Table 16.6).

The difference lies in the primary objective. In essence, CSR adds social objectives while still pursuing the main goal of making a profit. In contrast, many social entrepreneurship models, including the hybrid model, place equal emphasis on social and economic goals. An organization with a CSR strategy could reduce spending on its CSR program if it is struggling to meet revenues, whereas a social enterprise would prioritize its social goals even in the face of a reduction in profits.

Together, the biggest global firms spend more than $20 billion on CSR, and recent research suggests that some of these companies reap financial rewards as a result.[32] For example, consumers may be attracted to these companies because the CSR spending may indicate high-quality products; they also may want to buy the products as an indirect way to donate to the causes the corporation supports; and they may also look on the organization favorably (the "halo" effect) because of its good deeds.[33]

On the legal side, research also suggests that if a firm is sued and prosecuted, it may tend to receive more lenient penalties if it has a record of CSR activities. For example,

**Corporate social responsibility (CSR):** the efforts made by corporations to address the company's effects on environmental and social well-being in order to promote positive change.

**TABLE 16.6**

Corporate Social Responsibility Versus Social Entrepreneurship

| CORPORATE SOCIAL RESPONSIBILITY | SOCIAL ENTREPRENEURSHIP |
| --- | --- |
| Peripheral to mission | Core to mission |
| Side show | Main event |
| A department | The entire organization |
| Seeks to reduce harm | Measures social impact |
| Feel and look good | Do good |
| Stakeholder is the observer | Stakeholder is the customer |
| Consequence-driven | Purpose-driven |
| Image-motivated | Opportunity-motivated |

**FIGURE 16.5**

**CSR Makes Good Business Sense**

Good CSR helps to:

- engage more customers, especially if your firm is helping to support good causes
- lead to real innovations, such as environmentally safe products
- decrease costs by cutting packaging, travel, and energy expenses
- increase public image through the company's efforts to do good deeds
- bring people together by holding charity events such as sponsored walks and bake sales

**Source:** Adapted from Mitchell, R., Agle, B., & Wood, D. (1997). Toward a theory of stakeholder identification and salience: Defining the principle of who and what really counts. *Academy of Management Review, 22*(4), 853–866.

organizations with a focus on labor rights issues such as eliminating child labor or companies who increase CSR spending by 20% tend to be treated more leniently if they are prosecuted.[34]

Additional research also shows that CSR initiatives relating to sustainability, corporate foundations, employee volunteer programs, and donations to charity tend to attract and motivate employees.[35] However, if employees believe that companies are investing in CSR for the wrong reasons, such as boosting productivity or purely for financial gain, then they will disengage with the company and become less motivated.

A 2018 study lists corporations with the best CSR reputations, including Google, Microsoft, IKEA, Bosch, Natura, and LEGO.[36] One of Google's main principles is "doing good." For instance, the Google Green and Google Energy initiatives focus on investing more than $1 billion in renewable energy to reduce the costs of energy consumption of the Google Group of companies. Another example of its commitment to "doing good" is Google Person Finder, which helps track people down in the aftermath of major disasters.[37]

Although CSR has been mostly associated with large companies, it is also important to small to medium-sized companies. As Figure 16.5 shows, good CSR makes good business sense for small companies.

Smaller companies can also build a good reputation in the local community by volunteering at local libraries, hospitals, and schools and by supporting local sports teams or local charities. Being connected with ethical suppliers with positive CSR is also a bonus for a small company as it builds trust with new customers. Building trust and being socially responsible is important for all companies—big or small.

## 16.7 SOCIAL ENTREPRENEURSHIP AND AUDACIOUS IDEAS

>> **LO 16.7**   **Explore audacious ideas being pursued by social entrepreneurs today.**

It's tough to be a social entrepreneur; they may have groundbreaking ideas to save lives or improve the environment, but they still need funding to achieve their goals. This involves endless rounds of pitches to philanthropists or investors who may be hesitant to take the risk on a newly formed startup. Media organization TED is trying to narrow the gap between social entrepreneurs and philanthropists through a new model called The Audacious Project: Collaborative Philanthropy for Bold Ideas.[38] The Audacious Project invites social entrepreneurs to submit their ideas for creating global change, then carefully vets the ideas before choosing the ones with the most potential. These social entrepreneurs are given a platform to present their ideas to some of the most well-respected names in philanthropy.

More than $250 million has been raised to fund these ideas by a group of leading organizations including Virgin Unite, the Skoll Foundation, and The Bridgespan Group. Here are some of the 2018 Audacious Project awardees:[39]

## The Bail Project

The Bail Project is an organization set up to address the injustice of automatic imprisonment for those who can't afford bail, which typically affects low-income communities, women, and minorities. With the support of The Audacious Project, The Bail Project aims to post bail on behalf of 160,000 people over the next 5 years by working with public defenders and the impacted community members. The bail returned at the end of each case will be used to fund other affected people. If it proves successful, this idea could help to end mass incarceration and combat racial disparity.

Robin Steinberg, CEO of The Bail Project, said, "Pretrial detention is a key driver of mass incarceration in the United States, accounting for all of the net jail growth in the last 20 years. Thanks to The Audacious Project, we have an incredible opportunity to help turn the tide on this crisis. We have a proven model, strong local partners, and a growing team ready to give it their all until our work is no longer necessary."

## Environmental Defense Fund

Environmental Defense Fund (EDF) is a nonprofit environmental advocacy group that aims to reduce methane, a powerful greenhouse gas responsible for global warming. Although it is commonly known that the oil and gas industry is a major contributor to the tons of methane in our atmosphere, there hasn't been a way to measure the level of methane on a global scale or its original source.

With the support of The Audacious Project, EDF aims to build and launch low-cost satellite MethaneSAT, which tracks and measures emissions. The information gathered by MethaneSAT will provide companies and countries with the data they need to take steps to reduce and track their emissions.

"Cutting methane emissions from the global oil and gas industry is the fastest thing we can do right now to put the brakes on climate change," said Fred Krupp, EDF president. "MethaneSAT gives us the power to map and measure the problem, identify reduction opportunities, and track that progress over time."

## GirlTrek

GirlTrek is a health movement with a goal to improve the health and well-being of African American women through daily walking. Because of underemployment, lack of community safety, and chronic poverty, African American women are more likely to die of preventable diseases and at younger ages than any other groups of women in the United States.

With the support of The Audacious Project, GirlTrek aims to tackle poor health, including obesity, by training 10,000 people as public health activists to reach their goal of 1 million GirlTrek members.

"We are not a workout group. We are an army of women who, in the iconic words of Fannie Lou Hamer, are 'sick and tired of being sick and tired,'" said Vanessa Garrison, cofounder of GirlTrek and Chief Operating Officer.

## Sightsavers

Sightsavers is a UK-based nongovernmental international charity working to prevent avoidable blindness with a goal to combat the bacterial infection trachoma, which causes irreversible blindness. The charity aims to eliminate the disease by promoting the SAFE strategy (surgery, antibiotics, face-washing, and environmental improvements) endorsed by the World Health Organization (WHO), largely targeting people living in impoverished countries.

Dr. Caroline Harper, CEO of Sightsavers, said, "Trachoma traps the most vulnerable people in a vicious cycle of poverty. Together we can consign this awful disease to the history books, where it belongs. We'll free millions of people, today and for generations to come, from this scourge of the world's poorest communities."

## One Acre Fund

One Acre Fund is a nonprofit social enterprise working to provide African farmers with the opportunity to grow more food by offering access to agricultural training, tools, and asset-based financing. By learning the techniques to increase their produce, the farmers will be able to earn a higher income to support their families.

"The world's smallholder farmers are some of the hardest working people on the planet," said Andrew Youn, cofounder and executive director of One Acre Fund. "By working together and increasing access to financing, tools, and training, we envision a future where all farmers can achieve big harvests, healthy families, and rich soils."

Social entrepreneurs use the fundamental principles of entrepreneurship to build businesses of economic and social value. They improve the lives of whole communities by providing employment; they save the lives of premature babies; they educate people so they can make a living; they utilize our "trash" to create businesses that improve the lives of others; they offer loans to excluded members of society and give them confidence and a sense of purpose. There is no such thing as waste or hopelessness in the mind of a social entrepreneur. Social entrepreneurs bring hope and change lives. They are making the world a better place.

# 16.8 GLOBAL ENTREPRENEURSHIP

**>> LO 16.8    Illustrate the global diversity of entrepreneurship.**

Entrepreneurship is taking off on a global scale. Let's explore some data provided by The Global Entrepreneurship Monitor (GEM), a global research study founded by Babson College and the London Business School in 1999. Today the study is conducted by a consortium of universities around the world and measures entrepreneurial activity across 112 economies.[40]

According to the 2018/19 GEM report, more than 15% of Americans are entrepreneurs—the highest percentage on record. In fact, there are almost 500 million entrepreneurs worldwide, making entrepreneurship a global phenomenon.

The GEM study gathers its data according to different phases of entrepreneurship (see Figure 16.6). The process begins with potential entrepreneurs, who are individuals who believe they have the capacity and know-how to start a business without being burdened by the fear of failure. The next phase focuses on nascent entrepreneurs, who are individuals who have set up a business they will own or co-own that is less than 3 months old and has not yet generated wages or salaries for the owners. The third phase is the study of new business owners, who are former nascent entrepreneurs who have been actively involved in a business for more than 3 months but less than 3.5 years. The final phase explores established business owners—those who have been active in business for more than 3.5 years. Interestingly, the study found the reason that many of the established business entrepreneurs had discontinued the business after 3.5 years was not necessarily because they had failed; in fact, in many cases, the entrepreneurs had instead become serial entrepreneurs or joined other companies to become inside or corporate entrepreneurs.

The GEM study also looks at opportunity-based entrepreneurs and necessity-based entrepreneurs. Necessity-based entrepreneurs are individuals who are pushed into starting a business because of circumstance. Layoffs, threat of job loss, and inability to find a job are some factors that drive people to start a new business. In contrast,

**Potential entrepreneurs:** individuals who believe they have the capacity and know-how to start a business without being burdened by the fear of failure.

**Nascent entrepreneurs:** individuals who have set up a business they will own or co-own that is less than 3 months old and has not yet generated wages or salaries for the owners.

**New business owners:** individuals who are former nascent entrepreneurs and have been actively involved in a business for more than 3 months but less than 3.5 years.

**Established business owners:** the people who have been active in business for more than 3.5 years.

**Necessity-based entrepreneurs:** individuals who are pushed into starting a business because of circumstance such as redundancy, threat of job loss, and unemployment.

**FIGURE 16.6**

## Global Entrepreneurship Monitor Measuring Entrepreneurial Activity

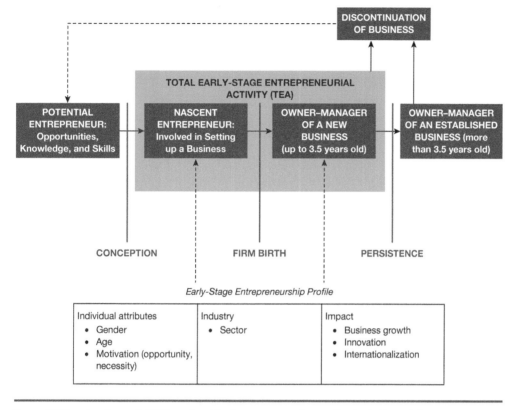

**Source:** GEM Report 2018-9: pg 16, GEM Consortium, http://www.gemconsortium.org/. Reprinted with permission.

opportunity-based entrepreneurs are individuals who make a decision to start their own businesses based on their ability to create or exploit an opportunity, and whose main driver for getting involved in the venture is being independent or increasing their income, rather than merely maintaining their income. Unlike necessity-based entrepreneurs, opportunity-based entrepreneurs freely make their own choice to get involved in a business.

One of the main focuses of the GEM study is the level of Total Entrepreneurial Activity (TEA) in different countries, which is the percentage of the population of each country between the ages of 18 and 64 who are either nascent entrepreneurs or owner—managers of a new business. For example, the early-stage TEA in the United States is just over 15% (Table 16.7). This means that just over 15% of the U.S. adult population from 18 to 64 years old is involved in some type of entrepreneurial activity, such as being in the process of starting a new business or owning and managing a business less than 3 years old.

Let's take a closer look at the age ranges of entrepreneurial activity in early stages of business across the world. North America is certainly perceived as being one of the most buoyant environments for entrepreneurship, but other geographical regions, such as Africa, Latin America, and the Caribbean, appear to have higher rates of entrepreneurial activity in certain age groups. Europe displays the lowest TEA rates over all, with Cyprus, Italy, Germany, and Poland, in particular, showing the lowest rates—5% or less of working adults begin or run new businesses. The low rates in some countries, particularly among the younger population, may be a consequence of compulsory military service or high college attendance.

Despite sub-Saharan Africa being a less well-developed region of the world than the United States, people living in some African countries tend to see opportunities to start their own businesses, have confidence in their own skills and abilities, and have less fear

**Opportunity-based entrepreneurs:** individuals who make a decision to start their own businesses based on their ability to create or exploit an opportunity, and whose main driver for getting involved in the venture is being independent or increasing their income, rather than merely maintaining their income.

**Total Entrepreneurial Activity (TEA):** the percentage of the population of each country between the ages of 18 and 64 who are either a nascent entrepreneur or owner—manager of a new business.

**TABLE 16.7**

Total Early-Stage Entrepreneurial Activity (TEA) Rates Among Adults (ages 18–64) in 49 Economies, in Four Geographic Regions

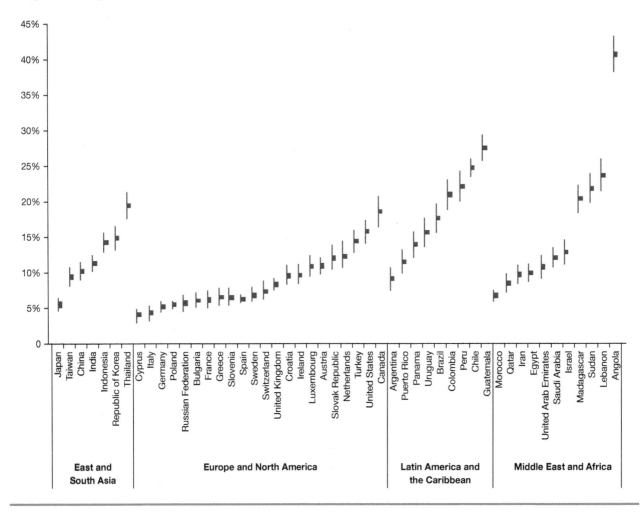

**Source:** GEM Report 2018-9: pg 16, GEM Consortium, http://www.gemconsortium.org/. Reprinted with permission.

of failure. These statistics prove that early-stage entrepreneurship is possible in poorer countries if the people are given the opportunity and support to grow their own businesses.

## Gender and Entrepreneurship

One of the greatest myths concerning entrepreneurship is that it is a male-only profession. As Table 16.8 shows, nothing could be farther from the truth.

Most countries studied have a similar proportion of men to women early-stage entrepreneurs, with the percentage of women in Vietnam, Panama, Qatar, Madagascar, Thailand, Angola, and Indonesia being equal to or exceeding their male counterparts. This shows that these countries are providing support for women-owned ventures.

Why do women want to become entrepreneurs? For the same reasons as men: to support themselves and their families, to attain the fulfillment of having started something on their own, and to satisfy their desire for financial independence.[41] Just like their male counterparts, women not only create jobs for themselves and others, but also work toward growing their businesses and constantly innovating new products and services.

However, in certain countries, there are some differences in what drives women to be entrepreneurs. For example, women in less-developed countries with higher rates of unemployment, poverty, and lack of choice in work are more likely to be driven by necessity, whereas women in more developed countries tend be more motivated by opportunity and innovation.

**TABLE 16.8**

Total Early-Stage Entrepreneurial Activity (TEA) Rates Among Men and Women (ages 18–64) in 49 Economies, in Four Geographic Regions

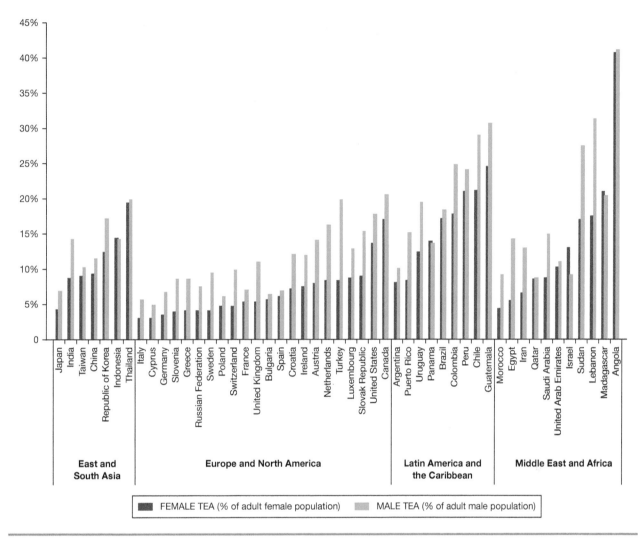

**Source:** GEM Report 2018-9: pg 16, GEM Consortium, http://www.gemconsortium.org/. Reprinted with permission.

## What Makes a Country Entrepreneurial?

What makes one country more entrepreneurial than another? The following are certain conditions that need to be put in place for small and medium businesses (SMEs) to flourish. Together, these conditions form the Entrepreneurship Ecosystem (Figure 16.7).

- Financial resources: Entrepreneurs need access to appropriate financing such as grants and subsidies, loans, private equity, angel investors, VC funds, and so on.

- Support from government: Entrepreneurs need support from government policies that incentivize entrepreneurship by tax incentives, lower interest rates, loans, and the like. Some countries also offer government entrepreneurship programs that provide entrepreneurs with access to tools, mentors, and educational resources.

- Entrepreneurship education: Certain countries provide entrepreneurship courses and training at primary and secondary levels and at higher education such as colleges, business schools, and other institutions.

- Research and development (R&D) transfer: The extent to which scientists and research will pass on their knowledge to entrepreneurs involved in innovation. Many SMEs do not have their own R&D department so it is important that they have the opportunity to access knowledge from other resources.

- Commercial and legal infrastructure: Entrepreneurs should be supported by a secure commercial and legal framework assisted by experts and advisors in property rights, accounting, law, investment banking, and technology.

- Entry regulation: Entrepreneurs should be able to meet the regulatory costs of starting a new business as well as undergoing administrative procedures. The extent of these costs and procedures is dependent on two factors: market dynamics—the annual rate of change in markets; and market openness—the degree to which new businesses have the freedom to enter new markets.

- Physical infrastructure: Entrepreneurs should be able to easily access or purchase at a reasonable price vital resources in the areas of communication, land, office space, and transportation.

- Cultural and social norms: Entrepreneurs tend to thrive more in an environment where they feel encouraged enough to start a business or have the confidence to choose entrepreneurship as a career path.

All these factors interact to create a very powerful force: New businesses are created, employment increases, new products hit the markets, competition is intensified, and productivity rises, all of which makes a huge contribution to social and economic development. This is why it is essential for every country in the world to build a climate where entrepreneurship can thrive. ●

## FIGURE 16.7

### Expert Ratings of the Entrepreneurial Framework Conditions

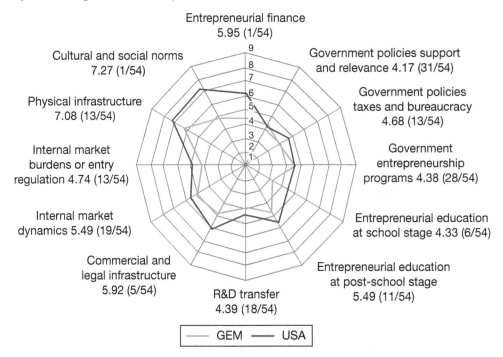

EFCs scale: 1 = very inadequate insufficient status, 9 = very adequate sufficient status
Rank out of 54 recorded in brackets

**$SAGE edge™**

Get the tools you need to sharpen your study skills. SAGE edge offers a robust online environment featuring an impressive array of free tools and resources.

- Access practice quizzes, eFlashcards, video, and multimedia at
  **edge.sagepub.com/neckentrepreneurship2e**

**16.1  Describe the role social entrepreneurship plays in society.**

Social entrepreneurship is the process of sourcing innovative solutions to social and environmental problems. Many companies strive simply to maximize shareholder value, but social entrepreneurs are often more committed to causes centered on preserving and protecting future generations.

**16.2  Explain how social entrepreneurship can help resolve wicked problems around the world that are connected to the United Nations Sustainable Development Goals.**

Social entrepreneurship can help resolve wicked problems such as those related to water shortages, education, health care, poverty, energy, forced migration, and global warming by creating innovative solutions that make a real impact on the lives and livelihoods of others.

**16.3  Identify the different types of social entrepreneurship.**

There are three primary types of social entrepreneurship: social purpose ventures, social consequence entrepreneurship, and enterprising nonprofits.

**16.4  Explain how social entrepreneurs can use capital markets to fund their ventures.**

Social entrepreneurs can seek funding from social venture capitalists (SVC) and community-funded VC to support operations. Microlending is another source of capital available for social entrepreneurs.

**16.5  Identify the primary attributes of stakeholders and how stakeholders can help or hinder a social entrepreneur.**

Stakeholders are all those involved in and affected by the activities of a social venture. Building relationships with key stakeholders is typically important for any entrepreneur, social or otherwise, but often social issues need additional support to gain traction with the majority of stakeholders.

**16.6  Distinguish between corporate social responsibility and social entrepreneurship.**

Corporate social responsibility and social entrepreneurship differ in one critical sense: the primary objective of the enterprise. Corporations seek to incorporate social initiatives into broader strategic and tactical objectives, while social entrepreneurs put those social issues front and center. To many corporations, social responsibility causes may just be another means to a successful business end.

**16.7  Explore audacious ideas being pursued by social entrepreneurs today.**

The Audacious Project: Collaborative Philanthropy for Bold Ideas is an initiative launched by media organization TED that provides social entrepreneurs with a platform to present their ideas to some of the most well-respected names in philanthropy.

**16.8  Illustrate the global diversity of entrepreneurship.**

There are hundreds of millions of entrepreneurs worldwide. Known as one of the most entrepreneurial nations on the planet, the United States is eclipsed by many world regions in terms of the percentage of the population engaged in entrepreneurship. Though entrepreneurs may be born out of necessity or to exploit opportunities, they all benefit from education, financial resources, accessible knowledge, and government support providing infrastructure that will enable the fledgling businesses to achieve success.

Corporate social responsibility (CSR)  445

Earned-income activities  436

Enterprising nonprofits  435

Established business owners  448

Hybrid model of social entrepreneurship  437

Nascent entrepreneurs  448

Necessity-based entrepreneurs  448

New business owners  448

## CASE STUDY

### Brandale Randolph, founder and CEO, 1854 Cycling Company

Before the 1854 Cycling Company started making state-of-the-art bicycles for law enforcement, Wharton graduate and founder Brandale Randolph was working as a commodities broker for a hedge fund in Los Angeles, California. When the financial crisis hit in 2008, Brandale's hedge fund lost 90% of its value in 48 hours. Brandale was interested in looking at PhD programs and attended a conference in Chicago called the PhD Project. Though he did not pursue a PhD, he met his future wife, Angela, at the conference. He followed her to Lubbock, Texas, where she started her PhD at Texas Tech University. Brandale started looking for work but could not find a brokerage house in Texas that could accommodate a seasoned broker. So, he started looking for something else to do.

Brandale took a low-wage job at Home Depot in Lubbock. As part of his job, he had to open the store, sometimes at 6 a.m. Because Lubbock was quite cold early in the mornings, he would stop at a fast-food restaurant to grab a cup of coffee. During one of these coffee runs, he saw a man throw a sandwich at a young man sitting outside the shop. A sandwich was thrown because the man felt that any money given would be used for alcohol or drugs. The sandwich hit the young person on his chest and fell to the ground. Brandale recalled, "I exchanged a few polite words with the gentleman but then starting talking to the young man sitting outside the coffee shop, and I learned that the boy was just a college student who needed money to get on a bus to get back home. Nobody knew that because nobody asked." This incident impacted Brandale and prompted him to do something for the poor people around Lubbock.

He started a nonprofit called Project Poverty that aimed to improve the lives of the poor. "I like numbers and created an algorithm that used 30 sets of data to discover pockets of poverty that were otherwise hidden." He identified the three most vulnerable groups in Lubbock: (1) soon-to-be-released incarcerated, (2) the chronically unemployed, and (3) at-risk young adults who don't have a stable home life. He started teaching these groups financial literacy and other life skills, yet he started to see the same people repeatedly. Brandale realized he was doing the same thing the man did outside the coffee shop—throwing the sandwich. "I was trying to beat poverty without fully understanding what the people wanted," said Brandale. "Upon revisiting the data and researching the problem, we realized that there were 30-odd internal and external factors that determined how much money a poor person had and how likely he or she was to keep it. Not just that, these people wanted different things. Soon-to-be-released offenders want to learn how to keep a job for more than 90 days and soon-to-be-released emancipated children wanted to learn how to make their money last longer. We started to teach them these things," Brandale says.

Through his experience, Brandale also learned it was very difficult to sustain a new nonprofit as it did not attract donations that were required to sustain the organization's activities. Although money was available, it usually went to bigger and older nonprofit organizations. Meanwhile, Brandale was reading about for-profit social organizations that were well positioned to provide well-paying jobs to people. He was inspired by Homeboy Bakery, a bakery that employs individuals who were previously incarcerated or gang-involved.

Brandale moved to Framingham, Massachusetts, in 2015 with his wife and kids when his wife took a faculty position after receiving her doctorate. Brandale began looking for a job. He submitted 82 job applications and got two interviews and zero job offers. His wife pointed out to him that if someone like him, with an Ivy League degree, found it difficult to get a job, the formerly incarcerated had it a lot tougher. He decided to apply the same algorithm he had developed for Project Poverty in Texas to the population in Framingham, Massachusetts. He discovered that Framingham had a disproportionate number of households led by formerly incarcerated women who had incomes below the poverty line. These women were also likely to have children under the age of 18. This was also the group that was least likely to revert to crime. Although women were less likely to revert to crime than men, they were more likely to live in poverty, with an average income of $11,500 per year. Brandale knew that if he wanted to make a lasting impact, he had to look for a for-profit model to tackle this problem.

At the same time, Brandale was looking to buy a new bike, and he couldn't find anything in the market that interested him. He then surfed the Internet and saw a number of beautiful bicycles that were being built in Europe. He decided to have a bike custom-made by Francisco Cornelio Jaquez of N+1 Cyclery in Framingham and custom leather maker Amar Sauza near Boston. Between the three of them, "The Garrison," the first bicycle by the 1854 Cycling Company, was born.

Through his research on the biking industry, Brandale discovered that bike mechanics at the time earned $13 an hour, which was above the minimum wage. On doing more research, he realized that there was also a demand in the market for master bike mechanics. Master bike mechanics are those that are "certified" to repair bicycles. Brandale saw the potential for a social, for-profit enterprise in the bike industry. He wanted to employ formerly incarcerated women he had identified in Framingham as master mechanics. Brandale believes that fair and stable employment is a good deterrent to crime. He would like to measure his company's success by the number of children of his employees who come from poverty and find their way to college. He believes that if the story is strong enough, people will not only pay for a world-class product but will also pay a premium, if they believe that their dollars are going to be used to help someone else.

To test the concept, he made a bike and tried to sell it. "We put this awesome bike on the market and sold exactly none of it. The lean business model that we used is based on creating a prototype to find market feedback before investing in unsellable inventory. We dodged a bullet because the unit cost for each bicycle was around $2,500." Talking with biking enthusiasts and retailers, attending local cycling events, and reading a trade publication called *Bicycle Retailer and Industry News*, he found out that he had not understood the Massachusetts cycling market at all. Most cyclists were vegan and anti-leather or felt that the weather in Framingham would crack the leather.

The company incorporated these learnings and started making bikes that customers wanted. They introduced single-speed bikes (called "The Craft") and cargo bikes (called "The Truth Cargo Bike"). In early 2018, they diversified into making electric bikes. "The demand for certified e-bike mechanics is very high and of the mechanics that were available, only 5% were women," he says. Brandale is now mostly focused on working with law enforcement officers to supply bikes equipped with the same technology in a squad car. Law enforcement—police—is now his primary target market. These bikes include radios and license plate scanners and enable the officers to ride the bikes on the street and do more community policing.

Brandale is also considering launching a motorbike by 2021. Apart from bikes, The 1854 Cycling Company now has its own set of merchandise that includes T-shirts, sweatshirts, hoodies, caps, and tank tops. The idea behind The 1854 Cycling Company is to create a brand that stands for a company that employs formerly incarcerated people and works toward reducing recidivism. They currently employ five women and produce 20 bikes a month.

The 1854 brand started off positioned as one of the first African American bike companies. "One of my best customers are white soccer moms. They buy my product, the merchandise, and also talk to their friends about the company. For every soccer mom customer, I get at least one more customer. In contrast, over the last 2 years, I've had only two white male customers, both of whom are my friends." Other customers include social activists, members of the #MeToo and the Black Lives Matter movements, and likewise. Today his primary customer is law enforcement. Brandale explains that his bikes are special to law enforcement because they see them as a way to give back to the community for some of their lapses of judgment toward African American people in the past.

Brandale is building a compelling story around the 1854 brand. He drew inspiration for the name of his company, The 1854 Cycling Company, from the first anti-slavery protest of the United States that happened in July 1854, at Framingham, Massachusetts. William Lloyd Garrison, a prominent abolitionist, burned the U.S. Constitution to protest the hypocrisy of celebrating independence while practicing slavery. This flame of the burning Constitution is part of their logo. He relates this protest to his company's fight against the "revolving doors of the criminal justice system where approximately 76.6% of all released prisoners will be rearrested within 5 years of their release." The brand stands for an opportunity for those people who did not have stable jobs and incomes to put food on the table and educate their children.

His advice to entrepreneurs who are planning on starting something that is potentially groundbreaking is "Do it slowly. Minimize and calculate your risk, but don't move too quickly because the industry is built to stomp companies like this into the ground."

## Critical Thinking Questions

1. What is the social mission of 1854 Cycling?

2. Does 1854 connect to any of the Sustainable Development Goals discussed in the chapter?

3. Articulate the story behind the company and evaluate its potential as a brand.

**Sources:**

Brandale Randolph (interview with Babson MBA graduate assistant Gaurav Khemka, October 25, 2018)

The 1854 Cycling Company. https://www.1854cycling.com/bicycles-2

Entrepreneurship for All. (2018). EforAll Summit 2018 Brandale Randolph full keynote [Video file]. *YouTube*. Retrieved from https://www.youtube.com/watch?v=sq-XSHBQ1d4

TEDx Talks. (2014). Stop throwing breakfast sandwiches at the poor [Video file]. *YouTube*. Retrieved from https://www.youtube.com/watch?v=v6ZWKSbeD9w

# GLOSSARY

**Accelerator:** an organization that provides tailored support in order to help new ventures scale and grow.

**Accounts payable:** money owed by a business to its suppliers.

**Accounts receivable:** money owed to the company for goods or services provided and billed to a customer.

**Accredited investors:** investors who earn an annual income of more than $200,000 or have a net worth of more than $1 million.

**Accrued expenses:** costs incurred by the company for which no payment has been made.

**Advertising revenue model:** generating revenue by advertising products and services.

**AEIOU framework:** acronym for *activities, environments, interactions, objects,* and *users*—a framework commonly used to categorize observations during fieldwork.

**Alertness:** the ability some people have to identify opportunities.

**All-benefits:** a type of value proposition that involves identifying and promoting all the benefits of a product or service to customer segments, with little regard for the competition or any real insight into what the customer really wants or needs.

**Analytical strategies:** actions that involve taking time to think carefully about a problem by breaking it up into parts, or looking at it in a more general way, in order to generate ideas about how certain products or services can be improved or made more innovative.

**Angel investor:** a type of investor who uses his or her own money to provide funds to young startup private businesses run by entrepreneurs who are neither friends nor family.

**Backlog:** orders that have been received but not delivered to the customer.

**Balance sheet:** a financial statement that shows what the company owes, what it owns, including the shareholder's stake, at a particular point in time.

**Behavior-focused strategies:** methods to increase self-awareness and manage behaviors, particularly when dealing with necessary but unpleasant tasks. These strategies include self-observation, self-goal setting, self-reward, self-punishment, and self-cueing.

**Benefit corporation (or B Corp):** a form of organization certified by the nonprofit B Lab that ensures strict standards of social and environmental performance, accountability, and transparency are met.

**Bonds:** the connections with family, friends, and others who have a similar cultural background or ethnicity.

**Bootstrapping:** the process of building or starting a business with no outside investment, funding, or support.

**Bottom-up analysis:** estimating potential sales using calculations in order to arrive at a total sales figure.

**Bottom-up (or build-up) method:** estimating revenues and costs from the smallest unit of sales, such as a day.

**Brand strategy:** a long-term plan to develop a successful brand; it involves how you plan to communicate your brand messages to your target customers.

**Branding:** the process of creating a name, term, design, symbol, or any other feature that identifies a product or service and differentiates it from others.

**Bridges:** the links that go further than simply sharing a sense of identity; for example, making connections with distant friends or colleagues who may have different backgrounds, cultures, and so on.

**Brokers:** the people who organize transactions between buyers and sellers.

**Bundled pricing:** a pricing strategy whereby companies package a set of goods or services together and then sell them for a lower price than if they were to be sold separately.

**Business model:** describes the rationale of how a new venture creates, delivers, and captures value.

**Business model canvas (BMC):** a one-page plan that divides the business model into nine components in order to provide a more thorough overview.

**Business plan:** the most formal of planning tools. It is typically a lengthy written document discussing the business concept, product mix, marketing plan, operations plan, development plan, and financial forecast.

**Buyer personas:** profiles or representations of ideal customers based on information and market research.

**C corporation:** (sometimes known as a "C-corp")—a separate legal and taxable entity created by the state government and owned by an unlimited number of shareholders.

**Capital stock:** the original amount the owners paid into the company plus any additional paid-in capital to purchase stock in the company.

**Cash conversion cycle (CCC):** the number of days a company's cash is tied up in the production and sales process.

**Cash flow statement:** a financial report that details the inflows and outflows of cash for a company over a set period of time.

**Cognitive comprehensiveness:** a process in which team members examine critical issues with a wide lens and formulate strategies by considering diverse approaches, decision criteria, and courses of action.

**Compensation policy:** The level of compensation and benefits for each type of position in the business.

**Competition-led pricing:** a pricing strategy that matches prices to other businesses selling the same or very similar products and services.

**Concept statement:** a written representation of your vision for your product or service.

**Constructive thought patterns:** models to help us to form positive and productive ways of thinking that can benefit our performance.

**Consumers:** Customers who actually use the product or service.

**Convergent thinking:** a thought process that allows us to narrow down the number of ideas generated through divergent thinking in an effort to identify which ones have the most potential.

**Convertible debt:** (also known as convertible bond or a convertible note)—a short-term loan that can be turned into equity when future financing is issued.

**Copyright:** a form of protection provided to the creators of original works in the areas of literature, music, drama, choreography, art, motion pictures, sound recordings, and architecture.

**Corporate entrepreneurship (or intrapreneurship):** a process of creating new products, ventures, processes, or renewal within large organizations.

**Corporate social responsibility (CSR):** describes the efforts taken by corporations to address the company's effects on environmental and social well-being in order to promote positive change.

**Cost of goods sold (COGS):** the direct cost of producing a product.

**Cost-led pricing:** a pricing strategy that involves calculating all the costs involved in manufacturing or delivering the product or service, plus all other expenses, and adding an expected profit or margin by predicting your sales volume to get the approximate price.

**Creation logic:** a form of thinking that is used when the future is unpredictable.

**Creativity:** the capacity to produce new ideas, insights, inventions, products, or artistic objects that are considered to be unique, useful, and of value to others.

**Credit policy:** The process and timing in which obligations to pay for products and services sold will be billed and collected.

**Crowdfunding:** the process of raising funding for a new venture from a large audience (the "crowd"), typically through the Internet.

**Crowdsourcing:** the process of using the Internet to attract, aggregate, and manage ostensibly inexpensive or even free labor from enthusiastic customers and like-minded people.

**Current assets:** cash and other assets that can be converted into cash within a year.

**Current liabilities:** bills that must be paid within 1 year of the date of the balance sheet.

**Customer:** someone who pays for a product or service.

**Customer journey map:** a visual representation that captures customer experience across multiple touchpoints.

**Customer value proposition (CVP):** a statement that describes why a customer should buy and use your product or service.

**Customer-led pricing:** a pricing strategy that asks customers how much they are willing to pay and then offers the product at that price.

**Customers:** people who populate the segments of a market served by the offering.

**Data revenue model:** generating revenue by selling high-quality, exclusive, valuable information to other parties.

**Days of inventory (DOI):** a measure of the average number of days it takes to sell the entire inventory of a company.

**Days payable outstanding (DPO):** a measure of the number of days it takes you to pay your bills.

**Days sales outstanding (DSO):** a measure of the number of days that it takes to collect on accounts receivable.

**Debt financing:** borrowing money to start a business that is expected to be paid back with interest at a designated point in the future.

**Decision makers:** customers similar to economic buyers who have even more authority to make purchasing decisions as they are positioned higher up in the hierarchy.

**Deliberate practice:** carrying out carefully focused efforts to improve current performance.

**Demand:** prospective customers' desire for the goods and services available.

**Design pathway:** a pathway that can uncover high-value opportunities because the entrepreneur is focusing on unmet needs of customers, specifically latent needs.

**Design thinking:** a human-centered approach to innovation that brings together what people need with what is technologically feasible and economically viable.

**Development strategies:** actions that involve enhancing and modifying existing ideas in order to create better alternatives and new possibilities.

**Deviance:** when an entrepreneur defies legal and ethical boundaries, leading to mismanagement of the venture.

**Direct cross-subsidies:** pricing a product or service above its market value to pay for the loss of giving away a product or service for free or below its market value.

**Divergent thinking:** a thought process that allows us to expand our view of the world to generate as many ideas as possible without being trapped by traditional problem-solving methods or predetermined constraints.

**Diversified market:** two or more customer segments with different needs and problems that bear no relationship to each other.

**Dramatic difference:** the uniqueness of your product or service in relation to other available options.

**Due diligence:** a rigorous process that involves evaluating an investment opportunity prior to the contract being signed.

**Early-stage financing:** a stage of financing that involves larger funds provided for companies that have a team in place and a product or service tested or piloted, but have little or no revenue.

**Earned-income activities:** the sale of products or services that are used as a source of revenue generation.

**Economic buyers:** the customers who have the ability to approve large-scale purchases, such as buyers for retail chains, corporate office managers, and corporate VPs.

**Effectuate pathway:** a pathway that involves using what you have (skills, knowledge, abilities) to uncover an opportunity that uniquely fits you.

**Effectuation theory:** an entrepreneurial approach to taking quick action using resources you have available to get early traction on new ideas.

**End users:** the type of customers who will use your product. Their feedback will help you refine and tweak the product.

**Enterprising nonprofits:** a form of social entrepreneurship where both the venture mission and the market impact are for social purposes.

**Entrepreneur:** an individual or a group who creates something new—a new idea, a new item or product, a new institution, a new market, a new set of possibilities.

**Entrepreneurial marketing:** a set of processes adopted by entrepreneurs based on new and unconventional marketing practices in order to gain traction in competitive markets.

**Entrepreneurial mindset:** the ability to quickly sense, take action, and get organized under uncertain conditions.

**Entrepreneurial self-efficacy (ESE):** the belief that entrepreneurs have in their own ability to begin new ventures.

**Entrepreneurs inside:** entrepreneurs who think and act entrepreneurially within organizations.

**Entrepreneurship:** a way of thinking, acting, and being that combines the ability to find or create new opportunities with the courage to act on them.

**Equity crowdfunding:** a form of crowdfunding that gives investors the opportunity to become shareholders in a company.

**Equity financing:** the sale of shares of stock in exchange for cash.

**Established business owners:** the people who have been active in business for more than 3.5 years.

**Evidence-based entrepreneurship:** the practice of hypothesizing, testing, and validating to create a business model.

**Experiment:** a method used to prove or disprove the validity of an idea or hypothesis.

**Exploratory experimentation:** a method whereby market tests are conducted to get early feedback and acquire important learning and information.

**Fair pricing:** the degree to which both businesses and customers believe that the pricing is reasonable.

**Family enterprise:** a business that is owned and managed by multiple family members, typically for more than one generation.

**Feasibility study:** a planning tool that allows entrepreneurs to test the possibilities of an initial idea to see if it is worth pursuing.

**Feedback interview:** an interview conducted to get feedback on an existing product or service.

**Financial viability:** defines the revenue and cost structures a business needs to meet its operating expenses and financial obligations.

**Find pathway:** a pathway that assumes that opportunities exist independent of entrepreneurs and are waiting to be found.

**Fixed mindset:** the assumption held by people who perceive their talents and abilities as set traits.

**Founders' agreement:** a clear agreement between founders on a number of key issues that their business might face.

**Founding team:** a group of people with complementary skills and a shared sense of commitment coming together in founding an enterprise to build and grow the company.

**Franchise:** a type of license purchased by a franchisee from an existing business called a franchisor to allow them to trade under the name of that business.

**Franchising revenue model:** earning revenue by selling franchises of an existing business to allow another party to trade under the name of that business.

**Freemium revenue model:** mixing free (mainly web-based) basic services with premium or upgraded services.

**General partnership:** a business owned by two or more people who have made a decision to comanage and share in the profits and losses.

**Goodwill:** the price paid for an asset in excess of its book value. You will see this on the balance sheet when the company has made one or more large acquisitions.

**Grit:** the quality that enables people to work hard and sustain interest in their long-term goals.

**Groupthink:** a phenomenon in which people share too similar a mindset, which inhibits their ability to spot gaps or errors.

**Growth mindset:** the assumptions held by people who believe that their abilities can be developed through dedication, effort, and hard work.

**Guerrilla marketing:** a low-budget strategy that focuses on personally interacting with a target group by promoting products and services through surprise or other unconventional means.

**Habit:** a sometimes unconscious pattern of behavior that is carried out often and regularly.

**Habit-breaking strategies:** actions that involve techniques that help to break our minds out of mental fixedness in order to bring about creative insights.

**Heterogeneous team:** a group of people with a mix of knowledge, skills, and experience.

**Homogenous team:** a group of people with the same or similar characteristics such as age, gender, ethnicity, experience, and educational background.

**Hybrid model of social entrepreneurship:** an organization with a purpose that equally emphasizes both economic and social goals.

**Hypothesis:** an assumption that is tested through research and experimentation.

**Ideation:** a creative process that involves generating and developing new ideas to address needs.

**Imagination-based strategies:** actions that involve suspending disbelief and dropping constraints in order to create unrealistic states or fantasies.

**Implementation:** a process involving the testing of assumptions of new ideas to continuously shape them into viable opportunities.

**Impression management:** paying conscious attention to the way people perceive you and taking steps to be perceived in the way you want others to see you.

**Improvisation:** the art of spontaneously creating something without preparation.

**Inattention:** when an entrepreneur becomes sidetracked from the core business.

**Inbound marketing:** bringing potential customers to your business by creating online content that addresses their needs, in order to build trust and brand awareness.

**Income statement (or profit and loss statement):** a financial report that shows revenue, expenses, and profit for a period of time, typically a month, quarter, or year.

**Incubator:** an organization that helps early stage entrepreneurs refine ideas, build out technology, and get access to resources.

**Influencers (or opinion leaders):** customers with a large following who have the power to influence our purchase decisions.

**Infrastructure:** the resources (people, technology, products, suppliers, partners, facilities, cash, etc.) that an entrepreneur must have in order to deliver the CVP.

**Initial public offering (IPO):** a company's first opportunity to sell stocks on the stock market to be purchased by members of the general public.

**Insight:** an interpretation of an observation or a sudden realization that provides us with a new understanding of a human behavior or attitude that results in the identification of a need.

**Inspiration:** the first phase of design thinking, when you develop the design challenge and acquire a deeper understanding of users.

**Intangible assets:** the value of patents, software programs, copyrights, trademarks, franchises, brand names, or assets that cannot be physically touched.

**Intellectual property (IP):** intangible personal property created by human intelligence, such as ideas, inventions, slogans, logos, and processes.

**Intelligent failures:** good failures that provide valuable new knowledge that can help a startup overcome hurdles and roadblocks.

**Interest expense:** the extent of the company's debt burden as well as representing any interest owed on borrowed money.

**Intermediation revenue model:** the different methods by which third parties such as brokers (or "middlemen") can generate money.

**Interpersonal strategies:** actions that involve group members generating ideas and building on each other's ideas.

**Introductory offer:** a pricing strategy to encourage people to try a new product by offering it for free or at a heavily discounted price.

**Inventory policy:** the level of various types of inventory (e.g., raw materials, work-in-process, finished goods) maintained and the speed with which inventory moves from the business to the customer.

**Investor model:** a crowdfunding model that gives backers an equity stake in the business in return for their funding.

**Lack of ability:** the lack of skillset to get the job done.

**Latent needs:** needs we don't know we have.

**Lean Canvas:** an adapted version of the BMC that was created to better address the needs of startup entrepreneurs.

**Lending model:** a crowdfunding model where funds are offered as loans with the expectation that the money will be repaid.

**Liabilities:** economic obligations of the company, such as money owed to lenders, suppliers, and employees.

**Licensing revenue model:** earning revenue by giving permission to other parties to use protected intellectual property (patents, copyrights, trademarks) in exchange for fees.

**Limited liability company (LLC):** a business structure that combines the taxation advantages of a partnership with the limited liability benefits of a corporation without being subject to the eligibility requirements of an S-corp.

**Linkages:** the connections to people or groups regardless of their position in an organization, society, or other community.

**Long-term debt:** obligation for debt that is due to be repaid in more than 12 months.

**Long-term investments:** assets that are more than 1 year old and are carried on the balance sheet at cost or book value with no appreciation.

**Loss leader:** a pricing strategy whereby a business offers a product or service at a lower price in an attempt to attract more customers.

**Market:** a place where people can sell goods and services (the supply) to people who wish to buy those goods and services (the demand).

**Market opportunity:** the degree of customer or market demand for a specific product application.

**Market sizing:** a method of estimating the number of potential customers and possible revenue or profitability of a product or service.

**Marketing:** a method of putting the right product in the right place, at the right price, at the right time.

**Marketing mix:** the combination of product, price, promotion, and placement of what a company is offereing.

**Mass market:** a large group of customers with very similar needs and problems.

**Metacognition:** our ability to understand and be aware of how we think and the processes we use to think.

**Microloan:** a very small, short-term loan often associated with entrepreneurs in developing countries.

**Multiparty business:** giving one party product or service free, but charging the other party (or parties).

**Multisided markets:** markets with two or more customer segments that are mutually independent of each other.

**MVP (minimum viable product):** a version of a new product that allows a team to collect the maximum amount of validated learning about customers with the least effort.

**Nascent entrepreneurs:** individuals who have set up a business they will own or co-own that is less than 3 months old and has not yet generated wages or salaries for the owners.

**Natural reward strategies:** types of compensation designed to make aspects of a task or activity more enjoyable by building in certain features or by reshaping perceptions to focus on the most positive aspects of the task and the value it holds.

**Necessity-based entrepreneurs:** individuals who are pushed into starting a business because of circumstance such as redundancy, threat of job loss, and unemployment.

**Need:** a lack of something desirable, useful, or required that is uncovered through the design process.

**Need-finding interview:** an interview conducted to better understand the problems or needs of people or validate what you think a need or problem may be.

**Net income:** indicates what is left after all costs, expenses, and taxes have been paid.

**New business owners:** individuals who are former nascent entrepreneurs and have been actively involved in a business for more than 3 months but less than 3.5 years.

**Niche market:** a small market segment that consists of customers with specific needs and requirements.

**Nondisclosure agreement (NDA):** a legal contract that outlines confidential information shared by two or more parties.

**Not-for-profit:** a tax status granted to companies performing functions deemed by Congress to be socially desirable that exempts them from income tax and, in some cases, allows them to receive tax-deductible donations.

**Observation:** the action of closely monitoring the behavior and activities of users/potential customers in their own environment.

**Offering:** what you are offering to a particular customer segment, the value generated for those customers, and how you will reach and communicate with them.

**Operating expenses:** the costs of running your business, including your rent, utilities, administration, marketing/advertising, employee salaries, and so on.

**Operating profit:** the amount left over from revenue once all costs and expenses are subtracted.

**Opportunity:** a way of generating profit through unique, novel, or desirable products or services that have not been previously exploited.

**Opportunity-based entrepreneurs:** individuals who make a decision to start their own businesses based on their ability to create or exploit an opportunity, and whose main driver for getting involved in the venture is being independent or increasing their income, rather than merely maintaining their income.

**Other current liabilities:** short-term liabilities that do not fall into a specific category, such as sales tax, income tax, and so forth.

**Outbound marketing:** promoting your product or service through traditional activities such as advertising, trade shows, and cold calling.

**Overt benefit:** the one big benefit for your customer.

**Packaging:** a process that explores every single visual element of the external appearance of an offering through the eyes of your customer.

**Passion:** an intense positive emotion, which is usually related to entrepreneurs who are engaged in meaningful ventures, or tasks and activities, and which has the effect of motivating and stimulating entrepreneurs to overcome obstacles and remain focused on their goals.

Patent: a grant of exclusive property rights on inventions through the U.S. and other governments.

Patronage model: a crowdfunding model where backers do not expect any direct return for their donation or investment..

Pattern recognition: the process of identifying links or connections between apparently unrelated things or events.

Payables policy: the process and timing in which obligations to pay for goods and services received by the business will be paid.

People: the people who are responsible for every aspect of sales and marketing.

Pilot experiment: a small-scale study conducted to assess the feasibility of a product or service.

Pitch: the act of clearly presenting and describing a product or service to others.

Pivot: a change in business direction.

Place: the location where the product is actually distributed to your target market; for example, trade fairs, retail stores, catalogs, mail order, online, and so forth.

Planning: a process of envisioning the future for a business, including what one plans to do and how one plans to do it.

Points-of-difference: a type of value proposition that focuses on the product or service relative to the competition and how the offering is different from others on the market.

Positioning: a marketing strategy that focuses on how your customers think or talk about product and company relative to competitors.

Potential entrepreneurs: individuals who believe they have the capacity and know-how to start a business without being burdened by the fear of failure.

Predictive logic: a form of thinking that sees entrepreneurship as a linear process in which steps are followed and outcomes are—ideally—predictable.

Prepaid expenses: the payments the company has already made for services not yet received.

Price: the amount that the customer is expected to pay for the product.

Pricing policy: how pricing will be determined for your products and services.

Primary research: refers to data gathered by yourself through sources such as focus groups, interviews, and surveys.

Prior knowledge: the information gained from a combination of life and work experience.

Process inadequacy: wrong (or missing) processes set up in the organization, causing communication breakdown.

Product: anything tangible or intangible (such as a service) offered by the company.

Product application: goods or services created to meet a demand, thereby providing a solution to a customer problem.

Product–market fit: an offering that meets the needs of customers.

Professional revenue model: earning revenue by providing professional services on a time and materials contract.

Promotion: the activities that involve all the ways in which companies tell their customers about their offering.

Psychological pricing: a pricing strategy intended to encourage customers to buy on the basis of their belief that the product or service is cheaper than it really is.

Purchasing policy: the price and timing of raw materials and other goods and services necessary to build, sell, and support products.

Real reason to believe: provides evidence to the customer that you will do as you promise.

Recommenders: people who may evaluate your product and tell the public about it, such as bloggers or experts in an industry.

Relationship-seeking strategies: plans of action that involve consciously making links between concepts or ideas that are not normally associated with each other.

Resonating-focus: a type of value proposition that describes why people will really like your product and focuses on the customers and what they really need and value.

Retained earnings: the cumulative amount of profit retained by the company and not paid out in the form of dividends to owners.

Revenue: the income gained from sales of goods or services.

Revenue model: a key component of the business model that identifies how the company will earn income and make profits.

Reward-based crowdfunding: a crowdfunding model that involves rewarding backers for supporting a project.

Royalties: a share of the income of a business paid by a franchisee to the franchisor.

S corporation: (sometimes known as an "S-corp")—a type of corporation that is eligible for, and elects, special taxation status.

SAM: serviceable available market; the section of the TAM that your product or service intends to target.

Search pathway: a pathway used when entrepreneurs are not quite sure what type of venture they want to start, so they engage in an active search to discover new opportunities.

Search strategies: actions that involve using a stimulus to retrieve memories in order to make links or connections based on personal experience that are relevant to the current problem.

Secondary research: refers to data gathered from external sources such as industry publications, websites, government agencies, and so on.

Seed-stage financing: a stage of financing in which small or modest amounts of capital are provided to entrepreneurs to prove a concept.

Segmented market: a market divided into groups according to customers' different needs and problems.

Self-cueing: the process of prompting that acts as a reminder of desired goals and keeps your attention on what you are trying to achieve.

Self–goal setting: the process of setting individual goals for ourselves.

Self-leadership: a process whereby people can influence and control their own behavior, actions, and thinking to achieve the self-direction and self-motivation necessary to build their entrepreneurial business ventures.

Self-observation: a process that raises our awareness of how, when, and why we behave the way we do in certain circumstances.

Self-punishment (or self-correcting feedback): a process that allows us to examine our mistakes before making a conscious effort not to repeat them.

Self-reward: a process that involves compensating ourselves when we achieve our goals. These rewards can be tangible or intangible.

**Self-selected stakeholders:** the people who "self-select" into a venture in order to connect entrepreneurs with resources in an effort to steer the venture in the right direction.

**Serial entrepreneurs (or habitual entrepreneurs):** entrepreneurs who start several businesses, either simultaneously or consecutively.

**Shareholder equity:** the money that has been invested in the business plus the cumulative net profits and losses the company has generated.

**Short-term debt:** the portion of long-term debt that must be paid within a year.

**Skimming:** a high pricing strategy, generally used for new products or services that face very little or even no competition.

**Social capital:** personal social networks populated with people who willingly cooperate, exchange information, and build trusting relationships with each other.

**Social consequence entrepreneurship:** a for-profit venture whose primary market impact is social.

**Social entrepreneurship:** the process of sourcing innovative solutions to social and environmental problems.

**Social purpose ventures:** businesses created by social entrepreneurs to resolve a social problem and make a profit.

**Sole proprietorship:** a business owned by one person who has full exposure to its liabilities.

**SOM:** share of market; the portion of SAM that your company is realistically likely to reach.

**Stakeholders:** the people or groups affected by or involved with the achievements of the social enterprise's objectives.

**Startup:** a temporary organization in search of a scalable business model.

**Startup financing:** a stage of financing in which the money is provided to entrepreneurs to enable them to implement the idea by funding product research and development.

**Storyboard:** an easy form of prototyping that provides a high-level view of thoughts and ideas arranged in sequence in the form of drawings, sketches, or illustrations.

**Subscription revenue model:** charging customers to gain continuous access to a product or service.

**Supply:** the sellers who compete for customers in the marketplace.

**Sweat equity:** a non-monetary investment that increases the value or ownership interest created by the investment of hard work for no compensation.

**TAM:** total available market; the total market demand for a product or service.

**Target-return pricing:** a pricing method whereby the price is based on the amount of investment you have put into your business.

**Top-down analysis:** determining the total market using demographic data and then estimating your share of the market.

**Total Entrepreneurial Activity (TEA):** the percentage of the population of each country between the ages of 18 and 64, who are either a nascent entrepreneur or owner—manager of a new business.

**Trade secret:** confidential information that provides companies with a competitive edge and is not in the public domain, such as formulas, patterns, compilations, programs, devices, methods, techniques, or processes.

**Trademark:** any word, name, symbol, or device used in business to identify and promote a product. Its counterpart for service industries is the service mark.

**True fans:** people who will buy anything you produce; they will wait in line for your products, drive for hours to attend one of your events, and preorder your next product without even knowing what it looks like.

**Uncertainty:** the lack of clarity about future events that can cause entrepreneurs to take unreasonable actions.

**Unicorn:** a tech startup company that has received a $1 billion valuation, as determined by private or public investment.

**Unit sales revenue model:** generating revenue by the number of items (units) sold by a company.

**Use case:** a methodology used in the software industry to illustrate how a user will interact with a specific piece of software.

**Utility and usage revenue model:** a pay-as-you-go model that charges customers fees on the basis of how often goods or services are used.

**Value-based pricing:** a pricing method that involves pricing a product based on how it benefits the customer.

**Venture capitalist (VC):** a type of professional investor who generally invests in early-stage and emerging companies because of perceived long-term growth potential.

**Venture philanthropy funding:** a combination of financial assistance such as grants with a high level of engagement by the funder.

**Vesting:** the concept of imposing equity forfeitures on cofounders over a certain period of time on a piecemeal basis should they not stay with the company.

**Wicked problems:** large, complex social problems where there is no clear solution; where there is limited, confusing, or contradictory information available; and where a whole range of people with conflicting values engage in debate.

# NOTES

## CHAPTER 1

1. Blank, S., & Dorf, B. (2012). *The startup owner's manual: The step-by-step guide for building a great company*. Pescadero, CA: K&S Ranch.

2. Neck, H. M., Greene, P. G., & Brush, C. B. (2014). *Teaching entrepreneurship: A practice-based approach*. Northampton, MA: Edward Elgar.

3. Sarasvathy, S. D. (2008). *Effectuation: Elements of entrepreneurial expertise*. Northampton, MA: Edward Elgar.

4. Sarasvathy, *Effectuation*.

5. Morris, M. H. (1998). *Entrepreneurial intensity: Sustainable advantages for individuals, organizations, and societies*. Westport, CT: Quorum.

6. Neck, H. M., & Greene, P. G. (2011). Entrepreneurship education: Known worlds and new frontiers. *Journal of Small Business Management, 49*, 55–70.

7. Brown, P. (2013, November 6). Entrepreneurs are "calculated" risk takers—The word that can be the difference between failure and success. *Forbes*. Retrieved from www.forbes.com/sites/actiontrumpseverything/2013/11/06/entrepreneurs-are-not-risk-takers-they-are-calculated-risk-takers-that-one-additional-word-can-be-the-difference-between-failure-and-success/

8. Schlesinger, L., Kiefer, C., & Brown, P. (2012). *Just start: Take action, embrace uncertainty, create the future*. Cambridge, MA: Harvard Business School Press.

9. Costello, C., Neck, H., & Williams, R. (2011). *Elements of the entrepreneur experience*. Babson Park, MA: Babson Entrepreneur Experience Lab. Retrieved from http://elab.businessinnovationfactory.com/sites/default/files/pdf/BabsonBIF-eLab-NVE-V1-2012rev.pdf

10. Rosen, A. (2015, May 7). *Why collaboration is essential to entrepreneurship*. Retrieved from https://www.entrepreneur.com/article/245599

11. Spors, K. K. (2007, January 9). Do start-ups really need formal business plans? Studies find often time wasted gathering data with no link to success. *Wall Street Journal*. Retrieved from http://www.wsj.com/articles/SB116830373855570835

12. Costello, Neck, & Williams, *Elements*.

13. Covin, J. G., & Miles, M. (1999). Corporate entrepreneurship and the pursuit of competitive advantage. *Entrepreneurship: Theory and Practice, 23*(3), 47–63.

14. Elkins, F. (2018, September 17). *The Corporate Entrepreneur Awards 2018: Recognizing the best in corporate innovation*. Retrieved from https://www.marketgravity.com/cea-celebrating-the-best-in-corporate-innovation/

15. Costello, C., Neck, H., & Dziobek, K. (2012). *Entrepreneurs of all kinds: Elements of the entrepreneurs inside experience*. Babson Park, MA: Babson Entrepreneur Experience Lab. Retrieved from http://elab.businessinnovationfactory.com/sites/default/files/pdf/babsonBIF-elab-EI-V2-2012rev.pdf

16. Ibid.

17. Judd, R. J., & Justis, R. T. (2007). *Franchising: An entrepreneur's guide* (4th ed.). Stamford, CT: Cengage Learning.

18. Retrieved from https://www.entrepreneur.com/franchises/500/2017

19. Mazareanu, E. (2019). Number of franchise establishments in the United States from 2007 to 2018. *Statista*. Retrieved from https://www.statista.com/statistics/190313/estimated-number-of-us-franchise-establishments-since-2007/

20. U.S. Small Business Administration. (n.d.). *Buy an existing business or franchise*. Retrieved from https://www.sba.gov/content/buying-existing-business

21. Chris Cranston, interview with the author.

22. Neck, H. M. (2010). Social entrepreneurship. In B. Bygrave & A. Zacharakis (Eds.), *The portable MBA in entrepreneurship* (pp. 411–436). Hoboken, NJ: Wiley.

23. Neck, H. M., Brush, C., & Allen, E. (2009). The landscape of social entrepreneurship. *Business Horizons, 52*, 13–19; Mair, J., & Marti, I. (2006). Social entrepreneurship research: A source of explanation, prediction and delight. *Journal of World Business, 41*, 36–44.

24. B Lab. (2019). *About B corps*. Retrieved from https://bcorporation.net/about-b-corps

25. Clifford, C. (2012, June 11). B corps: The next generation of company. *Entrepreneur*. Retrieved from www.entrepreneur.com/blog/223762

26. Smithers, R. (2016, January 22). Raise a toast and help tackle the problem of food waste. *The Guardian*. Retrieved from https://www.theguardian.com/uk-news/2016/jan/22/toast-ale-beer-surplus-bread-feedback-food-waste

27. Habbershon, T. G., Williams, M., & MacMillan, I. C. (2003). A unified systems perspective of family firm performance. *Journal of Business Venturing, 18*, 451–465.

28. Mars, V. (2017, April 19). *How does a family business survive?* Retrieved from https://insights.com.yale.edu/insights/how-does-family-business-survive

29. Ibid.

30. Featherstone, E. (2017, January 11). The women-led startups smashing the glass ceiling. *The Guardian*. Retrieved from https://www.theguardian.com/small-business-network/2017/jan/11/women-led-startups-smashing-glass-ceiling-investment

31. Blank & Dorf, *The startup owner's manual*.

32. McIntyre, G. (2019, March 20). What percentage of small businesses fail? (And other need-to-know stats). *Fundera*. Retrieved from https://www.fundera.com/blog/what-percentage-of-small-businesses-fail

33. Neck, H. M., & Greene, P. G. (2011). Entrepreneurship education: Known worlds and new frontiers. *Journal of Small Business Management, 49*, 55–70.

34. Neck, H. M., Greene, P. G., & Brush, C. B. (2014/2015). Practice-based entrepreneurship education using actionable theory. In M. Morris (Ed.), *Annals of entrepreneurship education and pedagogy* (pp. 3–20). Northampton, MA: Edward Elgar.

35. Blank & Dorf, *The startup owner's manual*.

36. Lehrer, J. (Host). (2006, November 22). Banker to the poor [Television broadcast]. In *The NewsHour With Jim Lehrer*. Arlington, VA: PBS. Retrieved from http://www.skaggsisland.org/sustainable/muhammadyunus.htm

37. Read, S., Sarasvathy, S., Dew, N., & Wiltbank, R. (2011). *Effectual entrepreneurship*. New York, NY: Routledge.

38. Mask, C. (2014, November 4). The 4 reasons why people start their own businesses. *The Business Journals.* Retrieved from http://www.bizjournals.com/bizjournals/how-to/growth-strategies/2014/11/4-reasons-why-people-start-their-own-businesses.html; Wells, C. (2015, May 26). Why some entrepreneurs feel fulfilled—But others don't: Money is only part of the equation; The latest research offers surprising insights into the path to satisfaction. *Wall Street Journal,* p. R.1.

39. Sarasvathy, *Effectuation.*

40. The concept of affordable loss is based on the previously cited words of Saras Sarasvathy.

41. Baron, R. A., & Henry, R. A. (2010). How entrepreneurs acquire the capacity to excel: Insights from research on expert performance. *Strategic Entrepreneurship Journal, 4,* 49–65.

42. Ibid.

43. Duvivier, R. J., van Dalen, J., Muijtjens, A. M., Moulaert, V., van der Vleuten, C., & Scherpbier, A. (2011). The role of deliberate practice in the acquisition of clinical skills. *BMC Medical Education, 11,* 101–108.

44. Clear, J. (2018). *The beginner's guide to deliberate practice.* Retrieved from https://jamesclear.com/beginners-guide-deliberate-practice

45. Ibid.

46. Ibid.

47. Wasserman, N. (2014, August 25). How an entrepreneur's passion can destroy a startup. *Wall Street Journal.* Retrieved from http://online.wsj.com/articles/how-an-entrepreneur-s-passion-can-destroy-a-startup-1408912044

48. Shen, J. (2017, May 31). The complete guide to deliberate practice. *Better Humans.* Retrieved from https://betterhumans.coach.me/the-complete-guide-to-deliberate-practice-3a70319be3af

49. Sarasvathy, *Effectuation.*

50. Dew, N., Read, S., Sarasvathy, S. D., & Wiltbank, R. (2009). Effectual versus predictive logics in entrepreneurial decision-making: Differences between experts and novices. *Journal of Business Venturing, 24,* 287–309.

## CHAPTER 2

1. McKean, E. (Ed.). (2005). *New Oxford American dictionary* (2nd ed.). New York, NY: Oxford University Press.

2. Walker, H. (2019, February 1). Is Cory Booker for real? Retrieved from https://www.huffpost.com/entry/cory-booker-real_n_5c54a758e4b08710475356a8

3. Taghavi, A. R. (2018, December 4). Cory Booker's mentor, Virginia Jones on being optimistic in the hardest times. Retrieved from https://medium.com/swlh/cory-bookers-mentor-virginia-jones-on-being-optimistic-in-the-hardest-times-9f3d4830755e

4. Dweck, C. (2006). *Mindset: The new psychology of success.* New York, NY: Random House.

5. Bronson, P. (2007, August 3). How not to talk to your kids. *New York Magazine.* Retrieved from http://nymag.com/news/features/27840/

6. Ibid.

7. Dweck, C. (2016). *Mindset: The new psychology of success* (2nd ed.). New York, NY: Random House.

8. Dweck, C. (2010). How can you change from a fixed mindset to a growth mindset? *Mindset.* Retrieved from http://mindsetonline.com/changeyourmindset/firststeps/

9. Ireland, R. D., Hitt, M. A., & Simon, D. G. (2003). A model of strategic entrepreneurship: The construct and its dimensions. *Journal of Management, 29,* 963–990.

10. Cardon, M. S., Vincent, J., Singh, J., & Drnovsek, M. (2009). The nature and experience of entrepreneurial passion. *Academy of Management Review, 34,* 511–532.

11. Warren, R. (2013, September 7). 101 best inspirational quotes for entrepreneurs. *Business Insider.* Retrieved from http://www.businessinsider.com/101-best-inspirational-quotes-for-entrepreneurs-2013-9

12. Cardon et al., The nature and experience.

13. Brännback, M., Carsrud, A., Elfying, J., & Krueger, N. (2006). *Sex, [drugs], and entrepreneurial passion? An exploratory study.* Paper presented at the Babson College Entrepreneurship Research Conference, Bloomington, IN.

14. Baron, R. A. (2008). The role of affect in the entrepreneurial process. *Academy of Management Review, 33,* 328–340.

15. Cardon et al., The nature and experience.

16. De Witte, M. (2018, June 18). Instead of "finding your passion," try developing it, Stanford scholars say. *Stanford News Service.* Retrieved from https://news.stanford.edu/press-releases/2018/06/18/find-passion-may-bad-advice/

17. Duhigg, C. (2012, February 27). How you can harness the power of habit. *NPR.* Retrieved from http://www.npr.org/2012/02/27/147296743/how-you-can-harness-the-power-of-habit

18. Information in this section taken from D'Intino, R. S., Goldsby, M. G.,

Houghton, J. D., & Neck, C. P. (2007). Self-leadership: A process for entrepreneurial success. *Journal of Leadership & Organizational Studies, 13*(4), 105–120.

19. Manz, C., & Neck, C. (2004). *Mastering self-leadership: Empowering yourself for personal excellence* (3rd ed.). Saddle River, NJ: Pearson Prentice Hall.

20. Neck, H. M. (2010). Idea generation. In B. Bygrave & A. Zacharakis (Eds.), *Portable MBA in entrepreneurship* (pp. 27–52). Hoboken, NJ: Wiley.

21. Kang, H. (2018, April 27). *Behold the winners of the 2018 Cartier Women's Initiative Awards.* Retrieved from website https://www.prestigeonline.com/sg/people-events/behold-winners-2018-cartier-womens-initiative-awards/

22. Hamidi, D. Y., Wennberg, K., & Berglund, H. (2008). Creativity in entrepreneurship education. *Journal of Small Business and Enterprise Development, 15*(2), 301–320.

23. Neck, Idea generation, 34–35.

24. Adams, J. (2001). *Conceptual blockbusting* (4th ed.). Cambridge, MA: Perseus.

25. Hayton, J., & Cacciotti, G. (2018, April 3). How fear helps (and hurts) entrepreneurs. *Harvard Business Review.* Retrieved from https://hbr.org/2018/04/how-fear-helps-and-hurts-entrepreneurs

26. Pink, D. H. (2005). *A whole new mind: Why right-brainers will rule the future.* New York, NY: Riverhead Books.

27. Nielsen, J. A., Zielinski, B. A., Ferguson, M. A., Lainhart, J. E., & Anderson, J. S. (2013). An evaluation of the left-brain vs. right-brain hypothesis with resting state functional connectivity magnetic resonance imaging. *PLoS ONE, 8*(8), e71275. doi:10.1371/journal.pone.0071275

28. Right brain, left brain? Scientists debunk popular theory. (2013, August 8). *Huffington Post.* Retrieved from http://www.huffingtonpost.com/2013/08/19/right-brain-left-brain-debunked_n_3762322.html

29. Csikszentmihalyi, M. (1996). *Creativity: Flow and the psychology of discovery and invention.* New York, NY: HarperCollins.

30. Hmieleski, K., & Corbett, A. (2008). The contrasting interaction effects of improvisational behavior with entrepreneurial self-efficacy on new venture performance and entrepreneur work satisfaction. *Journal of Business Venturing, 23,* 482–496.

31. Gotts, I., & Cremer, J. (2012). *Using improv in business.* Retrieved from http://iangotts.files.wordpress.com/2012/02/using-improv-in-business-e2-v1.pdf

32. Tutton, M. (2010, February 18). Why using improvisation to teach business skills is no joke. *CNN*. Retrieved from http://edition.cnn.com/2010/BUSINESS/02/18/improvisation.business.skills/

33. White, S. (2018, January 31). How an improv class can help develop essential business skills. *Financial Management*. Retrieved from https://www.fm-magazine.com/issues/2018/feb/improv-class-helps-develop-business-skills.html

34. Zagorski, N. (2008, Fall). The science of improv. *Peabody Magazine*. Retrieved from http://www.peabody.jhu.edu/past_issues/fall08/the_science_of_improv.html

35. Schwartz, K. (2014, April 11). Creativity and the brain: What we can learn from jazz musicians. *Mindshift*. Retrieved from http://blogs.kqed.org/mindshift/2014/04/the-link-between-jazz-improvisation-and-student-creativity/

36. McGee, J. E., Peterson, M., Mueller, S., & Sequeira, J. (2009). Entrepreneurial self-efficacy: Refining the measure. *Entrepreneurship Theory & Practice, 33*, 965–988.

37. Godwin, J. L., Neck, C. P., & D'Intino, R. S. (2016). Self-leadership, spirituality and entrepreneurial performance: A conceptual model. *Journal of Management, Spirituality, and Religion, 13*(1), 64–78.

38. DeMers, J. (2017, December 14). 5 entrepreneurs who started with nothing—and 3 lessons to learn: Sam Walton. George Soros. Kevin Plank. Jan Koum. What can these successful entrepreneurs teach you? *Entrepreneur*. Retrieved from https://www.entrepreneur.com/article/305990

39. Schwarzer, R., & Jerusalem, M. (1995). Generalized self-efficacy scale. In J. Weinman, S. Wright, & M. Johnston (Eds.), *Measures in health psychology: A user's portfolio. Causal and control beliefs* (pp. 35–37). Windsor, UK: NFER-NELSON. Scale retrieved from http://userpage.fu-berlin.de/~health/engscal.htm

## CHAPTER 3

1. Baron, R. A. (2006). Opportunity recognition as pattern recognition: How entrepreneurs "connect the dots" to identify new business opportunities. *Academy of Management Perspectives, 20*, 104–119.

2. Sheffield, H. (2017, July 26). Bios Urn: The startup that lets you grow a tree from human ashes. *The Independent*. Retrieved from https://www.independent.co.uk/Business/indyventure/startup-biodegradable-urn-grow-tree-human-remains-business-a7852446.html

3. History timeline: Post-it notes. (2014). *Post-it*. Retrieved from https://www.post-it.com/3M/en_US/post-it/contact-us/about-us/

4. From Crystal Pepsi to Colgate lasagna: Big companies' biggest product failures. (2019). *MSN*. Retrieved from https://www.msn.com/en-gb/money/companies/from-crystal-pepsi-to-colgate-lasagna-big-companies-biggest-product-failures/ss-BBSq6XA?li=AAnZ9Ug#image=13

5. Nguyen, T. C. (2018, March 29). 5 weird inventions that were surprisingly successful. *Liveaboutdotcom*. Retrieved from https://www.thoughtco.com/weird-inventions-4150072

6. Nova, A. (2017, December 11). 10 unlikely products that made millions of dollars. *CNBC*. Retrieved from https://www.cnbc.com/2017/12/11/10-unlikely-products-that-made-millions-of-dollars.html

7. Ibid.

8. Bizarre inventions that made serious bucks. (2016). *Business Management Degrees*. Retrieved from http://www.business-management-degree.net/bizarre-inventions-that-made-serious-bucks/

9. Thompson, D. (2012, June 15). Forget Edison: This is how history's greatest inventions really happened. *The Atlantic*. Retrieved from http://www.theatlantic.com/business/archive/2012/06/forget-edison-this-is-how-historys-greatest-inventions-really-happened/258-525/

10. Ibid.

11. Smith, G. F. (1998). *Quality problem solving* (pp. 133–135). Milwaukee, WI: ASQ Quality Press.

12. Climbing Mount Everest is work for supermen. (1923, March 18). *The New York Times*. Retrieved from http://graphics8.nytimes.com/packages/pdf/arts/mallory1923.pdf

13. This section is heavily sourced from four primary works: Alvarez, S. A., & Barney, J. B. (2007). Discovery and creation: Alternative theories of entrepreneurial action. *Strategic Entrepreneurship Journal, 1*, 11–26; Neck, H. (2018, August 22). Entrepreneurial intelligence [Video file]. Retrieved from https://www.youtube.com/watch?v=91APSwO9urc; Neck, H. M., Brush, C., & Corbett, A. C. (2018). *Entrepreneurial intelligence: Beyond the mindset* (Paper presented at Babson College); Townsend, D. M., Hunt, R. A., McMullen, J. S., & Sarasvathy, S. D. (2018). Uncertainty, knowledge problems, and entrepreneurial action. *Academy of Management Annals, 12*(2), 659–687.

14. Schumpeter, J. (1934/2004). *The theory of economic development: An inquiry into profits, capital, credit, interest and the business cycle*. Cambridge, MA: Harvard Business School.

15. Brush, C. B., Greene, P. G., & Hart, M. M. (2001). From initial idea to unique advantage: The entrepreneurial challenge of constructing a resource base. *Academy of Management Perspectives, 15*(1), 64–78.

16. Baron, Opportunity recognition as pattern recognition.

17. Fiet, J. O. (2000). The theoretical side of teaching entrepreneurship. *Journal of Business Venturing, 16*, 1–24; Fiet, J. O. (2002). *The systematic search for entrepreneurial discoveries*. Westport, CT: Quorum Books.

18. Marx, R. (2009). For Liddabit's Jen King and Liz Gutman, life is sweet. *Village Voice*. Retrieved from https://www.villagevoice.com/2009/11/16/for-liddabits-jen-king-and-liz-gutman-life-is-sweet/

19. Wilson, J. (2016). Liz Gutman & Jen King, Liddabit Sweets, women entrepreneurs. *Gotham Gal*. Retrieved from https://gothamgal.com/2016/02/liz-gutman-jen-king-luddabit-sweets-women-entrepreneurs/

20. Alvarez & Barney, Discovery and creation.

21. Kirzner, I. M. (1973). *Competition and entrepreneurship*. Chicago, IL: University of Chicago Press; Kirzner, I. M. (1997). Entrepreneurial discovery and the competitive market process: An Austrian approach. *Journal of Economic Literature, 35*, 60–85.

22. The invention of football—The story behind the ball we all know. (2015). *The Inventions Handbook*. Retrieved from http://www.inventions-handbook.com/invention-of-football.html

23. The concept of optimism and persistence is pervasive in entrepreneurship research. See Shane, S., Locke, E. A., & Collins, C. J. (2003). Entrepreneurial motivation. *Human Resource Management Review, 29*(2), 257–279; Cardon, M. S., & Kirk, C. P. (2015). Entrepreneurial passion as mediator of the self-efficacy to persistence relationship. *Entrepreneurship Theory and Practice, 39*(5), 1029–1050; Hmieleski, K. M., & Baron, R. A. (2009). Entrepreneurs' optimism and new venture performance: A social cognitive perspective. *Academy of Management Journal, 52*(3), 473–488.

24. Baron, Opportunity recognition as pattern recognition.

25. Shane, S. (2000). Prior knowledge and the discovery of entrepreneurial opportunities. *Organization Science, 11*, 448–469.

26. McKelvie, A., & Wiklund, J. (2004). How knowledge affects opportunity discovery and exploitation among

new ventures in dynamic markets. In J. E. Butler (Ed.), *Opportunity identification and entrepreneurial behavior* (pp. 219–239). Greenwich, CT: Information Age.

27. Glauser, M. (2016). 3 types of experiences that will help your startup succeed. *Entrepreneur.* Retrieved from https://www.entrepreneur.com/article/275091

28. Baron, Opportunity recognition as pattern recognition. The concept of pattern recognition comes from a rich research stream in cognition. See, for example, Matlin, M. W. (2002). *Cognition* (5th ed.). Fort Worth, TX: Harcourt College.

29. Baron, Opportunity recognition as pattern recognition.

30. Cutrin, M. (2018). 42 percent of startups fail for this 1 simple reason (it's not what you think). *Inc.* Retrieved from https://www.inc.com/melanie-curtin/the-no-1-reason-most-startups-fail-dont-make-this-mistake.html

31. Cohen, D., Shinnar, R. S., & Hsu, D. K. (2019). *Enhancing opportunity recognition skills in entrepreneurship education: A new approach and empirical test.* 2019 Babson College Entrepreneurship Research Conference, Babson Park, MA; Cohen, D., Pool, G., & Neck, H. (in press). *The IDEATE method: An empirically proven approach to generate high potential entrepreneurial ideas.* Thousand Oaks, CA: SAGE.

32. The great Pacific garbage patch. (2019). *The Ocean Cleanup.* Retrieved from https://www.theoceancleanup.com/great-pacific-garbage-patch/

33. Center for Disease Control and Prevention. (2017). *A look inside food deserts.* Retrieved from https://www.cdc.gov/features/fooddeserts/

## CHAPTER 4

1. Vredenburg, K. (2016). *Design vs design thinking explained.* Retrieved from https://www.karelvredenburg.com/home/2016/8/29/design-vs-design-thinking-explained

2. Design thinking defined. (n.d.). *IDEO.* Retrieved from https://designthinking.ideo.com/

3. Liedtka, J., & Ogilvie, T. (2011). *Designing for growth: A design thinking toolkit for managers.* New York, NY: Columbia University Press. [location 168 of 3511, Kindle.]

4. Brown, T., & Katz, B. (2009). *Change by design: How design thinking transforms organizations and inspires innovation* (p. 17). New York, NY: HarperCollins.

5. Neck, H. (2012, March 8). What is design thinking and why do

entrepreneurs need to care? *BostInno.* Retrieved from http://bostinno.streetwise.co/2012/03/08/what-is-design-thinking-and-why-do-entrepreneurs-need-to-care/

6. Berger, W. (2012, September 17). The secret phrase top innovators use. *Harvard Business Review.* Retrieved from https://hbr.org/2012/09/the-secret-phrase-top-innovato/

7. IDEO's human-centered design process: How to make things people love. (2018). *UserTesting.* Retrieved from https://www.usertesting.com/blog/how-ideo-uses-customer-insights-to-design-innovative-products-users-love/

8. A game-changing approach to sleep for athletes. (2016). *IDEO.* Retrieved from https://www.ideo.com/case-study/a-game-changing-approach-to-sleep-for-athletes

9. Hasso Plattner Institute of Design at Stanford. (n.d.). *An introduction to design thinking: Process guide.* Retrieved from https://dschool.stanford.edu/sandbox/groups/designresources/wiki/36873/attachments/74b3d/ModeGuideBOOTCAMP2010L.pdf

10. Ibid.

11. Brown, T., & Katz, B. (2019). How great design could fix the world's "wicked problems." *Fortune.* Retrieved from http://fortune.com/2019/02/15/change-by-design-new-excerpt-tim-brown/

12. MIT AgeLab. (2019). *AGNES (Age Gain Now Empathy System).* Retrieved from http://agelab.mit.edu/agnes-age-gain-now-empathy-system

13. Chion, J. (2013). What it's like to work at IDEO. *Medium.* Retrieved from https://medium.com/@jimmmy/what-its-like-to-work-at-ideo-6ca2c961aae4

14. The ladder example is borrowed from Dev Patnaik, cofounder of Jump Associates.

15. Patnaik, D. (2009). *Wired to care: How companies prosper when they create widespread empathy.* Upper Saddle River, NJ: FT Press.

16. Wheeler, R., & Osborn, A. F. (n.d.). The father of brainstorming. *RussellAWheeler.com.* Retrieved from http://russellawheeler.com/resources/learning_zone/alex_f_osborn/

17. Bell-Mayeda, M. (2018). 3 tips to help you prototype a service. *IDEO.* Retrieved from https://www.ideo.com/blog/3-tips-to-help-you-prototype-a-service

18. Mockplus. (2019, February 25). *What is rapid prototyping? A full guide for beginners.* Retrieved from https://www.mockplus.com/blog/post/what-is-rapid-prototyping

19. IDEO. (2015). *The field guide to human-centered design.* San Francisco, CA:

Author, 159. Retrieved from http://d1r3w4d5z5a88i.cloudfront.net/assets/guide/Field%20Guide%20to%20Human-Centered%20Design_IDEOorg_English-ee47a1ed4b91f3252115b83152828d7e.pdf

20. Gray, S. (2010, May 4). Insights—What are they really? *Quirk.* Retrieved from http://www.quirk.biz/resources/article/4878/insights

21. Ibid.

22. Williams, L. (2011, April 11). The key to design insights: See the world differently. *The Atlantic.* Retrieved from http://www.theatlantic.com/business/archive/2011/04/the-key-to-design-insights-see-the-world-differently/237117/

23. Sauro, J. (2015). 4 types of observational research. *MeasuringU.* Retrieved from https://measuringu.com/observation-role/

24. AEIOU framework. (n.d.). Retrieved from http://help.ethnohub.com/guide/aeiou-framework

25. Tool, K. (2011, March 28). Design thinking and three ways to improve our observation skills. *Design Due.* Retrieved from https://designdue.wordpress.com/2011/03/28/design-thinking-and-three-ways-to-improve-our-observation-skills/

26. Brown, T. (2012, November 27). One design thinking tip you can use right now. *Design Thinking.* Retrieved from http://designthinking.ideo.com/?p=784

27. Constable, G. (2014). *Talking to humans: Success starts with understanding your customers.* Retrieved from https://www.talkingtohumans.com/

28. Stocker Partnership. (2014). Innovation tools: Empathy mapping [slideshow]. *Slideshare.* Retrieved from http://www.slideshare.net/stockerpartnership/innovation-tools-empathy-mapping

29. Stanford Design School. (n.d.). *Empathy map.* Retrieved from http://dschool.stanford.edu/wp-content/themes/dschool/method-cards/empathy-map.pdf

30. Liedtka & Ogilvie. *Designing for growth.*

31. Design Sprints. (n.d.). *Transform the way your team works.* Retrieved from https://designsprintkit.withgoogle.com/introduction/overview

32. Liedtka & Ogilvie. *Designing for growth.*

## CHAPTER 5

1. Osterwalder, A., & Pigneur, Y. (2010). *Business model generation: A handbook for visionaries, game changers, and challengers.* Hoboken, NJ: Wiley.

2. Amit, R. (2014, November 18). The latest innovation: Redesigning the business model. *Knowledge@Wharton.* Retrieved

from http://knowledge.wharton.upenn .edu/article/redesigning-business-model/

3. Nunes, K. (2018). Product innovation central to General Mills' growth plans. *Food Business News*. Retrieved from https://www.foodbusinessnews.net/ articles/12141-product-innovation-central-to-general-mills-growth-plans

4. Johnson, M., Christensen, C., & Kagerman, H. (2008, December). Reinventing your business model. *Harvard Business Review*, 1–11; Osterwalder & Pigneur, *Business model generation*.

5. Info entrepreneurs. (n.d.). Price your product or service. Retrieved from https://www.infoentrepreneurs.org/en/ guides/price-your-product-or-service/

6. Shoot, B. (2018). How do you innovate a barbershop? Ask Great Clips franchisees. *Entrepreneur*. Retrieved from https://www.entrepreneur.com/ article/306749

7. Turn a 'no' into a winning solution [slideshow]. (n.d.). *Entrepreneur*. Retrieved from https://www.entrepreneur.com/ slideshow/281277#1

8. Amit, The latest innovation.

9. Anderson, J., Narus, J., & van Rossum, W. (2006, March). Customer value propositions in business markets. *Harvard Business Review*, 91–99.

10. Amit, The latest innovation.

11. Johnson et al., Reinventing your business model, 3.

12. Johnson, M. W. (2010, February 3). A new framework for business models strategy and innovation. *Innosight*. Retrieved from http://www.innosight .com/innovation-resources/a-new-framework-for-business-models.cfm

13. Hall, D. (2005). *Jump start your business brain: The scientific way to make more money*. Cincinnati, OH: Eureka! Institute.

14. Milne, R. (2018). IKEA vows "transformation" as it reshapes business model. *Financial Times*. Retrieved from https://www.ft.com/content/1a66c838-3cc1-11e8-b7e0-52972418fec4

15. Johnson et al., Reinventing your business model.

16. Osterwalder & Pigneur, Business model generation, 129.

17. Sundelin, A. (2009, December 10). Tata Motors—Inexpensive cars for modular distribution. *The Business Model Database*. Retrieved from http://tbmdb .blogspot.com/2009/12/business-model-example-tata-motors.html

18. Sundelin, Tata Motors; Fogarty, J. (2009, April 7). Tata's Nano: How'd they do it? *Seeking Alpha*. Retrieved from http://seekingalpha.com/ article/129832-tatas-nano-howd-they-do-it

19. No production of Tata Nano for third month in row, no sales in March. (2019). *Livemint*. Retrieved from https:// www.livemint.com/auto-news/ no-production-of-tata-nano-for-third-month-in-row-no-sales-in-march-1554219198846.html

20. Ghosh, K. (2018). It's time to say ta-ta to the world's cheapest car. *Quartz India*. Retrieved from https://qz.com/ india/1326635/tata-nano-the-slow-death-of-the-worlds-cheapest-car/

21. Ibid.

22. Freyer, F. (2015). It costs you $43 every time you wait for the doctor. *Boston Globe*. Retrieved from https://www.bostonglobe.com/ metro/2015/10/05/study-puts-dollar-value-time-spent-waiting-for-doctor/ If7KB4aU9mkY5qK8CqDYUO/story.html

23. Wartzman, R. (2013). The real face of healthcare reform. *Time*. Retrieved from http://business.time .com/2013/10/09/the-real-face-of-healthcare-reform/

24. Shah, H. (2017). How Grammarly quietly grew its way to 6.9 million daily users in 9 years. *Medium*. Retrieved from https://medium.com/swlh/ how-grammarly-quietly-grew-its-way-to-6-9-million-daily-users-in-9-years-88e417dbfbdf

25. Schroeder, J. (2018). How this 23-year-old college dropout built a $41m company. *Forbes*. Retrieved from https://www.forbes.com/sites/ julesschroeder/2018/01/25/how-this-23-year-old-college-drop-out-built-a-41m-company/#4416a4733aa7

26. Anderson, J., Narus, J., & van Rossum, W. (2006, March). Customer value propositions in business markets. *Harvard Business Review*, 91–99.

27. Blank, S., & Dorf, B. (2012). *The startup owner's manual: Step-by-step guide for building a great company* (pp. 87–88). California: K&S Ranch.

28. Rosemesh. (2014, May 31). Business model canvas customer segments [Video file]. Retrieved from https://www.youtube.com/ watch?v=VJdaCvviktk

29. Diet Coke vs. Coca-Cola Zero: What's the difference? (2017). *Huffington Post*. Retrieved from http://www .huffingtonpost.com/2012/01/11/ diet-coke-vs-coca-cola-zero_n_119 9008.html

30. Coke Zero ads aim clearly at the lads. (2006, July 8). *The Grocer*. Retrieved from http://www.thegrocer.co.uk/ fmcg/-coke-zero-ads-aim-clearly-at-the-lads/111665.article

31. Osterwalder & Pigneur, *Business model generation*, 21.

32. Ibid.

33. This section borrows heavily from Osterwalder & Pigneur, *Business model generation*.

34. Ash Maurya adapted the Business Model Canvas to better meet the needs of startup entrepreneurs. His version has been popularized as the Lean Canvas. Maurya, A. (2012). *Running lean* (2nd ed.). Sebastopol, CA: O'Reilly Media; Maurya, A. (2012). Why Lean Canvas vs Business Model Canvas? *Medium*. Retrieved from https://blog.leanstack.com/why-lean-canvas-vs-business-model-canvas-af62c0f250f0; Canvanizer. (n.d.). *Business model canvas vs. lean canvas*. Retrieved from https://canvanizer.com/how-to-use/business-model-canvas-vs-lean-canvas; Inspire9. (2017). Lean canvas is the new business plan. *Medium*. Retrieved from https://medium.com/@ inspire9/lean-canvas-is-the-new-business-plan-513dbfebbe8b

## CHAPTER 6

1. Nijssen, E. (2014). *Entrepreneurial marketing: An effectual approach* (p. 29). London: Routledge.

2. Moore, G. A. (2006). *Crossing the chasm: Marketing and selling high-tech products to mainstream customers*. New York: HarperCollins.

3. The Honest Kitchen. Retrieved from https://www.thehonestkitchen.com

4. Nijssen, *Entrepreneurial marketing*, 17.

5. Scocco, D. (2006). Users, purchasers and influencers [Blog post]. *Innovation Zen*. Retrieved from http://innovationzen.com/ blog/2006/12/06/users-purchasers-and-influencers

6. Blank, S., & Dorf, B. (2012). *The startup owner's manual* (pp. 87–88). California: K&S Ranch.

7. Baggs, M. (2019). Fyre Festival: Inside the world's biggest festival flop. *BBC*. Retrieved from https://www.bbc .co.uk/news/newsbeat-46904445

8. Blank, S. (2017). Everything you ever wanted to know about marketing communications [Blog post]. *Steve Blank*. Retrieved from https:// steveblank.com/2017/04/05/ everything-you-ever-wanted-to-know-about-marketing-communications/

9. Mullins, J. (2013). *The new business road test* (4th ed., p. 45). London, UK: Pearson.

10. Aulet, B. (2017). *Disciplined entrepreneurship workbook* (p. 49). Hoboken NJ: Wiley.

11. Berry, L. M. (2015). Know your customer [Blog post]. Retrieved from https:// leahmberry.com/know-your-customer-walk-in-your-customers-shoes/

12. Nijssen, *Entrepreneurial marketing*, 37.

13. Aulet, B. (2014). Launching a successful start-up #3: The beachhead market. *MIT Sloan Executive Education innovation@work Blog.* Retrieved from https://executive.mit.edu/blog/launching-a-successful-start-up-3-the-beachhead-market

14. Aulet, Launching a successful start-up.

15. Ibid.

16. Dixon, C. (2010). The bowling pin strategy. *Business Insider.* Retrieved from http://www.businessinsider.com/the-bowling-pin-strategy-2010-8

17. Revella, A. (2015). *Buyer personas: How to gain insight into your customer's expectations, align your marketing strategies, and win more business.* Hoboken, NJ: John Wiley & Son.

18. Pruitt, J., & Grudin, J. (2017). Personas: Practice and theory. *Microsoft.* Retrieved from https://www.microsoft.com/en-us/research/wp-content/uploads/2017/03/pruitt-grudinold.pdf

19. Vaughan, P. (2015). How to create detailed buyer personas for your business. *Hubspot Blog.* Retrieved from https://blog.hubspot.com/marketing/buyer-persona-research

20. Salesforce UK. (2016). What is customer journey mapping & why is it important? *Salesforce Blog.* Retrieved from https://www.salesforce.com/uk/blog/2016/03/customer-journey-mapping-explained.html

21. Ellis, A. (2017). How any startup can create a customer journey map [Video]. *Forget the Funnel.* Retrieved from https://forgetthefunnel.com/customer-journey-maps-for-startups/

22. Boag, P. (2019). What is customer journey mapping and how to start? *Boagworld.* Retrieved from https://boagworld.com/usability/customer-journey-mapping/

23. Morasky, M. (2017). Customer journey mapping: How to understand each stage of your customer's experience. *Startup Nation.* Retrieved from https://startupnation.com/grow-your-business/art-opportunity-customer-journey-mapping/

24. Boag, What is customer journey mapping?

25. Ibid.

26. Fisher, Y. (2016). TAM SAM and SOM are not good enough—stop relying on them. *Medium.* Retrieved from https://medium.com/value-your-startup/tam-sam-and-som-are-not-good-enough-stop-relying-on-them-f7e378850f4

27. Parker, D. (2015). TAM, SAM, SOM and LAM—What's your launch addressable market? *Techstars.* Retrieved from https://www.techstars.com/content/entrepreneur-resources/tam-sam-som-lam-whats-launch-addressable-market/

28. Zhuo, T. (2016). 5 strategies to effectively determine your market size. *Entrepreneur.* Retrieved from https://www.entrepreneur.com/article/270853

29. Ibid.

30. Haden, J. (2013). Best way to do a market analysis? *Inc.* Retrieved from https://www.inc.com/jeff-haden/bottom-up-or-top-down-market-analysis-which-should-you-use.html

## CHAPTER 7

1. Ries, E. (2011). *The lean startup* (p. 56). New York: Crown Business.

2. Dyer, J., Gregersen, H., & Christensen, C. (2011). *The innovator's DNA: Mastering the five skills of disruptive innovators* (p. 143/ibook). Boston, MA: Harvard Business Review Press.

3. Costa, R. (2019). 20 inspiring web and mobile wireframe examples. *Justinmind.* Retrieved from https://www.justinmind.com/blog/20-inspiring-web-and-mobile-wireframe-and-prototype-examples/

4. Kishfy, N. (2013). Button to nowhere. *Medium.* Retrieved from https://medium.com/@kishfy/button-to-nowhere-77d911517318

5. McCloskey, M. (2014). Turn user goals into task scenarios for usability testing. *Nielsen Norman Group.* Retrieved from https://www.nngroup.com/articles/task-scenarios-usability-testing/

6. The world's first monthly journal for living a great story. (2018). *Kickstarter.* Retrieved from https://www.kickstarter.com/projects/liveagreatstory/the-worlds-first-monthly-journal-for-living-a-grea

7. Buchenau, M., & Suri, J. F. (2000). Experience prototyping. In *DIS '00: Proceedings of the 3rd Conference on Designing Interactive Systems: Processes, practices, methods, and techniques* (pp. 424–433). doi:10.1145/347642.347802

8. Ries, E. (2011). *The lean startup: How today's entrepreneurs use continuous innovation to create radically successful businesses.* New York: Crown Business.

9. Chebanova, A. (n.d.). What is MVP and why is it necessary? *Steel Kiwi.* Retrieved from https://steelkiwi.com/blog/what-mvp-and-why-it-necessary/

10. Artemyan, M. (2018). What is the difference between a wireframe, mockup, prototype, and mvp? *Develandoo.* Retrieved from https://develandoo.com/blog/what-is-the-differencebetween-a-wireframe-prototype-and-mvp/

11. Dam, R., & Siang, T. (2019). Prototyping: Learn eight common methods and best practices. *Interaction Design.* Retrieved from https://www.interaction-design.org/literature/article/prototyping-learn-eight-common-methods-and-best-practices

12. Storyboarding. Retrieved from http://www.instructionaldesign.org/storyboarding.html

13. Bourque, A. (2012). 4 powerful reasons to storyboard your business. Retrieved from http://www.socialmediatoday.com/content/4-powerful-reasons-storyboard-your-business-ideas

14. Thorn, K. (2011). The art of storyboarding. Retrieved December 27, 2014, from http://elearnmag.acm.org/featured.cfm?aid=2024072

15. Bourque, 4 powerful reasons.

16. The Common Craft Blog. Retrieved from https://www.commoncraft.com/explainer-tip-creating-simple-storyboards

17. https://www.renttherunway.com/pages/about#about-definition

18. Roam, D. (2008). *The back of the napkin: Solving problems and selling ideas with pictures.* New York, NY: Penguin Books.

19. Blank, S. (2014). Keep calm and test the hypothesis. Retrieved from http://steveblank.com/2014/06/23/keep-calm-and-test-the-hypothesis-2-minutes-to-see-why/

20. Dyer et al., *The innovator's DNA*, 143.

21. Thomke, S., & Manzi, J. (2014, December). The discipline of business experimentation. *Harvard Business Review*, 70–79, at 72.

22. Steps of the scientific method. (2014, December 27). *Science Buddies.* Retrieved from https://www.sciencebuddies.org/science-fair-projects/science-fair/steps-of-the-scientific-method

23. Anderson, M. (2016). *The scientific method of entrepreneurship.* Retrieved from https://lassonde.utah.edu/the-scientific-method-of-entrepreneurship/

24. Buffer's 2018 in numbers (2019). *Buffer.* Retrieved from https://buffer.com/2018

25. 6 entrepreneurs share the brilliant, crazy ways they took their companies from pennies to profit. (2018). *Entrepreneur.* Retrieved from https://www.entrepreneur.com/article/311861

26. Anderson, E. T., & Simester, D. (2011, March). The step-by-step guide to smart business experiments. *Harvard Business Review*, 98–105.

27. Ibid.

28. Boehl, D. (2015). Why I ignored conventional wisdom and hired family members for my startup. *Forbes.*

Retrieved from https://www.forbes
.com/sites/theyec/2015/05/11/
why-i-ignored-conventional-wisdom-
and-hired-family-members-for-my-
startup/#46f7b419d58c

29. Lemley, P. (2018). I launched a tech startup in 2017: Here's everything I felt important enough to write down. *Medium.* Retrieved from https://medium.com/swlh/i-launched-a-tech-startup-in-2017-heres-every thing-i-felt-important-enough-to-write-down-4feb328b821f

30. Ries, *The lean startup*, 56.

31. Heller, C. (2018). *The intergalactic design guide: Harnessing the creative potential of social design* (pp. 71–82). Washington, DC: Island Press.

## CHAPTER 8

1. Tashakova, O. (2018). How networking can increase your business' net worth. *Entrepreneur.* Retrieved from https://www.entrepreneur.com/article/314496

2. Cope, J., Jack, S., & Rose, M. (2007). Social capital and entrepreneurship: An introduction. *International Small Business Journal, 25,* 213–219, at 213.

3. Ibid., 216.

4. Tsai, W., & Ghoshal, S. (1998). Social capital and value creation. The role of intrafirm networks. *Academy of Management Journal, 41,* 464–476.

5. Coleman, J. S. (1988). Social capital in the creation of human capital. *American Journal of Sociology: Supplement, Organizations and Institutions: Sociological and Economic Approaches to the Analysis of Social Structure, 94,* 95–120.

6. Al Muniady, R., Al Mamun, A., Mohamad, M. R., Permarupan, P. Y., & Zainol, N. R. B. (2015). The effect of cognitive and relational social capital on structural social capital and micro-enterprise performance. *Sage Open.* Retrieved from http://sgo.sagepub.com/content/5/4/2158244015611187

7. Uzzi, B. (1996). The sources and consequences of embeddedness for the economic performance of organizations: The network effect. *American Sociological Review, 61,* 674–698.

8. Covey, S. (2004). *The 7 habits of highly effective people.* New York: Free Press.

9. Ibid.

10. Al Muniady et al., The effect of cognitive and relational social capital.

11. Keeley, B. (2007). *Human capital: How what you know shapes your life.* Paris: OECD. Retrieved from http://www.oecd.org/insights/37966934.pdf

12. Ibid.

13. Uzzi, B., & Dunlap, S. (2005, December). How to build your network. *Harvard Business Review,* 52–60, at 53.

14. Cope et al., Social capital and entrepreneurship, 2–14.

15. Casson, M., & Della Giusta, M. (2007). Entrepreneurship and social capital: Analyzing the impact of social networks on entrepreneurial activity from a rational action perspective. *International Small Business Journal, 25,* 220–244, at 221.

16. Hoehn-Weiss, M., Brush, C., & Baron, R. (2004). Putting your best foot forward? Assessments of entrepreneurial social competence from two perspectives. *Journal of Private Equity, 7*(4), 17–26.

17. Guerrini, F. (2016). Study: For 78% of startups, networking is vital to entrepreneurial success. *Forbes.* Retrieved from https://www.forbes.com/sites/federicoguerrini/2016/11/10/study-for-78-of-startups-networking-is-the-key-to-entrepreneurial-success/#6f1ecc434195

18. Uzzi & Dunlap, How to build your network.

19. Science quotes by Linus Pauling. (n.d.). *Today in Science History.* Retrieved from https://todayinsci.com/P/Pauling_Linus/PaulingLinus-Quotations.htm

20. Murphy, W., & Kram, K. (2014). *Strategic relationships at work.* New York, NY: McGraw-Hill.

21. Neck, H. (2001). *An ethnographic study of entrepreneurship education: Trajectories connecting the classroom to the real world.* Unpublished working paper.

22. Willis, J., & Todorov, A. (2006). First impressions: Making up your mind after a 100-ms exposure to a face. *Psychological Science, 17*(7), 592–598.

23. Pentland, A., & Heibeck, T. (2009, October 31). Great ideas vs. confidence: Which counts more? *Psychology Today.* Retrieved from http://www.psychologytoday.com/blog/reality-mining/200910/great-ideas-vs-confidence-which-counts-more-0l

24. Hoehn-Weiss et al., Putting your best foot forward?

25. Understanding implicit bias. (2015). *The Kirwan Institute.* Retrieved from http://kirwaninstitute.osu.edu/research/understanding-implicit-bias/

26. Payne, K., Niemi, L., & Doris, J. (2018). How to think about "implicit bias." *Scientific American.* Retrieved from https://www.scientificamerican.com/article/how-to-think-about-implicit-bias/

27. Understanding implicit bias.

28. Ibid.

29. Which leading entrepreneurs met their business partners at school? (2013,

May 14). *Nerdwallet.* Retrieved from http://www.nerdwallet.com/blog/loans/student-loans/entrepreneurs-college-alumni-networks/

30. Sarasvathy, S. D. (2008). *Effectuation: Elements of entrepreneurial expertise.* Northampton, MA: Edward Elgar.

31. Loyd, T. (2018). Beyond autism awareness, Thorkil Sonne, Specialisterne. Retrieved from https://tonyloyd.com/beyond-autism-awareness-thorkil-sonne-specialisterne/

32. Senge, P. M. (1990). *The fifth discipline: The art and practice of the learning organization.* New York, NY: Doubleday/Currency.

33. Uzzi & Dunlap, How to build your network, 58.

34. Roberts, G. (2019). Runway East stories: How did you meet your co-founder? *Runway East.* Retrieved from https://runwayea.st/blog/how-did-you-meet-co-founder/

35. Extremely shy—Looking for friends. (n.d.). *Meetup.com.* Retrieved from http://www.meetup.com/extremely-shy-looking-for-friends/

36. Rahul, F. June 28, 2018. Decoding entrepreneurial meetups and their relevance in 2018. Entrepreneur India. Retrieved at https://www.entrepreneur.com/article/315905

37. Cremades, A. (2018). 10 startup accelerators based on successful exits. *Forbes.* Retrieved from https://www.forbes.com/sites/alejandrocremades/2018/08/07/top-10-startup-accelerators-based-on-successful-exits/#13ed6a84b3b9

38. Ibid.

39. Murphy, B. (2015, October 19). 9 smart habits of highly effective networkers. *Inc.* Retrieved from http://www.inc.com/bill-murphy-jr/9-smart-habits-of-highly-effective-networkers.html

40. Spencer, S. (2011, December 14). Business networking that works. It's called quid pro quo. *Forbes.* Retrieved from http://news.yahoo.com/business-networking-works-called-quid-pro-quo-190953397

41. Anderson, K. (2013, July 17). Pay it forward with the five-minute favor. *Forbes.* Retrieved from http://www.forbes.com/sites/kareanderson/2013/07/17/pay-it-forward-with-the-five-minute-favor/

42. Murphy, 9 smart habits.

43. Misner, I. (2009, January 14). You never know whom they know. *Entrepreneur.* Retrieved from http://www.entrepreneur.com/article/199542

44. Rollag, K. (2015). *What to do when you're new.* New York, NY: Amacom.

45. Kawasaki, G. (2015). *The art of the start* (p. 199). New York, NY: Penguin.

46. McClanahan, A. (2017). 6 entrepreneurs on why mentorship is the key to success. *Fundera*. Retrieved from https://www.fundera.com/blog/entrepreneurs-mentorship

47. Three famous billionaire entrepreneurs and their mentors. (2015, February 12). *Small Business BC*. Retrieved from http://smallbusinessbc.ca/article/three-famous-billionaire-entrepreneurs-and-their-mentors/

48. McClanahan, A. (2017). 6 entrepreneurs on why mentorship is the key to success. *Fundera*. Retrieved from https://www.fundera.com/blog/entrepreneurs-mentorship

49. Deutschman, A. (2004, December 1). The fabric of creativity. *Fast Company*. Retrieved from http://www.fastcompany.com/51733/fabric-creativity

50. Interview: Elizabeth Holmes. (2014). *The Academy of Achievement*. Retrieved from http://www.achievement.org/autodoc/page/holoint-6

51. Branson, R. (2012, July 24). Network early, network often. *Daily Monitor*. Retrieved from http://www.monitor.co.ug/Business/Prosper/Network-early--network-often/-/688616/1461204/-/1028mhh/-/index.html

52. Singh, N. (2018). How entrepreneurs can leverage LinkedIn to grow their business. *Entrepreneur India*. Retrieved from https://www.entrepreneur.com/article/310531

53. Koehn, E. (2017). 20 entrepreneurs to follow on Instagram in 2017. *Smart Company*. Retrieved from https://www.smartcompany.com.au/marketing/social-media/twenty-entrepreneurs-to-follow-on-instagram-in-2017/

54. VC4A. (n.d.). Connecting African startups to opportunities. Retrieved from https://vc4a.com/

55. Nsehe, M. (2015, March 1). Angel investors invest $27 million in African startups listed on VC4Africa. *Forbes*. Retrieved from http://www.forbes.com/sites/mfonobongnsehe/2015/03/01/angel-investors-invest-27-million-in-african-startups-through-vc4africa/

56. Uzzi & Dunlap, How to build your network.

57. Aldrich, H. E., & Kim, P. H. (2007). Small worlds, infinite possibilities? How social networks affect entrepreneurial team formation and search. *Strategic Entrepreneurship Journal, 1*, 147–165, at 149.

58. Timmons, J. A. (1994). *New venture creation: Entrepreneurship for the 21st century* (4th ed. p. 19). Burr Ridge, IL: Irwin; Cooper, A. C., & Daily, C. M. (1997). Entrepreneurial teams. In D. L. Sexton & R. W. Smilor (Eds.), *Entrepreneurship 2000* (pp. 127–150). Chicago, IL: Upstart.

59. Blank, S. (2013, July 29). Building great founding teams. Retrieved from http://steveblank.com/2013/07/29/building-great-founding-teams/

60. Cooper & Daily, Entrepreneurial teams.

61. Cooney, T. M. (2005). Editorial: What is an entrepreneurial team? *International Small Business Journal, 23*, 226–235, at 228.

62. Aldrich & Kim, Small worlds, infinite possibilities? 149.

63. Vozza, S. (2014, July 2). The only 6 people you need on your founding startup team. *Fast Company*. Retrieved from http://www.fastcompany.com/3032548/hit-the-ground-running/the-only-6-people-you-need-on-your-founding-startup-team

64. Houser, J. (2011, June 21). How to build an insanely great founding team. *Inc*. Retrieved from http://www.inc.com/articles/201106/how-to-build-an-insanely-great-team.html

65. Williams, G. (2017). It's a dirty job (and these entrepreneurs are doing it). *Success*. Retrieved from https://www.success.com/its-a-dirty-job-and-these-entrepreneurs-are-doing-it/

66. Rampton, J. (2019). 10 popular myths about leadership and how to overcome them. *Entrepreneur*. Retrieved from https://www.entrepreneur.com/article/330198

67. Rampton, J. (2016). 8 ways my ego killed my business. *Entrepreneur*. Retrieved from https://www.entrepreneur.com/article/278901

68. Spors, K. (2009, February 23). So, you want to be an entrepreneur. *Wall Street Journal/Small Business Reports*. Retrieved from http://www.wsj.com/articles/SB123498006564714189

69. Sommers, S. R., Warp, L. S., & Mahoney, C. (2008). Cognitive effects of racial diversity: White individuals' information processing in heterogeneous groups. *Journal of Experimental Social Psychology, 44*, 1129–1136.

70. Surowiecki, J. (2005). *The wisdom of crowds* (p. 36). New York, NY: Anchor Books.

71. Schwenk, C. R., & Cosier, R. A. (1980). Effects of the expert, devil's advocate, and dialectical inquiry methods on prediction performance. *Organizational Behavior and Human Performance, 26*, 409–424.

72. Chowdhury, S. (2005). Demographic diversity for building an effective entrepreneurial team: Is it important? *Journal of Business Venturing, 20*, 727–746.

73. Ibid.

74. Patrick Lencioni presentation at the World Business Forum, Oct. 6, 2009. For summary, see http://www.vault.com/blog/pink-slipped-make-your-layoff-pay-off/world-business-forum-building-winning-teams-with-patrick-lencioni/; see Lencioni, P. (2002). *The five dysfunctions of a team*. San Francisco, CA: Jossey-Bass.

75. Eisenhardt, K., Kahwajy, J., & Bourgeois, L. J., III. (1997, July–August). How management teams can have a good fight. *Harvard Business Review, 75*, 77–85.

76. Ibid.

77. The Keynote Group. (2016). Playing devil's advocate: Pushing your team to find solutions. Retrieved from https://thekeynotegroup.com/playing-devils-advocate/

78. Boulding, K. (1964). Further reflections on conflict management. In R. Kahn & E. Boulding, (Eds.), *Power and conflict in organizations*. New York, NY: Basic Books.

79. Eisenhardt et al., How management teams can have a good fight.

## CHAPTER 9

1. This section is adapted from Laniado, E. (2013). Revenue model types: The quick guide. *BMN!*. Retrieved from http://www.bmnow.com/revenue-models-quick-guide/

2. Chrisos, M. (2019). Razor and blades model: What is it and what benefits does it possess? *Techfunnel*. Retrieved from https://www.techfunnel.com/martech/razor-and-blades-model-what-is-it-and-what-benefits-does-it-possess/

3. Vanian, J. (2018). Amazon is now the 3rd largest digital ad platform in the US. *Fortune*. Retrieved from http://fortune.com/2018/09/19/amazon-facebook-google-digital-ads/

4. Jolly, W. (2019). The 6 most effective types of social media advertising in 2019. *Bigcommerce*. Retrieved from https://www.bigcommerce.co.uk/blog/social-media-advertising/#1-facebook-advertising

5. Melendez, S., & Pasternack, A. (2019). Here are the data brokers quietly buying and selling your personal information. *Fast Company*. Retrieved from https://www.fastcompany.com/90310803/here-are-the-data-brokers-quietly-buying-and-selling-your-personal-information

6. Wong, J. (2019). The Cambridge Analytica scandal changed the world, but it didn't change Facebook. *The Guardian*. Retrieved from https://www.theguardian.com/technology/2019/mar/17/the-cambridge-analytica-scandal-changed-the-world-but-it-didnt-change-facebook

7. Key, S. (2018). How this novelty gift company gets open innovation right. *Inc*. Retrieved from https://www.inc.com/stephen-key/love-to-create-fun-products-consider-novelty-gift-licensing.html

8. Starr, R. (2019). 10 weird franchises to stand out from the crowd. *Small Business Trends*. Retrieved from https://smallbiztrends.com/2017/09/weird-franchises.html

9. Laniado, Revenue model types.

10. Ibid.

11. The five best freemium business services. (n.d.). *Tech Donut*. Retrieved from https://www.techdonut.co.uk/business-software/essential-business-software/the-five-best-freemium-business-services

12. The concept was popularized by Anderson, C. (2009). *Free: The future of a radical price*. New York, NY: Hyperion.

13. Greenslade, R. (2011 January 26). Profitable Metro can't stop making money, but we still need 'proper' newspapers. *The Guardian*,

14. Osterwalder, A., & Pigneur, Y. (2010). *Business model generation: A handbook for visionaries, game changers, and challengers* (p. 104). Hoboken, NJ: Wiley.

15. The information in this section is heavily drawn from Zacharakis, A., & Santinelli, A. (2014). *Finance and financial models* [Working paper].

16. London's quirkiest cafes: in pictures. (2014, November 6). *The Telegraph*. Retrieved from http://www.telegraph.co.uk/travel/destinations/europe/united-kingdom/england/london/galleries/Londons-quirkiest-cafes/ziferblatcafe/

17. Carter, D. P. (2011, June 7). *The four fundamental drivers of revenue*. Retrieved from http://www.davidpaulcarter.com/2011/06/07/the-four-fundamental-drivers-of-revenue/

18. Clark, D. (2014, October 6). How to determine what you should charge customers. *Entrepreneur*. Retrieved from http://www.entrepreneur.com/article/238086

19. StartUpMe. (2010, January 29). 9 pricing rules for entrepreneurs [Video file]. *YouTube*. Retrieved from https://www.youtube.com/watch?v=redLOAIkEvI

20. Team, Y. S. (2010, July 27). *10 pricing strategies for entrepreneurs*. Retrieved from http://yourstory.com/2010/07/10-pricing-strategies-for-entrepreneurs-2

21. Evans, L. (2014). Inside five businesses that let customers name their own price. *Fast Company*. Retrieved from https://www.fastcompany.com/3024842/inside-five-businesses-that-let-customers-name-their-own-price

22. Riley, J. (2012, September 23). Pricing strategies (GCSE). *Tutor2u*. Retrieved from http://www.tutor2u.net/business/gcse/marketing_pricing_strategies.htm

23. Ibid.

24. Berry, T. (n.d.). What is a break-even analysis? *Bplans*. Retrieved from https://articles.bplans.com/break-even-analysis/

## CHAPTER 10

1. Brown, J. (2014). The top 10 dare devil entrepreneurs who embrace risk. #9 Elon Musk. *Addicted to Success*. Retrieved from http://addicted2success.com/entrepreneur-profile/the-top-10-dare-devil-entrepreneurs-who-embrace-risk/; An introduction to business plans. (2015). *Entrepreneur*. Retrieved from http://www.entrepreneur.com/article/38290

2. Herold, C. (2011). *Double double: How to double your revenue and profit in three years*. Austin, TX: Greenleaf Book Group Press.

3. Blank, S. (2013, May). Why the lean start-up changes everything. *Harvard Business Review*, 65–72.

4. Kolodny, L. (2017). Deere is paying over $300 million for a start-up that makes 'see-and-spray' robots. Retrieved from https://www.cnbc.com/2017/09/06/deere-is-acquiring-blue-river-technology-for-305-million.html

5. Kim, L. (2018). How this pitch deck raised $66 million in VC funding. *Inc.* Retrieved from https://www.inc.com/larry-kim/how-this-pitch-deck-raised-66-million-in-vc-funding.html

6. Berry, T. (2012, August 9). Should you create your business plan on Pinterest? *Entrepreneur*. Retrieved from http://www.entrepreneur.com/article/224157

7. Blank, S. (2013, May). Why the lean start-up changes everything. *Harvard Business Review*, 65–72.

8. Peterson, L. (2019). Example of a product concept statement. *Houston Chronicle*. Retrieved from https://smallbusiness.chron.com/example-product-concept-statement-13051.html

9. A guide to competitive analysis: It's not just about competitors. (n.d.). *Smartsheet*. Retrieved from https://www.smartsheet.com/competitive-analysis-examples

10. How to write a competitive analysis. (2017). *Expert Program Management*. Retrieved from https://expertprogrammanagement.com/2017/01/competitive-analysis-template/

11. Weinberger, J., & Hughes, L. (2014, March 2). Stay-at-home mom makes millions from pretzels. *CNBC*, 1.

12. Young Entrepreneur Council. (2013, January 13). The 10 reasons why you should write a business plan. *Small Business Trends*. Retrieved from http:// smallbiztrends.com/2013/01/10-reasons-write-business-plan.html

13. Timmons, J., Zacharakis, A., & Spinelli, S. (2004). *Business plans that work: A guide for small business*. New York, NY: McGraw-Hill.

14. Zwilling, M. (2013, November 6). The 10 reasons not to write a business plan. *Entrepreneur*. Retrieved from http://www.entrepreneur.com/article/229804

15. Neck, H. (2013, May 21). What comes before the business plan? Everything. *Forbes*. Retrieved from http://www.forbes.com/sites/babson/2012/05/21/what-comes-before-the-business-plan-everything/

16. Henricks, M. (2008). Do you really need a business plan? *Entrepreneur*. Retrieved from http://www.entrepreneur.com/article/198618

## CHAPTER 11

1. Hough, K. (2012, April 25). 10 greatest startup failures of all time. *Techli*. Retrieved from http://techli.com/2012/04/10-greatest-startup-failures/#

2. MacKay, J. (2017). 5 lessons to learn from the 10 biggest startup failures so far in 2017. *Inc.* Retrieved from https://www.inc.com/jory-mackay/5-lessons-to-learn-from-10-biggest-startup-failures-of-2017.html

3. Blank, S. (2014). *Do pivots matter?* Retrieved from https://steveblank.com/2014/01/14/whats-a-pivot/

4. Edmondson, A. C. (2011, April). Learning from failure. *Harvard Business Review*. Retrieved from https://hbr.org/2011/04/strategies-for-learning-from-failure

5. Stieg, C. (2019). What exactly was the Theranos Edison machine supposed to do? *Refinery29*. Retrieved from https://www.refinery29.com/en-us/2019/03/224904/theranos-edison-machine-blood-test-technology-explained

6. Solon, O. (2018). Theranos founder Elizabeth Holmes charged with criminal fraud. *The Guardian*. Retrieved from https://www.theguardian.com/technology/2018/jun/15/theranos-elizabeth-holmes-ramesh-balwani-criminal-charges

7. Vozza, S. (2015). Six millennial entrepreneurs share their lessons from early failure. *Fast Company*. Retrieved from https://www.fastcompany.com/3049841/six-millennial-entrepreneurs-share-their-lessons-from-early-failure

8. Cancialosi, C. (2015, April). 5 signs your organization has outgrown

you. *Forbes.* Retrieved from http://www.forbes.com/sites/chriscancialosi/2015/04/27/5-signs-your-organization-has-outgrown-you/#1faa91d6b917

9.   Burgess, W., & Lou, E. (2018). This growing company realized it was time for the founder to step aside. Here's how they made it work. *Entrepreneur.* Retrieved from https://www.entrepreneur.com/article/308498

10.  ReferralCandy. (2017). Why startups fail: 12 founders, and advice moving forward. *Medium.* Retrieved from https://medium.com/the-mission/why-startups-fail-12-founders-and-advice-moving-forward-edbcba80c522

11.  CB Insights. (2019). 298 startup failure post-mortems. Retrieved from https://www.cbinsights.com/research/startup-failure-post-mortem/

12.  Zissu, A. (2017). This founder created a genius way to do market testing on the cheap. *Entrepreneur.* Retrieved from https://www.entrepreneur.com/article/289144

13.  Sastray, A., & Penn, K. (2014). *Fail better: Design smart mistakes and succeed sooner* [p. 1 Kindle]. Cambridge, MA: Harvard Business Review Press.

14.  Curtin, M. (2018). 42 percent of startups fail for this 1 simple reason (It's not what you think). *Inc.* Retrieved from https://www.inc.com/melanie-curtin/the-no-1-reason-most-startups-fail-dont-make-this-mistake.html

15.  Shepherd, D. A. (2003). Learning from business failure: Propositions of grief recovery for the self-employed. *Academy of Management Review, 28,* 318–328; McGrath, R. (1999). Falling forward: Real options reasoning and entrepreneurial failure. *Academy of Management Review, 24,* 13–30.

16.  Taylor, M. (2018). Confessions of a recovering entrepreneur. *Forbes.* Retrieved from https://www.forbes.com/sites/meggentaylor/2018/03/18/confessions-of-a-recovering-entrepreneur/#6ac71681618f

17.  Singer, S., Amoros, J. E., & Moska, D. (2014). *Global Entrepreneurship Monitor 2014 global report.* Retrieved from http://www.gemconsortium.org/report

18.  McGregor, H. A., & Elliot, A. J. (2005). The shame of failure: Examining the link between fear of failure and shame. *Personality and Social Psychology Bulletin, 31,* 218–231, at 219.

19.  Spicker, P. (1984). Stigma and social welfare. Oxfordshire: Taylor & Francis.

20.  Walsh, Grace. S. (2017) Re-entry following firm failure: Nascent technology entrepreneurs' tactics for avoiding and overcoming stigma.

In J. A. Cunningham and C. O'Kane (Eds.), *Technology-based nascent entrepreneurship* (pp. 95–117). London: Palgrave Advances in the Economics of Innovation and Technology.

21.  Ibid., 229.

22.  Loder, V. (2014, October 30). How to conquer the fear of failure—5 proven strategies. *Forbes.* Retrieved from http://www.forbes.com/sites/vanessaloder/2014/10/30/how-to-move-beyond-the-fear-of-failure-5-proven-strategies/

23.  Patel, N. (2016). Why every entrepreneur should live with their parents. *Forbes.* Retrieved from https://www.forbes.com/sites/neilpatel/2016/11/10/why-every-entrepreneur-should-live-with-their-parents/#422a07e96200

24.  Heber, A. (2015, July 13). Chart: The fear of failure rates for entrepreneurs around the world. *Business Insider Australia.* Retrieved from http://www.businessinsider.com.au/chart-the-fear-of-failure-rates-for-entrepenuers-around-the-world-2015-7

25.  Griffith, E. (2014, December 2). Amazon CEO Jeff Bezos: "I've made billions of dollars of failures." *Fortune.* Retrieved from http://fortune.com/2014/12/02/amazon-ceo-jeff-bezos-failure/

26.  Edmondson, A. C. (2011, April). Strategy for learning from failure. *Harvard Business Review,* 48–55.

27.  Patel, S. (2017). What "failing fast" really looks like. Retrieved from https://sujanpatel.com/business/failing-fast-2/

28.  Temple, C. (2018). From dream to day job: Classy Llama Studios LLC. Retrieved from https://sbj.net/stories/from-dream-to-day-job-classy-llama-studios-llc,60603

29.  Seelig, T. (2009, July 28). Fail in order to succeed. *CreativyRulz.* Retrieved from http://creativityrulz.blogspot.com/2009/07/fail-in-order-to-suceed.html

30.  Avlani, S. (2018). Entrepreneurs cannot blame others for failures. *Livemint.* Retrieved from https://www.livemint.com/Leisure/pfrGN5YtX1joJMgWtwab4L/Entrepreneurs-cannot-blame-others-for-failures.html

31.  Porter, M. E., Lorsch, J. W., & Nohria, N. (2004, October). Seven surprises for new CEOs. *Harvard Business Review,* 62–72.

32.  Danner, J. (2015, May 11). How to make the other 'F' word work for you (not against you). *Fortune.* Retrieved from http://fortune.com/2015/05/11/how-to-make-the-other-f-word-work-for-you-innovation/

33.  Perkins-Gough, D. (2013, September). The significance of grit: A conversation with Angela Lee Duckworth.

*Educational Leadership, 71*(1). Retrieved from http://www.ascd.org/publications/educational-leadership/sept13/vol71/num01/The-Significance-of-Grit@-A-Conversation-with-Angela-Lee-Duckworth.aspx

34.  Del Giudice, M. (2014, October 14). Grit trumps talent and IQ: A story every parent (and educator) should read. *National Geographic.* Retrieved from http://news.nationalgeographic.com/news/2014/10/141015-angela-duckworth-success-grit-psychology-self-control-science-nginnovators/

35.  Perkins-Gough, The significance of grit.

36.  Del Giudice, Grit trumps talent and IQ.

37.  Fox, M. (2018). 5 entrepreneurs on how facing adversity helped them build successful businesses. *Forbes.* Retrieved from https://www.forbes.com/sites/meimeifox/2018/12/21/5-entrepreneurs-on-how-facing-adversity-helped-them-build-successful-businesses/#798ba0cc2469

38.  The Oracles. (2017). Never quit: Strategies on perseverance from 6 seasoned entrepreneurs. *Entrepreneur.* Retrieved from https://www.entrepreneur.com/article/299071

39.  Perlis, M. (2013, October 29). 5 characteristics of grit—How many do you have? *Forbes.* Retrieved from http://www.forbes.com/sites/margaretperlis/2013/10/29/5-characteristics-of-grit-what-it-is-why-you-need-it-and-do-you-have-it/

40.  Rao, M. (2018). Eight lessons in failure from Amani Institute's Fail Faire 2018. *Your Story.* https://yourstory.com/2018/05/eight-lessons-failure-amani-institutes-fail-faire-2018

41.  Fuckup Nights around the globe. (n.d.). Retrieved from https://fuckupnights.com/blog/fuckup-nights-around-world/

42.  Kanter, B. (2013, April 17). Go ahead, take a failure bow. *Harvard Business Review.* Retrieved from https://hbr.org/2013/04/go-ahead-take-a-failure-bow&cm_sp=Article-_-Links-_-End%20of%20Page%20Recirculation

43.  Ibid.

## CHAPTER 12

1.   National Venture Capital Association. (2019). 2019 yearbook. Retrieved from https://nvca.org/wp-content/uploads/delightful-downloads/2019/03/NVCA-2019-Yearbook.pdf

2.   Dinlersoz, E. (2018). Business formation statistics: A new Census Bureau product that takes the pulse of early-stage U.S. business activity. Retrieved from https://www.census.gov/newsroom/blogs/research-matters/2018/02/bfs.html

3. Mansfield, M. (2019). Startup statistics: The numbers you need to know. Retrieved from https://smallbiztrends.com/2019/03/startup-statistics-small-business.html

4. Sharp, G. (2014). *The ultimate guide to bootstrapping* [Kindle ed., LOC 173]. Real. Cool. Media.

5. Ibid., LOC 155.

6. Ibid., LOC 182.

7. Pilon, A. (2018). Don't have money? 17 entrepreneurs who bootstrapped their startups from nothing. Retrieved from https://smallbiztrends.com/2016/03/entrepreneurs-who-bootstrapped.html

8. Sharp, *The ultimate guide to bootstrapping*, LOC 147.

9. Mese, A. (n.d.). How to build a startup empire without selling your freedom. *Growth Supply*. Retrieved from https://growthsupply.com/build-bootstrapped-startup-without-investors/

10. Gooding, D. (2017). 16 bootstrapping tips and techniques from MailChimp. Retrieved from https://fourcolorsofmoney.com/16-bootstrapping-tips-techniques-mailchimp/

11. Garson, J. (2010). *How to build a business and sell it for millions.* New York, NY: St. Martin's Press.

12. Mese, How to build a startup empire.

13. Sharp, *The ultimate guide to bootstrapping*.

14. Steinberg, S. (2008). *The crowdfunding bible* [Kindle ed., LOC 78]. read.me Press.

15. Mollick, E. (2014). The dynamics of crowdfunding: An exploratory study. *Journal of Business Venturing, 29*, 1–16, at 2.

16. Yau, E. (2018). The ordinary people making medical breakthroughs via crowdsourcing: Solving problems that have doctors beat. Retrieved from https://www.scmp.com/lifestyle/health-wellness/article/2157627/how-crowdsourcing-helped-find-solutions-serious-health

17. Cohn, C. (2016). How crowdsourcing can help you with ideas, content and labor. *Entrepreneur*. Retrieved from https://www.entrepreneur.com/article/253959

18. Anderson, C. (2010, February). Atoms are the new bits. *Wired*, 59–67.

19. Owen, J. (2014, September 12). 3D-printed Wikihouse 4.0. *The Independent*. Retrieved from http://www.independent.co.uk/incoming/3dprinted-wikihouse-40-the-50000-house-you-can-download-from-the-internet-9727424.html

20. Mollick, The dynamics of crowdfunding, 3.

21. Zipkin, N. (2015, December 28). The 10 most funded Kickstarter campaigns ever. *Entrepreneur*. Retrieved from http://www.entrepreneur.com/article/235313

22. Goode, L. (2018). Fitbit will end support for Pebble smartwatches in June. Retrieved from https://www.theverge.com/2018/1/24/16928792/fitbit-smartwatch-pebble-end-support-date-june

23. Fundable. (n.d.). *Crowdfunding statistics.* Retrieved from https://www.fundable.com/crowdfunding101/crowdfunding-statistics

24. Kickstarter. (n.d.). *Kickstarter basics.* Retrieved from https://www.kickstarter.com/help/faq/kickstarter+basics?ref=footer

25. Kuppuswamy, V., & Bayus, B. (2014, January 29). *Crowdfunding creative ideas: The dynamics of project backers in Kickstarter.* (UNC Kenan-Flagler Research Paper No. 2013-15).

26. Kickstarter statistics listed on https://www.kickstarter.com/help/stats. These statistics change daily.

27. Kickstarter. (n.d.). *Our rules.* Retrieved from https://www.kickstarter.com/rules

28. Buck, S. (2012, May 13). 9 essential steps for a killer Kickstarter campaign. *Mashable*. Retrieved from http://mashable.com/2012/05/13/kickstarter-tips/

29. Kuppuswamy & Bayus, *Crowdfunding creative ideas*, 22.

30. Belleflamme, P., Lambert, T., & Schwienbacher, A. (2014). Crowdfunding: Tapping the right crowd. *Journal of Business Venturing, 29*, 585–609, at 589.

31. Statt, N. (2015, November 18). The Coolest Cooler is turning into one of Kickstarter's biggest disasters. *The Verge*. Retrieved from http://www.theverge.com/2015/11/18/9758214/coolest-cooler-amazon-kickstater-shipping-production-delay

32. Rogoway, M. (2018). Kickstarter fiasco Coolest Cooler has new plan to pay for 20,000 undelivered coolers. Retrieved from https://www.oregonlive.com/business/2018/06/kickstarter_fiasco_coolest_coo.html

33. Szabo, A. (2015). Two beards and a baby. *Indiegogo*. Retrieved from https://www.indiegogo.com/projects/two-beards-and-a-baby

34. Mollick, The dynamics of crowdfunding, 2.

35. Raphael, R. (2019). Equity crowdfunding platform OurCrowd has raised $1 billion in commitments. Retrieved from https://www.fastcompany.com/90316637/equity-crowdfunding-platform-ourcrowd-has-raised-1-billion-in-commitments

36. Mollick, The dynamics of crowdfunding.

37. Gomez, B. (2019). Patreon CEO says the company's generous business model is not sustainable as it sees rapid growth. Retrieved from https://www.cnbc.com/2019/01/23/crowdfunding-platform-patreon-announces-it-will-pay-out-half-a-billion-dollars-to-content-creators-in-2019.html

38. Benovic, C., & Oriando, S. (2015, April 16). Need some reward ideas? Here are 96 of them. Retrieved from https://www.kickstarter.com/blog/need-some-reward-ideas-here-are-96-of-them

39. Isbell, F. (2018). Veteran-owned Bottle Breacher cracking open $17M in sales after "Shark Tank." Retrieved from https://www.bizjournals.com/dallas/news/2018/08/15/veteran-owned-bottle-breacher-cracking-open-17m-in.html

40. Diallo, A. (2014, January 24). Crowdfunding secrets: 7 tips for Kickstarter success. *Forbes*. Retrieved from http://www.forbes.com/sites/amadoudiallo/2014/01/24/crowdfunding-secrets-7-tips-for-kickstarter-success/

41. Dewey, C. (2014, August 28). Ryan Grepper, inventor of the 'Coolest' Cooler, failed many times before raising $13 million on Kickstarter. *Washington Post*. Retrieved from http://www.washingtonpost.com/news/the-intersect/wp/2014/08/28/ryan-grepper-inventor-of-the-coolest-cooler-failed-many-times-before-raising-11-million-on-kickstarter/

42. Tarcomnicu, F. (2017). How to make a crowdfunding video people actually watch. Retrieved from https://www.entrepreneur.com/article/287665

43. Mollick, The dynamics of crowdfunding, 8.

44. Robinson, R. (2017). 5 crowdfunded side projects that became million-dollar companies. Retrieved from https://www.forbes.com/sites/ryanrobinson/2017/09/18/crowdfunded-side-projects-that-became-million-dollar-companies/#6af5241e3f1d

45. Flaherty, J. (2017). Despite billions in crowdfunding, only three "venture scale" exits. Retrieved from https://hackernoon.com/what-startups-can-learn-from-the-top-100-kickstarter-campaigns-6a0baf5bc31b

46. Mollick, The dynamics of crowdfunding, 2.

## CHAPTER 13

1. Mathisen, T. (2014, April 29). The list: CNBC first 25. *CNBC*. Retrieved from http://www.cnbc.com/2014/04/29/25-google-team--sergey-brin-larry-page-eric-schmidt.html

2. Moyer, M. (2012). Slicing pie: A guide to dividing up early-stage start-up equity. Retrieved from https://slicingpie.com/slicing-pie-a-guide-to-dividing-up-early-stage-startup-equity/

3. Ibid.

4. Venture capital. (n.d.). *Small Business Notes.* Retrieved from http://www.smallbusinessnotes.com/business-finances/venture-capital.html

5. Page, H. (2018). A timeline of investor interest in AR startup Magic Leap, which has raised $2.3B. Retrieved from https://news.crunchbase.com/news/a-timeline-of-investor-interest-in-ar-startup-magic-leap-which-has-raised-2-3b/

6. Shane, S. (2008, September). *The importance of angel investing in financing the growth of entrepreneurial ventures* (a working paper for the Small Business Association). Retrieved from http://www.angelcapitalassociation.org/data/Documents/Resources/AngelGroupResarch/1d%20-%20Resources%20-%20Research/19%20Angel_Investing_in_Financing_the_Growth_of_Entrepreneurial_Ventures.pdf

7. Retrieved from https://www.morphsuits.com/

8. Bailey, D. (2017). The secret formula for go-to-market. *Medium.* Retrieved from https://medium.dave-bailey.com/how-to-create-a-genius-go-to-market-strategy-89469ad9106d

9. Value of venture capital investment in the United States in 4th quarter 2018, by industry (in million U.S. dollars). Retrieved from https://www.statista.com/statistics/277506/venture-caputal-investment-in-the-united-states-by-sector/

10. What does unicorn mean? Retrieved from https://www.divestopedia.com/definition/5114/unicorn

11. Baston, N. (2018). 35 U.S. tech startups that reached unicorn status in 2018. *Inc.* Retrieved from https://www.inc.com/business-insider/35-us-tech-startups-that-reached-unicorn-status-in-2018.html

12. Asheesh, A. (2006, May 15). Raising money using convertible debt. *Entrepreneur.* Retrieved from http://www.entrepreneur.com/article/159520

13. Prive, T. (2013, March 12). Angel investors: How the rich invest. *Forbes.* Retrieved from http://www.forbes.com/sites/tanyaprive/2013/03/12/angels-investors-how-the-rich-invest/

14. Stengel, G. (2018). How women angels are good for innovation and the economy. *Forbes.* Retrieved from https://www.forbes.com/sites/geristengel/2018/06/06/women-are-different-and-thats-good-for-innovation-and-the-economy/#3985bcd1a3c5

15. Adams, P. (2014, January 12). How do angel investors differ from venture capitalists? [Rockies Venture Club blog.] Retrieved from http://www.rockiesventureclub.org/colorado-capital-conference/how-do-angel-investors-differ-from-venture-capitalists/

16. Hayden, B. (2015, March 20). Entrepreneurs can pay it forward through angel investing. *Entrepreneur.* Retrieved from http://www.entrepreneur.com/article/243759

17. Bygrave, W. (2010). Equity financing: Informal investment, venture capital, and harvesting. In B. Bygrave & A. Zacharakis (Eds.), *Portable MBA in entrepreneurship* (pp. 161–195). New York, NY: Wiley.

18. This section is sourced from: Finding an angel. (n.d.). *Small Business Notes.* Retrieved from http://www.smallbusinessnotes.com/business-finances/finding-an-angel.html

19. Stengel, How women angels are good.

20. Ibid.

21. Soper, T. (2017). Who are U.S. angel investors? Study shows 78% male; 87% white; 17% in California. *Geekwire.* Retrieved from https://www.geekwire.com/2017/u-s-angel-investors-study-shows-78-male-87-white-17-california/

22. Robehmed, N. (2013, October 16). There are few minority entrepreneurs, and they rarely get funding. *Forbes.* Retrieved from http://www.forbes.com/sites/natalierobehmed/2013/10/16/there-are-few-minority-entrepreneurs-and-they-rarely-get-funding/

23. Angel Capital Association. (n.d.). FAQ for angels & entrepreneurs. Retrieved from https://www.angelcapitalassociation.org/faqs/#How%20many%20angel%20investors%20are%20there%20in%20the%20U.S.

24. Kenton, W. (2017). Death Valley curve. *Investopedia.* Retrieved from https://www.investopedia.com/terms/d/death-valley-curve.asp

25. Timmons, J., & Spinelli, S. (2008). *New venture creation* (8th ed., p. 457). Boston, MA: McGraw-Hill Irwin.

26. Companies are raising bigger rounds across every investment stage. (2019). Retrieved from https://www.cbinsights.com/research/mega-rounds-venture-capital-2018/

27. Hadzima, J., Jr. (2005). All financing sources are not equal. *Boston Business Journal.* Retrieved from http://web.mit.edu/e-club/hadzima/all-financing-sources-are-not-equal.html

28. Frazier, D., Franklin, B., & Taylor, J. (2014). *National Venture Capital Association yearbook* (p. 13). New York, NY: Thomson Reuters.

29. Bygrave, Equity financing, 176.

30. Reich, D. (2014, January 4). Raising money from friends and family. *Forbes.com.* Retrieved from http://www.forbes.com/sites/danreich/2013/01/04/raising-money-from-friends-and-family/

31. Singerman, B. (2012, July 29). The paradox of VC seed investing. Retrieved from http://techcrunch.com/2012/07/29/the-paradox-of-vc-seed-investing/

32. Colombo, J. (n.d.). The dot-com bubble. *The Bubble Bubble.* Retrieved from http://www.thebubblebubble.com/dotcom-bubble/

33. Moon, A., & Franklin, J. (2019). Exclusive: Impossible Foods raises $300 million with investors eager for bite of meatless burgers. *Reuters.* Retrieved from https://www.reuters.com/article/us-impossible-foods-fundraising-exclusiv/exclusive-impossible-foods-raises-300-million-with-investors-eager-for-bite-of-meatless-burgers-idUSKCN1SJ0YK?il=0

34. Tyabji, H., & Sathe, V. (2010). Venture capital firms in America: Their caste system and other secrets. Retrieved from https://iveybusinessjournal.com/publication/venture-capital-firms-in-america-their-caste-system-and-other-secrets/

35. Timmons & Spinelli, *New venture creation,* 456.

36. Retrieved from http://www.angelblog.net/Venture_Capital_Exit_Times.html

37. Timmons & Spinelli, *New venture creation,* 458.

38. Jacob, L. (2018). 3 trends that prevent entrepreneurs from accessing capital. Retrieved from https://www.kauffman.org/currents/2018/07/3-trends-that-prevent-entrepreneurs-from-accessing-capital

39. Turits, M. (2018). 10 sources of financing for a startup or new small business to explore. Retrieved from https://www.fundera.com/blog/sources-of-financing-for-a-startup

40. Murray, J. (2018). Why do banks say no to business startup loans? Retrieved from https://www.thebalancesmb.com/why-do-banks-say-no-to-business-startup-loans-398025

41. Prithivi, S. (2011, August 24). Angel investing series part II: Due diligence, sealing the deal and post-investment relationship. *Tech.co.* Retrieved from http://tech.co/angel-investing-series-part-ii-2011-08

42. Lagorio-Chafkin, C. (2018). The 9 biggest—and most fascinating—startup acquisitions of 2018. *Inc.* Retrieved from https://www.inc.com/christine-lagorio/the-9-biggest-and-most-fascinating-startup-acquisitions-of-2018.html

43. Wasserman, N. (2008, February). The founder's dilemma. *Harvard Business Review*. Retrieved from https://hbr.org/2008/02/the-founders-dilemma

## SUPPLEMENT A

1. Buffet, M., & Clark, D. (2008). *Warren Buffet and the interpretation of financial statements* (p. 33). New York, NY: Scribner.

2. Ittelson, T. R. (2009). *Financial statements: A step-by-step guide to understanding and creating financial reports* (pp. 15–17). Pompton Plains, NJ: Career Press.

3. Ittelson, T. R. (2009). *Financial statements: A step-by-step guide to understanding and creating financial reports* (pp. 79–82). Pompton Plains, NJ: Career Press.

4. http://www.businessdictionary.com/definition/pro-forma.html

5. EZ Numbers website, http://www.eznumbers.com; Lonee Corporation website, http://marketing.lonee.com

6. Bizminer website, http://www.bizminer.com; IBISWorld website, http://www.ibisworld.com; Statista website, http://www.statista.com

7. Smith, R. L., & Smith, J. K. (2004). *Entrepreneurial finance* (pp. 144–146, 2nd ed.). Hoboken, NJ: Wiley.

## CHAPTER 14

1. Marinova, P. (2016). LegalZoom CEO: These are the biggest legal mistakes a startup can make. *Fortune*. Retrieved from http://fortune.com/2016/01/21/startup-legal-mistakes/

2. Abramowitz, Z. (2015, March 23). How lawyers can add value for startups *Above The Law* http://abovethelaw.com/2015/03/how-lawyers-can-add-value-for-startups/ retrieved on August 2, 2015.

3. Santa Clara University. (n.d.). The Entrepreneurs' Law Clinic. Retrieved from http://law.scu.edu/elc/

4. Source for legal research on the web. Retrieved from http://www.washlaw.edu/

5. Abramowitz, Z. (2015, March 23). How lawyers can add value for startups. *Above the Law*. Retrieved from http://abovethelaw.com/2015/03/how-lawyers-can-add-value-for-startups/

6. Successful entrepreneurs who started out as sole proprietors. (n.d.). *Gaebler.com*. Retrieved from http://www.gaebler.com/Successful-Entrepreneurs-Who-Started-Out-As-Sole-Proprietors.htm

7. http://www.inc.com/guides/2010/10/how-to-start-a-sole-proprietorship.html

8. http://www.moneyedup.com/2010/08/how-sole-proprietorship-works/

9. See, e.g., California Corporations Code Sections 2500, et seq., and Massachusetts General Laws Ch. 156E.

10. This section is heavily based on http://www.forbes.com/sites/allbusiness/2013/10/03/big-legal-mistakes-made-by-startups/

11. Prakash, P. (2019). Why a founders' agreement is important for every small business. *Fundera*. Retrieved from https://www.fundera.com/blog/founders-agreement

12. Intellectual property rights for innovative entrepreneurship. (n.d.). *The Innovation Policy Forum*. Retrieved from https://www.innovationpolicyplatform.org/content/intellectual-property-rights-innovative-entrepreneurship

13. Keating, R. J. (2013). *Unleashing small business through IP: Protecting intellectual property, driving entrepreneurship* (p. 36). Vienna, VA: Small Business & Entrepreneurship Council. Retrieved from http://www.sbecouncil.org/wp-content/uploads/2013/06/IP+and+Entrepreneurship+FINAL.pdf

14. Ibid.

15. Isaacson, W. (2011). *Steve Jobs* (p. 396). New York, NY: Simon & Schuster.

16. Cremades, A. (2018). 100 questions investors will ask entrepreneurs seeking funding. *Forbes*. Retrieved from https://www.forbes.com/sites/alejandrocremades/2018/08/14/100-questions-investors-will-ask-entrepreneurs-seeking-funding/#73bc397c4d81

17. McKenna, C. (2015, April 3). Do you really own all your intellectual property? *The National Law Review*. Retrieved from http://www.natlawreview.com/article/do-you-really-own-all-your-intellectual-property

18. Steele, A. (2013, June 11). Who owns Hackathon inventions? *Harvard Business Review*. Retrieved from https://hbr.org/2013/06/who-owns-hackathon-inventions

19. Purvis, S. (n.d.). The fundamentals of intellectual property for the entrepreneur. Presentation, U.S. Patent and Trademark Office, Department of Commerce. Retrieved from http://www.uspto.gov/sites/default/files/about/offices/ous/121115.pdf

20. Retrieved from www.copyright.gov/circs/circ61.pdf

21. Spotify settles $1.6bn lawsuit over songwriters' rights. (2018). *BBC*. Retrieved from https://www.bbc.co.uk/news/business-46646918

22. Miller, C. (2018). Clothing wars: Apparel giant Under Armour sends a cease and desist to local business. *Bendsource*. https://www.bendsource.com/bend/clothing-wars/Content?oid=8127194

23. Halligan, R. M., & Haas, D. (2010, February 19). The secret of trade secret success. *Forbes*. Retrieved from http://www.forbes.com/2010/02/19/protecting-trade-secrets-leadership-managing-halligan-haas.html

24. Quinn, G. (2009). Obscure patent: The dog umbrella & leash. *IPWatchdog*. Retrieved from https://www.ipwatchdog.com/2009/01/20/obscure-patent-the-dog-umbrella-leash/id=1634/

25. Quinn, G. (2014, February 15). Protecting ideas: Can ideas be protected or patented? *IPWatchdog*. Retrieved from http://www.ipwatchdog.com/2014/02/15/protecting-ideas-can-ideas-be-protected-or-patented/id=48009/

26. Keating, *Unleashing small business through IP*.

27. Twin, A. (2019). Non-disclosure agreement (NDA). *Investopedia*. Retrieved from https://www.investopedia.com/terms/n/nda.asp

28. Bornstein, A. (2018). Why you need to use NDAs to protect your business. *Entrepreneur*. https://www.entrepreneur.com/article/319362

29. Ibid.

30. Zwilling, M. (2017). How and when to pitch your idea without a signed NDA. *Inc.* Retrieved from https://www.inc.com/martin-zwilling/how-when-to-pitch-your-idea-without-a-signed-nda.html

31. Bizzo, G. (2017). Making non-disclosure agreements (NDA's) work for you. *Startups*. Retrieved from https://www.startups.com/library/expert-advice/making-non-disclosure-agreements-ndas-work-for-you

32. Watson, A. (2018). Media piracy: Statistics & facts. *Statista*. Retrieved from https://www.statista.com/topics/3493/media-piracy/

33. Sherman, E. (2019). One in five U.S. companies say China has stolen their intellectual property. *Fortune*. Retrieved from http://fortune.com/2019/03/01/china-ip-theft

34. Clark, G. (2018). What is intellectual property, and does China steal it? *Bloomberg*. Retrieved from https://www.bloomberg.com/news/articles/2018-12-05/what-s-intellectual-property-and-does-china-steal-it-quicktake

35. Bessen, J. (2014, November). The evidence is in: Patent trolls do hurt innovation. *Harvard Business Review*. Retrieved from https://hbr.org/2014/07/the-evidence-is-in-patent-trolls-do-hurt-innovation

36. Suneson, G. (2019). 10 most counterfeited products in America. *USA Today*. Retrieved

from https://eu.usatoday.com/story/money/2019/04/14/10-most-counterfeited-products-in-america/39327933/

37. Most of this section is based on Kotha, R., Kim, P. H., & Alexy, O. (2014, November). Turn your science into a business. *Harvard Business Review, 92*(11), 106–114.

38. Lococo, E. (2012, July 2). Apple pays Proview $60m to resolve iPad trademark dispute. *Bloomberg Business.* Retrieved from http://www.bloomberg.com/news/articles/2012-07-02/apple-pays-60-million-to-end-china-ipad-dispute-with-proview

39. U.S. Small Business Administration (n.d.). *Hire and manage employees.* Retrieved from https://www.sba.gov/business-guide/manage-your-business/hire-manage-employees

40. Burrow, S. (2015, June 10). Top ten worst countries for workers' rights: The ranking no country should want. *Huffington Post.* Retrieved from http://www.huffingtonpost.com/sharan-burrow/top-ten-worst-countries-f_b_7553364.html

41. Simon, R. (2019). The real danger of going on "Shark Tank": Copycats. *Wall Street Journal.* Retrieved from https://www.wsj.com/articles/the-real-danger-of-going-on-shark-tank-copycats-11556357401

42. U.S. Small Business Administration, *Hire and manage employees.*

43. See, e.g., Internal Revenue Service Publication 15-A, Employer's Supplemental Tax Guide 2016.

44. Wage and Hour Division (WHD). Retrieved from https://www.dol.gov/whd/regs/compliance/whdfs71.htm

45. See http://www.babson.edu/academics/centers-and-institutes/the-arthur-m-blank-center-for-entrepreneurship/john-e-and-alice-l-butler-launch-pad/beta-challenge

46. The specialty lines insurance market is the segment of the insurance industry where the more difficult and unusual risks are written. The specialty lines insurance market focuses on two types of products: unusual or difficult insurance and higher risk accounts.

## CHAPTER 15

1. *Entrepreneurial marketing.* (n.d.). Retrieved from http://www.marketing-schools.org/types-of-marketing/entrepreneurial-marketing.html

2. Egan, K. (2017). 11 things that make marketing in 2017 different from 2007. Retrieved from https://www.impactbnd.com/blog/11-things-that-make-marketing-in-2017-different-from-2007

3. Godin, S. (2009). First, organize 1,000. *Seth's Blog.* Retrieved from https://seths.blog/2009/12/first-organize-1000/

4. Much of this section is based on Manktelow, J. (n.d.). The marketing mix and the 4Ps of marketing. *MindTools.* Retrieved from http://www.mindtools.com/pages/article/newSTR_94.htm

5. Crane, F. G. (2012, September 12). *Marketing for entrepreneurs: Concepts and applications for new ventures,* p. 3. Thousand Oaks, CA: SAGE. [Kindle ed.]

6. Retrieved from http://www.entrepreneur.com/article/70824

7. Williams, J. (n.d.). The basics of branding. *Entrepreneur.* Retrieved from https://www.entrepreneur.com/article/77408

8. Retrieved from https://www.entrepreneur.com/article/219314

9. Pono, M. (2016, May 3). How industry leaders create strong brands. *Medium.* Retrieved from https://www.linkedin.com/pulse/how-industry-leaders-create-strong-brands-myk-pono

10. 12 marketing trends to take advantage of this year. (2018). *Forbes.* Retrieved from https://www.forbes.com/sites/forbescommunicationscouncil/2018/02/14/12-marketing-trends-to-take-advantage-of-this-year/#208dfca87401

11. Teitelman, M. (2018). 18 artificial intelligence marketing trends for 2018. *Medium.* Retrieved from https://medium.com/trapica/18-important-marketing-trends-for-2018-64922e2daff4

12. Wilson, M. (2017). Domino's Instagram is gross. That's by design. *Fast Company.* Retrieved from https://www.fastcompany.com/90138198/dominos-could-win-the-pizza-wars-by-being-grosser-than-everyone-else

13. 11 Influencer Marketing Campaigns to Inspire You to Start with Influencer Marketing in 2018. (2018). *Influencer Marketing Hub.* Retrieved from https://influencermarketinghub.com/11-influencer-marketing-campaigns-to-inspire-you-2018/

14. Meet the 25 highest-paid social media influencers. (2018). *Izea.* Retrieved from https://izea.com/2018/04/05/highest-paid-social-media-influencers/

15. Brenner, M. (2018). 4 creative experiential marketing examples that are raising the bar. Retrieved from https://marketinginsidergroup.com/strategy/4-creative-experiential-marketing-examples-raising-bar/

16. Ritchie, J. (2017, January 26). Five simple ways to educate your customers through content. Retrieved from https://www.forbes.com/sites/forbesagencycouncil/2017/01/26/five-simple-ways-to-educate-your-customers-through-content/#1697e35ad991

17. Ciotti, G. (2013, July 23). The new 4Ps of marketing. *Help Scout.* Retrieved from http://www.helpscout.net/blog/new-4ps-of-marketing/

18. Blendtec celebrates 10 years of viral marketing success. (2016). Retrieved from https://globenewswire.com/news-release/2016/11/07/887174/10165944/en/Blendtec-Celebrates-10-Years-of-Viral-Marketing-Success.html

19. MyLoupus. (2010, January 17). Guerrilla marketing by Loupus—Snow branding in Leipzig [Video file]. *YouTube.* Retrieved from https://www.youtube.com/watch?v=_JcuDxT88_Y

20. Botticello, C. (2018, July 18). 10 creative guerrilla marketing tactics to boost your brand, company, or cause. Retrieved from https://medium.com/side-hustle/10-creative-guerilla-marketing-tactics-to-boost-your-brand-company-or-cause-8dc02e43f02d

21. Pinegar, G. (2018). What is guerrilla marketing (+16 ideas and examples for innovative brands). Retrieved from https://learn.g2crowd.com/guerrilla-marketing

22. Pofeldt, E. (2018, July 8). How a fine artist built a million-dollar, one-person business that's true to her vision. Retrieved from https://www.forbes.com/sites/elainepofeldt/2018/07/08/how-a-fine-artist-built-a-million-dollar-one-person-business-thats-true-to-her-vision/#6c3a33617ddf

23. Agrawal, A. J. (2017, February 24). How to have rock star customer service on Twitter. Retrieved from https://www.forbes.com/sites/ajagrawal/2017/02/24/how-to-have-rockstar-customer-service-on-twitter/#6f08a7c3d918

24. Wertz, J. (2018, April 24). 4 entrepreneurs share which social media outlet garners the most business. Retrieved from https://www.forbes.com/sites/jiawertz/2018/04/24/4-entrepreneurs-share-which-social-media-outlet-garners-the-most-business/#7c2c479f4a21

25. Pink, D. (2012). *To sell is human* (p. 21). New York, NY: Penguin.

26. Black, W. (2013). Marketers, stop creating content and develop a point of view. Retrieved from https://e-m-marketing.com/blog/2013/12/marketers-stop-creating-content-and-develop-a-point-of-view/

27. Ibid.

28. Pepsi advert with Kendall Jenner pulled after huge backlash. (2017).

*Independent UK.* Retrieved from https://www.independent.co.uk/arts-entertainment/tv/news/pepsi-advert-pulled-kendall-jenner-protest-video-cancelled-removed-a7668986.html

29. Black, Marketers, stop creating content and develop a point of view.

30. Davidson, J. (2017, January 3). 3 ways how I get my followers to meaningfully engage with me. Retrieved from https://medium.com/startup-grind/3-ways-how-i-get-my-followers-to-meaningfully-engage-with-me-1fe886d9edc4

31. Hern, A. (2015, August 5). Smartphone now most popular way to browse internet—Ofcom Report. *The Guardian.* Retrieved from http://www.theguardian.com/technology/2015/aug/06/smartphones-most-popular-way-to-browse-internet-ofcom

32. Mintzer, R. (2014, May 27). The 10 most deadly mistakes in website design. *Entrepreneur.* Retrieved from http://www.entrepreneur.com/article/234129

33. Kelly, K. (2008). 1,000 true fans. *The Technium.* Retrieved from https://kk.org/thetechnium/1000-true-fans/

34. Welch, D. (2018, December 20). Musk's brother finds good use for Tesla Model 3 shortage. Retrieved from https://www.bloomberg.com/news/articles/2018-02-20/musk-s-brother-finds-good-use-for-tesla-model-3-shortage

35. Godin, First, organize 1,000.

36. Lewis, R. (2016). The long tail theory can be reality for traditional megabrands. Retrieved from https://www.forbes.com/sites/robinlewis/2016/05/31/the-long-tail-theory-can-be-reality-for-traditional-megabrands/#453fa026372b

37. Scott, D. M. (2017). *The new rules of marketing & PR* (p. 32). Hoboken, NJ: Wiley.

38. Gregoire, C. (2014, June 12). How to make the perfect first impression. *Huffington Post.* Retrieved from http://www.huffingtonpost.com/2014/05/30/the-science-and-art-of-fi_n_5399004.html

39. Mackay, J. (n.d.). The weird science behind first impressions. *Crew.* Retrieved from http://blog.crew.co/weird-science-first-impressions/

40. *Body language for entrepreneurs.* (n.d.). Retrieved from Udemy.com Course.

41. Ibid.

42. Payne, K. (n.d.). Personal branding for entrepreneurs. Retrieved from https://kevintpayne.com/personal-branding-for-entrepreneurs/

## SUPPLEMENT B

1. Pink, D. (2013). *To sell is human: The surprising truth about moving others.* New York, NY: Riverhead Books.

2. Ibid.

3. Clark, N. (2016). How Pixar can help you craft your 30-second pitch. Retrieved from https://www.linkedin.com/pulse/how-pixar-can-help-you-craft-your-30-second-pitch-nicholas-clark/

4. Monarth, H. "The irresistible power of storytelling as strategic business tool," Harvard Business Review.org (March 11, 2014) https://hbr.org/2014/03/the-irresistible-power-of-storytelling-as-a-strategic-business-tool/ retrieved on September 20, 2015

5. Neck, H. The entrepreneurial skillset of storytelling, *Forbes* (2015, July 14) http://www.forbes.com/sites/babson/2015/07/14/the-entrepreneurial-skillset-of-storytelling/ retrieved on September 20, 2015

6. Gallo, C. What Starbucks CEO Howard Schultz taught me about communication and success, *Forbes* (2013, December 19) http://www.forbes.com/sites/carminegallo/2013/12/19/what-starbucks-ceo-howard-schultz-taught-me-about-communication-and-success/ retrieved on September 20, 2015

7. Pink, D. (2012). *To sell is human,* New York: Penguin Group, p. 171.

8. Experiential Marketing and Event Staffing! Retrieved from https://www.attackmarketing.com/

9. Zwilling, M. Entrepreneurs who master storytelling win more, *Forbes* (2013, January 25) http://www.forbes.com/sites/martinzwilling/2013/01/25/entrepreneurs-who-master-storytelling-win-more/ retrieved on September 20, 2015

10. Pink, *To sell is human.*

11. See http://techcrunch.com/2010/11/02/365-days-10-million-3-rounds-2-companies-all-with-5-magic-slides/ (5 slides); http://avc.com/2010/06/six-slides/ (6 slides); http://guykawasaki.com/the-only-10-slides-you-need-in-your-pitch/ (10 slides); http://articles.bplans.com/what-to-include-in-your-pitch-deck/ (11 slides); http://www.forbes.com/sites/chancebarnett/2014/05/09/investor-pitch-deck-to-raise-money-for-startups/#5dcf25b84863 (12 slides); https://www.entrepreneur.com/article/240065 (15 slides); http://www.slideshare.net/Sky7777/the-best-startup-pitch-deck-how-to-present-to-angels-v-cs (30 slides).

12. http://techcrunch.com/2010/11/02/365-days-10-million-3-rounds-2-companies-all-with-5-magic-slides/

13. http://articles.bplans.com/what-to-include-in-your-pitch-deck/

14. http://www.slideshare.net/Sky7777/the-best-startup-pitch-deck-how-to-present-to-angels-v-cs

15. http://www.bridging-the-gap.com/what-is-a-use-case/

16. Sampson, M. (2011, March 23). Invest in people, not ideas. Retrieved from https://michaelsampson.net/2011/03/23/invest-people/

17. Question list was compiled from author experience, but some questions may be found at http://techcrunch.com/2012/04/27/be-concise-the-top-questions-asked-at-a-y-combinator-interview/; http://www.forbes.com/sites/allbusiness/2013/06/10/65-questions-venture-capitalists-will-ask-startups/#50987df18202

18. Behind the Scenes of TED Presenters. Retrieved from https://blog.powerspeaking.com/behind_the_scenes_of_ted_presenters

## CHAPTER 16

1. Sharir, M., & Lerner, M. (2006). Gauging the success of social ventures initiated by individual social entrepreneurs. *Journal of World Business,* 41, 6–20, at p. 7.

2. Churchman, C. W. (1967). Wicked problems. *Management Science,* 14(4), B-141 & B-142; Conklin, J. (2006). *Dialogue mapping: Building shared understanding of wicked problems.* Chichester, UK: Wiley. See also http://www.cognexus.org/id17.htm

3. Escher, A., Kolodny, L. (2017). Causes of the global water crisis and 12 companies trying to solve it. Retrieved from website https://techcrunch.com/2017/03/22/causes-of-the-global-water-crisis-and-12-companies-trying-to-solve-it/

4. Does Plastic Contribute to Global Warming. (2018) Retrieved from website https://www.envirotech-online.com/news/water-wastewater/9/breaking-news/does-plastic-contribute-to-global-warming/46942

5. Harvey, F. (2018). World must triple efforts or face catastrophic climate change, says UN. Retrieved from website https://www.theguardian.com/environment/2018/nov/27/world-triple-efforts-climate-change-un-global-warming

6. Schaffrath, M. (2018). 5 startups that prove tech can solve the world's biggest problems. Retrieved from website https://www.forbes.com/sites/maikoschaffrath/2018/06/17/5-startups-that-prove-tech-can-solve-the-worlds-biggest-problems/#1a81460512fd

7. Neck, H. M., Brush, C., & Allen, E. (2009). The landscape of social

entrepreneurship. *Business Horizons, 52*, 13–19.

8. Sword & Plough website https://www .swordandplough.com/pages/social-impact

9. Clark, M. (2018). Empowering women to be ABLE to thrive. Retrieved from website https://socialenterprise .us/2018/02/16/empowering-women-able-thrive/

10. Robin Hood website https://www .robinhood.org/

11. Harris, E. (2017) Robin Hood, favorite charity on Wall Street, gets new leader. *New York Times.* Retrieved from https://www.nytimes .com/2017/04/25/nyregion/robin-hood-foundation-charity-wes-moore.html

12. Luna, J. (2017). Jane Chen: Be courageous because you will fail. Retrieved from Stanford Business website https://www.gsb.stanford .edu/insights/jane-chen-be-courageous-because-you-will-fail

13. Retrieved from Goodwill website http://www.goodwill.org/about-us/

14. Blanding, M. (2013, August 12). Entrepreneurs and the "hybrid" organization. *Forbes Blog.* Retrieved from http://www.forbes.com/sites/ hbsworkingknowledge/2013/08/12/ entrepreneurs-and-the-hybrid-organization/

15. Sistare, H. (2013, February 28). Better World Books continues to innovate. *Triple Pundit.* Retrieved from http:// www.triplepundit.com/2013/02/ better-world-books-continues-to-innovate/

16. Retrieved from Better World Books website https://www.betterworld books.com/go/book-for-book

17. The Staff of Entrepreneur Media, Inc. (2017). How social entrepreneurs can land funding. Retrieved from website https://www.entrepreneur.com/ article/290808

18. Pi Slice Celebrates its second year. Retrieved from website https://www .pi-slice.com/en/news-from-the-field/article/pi-slice-celebrates-its-second-year

19. Gilber, J. (2017). Putting the impact in impact investing: 28 funds building a credible, transparent marketplace. Retrieved from https://www.forbes.com/sites/ jaycoengilbert/2017/10/09/putting-the-impact-in-impact-investing-28-funds-building-a-credible-transparent-marketplace/#2caf84523e5f

20. Cohen, R., & Bannick, M. (2014, September 20). Is social impact investing the next venture capital?" *Forbes.* Retrieved from http://www.forbes.com/sites/ realspin/2014/09/20/is-social-impact-investing-the-next-venture-capital/

21. Examples of impact investment funds, *Impactbase* Retrieved from http:// www.impactbase.org/info/examples-impact-investment-funds

22. VPP website. Retrieved from http:// www.vppartners.org/about-us

23. Retrieved from Venture Philanthropy Partners website http://www .vppartners.org/about/history/

24. https://sjfventures.com/our-portfolio/

25. Fehrenbacher, K. (2018). Meet 5 startups working on big energy ideas. Retrieved from website https:// www.greenbiz.com/article/meet-5-startups-working-big-energy-ideas

26. Yunus, M., & Jolis, A. 2007. *Banker to the poor: Micro-lending and the battle against world poverty.* New York: Public Affairs

27. Klich, T. (2018). The founder of Tala on her leap from finance to fundraising for her mission-driven startup. Retrieved from https://www.forbes .com/sites/tanyaklich/2018/07/18/ tala-founder-shivani-siroya-on-her-leap-from-finance-to-fundraising-for-her-mission-driven-fintech-startup/#2852129056f7

28. Mitchell, R., Agle, B., & Wood, D. (1997). Toward a theory of stakeholder identification and salience: Defining the principle of who and what really counts. *Academy of Management Review, 22*, 853–866.

29. Suchman, M. C. (1995). Managing legitimacy: Strategic and institutional approaches. *Academy of Management Review, 20*, 571–610.

30. Retrieved from http://www.c-e-o.org/ about-us

31. Rao, S. (2010, April 14). Moving from a "me" to an "other-centered" universe. *Huffpost Healthy Living.* Retrieved from http://www.huffingtonpost.com/ srikumar-s-rao/how-to-be-happy-moving-fr_b_570730.html

32. Meier, S., & Cassar, L. (2018). Stop talking about how CSR helps your bottom line. Retrieved from website https://hbr.org/2018/01/stop-talking-about-how-csr-helps-your-bottom-line

33. The halo effect. (2015, June 27). *The Economist.* Retrieved from http:// www.economist.com/news/ business/21656218-do-gooding-policies-help-firms-when-they-get-prosecuted-halo-effect

34. The halo effect. (2015, June 27). *The Economist.* Retrieved from http:// www.economist.com/news/ business/21656218-do-gooding-policies-help-firms-when-they-get-prosecuted-halo-effect retrieved on October 30, 2015.

35. Meier, S., and Cassar, L. (2018). Stop talking about how CSR helps your bottom line. Retrieved from website https://hbr.org/2018/01/stop-talking-about-how-csr-helps-your-bottom-line

36. Valet, V. (2018). The world's most reputable companies for corporate responsibility 2018. *Forbes.* Retrieved from https://www.forbes.com/ sites/vickyvalet/2018/10/11/the-worlds-most-reputable-companies-for-corporate-responsibility-2018/#3940c0003371

37. Half, R. (2017). 3 awesome CSR initiatives by top tech companies. Retrieved from website https://www .roberthalf.com.au/blog/employers/3-awesome-csr-initiatives-top-tech-companies

38. Anderson, C. (2018). Introducing . . . The Audacious Project, a new model to inspire change at scale. Retrieved from website https://ideas.ted.com/ the-audacious-project-a-new-model-to-inspire-change-at-scale/

39. TED. (2018). The Audacious Project [Press release]. Retrieved from https:// www.prnewswire.com/news-releases/ the-audacious-project-a-new-model-for-philanthropic-collaboration-announces-first-ever-recipients-live-from-the-ted-conference-300628424. html

40. Retrieved from https://www .gemconsortium.org/report

41. Kelley, D., Singer, S., & Herrington, M. (2015). *Global Entrepreneurship Monitor 2016 global report.* Retrieved from http://www.gemconsortium.org/ docs/download/3106

# NAME INDEX

# SUBJECT INDEX